JUDAISM

This all-encompassing textbook is an unrivalled guide to the history, beliefs and practice of Judaism. Beginning with the ancient Near Eastern background, it covers early Israelite history, the emergence of classical rabbinic literature and the rise of medieval Judaism in Islamic and Christian lands. It also includes the early modern period and the development of Jewry in the nineteenth and twentieth centuries. Extracts from primary sources are used throughout to enliven the narrative and provide concrete examples of the rich variety of Jewish civilization.

Specially designed to assist learning, *Judaism*:

- *Introduces* texts and commentaries, including the Hebrew Bible, rabbinic texts, mystical literature, Jewish philosophy and Jewish theology

- *Provides* the skills necessary to understand these step-by-step with the help of a companion website

- *Explains* how to interpret the major events in nearly four thousand years of Jewish history

- *Supports* study with discussion questions on the central historical and religious issues, and includes key reading for each chapter, an extensive glossary and index

- *Illustrates* the development of Judaism, its concepts and observances, with 75 maps and 94 photos, paintings and engravings

- *Links* each chapter to a free companion website which provides things to think about, things to do and tips for teachers as well as other online resources

Dan Cohn-Sherbok is an American-born rabbi and Professor of Judaism at the University of Wales, Lampeter. He is a prolific and respected writer and the author of Routledge's *Atlas of Jewish History*, *Fifty Key Jewish Thinkers*, and *Judaism* in the Religion of the World series. As a teacher and rabbi he is in a unique position to provide guidance for college and university students on the history and practice of Judaism.

Judaism

History, Belief and Practice

Dan Cohn-Sherbok

Routledge
Taylor & Francis Group
LONDON AND NEW YORK

With free companion website at
http://www.routledge.com/textbooks/0415236614

For Lavinia

First published 2003
by Routledge
2 Park Square, Milton Park, Abingdon, Oxon OX14 4RN

Simultaneously published in the USA and Canada
by Routledge
711 Third Avenue, New York, NY 10017

Routledge is an imprint of the Taylor & Francis Group,
an informa business

© 2003 Dan Cohn-Sherbok

Reprinted 2008 (twice), 2009

Designed and Typeset in Garamond and Univers by
Keystroke, Jacaranda Lodge, Wolverhampton

British Library Cataloguing in Publication Data
A catalogue record for this book is available from the
British Library

Library of Congress Cataloging in Publication Data
Cohn-Sherbok, Dan.
  Judaism : history, belief, and practice /
Dan Cohn-Sherbok.
  Includes bibliographical references and index.
  1. Judaism. I. Title.

BM562 .C64 2003
296–dc21   2002036646

  ISBN 978–0–415–23660–7 (hbk)
  ISBN 978–0–415–23661–4 (pbk)

Contents

BELIEF

PRACTICE

Maps

Figures

Preface

Who are the Jews? What do they believe? What do they practise? This volume is designed to provide a comprehensive picture of Jewish life and thought from ancient times to the present. Throughout students are encouraged to gain an appreciation of traditional Judaism as it has been understood and practised through the centuries, as well as an awareness of modern critical scholarship. Divided into two major parts – Jewish history, and Jewish belief and practice – it begins with an account of the history and religion of the ancient Near East, focusing on the influence of ancient Near Eastern civilization on the Hebrew Scriptures. The book goes on to examine ancient Israelite history, the patriarchs, the exodus from Egypt, the rise of monarchy and the emergence of prophecy. It then surveys later Biblical history, the development of Judaism in Hellenistic times, and the emergence of classical rabbinic literature and theology. The medieval period in Islamic and Christian lands is also explained in detail, with special attention to the rise of Jewish philosophy, theology and mysticism. In the modern world, the emergence of religious reform and the rise of *Hasidism* are both analysed. Finally, the book concentrates on the development of Jewry in the nineteenth and twentieth centuries.

This presentation of Jewish history is followed by an extensive outline of Jewish belief and practice, beginning with a discussion of the primary religious doctrines of Judaism. Each chapter highlights Biblical teaching and traces its development from rabbinic times to the present. Commencing with a survey of Jewish belief about God's unity, the book goes on to examine the traditional doctrines about God's nature, including such concepts as divine transcendence, eternal existence, omniscience and omnipotence. Turning to a consideration of God's action in the world, the subsequent chapters focus on creation, providence, divine goodness and revelation. There then follows an

exploration of ideas specifically connected with God's relation to Israel: Torah, *mitzvah*, sin and repentance, the chosen people, the promised land, prayer, and the love and fear of God. This discussion concludes with an exploration of Jewish eschatology. The next section, dealing with Jewish practice, commences with a depiction of the Jewish community, its literature, and the process of education as it has emerged over the centuries. This is followed by an outline of the Jewish calendar, and Jewish worship embracing such institutions as the sanctuary, Temple and synagogue as well as the major festivals in the yearly cycle: Sabbath, Pilgrim Festivals, New Year, Day of Atonement, Days of Joy, and Fast Days. The next chapters discuss major events in the Jewish life cycle including marriage, divorce, death and mourning. In the following chapter some of the central characteristics of Jewish morality are highlighted, and the book concludes with a depiction of the conversion procedure. This volume also contains an extensive list of reference material – including a list of encyclopedias, dictionaries, atlases, journals, newspapers and internet sites – and a glossary of terms.

Each of the ninety chapters of the book is composed of a discussion of the topic, illustrative texts, questions for students, and further books dealing with the subject. Sources used throughout the book contain the author, title and work where the source is cited. Biblical references are from the RSV (Revised Standard Version). Throughout readers are encouraged to engage with the material and to reflect on the issues that emerge. In order to facilitate this process, this book is supplemented by a separate *Companion Website*. This accompanying Companion is divided into ninety chapters which parallel the contents of the book. In each chapter students are given additional information as well as suggestions how to approach the material. This *Judaism*

Companion Website is also designed for teachers, and each chapter contains a separate section: tips for teachers. The aim of *Judaism: History, Belief and Practice* and the *Judaism Companion Website* is thus to provide students – no matter what their religious background or orientation – with a comprehensive picture of the Jewish faith as it emerged over nearly four thousand years of history.

Tips for students

- This volume is divided into three sections: history, belief and practice. If your teacher has assigned *Judaism: History, Belief and Practice* as the textbook for the course, you will be given instructions on how to use it. Otherwise, you should use the relevant sections of the book to help you understand what you are covering in class.

- As you read each chapter, be sure to look at the *Judaism Companion Website* which is on the Internet at www.routledge.com/textbooks/0415 236614. This is divided into ninety chapters which parallel the chapters in this book and contains things to think about and things to do (as well as tips for teachers). This information supplements the book, focuses on key issues, and provides a wealth of suggestions to support your study.

- Every chapter contains a list of books for further reading. Some of these books are introductory in character; others are more advanced. Of course not all the books listed will be in your library, but some may be. In any event, you should also use amazon.com (amazon.co.uk) to look for other books dealing with the topics you are studying. Go to Amazon.com and type in the relevant topics. The *Judaism Companion Website* gives advice on how to do this. In addition, you should be sure to use the web to look at books in your university or college library.

- Take advantage of resources in your local community to supplement the material found in this book. If there is a synagogue, visit it. Go to a Sabbath service or to a festival service. The *Companion Website* will help you to know what is important. If possible, contact local rabbis and tell them you are doing a course on Judaism and would like to have contact with Jews in your area.

- Hebrew is very important in understanding the tradition. As you read this book, you will come across a wide range of Hebrew terms. You should consider taking an elementary Hebrew course either at your university or college, or possibly at a local synagogue. At the very least, you should learn the Hebrew alphabet.

- Judaism is a living religion. You should therefore make an attempt to get to know Jews of all persuasions. Some of your friends may be Jewish. If so, ask them about what you are studying in this book. You should also pay special attention to articles in newspapers and magazines as well as to television programmes which relate to what you are learning.

- Supplement your academic work with novels and films dealing with Jewish life. Novels concerning all aspects of Jewish existence will enrich your understanding of the tradition. Search for these on amazon.com and amazon.co.uk. This will give you an idea what is available. You could then use the web to see if your local library, university or college libraries have the novels that interest you. The same applies to videos. Go to your local video shop and ask if there are films with Jewish themes.

- Subscribe to your local Jewish newspaper. This will give you an insight into contemporary Jewish life in the diaspora and Israel. You will gain a wealth of information about Judaism past and present. If your community does not have a local newspaper, go to Google and type 'Jewish newspapers'. You will find that there are many to choose from. You could then subscribe to any of these.

- Note that in this volume all books and foreign words are in italics. In addition, words that are in

bold typeface relate to the key readings that are included in each chapter. You should pay special attention to the index which will direct you to the topics contained in this book. The glossary at the end of the book gives definitions of all Hebrew terms, and you should use this as you read the book.

- In addition to the further reading for every chapter, there is a reference bibliography at the end of the book which lists important dictionaries, encyclopedias and atlases, as well as electronic texts and Jewish journals. Be sure to consult these reference books to supplement this volume. Don't forget to use the *Judaism Companion Website* as you read this book to increase your knowledge of the topics you are studying.

- Each chapter contains topics for discussion – these are also subjects for you to think about as you reflect on material in the chapter. Dialogue is vital, and you should make every attempt to explore the topics that interest you with other students in your class or with friends who are similarly interested in Jewish history and thought. The *Companion Website* also focuses on key issues in each chapter of the book and poses questions to consider.

- You will see that there are a number of activities that are recommended in the *Judaism Companion Website*. Even if your teacher does not require you to undertake these activities, you should consider whether they might help to increase your understanding of the Jewish tradition and way of life.

Sources

Works cited in this book are found in the following sources:

A   Dan Cohn-Sherbok, *Anti-Semitism*, Sutton, 2002.
ADPB   *The Authorized Daily Prayer Book*, Bloch, 1984.
BDDH   Bahya Ibn Paquda, *Book of the Directions of the Duties of the Heart*, Littman Library, 1973.
BK   Judah Halevi, *Book of the Kuzari*, New York, 1949.
BRJ   Jacob Neusner and Alan J. Avery-Peck (eds), *The Blackwell Reader in Judaism*, Blackwell, 2001.
C   Sherwin Wine, *Celebration*, Prometheus, 1988.
CJ   Dan Cohn-Sherbok, *The Crucified Jew*, HarperCollins, 1992.
CJL   Simon Ganzfried, *Code of Jewish Law*, Hebrew Publishing Co., 1963.
DOTT   D. Winton Thomas (ed.), *Documents from Old Testament Times*, Harper and Row, 1961.
DPB   Joseph Hertz, *Daily Prayer Book*, Bloch, 1948.
DSS   Geza Vermes, *The Dead Sea Scrolls in English*, Penguin, 1995.
EJ   Cecil Roth and Geoffrey Wigoder (eds), *Encyclopedia Judaica*, Coronet Books, 2002.
EJCG   George Robinson, *Essential Judaism: A Complete Guide to Beliefs, Customs and Rituals*, Pocket Books, 2000.
FJ   Dan Cohn-Sherbok, *The Future of Judaism*, T. and T. Clark, 1994.
FJT   Dan Cohn-Sherbok, *Fifty Jewish Thinkers*, Routledge, 1997.
GP   Moses Maimonides, *The Guide for the Perplexed*, Chicago, 1964.
GP: NUPB   *Gates of Prayer: The New Union Prayer Book*, CCAR, 1975.
GS   *Gates of the Seasons*, CCAR, 1983.
H   Hyman Goldin, *Hamadrich*, Hebrew Publishing Company, 1956.
HA   Léon Poliakov, *History of Anti-Semitism*, Littman Library, 4 vols, 1974–85.
HDJ   Norman Solomon, *Historical Dictionary of Judaism*, Scarecrow Press, 1998.
HJPMA   Collette Sirat, *A History of Jewish Philosophy in the Middle Ages*, Cambridge University Press, 1995.
HT   Dan Cohn-Sherbok, *Holocaust Theology: A Reader*, Exeter University Press, 2002.
I   Dan Cohn-Sherbok, *Israel: The History of an Idea*, SPCK, 1992.
ICJ   Dan Cohn-Sherbok, *Issues in Contemporary Judaism*, Macmillan, 1991.
JF   Dan Cohn-Sherbok, *Jewish Faith*, SPCK, 1993.
JL   Louis Jacobs, *Jewish Law*, Behrman House, 1996.
JM   Dan Cohn-Sherbok, *Jewish Mysticism: An Anthology*, Oneworld, 1995.
JMW   Paul Mendes-Flohr and Jehuda Reinharz (ed.), *The Jew in the Modern World*, Oxford University Press, 1995.
JMedW   Jacob Rader Marcus (ed.), *The Jew in the Medieval World*, Athenaeum, 1977.
JOF   Dan Cohn-Sherbok, *Judaism and Other Faiths*, Macmillan, 1994.
JP   John Bowker, *Jesus and the Pharisees*, Cambridge University Press, 1973.
JT   Hyam Maccoby, *Judaism on Trial*, London, 1982.
JTheo   Louis Jacobs, *A Jewish Theology*, Behrman House, 1973.

KC	Solomon ibn Gabirol, *The Kingly Crown*, London, 1961.
KH	*Kol Haneshamah, Shabbat Vehasim*, The Reconstructionist Press, 2000.
KSO	*Kitzur Shulkhan Arukh*, Moznaim, 1991.
M	*Mahzor for Rosh Hashanah and Yom Kippur*, Rabbinical Assembly, 2000.
MJ	Dan Cohn-Sherbok, *Modern Judaism*, Macmillan, 1996.
MI	Philip Blackman, *Mishnayoth*, vol. 4, Judaica Press, 1965.
MMZ	S. Avineri, *The Making of Modern Zionism*, Basic Books, 1984.
MRHYK	*Mahzor for Rosh Hashanah and Yom Kippur*, The Rabbinical Assembly, 2000.
PBHV	T. Carmi (ed.), *The Penguin Book of Hebrew Verse*, Penguin, 1981.
PJF	Louis Jacobs, *Principles of the Jewish Faith*, Jason Aaronson, 1988.
RA	Herbert Loewe, Claud Montefiore, *A Rabbinic Anthology*, Schocken, 1974.
RJ	Dow Marmur (ed.), *Reform Judaism*, Reform Synagogues of Great Britain, 1973.
SBW	A. C. Bouquet, *Sacred Books of the World*, London, Penguin, 1959.
SHJ	Lavinia and Dan Cohn-Sherbok, *A Short History of Judaism*, Oneworld, 1997.
SIJ	Lavinia and Dan Cohn-Sherbok, *A Short Introduction to Judaism*, Oneworld, 1997.
SRJ	Lavinia and Dan Cohn-Sherbok, *A Short Reader of Judaism*, Oxford, Oneworld, 1997.
SSS	*Siddur Sim Shalom*, Rabbinical Assembly, United Synagogue of Conservative Judaism, 1985.
TJM	Dan Cohn-Sherbok, *The Jewish Messiah*, T. and T. Clark, 1997.
TJP	Hans Lewy (ed.), *Three Jewish Philosophers: Philo, Saadya Gaon, Jehuda Halevi*, Macmillan, 1972.
TSSJ	Philip Alexander, *Textual Sources for the Study of Judaism*, Manchester University Press, 1984.
UH	Dan Cohn-Sherbok, *Understanding the Holocaust*, Continuum, 1999.
TUH	*The Union Haggadah*, CCAR Press, 1923.
WI	Lewis Browne, *The Wisdom of Israel*, Michael Joseph, 1949.
ZI	A. Hertzberg, *The Zionist Idea: A Historical Analysis and Reader*, Atheneum, 1959.

Rabbinic sources

The following rabbinic sources have been used throughout this book:

Genesis Rabbah: Midrash on Genesis.

Exodus Rabbah: Midrash on Exodus.

Hekhalot Rabbati: Mystical works containing descriptions of the ascent to Heaven to behold the *Merkavah* (chariot).

Leviticus Rabbah: Midrash on Leviticus.

Mekhilta: Term applied to various *midrashic* works.

Mekhilta, Pisha: Tractate of the *Mekhilta*.

Midrash Rabbah: Midrash on the Pentateuch and the Five *Megillot* (Song of Songs, Ruth, Lamentations, Ecclesiastes and Esther).

Midrash, Lamentations: Midrash on Lamentations.

Midrash, Psalms: Midrash on Psalms.

Mishnah: Early rabbinic legal code compiled by Judah ha-Nasi in the second century.

Mishnah, Berakhot: Tractate of the *Mishnah* dealing with blessings and prayer.

Mishnah, Eduyot: Tractate of the *Mishnah* dealing with a variety of laws.

Mishnah, Gittin: Tractate of the *Mishnah* dealing with divorce.

Mishnah, Sanhedrin: Tractate of the *Mishnah* dealing with courts of justice and judicial procedure.

Mishnah, Pirke Avot (Sayings of the Fathers): Tractate of the *Mishnah*.

Pesikta de Rav Kahannah: Collection of *midrashic* homilies for holidays and special Sabbaths.

Sefer Yetsirah: Early mystical work.

Sifra: *Halakhic midrash* on Leviticus.

Sifre: *Halakhic midrash* on Numbers and Deuteronomy.

Shulkhan Arukh: Code of Jewish Law.

Talmud: Name of the two collections of the discussion of Jewish law by scholars from *c.* 200–500.

Talmud, Berakot: Tractate of the *Talmud* dealing with blessings and prayers.

Talmud, Baba Metzia: Tractate of the *Talmud* dealing with losses, loans and wage contracts.

Talmud, Eduyot: Tractate of the *Talmud* dealing with a variety of laws.

Talmud, Eruvin: Tractate of the *Talmud* dealing with laws establishing permissible limits for carrying on the Sabbath.

Talmud, Ketuvot: Tractate of the *Talmud* dealing with marriage contracts.

Talmud, Megillah: Tractate of the *Talmud* dealing with laws regarding *Purim*.

Talmud, Pesakhim: Tractate of the *Talmud* dealing with Passover.

Talmud, Sanhedrin: Tractate of the *Talmud* dealing with courts of justice and judicial procedure.

Talmud, Shabbat: Tractate of the *Talmud* dealing with the Sabbath.

Talmud, Sukkah: Tractate of the *Talmud* dealing with *Sukkot*.

Talmud, Yoma: Tractate of the *Talmud* dealing with the Temple service on *Yom Kippur*.

Tanhuma: Palestinian *midrashic* collection attributed to Tanhuma bar Abba.

Tosefta: Collection of rulings and maxims of early rabbinic sages.

Zohar: Medieval mystical commentary on the Pentateuch and parts of the Hagiographa.

ACKNOWLEDGEMENTS

Acknowledgement should be given to these important books from which I have gained information and source material: Louis Jacobs (1973), *A Jewish Theology*, Behrman House, New York; Robert Seltzer, *Jewish People Jewish Thought*, Macmillan, New York.

I would like to thank the authors and publishers of titles given below for permission to use their works. Sutton, Stroud, for Dan Cohn-Sherbok (2002) *Anti-Semitism*; Bloch Publishing Company, Inc., New York for *The Authorized Daily Prayer Book* (1984); Blackwell for Jacob Neusner and Alan J. Avery-Peck (eds) (2001) *The Blackwell Reader in Judaism*; Prometheus for Sherwin Wine (1988) *Celebration*; Harper Collins for Dan Cohn-Sherbok (1992) *The Crucified Jew*; Harper and Row for D. Winton Thomas (ed.) (1961) *Documents from Old Testament Times*; Bloch Publishing Company, New York for Joseph Hertz (1948) *Daily Prayer Book*; Penguin Books for Geza Vermes (1995) *The Dead Sea Scrolls* in English; T. Carmi (ed.) (1981) *The Penguin Book of Hebrew Verse* and A.C. Bouquet (1959) *Sacred Books of the World: A Companion Source-Book to Comparative Religion*, copyright 1954 to A.C. Bouquet; Pocket Books for George Robinson (2000) *Essential Judaism: A Complete Guide to Beliefs, Customs and Rituals*; T. & T. Clark, part of the Continuum Publishing Group, Ltd, London and New York for Dan Cohn-Sherbok (1994) *The Future of Judaism* and Dan Cohn-Sherbok (1997) *The Jewish Messiah*; Routledge for Dan Cohn-Sherbok (1997) *Fifty Jewish Thinkers*; University of Chicago Press for Moses Maimonides, *The Guide for the Perplexed*, trans. Pines, (1964); Central Conference of American Rabbis (CCAR) for *Gates of Prayer: The New Union Prayer Book*, copyright 1975, and *Gates of the Seasons*, copyright 1983; Hebrew Publishing Company for Hyman Goldin (1956) *Hamadrich*; Littman Library for Leon Poliakov (1980) *History of Anti-Semitism*; Scarecrow Press for Norman Solomon (1998) *Historical Dictionary of Judaism*; Cambridge University Press for selected extracts from the translated medieval works from Colette Sirat (1995) *A History of Jewish Philosophy in the Middle Ages*; Exeter University Press for Dan Cohn-Sherbok (2002) *Holocaust Theology: A Reader*; SPCK for Dan Cohn-Sherbok (1992) *Israel: The History of an Idea*, and (1993) the same author's *Jewish Faith*; Behrman House for Louis Jacobs (1996) *Jewish Law* and (1973) *A Jewish Theology*; Oneworld; Oxford for Dan Cohn-Sherbok (1995) *Jewish Mysticism: An Anthology* also for Lavinia and Dan Cohn-Sherbok (1997) *A Short Introduction to Judaism* and the same authors, (1997) *A Short Reader of Judaism*; Oxford University Press for Paul Mendes-Flohr and Jehuda Reinharz (eds) (1995) *The Jew in the Modern World*; Athenaeum for Jacob Rader Marcus (ed.) (1977) *The Jew in the Medieval World*; Cambridge University Press for John Bowker (1973) *Jesus and the Pharisees*; Littman Library, for Hyam Maccoby (1982) *Judaism on Trial*; The Reconstructionist Press for (2000) *Kol Haneshamah: Shabbat Vehagim*; The Rabbinical Assembly for *Mahzor* for *Rosh Hashanah* and *Yom Kippur*, (2000), edited by Rabbi Jules Harlow, copyright 1972; Macmillan for Dan Cohn-Sherbok (1996) *Modern Judaism* and Hans Lewy (ed.) (1972) *Three Jewish Philosophers: Philo, Saadya Gaon, Jehuda Halevi*; Jason Aaronson for Louis Jacobs (1988) *Principles of the Jewish Faith*; Schocken Books, a division of Random House, Inc., for Herbert Loewe, Claud G. Montefiore, *A Rabbinic Anthology*, copyright 1974; Reform Synagogues of Great Britain for Dow Marmur (ed.) (1973) *Reform Judaism*; Rabbinical Assembly, United Synagogue of Conservative Judaism for *Siddur Sim Shalom*, 1985; Manchester University Press for Philip Alexander (1984) *Textual Sources for the Study of Judaism*; Continuum for Dan Cohn-Sherbok (1999) *Understanding the Holocaust*; Michael Joseph for Lewis Browne (1949) *The Wisdom of Israel*; The Jewish Publication Society for A. Hertzberg (1959) *The Zionist Idea: A Historical Analysis and Reader*, New York, reprinted from *The Zionist Idea*, copyright 1977 to Arthur Hertzberg.

My grateful thanks are due to those readers who reviewed an early draft of the book and companion website: Rabbi Alan Unterman, Professor Oliver Leaman, Dr Melissa Raphael, Professor W.D. Rubinstein. I would also like to thank Moira Taylor for her invaluable help with this book and with the companion website, Ruth Jeavons, production editor, Sarah Worsfold, marketing executive, Leigh Hurlock, cover designer, and Alan Foster, copy editor.

Professor Rabbi Dan Cohn-Sherbok

PART I HISTORY

This survey of Jewish history traces the evolution of Judaism from Biblical times to the present day. Throughout this account the major developments of the faith as well as the central turning points of Jewish history are discussed in detail. The narrative includes such topics as the patriarchs, the Exodus, the period of the judges, the rise of monarchy, the prophets, the rise of rabbinic Judaism, Jews under Islamic rule, medieval Jewish philosophy and mysticism, Judaism in the early modern period, the Enlightenment, the emergence of Hasidism, the growth and development of Reform Judaism, Jewish life in the nineteenth and early twentieth century, the Holocaust and aftermath, and modern Jewish thought.

CHAPTER 1

Ancient Mesopotamian Civilization

Timeline:

c. 3100 BCE Invention of cuneiform writing by the Sumerians in Mesopotamia

c. 2615–2175 BCE Old Kingdom period of Egyptian history

c. 2360–2180 BCE First large-scale territorial empire of Mesopotamian history

21st–19th centuries BCE Movement of Amorites and other peoples into Mesopotamia and Canaan

21st–15th century BCE Middle Bronze Age in Canaan

2060–1950 BCE Third Dynasty of Ur

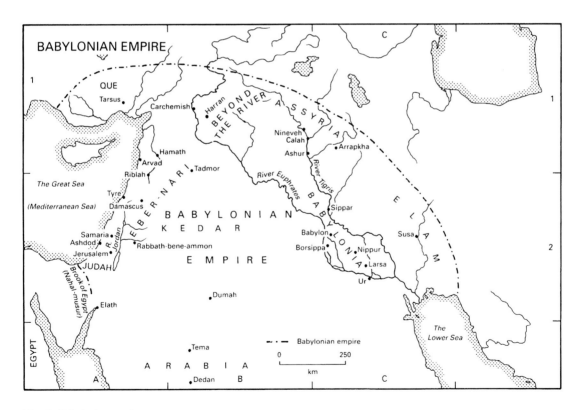

Map 1 Babylonian empire

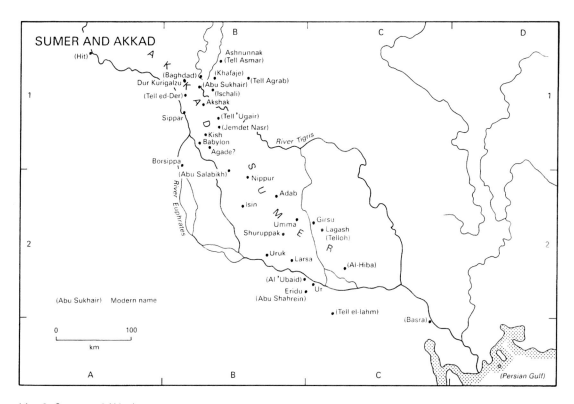

Map 2 Sumer and Akkad

In about 7000 BCE ancient peoples began to engage in agriculture, domesticate animals and establish urban communities – their dwellings have been traced to the hills of western Iran and Anatolia, to the shores of the Caspian Sea and Palestine. Later at the end of the fourth millennium, the Sumerians – a people who produced the first written script, the cuneiform system of wedge-shaped signs – created city states in southern Mesopotamia. Each city had its local god. In Uruk – the best known from archaeological excavations – there were two main temples: one was for Anu, the supreme god of heaven; the other was for Inanna, the mother goddess of fertility, love and war. In addition to these two gods deities were worshipped at other sites. Enlil, lord of the atmosphere, was worshipped at Nippur; Enki, ruler of the fresh waters beneath the earth, at Eridu; Utu, the sun god, at Larsa; Nanna, the moon god, at Ur.

Each of these gods had a family and servants who were also worshipped at other shrines. The temple itself was placed on a high platform and housed in a holy room a statue of the god. Sumerian priests recounted stories about these gods whose actions were restricted to various spheres of influence. Often they were portrayed as quarrelling over their areas of power; they also engaged in trickery, expressing every type of human emotion and vice. In addition, the Sumerian legends contain accounts of creation. According to the **Sumerian epics**, Enlil, the lord of the atmosphere, separated heaven from earth, and Enki, the ruler of fresh waters beneath the earth, created human beings to grow food for himself and the gods.

During the third millennium, a Semitic people – the Akkadians – settled amidst the Sumerians and adopted their writing and culture. In 2300 BCE King Sargon of Akkad established the first Akkadian empire, and the Akkadians dominated Mesopotamia. At this time the Sumerian myths were written in the Semitic script Akkadian rather than in Sumerian cuneiform. These Semites identified some of their

Figure 1 God Ningirso as lion-headed eagle, lapis lazuli with gold leaf, from treasure of Ur (Sumerian capital of Mesopotamia. Copyright The Art Archive/ National Museum Damascus Syria/Dagli Orti.

gods with the Sumerian ones: Anu was equated with El (the chief god); Inanna with Ishtar; Enki with Ea. In Akkadian schools epics of the gods were recorded. The **Gilgamesh Epic**, for example, tells of King Gilgamesh who ruled in Uruk in about 2700 BCE. According to legend, Gilgamesh embarked on a quest for immortality; eventually he encountered an old man – Ut-napishtim – who told Gilgamesh how he had become immortal. The gods, he explained, created man, but were disturbed by his noise. Unable to quell this tumult, they decided to destroy man by a great flood. Enki, who had created man in the first place, told Ut-napishtim to build a large boat in which he could escape. After the flood, the boat was grounded on a mountain, and the gods rewarded Ut-napishtim with immortality. Ut-napishtim told Gilgamesh to get a plant that could make him young again. Although Gilgamesh discovered it, he put it on the ground when he went swimming. Later it was eaten by a snake and Gilgamesh returned home empty-handed.

In Sumerian and Akkadian mythology, life was under the control of the gods. To obtain happiness, it was vital to keep the gods in good humour through sacrifice and worship. Nonetheless, the gods were unpredictable, and this gave rise to the use of omens. In the birth of monstrosities, in the movements of animals, in the shapes of cracks in the wall, and in oil poured into a cup of water, these ancient peoples were able to see the fingers of the gods pointing to the future. Hence, if a person wanted to marry, or a king wished to go to war, they would consult the gods. One common practice was to examine the liver of a sacrificed animal, and a special class of priests was trained to interpret these signs.

At its height the empire of Sargon and his descendants stretched from the Persian coast to the Syrian shores of the Mediterranean. However, in about 2200 BCE this empire collapsed through invasion and internal conflict. Among the new arrivals in Mesopotamia were the Amorites who dwelt in Mesopotamian cities such as Mari and Babylon; there they integrated into Sumero-Akkadian civilization. Other Amorites penetrated into Syria–Palestine (ancient Canaan). There they retained their separate tribal structure. The collapse of the Akkadian empire was followed by a Sumerian revival in the Third Dynasty of Ur (2060–1950 BCE). One of the greatest rulers was Hammurabi of Babylon who reigned from 1792 to 1750 BCE. In his honour the *Enuma Elish* (the Babylonian creation story) was composed. Several centuries later, in about 1400 BCE the state of Assyria became powerful in northern Mesopotomia, and after an interval became the dominant power in the Near East. The Assyrian kings copied the Babylonians; they worshipped the same gods, but their chief god was Ashur. When the Assyrians went to battle, it was at Ashur's command, and it was to defend or expand his frontiers that they fought.

In the second millennium, the inhabitants of Canaan consisted of a mixture of races, largely of Semitic origin. Excavations have unearthed the remains of small temples in Canaanite towns which contained cultic statues in niches opposite doorways. Where temples had courtyards, it appears that worshippers stood outside while priests entered the sanctuary. Archaeological discoveries have revealed that a large altar was in all likelihood placed in the courtyard with a smaller one inside the temple. Animal remains suggest that sacrifices consisted mainly of lambs and kids. Liquid offerings of wine and oil were made and incense was burned. In some temples, stone pillars stood as memorials to the dead; other pillars were symbols of gods. Statues of gods and goddesses were carved in stone or moulded in metal; they were then overlaid with gold, dressed in expensive garments, and decorated with jewellery.

In the north of ancient Canaan, excavations at Ugarit have provided information about the local religion. The texts of Ugarit illustrate that the gods of Canaan were similar to many others of the ancient Near East. El was the father of gods and men; his wife was Asherah, the mother goddess. El had a daughter Anat who personified war and love; she is described in some accounts as the lover of her brother, Baal, the god of weather. These Ugaritic texts depict Baal's victory over Yam (the sea) and against Mot (the god of death). Other gods include Shapash, the sun goddess; Yarikh, the moon god; Eshmun, the healer. The Canaanite religious structure as well as the earlier Sumerian and Akkadian religions set the backdrop for the emergence of the religion of the ancient Israelites. The earliest stories in the Torah (Genesis, Exodus, Leviticus, Numbers and Deuteronomy) contain centuries-old legends, composed in the light of Mesopotamian myths. Jewish civilization thus did not emerge in a vacuum. Rather it was forged out of the essential elements of an extensive Mesopotamian cultural heritage.

SOURCES

Babylonian Creation Myth

For the ancient Babylonians, the Creation Myth provided a religious framework for the understanding of the cosmos. Unlike the account of creation in Genesis which is monotheistic in character, this Babylonian epic portrays the actions of the gods of the ancient Near East:

> When above the heaven was not yet named,
> And the land beneath bore no name,
> And the primeval Apsu (abyss) their begetter,
> And chaos, Tiamat, the mother of them both –
> Their waters were mingled together,
> And no field was formed, nor marsh was to be seen;
> When of the gods still none had been produced,
> No name had yet been named, no destiny yet fixed;
> Then were created the gods in the midst of heaven . . .

> He (Marduk) made the stations for the great gods,
> As stars resembling them he fixed the signs of the zodiac,
> He ordained the year, defined divisions,
> Twelve months with stars, three each he appointed.
> He caused the moon-god to shine forth, entrusted to him the night:
> Appointed him as a night body to determine the days.

(*The Babylonian Creation-Epic*, Tablet I in SBW, pp. 47–48).

Babylonian Flood Story

The story of the Flood is one of the greatest of the Babylonian myths. It is told in the eleventh of the twelve tablets which make up the *Epic of Gilgamesh*:

I put on board all my family and relatives,
The cattle of the field, the beasts of the field,
Craftsmen all of them, I put on board.
A fixed time had Shamash appointed (saying):
'When the ruler of darkness (?) sends a heavy rain in the evening,
Then enter into the ship, and shut thy door.'
The appointed time arrived,
The ruler of darkness at eventide sent a heavy rain.
The appearance of the weather I observed,
I feared to behold the weather,
I entered the ship and shut my door.
To the ship's master, to Puzur-Amurri, the boatman,
The great structure I handed over with its goods.
When the first light of dawn appeared
There came up from the horizon a black cloud,
Adad in the midst thereof thundered
While Nabu and Sharru (i.e. Marduk) went before.
They passed like messengers over mountain and plain,
Nergal tore away the anchor cable (?).
Ninib goes on, the storm he makes to descend.
The Anunnaki lifted up their torches,
And with their brightness they lit up the land.
The raging of Adad reached into heaven,
All light was turned into darkness.
It (flooded) the land like . . .
One day, the tempest . . .
Hard it blew and . . .
Like an onslaught in battle it rushed in on the people.
No man beheld his fellow,
No longer could men know each other. In heaven
The gods were dismayed at the flood,
They retreated, they went up to the heaven of Anu
The gods cowered like dogs, they crouched by the walls . . .
For six days and nights
The wind blew, the flood, the tempest overwhelmed the land.
When the seventh day drew near, the tempest, the flood, ceased from the battle in which it had fought
  like a host.
Then the sea rested and was still, and the wind-storm and the flood ceased.
When I looked upon the sea, the uproar had ceased,
And all mankind was turned to clay.
The tilled land was become like a swamp. I opened the window and daylight fell upon my face.
I bowed myself down and sat a-weeping;
Over my face flowed my tears.
I gazed upon the quarters (of the world) – terrible (?) was the sea.
After twelve days, an island arose,
To the land of Nisir the ship took its course.

(*The Babylonian Flood Story*, Canto 11, in SBW, pp. 49–50).

DISCUSSION

1. What was the role of the gods in the religions of the ancient Near East?

2. Compare and contrast the Babylonian creation myth and the account of the flood with the Biblical account of creation and the flood.

FURTHER READING

Guillermo, Algaze, *The Uruk World System: The Dynamics of Expansion of Early Mesopotamian Civilization*, Chicago University Press, 1993.

Black, Jeremy, Green, Anthony, Richards, Tessa, *Gods, Demons and Symbols of Ancient Mesopotamia: An Illustrated Dictionary*, University of Texas Press, 1992.

Dalley, Stephanie (ed.), *Myths from Mesopotamia, Creation, the Flood, Gilgamesh, and Others*, Oxford University Press, 1998.

Downey, Susan B., *Mesopotamian Religious Architecture: Alexander Through the Parthians*, Princeton University Press, 1988.

De Mieroop, Marc Van, *The Ancient Mesopotamian City*, Oxford University Press, 1999.

Fairservis, Walter Ashlin, *Mesopotamia, the Civilization that Rose Out of the Clay*, Macmillan, 1964.

Foster, Benjamin R., *From Distant Days: Myths, Tales, and Poetry of Ancient Mesopotamia*, Capital Decisions Ltd, 1995.

Kurht, Amélie, *The Ancient Near East; c. 3000–330 BC*, Routledge, 1997.

Moorey, P.R.S., *Ancient Mesopotamian Materials and Industries: The Archaeological Evidence*, Clarendon, 1997.

Potts, D.T., *Mesopotamian Civilization: The Material Foundations*, Cornell University Press, 1996.

Roaf, Michael, *The Cultural Atlas of Mesopotamia and the Ancient Near East*, Checkmark Books, 1990.

Saggs, H.W.F., *Civilization Before Greece and Rome*, Yale University Press, 1991.

Sandars, N.K., *The Epic of Gilgamesh: An English Version with an Introduction*, Penguin, 1972.

Woolley, Leonard *et al.*, *Ur of the Chaldees: A Revised and Updated Edition of Sir Leonard Woolley's Excavations at Ur*, Cornell University Press, 1982.

CHAPTER 2

The Bible and Ancient Near Eastern civilization

Timeline:

1678–1570 BCE Canaan and Egypt ruled by the Hyksos

1570–1304 BCE New Kingdom or Empire period of Egyptian history

1450–1200 BCE Hittite empire in Asia Minor and Syria

13th–12th century BCE Wave of invasions in Syria and Palestine

Figure 2 Gilgamesh, or the Lion Spirit, Stone relief, Assyrian, from Khorsabard, eighth century BCE. Copyright The Art Archive/Musée du Louvre Paris/Dagli Orti.

From what is known of the religion of the ancient Near East, we can see that the Bible reflects various aspects of Mesopotamian culture. The physical structure of the universe as outlined in Genesis parallels what is found in Near Eastern literature: the earth is conceived as a thin disk floating in the surrounding ocean; the heavens are a dome holding back the upper waters; under the earth is located the domain of the dead. Like the gods of ancient literatures, the God of Israel is conceived anthropomorphically. As with other peoples, the Israelites accepted **magical** procedures (Exodus 7:9–12), recognized the power of **blessings and curses** (Numbers 22–24), and believed that God's will can be known through dreams, dice and oracles. Further, as in other cultures, holy men, kings and priests were revered, and there was a preoccupation with ritual uncleanliness and purity as well as priestly rites.

In addition to these similarities, there are strong parallels between the Hebrew Bible and the literature of the ancient Near East. Genesis, for example, appears to borrow details from the Babylonian Epic of Gilgamesh in connection with the legend of the flood. Biblical law bears a striking resemblance to ancient legal codes, in particular the Assyrian treaties between a king and his vassals which are very like the covenantal relationship between God and Israel. Yet despite such parallels, Israelite monotheism transformed these mythological features – themes retained in the Bible (such as the marriage of divine beings with women) are only briefly mentioned; Biblical heroes are not worshipped; nor is the underworld a subject for speculation. The cult is free of rites to placate ghosts and demons, and there is no ancestor worship. Further, divination (such as investigating the livers of sacrificial animals) is forbidden. In essence, the Biblical narratives are simplified and demythologized. There are no myths of the birth of gods, their rivalries, sexual relations or accounts of death and resurrection. Moreover, there is no mention of fate to which both men and gods are subject. Rather, the Hebrew Bible concentrates on the moral condition of humankind within the context of divine providence.

Such demythologization is a particular feature of the Biblical narratives. According to modern scholarship, the priestly editors composed a **creation** account (Genesis 1–2:4) markedly different from the Babylonian narrative. In the *Enuma Elish* – a reworking of old Sumerian themes – the primordial powers Tiamat (salt water) and Apsu (sweet water) gave birth to a pair of forces which engendered other gods such as Anu (the god of heaven) and Ea (the god of running waters). Later Tiamat with her second husband and an army of gods and monsters attack the younger gods. Marduk, the god of Babylonia, however slaughters

Tiamat and from her corpse fashions the cosmos and from the blood of her consort Ea makes man.

Though there are echoes of this mythology in the Bible, Genesis decrees that God created the universe without any struggle against other gods. The entities created by God's fiat have no divine aspect. Further, the abyss (in Hebrew *tehom* which is etymologically related to Tiamat) simply refers to the original state of the universe after a primary substance – an unformed and watery chaos – came into existence. Turning to the flood story – a central element of Mesopotamian myth – the Bible ignores such details as the gods' terror at the cataclysms accompanying the flood. In the Epic of Gilgamesh the flood is seen as the god Enlil's remedy to reduce the level of human noise in the world. The Bible, however, proclaims that man's wickedness is its cause; and when the flood comes, God gives laws to restrain future human evil and promises that this devastation will never happen again. A comparison of texts from the Babylonian flood story and the Hebrew Bible forcefully illustrates the demythologizing intention of the Biblical authors:

SOURCES

Creation

In these passages the Hebrew writer has reshaped this myth to emphasize God's dominion over the cosmos as well as his concern for human morality. By refashioning the myths of the ancient Near East, the Israelites proclaimed the God of Israel as the creator and ruler over all things.

Gilgamesh Epic (eleventh canto)

I sent forth a dove and let her go,
The dove went to and fro,
But there was no resting place, and she returned.
Then I sent forth a raven and let her go.
The raven flew away, she beheld the abatement
  of waters,
And she came near, wading and croaking, but did
  not return.
Then I sent everything forth to the four quarters of
  heaven, I offered sacrifice,
I made a libation on the peak of the mountain.
By sevens I set out the vessels,
Under them I heaped up reed and cedarwood and
  myrtle,

The gods smelt the sweet savour,
The gods gathered like flies about him that offered
  up the sacrifice.

Genesis 8

Then he sent forth a dove from him to see if the waters had subsided from the face of the ground; but the dove found no place to set her foot, and she returned to him . . .

He waited another seven days, and sent forth the dove . . . and she did not return to him any more . . .

So Noah went forth and his sons and his wife and

his sons' wives went with him. And every creeping thing, and every bird, everything that moves upon the earth, went forth by families out of the ark.

Then Noah built up an altar to the Lord, and took of every clean animal and of every clean bird, and offered burnt offerings on the altar.

And when the Lord smelled the pleasing odour, the Lord said in his heart, 'I will never again curse the ground because of man, for the imagination of man's heart is evil from his youth; neither will I ever again destroy every living creature as I have done'.

[*Gilgamesh Epic*, in SBW, p. 51]

Magic

Like the peoples of the ancient Near East, the Israelites believed in miraculous powers:

> When Pharaoh says to you, 'Prove yourselves by working a miracle', then you shall say to Aaron, 'Take your rod and cast it down before Pharaoh, that it may become a serpent'. So Moses and Aaron went to Pharaoh and did as the Lord commanded; Aaron cast down his rod before Pharaoh and his servants, and it became a serpent. Then Pharaoh summoned the wise men and the sorcerers; and they also, the magicians of Egypt, did the same by their secret arts. For every man cast down his rod, and they became serpents. But Aaron's rod swallowed up their rods.

(Exodus 7:9–12)

Blessings and Curses

The ancient Israelites, like those among whom they lived, believed in the power of blessings and curses:

> And Balaam took up his discourse and said,
> 'From Aram Balak has brought me,
> the king of Moab from the eastern mountains:
> "Come, curse Jacob for me,
> and come, denounce Israel!"
> How can I curse whom God has not cursed?
> How can I denounce whom the Lord has not denounced?
> For from the top of the mountains I see him,
> from the hills I behold him;
> lo, a people dwelling alone,
> and not reckoning itself among the nations!
> Who can count the dust of Jacob,
> or number the fourth part of Israel?
> Let me die the death of the righteous,
> and let my end be like his!'

And Balak said to Balam, 'What have you done to me? I took you to curse my enemies, and behold you have done nothing but bless them.' And he answered, 'Must I not take heed to speak what the Lord puts in my mouth?'

(Numbers 23:7–12)

Creation

In these passages the Hebrew writer has reshaped this myth to emphasize God's dominion over the cosmos. By refashioning the myths of the ancient Near East, the Israelites proclaimed the God of Israel as the creator and ruler of all things:

In the beginning God created the heavens and the earth. And the earth was without form and void, and darkness was upon the face of the deep, and the Spirit of Good was moving over the face of the waters. And God said, 'Let there be light'; and there was light. And God saw the light was good; and God separated the light from the darkness. God called the light Day, and the darkness he called Night. And there was evening and there was morning, one day. And God said, 'Let there be a firmament in the midst of the waters, and let it separate the waters from the waters.' And God made the firmament and separated the waters which were under the firmament from the waters which were above the firmament. And it was so. And God called the firmament Heaven. And there was evening and there was morning, a second day. And God said, 'Let the waters under the heavens be gathered together into one place, and let the dry land appear.' And it was so. God called the dry land Earth, and the waters that were gathered together he called Seas. And God saw that it was good. And God said, 'Let the earth put forth vegetation, plants yielding seed, and fruit trees bearing fruit in which is their seed, each according to its kind upon the earth.' And it was so. The earth brought forth vegetation, plants yielding seed according to their own kinds, and trees bearing fruit in which is their seed, each according to its kind. And God saw that it was good. And there was evening and there was morning, a third day. And God said, 'Let there be lights in the firmament of the heavens to separate the day from the night; and let them be for signs and for seasons and for days and years, and let them be lights in the firmament of the heavens to give light upon the earth.' And it was so. And God made the two great lights, the greater light to rule the day, and the lesser light to rule the night; he made the stars also. And God set them in the firmament of the heavens to give light upon the earth, to rule over the day and over the night, and to separate the light from the darkness. And God saw that it was good. And there was evening and there was morning, a fourth day. And God said, 'Let the waters bring forth swarms of living creatures, and let birds fly above the earth across the firmament of the heavens.' So God created the great sea monsters and every living creature that moves, with which the waters swarm, according to their kind. And God saw that it was good. And God blessed them, saying, 'Be fruitful and multiply and fill the waters in the seas, and let the birds multiply on the earth.' And there was evening and there was morning, a fifth day. And God said, 'Let the earth bring forth living creatures according to their kinds: cattle and creeping things and beasts of the earth according to their kinds.' And it was so. And God made the beasts of the earth, each according to its kind. And God saw that it was good. Then God said, 'Let us make man in our image, after our likeness, and let them have dominion over the fish of the sea, and over the birds of the air, and over the cattle, and over all the earth, and over every creeping thing that creeps upon the earth.' So God created man in his own image, in the image of God he created him; male and female he created them. And God blessed them, and God said to them, 'Be fruitful and multiply, and fill the earth and subdue it; and have dominion over the fish of the sea and over the birds of the air and over every living thing that moves upon the earth.' And God said, 'Behold, I have given you every plant yielding seed which is upon the face of all the earth, and every tree with seed in its fruit; you shall have them for food. And to every beast of the earth, and to every bird of the air, and to everything that creeps upon the earth, everything that has the breath of life, I have given every green plant for food.' And it was so. And God saw everything that he had made, and behold, it was very good. And there was evening and there was morning, a sixth day.

(Genesis 1:1–31)

DISCUSSION

1. How did the ancient Israelites demythologize the Babylonian epics?

2. Discuss the nature of miracles in the Five Books of Moses.

FURTHER READING

Arnold, Bill T., Beyer, Bryan (eds), *Readings from the Ancient Near East: Primary Sources for Old Testament Study*, Baker Book House, 2002.

Benjamin, Don C., Matthews, Victor Harold, *Old Testament Parallels: Laws and Stories from the Ancient Near East*, Paulist Press, 1997.

Clifford, Richard J., *Creation Accounts in the Ancient Near East and in the Bible*, Catholic Biblical Association, 1994.

Epstein, Leon, *Social Justice in the Ancient Near East and the People of the Bible*, Trinity Press International, 1986.

Gordon, Cyrus H., Rendsburg, Gary A., *The Bible and the Ancient Near East*, W.W. Norton and Co., 1998.

Greenspahn, Fred (ed.), *Essential Papers on Israel and the Ancient Near East*, New York University Press, 1991.

Huong, Xuan Thi Pham, *Mourning in the Ancient Near East and the Hebrew Bible*, Sheffield Academic Press, 2001.

Kang, Sa-Moon, *Divine War in the Old Testament and in the Ancient Near East*, Walter de Gruyter, 1989.

Matthews, Victor Harold, Levinson, Bernard M., Frymer-Kensky, Tikva (eds), *Gender and Law in the Hebrew Bible and the Ancient Near East*, Sheffield Academic Press, 1998.

Pritchard, James Bennett (ed.), *Ancient Near East in Pictures Relating to the Old Testament with Supplement*, Princeton University Press, 1965.

Pritchard, James Bennett (ed.), *Ancient Near East: An Anthology of Texts and Pictures*, Princeton University Press, 1965.

Vaux, Roland de, *The Bible and the Ancient Near East*, Darton, Longman and Todd, 1972.

Weinfeld, Moshe, *Social Justice in Ancient Israel and in the Ancient Near East*, Fortress Press, 1995.

Wold, Donald J., *Out of Order: Homosexuality in the Bible and the Ancient Near East*, Baker Book House, 1998.

Wright, Ernest G., *Bible and the Ancient Near East: Essays in Honor of William Foxwell Albright*, Eisenbrauns, 1979.

CHAPTER 3

Israelite Monotheism and Law

Timeline:

c. 1275–1250 BCE Exodus from Egypt

13th–12th century BCE Wave of invasions in Syria and Palestine

Figure 3 Code of Hammurabi. The code of this famous reformer and legislator was carved on this stele. Copyright photo RMN-Hervè Lewandowski. (In the Louvre.)

According to some scholars, the beginnings of Israelite monotheism stemmed from a disillusionment with Mesopotamian religion in the second millennium.

These scholars attribute this radical break to Abraham's discovery that the concept of universal justice must rest on the belief in one supreme God. Other scholars see Moses as the principal architect of Israelite monotheism; they point out that before Moses there was evidence of monotheistic belief in the religious reforms of the Egyptian Pharaoh Akhenaton in the fourteenth century BCE. In this light, Moses is seen as following the path of this Egyptian revolutionary figure. However, other scholars contend that it is unlikely that monotheism can be attributed to Abraham or Moses. Such a view, they insist, conflicts with the Biblical narratives of the tribal and monarchial periods that give evidence of a struggle on the part of some Israelites to remain faithful to God in the face of competing deities. For these writers, monotheism should be understood as the result of a clash of cults and religious concepts.

According to this latter view, Israelite religion was not monotheism but monolatry: the worship of one God despite the admitted existence of other gods. This may have been the meaning of Deuteronomy 6:4 ('Hear, O Israel: the Lord our God is one Lord'). With this view, the God of Israel was conceived as the divine being who revealed his will to Israel, inspired its leaders, protected the Israelites in the wanderings, and led them to the Promised Land. The worship of any other deity was betrayal and blasphemy. Instead of symbolizing the cycle of nature like the Canaanite deities, the Israelite God was a redeemer who liberated his people from slavery. It was this God, not the

Canaanite El, who was the creator of heaven and earth. He, not Baal, was the source of rain and agricultural fertility. Through his action – rather than that of Ashur or Marduk – the Assyrian and Babylonian conquest took place.

Monotheism was thus a later development in the history of Israel; it occurred when foreign gods were seen as simply the work of men's hands. Possibly this was the view of Elijah in the ninth century BCE when, confronting the prophets of Baal, he declared: 'The Lord, he is God; the Lord he is God.' (l Kings 18:39). Certainly by the time of Jeremiah (several decades before the Babylonian exile), monotheism appears to have taken a firm hold on the Israelite community. In the words of Jeremiah: 'Their idols are like scarecrows in a cucumber field, and they cannot speak; they have to be carried for they cannot walk. Be not afraid of them, for they cannot do evil, neither is it in them to do good' (Jeremiah 10:5). According to some scholars, Psalm 82 gives evidence of this transition from monolatry to monotheism. Here the psalmist declares that God rebukes the other gods for their injustice and deprives them of divine status and immortality.

Turning from this issue to that of law, Biblical scholars have become increasingly aware of the degree to which the Biblical writers utilized ancient **Near Eastern treaties** as models for legal codes. Israel's covenant with God, for example, has been traced back to king–vassal treaties of the Hittites in the second millennium BCE and of the Assyrians in the first millennium BCE. These political documents usually include a historical prologue describing the benevolent acts of the rulers, as well as stipulations that the vassal accepts the provision for the deposit of the treaty in the sanctuary, an agreement about its periodic recitation, and an indication of the punishments if the agreement is broken and of rewards if it is kept. As Biblical scholars stress, such features are also present to some degree in the central collections of law in the Five Books of Moses.

The older corpus of Biblical law is found in the Book of the Covenant (Exodus 20–23). God's speech in Exodus 19:4–6 serves as an introduction; the specific laws that follow are the covenantal stipulations that Israel agrees to follow: the sacrificial meal of Exodus 24:9–11 is a ceremony of acceptance; Deuteronomy 12–26 is the second collection of law, and is largely a revision of the Book of the Covenant. The law is presented as a speech by Moses to the people on the plains of Moab just before his death. It is prefaced by a review of what God has done for Israel, and is followed by a list of blessings and curses which will befall the people for their loyalty or disobedience to God's decrees. The third corpus of law is the priestly material (Exodus 25 to Numbers 10) which contains the Holiness Code (Leviticus 17–26).

Despite differences in detail, these three legal collections have much in common. All condemn murder, robbery, incest and adultery; each requires respect for parents and strict justice in the courts. The laws protect the rights of the stranger and the impoverished. There is provision made for the liberation of slaves and rest for the soil. Certain locations are to be set aside as refuges for those who unintentionally committed manslaughter. Destruction of idols and a ban on divination are also stipulated. Observance of the Passover and festivals is required. Tithes are to be given to priests and Levites. The first-born of animals and men belong to God but may be redeemed. As scholars have noted, this compilation of moral, civil and criminal law draws extensively on ancient Near Eastern precedent in various spheres. First, the civil and criminal code borrows from Mesopotamian legislation, reshaping laws according to the characteristic features of the religion of ancient Israel. A second feature of the Mesopotamian law code – the protection of the dignity and purity of the family – was also a central aspect of Biblical legislation. Severe punishments were enjoined against acts that undermine family life (such as incest, sodomy and bestiality).

A third area of borrowing from Near Eastern culture deals with the dichotomy between the holy and the profane. All Near Eastern cultures subscribed to the conviction that the sacred is a source of danger, and Biblical writers similarly were convinced that supernatural danger stems from God. 1 and 2 Samuel, for example, emphasize the power inherent in the Ark of the Covenant. The Pentateuch focuses on dangers faced by priests in handling holy objects in the sanctuary. Diseases and plagues are brought about by God. In priestly law there is a contaminating substance that adheres to things and people and can only be eliminated through religious rites. The impure must be kept from contact with sanctuary vessels, offerings, priests, the holy city and the holy land, yet through the passage of time and immersion in water such pollution can be removed.

The sacrificial system is a fourth area of borrowing from the ancient Near East. Yet, unlike the myths of Mesopotamia, God in the Bible is not dependent on nourishment from sacrifices. Instead, sacrifice serves as a means by which the Israelites are able to establish a relationship with their God. Some offerings express thanksgiving, gratitude and reverence, whereas others effect expiation through blood poured on the altar. Since blood was understood as the principle of life, the blood of an actual victim symbolized atonement for the guilt of the offender. Unless such offerings were made, the wrath of God could be kindled with terrible consequences.

A final sphere of borrowing concerned the major festivals. All the Israelites' agricultural celebrations seem to have been adopted from Canaanite practices and were transformed into occasions of pilgrimage to God's sanctuary in order to celebrate his role in bestowing fertility on nature.

From this survey it is clear that law in Torah was drawn and modified from the legal collections and political treaties of neighbouring peoples. The Biblical writers utilized concepts of election and covenant to give authority to their legal system. God was conceived as supreme and worthy of worship. Israel was obligated to serve him with fidelity. In such a context, justice was a cardinal obligation imposed on the leaders of the people, and Israelite society as a whole as a result of their relationship with God. Law in ancient Israel was not simply the concern of the elite as in the ancient Near East. Rather, legal obligations were at the centre of public life. In numerous cases no reasons were given why laws should be obeyed. They were simply decrees to be followed by all. As a result, the study and interpretation of law came to be a central preoccupation in the religious life of the nation.

SOURCES

Code of Hammurabi

The *Code of Hammurabi* was discovered in 1901. Hammurabi is believed to be the Amraphel referred to in Genesis 14:1; his date has been given as about 2130–2088 BCE. There are parallels between this *Code* and the laws of the ancient Israelites.

> If a physician operate on a man for a severe wound (or make a severe wound upon a man) with a bronze lancet and save the man's life; or if he open an abscess (in the eye) of a man with a bronze lancet and save that man's eye, he shall receive 10 shekels of silver (as his fee).
>
> If he be a freeman, he shall receive 5 shekels.
>
> If he be a man's slave, the owner of the slave shall give 2 shekels of silver to the physician.
>
> If a physician operate on a man for a wound with a bronze lancet and cause the man's death; or open an abscess (in the eye) of a man with a bronze lancet and destroy the man's eye, they shall cut off his fingers.
>
> If a physician operate on a slave of a freeman for a severe wound with a bronze lancet and cause his death, he shall restore a slave of equal value.
>
> If he open an abscess (in his eye) with a bronze lancet, and destroy his eye, he shall pay silver to the extent of one-half of his price.
>
> If a physician set a broken bone for a man or cure his diseased bowels, the patient shall give 5 shekels of silver to the physician.

If he be a freeman, he shall give 3 shekels of silver.

If it be a man's slave, the owner of the slave shall give 2 shekels of silver to the physician.

If a man hire a man to oversee his farm and furnish him with seed-grain and entrust him with oxen and contract with him to cultivate the field, and that man steal either the seed or the crop and it be found in his possession, they shall cut off his fingers.

If he take the seed-grain and overwork the oxen, he shall restore the quantity of grain which has been hoed.

If he let the oxen of the man on hire, or steal the seed-grain and there be no crop in the field, they shall call that man to account, and he shall measure out 60 *gur* of grain per *gan*.

If he be not able to meet his obligation, they shall leave him in that field with the cattle.

If a man hire a field-labourer, he shall pay him 8 *gur* of grain per year.

If a man hire a herdsman, he shall pay him 6 *gur* of grain per year.

If a man steal a watering-machine in a field, he shall pay 5 shekels of silver to the owner of the watering-machine.

If a man steal a watering bucket or a harrow, he shall pay 3 shekels of silver.

If a man hire a herdsman to pasture oxen or sheep, he shall pay him 8 *gur* of grain per year.

(*Code of Hammurabi* in SBW, pp. 44–45)

DISCUSSION

1. Compare the *Code of Hammurabi* with law in the Bible.

2. Discuss the traditional Jewish belief that Moses was the author of the Five Books of Moses.

FURTHER READING

Ball, Milner S., *Called by Stories: Biblical Sagas and Their Challenge for Law*, Duke University Press, 2000.

Blenkinsopp, Joseph, *Wisdom and Law in the Old Testament: The Ordering of Life in Israel and Early Judaism*, Oxford University Press, 1995.

Brin, Gershon, *Studies in Biblical Law: From the Hebrew Bible to the Dead Sea Scrolls*, Sheffield Academic Press, 1994.

Brueggemann, Patrick Miller, D. (eds), *The Covenanted Self: Explorations in Law and Covenant*, Fortress, 1999.

Falk, Zeev, *Hebrew Law in Biblical Times: An Introduction*, FARMS, 2001.

Horowitz, George, *The Spirit of Jewish Law: A Brief Account of Biblical and Rabbinic Jurisprudence, with a Special Note on Jewish Law and the State of Israel*, Associated Faculty Press Inc., 1985.

Jackson, Bernard S., *Studies in the Semiotics of Biblical Law*, Sheffield Academic Press, 2001.

Marshall, Jay W., *Israel and the Book of the Covenant: An Anthropological Approach to Biblical Law*, Society of Biblical Literature, 1993.

Matthews, Victor Harold, Levinson, Bernard M., Frymer-Kensky, Tikva (eds), *Gender and Law in the Hebrew Bible and the Ancient Near East*, Sheffield Academic Press, 1998.

Smith, John Merlin Powis, *The Origin and History of Hebrew Law*, Hyperion Press, 1990.

Versteeg, Russ (ed.), *Early Mesopotamian Law*, Carolina Academic Press, 2000.

Westbrook, Raymond, *Studies in Biblical and Cuneiform Law*, J. Gabalda Tobi Roth, Martha, Law Collections from Mesopotamia and Asia Minor, Society of Biblical Literature, 1997.

CHAPTER 4

The Patriarchs

Timeline:

c. 1900–1600 BCE Patriarchal period

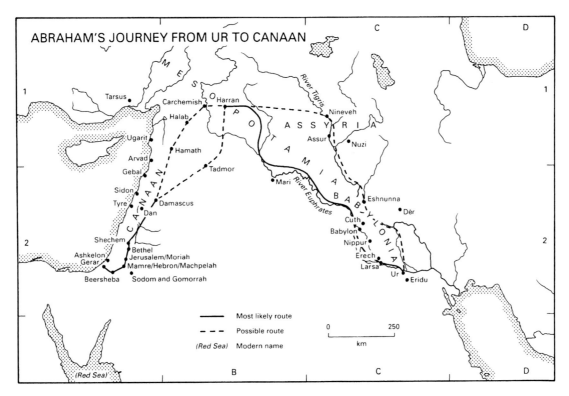

Map 3 Abraham's journey from Ur to Canaan

According to the Biblical narrative, Abraham was the father of the Jewish nation. Originally known as Abram, he came from Ur of the Chaldaeans, a Sumerian city of Mesopotamia. Together with his father Terah, his wife Sarai, and his nephew Lot, he travelled to Harran, a trading centre in northern Syria. There his father died, and God called him to go to Canaan: 'Go from your country and your kindred and your father's house to the land I will show you. And I will make of you a great nation' (Genesis 12:1–2). During a famine in Canaan, he went to Egypt, and then proceeded to the Negeb. Finally he settled in the plains near Hebron. Here he experienced a revelation which confirmed that his deliverance from Ur was an

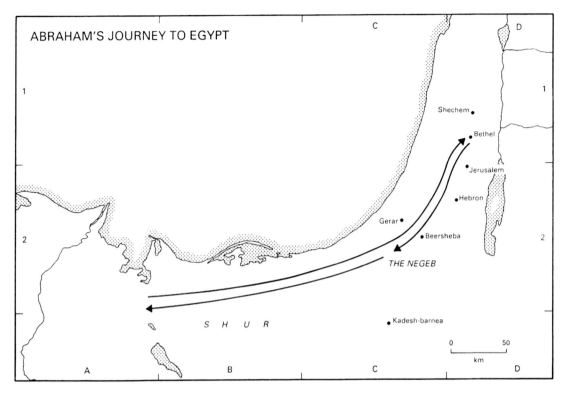

Map 4 Abraham's journey to Egypt

act of providence: 'I am the Lord who brought you from Ur of the Chaldaeans to give you this land to possess' (Genesis 15:7).

The Bible relates that since Sarai had not given birth to children, Abram had relationship with her servant girl, Hagar, who gave birth to Ishmael. However, when Abram was ninety-nine and Sarai ninety, God granted them a son, Isaac. It was then that Abram was given his new name, Abraham ('the father of a multitude'), and Sarai was renamed Sarah ('princess'). When Isaac was born, Abraham sent Hagar and Ishmael away at Sarah's request.

During this time God made a covenant with Abraham symbolized by an act of circumcision: 'You shall be circumcised in the flesh of your foreskins and it shall be a sign of the covenant between me and you' (Genesis 17:11). Later God tested Abraham's dedication by ordering him to sacrifice **Isaac**, only telling him at the last moment to refrain. When Isaac became older, Abraham sent a servant to his kinsfolk in Hebron to find a wife, and the messenger returned

with Rebecca. After many years, God answered Isaac's prayers for a son, and twins – Esau and Jacob – were born.

Jacob bought his brother's birthright for food, and with his mother's help secured Isaac's blessing, thereby incurring Esau's wrath. Fleeing from his brother, Jacob travelled northwards towards Harran; en route he had a vision of a ladder rising to heaven and heard God speak to him promising that his offspring would inherit the land and fill the earth:

And he dreamed that there was a ladder set up on the earth, and the top of it reached to heaven; and behold, the angels of God were ascending and descending on it! And behold, the Lord stood above it and said, 'I am the Lord, the God of Abraham your father and the God of Isaac; the land on which you lie I will give to you and to your descendants; and your descendants shall be like the dust of the earth.'

(Genesis 28:12–14)

After arriving in Harran, Jacob worked for twenty years as a shepherd for his uncle Laban. There he married Laban's daughters, Rachel and Leah, and they and their maids (Bilhah and Zilpah) bore twelve sons and a daughter. When he eventually returned to Canaan, Jacob wrestled with a mysterious stranger in the gorge of the Jabbok river, a tributary of the Jordan, where God bestowed upon him the new name 'Israel'.

> When the man saw that he did not prevail against Jacob, he touched the hollow of his thigh; and Jacob's thigh was put out of joint as he wrestled with him. Then he said, 'Let me go, for the day is breaking.' But Jacob said, 'I will not let you go, unless you bless me.' And he said to him, 'What is your name?' And he said, 'Your name shall no more be called Jacob, but Israel for you have striven with God and with men and have prevailed.'
>
> (Genesis 32:25–28)

Jacob was welcomed by Esau in Edom, but then the brothers parted. Jacob lived in Canaan until one of his sons, Joseph, invited him to settle in Egypt where he died at the age of 147.

For some time scholars have sought to relate these patriarchal stories to the Biblical period. In particular they emphasized, on the basis of ancient documents found at the Mesopotamian sites of Mari and Nuzi, that the accounts of the Hebrew patriarchs accurately reflect the conditions of the Middle Bronze Age period (2000–1500 BCE). Names like Abraham, Isaac and Jacob, for example, have been found in numerous texts – they appear to have been especially popular among the Amorites. Other names from Genesis as well (such as Terah and Ishmael) were also widely used. Furthermore, these ancient documents illustrate that the wandering of the patriarchs mirrors what is known of life in the early part of the second millennium BCE.

The legal documents found at Nuzi also help to explain patriarchal customs. For example, the story of Sarai presenting Abraham with a slave girl by whom to have a child is paralleled by a text from Nuzi which explains how in certain marriage contracts a childless wife could be required to provide her husband with a substitute. Again, Nuzi law stipulates that childless couples could ensure the continuation of their family by adopting a slave who would take the place of a son. This child would then inherit their property, but if a natural son were eventually born the slave son would lose his inheritance rights. Such a law is paralleled by Genesis 15:1–4 where Abraham expresses a fear that his slave Eliezer could succeed him. Though these Mari and Nuzi texts do not specifically refer to the patriarchs themselves, it is apparent that Genesis legends are in accord with some of the laws and customs of the second millennium BCE. Thus there is good reason to believe that the Genesis narrative may have preserved an accurate picture of the earliest ancestors of the Jewish people.

This history of the three patriarchs is followed by the cycle of stories about Jacob's son **Joseph**. As a young boy, Joseph was presented with a special coat (or a long sleeved robe) of many colours as a sign that he was his father's favourite. When he was in Shechem helping his brothers tend his family's flocks he angered them by recounting dreams in which they bowed down before him. They reacted by plotting his death, but one of his brothers (Reuben) persuaded them to wait, and another (Judah) suggested that they should sell him as a slave rather than kill him. Eventually Joseph was taken to Egypt; his brothers dipped his coat in a kid's blood and declared to their father that he had been mauled by a wild animal.

In Egypt Joseph served in the house of Potiphar but was falsely accused by **Potiphar's wife** of rape and incarcerated in prison. Some time later he was set free by the reigning pharaoh to interpret his dreams and subsequently became chief minister of the land. After a famine, he made the country rich and later encountered his brothers who came before him to buy grain. Movingly he revealed to them his true identity, and God's providential care. Joseph died when he was 110, and his family remained and flourished in Egypt. But with the reign of a new pharaoh 'who did not know Joseph' (Exodus 1:8), the Jewish people were oppressed and persecuted and forced to work as slaves on the construction of the royal cities of Pithom and Raamses. Finally the pharaoh declared that all male offspring should be killed at birth.

Scholars point out that the Joseph legends consist of a collection of stories which were woven together into a complex form. Yet it is recognized that Semitic speaking groups had for centuries been emigrating into

Egypt to escape the adverse conditions in the north as well as to find food and engage in trade. The tomb-paintings of 1900–1890 BCE at Beni-Hasan, for example, portray a group of such aliens led by Ibsha (or Abishar) and accompanied by donkeys bringing lead sulphide from the Red Sea. From the later eighteenth century BCE onwards such immigration appears to have been widespread as is evidenced by the Canaanite influence on Egyptian culture and ritual. It is possible that the Joseph legends derive from such a pattern of immigration. Some scholars have pointed out that if the story of Joseph took place in the time of the Hyksos empire in Egypt, it is possible that these non-Egyptian Semitic-speaking rulers were more likely to appoint an alien like Joseph to a position of authority. The new king who did not know Joseph might have been a native Egyptian pharaoh who came to power after the Hyksos had been overthrown.

Other scholars date the Joseph story much later; they suggest that the ancient Hebrews may have migrated to Egypt during the reign of Pharaoh Seti I (1304–1290 BCE), the son of Rameses I. Seti re-established Egyptian dominance over Canaan; it was he who moved his capital to Tanis in the eastern delta where, according to the Psalms, Joseph and his followers resided (Psalm 78:12, 43). In either case, the pharaoh 'who did not know Joseph' may have been Rameses II (1290–1224 BCE) who, scholars believe, built the cities of Pithom and Raamses. The successor of Rameses II was Merneptah (1224–1211 BCE). On a large black granite stele of Merneptah is inscribed an account of an alleged military victory mentioning Israel: 'Israel is laid waste; its (grain) seed is not'. It is possible that this inscription provides historical corroboration for the existence of the house of Joseph in Egypt at this time.

SOURCES

The Sacrifice of Isaac

The Book of Genesis records the sacrifice of Isaac; here Abraham is willing to offer his son to God as a sacrifice out of obedience to the Lord:

After these things God tested Abraham, and said to him, 'Abraham!' And he said, 'Here am I.' He said, 'Take your son, your only son Isaac, whom you love, and go to the land of Moriah, and offer him there as a burnt offering upon one of the mountains of which I shall tell you.' So Abraham rose early in the morning, saddled his ass, and took two of his young men with him, and his son Isaac; and he cut the wood for the burnt offering, and arose and went to the place of which God had told him. On the third day Abraham lifted up his eyes and saw the place afar off. Then Abraham said to his young men, 'Stay here with the ass; I and the lad will go yonder and worship, and come again to you.' And Abraham took the wood of the burnt offering, and laid it on Isaac his son; and he took in his hand the fire and the knife. So they went both of them together. And Isaac said to his father Abraham, 'My father!' And he said, 'Here am I, my son.' He said, 'Behold, the fire and the wood; but where is the lamb for a burnt offering?'

Abraham said, 'God will provide himself the lamb for a burnt offering, my son.' So they went both of them together. When they came to the place of which God had told him, Abraham built an altar there, and laid the wood in order, and bound Isaac his son, and laid him on the altar, upon the wood. Then Abraham put forth his hand, and took the knife to slay his son. But the angel of the Lord called to him from heaven, and said, 'Abraham, Abraham!' And he said, 'Here am I.' He said, 'Do not lay your hand on the lad or do anything to him; for now I know that you fear God, seeing you have not withheld your son, your only son, from me.' And Abraham lifted up his eyes and looked, and behold, behind him was a ram, caught in a thicket by his horns; and Abraham went and took the ram, and offered it up as a burnt offering instead of his son. So Abraham called the name of that place 'the Lord will provide'; as it is said to this day, 'On the mount of the Lord it shall be provided.' (Genesis 22:1–14)

Figure 4 The Sacrifice of Isaac, fresco, 1726–28. Artist: Tiepolo, Giambattista: 1696–1770: Italian. Copyright The Art Archive/Palazzo dello Arcivescovado Udine/Dagli Orti.

Joseph and His Brothers

Out of hatred for their brother Joseph, his brothers captured him and sold him to a travelling group of merchants who were on their way to Egypt:

Joseph, being seventeen years old, was shepherding the flock with his brothers; he was a lad with the sons of Bilhah and Zilpah, his father's wives; and Joseph brought an ill report of them to their father. Now Israel loved Joseph more than any other of his children because he was the son of his old age; and he made him a long robe with sleeves. But when his brothers saw that their father loved him more than all his brothers, they hated him, and could not speak peaceably to him. Now Joseph had a dream, and when he told it to his brothers they only hated him the more. He said to them, 'Hear this dream which I have dreamed: behold, we were binding sheaves in the field, and lo, my sheaf arose and stood upright; and behold, your sheaves gathered round it, and bowed down to my sheaf.' His brothers said to him, 'Are you indeed to reign over us? Or are you indeed to have dominion over us?' So they hated him yet more for his dreams and for his words. Then he dreamed another dream, and told it to his brothers, and said, 'Behold I have dreamed another dream; and behold, the sun, the moon, and eleven stars were bowing down to me.' But when he told it to his father and to his brothers, his father rebuked him, and said to him, 'What is this dream that you have dreamed. Shall I and your mother and your brothers indeed come to bow ourselves to the ground before you?' And his brothers were jealous of him, but his father kept the saying in mind. Now his brothers went to pasture their father's flock near Shechem. And Israel said to Joseph, 'Are not your brothers pasturing the flock at Shechem? Come, I will send you to them.' And he said to him, 'Here I am.' So he said to him, 'Go now, see if it is is well with your brothers, and with the flock; and bring me word again.' . . . So Joseph went after his brothers, and found them at Dothan. They saw him afar off, and before he came near to them they conspired against him to kill him. They said to one another, 'Here comes this dreamer. Come now, let us kill him and throw him into one of the pits; then we shall say that a wild beast has devoured him, and we shall see what will become of his dreams.' But when Reuben heard it, he delivered him out of their hands, saying, 'Let us not take his life.' And Reuben said to them, 'Shed no blood; cast him into this pit here in the wilderness, but lay no hand upon him' – that he might rescue him out of their hand, to restore him to his father. So when Joseph came to his brothers, they stripped him of his robe, and the long robe with sleeves that he wore; and they took him and cast him into a pit. The pit was empty, there was no water in it. Then they sat down to eat; and looking up they saw a caravan of Ishmaelites coming from Gilead, with their camels bearing gum, balm, and myrrh, on their way to carry it down to Egypt. Then Judah said to his brothers, 'What profit is it if we slay our brother and conceal his blood? Come, let us sell him to the Ishmaelites, and let not our hand be upon him, for he is our brother, our own flesh.' And his brothers heeded him. Then Midianite traders passed by; and they drew Joseph up and lifted him out of the pit, and sold him to the Ishmaelites for twenty shekels of silver; and they took Joseph to Egypt. When Reuben returned to the pit and saw that Joseph was not in the pit, he rent his clothes and returned to his brothers, and said, 'The lad is gone; and I, where shall I go? Then they took Joseph's robe, and killed a goat, and dipped the robe in the blood; and they rent the long robe with sleeves and brought it to their father, and said, 'This we have found; see now whether it is your son's robe or not.' And he recognized it, and said, 'It is my son's robe; a wild beast has devoured him; Joseph is without doubt torn in to pieces.' Then Jacob rent his garments, and put sackcloth upon his loins, and mourned for his son many days.

(Genesis 37:2–14, 17–34)

Potiphar's Wife

In Egypt Joseph was employed in Potiphar's house; there Potiphar's wife sought to seduce him:

Now Joseph was handsome and good-looking. And after a time his master's wife cast her eyes upon Joseph, and said, 'Lie with me.' But he refused and said to his master's wife, 'Lo, having me my master has no concern about anything in the house, and he has put everything that he has in my hand; he is not greater in this house than I am, nor has he kept back anything from me except yourself, because you are his wife; how then can I do this great wickedness, and sin against God?' And although she spoke to Joseph day after day, he would not listen to her, to lie with her or to be with her. But one day, when he went into the house to do his work and none of the men of the house were there in the house, she caught him by his garment, saying, 'Lie with me'; But he left his garment in her hand, and fled and got out of the house. And when she saw that he had left his garment in her hand, and had fled out of the house, she called to the men of her household and said to them, 'See, he has brought among us a Hebrew to insult us; he came in to me to lie with me, and I cried out with a loud voice; and when he heard that I lifted up my voice, and cried, he left his garment with me, and fled and got out of the house.' Then she laid up his garment by her until his master came home, and she told him the same story, saying, 'The Hebrew servant, whom you have brought among us, came in to me to insult me; but as soon as I lifted up my voice and cried, he left his garment with me, and fled out of the house.' When his master heard the words which his wife spoke to him, 'This is the way your servant treated me', his anger was kindled. And Joseph's master took him and put him into the prison.

(Genesis 39:6–20)

DISCUSSION

1. Discuss the historicity of the patriarchal narratives.

2. In what ways does Scripture present God as involved with his chosen people in the patriarchal narratives?

FURTHER READING

Jordan, James B., *Primeval Saints: Studies in the Patriarchs of Genesis*, Canon Press, 2001.

Malamat, Abraham, *Mari and the Bible*, Brill Academic Publishers, 1998.

McKane, William, *Studies in the Patriarchal Narratives*, Longwood Pr Ltd, 1979.

Pagolu, Augustine, *The Religion of the Patriarchs*, Sheffield Academic Press, 1998.

Shanks, Hershel (ed.), *Abraham and Family: New Insights into the Patriarchal Narratives*, Biblical Archaeology Society, 2000.

Thompson, Thomas L., *The Historicity of the Patriarchal Narratives: The Quest for the Historical Abraham*, Trinity Press International, 2002.

Van Seters, John, *Abraham in History and Tradition*, Yale University Press, 1975.

Westermann, Claus, *The Promises to the Fathers: Studies on the Patriarchal Narratives*, Fortress Press, 1980.

Wiseman, D.J. (ed.), *Essays on the Patriarchal Narratives*, Eisenbrauns, 1983.

Williamson, Paul R., Willard, Paul R., *Abraham, Israel and the Nations: The Patriarchial Promise and its Covenantal Development in Genesis*, Sheffield Academic Press, 2001.

CHAPTER 5

Exodus

Timeline:

c. 1275–1250 BCE Exodus of Israelites from Egypt   *c.* 1250–1200 BCE Israelite conquest in Canaan

The Biblical narrative continues with an account of the deliverance of the Jews from Egyptian bondage. Exodus relates that a son had been born to Amram of the House of Levi and his wife Jochebed. When he was three months old, his parents concealed him among the reeds growing on the banks of the Nile to save him from Pharaoh's decree. Pharaoh's daughter found the child and adopted him as her son, Moses. When he became older, he was incensed and killed a taskmaster who was oppressing a Hebrew slave and fled into the desert. There he lived with Jethro, a priest of Midian, and married his daughter, Zipporah. Eventually God revealed himself to Moses, and commanded that he deliver the chosen people from bondage: 'I am the God of your father, the God of Abraham, the God of Isaac, and the God of Jacob . . . I have seen the affliction of my people who are in Egypt, and have heard their cry because of their taskmasters. I know their sufferings . . . Come, I will send you to Pharaoh that you may bring forth my people, the sons of Israel, out of Egypt (Exodus 3:6–7, 10).

In order to persuade Pharaoh that he should let the Jewish people go, God sent ten plagues on the Egyptians culminating in the slaying of every Egyptian first-born son. The first-born of the Israelites were spared as each family slaughtered a lamb and smeared its blood on the doorposts of their homes. Seeing this, the Angel of Death passed over their household. After this final plague, Pharaoh released the Israelites, and they fled without even waiting for their bread to rise. However, the perils did not end. Pharaoh changed his mind and sent his forces in pursuit. When the Israelites came to an expanse of water, it seemed that they were trapped. Miraculously it was converted to dry land by

a strong wind so they were able to escape. The Egyptians, however, were drowned as they chased after them: 'The Egyptians pursued, and went in after them into the midst of the sea, all Pharaoh's horses, his chariots and the horsemen . . . The waters returned and covered the chariots and the horsemen and all the host of Pharaoh that had followed them into the sea; not so much as one of them remained (Exodus 14:23, 28).

The band of free people then entered the wilderness of Sinai where Moses performed miracles to provide them with food and water (Exodus 16–17). After travelling for about ninety days, they encamped before **Mt Sinai**. God called Moses up to the top of the mountain and told him that if his people would listen to him and keep his covenant, they would become God's special people. They were commanded to wash and purify themselves for two days; on the third day they came to the foot of the mountain amongst thunder, lightning and the sound of a ram's horn to hear God's voice. Alone Moses climbed the mountain again where he remained for forty days. At the end of this period, he returned with two tablets of stone on which were inscribed **God's laws**. But on his return, Moses discovered the people had forsaken him and their God, and in anger he smashed the tablets of stone, only later carving new ones. Subsequently the Jews moved on and came to Kadesh-barnea, near the border of Canaan. There Moses saw the Promised Land from a distance: 'And Moses went up from the plains of Moab to the top of Pisgah, which is opposite Jericho. And the Lord showed him all the land . . . And the Lord said to him, "This is the land of which I swore to Abraham, to Isaac, and to Jacob, 'I will give it to

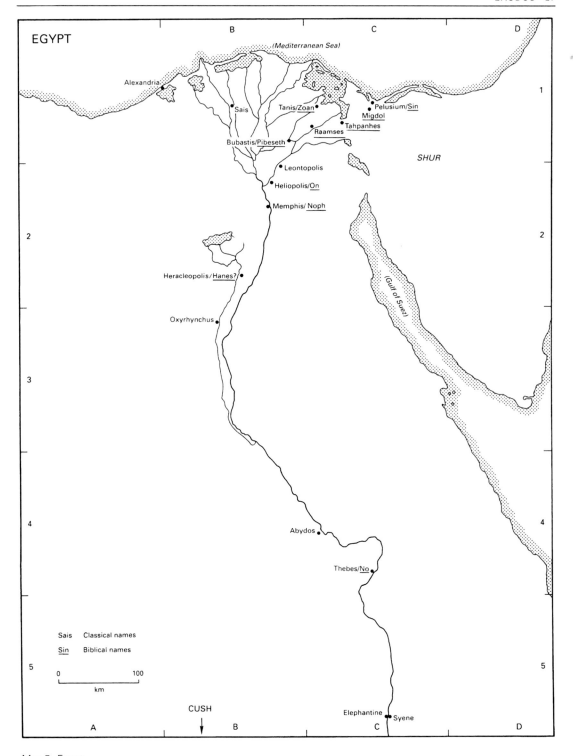

Map 5 Egypt

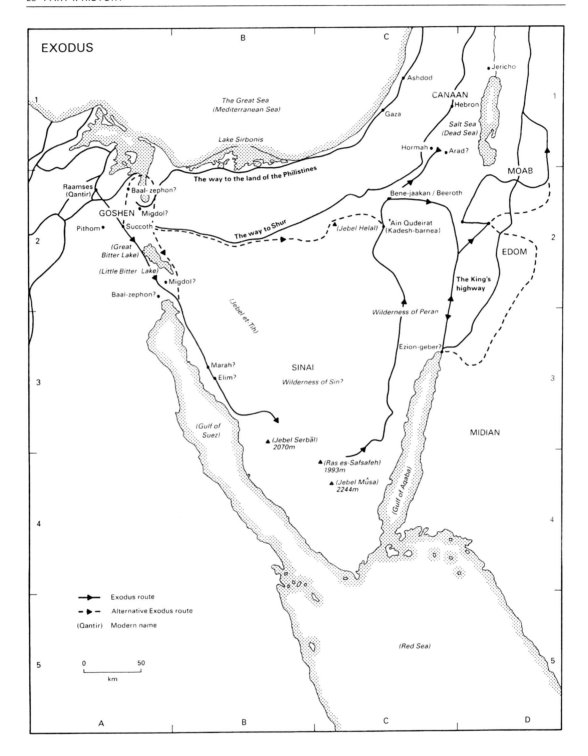

Map 6 Exodus

your descendants.' I have let you see it with your eyes, but you shall not go over there'" (Deuteronomy 34:1, 4).

From a geographical standpoint, there is considerable uncertainty about the details of this narrative account of the Exodus. Some scholars have suggested that the crossing of the Red Sea (or Reed Sea) took place, not at the head of the Gulf of Suez which is a long way from the Israelites' point of departure, but at one of the lakes now joined by the Suez Canal. Other suggestions include the head of the Gulf of Aqaba or alternatively Lake Sirbonis. The mountain where God revealed himself to Moses has traditionally been identified with Jebel Musa in the south of Sinai, but it has been objected that such a location would have taken the Israelites dangerously near the route the Egyptians used to reach copper and turquoise mines in that area. Another suggestion is that the occurrences on the mountain suggest volcanic activity. Since no mountain in the Sinai peninsula is volcanic, it has been advanced that the site was in north-western Arabia, east of the Gulf of Aqaba. Thus the Bible does not enable us to trace the route of the Jewish people in the wilderness. Regarding the date of the Exodus, 1 Kings 6:1 ('In the four hundred and eightieth year after the people of Israel came out of the land of Egypt, in the fourth year of Solomon's reign over Israel, in the month of Ziv, which is the second month, he began to build the house of the Lord') states that it took place 480 years before Solomon founded the Temple (in the fourth year of his reign). Assuming Solomon came to the throne in 961 BCE, the Exodus would have taken

Figure 5 Moses with Tablet of the Law. Artist: Ghent, Justus van: 1410–80?: Flemish. Copyright The Art Archive/ Palazzo Ducale Urbino/Dagli Orti (A).

place in 1438 BCE. But, if the Israelites laboured at Pithom and Raamses as Scripture relates, the Exodus would have taken place much later. Thus it can be seen that from a historical viewpoint, the Exodus narrative poses a number of serious difficulties.

SOURCES

Mount Sinai

For the ancient Israelites, the revelation on Mount Sinai served as the basis of legal obligations:

On the morning of the third day there were thunders and lightnings, and a thick cloud upon the mountain, and a very loud trumpet blast, so that all the people who were in the camp trembled. Then Moses brought the people out of the camp to meet God; and they took their stand at the foot of the mountain. And Mount Sinai was wrapped in smoke, because the Lord descended upon it in fire; and the smoke of it went up like the smoke of a kiln, and the whole mountain quaked greatly. And as the sound of the trumpet grew louder and louder, Moses spoke, and God answered him in thunder. And the Lord came down upon Mount Sinai, to the top of the mountain, and Moses went up. And the Lord said to Moses, 'Go down and warn the people, lest they break through to the Lord to gaze and many of them perish. And also let the priests who come near to the Lord consecrate themselves, lest the Lord break out upon them.' And Moses said to the Lord, 'The people cannot come up to Mount Sinai; for thou thyself didst charge us, saying, "Set bounds about the mountain, and consecrate it."' And the Lord said to him, 'Go down, and come up bringing Aaron with you; but do not let the priests and the people break through to come up to the Lord, lest he break out against them.' So Moses went down to the people and told them.

(Exodus 19:16–25)

The Ten Commandments

The Ten Commandments were revealed by God to Moses on Mt Sinai and have played a central role in the life of the Jewish people:

And God spoke all these words, saying, 'I am the Lord your God, who brought you out of the land of Egypt, out of the house of bondage. You shall have no other gods before me. You shall not make for yourself a graven image, or any likeness of anything that is in heaven above, or that is in the earth beneath, or that is in the water under the earth; you shall not bow down to them or serve them; for I the Lord your God am a jealous God, visiting the iniquity of the fathers upon the children to the third and the fourth generation of those who hate me, but show-ing steadfast love to thousands of those who love me and keep my commandments.

You shall not take the name of the Lord your God in vain; for the Lord will not hold him guiltless who takes his name in vain.

Remember the sabbath day to keep it holy. Six days you shall labour, and do all your work; but the seventh day is a sabbath to the Lord your God; in it you shall not do any work, you, or your son, or your daughter, your manservant, or your maidservant, or your cattle, or the sojourner who is within your gates; for in six days the Lord made heaven and earth, the sea, and all that is in them, and rested the seventh day; therefore the Lord blessed the sabbath day and hallowed it.

Honour your father and your mother, that your days may be long in the land which the Lord your God gives you.

You shall not kill.

You shall not commit adultery.

You shall not steal.

You shall not bear false witness against your neighbour.

You shall not covet your neighbour's house; you shall not covet your neighbour's wife, or his manservant, or his maidservant, or his ox, or his ass, or anything that is your neighbour's.

(Exodus 20:1–17)

DISCUSSION

1. What are the theological perplexities connected with the Scriptural account of God's hardening Pharaoah's heart?

2. Discuss the historical evidence for the Exodus.

FURTHER READING

Childs, Bernard S., *The Book of Exodus: A Critical Theological Commentary*, Westminster John Knox Press, 1974.

Clements, Ronald E. (ed.), *The World of Ancient Israel: Sociological, Anthropological and Political Perspectives*, Cambridge University Press, 1991.

Coggins, Richard, *The Book of Exodus*, Epworth Press, 2000.

Dobson, John H., *Guide to Exodus*, SPCK, 2000.

Fretheim, Terence E., *Exodus (Interpretation): A Bible Commentary for Teaching and Preaching*, Westminster John Knox Press, 1991.

Ginzberg, Louis, Szdd, Henrietta, Radin, Paul, *The Legends of the Jews: Notes to Volumes 1 and 2: From the Creation to the Exodus*, Vol. 5, Johns Hopkins University Press, 1998.

Hayes, John Haralson and Miller, James Maxwell (eds), *Israelite and Judaean History*, University of Pennsylvania Press, 1977.

Mills, Watson E. (ed.), *Bibliographies for Biblical Research: Periodical Literature for the Study of the Old Testament, Vol. II: Exodus-Leviticus*, Edwin Mellen Press, 2002.

Petrie, W.M. Flinders, *Tell El-Amarna*, Aris and Phillips, 1974.

Pfeiffer, Charles F., *Tell El-Amarna and the Bible*, Baker Book House, 1963.

Sarna, Nahum M., *Exploring Exodus: The Origins of Biblical Israel*, Schocken Books, 1996.

Sarna, Nahum M., *Exodus: The Traditional Hebrew Text with the New JPS Translation*, Jewish Publication Society, 1991.

Van Setters, John, *The Life of Moses: The Yahwist as Historian in Exodus-Numbers*, Westminster John Knox Press, 1994.

Wildsmith, Brian, *Exodus*, Oxford University Press, 1999.

CHAPTER 6

Conquest and Settlement

Timeline:

c. 1250–1200 BCE Israelite conquest in Canaan. Leadership by judges

c. 1100 BCE Iron Age. Rise of Philistine league of cities

c. 1050 BCE Victory of Philistines over Israel at Aphek

After the death of Moses, Joshua was commanded by God to lead the Jewish people into the Promised Land. After crossing the Jordan river, he captured Jericho and Ai. Subsequently he defeated both southern and northern kings. The second part of the Book of Joshua begins with a list of areas which had not been conquered in the plain and valley regions as well as on the coast. To encourage the people, Joshua delivered speeches enjoining them to remain steadfast in their faith. Recalling God's past mercies, he ordered them to be obedient to the covenant. After Joshua's death at the age of 110, the people began to form separate groups. Initially there were twelve tribes named after the sons of Jacob: Joshua and Benjamin (the sons of Rachel), Levi, Simeon, Reuben, Judah, Issachar, Zebulun (the sons of Leah), Dan and Napthali (the sons of Bilhah), God and Asher (the sons of Zilpah). When Levi became a special priestly group excluded from this territorial division, the tribe of Joseph was divided into two, named after his sons, Ephraim and Manasseh.

The Book of Judges also tells the story of the twelve national heroes who served as judges of the nation after Joshua's death. The sagas of six major judges – Othniel, Ehud, Deborah, Gideon, Jephthah and Samson – are recounted at length. The judges were tribal and attached to particular regions; their fragmented reign continued for more than 150 years during the twelfth and eleventh centuries BCE. During quiet periods, the tribes were governed by councils of

elders; it was only at times of emergency that the judges took control. From a religious perspective, the era of the judges was of central significance. The Covenant between God and the Israelites, first formulated by Moses, was repeatedly proclaimed at gatherings in such national shrines as Shechem. Such an emphasis on covenantal obligations reinforced the belief that the Jews were the recipients of God's loving kindness: they were his chosen people.

In a more settled existence, the Covenant expanded to include additional legislation. Mosaic law consisted largely of unconditional obligations. However, as time passed, provisions for every kind of situation were included within the system. Many of these provisions were needed for an agricultural community, and seem to date back to the time of the judges. It also became clear to the Jewish nation that the God of the Covenant directed human history. The Exodus and the entry into the Promised Land were seen as the unfolding of a divine plan. Unlike their Canaanite neighbours who worshipped local gods, the people of Israel stressed their detachment from place-related ties by revering a mobile shrine which they carried from place to place. In all likelihood this tent or tabernacle was the repository of the sacred Ark.

The rejection of Canaanite religions was reinforced by the Israelite disapproval of such rites as magic fertility rituals, making images of gods, temple prostitution, and the human sacrifice of children. However, the Israelites adapted the three Canaanite agricultural

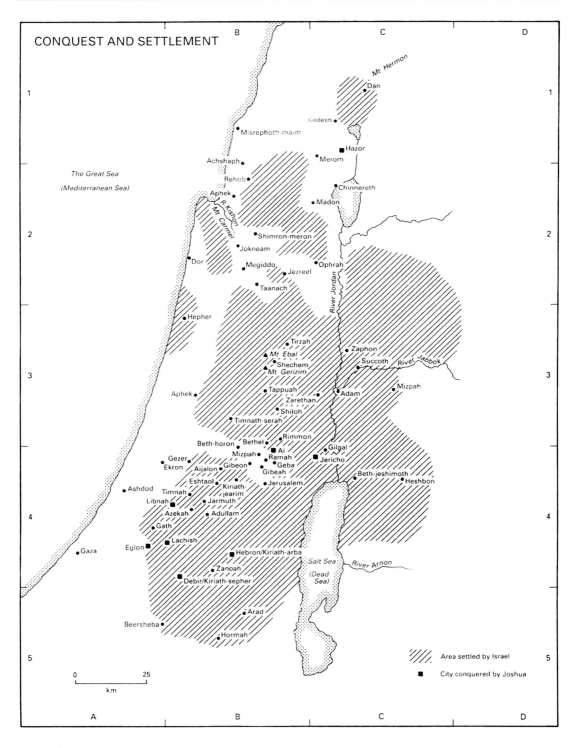

Map 7 Conquest and settlement

festivals to suit their own religious aims. The spring festival was transformed into *Pesach* (Passover) to commemorate the Exodus from Egypt. The autumn festival became *Sukkot* (Booths), a celebration of the dwelling in tents during the sojourn in the desert. The early summer festival was changed to *Shavuot* (Weeks) to bear witness to the giving of law on Mt Sinai. The three festivals eventually became occurrences of pilgrimage to remind the Jewish nation of their former sufferings, liberation and dedication to the Covenant, but they had their origins in the Canaanite agricultural rhythms.

Though the results of archaeological investigation do not conclusively demonstrate the accuracy of the account of the conquest as portrayed in the Book of Joshua, archaeological findings do cast light on certain features of this period. The **Tell el-Amarna letters** dating from the early fourteenth century BCE, which were written by various rulers in Canaan and Syria to Pharaoh Amenhotep III (1398–1361 BCE) and his successor Akhen-aten (1369–1353 BCE) complain of the *Habiru* who caused havoc in the countryside. Previous scholars identified the *Habiru* with the Hebrew nation and equated the invasions into southern Canaan with Joshua's incursions. Nowadays there is some doubt about this theory; it is argued instead that these letters reflect a more generalized migration of foreign peoples into Canaan. It is possible to see the Israelites as part of this movement, although this would imply a very early date for the Exodus and conquest. However, there is the possibility that some of the Israelites immigrated to Canaan prior to the liberation from Egyptian bondage.

Regarding the Biblical claim that Joshua conquered several Canaanite cities, an excavation of Jericho was thought to prove that the city was in fact captured by the Israelites. The walls appeared to have collapsed and there was evidence of considerable destruction by fire. Investigations by later archaeologists, however,

cast serious doubt on this theory. The remains have been shown to have been at a lower level and to date from the latter part of the third millennium BCE. On the other hand, evidence from different sites such as the city of Hazor shows that there was widespread devastation during the thirteenth century BCE. Some scholars argue that this had nothing to do with Joshua; they believe it was the result of feuding between Canaanite city states. Others maintain that the destruction was caused by foreign invaders such as Philistines and Amorites. Nevertheless, the fact that parts of Canaan were destroyed during this period provides some corroboration for the accuracy of the Joshua account.

Archaeological evidence has cast considerable light on Canaanite religion. The tell of Ras-esh-Shamra on the coast of Syria was the site of the citadel of Ugarit which flourished in the fifteenth and fourteenth centuries BCE. In an annexe to the temple, archaeologists discovered a collection of thirteenth-century clay tablets describing the exploits of Baal and other Canaanite gods and goddesses. El is portrayed as chief of the gods with his female consort Asherah, but they appear to be subservient to Baal, the weather god, and his lover Anat. One story relates that Baal was attacked by Mot, the god of barrenness and sterility. He was overcome and his body scattered to the four corners of the earth. But Anat took her revenge.

Baal's power returned when he engaged in sexual relations with Anat; this ensured the fertility of the earth. In Canaanite religion this was crucial since rainfall was vital for agriculture. Some scholars believe that the story of Baal's revival was the high point of the autumn New Year Festival: the King and a temple prostitute would act out the story of Baal and Anat. Such a mixture of sexual activity and fertility presented a major challenge to the Israelite concept of God who demands moral and ritual obedience to his decree.

Figure 6 Joshua before Jericho. On the right, Rahab lowers Joshua's escaping emissaries over the ramparts. On the left, the emissaries come before Joshua, who is commanding his armoured horsemen. Illustrated manuscript of the Alba Bible from the Palace de Liria, Madrid. Facsimile. Copyright the Beth Hatefutsoth collection, Tel Aviv.

SOURCES

Tell el-Amarna Letter

This is a letter from Abdiheba, governor of Jerusalem, to the Pharaoh Akhenaton concerning the *Habiru*.

(To the kin)g, my lord, (say: Thus says) Abdiheba, thy servant. (At) the feet of my lord seven t(imes and seven times I fall. I have heard a(ll) the words the king, my lord, has sent in to me concerning (?) . . . (Behold,) the deed which t (the Habiru (?) have) done . . . of bronze . . . the word . . . brought in to (Kelia)h (?). Let the (kin)g know that all the lands are at peace but there is hostility against me; so let the king take thought about his land. Behold the land of (G)ezer, the land of Ashkelon and Lachish (?) have given them food, oil and all their needs; so let the king take thought about archers; let him send archers against the men who are committing a crime against the king, my lord. If this year there are archers, then the lands (and) the regent will belong to the king my lord, (but) if there are no archers, the lands and the regents will not belong to the king. Behold, this land of Jerusalem, neither my father nor my mother gave it to me; the mighty arm (of the king) gave it to me. Behold this deed is the deed of Milkilu and the deed of the sons of Labaya who have given the land to the king to the *Habiru*. Behold, O king, my lord, I am in the right. As for the Cushites, let the king ask the commissioners if the house is (really) very strong; for they attempted a grave and serious crime; they took their implements and broke through the . . . of the roof . . . sent into the land . . . came up (?) with . . . servants. Let the king take thought about them . . . gone forth (?) . . . the lands into their hand, (so) let the king demand (satisfaction) from them – abundance of food, abundance of oil and abundance of clothing, until Pauru, the commissioner of the king, comes up to the land of Jerusalem. Addaya has left with the men of the warden's garrison (which) the king gave me. Let the king know. Addaya said to me: 'Behold, I am leaving, but thou shalt not abandon it.' This (year) send me a garrison (and) send me a commissioner of the king. Even as we are (?), I send (gift)s (?) to the king, (my) lord, . . . captives, five thousand (shekels of silver (?) and (?) eight (?) bearers (in) caravans for the king, but they were captured in the open country at Aijalon. Let the king, my lord, know. I am not able to send a caravan to the king, my lord, – that thou mayest know. Behold the king has set his name in the land of Jerusalem for ever, so he cannot abandon the lands of Jerusalem.

(*Tell el-Amarna Letter*, in DOTT, pp. 39–40)

Tell el-Amarna Letter

This is a letter from Abdiheba, the governor of Jerusalem, to the Pharaoh Akhenaton about the conquests of the *Habiru*:

To the king, my lord, my Sun-god, say: Thus says Abdiheba, thy servant. At the feet of the king, my lord, seven times and seven times I fall. Behold, the king, my lord, has set his name at the rising of the sun and at the setting of the sun. It is outrageous what they committed against me. Behold, I am not a regent, but I am a warden to the king, my lord. Behold, I am a shepherd of the king, and a tribute-bringer of the king am I. Neither my father nor my mother but the mighty arm of the king set (me) in the house of (my) father . . . (Behold) . . . came to me . . . I gave ten servants (into his h)and. Shuta, the commissioner of the king, came to me. Twenty-one maidens (and eigh)ty (male) captives I gave into the hand of Shuta as a gift to the king, my lord. Let the king take counsel for his land. The land of the king is lost; all of it is taken away from me. There is hostility against me as far as the lands of Seir and as far as Gath-carmel. There is peace to all the regents, but there is hostility against me. I am treated like a *Hibru*, and I do not see the eyes of the king, my lord, for there is hostility against me. I am made like a ship in the midst of the sea. The mighty arm of the king may take Naharaim and Cush, but now the *Habiru* have taken the cities of the king. No regent is left to the king, my lord; all are lost. Behold, Turbazu has been killed in the city-gate of Zilu, yet the king holds back. Behold, Zimrida at Lachish – his servants have smitten him and have made themselves over to the *Habiru*. Yaptihadda has been killed in the city-gate of Zilu, yet (the king) holds back and does not demand

(satisfaction) from them. (So) let the king take thought (about his land and) let the king give his attention to (sending) archers for his (?) land. (For) if there are no archers this year all the lands of the king, my lord, will be lost. They are not reporting in the presence of the king, my lord, that the land of the king, my lord is lost and all the regents are lost.

(*Tell el-Amarna Letter*, in DOTT, p. 43)

DISCUSSION

1. What are the moral as well as religious difficulties connected with the Biblical account of the conquest?

2. If the ancient Israelites were commanded by God to conquer the Canaanites in ancient times, does this give licence to modern Israel's treatment of the Palestinian people?

FURTHER READING

Anderson, George Wishart, *The History and Religion of Israel*, Oxford University Press, 1966.

Bright, John, *A History of Israel*, Westminster Press, 1972.

De Vaux, Roland, *Ancient Israel*, Vols 1–2, McGraw-Hill, 1965.

Finkelstein, Israel, Silberman, Neil Asher, *The Bible Unearthed: Archaeology's New Vision of Ancient Israel and the Origin of its Sacred Texts*, Touchstone Books, 2002.

Finkelstein, Israel, *The Archaeology of the Israelite Settlement*, Brill Academic Publishers, 1988.

Garbini, Giovanni, *History and Ideology in Ancient Israel*, XPRESS Reprints, 1997.

Gottwald, Norman K., *The Politics of Ancient Israel*, Westminster John Knox Press, 2000.

King, Philip, Stager, Lawrence, Knight, Lawrence A., *Life in Biblical Israel*, Westminster John Knox Press, 2002.

Lange, Nicholas de, Gerber, Jane S., Long, N.R.M. de (eds), *The Illustrated History of the Jewish People*, Harcourt, 1997.

Matthews, Victor, H., *A Brief History of Ancient Israel*, Westminster John Knox Press, 2002.

Mendenhall, George E., Herion, Gary A. (eds), *Ancient Israel's Faith and History: An Introduction to the Bible in Context*, Westminster John Knox Press, 2001.

Miller, Patrick D., Knight, Douglas A., *The Religion of Ancient Israel*, SPCK, 2000.

Nakhai, Beth Alpert, *Archaeology and the Religions of Canaan and Israel*, American Schools of Oriental Research, 2001.

Noth, Martin, *The History of Israel*, HarperCollins, 1960.

Soggin, J. Alberto, *An Introduction to the History of Israel and Judah*, SCM, 1999.

Thompson, Thomas L., *Early History of the Israelite People: From the Written and Archaeological Sources*, Brill, 2000.

Whitelam, Keith W., *The Invention of Ancient Israel: The Silencing of Palestinian History*, Routledge, 1997.

Zevit, Ziony, *The Religions of Ancient Israel*, Continuum, 2000.

CHAPTER 7

The Rise of Monarchy

Timeline:

c. 1050 BCE Victory of Philistines over Israelites at Aphek

c. 1020–1000 BCE   Saul, king of Israel

c. 1000–961 BCE David, king of Israel

c. 961–922 BCE Solomon, king of Israel

During the period of the Judges, God was viewed as the supreme monarch. When some tribes suggested to Gideon that he deserved a formal position of power, he declared it was impossible for the nation to be ruled by both God and a human king (Judges 8:22–23). The political associations of the Israelites were composed of a loose confederation united for common welfare. During Samuel's lifetime, however, the people found tribal alliances and simple trust in God's power inadequate. Politically and militarily, Israel was less well organized than the Philistines (who occupied southern Canaan), and could offer no effective resistance to invading armies.

After a defeat at Aphek, the leaders of the nation realized they were powerless and decided to make certain God would be with them in battle. This plan was unsuccessful; the Ark was captured; its shrine destroyed, and the Israelite army overwhelmed. Though the Ark was later returned, this defeat crushed the people's confidence. The Israelites needed a king, but in the chapters which describe Saul's election to kingship (1 Samuel 8–12), there appear to be at least two strands of tradition. The first (1 Samuel 9:1–10: 16) represents Saul as God's instrument for deliverance as evidenced by his leadership of the Israelite army against the Ammonites. The other strand (1 Samuel 8:10–17:12), however, presents the people's desire for a king as a rejection of God's authority. Here Samuel's warning against the dangers of kingship was expressed:

And now behold the king whom you have chosen, for whom you have asked; behold, the Lord has set a king over you. If you will fear him and hearken to his voice and not rebel against the commandment of the Lord, and if both you and the king who reigns over you will follow the Lord your God, it will be well; but if you will not hearken to the voice of the Lord, but rebel against the commandment of the Lord, then the hand of the Lord will be against you and your king.

(1 Samuel 12:13–15)

Samuel's forebodings proved to be correct: Saul's reign was plagued by a number of difficulties. His first problem was that he soon lost the support of Samuel. When Saul was instructed to take neither prisoners nor spoil in a campaign against the Amalekites, these instructions were not strictly followed. As a consequence, Samuel denounced the king and declared he had been rejected by God (1 Samuel 15). The second problem concerned Saul's moods of gloom and violence. After his anointing, God's spirit came upon Saul and imparted to him prophetic frenzy so that he could lead Israel to victory. As is known from the eighteenth-century BCE letters from Mari, prophetic ecstasy linked with military triumph was a feature of the ancient Near East. But for Saul such emotional activity took a toll on his mental state. To relieve him from depression, David joined his retinue so that he might bring relief through music. Yet this was no solution. Saul became jealous of David's popularity and success. Much of the account of Saul's reign is

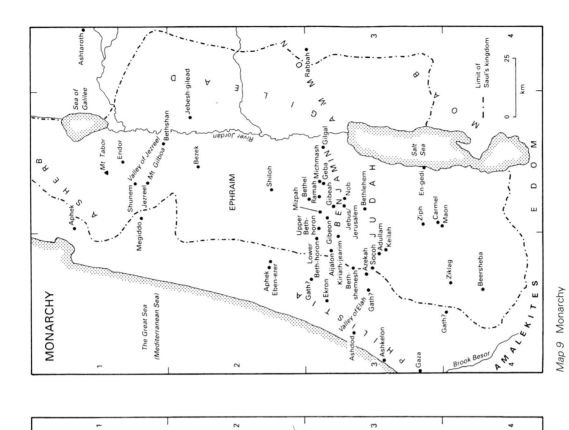

Map 9 Monarchy

Map 8 Battles of the judges period

concerned with the deteriorating relationship between the two men. Saul's reign thus began with a successful military action reminiscent of the exploits of the judges, but it ended in madness and defeat.

After joining Saul's entourage, David (1010–970 BCE) quickly gained a reputation as a successful warrior as is reflected in the account of his victory over the giant Goliath. Later he married Saul's daughter Michal, buying her hand with the foreskins of a hundred slaughtered Philistines. But David's military exploits and general popularity evoked Saul's anger. On the advice of Saul's son Jonathan, David fled for safety to the cave of Adullam in the southern wilderness. When Saul, along with his son Jonathan, was killed at Mt Gilboa, David became the leader of the southern tribes; at Hebron he was anointed King of Judah. In the north, Saul's son Ishbaal was appointed king. Later, however, David supplanted Ishbaal and became king over the entire country.

One of David's first victories was over the Jebusites

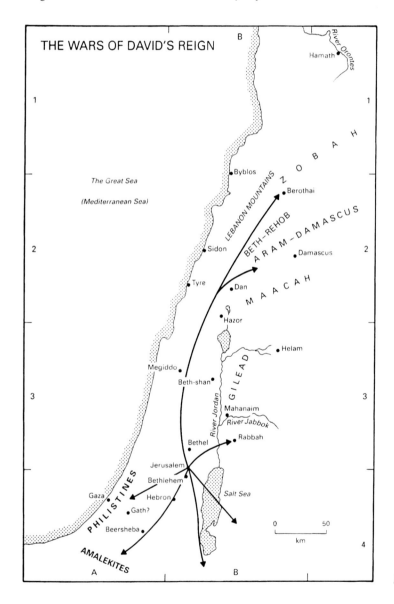

Map 10 The wars of David's reign

in Jerusalem which he declared the new capital. Very little exists of the Jerusalem of David's reign, but there is no question that David transformed the city into a major administrative centre. Employing foreign craftsmen, he built new fortifications and a palace. To Jerusalem he also brought the Ark of the Covenant, and by this act symbolically transferred power away from the tribes.

Despite his glory as a conqueror and leader, Scripture bemoans David's moral failings. After he had committed adultery with Bathsheba and caused the death of her husband Uriah, the court prophet Nathan denounced David and demanded repentance; even the king was subject to God's moral dictates. Yet for all his immorality, David was assured that his dynasty would continue. As God declared: 'When your days are fulfilled and you lie down with your fathers, I will raise up your offspring after you, who shall come forth from your body, and I will establish his kingdom. He shall build a house for my name, and I will establish the throne of his kingdom forever' (2 Samuel 7:12–13).

Towards the end of David's life, rivals for the throne battled against one another. Revolts led by his son Absalom and by Sheba from the tribe of Benjamin were suppressed; by the time of David's death, his son Adonijah seemed the likely successor. Although Adonijah was supported by the priest Abiathar and the army general Joab, another son, Solomon (970–930 BCE), had still more powerful allies. Solomon's mother, Bathsheba, had been David's favourite wife, and was supported by the prophet Nathan, Zadok the priest and Benaiah, another army commander. Eventually Solomon was victorious. Adonijah and his supporters were killed and Abiathar was exiled. But,

unlike David, Solomon was concerned more with his own security than the defence of the nation. Enormous resources were directed into a personal army consisting of 12,000 men and horses, and 1,400 chariots.

Figure 7 David with head of Goliath. Artist: Reni, Guido: 1575–1642: Italian. Copyright The Art Archive/Musée du Louvre Paris/Dagli Orti (A).

SOURCES

Kingship

Despite Samuel's reluctance, the institution of the monarchy was established in ancient Israel:

When Samuel became old, he made his sons judges over Israel. The name of his first-born son was Joel, and the name of his second, Abijah; they were judges in Beer-sheba. Yet his sons did not walk in his ways, but turned aside after gain; they took bribes and perverted justice.

Then all the elders of Israel gathered together and came to Samuel at Ramah, and said to him, 'Behold, you are old and your sons do not walk in your ways; now appoint for us a king to govern us like all the nations.' But the thing displeased Samuel when they said, 'Give us a king to govern us.' And Samuel prayed to the Lord. And the Lord said to Samuel, 'Hearken to the voice of the people in all that they say to you; for they have not rejected you, but they have rejected me from being king over them. According to all the deeds which they have done to me, from the day I brought them up out of Egypt even to this day, forsaking me and serving other gods, so they are also doing to you. Now then, hearken to their voice; only, you shall solemnly warn them, and show them the ways of the king who shall reign over them.'

So Samuel told all the words of the Lord to the people who were asking a king from him. He said, 'These will be the ways of the king who will reign over you: he will take your sons and appoint them to his chariots; and he will appoint for himself commanders of thousands and commanders of fifties, and some to plough his ground and to reap his harvest, and to make his implements of war and the equipment of his chariots. He will take your daughters to be perfumers and cooks and bakers. He will take the best of your fields and vineyards and olive orchards and give them to his servants. He will take the tenth of your grain and of your vineyards and give it to his officers and to his servants. He will take your menservants and maidservants, and the best of your cattle and your asses, and put them to his work. He will take the tenth of your flocks, and you shall be his slaves. And in that day you will cry out because of your king, whom you have chosen for yourselves; but the Lord will not answer you in that day.'

But the people refused to listen to the voice of Samuel; and they said, 'No! but we will have a king over us, that we also may be like all the nations, and that our king may govern us and go out before us and fight our battles.'

(1 Samuel 8:1–20)

David and Goliath

In a confrontation with the Philistines, David demonstrated his courage:

When the Philistine arose and came and drew near to meet David, David ran quickly toward the battle line to meet the Philistine. And David put his hand in his bag and took out a stone, and slung it, and struck the Philistine on his forehead; the stone sank into his forehead, and he fell on his face to the ground. So David prevailed over the Philistine with a sling and with a stone, and struck the Philistine, and killed him; there was no sword in the hand of David. Then David ran and stood over the Philistine, and took his sword and drew it out of its sheath, and killed him, and cut off his head with it.

(1 Samuel 17:48–51)

The Hatred of Saul

Jealous of David, Saul expressed his displeasure:

As they were coming home, when David returned from slaying the Philistine, the women came out of all the cities of Israel, singing and dancing, to meet King Saul, with timbrels, with songs of joy, and with instruments of music. And the women sang to one another as they made merry,

'Saul has slain his thousands,
and David his ten thousands.'

And Saul was very angry, and this saying displeased him; he said, 'They have ascribed to David ten thousands, and to me they have ascribed thousands; and what more can he have but the kingdom?' And Saul eyed David from that day on.

(1 Samuel 18:6–9)

David and Bathsheba

Desirous of Bathsheba, King David violated the moral law:

It happened, late one afternoon, when David arose from his couch and was walking upon the roof of the king's house, that he saw from the roof a woman bathing; and the woman was very beautiful. And David sent and inquired about the woman. And one said, 'Is not this Bathsheba, the daughter of Eliam, the wife of Uriah the Hittite?' So David sent messengers, and took her; and she came to him, and he lay with her. (Now she was purifying herself from her uncleanness.) Then she returned to her house. And the woman conceived, and she sent and told David, 'I am with child.' . . . In the morning David wrote a letter to Joab, and sent it by the hand of Uriah. In the letter he wrote, 'Set Uriah in the forefront of the hardest fighting, and then draw back from him, that he may be struck down, and die. And as Joab was besieging the city, he assigned Uriah to the place where he knew there were valiant men. And the men of the city came out and fought with Joab; and some of the servants of David among the people fell. Uriah the Hittite was slain also. Then Joab sent and told David all the news about the fighting . . .

(2 Samuel 11:2–5, 14–18)

Nathan and David

The prophet Nathan confronted the king and rebuked him for his sinfulness:

And the Lord sent Nathan to David. He came to him, and said to him, 'There were two men in a certain city, the one rich and the other poor. The rich man had very many flocks and herds; but the poor man had nothing but one little ewe lamb, which he had bought. And he brought it up, and it grew up with him and with his children; it used to eat of his morsel, and drink from his cup, and lie in his bosom, and it was like a daughter to him. Now there came a traveller to the rich man, and he was unwilling to take one of his own flock or herd to prepare for the wayfarer who had come to him, but he took the poor man's lamb and prepared it for the man who had come to him.' Then David's anger was greatly kindled against the man; and he said to Nathan, 'As the Lord lives, the man who has done this deserves to die; and he shall restore the lamb fourfold, because he did this thing, and because he had no pity.'

(2 Samuel 12:1–6)

DISCUSSION

1. What were the central objections to the establishment of the monarchy?

2. Compare and contrast the role of the prophets in the ancient Near East and ancient Israel.

FURTHER READING

Finkelstein, Israel, Na'Aman, Nadav (eds), *From Nomadism to Monarchy: Archaeological and Historical Aspects of Early Israel*, Biblical Archaeology Society, 1994.

Finkelstein, Israel (ed.), *From Nomadism to Monarchy*, Yad Izhak Ben-Zvi, 1999.

Halpern, Baruch, *Constitution of the Monarchy in Israel*, Scholars Press, 1982.

Rogerson, John W. *Chronicle of the Old Testament Kings: The Reign-By-Reign Record of the Rulers of Ancient Israel*, Thames and Hudson, 1999.

Torijano, Pablo A., *Solomon the Esoteric King: From King to Magus, Development of a Tradition*, Brill, 2002.

CHAPTER 8

Solomon and the Divided Monarchy

Timeline:

c. 961–922 BCE Solomon, king of Israel

c. 922 BCE Succession of northern tribes. Division into the Northern Kingdom (Israel) and Southern Kingdom (Judah)

In foreign affairs, Solomon traded with Phoenicia, Arabia and Syria, Cilicia and probably with north and east Africa as well. By marrying an Egyptian princess he linked himself with Egypt. One of Solomon's close contacts was with Hiram, King of Tyre. The Phoenicians had extensive trading links in the Mediterranean, and through this alliance Solomon was able to develop his own trade in the Red Sea and the Indian Ocean. In all likelihood the Phoenicians also helped him build and operate his copper refineries on the Gulf of Aqaba. In addition, it appears that Solomon traded horses with the Egyptians in the south and the Hittites in the north.

As a result of this activity, Solomon was able to build a new palace for himself, another for his Egyptian wife, a hall for state occasions, a judgement chamber and, most importantly, the Temple. Originally David wanted to build a temple to house the Ark of the Covenant, but this became Solomon's greatest triumph. The best material was transported (such as timber from the King of Tyre), and skilled craftsmen from Phoenicia were employed. Scholars have pointed out that the actual plan of the Temple was identical to the temples of Baal which have been discovered by archaeologists, and they note that the Jerusalem Temple was consecrated at exactly the same time in the year as the Baal temple at Ugarit (before the autumn rains). Yet whether or not Solomon attempted to initiate Canaanite worship, he did play an active part in the Israelite cult, offering sacrifices and blessing the

people – actions Saul and David had been expressly forbidden from performing.

In addition to his architectural achievements, Solomon was universally recognized as a wise ruler. In the words of 1 Kings: 'Solomon's wisdom surpassed the wisdom of all the people of the east, and all the wisdom of Egypt' (1 Kings 4:30). According to tradition, he was able to recite 'three thousand proverbs; and his songs were a thousand and five. He spoke of trees, from the cedar that is in Lebanon to the hyssop that grows out of the wall; he spoke also of beasts, and of birds, and of reptiles, and of fish' (1 Kings 4:32–33). Scholars have recognized that such wisdom was part of an intellectual movement of the time, and Solomon's achievement is akin to the pursuits of kings and philosophers in ancient Egypt and Mesopotamia. It has been argued that it was as a reaction to such artistic and cultural interests that scribes during Solomon's reign wove together Israel's early history. Their purpose was to point out that heroes such as Abraham and Moses prospered as a result of God's grace and loving kindness, not because of their own efforts.

To support Solomon's many projects, an elaborate system of taxation had been developed – each of the twelve districts of the territory was obligated to support the court for one month a year. Not surprisingly, this taxation evoked a strong reaction. The notion of a privileged elite supported by the general population conflicted with the egalitarian tribal organization. In

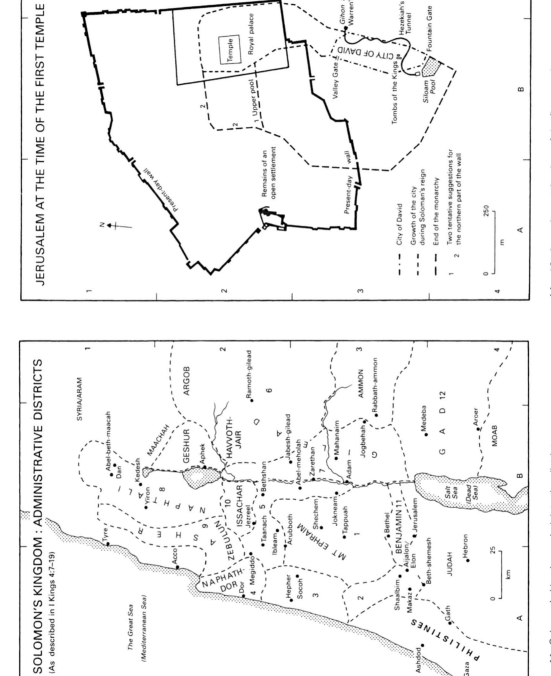

Map 12 Jerusalem at the time of the first temple

Map 11 Solomon's kingdom: administrative districts

Figure 8 King Solomon overseeing construction of the Temple, Jerusalem, folio 263 of 1526–29 manuscript Latin Bible from Abbey of St Amand, France. Copyright The Art Archive / Bibliothèque Municipale Valenciennes/Dagli Orti.

place of twelve tribes serving God, twelve districts served the king. Moreover, the fact that the Canaanites adopted a similar financial system emphasized the foreignness of this arrangement. But even such taxation was insufficient to support Solomon's projects. To meet his expenses he instituted forced labour. This provision provoked a revolt led by the northern army leader Jeroboam, but his plot was uncovered and he fled to Egypt. The northern tribes remained dissatisfied, but the southern tribes were loyal to the house of David. Not only were David and his son southerners by birth, but they also favoured the southern tribes. Judah and Benjamin seem to have been excluded from the taxation burden.

After Solomon's death, his son Rehoboam (930–908 BCE) became king and sought the allegiance of the northern tribes. When he went to Shechem from Jerusalem to meet them, they outlined the terms on which they would accept the monarchy. Rehoboam refused to listen and arrogantly proclaimed, 'My father made your yoke heavy, but I will add to your yoke; my father chastised you with whips, but I will chastise you with scorpions' (1 Kings 12:14). As a consequence of Rehoboam's policies, the northern tribes revolted against him and chose instead Jeroboam I (930–910 BCE) as their monarch: 'When all Israel heard that Jeroboam had returned, they sent and called him to the assembly and made him king over all Israel (1 Kings 12:20). Shechem initially served as Jeroboam's administrative centre, but he later made Tirzah his capital. No major battle appears to have taken place between the northern kingdom (Israel) and the southern kingdom (Judah), but later border clashes resulted from Judah's retention of the territory of Benjamin.

As the kingdom divided, the aggressor who threatened the nation was Shoshenk I (945–924 BCE), the first pharaoh of the twenty-second dynasty who invaded the land and forced Rehoboam to pay tribute. An inscription of the Temple of Amun at Thebes refers to this conquest. Shoshenk does not mention any towns in Judah being captured, but he does refer to some cities in the northern kingdom. Another inscription found at Megiddo suggests that the Egyptian incursion must have enveloped most of the territory. In the north the external danger was matched by an internal threat; the tribes keenly felt the loss of the Temple and desired to make pilgrimage to Jerusalem. To stem such disloyalty, Jeroboam I set up alternative shrines at old centres of Canaanite worship, Dan and Bethel. There he placed golden bulls in an attempt to reconcile the faith of Israel with features of Canaanite belief, a policy which he believed to be necessary since there was a sizeable Canaanite population within his territory. The Canaanite elements would have no difficulty in associating these idols with their own god Baal (who was often represented as a bull); the Israelites could regard them as thrones for their God (like the throne in the Temple).

SOURCE

Kingship

When the northern tribes complained to Rehoboam, he refused to heed their demands:

Rehoboam went to Shechem, for all Israel had come to Shechem to make him king. And when Jeroboam the son of Nebat heard of it (for he was still in Egypt, whither he had fled from King Solomon), then Jeroboam returned from Egypt. And they sent and called him; and Jeroboam and all the assembly of Israel came and said to Rehoboam, 'Your father made our yoke heavy. Now therefore lighten the hard service of your father and his heavy yoke upon us, and we will serve you.' He said to them, 'Depart for three days, then come again to me.' So the people went away.

Then King Rehoboam took counsel with the old men, who had stood before Solomon his father while he was yet alive, saying, 'How do you advise me to answer this people?' And they said to him, 'If you will be a servant to this people today and serve them, and speak good words to them when you answer them, then they will be your servants for ever.' But he forsook the counsel which the old men gave him, and took counsel with the young men who had grown up with him and stood before him. And he said to them, 'What do you advise that we answer this people who have said to me, "Lighten the yoke that your father put upon us"? And the young men who had grown up with him said to him, 'Thus shall you speak to this people who said to you, "Your father made our yoke heavy, but do you lighten it for us"; thus shall you say to them, "My little finger is thicker than my father's loins. And now, whereas my father laid upon you a heavy yoke, I will add to your yoke. My father chastised you with whips, but I will chastise you with scorpions."'

(I Kings 12:1–11)

DISCUSSION

1. What were the causes of the division of the monarchy?

2. Discuss the nature of Israelite syncretism in the Northern Kingdom.

FURTHER READING

Barnes, William Hamilton, *Studies in the Chronology of the Divided Monarchy of Israel*, Scholars Press, 1991.

Bendor, S., *The Social Structure of Ancient Israel: The Institution of the Family from the Settlement to the End of the Monarchy*, Eisenbrauns, 1996.

Coutts, John I., *Prophets and Kings of Israel: A History of Israel from the Institution of the Monarchy to the Fall of Samaria*, Longmans, 1969.

Crockett, William Day, *Harmony of the Books of Samuel, Kings and Chronicles, the Books of the Kings of Judah and Israel*, Baker Book House, 1985.

Finkelstein, Israel and Na'Aman, Nadav (eds), *From Nomadism to Monarchy: Archaeological and Historical Aspects of Early Israel*, Biblical Archaeology Society, 1994.

Handy, Lowell (ed.), *The Age of Solomon: Scholarship at the Turn of the Millennium*, Brill, 1997.

Lemche, Niels Peter, *Early Israel: Anthropological and*

Historical Studies on the Israelite Society Before the Monarchy, Brill, 1986.

Miller, James Maxwell, Hayes, John Haralson, *A History of Ancient Israel and Judah*, Westminster John Knox Press, 1986.

Shanks, Hershel, *Ancient Israel: From Abraham to the Roman Destruction of the Temple*, Prentice-Hall, 1999.

Tor, Amnon Ben-Tor (ed.), *The Archaeology of Ancient Israel*, Yale University Press, 1994.

CHAPTER 9

Kings of Israel and Judah

Timeline:

875–842 BCE Dynasty of Omri. Religious conflict during reign of Ahab, or of Omri, involving Elisha and Elijah

873–849 BCE Jehosaphat, king of Judah, allied with Israel and Tyre

842 BCE Jehu overthrows Omri dynasty

836 BCE Overthrow of Ahab's daughter, Athaliah. Restoration of Davidic dynasty

Jeroboam I's successor was his son Nadab (910–909 BCE) who was followed by Baasha (909–886 BCE). Like Jeroboam I, he encouraged a mixture of Canaanite and Israelite religions or, as the Biblical writers put it, he 'made Israel to sin' (1 Kings 15:34). When he died, his son Elah (886 BCE) attempted to succeed him but was assassinated, and Zimri, the army commander (886 BCE), usurped the throne. Zimri's reign lasted only seven days; he was followed by another general, Omri (885–874 BCE) and his son Ahab (874–852 BCE). Under the rule of these later two kings, the position of the northern kingdom was greatly strengthened. They ended the conflict with Judah, and the alliance of the kingdoms was sealed by the marriage of Ahab's daughter, Athaliah, to Jehoram (851–842 BCE), the son of Jehosaphat (875–851 BCE), king of Judah. Israel also made peace with the powerful kingdom of Phoenicia and Ahab himself married the Phoenician princess, Jezebel. Further, Omri gained control over Moab. This victory is mentioned in a large stone inscription erected by King Mesha of Moab after he had released his kingdom from Israel's grasp after Ahab's death. Much of the inscription concerns Mesha's victory, but the text states 'Omri, king of Israel, humbled Moab for many years'. To solidify his position, Omri built a new administrative centre and shrine in Samaria. Like Jeroboam, Ahab incorporated Canaanite religious features. He provided for the worship of Baal, and thereby incurred the condemnation

of Scripture: 'He did evil in the sight of the Lord more than all that were before him. And as if it had been a light thing for him to walk in the sins of Jeroboam . . . and went and served Baal and worshipped him' (1 Kings 16:30–31).

Such idolatrous practice was encouraged by Jezebel who wanted Baal to become the God of Israel. To combat this threat, the prophet **Elijah** was determined to prove the God of Israel was supreme. Thus he challenged 450 prophets of Baal and 400 prophets of Asherah to a contest on Mt Carmel, near Phoenician territory. This had once been the site of an altar to the Israelite God, but it had been displaced by a shrine to Baal. There he and the Canaanite prophets prepared sacrifices and prayed to their respective gods to send fire from Heaven to ignite the offerings. Although the prophets of Baal and Asherah cried aloud in ecstatic frenzy and cut themselves with swords, no answer was forthcoming. But Elijah's supplication was successful: 'the fire of the Lord fell and consumed the burnt offering, and the wood and the stones, and the dust and licked up the water that was in the trench. And when all the people saw it, they fell on their faces; and they said, "The Lord, he is God; the Lord, he is God"' (1 Kings 18:38–39). Despite Elijah's victory, Jezebel encouraged Ahab to follow Phoenician customs. She regarded the life and property of every subject as belonging to the king, and so had no hesitation in having the Israelite Naboth killed in order that Ahab

Map 13 The kingdoms of Israel and Judah

could take possession of his property. But Elijah denounced the foreign queen, just as Nathan had previously rebuked David for similar unscrupulousness. For these early prophets, religion was bound up with life and politics, and not even the royal couple were above God's law.

Ahab was succeeded by his two sons, Ahaziah (852–850 BCE) and Joram (850–842) BCE), but it was not long before those loyal to the faith of Israel rebelled. These devotees, inspired by the prophet Elisha, Elijah's successor, chose an army officer, Jehu (842–815 BCE), to be the next king of Israel. During a battle between Israel and Syria, Joram was wounded and returned to recuperate in Jezreel. Jehu followed him there where he discovered Ahaziah (842 BCE), king of Judah, who was paying him a visit. Jehu assassinated both kings as well as Jezebel, the queen mother, and appealed to the city rulers of Samaria to pay allegiance to him. This they did by presenting him with the heads of seventy members of Ahab's family. But Jehu was less successful politically. Since he had killed the Phoenician princess Jezebel, he could no longer rely on the support of a Phoenician alliance. And by killing the king of Judah, he also lost the loyalty of the southern kingdom. In Judah Athaliah, Ahab's sister (842–837 BCE), seized control and murdered all claimants for the throne except for one child, Joash (837–800 BCE), who was rescued by the priest Jehoiada. Athalia reigned for six years, but was deposed in a coup led by Jehoiada. Joash was then installed as king.

During this period the Syrians had been engaged in war with the Assyrian king Shalmaneser III (859–824 BCE) who was intent on expanding his empire. After Jehu came to power, Shalmaneser invaded Syria and besieged Damascus; Phoenicia and Israel were forced to pay tribute so as to avoid being conquered by Assyria. On the **Black Obelisk** of Shalmaneser III, Jehu is depicted as a leader of a vassal state paying tribute. At the end of Shalmaneser III's reign, a revolt took place in Nineveh which weakened the Assyrian empire and gave the king of Damascus, Hazael (843–796 BCE), an opportunity to invade Israel. Under Jehu's son Jehoahaz (815–801 BCE), Israel became almost a province of Syria. The entire country east of the Jordan was occupied, and the Syrians continued their attack into Judah. But Joash offered Hazael treasure from the Temple to dissuade him from invading Jerusalem.

By the time Jehu's grandson Jehoash (801–786 BCE) became king, Assyria had grown in power under Shalmaneser's grandson, **Adad-Nirari III** (810–783 BCE). According to Assyrian records, Israel was forced to pay tribute to Assyria along with the Edomites and Philistines. Damascus was devastated by the Assyrian advance. When Scripture states 'The Lord gave Israel a saviour so that they escaped from the hand of the Syrians' (2 Kings 13:5), some scholars contend that this refers to Adad-Nirari. The Assyrian attack on Syria gave Jehoash the opportunity to recover Israel's lost territory; Amaziah the king of Judah (800–783 BCE) similarly captured his land from the Edomites. At this stage Amaziah declared war also on the northern kingdom, but Judah was defeated and Jehoash raided Jerusalem. As a consequence, Amaziah lost favour and was assassinated, to be succeeded by his son Uzziah (783–742 BCE).

SOURCES

Elijah and the Prophets of Baal

In the conquest between Elijah and the prophets of Baal, Elijah sought to demonstrate the supremacy of the God of Israel:

So Ahab sent to all the people of Israel, and gathered the prophets together at Mt Carmel. And Elijah came near to all the people, and said, 'How long will you go limping with two different opinions? If the Lord is God, follow him; but if Baal, then follow him.' And the people did not answer him a word. Then Elijah said to the people, 'I, even I only, am left a prophet of the Lord; but Baal's prophets are four hundred and fifty men. Let two bulls be given to us; and let them choose one bull for themselves, and cut it in pieces and lay it on the wood, but put no fire to it; and I will prepare the other bull and lay it on the wood, and put no fire to it. And you call on the name of your god and I will call on the name of the Lord; and the God who answers by fire, he is God.' And all the people answered, 'It is well spoken.' Then Elijah said to the prophets of Baal, 'Choose for yourselves one bull and prepare it first, for you are many; and call on the name of your god, but put no fire to it.' And they took the bull which was given them, and they prepared it, and called on the name of Baal from morning until noon, saying, 'O, Baal, answer us!' But there was no voice, and no one answered. And they limped about the altar which they had made. And at noon Elijah mocked them, saying, 'Cry, aloud, for he is a god; either he is musing, or he has gone aside, or he is on a journey, or perhaps he is asleep and must be awakened.' And they cried aloud, and cut themselves after their custom with swords and lances, until the blood gushed out upon them. And as midday passed, they raved on until the time of the offering of the oblation, but there was no voice; no one answered, no one heeded.

Then Elijah said to all the people, 'Come, near to me'; and all the people came near to him. And he repaired the altar of the Lord that had been thrown down; Elijah took twelve stones, according to the number of the tribes of the sons of Jacob, to whom the word of the Lord came, saying, 'Israel shall be your name'; and with the stones he built an altar in the name of the Lord. And he made a trench about the altar, as great as would contain two measures of seed. And he put the wood in order, and cut the bull in pieces and laid it on the wood. And he said, 'Fill four jars with water, and pour it on the burnt offering, and on the wood.' And he said, 'Do it a second time' and they did it a second time. And he said, 'Do it a third time'; and they did it a third time. And the water ran round about the altar, and filled the trench also with water.

And at the time of the offering of the oblation, Elijah the prophet came near and said, 'O Lord, God of Abraham, Isaac, and Israel, let it be known this day that thou art God in Israel, and that I am thy servant, and that I have done all these things at thy word. Answer me, O Lord, answer me, that this people may know that thou, O Lord, art God, and that thou hast turned their hearts back. Then the fire of the Lord fell, and consumed the burnt offering, and the wood, and the stones, and the dust, and licked up the water that was in the trench. And when all the people saw it, they fell on their faces; and they said, 'The Lord he is God; the Lord, he is God.'

(1 Kings 18:20–39)

The Black Obelisk

The Black Obelisk of Shalmaneser III depicts the leader of a vassal state paying tribute:

In my eighteenth regal year I crossed the River Euphrates for the sixteenth time. Hazael of Aram put his trust in the numerical strength of his army and called out his army in great numbers. He made Sanir, a mountain-peak which stands out in front of the Lebanon, his strong position, (but) I fought with him and defeated him, smiting with weapons 16,000 of his experienced troops. I snatched away from him 1,121 of his chariots and 470 of his cavalry horses together with his baggage train. He went off to save his life, (but) I followed after him and surrounded him in Damascus, his capital city. I cut down his plantations (and then) marched as far as the mountains of the Hauran. I destroyed, tore down, and burnt with fire numberless villages, carrying away innumerable spoil from them. I marched as far as the mountains of Ba'ali-ra'si, a headland by the sea, and put up on it a representation of my royal person. At that time I received the tribute of the people of Tyre, Sidon, and of Jehu, son of Omri.

The tribute of Jehu, son of Omri. Silver, gold, a golden bowl, a golden vase, golden cups, golden buckets, tin, a staff for the royal hand (?), puruhati-fruits.

(*The Black Obelisk*, in DOTT, p. 48)

Figure 9 Black obelisk from the city of Nimrud during the reign of King Shalmaneser III, showing scene of the king of Israel bringing tribute to the king. Copyright The British Museum.

Adad-Nirari III's Expedition to Syria and Palestine

The following text depicts Adad-Nirari III's expedition to Syria and Palestine:

Building by Adad-Nirari the great king, the mighty king, king of the world, king of Assyria, the king whom Ashur, king of the gods of the Upper World, chose while still in his youth and granted him an unrivalled princeship. He whose shepherding they made (to be) as good for the people of Assyria as (is) the plant of life and whose throne they founded securely; the holy priest, unceasing preserver of the Esharra-temple, who fulfils the ritual of the temple, who moves about by the support of Ashur his lord, making to submit at his feet the princes of the four world-regions; conqueror from Mount Siluna in the East, the countries Saban (?), Ellipi, Harhar, Araziash, Mesu, Media, Gilzilbunda in its whole area, Munna,

Parsua, Allabria, Apdadana, Nairi in its whole district, Anidu whose location is far off, a mountain fastness in its whole district, overlooking the great Sea of the Rising Sun, from (the districts) above the Euphrates, Hatti-land, Amorite-land in its border (regions), Tyre, Sidon, Israel, Edom, Philistia, as far as the great Sea of the Setting Sun, I made to bow at my feet (and) I imposed a heavy tribute upon them. I marched to Aram and shut up Mari', king of Aram, in Damascus his capital city. The awful splendour of the god Ashur his lord overwhelmed him and he seized my feet, expressing submission, 2,300 talents of silver, 20 talents of gold, 300 talents of copper, 5,000 talents of iron, embroidered linen garments, an ivory bed, a couch embossed and inlaid with ivory, countless of his goods and possessions. I received in his own palace at Damascus, his capital city. All the individual rulers of Kaldu-land expressed their submission, so I imposed heavy tribute upon them (which was inscribed in tablets).

(*Adad-Nirari's Expedition to Syria and Palestine*, in DOTT, p. 51)

DISCUSSION

1. Does Elijah's contest with the prophets of Baal constitute proof of God's existence?

2. Do archaeological discoveries from this period demonstrate the historicity of the biblical account?

FURTHER READING

Galil, Gershon, *The Chronology of the Kings of Israel and Judah*, Brill, 1996.

Gottwald, Norman, *The Politics of Ancient Israel*, Westminster John Knox Press, 2001.

Grant, Michael, *The History of Ancient Israel*, Weidenfeld and Nicolson, 1984.

Isserlin, B.S.J., *The Israelites*, Thames and Hudson, 1998.

McNutt, Paula H., *Reconstructing the Society of Ancient Israel*, Westminster John Knox Press, 1999.

Mendenhall, George, Herton, Gary (eds), *Ancient Israel's Faith and History: An Introduction to the Bible in Context*, Westminster John Knox Press, 2001.

Miller, Patrick D., Knight, Douglas A., *The Religion of Ancient Israel*, Westminster John Knox Press, 2000.

Rogerson, J.W., *Chronicle of the Old Testament Kings: The Reign-By-Reign Record of the Rulers of Ancient Israel*, Thames and Hudson, 1999.

Toews, Wesley, *Monarchy and Religious Institution in Israel under Jeroboam* I, Society of Biblical Literature, 1983.

Vaux, Roland de, *Ancient Israel: Its Life and Institutions*, Eerdmans, 1997.

CHAPTER 10

Jeroboam II to the Fall of the Northern Kingdom

Timeline:

Under Uzziah in Judah and Jeroboam II (786–746 BCE) in Israel, the nation prospered for the next forty years. Uzziah repaired the fortifications in Jerusalem, reorganized the army, and equipped it with new weapons. He also instituted new agricultural methods and reopened parts of Solomon's copper refineries on the Gulf of Aqaba. In the northern kingdom Jeroboam II constructed new buildings and engaged in international trade. As the nation grew richer, the people became more religious – they believed their wealth was a sign of God's favour. Yet some dissenters thought that the quest for riches was incompatible with God's covenant. According to some scholars, a new edition of Israel's early history was written at this time as a reaction against such high living. This reflected northern traditions and emphasized the role of Moses. Many of these stories, they believe, came to form a part of the Hebrew Bible, particularly the books of Genesis and Exodus.

Towards the end of Jeroboam's II reign, **Amos**, a shepherd from Tekoa who firmly differentiated himself from the official cultic prophets, expressed his dissatisfaction – he proclaimed that Israelite society had become morally corrupt. Many Israelites had become rich, but at the expense of the poor. Israel had sinned, he declared,

Figure 10 (a) The prophet Amos, folio 194v of the late twelfth century Couvigny Bible. Copyright The Art Archive/ Bibliothèque Municipale Moulins/Dagli Orti.

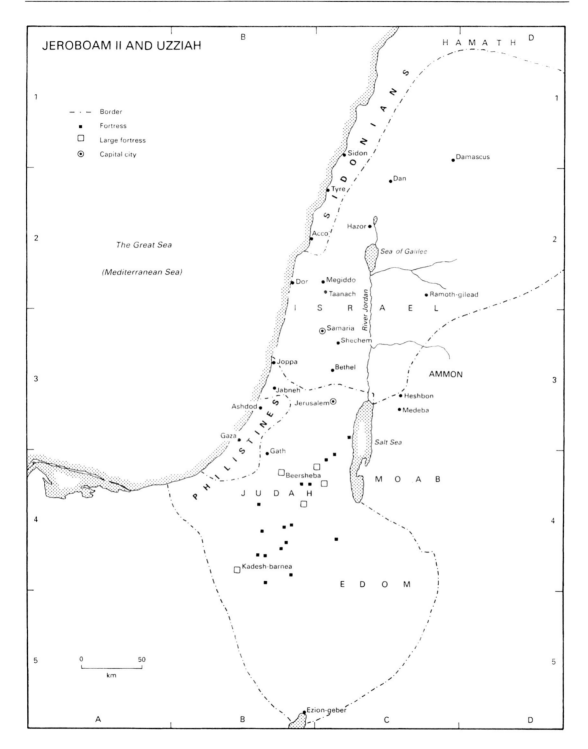

Map 14 Jeroboam II and Uzziah

because they sell the righteous for silver
and the needy for a pair of shoes –
they that trample the head of the poor
into the dust of the earth,
and turn aside the way of the afflicted.

(Amos 2:6–7)

Shrines like Bethel were full of worshippers, but
such ritual was empty. The 'day of the Lord', Amos
announced, would be a time of punishment for the
nation:

Woe to you who desire the day of the Lord . . .
It is darkness and not light . . .
I hate, I despise your feasts, and I take no delight
    in your solemn assemblies.
Even though you offer me your burnt offerings
    and cereal offerings, I will not accept them . . .
Therefore I will take you into exile beyond
Damascus, says the Lord, whose name is the God
    of Hosts.

(Amos 5:18–19, 21–22, 27)

His later contemporary, the prophet **Hosea**, echoed
these dire predictions. Israel had gone astray and would
be punished. Yet through personal tragedy – the
infidelity of his wife Gomer – Hosea was able to offer
words of consolation and hope. Just as his love for his
wife had been rejected, so God's love for Israel had
been despised. But despite the coming devastation,
God would not cease to love his chosen people. Just as
Hosea could not give up his wife, God could not
abandon Israel: 'How can I hand you over, O Israel!
. . . My heart recoils within me, my compassion grows
warm and tender' (Hosea 11:8).

It was not long before these prophecies of destruction were fulfilled. The Asssyrian king **Tiglath-Pileser
III** (745–727 BCE) embarked on a policy of expansion
during the reign of Menahem, king of Israel (746–738
BCE). Israel's government was unstable at the time
anyway.

Menahem's son Pekahiah (738–737 BCE) held his
throne for two years by paying tribute to the Assyrian
king, but was overthrown by his rival Pekah (737–732
BCE). The new Israelite king formed an alliance
with the king of Syria against the Assyrians. Together
they attempted to persuade Jotham, king of Judah
(742–735 BCE), to join them; when he refused they
declared war on Judah. In the face of this danger, the
southern prophet Isaiah declared to Ahaz (735–715
BCE), Jotham's successor, that this threat would come
to naught: both Israel and Syria would collapse. But
Ahaz was unconvinced. He attempted to placate the
Assyrians and went to Damascus (which the Assyrians
had just conquered) to pay homage to Tiglath Pileser
III. He returned with the plans for an altar to be erected
in the Temple as a sign of Judah's submission.

In the northern kingdom, Pekah's position was
weakened as the Assyrians pressed forward, and he
was assassinated by Hoshea (732–722 BCE) who
surrendered to the Assyrians. When Shalmaneser V
(727–722 BCE) replaced Tiglath-Pileser III, Egyptian
forces were powerless to help, and Shalmaneser V
conquered Israel's capital Samaria after a siege of two
years. The annals of Shalmaneser's successor, Sargon II
(722–705 BCE), record that 27,290 Israelites were
deported as a result of this conquest. This marked the
end of the northern kingdom.

Figure 10(b) Assyrian relief, eighth
century BCE, from the city of Nimrud
during the reign of King Tiglath-Pileser III,
showing a scene from the capture of the
city of Astartu. Copyright The British
Museum.

SOURCES

Amos' Prophecy Against Israel and Judah

Declaring devastation for iniquity, the prophet Amos predicted that both Israel and Judah would be destroyed because of their sins:

> Thus says the Lord:
> For three transgressions of Judah,
> and for four, I will not revoke the punishment;
> because they have rejected the law of the Lord,
> and have not kept his statutes,
> but their lies have led them astray,
> after which their fathers walked.
> So I will send a fire upon Judah,
> and it shall devour the strongholds of Jerusalem.
> Thus says the Lord:
> For three transgressions of Israel,
> and for four, I will not revoke the punishment;
> because they sell the righteous for silver,
> and the needy for a pair of shoes –
> and that trample the head of the poor and the dust of the earth,
> and turn aside the way of the afflicted;
> a man and his father go in to the same maiden,
> so that my holy name is profaned;
> they lay themselves down beside every altar upon garments taken in pledge;
> and in the house of their God they drink
> the wine of those who have been fined.
>
> (Amos 2:4–8)

Hosea's Marriage to Gomer

Like Amos, Hosea prophesied doom for the nation, comparing his own personal situation to that of Israel:

When the Lord first spoke through Hosea, the Lord said to Hosea, 'Go, take to yourself a wife of harlotry and have children of harlotry, for the land commits great harlotry by forsaking the Lord.' So he went and took Gomer the daughter of Diblaim, and she conceived and bore him a son.

And the Lord said to him, 'Call his name Jezreel; for yet a little while, and I will punish the house of Jehu for the blood of Jezreel, and I will put an end to the kingdom of the house of Israel. And on that day, I will break the bow of Israel in the valley of Jezreel.' She conceived again and bore a daughter. And the Lord said to him, 'Call her name Not pitied, for I will no more have pity on the house of Israel, to forgive them at all. But I will have pity on the house of Judah, and I will deliver them by the Lord their God; I will not deliver them by bow, nor by sword, nor by war, nor by horses, nor by horsemen.'

When she had weaned Not pitied, she conceived and bore a son. And the Lord said, 'Call his name Not my people, for you are not my people and I am not your God.'

(Hosea 1:2–8)

Tiglath-Pileser III in Syria and Palestine

Tiglath-Pileser III's conquest of Syria and Palestine is recorded in Assyrian records:

The town of Hatarikka as far as Mount Saue . . . the towns of Gebal, Simirra, Arga, Zimarra . . . Usnu, Ri'raba, Ri'sisu . . towns of the Upper (Sea) I brought (under my control), six of my officials . . . I set (as district-governors over) them; the town of Kashpuna on the coast of the Upper Sea . . . (the towns . . .)nite, Gal'za, Abilakka which are on the border of Israel (the widespread territory of Damascus Bit-Haza'i)li in its whole extent I restored to the border of Assyria. My (official) I set (over them) as district~governor. As for Hanunu of Gaza who had fled before my weapons and run off to Egypt, the town of Gaza (I conquered, his . . . and his possessions, his gods (I carried off and an image of the god Ashur), my lord, and an image of my own royal person (. . . I set up) within his palace and reckoned them as the gods of their country. I imposed upon them (a heavy tribute . . . silver) I tore out, like a bird . . . he fled. I restored him to his place and (imposed a heavy tribute upon him; gold), silver, linen garments with embroidery . . . great, . . . I received Israel (*Bit-Humria*) . . . the total of its inhabitants (together with their possessions) I led off to Assyria. Pekah their king they deposed and Hoshea I set (as king) over them. I received from them their (tribute)?) 10 talents of gold and . . . talents of silver and brought (them to Assyria).

(*Tiglath-Pileser III in Syria and Palestine*, in DOTT, p. 55)

DISCUSSION

1. According to the eighth-century prophets, what was Israel's sin?

2. Does it make sense to believe that God uses foreign powers to punish Israel for her transgressions?

FURTHER READING

Blenkinsopp, Joseph, *A History of Prophecy in Israel*, Westminster John Knox Press, 1996.

Blenkinsopp, Joseph, Knight, Douglas A., (eds), *Sage, Priest and Prophet: Religious and Intellectual Leadership in Ancient Israel*, Westminster John Knox Press, 1995.

Grabbe, Lester L., *Priests, Prophets, Diviners, Sages: A Socio-Historical Study of Religious Specialists in Ancient Israel*, Trinity Press International, 1995.

Knoppers, Gary N., *Two Nations Under God: The Deuteronomistic History of Solomon and the Dual Monarchies: The Reign of Jereboam, the Fall of Israel, and the Reign of Josiah*, Scholars Press, 1994.

Mowinckel, Sigmund, Hanson, K.C. (eds), *The Spirit and the Word: Prophecy and Tradition in Ancient Israel*, Fortress Press, 2002.

Silver, Morris, *Prophets and Markets: The Political Economy of Ancient Israel*, Kluwer Academic Publishers, 1982.

Soggin, J. Alberto, *Israel in the Biblical Period: Institutions, Festivals, Ceremonies, Rituals*, T. and T. Clark, 2002.

Tadmor, Hayyim, *The Inscriptions of Tiglath-Pileser III, King of Assyria*, Eisenbrauns, 1994.

Wilson, Robert, *Prophecy and Society in Ancient Israel*, Fortress Press, 1980.

Zucker, David J., *Israel's Prophets: An Introduction for Christians and Jews*, Paulist Press, 1994.

CHAPTER 11

Ahaz and Hezekiah

Timeline:

735–715 BCE Ahaz, King of Judah, refuses to join anti-Assyrian alliance

c. 715–687 BCE Reign of Hezekiah. Isaiah and Micah

701 BCE Assyrian siege of Jerusalem

With the collapse of the northern kingdom, Judah was under threat. To avoid a similar fate in the south, King Ahaz (735–715 BCE) continued to pay tribute to Assyria and to encourage the nation to worship Assyrian gods. However the prophet **Isaiah** was deeply concerned about such idolatrous practices. He believed that the collapse of Israel was God's punishment for sinfulness, and he foresaw a similar fate for Judah. Echoing the words of Amos, Isaiah warned his countrymen that God was not satisfied with empty ritual:

> What to me is the multitude of your
> sacrifices? says the Lord.
> I have had enough of burnt offerings of rams
> And the fat of fed beasts;
> I do not delight in the blood of bulls,
> or of lambs, or of he-goats.
>
> (Isaiah 1:11)

A contemporary of Isaiah, the prophet Micah, also criticized the people for their iniquity and foretold destruction:

> Hear this, you heads of the house of Jacob
> and rulers of the house of Israel,
> who abhor justice and pervert all equity . . .
> because of you Zion shall be ploughed as a field;
> Jerusalem shall become a heap of ruins.
>
> (Micah 3:9,12)

Ahaz refused to listen to these words; trusting in his own political alliances, he believed his kingdom was secure.

By the time Hezekiah (715–687 BCE) succeeded Ahaz, the Assyrian king, **Sargon II**, had turned his attention to problems in other parts of the empire. This gave Egypt and Philistia an opportunity to join ranks to throw off Assyrian domination. Seeking the help of Judah, the Philistine ambassadors tried to secure Hezekiah's support. But the prophet Isaiah warned that such an alliance would be of no avail. Assyria could not be stopped, and to dramatize the inevitable devastation, Isaiah walked naked around Jerusalem. 'So', he said, 'shall the king of Assyria lead away the Egyptian captives, and the Ethiopian exiles, both the young and the old, naked and barefoot, with buttocks uncovered, to the shame of Egypt' (Isaiah 20:4). Fortunately Hezekiah heeded Isaiah's prediction. Assyria quickly conquered the Philistine and Egyptian nations.

After this conquest Hezekiah attempted to establish his independence from Assyrian domination by reforming the religious practices of the people. As well as removing the altar to Assyrian gods in the temple which his father Ahaz had erected, he tried to close down local shrines in order to centralize the cult in Jerusalem. Further, he sent a message to those who remained in the former northern kingdom urging them to come south to worship. Hezekiah also

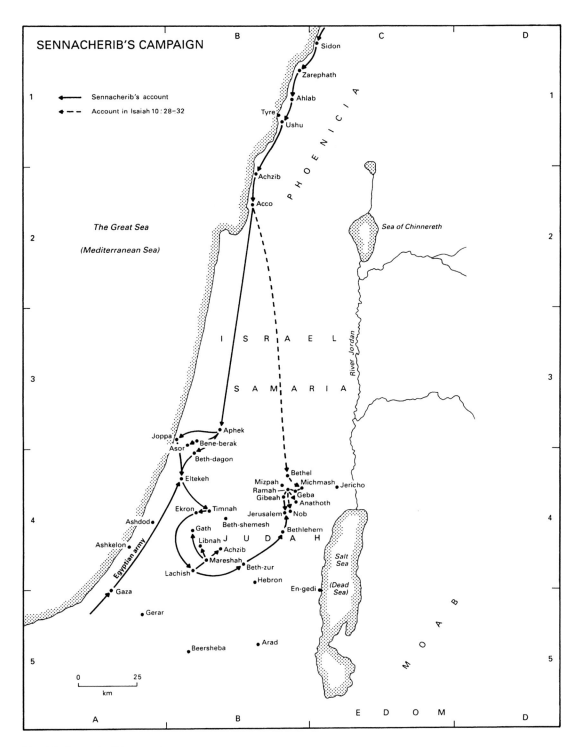

Map 15   Sennacherib's campaign

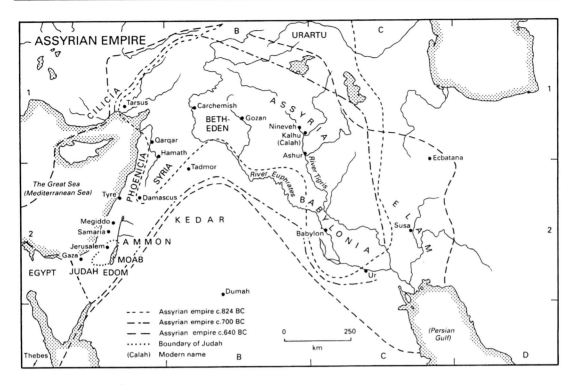

Map 16 Assyrian empire

prepared his kingdom for an Assyrian onslaught: he created new defences, restructured the army, established new store cities, and rationalized the civil service. In Jerusalem he built the Siloam Tunnel to ensure that the city would have a water supply if it were besieged. A surviving Hebrew inscription from this period etched on this tunnel describes its construction.

After the death of Sargon II, the kings of Babylon and Egypt asked Hezekiah to help overthrow the Assyrians. Isaiah cautioned against joining such an alliance, but Hezekiah took no notice. Sargon's successor **Sennacherib** (705–681 BCE) quickly acted to suppress this revolt. He subdued Babylon, Phoenicia and Philistia, and then moved against the kingdom of Judah in 701 BCE. According to an account of this assault in the annals of Sennacherib, the Assyrian army besieged and captured forty-six of Hezekiah's 'strong walled cities as well as the small cities in their neighbourhood'. Though the Assyrian records do not list the names of these places, the defeat of Lachish was depicted by Assyrian royal artists and placed in Sennacherib's palace at Nineveh. These surviving reliefs carved on stone portray the attack on Lachish and its eventual conquest.

The next step in the Assyrian campaign was the assault on Jerusalem. According to Sennacherib's records, Hezekiah was shut up in the city like a bird in a cage. Seeing no way of escape, he sent gold and silver as tribute to Sennacherib who was encamped at Lachish. It is unclear what events occurred next. 2 Kings contains an account of a siege of Jerusalem which ended in failure: the Asssyrian army camped outside the city, but just as their victory seemed imminent, the Assyrians withdrew. Many soldiers seem to have died. Though there are scholars who accept this story as authentic, they disagree about its dating. Some believe it was part of Sennacherib's invasion; others contend it refers to a second Assyrian campaign, since the narrative mentions King Tirhakah of Sudan who ruled in Egypt from about 689 BCE. Sennacherib's annals, however, contain no mention of this defeat – thus the Biblical account may be no more than a pious legend.

(a)

(b)

(c)

Figure 11(a) Surrender of the city of Lachish after the Assyrian siege by King Sennacherib, 701 BCE. Print after Assyrian base reliefs. (b) Relief, eighth century BCE, of two soldiers from Nineveh during the reign of King Sennacherib. (c) Relief, eighth century BCE from the South West Palace at Nineveh from the reign of King Sennacherib, showing the king inspecting the booty from Lachish. All images Copyright The British Museum.

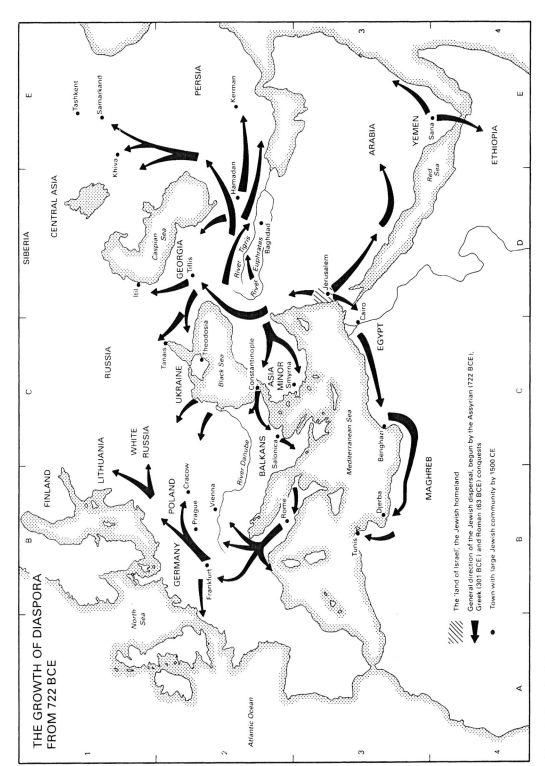

THE GROWTH OF DIASPORA
FROM 722 BCE

SIBERIA

CENTRAL ASIA

- Tashkent
- Samarkand

PERSIA

- Khiva
- Kerman

- Hamadan

FINLAND

LITHUANIA

WHITE RUSSIA

Itil

Caspian Sea

GEORGIA

- Tiflis

River Tigris

River Euphrates

Baghdad

RUSSIA

UKRAINE

Tanais

Theodosia

Black Sea

POLAND

- Cracow

GERMANY

- Prague
- Vienna

Constantinople

ASIA MINOR

Smyrna

Jerusalem

Cairo

EGYPT

ARABIA

YEMEN
Sana

Red Sea

ETHIOPIA

Frankfurt

River Danube

BALKANS

Salonica

Rome

Mediterranean Sea

Benghazi

MAGHREB

Djerba

North Sea

Atlantic Ocean

Tunis

The 'land of Israel'; the Jewish homeland

General direction of the Jewish dispersal, begun by the Assyrian (722 BCE),
Greek (301 BCE) and Roman (63 BCE) conquests

- Town with large Jewish community by 1500 CE

1 2 3 4

A B C D E

Map 17 Growth of diaspora

SOURCES

Isaiah's Vision

The prophet Isaiah experienced God's presence in the Temple in Judah:

> In the year that King Uzziah died I saw the Lord sitting upon a throne, high and lifted up; and his train filled the temple.
>
> Above him stood the seraphim; each had six wings; with two he covered his face, and with two he covered his feet, and with two he flew. And one called to another and said:
>
> > 'Holy, holy, holy is the Lord of hosts;
> > the whole earth is full of his glory.'
>
> (Isaiah 6:1–3)

Micah's Prophecy of Destruction of Samaria and Judah

Like earlier prophets, the prophet Micah also predicted destruction of both the northern and southern kingdoms for their sinfulness:

> Hear, you peoples, all of you;
> hearken, O earth, and all that is in it;
> and let the Lord God be a witness against you,
> the Lord from his holy temple.
> For behold, the Lord is coming forth out of his place,
> and will come down and tread upon the high places of the earth.
> And the mountains will melt under him
> and the valleys will be cleft,
> like wax before the fire,
> like waters poured down a steep place.
> All this is for the transgression of Jacob
> and for the sins of the house of Israel.
>
> (Micah 1:2–5)

Sargon II's Capture of Samaria

The annals of Shalmaneser record the victory of Sargon II:

At the beginning (of my rule . . . the city of the Sa)marians I (besieged and conquered . . .) who let me achieve my victory . . . carried off prisoners (27,290 of the people who dwelt in it; from among them I equipped 50 chariots for my royal army units . . . the city of Samaria) I restored and made it more habitable than before. (I brought into it) people of the countries conquered by my own hands. (My official I set over them as district governor and) imposed upon them tribute as on an Assyrian (city) . . . I made to mix with each other; the market price . . .

(*Annals of Shalmaneser*, in DOTT, p. 59)

Sennacherib's Siege of Jerusalem

Assyrian records also record Sennacherib's siege of Jerusalem:

But as for Hezekiah, the Jew, who did not bow in submission to my yoke, forty-six of his strong walled towns and innumerable smaller villages in their neighbourhood I besieged and conquered by stamping down earth-ramps, and then by bringing up battering rams, by the assault of foot-soldiers, by breaches, tunnelling and sapper operations. I made to come out from them 200,150 people, young and old, male and female, innumerable horses, mules, donkeys, camels, large and small cattle, and counted them as the spoils of war. He himself I shut up like a caged bird within Jerusalem, his royal city.

(Sennacherib's Siege of Jerusalem in DOTT, p. 67)

DISCUSSION

1. How did the symbolic actions of the prophets illustrate Israel's fate?

2. Do Assyrian records confirm the Biblical account of Sennacherib's conquests?

FURTHER READING

Cross, Frank Moore Jr, *From Epic to Canon: History and Literature in Ancient Israel,* Johns Hopkins University Press, 2000.

Dearman, John Andrew, *Religion and Culture in Ancient Israel,* Hendrickson Publishers, 1999.

Fox, Nili Sacher, *In the Service of the King: Officialdom in Ancient Israel and Judah,* Hebrew Union College, 2000.

Gallagher, William R., *Sennacherib's Campaign to Judah: New Studies,* Brill, 1999.

Gerstenberger, Erhard S., *Theologies of the Old Testament: Pluralism and Syncretism in Ancient Israel's Faith,* Fortress Press, 2002.

Irvine, Stuart, *Isaiah, Ahaz and the Syro-Ephraimitic Crisis,* Scholars Press, 1990.

Keel, Othmar, Wehlinger, Christoph, Trapp, Thomas H., *Gods, Goddesses and Images of God in Ancient Israel,* Continuum, 1998.

King, Philip, Stager, Lawrence, Knight, Douglas, *Life in Biblical Israel,* Westminster John Knox Press, 2002.

Provan, Ian, *Hezekiah and the Books of Kings,* Walter de Gruyter, 1988.

Vaughn, Andrew G., *Theology, History, and Archaeology in the Chronicler's Account of Hezekiah,* Scholars Press, 1999.

Weinfeld, Moshe, *Social Justice in Ancient Israel and in the Ancient Near East,* Fortress Press, 1995.

CHAPTER 12

From Manasseh to Babylonian Captivity

Timeline:

640–609 BCE Reign of Josiah. Judean independence. Deuteronomic movement for reform. Jeremiah

625–605 BCE Reign of Narbopolassar, the last Assyrian ruler. Assyrian empire collapses

Early 6th century BCE Division of the Assyrian empire between Babylonians and Medes

586 BCE Babylonian conquest. Deportations of Judeans to Babylonia

Following the invasion of Judah, Sennacherib was murdered. He was succeeded by **Esarhaddon** (681–669 BCE) who was a successful ruler. When he died the empire was divided between his two sons – Ashurbanipal (669–627 BCE) who reigned in Nineveh, and Shamash-Shanakin who had headquarters in Babylon. During this period Assyria was victorious against the Egyptians and became the dominant force in Mesopotamia. Under Ashurbanipal Nineveh emerged as a cultural centre. Here artists produced works of great merit and scribes collected together the literary treasures of Mesopotamian culture. In the kingdom of Judah, Hezekiah's successor, Manasseh (687–642 BCE), was completely under Assyrian domination. The nation's faith was neglected and pagan ceremonies again became prevalent. Like Ahaz, Manasseh was forced to worship Assyrian gods as a sign of submission, and his son and successor, Amon (642–640 BCE), continued his father's policies.

Despite its prominence, Assyria came under increasing threat from the kingdom of Lydia in the north-west, the Medes in the east and the Scythians in the north. This weakening of the Assyrian empire brought about a nationalistic revival in Judah.

The prophet **Jeremiah** warned that the southern kingdom would eventually be devastated by foreign powers. The new king, Josiah (640–609 BCE), believed he could restore Judah to its former glory through territorial expansion and religious reform. Josiah banned the symbols of Assyrian domination in the former

northern kingdom, destroyed the sanctuary at Bethel established by Jeroboam I and removed many local shrines and their priests. Most importantly, there was found in the Temple a forgotten book – in all likelihood the Book of Deuteronomy – which asserted that a single God should be worshipped in a central place by a united people. Some scholars argue that this text was not discovered but was commissioned by Josiah to support his policies. In any event, it had a profound effect on the nation. In a solemn ceremony, the people pledged their allegiance to God: 'And the king stood by the pillar and made a covenant before the Lord, to walk after the Lord and to keep his commandments and his testimonies and his statutes, with all his heart and all his soul, to perform the words of this covenant that were written in this book; and all the people joined in the covenant' (2 Kings 23:3).

While these events took place in Judah, the Babylonians advanced against Assyria and captured all its main cities. Some years after Josiah's reform, in 609 BCE the Assyrians made a final attempt to regain the town of Harran. Embroiling himself in this struggle, Josiah tried to halt the Egyptian army which had been summoned by the Assyrians to come to their aid. In the ensuing battle Josiah was mortally wounded, and Judah came under the domination of Egypt. Eventually, however, the Assyrian empire collapsed and the Babylonians succeeded in conquering the Egyptians at **Carchemish** in 605 BCE. At this King Jehoiakim (609–598 BCE), who had been put in power by

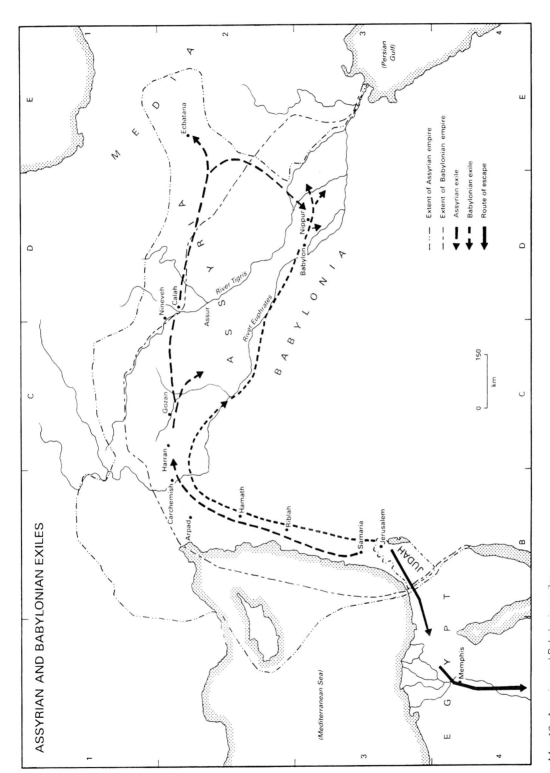

Map 18 Assyrian and Babylonian exiles

the Egyptians, transferred his allegiance to King Nebuchadnezzar II of Babylon (605–562 BCE). During the reign of Jehoiakim, Jeremiah continued to prophesy disaster – Jerusalem and the Temple itself, he declared, would be destroyed. His contemporary the prophet **Habakkuk** echoed the prediction that God would use foreign nations as instruments of his wrath. Jehoiakim was undeterred by this message; he believed he could eventually assert his independence from foreign rule.

When Babylon was defeated by Egypt several years later, Jehoaikim decided the time was ripe for rebellion. Nebuchadnezzar, however, quickly responded by invading the country and conquering Jerusalem. In this siege Jehoiakim was killed and replaced by his son Jehoiachin (597 BCE) who was captured. Along with other important citizens he was led into captivity, and the treasures of the palace and Temple were plundered. A new king, Zedekiah (597–586 BCE) was placed on the throne by Nebuchadnezzar in 597 BCE. Jeremiah counselled the king to accept Babylonian domination, but he was persuaded to join a rebellion led by Egypt. After a siege of eighteen months, **Jerusalem** was conquered in 586 BCE; all the main buildings were destroyed, and Zedekiah was blinded and exiled to Babylon. The last days of Judah just before the conquest of Jerusalem are described in a collection of potsherds (*ostrica*) written by Hoshayahu, who appears to have been the officer in charge of a military outpost to the north of Lachish. These fragments were addressed to Yaush, who was probably the military commander of Lachish. The value of these records is the insight they give into the reaction of the inhabitants of the land as they faced the end of their kingdom at the hands of the Babylonian army.

SOURCES

Jeremiah's Prophecy of the Destruction of the Southern Kingdom

Like the northern prophets, the prophet Jeremiah predicted destruction of the southern kingdom because of its iniquities:

For thus says the Lord to the men of Judah and to the inhabitants of Jerusalem:

'Break up your fallow ground
and sow not among thorns.
Circumcise yourselves to the Lord, remove the foreskins of your hearts,
O men of Judah and inhabitants of Jerusalem;
lest my wrath go forth like fire
and burn with none to quench it,
because of the evil of your doings.'
Declare in Judah, and proclaim in Jerusalem, and say,
"Blow the trumpet through the land";
cry aloud and say,
"Assemble and let us go into the fortified cities!"
Raise a standard toward Zion,
flee for safety, stay not,
for I bring evil from the north,
and great destruction.

(Jeremiah 4:3–6)

Habakkuk's Prediction of God's Destruction of Judah

The prophet Habakkuk similarly repeated this warning to the nation:

> Look among the nations, and see;
> wonder and be astounded.
> For I am doing a work in your days
> that you would not believe if told.
> For lo, I am rousing the Chaldeans,
> that bitter and hasty nation
> who march through the breadth of the earth,
> to seize the habitations not their own.
> Dread and terrible are they.

(Habakkuk 1:5–7)

Esarhaddon's Syro-Palestinian Campaign

Esarhaddon's Syro-Palestinian campaign is also recorded in ancient Near Eastern texts:

I called out the kings of the Hatti-land and the Trans-Euphrates area; Ba'al, king of Tyre, Manasseh, king of Judah, Qaushgabri, king of Edom, Musuri, king of Moab, Sil-Bel, king of Gaza, Metinti, king of Ashkelon, Ikasu, king of Ekron, Milki-ashapa, king of Gebal, Matan-ba'al, king of Arvad, Abi-ba'al, king of Samsimuruna, Pudu-il, king of Beth-Ammon, Ahi-milki, king of Ashdod – 12 kings of the sea coast. Ekistura, king of Edi'il (Idalion), Pilagura, king of Kitrusi (Chytrus), Kisu, king of Siollu'a (Soli), Ituandar, king of Pappa (Paphos), Erisu, king of Silli, Damasu, king of Kuri (Curium), Atmesu, king of Tamesi, Damusi, king of Qartihadsati, Unasagusuk, king of Ledir (Ledra), Bususu, king of Nuria – 10 kings of Iadnana (Cyprus), an island; – a total of 22 kings of the Hatti-land, the sea-shore and the island. I sent all of these to drag with pain and difficulty to Nineveh, the city of my dominion, as supplies needed for my palace, big beams, long posts and trimmed planks of cedar and cypress wood, products of the Sirara and Lebanon mountains, where for long they had grown tall and thick; also from their place of origin in the mountains the forms of winged bulls and colossi made of ashman stone . . .

(*Esarhaddon's Syro-Palestinian Campaign*, in DOTT, p. 74)

The Battle of Carchemish

The Battle of Carchemish is also recorded in ancient Near Eastern texts:

In the twenty-first year the king of Babylon stayed in his own country while the crown prince Nebuchadrezzar, his eldest son, took personal command of his troops and marched to Carchemish which lay on the bank of the River Euphrates. He crossed the river (to go) against the Egyptian army which was situated in Carchemish and . . . they fought with each other and the Egyptian army withdrew before him. He defeated them (smashing) them out of existence. As for the remnant of the Egyptian army which had escaped from the defeat so (hastily) that no weapon had touched them, the Babylonian army overtook and defeated them in the district of Hamath, so that not a single man (escaped) to his own country.

(*The Battle of Carchemish*, in DOTT, pp. 78–79)

The Capture of Jerusalem

Ancient Near Eastern sources similarly record the capture of Jerusalem by the Babylonian army:

> In the seventh year, in the month of Kislev, the Babylonian king mustered his troops, and having marched to the land of Hatti, besieged the city of Judah, and on the second day of the month of Adar took the city and captured the king.
>
> (*The Capture of Jerusalem*, in DOTT, p. 80)

DISCUSSION

1. Why did Josiah institute a series of reforms?

2. What was the nature of the final days of the Kingdom of Judah?

FURTHER READING

Becking, Bob, *The Fall of Samaria: An Historical and Archaeological Study*, Brill, 1992.

Christensen, Duane L., *Prophecy and War in Ancient Israel: Studies in the Oracles Against the Nations*, Sheffield Academic Press, 1989.

Gordon, Cyrus H., Rendsburg, Gary A., *The Bible and the Ancient Near East*, W.W. Norton and Company, 1998.

Healey, Mark, *Ancient Assyrians*, Osprey Publications, 2000.

Lindblom, Johannes, *Prophecy in Ancient Israel*, Fortress Press, 1962.

Newsome, James D., *By the Waters of Babylon: An Introduction to the History and Theology of the Exile*, Westminster John Knox Press, 1979.

Oppenheim, A. Leo, *Ancient Mesopotamia: Portrait of a Dead Civilization*, University of Chicago Press, 1977.

Pritchard, James Bennett, *Ancient Near East*, Princeton University Press, 1965.

Roaf, Michael, *The Cultural Atlas of Mesopotamia and the Ancient Near East*, Checkmark Books, 1990.

Saggs, Henry W. F., *Babylonians*, University of California Press, 2000.

Smith, Daniel L., *The Religion of the Landless: The Social Context of the Babylonian Exile*, HarperCollins, 1989.

Snell, Daniel, *Life in the Ancient Near East: 3100–332 BCE*, Yale University Press, 1998.

Wilson, Robert, *Prophecy and Society in Ancient Israel*, Fortress Press, 1980.

Weinfeld, Moshe, *Social Justice in Ancient Israel and in the Ancient Near East*, Fortress Press, 1995.

CHAPTER 13

Aftermath of the Fall of Judah

Timeline:

587 BCE Fall of Jerusalem

546–530 BCE Cyrus, king of Persia, overthrows Median kings, conquers Babylonian empire. Persia dominates ancient Near East

538 BCE Cyrus' edict permits Jews to return to Judah and rebuild the Temple

c. 515 BCE Completion of Second Temple in Jerusalem. Haggai and Zechariah. Judah a semiautonomous province of the Persian empire

Figure 12 Cyrus cylinder, fifth century BCE, from the period. It describes events from the reign of Cyrus, King of Persia, including various decrees relating to people he had freed. It includes detail of Cyrus returning the Israelites to their place of origin. Copyright The British Museum.

The anguish of the people facing the tragedy of Babylonian conquest and captivity is reflected in the Book of Lamentations. Here the exiles bemoaned the plight of Jerusalem:

> How lonely sits the city that was full of people!
> How like a widow she has become,
> She that was great among the nations! . . .
> The roads to Zion mourn,
> for none come to the appointed feasts;
> all her gates are desolate,
> her priests groan;
> her maidens have been dragged away
> and she herself suffers bitterly.
>
> (Lamentations 1:1, 4)

In 586 BCE Gedaliah, a palace official, was appointed governor of Judah and his capital was established at Mizpah. His appointment, however, aroused fierce opposition and Gedaliah was killed by Ishmael, a member of the former royal family. Fearing Babylonian vengeance, those who supported this rebellion fled to Egypt taking the prophet Jeremiah with them against his will. In exile these rebels were convinced that the Babylonian invasion was the fault of prophets like **Jeremiah** who had discouraged the people from worshipping foreign gods. The way to renewed prosperity, they believed, consisted in a return to the worship of Baal: 'But we will do everything that we have vowed', they declared, 'burn incense to the queen of heaven and pour our libations to her . . . since we left off burning incense to the queen of heaven and pouring out libations to her, we have lacked everything and have been consumed by the sword and the famine' (Jeremiah 44:17–18). For Jeremiah such a view was utter blasphemy; it was just such worship that brought about the downfall of Judah. Eventually Jeremiah's view became the basis for restructuring Jewish life, and some scholars argue that the books of Deuteronomy, Joshua, Judges, Samuel and Kings were gathered together at this time to form an epic history of Israel based on this vision of God's dealings with his chosen people.

Those exiles who settled in Babylon appear to have established a relatively prosperous community, keeping the faith alive in the synagogues. According to Scripture, the Babylonian king Nebuchadnezzar's successor Amel-Marduk (562–560 BCE) released Jehoiachin from prison in Babylon and offered him a position in the Babylonian court. However, despite their affluence, the exiles lamented the loss of their homeland as Psalm 137 records:

> By the waters of Babylon, there we sat down
> and wept,
> When we remembered Zion . . . How shall we
> sing the Lord's song in a foreign land?
>
> (Psalm 137:1, 4)

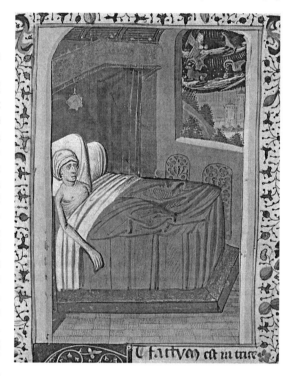

Figure 13 The vision of Ezekiel, miniature, folio 76r, tome 2, fifteenth century manuscript Bible said to be of Pope John XXII, reigned 1334–42, from Papal Palace, Avignon, France. Copyright The Art Archive/Musée Atger Montpellier/Dagli Orti.

The prophet **Ezekiel**, however, counselled those in Babylon not to despair. God, he believed, would restore the fallen nation. Though they were scattered, he would gather them up again:

> I will rescue them from all places where they have been scattered on a day of clouds and thick

darkness. And I will bring them out from the peoples, and gather them from the countries, and will bring them into their own land.

(Ezekiel 34:12–13)

During the decades that followed, Babylonia was ruled by a succession of weak and inept rulers. The Bible records that this was a difficult period for the Jewish community. The Book of Daniel, for example, relates how Daniel and his friends were subject to harsh treatment by Belshazzar, the king of Babylon. Such persecution is found also in the non-canonical books of Judith and Tobit.

As the Babylonian empire began to disintegrate, the kingdom of Persia grew in strength. In 539 BCE Cyrus of Persia (539–530 BCE) conquered Babylon and set about rebuilding the city. Though he himself worshipped the god Marduk, Cyrus believed that all peoples should be free to worship their own gods and live where they wished – the surviving Cyrus cylinder depicts this religious innovation. As far as the Jews were concerned, the Book of Ezra records Cyrus's pronouncement allowing them to return to Zion:

Concerning the house of God at Jerusalem, let the house be rebuilt, the place where sacrifices are offered and burnt offerings are brought; its height shall be sixty cubits and its breadth sixty cubits, with three courses of great stones and one course of timber; let the cost be paid from the royal treasury. And also let the gold and silver vessels of the house of God, which Nebuchadnezzar took out of the temple that is in Jerusalem and brought to Babylon, be restored and brought back to the temple which is in Jerusalem, each to its place; you shall put them in the house of God . . . let the governor of the Jews and the elders of the Jews rebuild this house of God on its site.

(Ezra 6:3–7)

In the latter part of the Book of Isaiah (which scholars attribute to a **second Isaiah**), this return is described as leading to a universal redemption for all people in which Israel will have a special role:

I will give you as a light to the nations, that my salvation may reach to the end of the earth.

(Isaiah 49:6)

SOURCES

Jeremiah's Condemnation of Idolatry in Egypt

Incensed at the apostasy of his fellow Jews living in Egypt, he castigated them for their waywardness:

Why do you provoke me to anger with the works of your hands, burning incense to other gods in the land of Egypt where you have come to live, that you may be cut off and become a curse and a taunt among all the nations of the earth? Have you forgotten the wickedness of your fathers, the wickedness of their wives, your own wickedness, and the wickedness of your wives, which they committed in the land of Judah and in the streets of Jerusalem? They have not humbled themselves even to this day, nor have they feared, nor walked in my law and my statutes which I set before you and before your fathers. 'Therefore thus says the Lord of hosts, the God of Israel: Behold I will set my face against you for evil, to cut off all Judah. I will take the remnant of Judah who have set their faces to come to the land of Egypt to live, and they shall all be consumed; in the land of Egypt they shall fall; by the sword and by famine they shall be consumed; for the least to the greatest, they shall die by the sword and by famine; and they shall become an execration, a horror, a curse and a taunt. I will punish those who dwell in the land of Egypt, as I have punished Jerusalem, with the sword, with famine, and with pestilence, so that none of the remnant of Judah who have come to live in the land of Egypt shall escape or survive or return to the land of Judah.'

(Jeremiah 44:8–14)

Ezekiel's Vision of the Chariot

In Babylonia the prophet Ezekiel had a vision of the divine chariot; this experience served as the basis for later rabbinic mysticism:

As I looked, behold, a stormy wind came out of the north, and a great cloud, with brightness round about it, and fire flashing forth, continually, and in the midst of the fire, as it were gleaming bronze. And from the midst of it came the likeness of four living creatures. And this was their appearance: they had the form of men, but each had four faces, and each of them had four wings. Their legs were straight, and the soles of their feet were like the sole of a calf's foot; and they sparkled like burnished bronze. Under their wings on their four sides they had human hands. And the four had their faces and their wings thus: their wings touched one another; they went every one straight forward, without turning as they went. As for the likeness of their faces, each had the face of a man in front . . . Now as I looked at the living creatures, I saw a wheel upon the earth beside the living creatures, one for each of the four of them. As for the appearance of the wheels and their construction: their appearance was like the gleaming of a chrysolite; and the four had the same likeness, their construction being as it were a wheel within a wheel.

(Ezekiel 1:4–10, 15–16)

Second Isaiah's Prophecy of the Suffering Servant

The prophet Isaiah predicted that a suffering servant would appear who would be despised and rejected; traditionally this figure has been understood as a symbol of the Jewish nation:

He was despised and rejected of men;
a man of sorrows, and acquainted with grief;
and as one from whom men hide their faces
he was despised, and we esteemed him not.
Surely he has borne our griefs
and carried our sorrows;
yet we esteemed him stricken,
smitten by God, and afflicted.
But he was wounded for our transgresssions,
he was bruised for our iniquities;
upon him was the chastisement that made us whole,
and with his stripes we are healed.
All we like sheep have gone astray;
we have turned every one to his own way;
and the Lord has laid on him
the iniquity of us all.
He was oppressed, and he was afflicted,
yet he opened not his mouth;
like a lamb that is led to the slaughter,
and like a sheep that before its shearers is dumb,
so he opened not his mouth.

(Isaiah 53:3–7)

DISCUSSION

1. Why were the Babylonian captives devastated by the fall of their kingdom?

2. What was the nature of Jewish life in Babylonia?

FURTHER READING

Anderson, Jeff S., *The Internal Diversification of Second Temple Judaism: An Introduction to the Second Temple Period*, University Press of America, 2002.

Bruce, Frederick Fyvie, Payne, David F., *Israel and the Nations: The History of Israel from the Exodus to the Fall of the Second Temple*, Intervarsity Press, 1998.

Carson, D.A., O'Brien, Peter T., Seifrid, Mark (eds), *Justification and Variegated Nomism: The Complexities of Second Temple Judaism*, Baker, 2001.

Castel, Francois, *History of Israel and Judah: In Old Testament Times*, Paulist, 1986.

Davies, Philip R. (ed.), *Second Temple Studies 1: Persian Period*, Continuum, 1991.

Davies, Philip, Halligan, John, *Second Temple Studies Vol. 3*, Continuum, 2002.

Eskenazi, Tamara C., Richards, Kent H., *Second Temple Studies Part 2: Temple and Community in the Persian Period*, Continuum, 1994.

Hayes, John, Hooker, Paul, *New Chronology for the Kings of Israel and Judah: And its Implications for Biblical History and Literature*, Westminster John Knox Press, 1988.

Helyer, Larry R., *Exploring Jewish Literature of the Second Temple Period: A Guide for New Testament Students*, Intervarsity Press, 2002.

Matthews, Victor H., *A Brief History of Ancient Israel*, Westminster John Knox Press, 2002.

Miller, James Maxwell, Hayes, John Harlason, *A History of Ancient Israel and Judah*, Westminster John Knox Press, 1986.

Rogerson, John W. *Chronicle of the Old Testament Kings*, Thames and Hudson, 1999.

Sacchi, Paolo, *History of the Second Temple Period*, Continuum, 1999.

Schiffman, Lawrence H., *From Text to Tradition: A History of Second Temple and Rabbinic Judaism*, KTAV, 1991.

Soggin, J. Alberto, *An Introduction to the History of Israel and Judah*, Trinity Press International, 1994.

Stone, Michael E. (ed.) *Jewish Writings of the Second Temple Period*, Fortress Press, 1984.

CHAPTER 14

Return and Restoration

Timeline:

c. 450s–440s BCE Israelites return to Judah from
Babylonia under Nehemiah and Ezra. Social reform
in Judah

c. 333 BCE Alexander the Great's army occupies
Judaea

To implement their policy of repatriation, the Persians
appointed Sheshbazzar as governor of Judah. Other
returning exiles included Joshua the priest and Zerubbabel, the grandson of Jehoiachin, who supervised the
repair and restoration of the Temple. According to
the Book of Jeremiah, after Nebuchadnezzar's invasion
worshippers continued to make a pilgrimage to the
Temple site. These Jews offered their assistance to
Zerubbabel, but he refused since he did not regard
them as real Jews: they were of uncertain racial origins
and their worship was suspect. These Judaean inhabitants and the people of Samaria recognized that the
returning exiles were intent on forming a state in which
they would have no role. Having their offer of co-
operation rejected, they persuaded the Persian officials
responsible for the western empire that the plans of
restoration were illegal, thereby delaying work on the
Temple for ten years or more. This was the start of
the enmity between the Jews and the Samaritan people
which continued for many hundreds of years and is
reflected in the New Testament.

Zerubbabel and Joshua were encouraged in their
labours by the prophets **Haggai** and **Zechariah**.
During the early part of the reign of the Persian king,
Darius I (522–486 BCE), Haggai urged the people to
make the rebuilding of the Temple a major priority.
Once the Temple walls were restored, he proclaimed,
a new era in Jewish history would dawn. Zerubbabel
was God's chosen ruler in this task of rebuilding: 'On

that day, says the Lord of Hosts, I will take you, O
Zerubbabel, my servant, the son of Shealtiel . . . and
make you like a signet-ring; for I have chosen you'
(Haggai 2:23). At the same time the prophet Zechariah
encouraged the completion of the Temple. He too
stressed that God was with Zerubbabel: 'Moreover the
word of the Lord came to me, saying, "The hands of
Zerubbabel have laid the foundation of this house:
his hands shall also complete it. Then you will know
that the Lord of Hosts has sent me to you"' (Zechariah
4:8–9).

In 515 BCE the Temple was completed, but little
is known about the period from 515 to 444 BCE. The
Book of Malachi, however, does depict a widespread
disregard for Temple worship. The priests appear to
have been negligent in their duties, and the faith of
Israel seems to have been polluted by magical practices.
In addition, social evil had become rampant. According to **Malachi**, God would eventually judge those
who were corrupt. Malachi also complained that
Jewish men were marrying women who belonged to
the racially mixed population of the country. By the
middle of the fifth century BCE, important steps were
taken by **Nehemiah** and Ezra to reform the life of the
Jewish community. According to modern scholars, it
is difficult to determine the chronological sequence
of their activity. It may be that the Biblical order
should be reversed and that Ezra should be placed after
Nehemiah. In any case, it appears that Nehemiah was

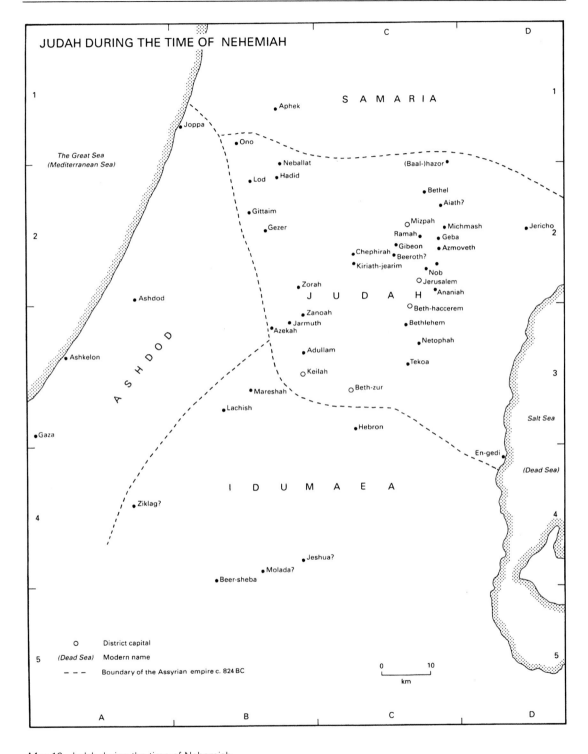

JUDAH DURING THE TIME OF NEHEMIAH

S A M A R I A

Aphek

Joppa

The Great Sea
(Mediterranean Sea)

Ono

Neballat

(Baal-)hazor

Lod   Hadid

Bethel

Aiath?

Gittaim

Mizpah   Michmash

Gezer

Ramah   Geba

Gibeon   Azmoveth

Chephirah   Beeroth?

Kiriath-jearim

Nob

Zorah   Jerusalem

J U D A H   Ananiah

Ashdod

Beth-haccerem

Zanoah   Bethlehem

Jarmuth

Azekah   Netophah

A S H D O D   Adullam

Tekoa

Ashkelon   Keilah

Beth-zur

Mareshah

Salt Sea

Lachish

Gaza   Hebron

En-gedi

(Dead Sea)

I D U M A E A

Ziklag?

Jeshua?

Molada?

Beer-sheba

O   District capital

(Dead Sea)   Modern name

– – –   Boundary of the Assyrian empire c. 824 BC

0   10
km

Map 19   Judah during the time of Nehemiah

appointed by the Persian King Artaxerxes I (464–423 BCE) as governor of Judah. Previous governors had been more concerned with their own comfort than with the welfare of the people, but Nehemiah was dedicated to the welfare of all. When he arrived from Persia, he discovered that Jews had intermarried with peoples of other races, and that the rich were exploiting the poor. To combat such laxity, he asserted that the community must purify itself by concentrating Jewish life within the confines of Jerusalem, and he initiated a policy of rebuilding and fortification. Such plans were opposed by Sanballat – the governor of Samaria, Tobiah – a prominent Ammonite, and others who feared that Israelites of mixed stock would be excluded from such plans. Despite such opposition, Nehemiah prevailed and Jerusalem was restored, kindling a new sense of religious identity.

In this policy of reform and renewal, Nehemiah was joined by the priest Ezra. Like Nehemiah, Ezra was a Persian state official who had come to Judah with royal authorization to reorganize religious affairs. Accompanied by other exiles who carried with them substantial financial contributions to the Temple, Ezra was determined to bring the people back to the covenant. For the exiles, covenantal law had taken on supreme importance, but this was not so in Judah. Traditional worship was frequently neglected. To remedy this situation, Ezra insisted on reading the law to the people, translated by the priests; this was necessary because the law was written in Hebrew but the inhabitants of the land spoke only Aramaic, the official language of the Persian empire. It is not clear exactly what this law was, but probably it was an early version of the Five Books of Moses as we know it today and included the priestly codes of Leviticus. When the nation heard these words, they were profoundly moved and vowed to observe the religious practices and festivals of their ancestors as recorded in Scripture, such as the pilgrim festivals – *Pesach*, *Shavuot* and *Sukkot* – and the New Year celebrations – *Rosh Hashanah* and *Yom Kippur*. The pilgrim festivals in particular provided a reason for the Jews who lived outside the land of Israel to visit Jerusalem regularly and regard it as their spiritual home.

During this period Jews lived in many parts of the world other than Judah and Babylonia where they asserted their religious identity in the synagogues. The

Figure 14 'Ezra in Prayer'. Wood engraving after the drawing by Gustave Doré. From a series of 230 Pictures of the Bible, 1865. German edition, Stuttgart (E. Hallberger), undated. Copyright AKG, London.

story of Esther, which is recited every spring at the festival of Lots (**Purim**) provides a vivid picture of the Jewish community during this period. A number of Aramaic documents discovered on the island of Elephantine also illustrate the habits of another Jewish group settled in Egypt. Like Judah, Egypt was then part of the Persian empire, and it appears that a Jewish military force was sent to Elephantine to guard the southern frontier. In this collection of papyrus documents there are deeds of property, marriage contracts and accounts of religious practices. Despite the Deuteronomic law forbidding sacrificial worship outside Jerusalem, there was a Jewish temple on this island where sacrifices were offered. Here the priests were neither Levites nor did they seem to be knowledgeable about Jewish law. Moreover, though this temple was dedicated to the God of Israel, other gods and goddesses were part of the cult. Though scholars disagree about the origins of this group it is clear that these Jews believed it was possible to be pious without following the guidelines established in Jerusalem.

In the years following Ezra, the inhabitants of Judah appear to have carried out his reforms, although some scholars believe the books of Ruth and Jonah were written as propaganda against his xenophobic policies. In contrast the books of Chronicles seem to support Jewish nationalism. They look back to the reigns of David and Solomon as a golden era and blame the subsequent disasters on the corruption of later kings, particularly on their neglect of temple worship. These books may be seen against the reforming background of the post-exilic period. The peoples of Samaria, on the other hand, came to realize that they would not be allowed to worship God in Jerusalem. As a consequence, they developed their own beliefs and culture, built their own temple on Mt Gerizim, and eventually established a strong national identity. In 333 BCE the Persian king, Darius III Codomannus (336–331 BCE) was defeated by Alexander the Great (331–323 BCE) from Macedonia. After this victory, Alexander advanced toward Egypt, but the Egyptians did not attempt to repulse his advance. Alexander subsequently died in 323 BCE. After a power struggle among his generals, both Egypt and Judah (then called Judaea) came under the jurisdiction of the Ptolemaic dynasty which lasted from 320 BCE until 198 BCE. During this period the Ptolemies were generally tolerant of the Jewish population, and it was at this stage that the Septuagint, the Greek translation of the Torah, was completed.

SOURCES

Haggai's Prediction of Restoration

The prophet Haggai returned to Judah after the exile and together with Zerubbabel engaged in the rebuilding of the Temple:

The word of the Lord came a second time to Haggai on the twenty-fourth day of the month, 'Speak to Zerubbabel, governor of Judah, saying, I am about to shake the heavens and the earth, and to overthrow the throne of kingdoms; I am about to destroy the strength of the kingdoms of the nations, and overthrow the chariots and their riders; and the horses and their riders shall go down, every one by the sword of his fellow. On that day, says the Lord of hosts, I will take you, O Zerubbabel my servant, the son of She-al'ti-el, says the Lord, and make you like a signet ring; for I have chosen you, says the Lord of hosts.'

(Haggai 2:20–23)

Zechariah's Prophecy of Redemption

The prophet Zechariah prophesied the eventual redemption of the nation:

So the angel who talked with me said to me, 'Cry out, Thus says the Lord of hosts: I am exceedingly jealous for Jerusalem and for Zion. And I am very angry with the nations that are at ease; for while I was angry but a little they furthered the disaster. Therefore, thus says the Lord, I have returned to Jerusalem with compassion; my house shall be built in it, says the Lord of hosts, and the measuring line shall be stretched out over Jerusalem. Cry again, Thus says the Lord of hosts: My cities shall again overflow with prosperity, and the Lord will again comfort Zion and again choose Jerusalem.'

(Zechariah 1:14–17)

Malachi's Condemnation of the Nation

Like earlier prophets, Malachi condemned the nation for its iniquity:

You cover the Lord's altar with tears, with weeping and groaning, because he no longer regards the offering or accepts it with favour at your hand. You ask, 'Why does he not?' Because the Lord was witness to the covenant between you and the wife of your youth, to whom you have been faithless, though she is your companion and your wife by covenant. Has not the one God made and sustained for us the spirit of life? And what does he desire? Godly offspring. So take heed to yourselves, and let none be faithless to the wife of his youth. 'For I hate divorce, says the Lord the God of Israel.'

(Malachi 2:13–16)

The Commemoration of *Purim*

The Book of Esther declares that the festival of *Purim* should be commemorated yearly:

Therefore they called these days *Purim* after the term, *Pur*. And, therefore, because . . . of what they had faced in this matter, and of what had befallen them, the Jews ordained and took it upon themselves and their descendants and all who joined them, that without fail they would keep these two days according to what was written and at the time appointed every year, that these days should be remembered and kept throughout every generation, in every family, province, and city, and that these days of *Purim* should never fall into disuse among the Jews, nor should the commemoration of these days cease among their descendants.

(Esther 9: 26–28)

Nehemiah's Description of Ezra

The prophet Nehemiah described Ezra's activity in Judah:

And Ezra the priest brought the law before the assembly, both men and women and all who could hear with understanding, on the first day of the seventh month. And he read from it facing the square before the Water Gate from early morning until midday, in the presence of the men and the women and those who could understand; and the ears of all the people were attentive to the book of the law. And Ezra the scribe stood on a wooden pulpit which they had made for the purpose . . . And Ezra opened the book in the sight of all the people, for he was above all the people, and when he opened it all the people stood. And Ezra blessed the Lord, the great God; and all the people answered, 'Amen, Amen.'

(Nehemiah 8: 2–6)

DISCUSSION

1. Why did King Cyrus allow the Jews to return from exile?

2. How does the Book of Esther symbolize the victory of the Jews against their enemies?

FURTHER READING

Bickerman, Elias, *From Ezra to the Last of the Maccabees: Foundations of Postbiblical Judaism*, Schocken, 1981.

Blenkinsopp, Joseph, *Prophecy and Canon: A Contribution to the Study of Jewish Origins*, Notre Dame Press, 1977.

Kaufmann, Yehezkel, *History of the Religion of Israel: From the Babylonian Captivity to the End of Prophecy*, KTAV, 1977.

Nickelsburg, George W.E., *Jewish Literature Between the Bible and the Mishnah*, Fortress Press, 1981.

Smith, Morton, *Palestinian Parties and Politics that Shaped the Old Testament*, Columbia University Press, 1971.

CHAPTER 15

The Rise of Hellenism

Timeline:

3rd century BCE Judaea under the Ptolemies, Hellenistic rulers in Egypt. Rise of Jewish community in Alexandria

201–198 BCE Judaea under rule of Seleucids with Syria, Mesopotamia and other lands

175–163 BCE Reign of Antiochus IV Epiphanes, king of Seleucids

175 BCE Hellenizing Jews dominant in Jerusalem

167 BCE Antiochus IV turns the Temple into a pagan shrine. Maccabean revolt

164 BCE Victory of the Maccabees over the Seleucids. Temple rededicated

163–140 BCE Maccabean stuggle against the Seleucids

161 BCE Judah Maccabee killed. Jonathan, his brother, becomes leader of the Maccabees

146 BCE Roman control of Greece and Macedonia

140 BCE Jonathan killed. Assembly in Jerusalem recognizes Simon, his brother, as high priest and *ethnarch* of Judaea

134–104 BCE Rule of John Hyrcanus, Simon's son

104–103 BCE Rule of Judah Aristobulus, John Hyrcanus' son

Though Ptolemy was victorious in securing Judaea, another of Alexander's generals, Seleucus, was dissatisfied with this outcome. Throughout the third century BCE his successors were involved in a series of battles to determine sovereignty over the country. In 198 BCE the issue was settled when the Seleucid king, Antiochus III (223–187 BCE), defeated Scopus, the general of the Egyptian king, Ptolemy V. Initially Antiochus III had a positive attitude toward the Jews – he reduced their taxes and made a donation to the Temple. In time he reversed these policies, but in 190 BCE he was defeated in a battle against the Romans at Magnesia near Ephesus. In the peace treaty he was forced to hand over his territory in Asia Minor, the richest part of the empire. A year later Antiochus III was killed while robbing a temple to increase revenue, and was succeeded by his son, Seleucus IV (187–175 BCE), who dispatched his chancellor Heliodorus to plunder the Jerusalem Temple.

During the reign of the Seleucids in the second century, two families engaged as rivals in the Judaean Jewish community – the Tobiads and Oniads. When Seleucus IV was murdered in 175 BCE and succeeded by Anitochus IV Epiphanes (175–163 BCE), Jason, a member of the Oniad family, bribed Antiochus IV to make him high priest in place of his brother Onias. When he was appointed to this position, Jason attempted to Hellenize Jerusalem. This involved the introduction of Greek games in which the athletes competed naked, a sight shocking to traditional sensibilities. Many Jews found these changes abhorrent, and Jason was deposed from the throne and replaced by Menelaus, a member of the Tobiad family.

While this internal conflict took place in Judaea, Antiochus IV advanced against Egypt and defeated the Egyptian king, Ptolemy VI; on his return he robbed the Jerusalem Temple. In 168 BCE Antiochus IV again invaded Egypt, but this time he encountered the Romans, who drove back his onslaught. In Jerusalem it was rumoured that Antiochus IV had been killed,

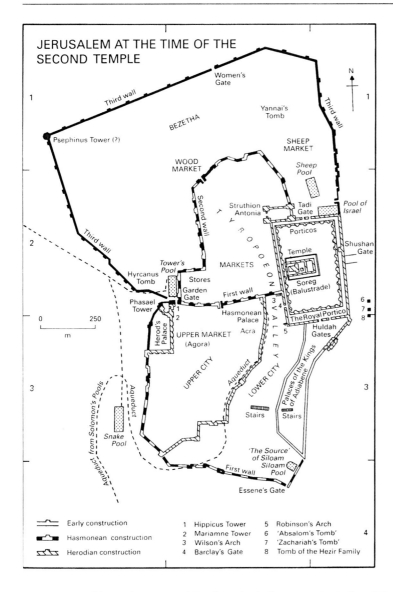

JERUSALEM AT THE TIME OF THE SECOND TEMPLE

Third wall

Women's Gate

BEZETHA

Yannai's Tomb

Third wall

Psephinus Tower (?)

SHEEP MARKET

WOOD MARKET

Sheep Pool

Second wall

Struthion Antonia

Tadi Gate

Pool of Israel

T Y R O P O E O N

Porticos

Third wall

Temple

Shushan Gate

Tower's Pool

MARKETS

Hyrcanus Tomb

Stores

Soreg (Balustrade)

Garden Gate

First wall

6
7
8

Phasael Tower

1

Hasmonean Palace

The Royal Portico

0   250

2

Acra

Huldah Gates

m

Herod's Palace

UPPER MARKET (Agora)

V A L L E Y

UPPER CITY

Aqueduct

LOWER CITY

Palaces of the Kings of Adiabene

Aqueduct from Solomon's Pools

Aqueduct

Stairs

Stairs

Snake Pool

'The Source' of Siloam

Siloam Pool

First wall

Essene's Gate

Early construction	
Hasmonean construction	
Herodian construction	

1 Hippicus Tower
2 Mariamne Tower
3 Wilson's Arch
4 Barclay's Gate

5 Robinson's Arch
6 'Absalom's Tomb'
7 'Zachariah's Tomb'
8 Tomb of the Hezir Family

4

Map 20 Jerusalem at the time of the Second Temple

and Jason quickly tried to remove Menelaus. Antiochus IV however acted speedily to crush this rebellion. He conquered Jerusalem and led off some of the people as slaves. In addition he banned circumcision, Sabbath observance and the reading of the Torah. He also decreed that the Temple should be dedicated to the worship of the Greek god Zeus, that pigs should be sacrificed on the altar, and that all people, including non-Jews, should be allowed to worship there. Hellenism, which previously was encouraged by the Seleucids, thus became official policy.

Antiochus IV underestimated Jewish resistance to his reforms; many Jews were prepared to die rather than violate their traditions. Eventually a guerrilla band, led by a priest Mattathias and his five sons, engaged in armed revolt. After Mattathias's death, this movement was spearheaded by his son Judas. Some Jews – the Hasideans – were opposed to armed struggle and retreated into the Judaean desert where they were slaughtered by the Seleucids when they refused to fight in battle on the Sabbath. The event drew other Jews to the side of the rebels, and after a series of military

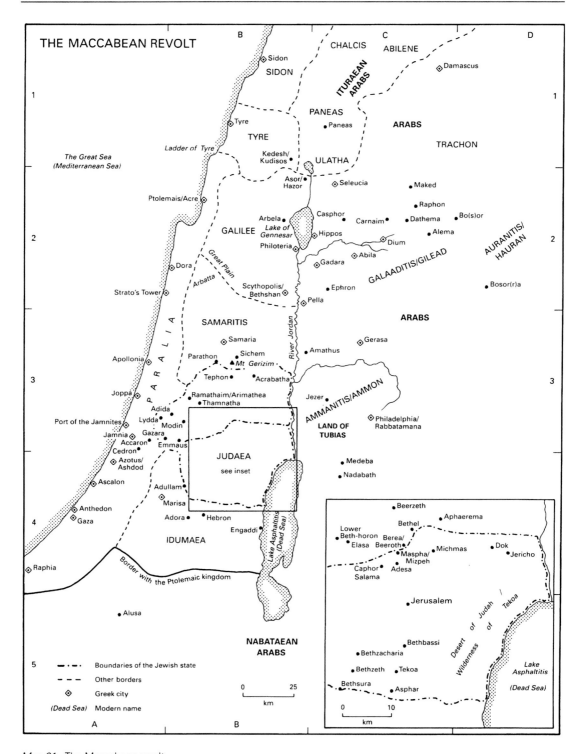

Map 21 The Maccabean revolt

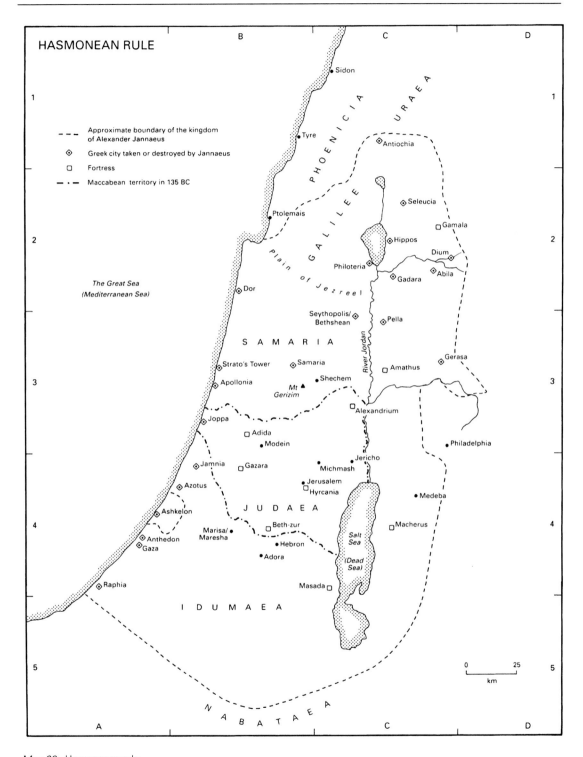

HASMONEAN RULE

- - - - Approximate boundary of the kingdom of Alexander Jannaeus

⊗ Greek city taken or destroyed by Jannaeus

□ Fortress

- · - Maccabean territory in 135 BC

The Great Sea
(Mediterranean Sea)

Sidon

Tyre

Antiochia

P H O E N I C I A

U R A E A

Seleucia

Gamala

Ptolemais

G A L I L E E

Hippos

Dium

Philoteria

Abila

Plain of Jezreel

Gadara

Dor

Scythopolis/
Bethshean

Pella

S A M A R I A

Gerasa

Strato's Tower

Samaria

Amathus

River Jordan

Apollonia

Mt Gerizim

Shechem

Alexandrium

Joppa

Adida

Modein

Philadelphia

Jamnia

Gazara

Jericho

Michmash

Azotus

Jerusalem
Hyrcania

Medeba

Ashkelon

J U D A E A

Anthedon

Marisa/
Maresha

Beth-zur

Salt
Sea

Macherus

Gaza

Hebron

Adora

(Dead
Sea)

Raphia

I D U M A E A

Masada

0   25
km

N A B A T A E A

Map 22   Hasmonean rule

engagements the oppressive policies of the Seleucids were reversed. Jewish law was reinstituted, and the Temple was restored and rededicated on 14 December 164 BCE, an event subsequently commemorated by the festival of lights (*Hanukkah*). This victory enabled Judas's clan (the Hasmoneans) to establish themselves as the ruling family in Judaea.

Following the campaign against the Seleucids, Judas made a treaty with the Roman Republic. But in 160 BCE he fell in battle and was succeeded by his brother Jonathan. On the death of the high priest, Jonathan was appointed supreme pontiff even though he lacked hereditary qualification. He was later formally recognized as governor of Judaea. The last surviving brother, Simon, who succeeded Jonathan, asserted formal independence from the Seleucid empire. He expelled the Seleucid garrison from the Jerusalem citadel in 142–141 BCE, captured the fortress of Gazara and compelled the Seleucid monarch to acquiesce. The Maccabean rebellion thus finally triumphed, and Simon took on the hereditary title of *ethnarch*, a desig-

nation which signified the ruler of an *ethnos* (nation). Many scholars believe that the Book of **Daniel** was written during this period of rebellion as a message of encouragement against the Seleucids, although it ostensibly deals with events belonging to the reign of Jehoiakim in the sixth century BCE.

In 135 BCE Simon was murdered in a palace intrigue, and his son, John Hyrcanus I (134–104 BCE) became high priest and ethnarch. During the early part of his reign, the Seleucids besieged Jerusalem and John Hyrcanus I was forced to give up some territory and join the Seleucid king in an unsuccessful campaign against the Parthians. Subsequently John Hyrcanus I conquered large areas of Transjordan and Samaria where he razed the Samaritan temple on Mt Gerizim. He also conquered Idumea and compelled the inhabitants to convert to Judaism. One of his sons, Aristobulus I (104–103 BCE) completed the conquest of Galilee, and his second son, Alexander Janneus (102–76 BCE) annexed nearly all the Hellenized cities of the coastal region and northern Transjordan.

SOURCES

Belshazzar's Feast

The Book of Daniel records Belshazzar's feast during which his downfall was predicted:

King Belshazzar made a great feast for a thousand of his lords, and drank wine in front of the thousand. Belshazzar, when he tasted the wine, commanded that the vessels of gold and of silver which Nebuchadnezzar his father had taken out of the temple in Jerusalem be brought that the king and his lords, his wives, and his concubines might drink from them. They brought in the golden and silver vessels which had been taken out of the temple, the house of God in Jerusalem; and the king and his lords, his

wives, and his concubines drank from them. They drank wine, and praised the gods of gold and silver, bronze, iron, wood and stone. Immediately the fingers of a man's hand appeared and wrote on the plaster of the wall of the king's palace, opposite the lampstand: and the king saw the hand as it wrote. Then the king's colour changed, and his thoughts alarmed him; his limbs gave way, and his knees knocked together.

(Daniel 5:1–6)

DISCUSSION

1. Discuss the conflict between Jewish Hellenizers and their opponents.

2. In what ways did Antiochus Epiphanes IV violate Jewish sensibilities?

Figure 15 Belshazzar's Feast, painting by Rembrandt. Copyright The National Gallery, London.

FURTHER READING

Box, G.H., *Judaism and Hellenism*, Church History, 2001.

Collins, John J., Sterling, Gregory (eds), *Hellenism in the Land of Israel*, Notre Dame Press, 2001.

Goodman, Martin (ed.), *Jews in a Graeco-Roman World*, Clarendon Press, 1999.

Hengel, Martin, *Judaism and Hellenism: Studies in their Encounter in Palestine During the Early Hellenistic Period*, Fortress Press, 1975.

Kugel, James (ed.), *Shem in the Tents of Japhet: Essays on the Encounter of Judaism and Hellenism*, Brill, 2002.

Levine, Lee I., *Judaism and Hellenism in Antiquity: Conflict or Confluence?*, Hendrickson Publishers, 1999.

Rajak, Tessa, *The Jewish Dialogue with Greece and Rome: Studies in Cultural and Social Interaction*, Brill, 2001.

Schalit, Abraham (ed.), *The Hellenistic Age: Political History of Jewish Palestine from 332 BCE to 67 CE*, Rutgers University Press, 1972.

Schurer, Emil, Vermes, Geza, Millar, Fergus, Goodman, Martin (eds), *The History of the Jewish People in the Age of Jesus Christ*, Vols 1–2, T. and T. Clark, 1987.

Smith, Morton, Cohen, Shaye J. D. (eds), *Studies in the Cult of Yahweh: Studies in Historical Method, Ancient Israel, Ancient Judaism*, Brill, 1997.

Tcherikover, Victor, *Hellenistic Civilization and the Jews*, Hendrickson Publishers, 1999.

Zeitlin, Solomon, *The Rise and Fall of the Judean State*, Vols l–3, Jewish Publication Society, 1962–78.

CHAPTER 16

Judaism under Hellenism

Timeline:

103–76 BCE Rule of Alexander Janneus, second son of John Hyrcanus. Extension of Judaean control over Palestine and Transjordan. Conflict between John Hyrcanus and Pharisees

76–67 BCE Rule of Salome Alexandra, wife of Alexander Janneus

67–63 BCE Struggle between Salome's sons (John Hyrcanus II and Aristobulus II) for the throne

65 BCE Pompey's victory over king of Pontus results in Asia Minor and Syria under Roman control

63 BCE Pompey supports Hyrcanus and captures Jerusalem. John Hyrcanus II becomes high priest. Antipater, his adviser, becomes administrator in Judaea

48 BCE Julius Caesar defeats Pompey

44 BCE Assassination of Julius Caesar

42 BCE Mark Antony and Octavian defeat the anti-Caesar party. Antony rules over eastern half of the Roman empire. Octavian rules over the western half.

40 BCE Parthians invade Judaea. Antipater's son Herod flees to Rome where he is viewed as king of Judaea

37 BCE Herod captures Jerusalem with the help of the Roman army

37–4 BCE Reign of Herod as king of Judaea

31 BCE Octavian defeats Antony at Actium. Octavian becomes emperor

4 BCE Division of Herod's kingdom between three of his sons

Although all Jews professed allegiance to the Torah, the Jewish community in Judaea at this time was divided into various sects. According to the first century CE historian, Josephus, the three most important groups were the **Sadducees**, the **Pharisees** and the Essenes. The Sadducees consisted of a small group of influential individuals including the hereditary priests who controlled Temple worship. Possibly their name derives from King David's priest Zadok. For these Jews there was no reason to interpret and expand the written law, and they rejected any speculation about a future life. The second group consisted of the Pharisees – their name seems to derive from a Hebrew term *parush* (meaning 'separated'). Some scholars suggest that this name was applied to them because they separated themselves from the masses for the sake of holiness; others surmise that it was given by opponents who charged that they had separated themselves from the Sadducean interpretation of Scripture. Their rise appears to date from the Hasideans who broke from the Hasmonean regime in the second century because of its irreligious character. Initially they were not political activists; instead they advocated submission to God's will. Unlike the Sadducees, the Pharisees believed in the resurrection of the body and the world to come. Moreover, they were anxious to make Biblical law applicable to contemporary circumstances by offering oral expositions of the text. This procedure, they believed, had been commanded by God to Moses on Mt Sinai when he received the written commandments. For example, the fourth commandment forbade work on the Sabbath; the Pharisees devised thirty-nine categories of labour so that everyone was clear what it was that had to be avoided. In contrast to the Sadducees who were involved in the Temple cult, the Pharisees centred their activities on the synagogue. It was from this sector of society that the scribes emerged as an important force in Jewish life. Although there appear to have been scribes from the time of Jeremiah (such as the prophet's secretary, Baruch), they came to form a recognizable class who copied the law and decided how its prescriptions could be put into effect. Both the Pharisees and the Sadducees were involved in the Great Sanhedrin, the central religious and legislative body of the Judaean community.

The third principal sect were the Essenes who may also have been an offshoot of the Hasideans. Their name possibly derives from the Aramaic word '*hasa*' (pious). According to the Essenes, the Hellenizers and worldly Sadducees were violators of God's law. The most important characteristic which differentiates this group from Pharisees and Sadducees concerned their lifestyle: rejecting the corruption of town life, they congregated in semi-monastic communities. Most scholars believe it was this sect who produced the **Dead Sea Scrolls**. This literature was the work of a devoted community based near the Dead Sea who wrote about

Figure 16 Dead Sea Scrolls. Written documents which were recovered from these caves in Wadi Qumran in the desert hills close to the shores of the Dead Sea.

an ideal Teacher of Righteousness as their leader. The Essenes believed that they alone were members of the new covenant prophesied by Jeremiah. In their community rule (the Manual of Discipline) and war rule, a cataclysmic end of the world is described, to be preceded by a struggle against good and evil in which Israel will emerge victorious.

During the reign of Alexander Jannaeus a number of Pharisees revolted against his Hellenizing influence. It appears that they seized Jerusalem and the royal mint, issuing coins of their own in the name of the Council of Elders. But this rebellion failed, resulting in the loss of many lives. After the death of Alexander Jannaeus, his widow Salome Alexandra (76–67 BCE) succeeded him and reversed his religious policies, treating the Pharisees with favour. On her death, her two sons John Hyrcanus II and Aristobulus II struggled for power. A chieftain from Idumea, Antipater attempted to assist John Hyrcanus II's cause by inviting his allies the Nabateans to march on Jerusalem. But it was left to the Roman leader Pompey, who had recently annexed Syria, to decide the matter of the Hasmonean succession. Pompey marched into Jerusalem, killed many of its inhabitants, and stepped inside the Holy of Holies in the Temple – an act of blasphemy in the eyes of the Jewish populace. Judaea became a client state of Rome, and John Hyrcanus II was appointed high priest and *ethnarch* of Judaea and Galilee (territory in the north). In addition he was given the right to intervene in matters relating to the Jewish communities abroad (the Jewish diaspora). After five years, however, he was deprived of his position as *ethnarch*, and the country was divided into five districts, each under a court of local dignitaries drawn largely from the Sadducees. Antipater was put in charge of Idumea but retained special powers in Jerusalem such as tax-collecting.

After Pompey's death in 48 BCE, John Hyrcanus II and Antipater gave assistance to Julius Caesar in his battle against the Egyptian forces. As a reward Caesar enlarged John Hyrcanus II's former state and recognized Antipater as chief minister. Caesar also introduced a number of measures to safeguard the security of Jewish communities outside Judaea: they were allowed liberty of religious observance, freedom to send gifts to the Jerusalem Temple, exemption from military duty and the right to their own jurisdiction.

Antipater's son Phasael was made governor of Jerusalem, and his other son Herod became governor of Galilee. When Herod successfully crushed a Galilean revolt, he was censured by the Great Sanhedrin for his brutal behaviour towards those he conquered and was forced to leave Judaea. Nevertheless the new governor of Syria entrusted him with an important military command, as did Cassius when

Caesar was assassinated. After Mark Antony and Octavian had avenged Caesar's death, they confirmed the appointments of Phasael and Herod as *tetrarchs* (subordinate rulers) of Judaea despite Jewish resistance. Yet it was not long before the Parthians invaded Roman Asia Minor, Syria and Judaea. John Hyrcanus II was dethroned in favour of his nephew Antigonus; Phasael was killed; and Herod forced to escape.

SOURCES

Sadducees

Flavius Josephus was a Palestinian historian and soldier in the first century CE. Born in Jerusalem, he went to Rome in 64 CE on a mission to secure the release of several priests. At the outbreak of the Jewish rebellion against Rome in 66 CE, he was appointed commander of Galilee; when the Romans attacked the province in 67 CE, he directed the resistance. He surrendered to the Romans after Jotapata was captured. Later he accompanied Vespasian and Titus during the siege of Jerusalem. In his writings he describes the nature of the Saducean movement.

The Sadducees hold that the soul perishes along with the body. They own no observance of any sort apart from the laws; in fact, they reckon it a virtue to dispute with the teachers of the path of wisdom that they pursue. There are but few men to whom this doctrine has been made known, but these are men of the highest standing. They accomplish practically nothing, however. For whenever they assume some office, though they submit unwillingly and perforce, yet submit they do to the formulas of the Pharisees, since otherwise the masses would not tolerate them.

(*Antiquities*. xviii.16, in JP, p. 89)

The Sadducees, the second of the orders, do away with fate altogether, and remove God beyond, not merely the commission, but the very sight, of evil. They maintain that man has the free choice of good or evil, and that it rests with each man's will whether he follows the one or the other. As for the persistence of the soul after death, penalties in the underworld and rewards, they will have none of them.

(*War* ii.164, JP, p. 93–94)

Pharisees

In his writings, Josephus also describes the nature of Pharisaic belief.

There was also a group of Jews priding itself on its adherence to ancestral custom and claiming to observe the laws of which the Deity approves, and by these men, called Pharisees, the women (of the court) were ruled.

(*Antiquities* xvii.41, in JP, p. 85)

The Pharisees simplify their standard of living, making no concession to luxury. They follow the guidance of

that which their doctrine has selected and transmitted as good, attaching the chief importance to observance of those commandments which it has seen fit to dictate to them. They show respect and deference to their elders, nor do they rashly presume to contradict their proposals. Though they postulate that everything is brought about by fate, still they do not deprive the human will of the pursuit of what is in man's power, since it was God's good pleasure that there should be a fusion and that the will of the man with his virtue and vice should be admitted to the council-chamber of fate. They believe that souls have power to survive death and that there are rewards and punishments under the earth for those who have led lives of virtue or vice: eternal punishment is the lot of evil souls, while the good souls receive an easy passage to a new life. Because of these views they are, as a matter of fact, extremely influential among the townsfolk; and all prayers and sacred rites of divine worship are performed according to their exposition. This is the great tribute that the inhabitants of the cities, by practising the highest ideals both in their way of living and in their discourse, have paid to the excellence of the Pharisees.

(*Antiquities* xviii.12–13, in JP, p. 89)

The Pharisees, who are considered the most accurate interpreters of the Laws, and hold the position of the leading sect, attribute everything to fate and to God; they hold that to act rightly or otherwise rests, indeed, for the most part with men, but that in each action fate co-operates. Every soul, they maintain, is imperishable, but the soul of the wicked suffer eternal punishment.

(*War* ii.162–163, in JP, p. 93)

The Pharisees are affectionate to each other and cultivate harmonious relations with the community.

(*War* ii.166, in JP, p. 166)

Dead Sea Scrolls

The Hymn Scroll parallels the Psalms and contains references to the experiences of a teacher who is abandoned by his friends and persecuted by enemies. Some scholars ascribe the authorship of these texts to the Teacher of Righteousness:

> Thou are long-suffering in Thy judgements
> and righteous in all Thy deeds.
>
> By Thy wisdom (all things exist from eternity),
> and before creating them Thou knewest their works for ever and ever.
> (Nothing) is done (without Thee)
> and nothing is known unless Thou desire it.
>
> Thou hast created all the spirits
> (and hast established a statute) and law
> for all their works.
> Thou hast spread the heavens for Thy glory
> and hast (appointed) all (their hosts)
> according to Thy will;
> the mighty winds according to their laws
> before they became angels (of holiness)
> . . . and eternal spirits in their dominions;
> the heavenly lights to their mysteries,
> the stars to their paths,
> (the clouds) to their tasks,
> the thunderbolts and lightnings to their duty,
> and the perfect treasuries (of snow and hail)
> to their purposes,
> . . . to their mysteries.

Thou hast created the earth by Thy power
and the seas and deeps (by Thy might).
Thou hast fashioned (all their) inhabitants
according to Thy wisdom,
and hast appointed all that is in them
according to Thy will.

(And) to the spirit of man
which Thou hast formed in the world,
(Thou hast given dominion over the works of Thy hands)
for everlasting days and unending generations.
. . . in their ages
Thou hast allotted to them tasks
during all their generations,
and judgement in their appointed seasons
according to the rule (of the two spirits.
For Thou hast established their ways)
for ever and ever,
(and hast ordained from eternity)
their visitation for reward and chastisements;
Thou hast allotted it to all their seed
for eternal generations and everlasting years . . .
In their wisdom of Thy knowledge
Thou didst establish their destiny before ever they were,
All things (exist) according to (Thy will)
and without Thee nothing is done.

These things I know
by the wisdom which comes from Thee
for Thou hast unstopped my ears
to marvellous mysteries.

And yet, I, a shape of clay
kneaded in water,
a ground of shame
and a source of pollution,
a melting-pot of wickedness
and an edifice of sin,
a straying and perverted spirit
of no understanding,
fearful of righteous judgements,
what can I say that is not foreknown,
and what can I utter that is not foretold?
All things are graven before Thee
on a written Reminder
for everlasting ages,
and for the numbered cycles
of the eternal years
in all their seasons;
they are not hidden or absent from Thee.

(*The Hymn Scroll*, I in DSS, pp. 150–151)

DISCUSSION

1. What were the major differences between the Sadducees, Pharisees and Essenes?

2. Why did the Essenes separate themselves from city life?

FURTHER READING

Fenn, Richard, *The Death of Herod: An Essay in the Sociology of Religion*, Cambridge University Press, 1992.

Grant, Michael, *Herod the Great*, Weidenfeld and Nicolson, 1971.

Green, Robert, *Herod the Great*, Franklin Watts, 1996.

Hengel, Martin, *The Zealots: Investigations into the Jewish Freedom Movement in the Period from Herod I until 70 AD*, T. and T. Clark, 1997.

Richardson, Peter, *Herod: King of the Jews and Friend of the Romans*, Fortress Press, 1999.

Roller, Duane W., *The Building Program of Herod the Great*, University of California Press, 1998.

Ritmeyer, Kathleen, *Temple Mount: Reconstructing Herod's Temple Mount in Jerusalem*, Biblical Archaeology Society, 1990.

Shanks, Herschel, Cole, Dan (eds), *Archaeology and the Bible: The Best of Bar: Archaeology in the World of Herod, Jesus and Paul*, Biblical Archaeology Society, 1990.

Shatzman, Israel, *Armies of the Hasmonaeans and Herod: From Hellenistic to Roman Frameworks*, Coronet, 1990.

Snaith, Norman H., *Jews: From Cyrus to Herod*, Abingdon, 1956.

Yadin, Yigael, *Masada: Herod's Fortress and the Zealots' Last Stand*, Welcome Rain, 1998.

CHAPTER 17

The Kingship of Herod

Timeline:

37–4 BCE Reign of Herod as king of Judaea

31 BCE Octavian defeats Anthony at Actium. Octavian becomes emperor

4 BCE Division of Herod's kingdom between three of his sons

After the Parthian victory, Herod set off for Rome to meet Mark Antony who had secured the eastern provinces from Octavian in the division of the empire. Through Mark Antony's influence the Roman government made a treaty with Herod establishing him as king of Judaea. By this means the Romans hoped to depose Antigonus, the nominee of the Parthians. With a Roman army Herod conquered Judaea; after a five-month siege Jerusalem fell in 37 BCE. Herod unified the country by incorporating Samaria, and replaced the council of elders by an advisory body similar to the privy councils of Hellenistic monarchs. Remembering that the Great Sanhedrin had previously censured him and had also supported the cause of Antigonus against his own, Herod executed forty-five of its seventy-one members, including many Sadducees who supported the Hasmonean dynasty. He did, however, spare the two leaders of the Great Sanhedrin – the Pharisees **Hillel** and Shammai – who continued to exert a profound influence through their schools on the direction of Pharisaic thought.

Since Herod was from an Idumite family – descendants of the Edomites who were converted to Judaism by the Hasmoneans – he was ineligible for the high priesthood and bestowed this office upon Hananel, a Babylonian Jew who claimed descent from the Zadokite house. According to Herod, Hananel's claims were better than had ever been offered by any Hasmonean ruler. Herod, however, had married a Hasmonean princess, Mariamne, and her mother

Alexandra (daughter of John Hyrcanus II) complained to the Egyptian Queen Cleopatra about this nomination. As a result, Herod was forced to appoint Alexandra's younger son Aristobulus instead. But he soon died, and Hananel was reinstated.

When Antony and Cleopatra were defeated by Octavian's admiral Marcus Agrippa at the battle of Actium in 31 BCE, Herod pledged his loyalty to Octavian (later known as Augustus). His declaration was accepted and he received back most of the territory Pompey had taken from Judaea in 63 BCE as well as two Greek cities across the Jordan – Hippos and Gadara. Alexandra and her daughter, Herod's wife Mariamne, were put to death along with Costobarus (governor of Idumaea) for plotting against Herod. For the next twenty-seven years Herod acted as Augustus' agent. He initiated games in honour of the victory at Actium, constructed a Greek theatre and amphitheatre in Jerusalem, transformed Samaria into a Graeco-Samaritan city and built the port of Caesarea. In addition, he created citadels and palaces at such strategic sites as Jericho, Herodium near Jerusalem and Masada on the Dead Sea. The great achievement of his reign was the rebuilding of the Jerusalem Temple on a magnificent scale. All that remains of this Temple are the foundations of the western wall which served as a meeting place, a market centre and a platform for preachers. Inside the court of the gentiles was another gateway through which only Jews could enter. This opened into the court of women, and beyond this was

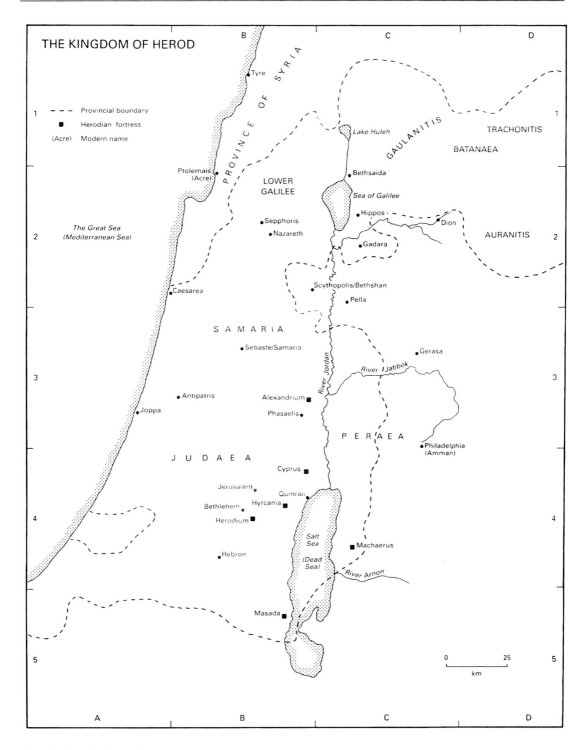

Map 23 The kingdom of Herod

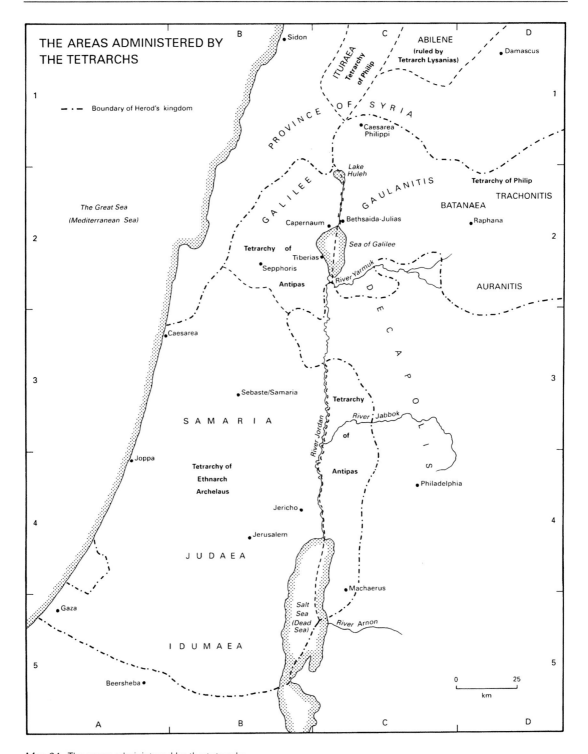

THE AREAS ADMINISTERED BY
THE TETRARCHS

— · — Boundary of Herod's kingdom

Sidon

ITURAEA
Tetrarchy
of Philip

ABILENE
(ruled by
Tetrarch Lysanias)

Damascus

PROVINCE OF SYRIA

Caesarea
Philippi

Lake
Huleh

GALILEE

GAULANITIS

Tetrarchy of Philip

TRACHONITIS

BATANAEA

Raphana

The Great Sea
(Mediterranean Sea)

Capernaum

Bethsaida-Julias

Sea of Galilee

Tetrarchy of

Tiberias

Sepphoris

Antipas

River Yarmuk

D
E
C
A
P
O
L
I
S

AURANITIS

Caesarea

Sebaste/Samaria

Tetrarchy

River Jabbok

S A M A R I A

of

Antipas

Philadelphia

Joppa

Tetrarchy of
Ethnarch
Archelaus

River Jordan

Jericho

Jerusalem

J U D A E A

Machaerus

Salt
Sea
(Dead
Sea)

River Arnon

Gaza

I D U M A E A

0   25

km

Beersheba

Map 24 The areas administered by the tetrarchs

the court of priests where the Sadducees conducted the sacrifices witnessed by Jewish men over the age of thirteen. The most sacred place in the Temple was the Holy of Holies which was only entered by the high priest on the Day of Atonement (*Yom Kippur*).

In the years that followed, Herod managed to obtain two large regions of southern Syria from Augustus. He also intervened with the Romans to stop Greek cities from withholding the privileges to which Jews in the diaspora were entitled. Yet despite such successes, Herod evoked Augustus's displeasure by his executions of those he suspected of intrigue as well as by his attack on his foes, the Nabataeans. To pacify the emperor, Herod ordered that all Jews in Judaea must swear an oath of loyalty to the Roman ruler and to himself. Such a practice was common in Roman client-monarchies, but a number of Pharisees feared it might involve worship of the emperor's statues and refused to comply. Increasingly these objectors began to indulge in messianic speculation. Previously such eschatological expectation had not been favoured in Pharisaic circles, but these Pharisees were persuaded that the period of messianic redemption was at hand. A few even succeeded in persuading Bagoas (a royal court official) that he was to be the father of the messianic king. Herod regarded such talk as high treason, and he executed Bagoas and others in 5 BCE. In the following year a number of Pharisaic scholars instigated demonstrations against the erection of an eagle, a forbidden image, over the main gate of the Temple. The rioters pulled it down, and were put to death for this insurrection. After these final years of upheavals, Herod himself died in 4 BCE.

Figure 17 Herod's Banquet, from Altarpiece of Saint John the Baptist and Saint Catherine, lower left side panel (previously attributed to Master of Siguenza). Artist: Peralta, Juan de (Hispalense): fifteenth century: Spanish. Copyright The Art Archive/Museo del Prado Madrid/Dagli Orti.

SOURCES

Hillel

Hillel used to say: 'Be among the disciples of Aaron, loving peace, cherishing mankind, and bringing (people) ever closer to the Law.' (Also) he would say: 'He who advertises his name, loses it; he who does not increase (knowledge), diminishes it; he who refuses to learn, merits extinction; and he who puts his talent to selfish use, commits spiritual suicide.' (Also) he would say: 'If I am not self-reliant, on whom shall I rely? But if I am selfish, what (good) am I? And if (the time for action is) not now, when (is it)?'

(*Pirke Avot* 1:12–14 in WI, p. 127)

Hillel (also) said: 'Don't keep aloof from the people; and don't be (too) sure of yourself till the day you die; and don't condemn your comrade till you are in his place; and . . . don't say "I shall study when I find the time", because you may never find it.'

He (also) said: 'A boor does not fear sin, and a vulgar man cannot be a saint. A bashful man cannot learn, an ill-tempered man cannot teach, and one who preoccupies himself with worldly affairs, cannot impart wisdom. Moreover, in a place where there are no men, show yourself a man.'

On another occasion, he saw a skull floating, and he said: 'Because you drowned others, you were drowned, and in the end they that drowned you shall likewise be drowned.'

He used to say:

'More flesh, more worms;
More wealth, more worry;
More women, more witchcraft;
More concubines, more lechery;
More slaves; more thievery.

(But) More law; more life;
More study, more wisdom;
More counsel, more enlightenment;
More righteousness; more peace.
He who acquires a good name, acquires it for himself,
He who acquires knowledge of the Law, acquires life in the world to come.

(*Pirke Avot* 2:5–8 in WI, pp. 127–128)

Once when Hillel left his disciples, they said to him, 'Where are you going?' He replied, 'To do a pious deed.' They said, 'What may that be?' He said, 'To take a bath.' They asked, 'Is that a pious deed?' He answered, 'Yes, for if the man who is appointed to tend and wash the images of kings where they are set up in theatres and circuses, receives his rations for so doing, and is even raised up to be regarded as among the great ones of the kingdom, how much more is it obligatory on me to tend and wash my body, since I have been created in the image of God.'

(*Leviticus Rabbah* 34:3 in WI, p. 128)

A heathen came to Shammai, and said to him, 'Accept me as a convert on the condition that you teach me the whole Law while I stand on one foot.' Then Shammai drove him away with the rod which he held in his hand. Whereupon he went to Hillel, who received him as a convert and said to him, 'What is hateful to you do not to your fellow: that is the whole Law; all the rest is its interpretation. Go and learn.'

(*Shabbat* 31b in WI, p. 129)

DISCUSSION

1. How did Herod manage to become king of Judaea?

2. What factors led to an intensification of messianic fervour?

FURTHER READING

Appelbaum, Shimon, Neuser, Jacob, *Judaea in Hellenistic and Roman Times: Historical and Archaeological Essays*, Brill, 1989.

Borgen, Peder, Giversen, Soren (eds), *The New Testament and Hellenistic Judaism*, Aarhus University Press, 1995.

Collins, John J., *Between Athens and Jerusalem: Jewish Identity in the Hellenistic Diaspora*, Eerdmans, 1999.

Collins, John, *Jewish Wisdom in the Hellenistic Age*, Continuum, 1998.

Daube, David, *The New Testament and Rabbinic Judaism*, Hendrickson, 1994.

Davies, William David, *Paul and Rabbinic Judaism: Some Rabbinic Elements in Pauline Theology*, Fortress, 1980.

Davies, William David, Finkelstein, Louis (eds), *The Cambridge History of Judaism: The Hellenistic Age Vol. 2*, Cambridge University Press, 1990.

Fischel, Henry A., *Rabbinic Literature and Greco-Roman Philosophy: A Study of Epicura and Rhetorica in Early Midrashic Writing*, Brill, 1997.

Green, William Scott (ed.), *Persons and Institutions in Early Rabbinic Judaism*, Scholars Press, 1977.

Hengel, Martin, *Judaism and Hellenism: Studies in Their Encounter in Palestine During the Early Hellenistic Period*, Fortress Press, 1975.

Richardson, Peter, *Herod: King of the Jews and Friend of the Romans*, Fortress Press, 1999.

Talmon, Shemaryahu (ed.), *Jewish Civilization in the Hellenistic-Roman Period*, Trinity Press International, 1992.

CHAPTER 18

Rebellion Against Rome

Timeline:

4 BCE Division of Herod's kingdom between Herod's three sons

6 CE Roman government rules over Judaea

Early first century CE Death of Hillel and Shammai

c. 20 BCE–c. 50 CE Philo

14–37 Tiberius Roman emperor

26–36 Pontius Pilate Roman governor of Judaea

c. 30 Crucifixion of Jesus

37–41 Caligula Roman emperor

41–54 Claudius Roman emperor

66–70 Jewish revolt against Rome

74 Fall of Masada

70s Sanhedrin established in Yavneh

After Herod's death, Augustus divided Judaea between three of Herod's sons: Archelaus as *ethnarch* (4 BCE to 6 CE) was to rule the central region of Judaea including Samaria; Herod Antipas as *tetrarch* (4 BCE to 39 CE) was given Galilee and Peraea; Philip also as *tetrarch* (4 BCE to 34 CE) was to reign over the newly acquired lands in Southern Syria. Archelaus' rule lasted only ten years; he was deposed and exiled by Augustus after he received complaints from Jews and Samaritans about his high-handedness. Judaea thereby became a small-scale Roman province administered by governors with the title of prefect (later called procurator). When the Romans instituted a census of the population, they provoked Jewish resentment since census-taking was contrary to Jewish law. Under the leadership of Judas the Galilean, a resistance movement (the Zealots) became active. At the same time there appeared a number of messianic aspirants who were regarded with suspicion by the authorities. The Sadducees, however, collaborated with the Romans who continued to appoint high priests from their ranks. Under the prefects, the Sanhedrin was resuscitated (in place of Herod's advisory body) and played an important role in the administration of the country.

Following his accession in 14 CE, the emperor Tiberius relied more and more on the advice of Sejanus, the commander of his bodyguard. Sejanus appears to have been ill-disposed to the Jewish population since two Jews – Hasinai and Hanilai – had set up an autonomous community at Nehardea in Parthian Babylonia. Sejanus feared that such aspirations might spread to Judaea. The fourth prefect of Judaea, Pontius Pilate (25–36 CE) experienced a number of difficulties with the Jewish community. They regarded his military standards bearing medallions of the emperor as idolatrous. Following demonstrations in Jerusalem, protesters encamped in front of Pilate's official residence at Caesarea Maritima and then in the stadium. Pilate also caused considerable consternation when he used a Jewish religious fund to pay for an aqueduct, and again when he set up gilded shields inscribed with both his and the emperor's names in the former palace of Herod.

Under Tiberius' nephew and successor Caligula (37–41 CE), the Jews of Alexandria became embroiled in a conflict with the Roman authorities. These Jews had put forward a claim for full citizenship rights, thereby evoking a violent reaction from the gentile

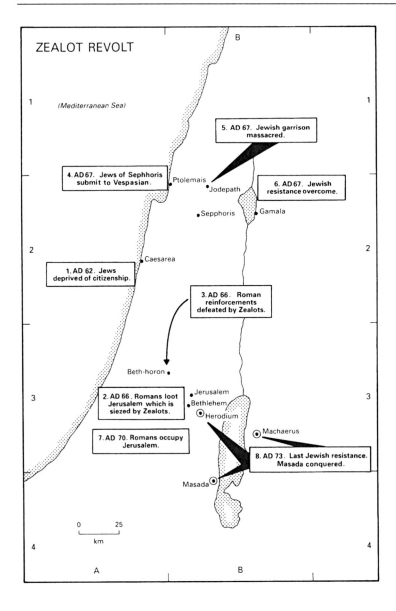

ZEALOT REVOLT

(Mediterranean Sea)

5. AD 67. Jewish garrison massacred.

4. AD 67. Jews of Sephhoris submit to Vespasian.

Ptolemais

Jodepath

6. AD 67. Jewish resistance overcome.

Sepphoris

Gamala

Caesarea

1. AD 62. Jews deprived of citizenship.

3. AD 66. Roman reinforcements defeated by Zealots.

Beth-horon

2. AD 66. Romans loot Jerusalem which is siezed by Zealots.

Jerusalem

Bethlehem

Herodium

Machaerus

7. AD 70. Romans occupy Jerusalem.

8. AD 73. Last Jewish resistance. Masada conquered.

Masada

0   25

km

A   B

Map 25 Zealot revolt

Greek community. Mobs broke into synagogues and set up statues of the emperor. The Roman governor of Egypt, Aulus Avillius Flaccus, ordered thirty-eight members of the Jewish council to be flogged in the theatre while Jewish women were forced to eat pork. To calm the situation Agrippa I – the grandson of Herod who had been appointed king after the death of Philip and the disgrace of Herod Antipas – secured the recall of Avillius Flaccus.

In 40 CE both the Greek and Jewish communities sent delegations to Rome to plead their cases before Caligula. According to an account written by the leader of the Jewish group, the neo-Platonic philosopher **Philo** from Alexandria, Caligula regarded the Jews' failure to recognize his divinity as lunacy. Meanwhile, at Javneh on the coast of Judaea, the Greek community erected an altar in honour of Caligula. The Jewish community of Jamnia regarded this act as a deliberate

Figure 18 Portrait of Caligula, 12–41 AD, marble bust. Copyright The Art Archive/Museo Capitolino Rome/Dagli Orti.

provocation, and destroyed it. As a consequence, the emperor and his advisers decided to revive the policy of Antiochus IV Epiphanes: the Temple and all synagogues were to be transformed into shrines of the imperial cult. Orders were given to the governor of Syria, Publius Pettronius, to construct a large statue of Caligula in the guise of Jupiter to be set up in Jerusalem. The governor decided he would need two

legions to perform this task, but Agrippa I persuaded him not to carry out his plans on the condition that the Jews would cease trying to stop gentiles from engaging in imperial worship. A short time later Caligula was murdered, and the Jews celebrated this day as a joyful feast.

Claudius (41–54 CE) who succeeded Caligula immediately had to deal with renewed conflict between Jews and Greeks in Alexandria. In his surviving letter to both groups, he urged them to be tolerant of one another; specifically he urged the Jews not to behave with contempt towards the gods of other peoples. In Judaea itself Claudius abolished direct Roman rule and allowed the country the status of a self-governing client kingdom. Agrippa I was permitted to add the Roman province of Judaea to the territories he had already been given where he reigned as king.

But Agrippa I's death in 44 CE ended this period of relative tranquillity as Judaea reverted to the status of a Roman province. Under the governors that followed, various problems became apparent: tensions developed between the rich and the poor; rebels, self-styled prophets and holy men roamed the country; and insurrections occurred in many localities. The procurator Tiberius Julius Alexander (46–48 CE) had to deal with an extensive famine; Ventidius Cumanus (48–52 CE) witnessed riots, a massacre at the Temple and conflict between Samaritans and Galileans; and Antonius Felix (52–60 CE) was confronted by bands of freedom fighters and miracle workers who preached a message of nationalism and messianic expectation.

SOURCES

Philo

The Alexandrian philosopher Philo (*c.* 20 BCE–50 CE) attempted to combine Jewish and Hellenistic thought in presenting his interpretation of Scripture:

For God, not wishing to come down to the external senses, sends his own words (*logoi*) or angels in order to give assistance to those who love virtue. They attend like physicians to the diseases of the soul, apply themselves to heal them, offer sacred recommendations like sacred laws, and invite humans to practise the duties inculcated by them.

Like the trainers of wrestlers, they implant in their pupils strength and power and irresistible vigour. Very properly therefore, when he (Jacob) arrived at the external sense, he was represented no longer as meeting God, but only the divine word.

(Philo, *On Dreams*, 1:12, in JM, p. 56–57)

For Philo angels are representative of God among human beings. Using this theoretical framework, he expounded the meaning of Scripture where God is depicted as acting in the world:

These men pray to be nourished by the word (*logos*) of God. However, Jacob, raising his head above the word, says that he is nourished by God himself. His words are as follows: 'The God in whom my father Abraham and Isaac were well pleased, the God who has nourished me from my youth to this day; the angel who delivered me from all my evils, bless these children.' Being a symbol of a perfect disposition, he now thinks God himself his nourisher, and not the word; he speaks of the angel, which is the word, as the physician of his evils, thereby speaking most naturally. The good things which he has previously mentioned are pleasing to him, in as much as the living and true God gave them to him face to face. However, the secondary good things have been given to him by the angels and by the word of God. On this account I think that God alone gives men pure good health which is not preceded by any disease in the body; but that health which is an escape from disease, he gives through the medium of skill and medical science. It is attributed to science, and whoever can apply it skilfully even though in truth it is God himself who heals both by these means, and without these means. The same is the case with regard to the soul – the good things, namely, food, he gives to men by his power alone, but those which contain in them a deliverance from evil he gives by means of his angels and his word.

(Philo, *Allegories of Shared Laws*, 3:62, in JM, p. 57)

DISCUSSION

1. What was the nature of the Jewish revolt against Roman rule?

2. How did the creation of the academy at Jamnia succeed in preserving the Jewish faith?

FURTHER READING

Donfried, Karl P., Richardson, Peter (eds), *Judaism and Christianity in First-Century Rome*, Eerdmans, 1998.

Goodman, Martin, *The Ruling Class of Judaea: The Origins of the Jewish Revolt Against Rome AD 66–70*, Cambridge University Press, 1993.

Gruen, Erich S., *Diaspora: Jews Amidst Greeks and Romans*, Harvard University Press, 2002.

Horbury, William, Noy, David (eds), *Jewish Inscriptions of Graeco-Roman Egypt, With an Index of the Jewish Inscriptions of Egypt and Cyrenaica*, Cambridge University Press, 1992.

Leon, Harry J., Osiek, Carolyn A., *The Jews of Ancient Rome*, Hendrickson Publishers, 1995.

Reinhold, Meyer, *Diaspora, The Jews among the Greeks and Romans*, Stevens, Samuel & Company, 1983.

Sicker, Martin, *Between Rome and Jerusalem: 300 Years of Roman-Judaean Relations*, Praeger, 2001.

Smallwood, E. Mary, *The Jews Under Roman Rule: From Pompey to Diocletian: A Study in Political Relations*, Prometheus, 2001.

Sussman, Varda, *Ornamented Jewish Oil-Lamps: From the Destruction of the Second Temple through the Bar-Kokhba Revolt*, Aris and Phillips, 1982.

Whittaker, Molly, *Jews and Christians: Graeco-Roman Views*, Cambridge University Press, 1985.

Williams, Margaret H. (ed.), *The Jews Among the Greeks and Romans: A Diasporan Sourcebook*, Gerald Duckworth & Co., 1998.

CHAPTER 19

The Rise of Christianity

Timeline:

26–36 Pontius Pilate Roman governor of Judaea

c. 30 Crucifixion of Jesus

c. 65 Death of Paul

From the gospels of the New Testament as well as information from Jewish, Greek and Roman sources, it appears that a Jewish sect of Christians emerged during the years of unrest following Herod's death in 4 BCE. In consonance with messianic expectations of this period, these believers expected their messiah to bring about the fulfilment of human history. According to the Christian scriptures, **Jesus** of Nazareth spent most of his life in Galilee where he acted as a healer, exorcist and itinerant preacher who proclaimed the imminent arrival of the Kingdom of God. After a brief association with John the Baptist he attracted disciples from among the most marginalized sectors of society but soon aroused suspicion and hostility and was put to death during the reign of Pontius Pilate in about 30 CE. Afterwards his followers believed he had risen from the dead, appeared to them, and promised to return to usher in the period of messianic rule.

There has been considerable scholarly debate about Jesus' relationships with such groups as Sadducees, Pharisees, Essenes, scribes, priests and Roman officials. It is unclear, for example, if Jesus intended to violate Jewish law, whether the titles he used, such as 'Son of God'; and 'Son of Man' simply reflect his own messianic consciousness or point to an acknowledgement of his divine nature. Further, scholars are undecided about who was responsible for his trial and crucifixion. Nevertheless, there is no doubt that Jesus inspired a considerable number of Jewish followers. According to the Acts of the Apostles, Jews who accepted Jesus as their Saviour in the 30s and 40s continued to pray at the Temple, observed Jewish laws, and considered themselves members of the Jewish people.

Figure 19 Saint Paul, from mosaic depicting the apostles, twelfth century, in apse. Copyright The Art Archive/Basilica San Giusto Trieste/Dagli Orti.

In the spreading of the gospel, **Paul** – a diaspora Jew from Tarsus in Asia Minor – played a pivotal role. His letters to scattered Christian communities provide first-hand evidence of the growth of this new religion. In his epistles to the Galatians, Paul describes himself as a Pharisee who had persecuted Christians until he had a revelation from God in which he was transformed into an apostle:

> For you have heard of my former life in Judaism, how I persecuted the church of God violently and tried to destroy it; and I advanced in Judaism beyond many of my own age among my people, so extremely zealous was I for the traditions of my fathers. But when he who had set me apart before I was born, and had called me through his grace, was pleased to reveal his Son to me, in order that I might preach him among the gentiles . . .
>
> (Galatians 1:13–16)

Subsequently Paul travelled around Asia Minor and Greece as a Christian missionary.

For some time scholars have debated Paul's relationship with the Jewish faith, but it is likely that Paul's thought is largely a fusion of elements of Pharisaic and Hellenistic Judaism. According to Paul, the new era was at hand, but he distinguished between the period before the coming of Christ and the time afterwards in terms of two states of being. The first, fleshly state is the realm of death, bondage and the rule of sin; the second, the spiritual state, is a condition of eternal life, freedom and the right relationship with God. The crucifixion and resurrection represent the inbreaking of the eschaton, and even though the day of final judgement has not yet arrived, those who accept Christ are redeemed from the burden of evil, death and sin. Jesus was sent to conquer death, and as God's son, he humbled himself so that all could come to the Father. Central to this theology is the distinction between 'works' and 'faith'. Faith, Paul believed, is a gift, the sign of divine grace. Salvation cannot be earned by observing the law but 'he who through faith is righteous shall live' (Galatians 3:11).

In his epistles, Paul differentiates the new life in Christ from licentiousness as well as from the belief that all things are permitted to those who believe. On the basis of this belief, Paul stresses the importance of love – just as God's act in Christ was motivated by love, so love is the supreme spiritual gift. A second theme in Paul's letters is his rejection of the demands of the Mosaic law: it is unnecessary, he argues, for Christians to be circumcised and to follow Jewish food regulations. Underlying these attitudes was Paul's conception of an apocalyptic history of salvation. Through Adam's transgression, sin and death entered the world. Abraham's trust in God illustrates that faith is more important than law. Mosaic legislation was binding only for a limited period. It cannot by itself bestow justification. The more one attempts to observe legal prescriptions, the greater one is conscious of sin. Thus God made Christ available to overcome man's evil propensity. In this context Paul interprets Abraham's two sons – Ishmael and Isaac – allegorically. Ishmael symbolizes the old covenant; Isaac represents the new dispensation. Now that Christ has come, it is not simply Jews who are Israel; instead, all those whom God has called through Christ are the true Israel.

The next stage in the development of Christianity took place in the decades following Paul's death. As time passed traditions about Jesus circulated and eventually formed the basis of the synoptic gospels and Acts which were written down in approximately the last quarter of the first century CE. Each gospel was composed with different religious intentions and concerns. Mark appears to be the earliest of the gospels and portrays Jesus as a divinely appointed figure whose task was to bring about God's kingdom on earth. In the Gospel of Matthew Jesus is presented as a lawgiver instructing the people in the principles of moral living. The Gospel of Luke and the Acts of the Apostles depict Jesus as the fulfilment of the Old Testament and portray the subsequent transference of the Church to the gentiles of the Graeco-Roman world. In the Gospel of John (in likelihood later than the synoptic gospels) Jesus is described as the divine *Logos* who is 'the way, the truth, and the life'. Not surprisingly the messsage of the New Testament was firmly rejected by mainstream Judaism, and the Jewish community responded to the challenge of Christianity by anathematizing its followers.

SOURCES

Jesus and the Sadducees

The conflict between Jesus and the Sadducees concerned the doctrine of the resurrection of the dead:

The same day Sadducees came to him, who say that there is no resurrection; and they asked him a question, saying, 'Teacher, Moses said, "If a man dies, having no children, his brother must marry the widow, and raise up children for his brother." Now, there were seven brothers among us; the first married, and died, and having no children left his wife to his brother. So too the second and third, down to the seventh. After them all, the woman died. In the resurrection, therefore, to which of the seven will she be the wife? For they all had her." But

Jesus answered them, 'You are wrong, because you know neither the scriptures nor the power of God. For in the resurrection they neither marry nor are given in marriage, but are like angels in heaven. And as for the resurrection of the dead, have you not read what was said to you by God, "I am the God of Abraham, and the God of Isaac; and the God of Jacob"? He is not the God of the dead, but of the living.' And when the crowd heard it, they were astonished at his teaching.

(Matthew 22:23–33)

Jesus and the Pharisees

According to the Pharisees, Jesus was a violator of the law:

At that time Jesus went through the grainfields on the Sabbath; his disciples were hungry, and they began to pluck heads of grain and to eat. But when the Pharisees saw it, they said to him, 'Look, your disciples are doing what is not lawful to do on the Sabbath.' He said to them, 'Have you not read what David did, when he was hungry, and those who were with him: how he entered the house of God and ate the bread of the Presence, which it was not lawful for him to eat nor for those who were with him, but only for the priests? Or have you not read in the law how on the Sabbath the priests in the temple profane the Sabbath, and are guiltless? I tell you, something greater than the temple is here. And if you had known what this means, 'I desire mercy, and not sacrifice', you would not have

condemned the guiltless. For the Son of Man is lord of the Sabbath.'

And he went on from there, and entered their synagogue. And behold, there was a man with a withered hand. And they asked him, 'Is it lawful to heal on the sabbath?' so that they might accuse him. He said to them, 'What man of you, if he has one sheep and it falls into a pit on the sabbath, will not lay hold of it and lift it out? Of how much more value is a man than a sheep! So it is lawful to do good on the Sabbath.' Then he said to the man, 'Stretch out your hand.' And the man stretched it out, and it was restored, whole like the other. But the Pharisees went out and took counsel against him, how to destroy him.

(Matthew 12:1–14)

Paul and the Jews

Born in Tarsus, Paul recounts that he studied under Rabban Gamaliel in Jerusalem. In the *Epistle to the Romans*, he discusses God's plan for the Jewish nation:

I ask, then, has God rejected his people? By no means! I myself am an Israelite, a descendant of

Abraham, a member of the tribe of Benjamin. God has not rejected his people whom he foreknew. Do you not know what the scripture says of Elijah, how he pleads with God against Israel? 'Lord, they have killed thy prophets, they have demolished thy altars, and I alone am left, and they seek my life.' But what is God's reply to him? 'I have kept for myself seven thousand men who have not bowed the knee to Baal.' So too at the present time there is a remnant, chosen by grace. But if it is by grace, it is no longer on the basis of works; otherwise grace would no longer be grace.

What then? Israel failed to obtain what it sought. The elect obtained it, but the rest were hardened, as it is written, 'God gave them a spirit of stupor, eyes that should not see and ears that should not hear, down to this very day.' And David says, 'Let their table become a snare and a trap, and a pitfall and a retribution for them; let their eyes be darkened so that they cannot see, and bend their backs for ever.' So I ask, have they stumbled so as to fall? By no means! But through their trespass salvation has come to the Gentiles, so as to make Israel jealous. Now if their trespass means riches for the world, and if their failure means riches for the Gentiles, how much more will their full inclusion mean! . . .

But if some of the branches were broken off, and you, a wild olive shoot, were grafted in their place to share the richness of the olive tree, do not boast over the branches. If you do boast, remember it is not you that support the root, but the root that supports you. You will say 'Branches were broken off so that I might be grafted in.' That is true. They were broken off because of their unbelief, but you stand fast only through faith. So do not become proud, but stand in awe. For if God did not spare the natural branches, neither will he spare you . . .

And even the others, if they do not persist in their unbelief, will be grafted in, for God has the power to graft them in again.

(Romans 11:1–12; 17–21; 23)

DISCUSSION

1. Did Jesus view himself as the Messiah?

2. Did Paul remain faithful to the Jewish faith?

FURTHER READING

Davies, W.D., *Christian Origins and Judaism*, Darton, Longman & Todd, 1962.

Donfried, Karl, Richardson, Peter (eds), *Judaism and Christianity in First-Century Rome*, Eerdmans, 1998.

Dunn, James, *Jews and Christians: The Parting of the Ways, AD 70–135;* The Second Durham–Tubingen Research Symposium on earliest Christianity and Judaism, Eerdmans, 1999.

Flusser, David, Leibowitz, Yeshaiahu, *Jewish Sources in Early Christianity*, Jewish Lights, 1996.

Hengel, Martin, Barrett, C.K., Hagner, Donald A. (eds), *Conflicts and Challenges in Early Christianity*, Trinity Press International, 1999.

Martin, Vincent, *A House Divided: The Parting of the Ways Between Synagogue and Church*, Paulist Press, 1995.

Sanders, E.P., *Jewish Law from Jesus to the Mishnah: Five Studies*, Trinity Press International, 1990.

Sanders, E.P., *The Historical Figure of Jesus*, Penguin, 1996.

Sanders, E.P., *Paul and Palestinian Judaism: A Comparison of Patterns of Religion*, Fortress Press, 1983.

Segal, Alan, *Rebecca's Children: Judaism and Christianity in the Roman World*, Harvard University Press, 1989.

Shanks, Hershel (ed.), *Christianity and Rabbinic Judaism: A Parallel History of their Origins and Early Development*, Biblical Archaeological Society, 1992.

Sharpe, Eric, *Memory and Manuscript: Oral Tradition and Written Transmission in Rabbinic Judaism and Early Christianity*, Eerdmans, 1998.

Skarsaune, Oskar, *In the Shadow of the Temple: Jewish Influences on Early Christianity*, Intervarsity Press, 2002.

Weiss-Rosmarin, Trude, *Judaism and Christianity: The Differences*, Jonanthan David, 1997.

CHAPTER 20

Roman Jewish War and Aftermath

Timeline:

66–70 Jewish revolt against Rome

69–79 Vespasian Roman emperor

74 Fall of Masada

70s Sanhedrin assembles at Yavneh (Jabneh)

79–81 Titus Roman emperor

Two decades of procurators after the death of Agrippa I marked a period of constant friction between Roman rulers and the Jewish population. Under the procurator Florus (64–66 CE), fighting took place between Greeks and Jews in Caesarea Maritima. The procurator adopted an anti-Jewish stance and allowed his troops to riot in Jerusalem and execute a number of eminent Jews. After Florus returned to Caesarea, pro-Roman Jews as well as a small Roman legion in Judaea were killed by Jewish rebels and sacrifices on behalf of the Roman people and the emperor were stopped. To quell this revolt, the governor of Syria and an army marched to Jerusalem. He began a siege of the Temple, but was met with resistance and retreated to the sea coast.

This success drove out the Roman military presence in Judaea and in its place a provisional government was established. To pacify the country the general Vespasian, acting under the emperor Nero's orders, assembled an army in the north in 67 CE. Sepphoris in Galilee refused to join in the revolt, and the Jewish rebels were unable to stand against the Roman legions. Though the fortress of Jotapata held out for forty-seven days, it eventually fell and the Romans slaughtered most of the population. During the winter of 67–68 CE the Zealots overthrew the moderate government in Jerusalem. Those suspected of aiding the Romans were arrested or killed, and anti-Roman groups occupied the city. But in March 67 CE, Vespasian marched against the Jewish population. He subjugated Transjordan, western Judaea, Idumea,

Samaria and Jericho. The only parts of the country remaining in Jewish hands were Jerusalem and several Herodian fortresses in other parts of the country. When Nero committed suicide in 68 CE the Roman military effort ceased.

During the next year Roman armies in different parts of the empire elevated three generals to the throne; in July 69 CE the eastern provinces proclaimed Vespasian. Before long Vespasian put his son Titus in charge of the Judaean campaign. Just before Passover in April 70 CE, Titus encamped outside the walls of Jerusalem. In late May the Romans occupied the newer part of Jerusalem, north of the Temple. By the end of July they took the citadel adjacent to the Temple; on 6 August the sacrifices were suspended. A week later the porticos surrounding the Temple courtyards were burned, and on 28 August the Temple went up in flames during the fighting. After another month the Romans captured the upper city west of the Temple, and thus the entire city was taken although with considerable effort. All resistance ceased, and Titus ordered that Jerusalem be devastated except for the towers of Herod's palace.

For the rest of the year Titus held celebrations in various cities of the Near East during which Jewish prisoners were thrown to wild animals or were forced to fight with gladiators. In 71 CE, Titus and Vespasian held a triumphal procession in which ritual objects and rebel leaders were exhibited; the surviving Arch of Titus in Rome depicts the *menorah* and other objects

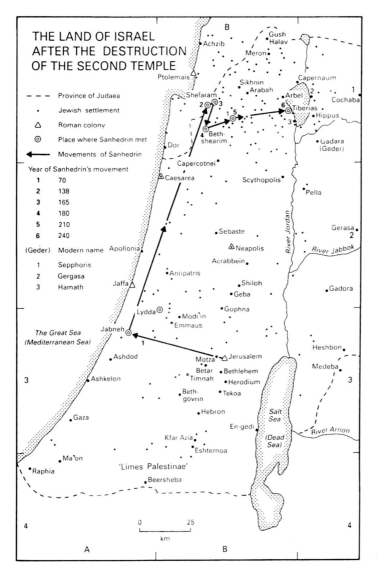

THE LAND OF ISRAEL
AFTER THE DESTRUCTION
OF THE SECOND TEMPLE

- - - Province of Judaea

·   Jewish settlement

△   Roman colony

◎   Place where Sanhedrin met

◀   Movements of Sanhedrin

Year of Sanhedrin's movement

1	70
2	138
3	165
4	180
5	210
6	240

(Geder)	Modern name
1	Sepphoris
2	Gergasa
3	Hamath

The Great Sea
(Mediterranean Sea)

Map 26 The land of Israel after the
destruction of the Second Temple

that were taken from the Temple. Over the next few years the Romans captured the remaining fortresses including Masada which fell in April 74 CE when its defenders committed suicide rather than surrender to the Romans. The historian **Josephus** describes the end of the rebels in vivid detail, and the tale has been an inspiration to Jews struggling against oppression ever since. Archaeologists have excavated the site and have learned a great deal both about King Herod's original fortress and the day-to-day existence of the revolutionaries.

The Roman conquest of Judaea brought about enormous destruction and the enslavement of thousands of Jews. Nevertheless, reconstruction began immediately and the Jews continued as the largest population in the country. Though the Romans heavily taxed the Jewish community, they recognized Judaism as a lawful religion, and exempted Jews from emperor worship and other religious duties. During this period it appears that the Sadducees and Essenes disappeared. In their place the Pharisees became the dominant religious group led by Rabban Johanan ben

Figure 20 Arch of Titus – the triumphal arch on the Roman Forum built 81 CE in honour of Titus's victory over the Jews in 70 CE. Detail shows a triumphal procession with the seven-branched candelabrum of the Temple of Solomon. Copyright AKG, London.

Zakkai, who escaped from Jerusalem during the siege. In the town of Yavneh near the Judaean sea coast he assembled a group of distinguished Pharisaic scholars (known as *Tannaim*). There these sages engaged in the development of the legal tradition. Under Johanan ben Zakkai and later in the century under Rabban Gamaliel II, the rabbinic assembly (Sanhedrin) summarized the teachings of the earlier schools of Hillel and Shammai. In addition, they determined the canon of Scripture, organized the daily prayers, and transferred to the synagogue some of the observances of the Temple such as the rituals associated with the pilgrim festivals, the Passover *seder* and the blowing of the ram's horn at the New Year. They also instituted a procedure of rabbinic ordination (*semikhah*).

Though this body was presided over by a head (*nasi*), the rabbis collectively reached decisions which were binding on the populace. Its members were drawn from all sectors of society and they attracted numerous students to hear their oral teachings. The first generation of sages (including such figures as R. Eliezer ben Hyrcanus, R. Elazar ben Azaria and R. Joshua ben Haninah) was followed by a second generation of eminent scholars such as R. Hananiah ben Taradion, R. Tarphon and R. Ishmael ben Elisha. The most prominent scholar of the first decades of the second century was R. Akiva ben Joseph (50–135 CE) who was an exegete, mystic and legal systematizer as well as a pioneer of a method of Scriptural interpretation based on the view that no word in Scripture is redundant.

SOURCES

Josephus

Josephus served as a commander of the Jewish army which rebelled against Rome in the first century CE. Later he composed a history of the Roman War. The following is a speech which Josephus puts into the mouth of one of the Jewish commanders in this struggle:

And as for those who have died in the war, we should deem them blessed, for they are dead in defending, and not in betraying, their liberty: but as to the multitude of those that have submitted to the Romans, who would not pity their condition? And who would not make haste to die before he would suffer the same miseries? Where is now that great city, the metropolis of the Jewish nation, which was fortified by so many walls round about, which had so many fortresses and large towers to defend it, which could hardly contain the instruments prepared for war, and which had so many myriads of men to fight for it? Where is this city that God Himself inhabited? It is now demolished to the very foundations; and hath nothing but that monument of it preserved, I mean the camp of those that have destroyed it, which still dwells upon its ruins. Some unfortunate old men also lie upon the ashes of the Temple, and a few women are there preserved alive by the enemy for our bitter shame and reproach.

(Josephus, *War of the Jews*, 7:8, in WI, p. 135)

DISCUSSION

1. What effect did the destruction of the Second Temple have on Jewish life?

2. Discuss the process whereby the *Tannaim* expanded Biblical law.

FURTHER READING

Feldman, Louis, Reinhold, Meyer (eds), *Jewish Life and Thought Among Greeks and Romans: Primary Readings*, Fortress Press, 1996.

Gruen, Erich S., *Diaspora: Jews Amidst Greeks and Romans*, Harvard University Press, 2002.

Horbury, William, *Jews and Christians in Contact and Controversy*, T. and T. Clark, 1998.

Horbury, William, *Jewish Messianism and the Cult of Christ*, Morehouse, 1998.

Horbury, William, Davies, W.D., Sturdy, John (eds), *The Cambridge History of Judaism, Vol. 3: The Early Roman Period*, Cambridge University Press, 1999.

Neusome, James D., *Greeks, Romans, Jews: Currents of Culture and Belief in the New Testament World*, Trinity Press International, 1992.

Reinhold, Meyer, *Diaspora: The Jews Among the Greeks and Romans*, Samuel Stevens, 1983.

Rutgers, Leonard Victor, *The Hidden Heritage of Diaspora Judaism*, Peeters, 1998.

Williams, Margaret, *The Jews Among the Greeks and Romans: A Diasporan Sourcebook*, Johns Hopkins Press, 1998.

CHAPTER 21

Jews in the Roman Empire

Timeline:

114–117 Revolt of Jews in Egypt, Cyrene, Cyprus

117–138 Hadrian Roman emperor

132–135 Jewish revolt in Judaea under Simeon Bar Kochba

135 Beginning of anti-Jewish persecutions in Palestine

140s or 150s End of anti-Jewish persecutions. Sanhedrin reassembles in Galilee

c. 170–217 Judah I is *nasi*. *Mishnah* compiled

193–235 Severian dynasty of Roman emperors

225–255 Sanhedrin reassembles in Tiberius

235–283 Political and economic disorder of Roman empire

284–305 Diocletian Roman emperor establishes order. Persecution of Christians

306–337 Constantine Roman emperor makes Christianity the legal religion of the Roman empire

Early 4th century First restrictions on Jewish legal rights

Middle 4th century Redaction of the Palestinian *Talmud* begins in Galilee

527–565 Justinian Roman emperor conquers western Mediterranean. Justianian Code

Despite the devastating victory of the Romans, Jewish revolts continued into the second century CE. When the emperor Trajan (98–117 CE) invaded the east up to the Persian coast, uprisings among Babylonian Jews took place. Moreover, riots occurred in many parts of the Roman diaspora. Between 114 and 117 CE Jewish centres in Alexandria, Cyrenaica, Egypt and Cyprus were decimated. After Trajan's death his successor Hadrian (117–138 CE) abandoned the effort to extend the empire eastwards, leaving the Jewish diaspora in Babylonia free from Roman domination.

In Judaea a messianic revolt was led in 132 CE by Simeon Bar Kochba which appears to have been aided by Rabbi Akiva and other scholars from **Yavneh** and touched off by Hadrian's programme of Hellenization. This Jewish revolt was inspired by the conviction that God would empower the Jews to regain control of their country and rebuild the Temple. Yet despite the valiant efforts on the part of the rebels, the Romans crushed this uprising. In addition to archaeological evidence –

including coins issued by Bar Kochba's government as well as letters sent to him by deputies – the third-century historian Dio Cassius provides information about this period. According to his account, hundreds of thousands of Jews were killed and Judaea was almost completely devastated. In 135 CE the rebellion came to an end with the fall of Bethar, south-west of Jerusalem. According to tradition, this event occurred on the 9th of *Av*, the same day as the destruction of the First and Second Temples, later commemorated by *Tisha B'Av*. During the course of the campaign Bar Kochba was killed in battle, and Rabbi Akiva was later flayed alive.

Following the Bar Kochba war, Hadrian outlawed Judaism throughout the land, but after his death in 138 CE prohibitions against the religion were rescinded. As far as the Jews were concerned, their defeat under Bar Kochba initiated a conciliatory policy towards the Roman authorities resulting in the flourishing of rabbinic learning. The centre of Jewish life was transferred to Galilee, and under the disciples of Rabbi Akiva, the Sanhedrin reassembled at Usha. The outstanding **scholars** of this period included Rabban Simeon ben Gamaliel II (who served as *nasi*), R. Elazar ben Shammua, R. Jose ben Halafta, R. Judah bar Illai, R. Simeon bar Yohai and R. Meir. Under these sages, the Sanhedrin emerged as the decisive force in Jewish life; through its deliberations the legal decisions of previous generations were systematized and disseminated.

By the third century economic conditions in Galilee had improved and the Jewish population attained a harmonious relationship with the Roman administration. The Severan dynasty of Roman emperors entrusted the *nasi* with the authority to appoint judges for Jewish courts, collect taxes and send messengers to diaspora communities. The most important *nasi* of this epoch was **Judah ha-Nasi** whose main achievement was the redaction of the **Mishnah**. This volume consisted of the discussions and rulings of scholars whose teachings had been transmitted orally. The *Mishnah* itself is almost entirely halalchic in content, consisting of six sections (or orders) comprising a series of chapters (known as tractates) on specific subjects. The first order (Seeds) begins with a discussion of benedictions and prayers and continues with the other tractates dealing with various matters (such as the tithes of the harvest to be given to priests, Levites and the poor). The second order (Set Feasts) contains twelve tractates dealing with the Sabbath, Passover, the Day of Atonement and other festivals as well as shekel dues and the proclamation of the New Year. In the third section (Women) seven tractates consider matters affecting women (such as bethrothal, marriage contracts and divorce). The fourth section (Damages) contains ten tractates concerning civil law: property rights, legal procedures, compensation for damage, ownership of lost objects, treatment of employees, sale and purchase of land, Jewish courts, punishments, criminal proceedings, etc. In addition a tractate of rabbinic moral maxims (**Sayings of the Fathers**) is included in this order. In the fifth section (Holy Things) there are eleven tractates on sacrificial offerings and other temple matters. The final section (Purifications) treats in twelve tractates the various types of ritual uncleanliness and methods of purification. According to some scholars this comprehensive collection of

Jewish law based on Scriptural precedent was indirectly influenced by a similar codification of Roman law undertaken by Latin jurists in the reign of Hadrian.

The Sanhedrin which had been so fundamental in the compilation of this work met in several cities in Galilee, but later settled in the Roman district of Tiberias. The *nasi* remained the head of the Sanhedrin but other scholars established their own schools in other parts of the country where they applied the *Mishnah* to everyday life together with old rabbinic teachings (*beraitot*) which had not been incorporated in the *Mishnah*.

By the 230s, the Roman empire was encountering numerous difficulties including inflation, population decline and a lack of technological development to support the army. In the next few decades rival generals struggled against one another for power and the government became increasingly inefficient. During this time of upheaval, the Jewish community underwent a parallel decline as a result of famine, epidemics and plunder.

At the end of the third century CE, the emperor Diocletian (284–305 CE) inaugurated reforms that strengthened the empire. Under his reign the republican veneer of Roman rule was replaced by an absolutist structure. An elaborate system of prices, offices and occupations was introduced to halt economic decline. In addition, Diocletian introduced measures to repress the spread of Christianity which had become a serious challenge to the official religion of the empire. Diocletian's successor, Constantine the Great (306–337 CE), reversed his predecessor's hostile stance and extended official toleration to Christians in 313. By this stage Christianity had succeeded in gaining a substantial number of adherents among the urban population; eventually Constantine became more involved in Church affairs, and just before his death he himself was baptized. The Christianization of the empire continued throughout the century and by the early 400s, Christianity was fully established as the state religion. This merger of the Roman government and the Church did not affect the legal rights of the Jews, but it did provide an important channel for anti-Jewish hostility.

By the first half of the fourth century, Jewish scholars in Israel had collected together the teachings of generations of rabbis in the academies of Tiberias,

Figure 21 Declaration of loyalty by the 'Parnas' of a synagogue, who also served as the municipal customs director for the Roman empire. Inscription on stone found in Dunaujvaros, Pannonia, third century. Pannonia was a province in the Roman empire corresponding to present-day western Hungary, parts of eastern Austria, Slovenia and north Yugoslavia. Copyright Beth Hatefutsoth Photo Archive.

Caesarea and Sepphoris. These extended **discussions** of the *Mishnah* became the Palestinian *Talmud.* The text of this multi-volume work covered four sections of the *Mishnah* (Seeds, Set Feasts, Women and Damages) but here and there various tractates were missing. No doubt the discussions in these academies included matters in these missing tractates, but it is not known how far the recording, editing and arrangement of these sections had progressed before they were lost. The views of these Palestinian teachers (*Amoraim*) had an important influence on scholars in Babylonia, though this work never attained the same prominence as that of the Babylonian *Talmud.*

Although Jewish scholarship prospered during this time, the Jews were facing new legal handicaps.

When Christianity became the dominant religion of the Roman empire, Judaism was relegated to a position of legal inferiority. Imperial laws of the middle of the fourth century prohibited conversion to Judaism as well as intermarriage between Jews and Christians. At the beginning of the fifth century Jews were formally barred from government positions, and this attitude continued throughout the rest of the century and was reinforced by the emperor Justinian's (525–565 CE) decrees. The official stance of the Church was to attempt to bring Jews to the true faith. Judaism was allowed to continue because the existence of the Jewish people was seen as a testimony to the truth of Scripture. According to Church teaching, the Jews would eventually recognize Jesus' messiahship and sovereignty.

SOURCES

Chain of Tradition

Johanan ben Zakkai managed to escape from Jerusalem during the siege. He settled in the town of Yavneh and gathered around him a group of scholars (*Tannaim*):

Moses received the Torah on Mount Sinai and passed it on to Joshua, and Joshua to the elders and the elders to the prophets and the prophets to the men of the Great Assembly . . . Simon the righteous was one of the last members of the Great Assembly . . . Antigonus of Solcho received the Torah from Simon the Righteous . . . Yose ben Yoezer of Zeredah and Yose ben Yohanan of Jerusalem received the Torah from them . . . Joshua ben Perahyah and Nittai the Arbelite received the Torah from them . . . Judah ben Tabbai and Simeon ben Shetah received the Torah from them . . . Shemayah and Avtalyon received the Torah from them . . . Hillel and Shammai received the Torah from them . . . Rabban Johanan ben Zakkai received the Torah from Hillel and Shammai; he used to say: If you have learned much Torah, do not give yourself any credit, for this was the purpose of your creation.

(*Mishnah, Sayings of the Fathers*, 1:1, in SRJ, p. 63)

Rabbi Eliezer

In their debates about the meaning of law, scholars relied on argument rather than appealing to miraculous events.

On that day Rabbi Eliezer brought forward all the arguments in the world to support his view, but they refused to accept them. He said to them: 'If the *halakhah* agrees with me, let this carob tree prove it'. The carob tree was uprooted and hurled from its place a hundred cubits. . . . 'No proof can be brought from a carob tree', they said to him. Again, he said to them: 'If the *halakhah* agrees with me, let this stream of water prove it'. The stream flowed backwards. 'No proof can be brought from a stream of water', said they. Again he said to them: 'If the *halakhah* agrees with me, let the walls of the school house prove it'. The walls started to lean as if about to fall. Rabbi Joshua rebuked them and said: 'When the pupils of the Sages are disputing about *halakhah* what business have you to interfere?' The walls did not fall, for the sake of Rabbi Joshua's honour, nor did they resume the upright for the sake of Rabbi Eliezer's honour . . . Again Rabbi Eliezer said: 'If the *halakhah* agrees with me, let it be proved from heaven'. A *bat kol* (voice from heaven) went forth and said: 'Why do you dispute with Rabbi Eliezer, seeing that in every case the *halakhah* agrees with him!' But Rabbi Joshua stood up and exclaimed: 'It is not in heaven!' (Deut. 30:12) What did he mean by this? Rabbi Jeremiah said: 'He meant: The Torah has already been given on Mount Sinai, so we pay no attention to a *bat kol*, since you long ago wrote in the Torah at Mount Sinai: "You must follow the majority opinion"' (Exod. 23:2).

(*Talmud, Baba Mezia*, 59a–b, in TSSJ, pp. 80–81)

Judah Ha-Nasi

The *Mishnah* was compiled by Judah Ha-Nasi who is generally referred to as Rabbi. His learning and sanctity were undisputed:

> At the time of his dying, Rabbi raised ten fingers to Heaven and said, 'Lord of the Universe, you know and it has been revealed to you that I have laboured in the study of the Torah with my ten fingers and that I did not enjoy any worldly advantage even with my little finger. May there be peace in my resting place, according to your will.' A voice from Heaven echoed, saying, 'He shall enter into peace.'
>
> (*Talmud, Ketuvot*, CIV, in SRJ, p. 68)

Mishnah

The *Mishnah* was compiled in the second century CE by Judah ha-Nasi. It contains a wide range of oral law formulated by early sages:

> These are the ways in which the School of Shammai and the School of Hillel differ in the conduct of a meal. The School of Shammai first say the benediction of the day and then the benediction for the wine, whereas the School of Hillel first say the benediction for the wine and then the one for the day.
>
> The School of Shammai say: First wash the hands and then mix the cup.
>
> The School of Hillel say: First mix the cup and then wash the hands.
>
> The School of Shammai say: A man wipes his hands with a napkin and then lays it on the table, but the School of Hillel say: He lays it on a cushion.
>
> (*Mishnah, Berakot*, VIII, SRJ, p. 66)

In the *Mishnah* the usual format is that the minority opinion is placed first followed by the accepted view:

> If a man divorces his wife because of her bad reputation, he may not take her back; and if because of a vow, he may not take her back. R. Judah says: If he divorced her because of a vow that many people know about, he may not take her back, but if only a few people know about it, then he may take her back. R. Meir says: He may not take her back if the vow needed the opinion of a sage to revoke, but for any vow that he could revoke himself, he could take her back . . . R. Jose b. R. Judah said: Once in Sidon a man said to his wife, 'I will give everything away if I do not divorce you!' and he disgraced her. But the sages allowed him to take her back as a precaution for the good of everyone. If a man divorces his wife because she is barren, R. Judah says: He may not take her back. But the sages say: He may take her back.
>
> (*Mishnah, Gittin*, IV, SRJ, p. 66)

Sayings of the Fathers

The Sayings of the Fathers (*Pirke Avot*) are contained in the *Mishnah* and consist of maxims from the early rabbinic period:

> Simeon the Just was one of the last members of the Great Assembly. He used to say: Upon three things the world stands – on the Torah, on the Temple service, and on acts of kindness.

> Antigonus of Sokho received Torah from Simeon the Just. He used to say: Do not be like slaves who serve their master only in order to receive their allowance, but be like slaves who serve their master with no thought of receiving an allowance; and let the fear of heaven be upon you.

> Yose ben Yoezer of Zeredah and Yose ben Yohanan of Jerusalem received Torah from them. Yose ben Yoezer says: Let your house be a meeting-place for the Sages; sit in the dust at their feet, and drink in their words thirstily.

> Yose ben Yohanan of Jerusalem says: Let your house be opened wide, and let the poor be members of your household, and avoid talking too much with women. This was meant to apply to a man's own wife; how much more, then, to the wife of a friend! Hence the sages said: Whenever a man talks much with a woman, he brings evil upon himself, neglects the words of the Torah, and ends by inheriting *Gehinnom* (Hell).

> Joshua ben Perahyah and Nittai the Arbelite received Torah from them. Joshua ben Perahyah says: Provide yourself with a teacher, and study along with another student; and when you judge anyone, give him the benefit of the doubt.

> Nittai the Arbelite says: Keep your distance from a bad neighbour, avoid the company of a wicked man, and do not lose all hope of retribution.

> Judah ben Tabbai and Simeon ben Shetah received Torah from them. Judah ben Tabbai says: Do not play the part of advocate, and when the litigants stand before you, regard them as guilty, but when they have left the court regard them as innocent, provided they have acquiesced in the sentence.

> Simeon ben Shetah says: Examine witnesses thoroughly, and choose your words carefully, lest from them they learn to lie.

> Shemayah and Avtalyon received Torah from them. Shemayah says: Love work, shun office, and see that you do not become known to the authorities.

> Avtalyon says: Sages, take care what you say lest you incur the penalty of exile, and go into exile to a place of evil waters, and your students who follow after you drink them and die, and thus the name of Heaven be profaned.

> Hillel and Shammai received Torah from them. Hillel says: Be one of Aaron's disciples, loving peace and pursuing peace, loving mankind and bringing them near to the Torah.

> He used to say: He who promotes his own name destroys his name; he who does not increase decreases; he who does not learn deserves death; he who exploits the crown to his own advantage perishes.

> He used to say: If I am not for myself, who, then, is for me? And when I alone am for myself, what am I? And if not now, when?

Shammai says: Make your study of the Torah a fixed habit; say little and do much, and greet everyone with a cheerful look on your face.

Rabban Gamaliel says: Provide yourself with a teacher and remove yourself from doubt, and do not get into the habit of tithing by guesswork.

Simeon his son says: All my days I grew up among the Sages and I found nothing better for a man than silence. Expounding (the Torah) is not the chief thing, but fulfilling it. Whoever multiplies words occasions sin.

Rabban Simeon ben Gamaliel says: On three things the world stands: on justice, on truth and on peace, as it is written: 'Excuse the judgement of truth and peace in your gates' (Zech. 8:16)

(*Mishnah, Sayings of the Fathers* 1:2–18 in ml, pp. 490–496)

Rules of Exegesis

In the second century CE Rabbi Ishmael expounded thirteen rules of Biblical exegesis based on Hillel's seven rules formulated in the previous century:

1. Inference from a less important to a more important case . . . Since the daily offering . . . overrides the Sabbath, then is it not logical that the Passover offering will override the Sabbath?

2. Inference from an identical word or phrase. '*Be-moado* (in its set time) is stated in connection with the Passover and . . . in connection with the daily sacrifice. '*Be-moado*' . . . with the daily sacrifice overrides the Sabbath so '*Be-moado*' . . . with the Passover overrides the Sabbath . . .

3. Construction of a general principle from one verse and from two verses. 'If he knocks out the tooth of a slave' (Exodus 21:27) could be understood to mean either a milk tooth or a permanent tooth, but scripture also says, 'When a man strikes the eye of a slave and destroys it' (Exodus 21:26). Just as the eye is an organ which does not grow back again, so too must the tooth be one which does not grow back again . . .

4. General and specific . . . Rava objected: If it had just said, when any man of you brings an offering to the Lord, you shall bring your offering of cattle ('*behamah*', Leviticus 1:2), I would agree that wild creatures are included in the category *behamah* . . . but the text goes on to state 'from the herd or from the flock' (Leviticus 1:2); so sacrifices of the herd and flock have been commanded, not of the wild beasts. . . .

13. Two contradictory passages stand as they are until a third passage can be found to decide between them. R. Akiva says: One passage says: 'You shall offer the Passover sacrifice to the Lord your God from the flock ('*zon*') or the herd, ('*vaqar*', Deuteronomy 16:2), and another says: 'You shall take it from the sheep ('*kevasim*') or from the goats ('*izzim*', Exodus 12:5). How can both these verses stand . . . ? Now the passage: 'Select lambs (*zon*) for yourself according to your families (Exodus 12:21) decides in this instance since it demonstrates that only from the flock (*zon*) . . . can the Passover offering come.

(*Mekhilta, Pisha* 4, in SRJ, pp. 69–70)

DISCUSSION

1. What was the nature of Jewish life in Judaea after the Roman victory in the first century?

2. Discuss the nature of rabbinic debate in the Palestinian academies during the *Tannaitic* and *Amoraic* periods.

FURTHER READING

Dubnov, Simon, *History of the Jews: From the Roman Empire to the Early Medieval Period*, Cornwall Books, 1980.

Edward, Mark J., Goodman, Martin, Price, Simon, Rowland, Chris (eds), *Apologetics in the Roman Empire: Pagans Jews and Chrstians*, Clarendon Press, 1999.

North, John, Rajak, Tessa, Lieu, Judith M. (eds), *The Jews Among Pagans and Christians: In the Roman Empire*, Routledge, 1994.

Rabello, Alfredo Mordechai, *The Jews in the Roman Empire: Legal Problems from Herod to Justinian*, Variorum, 2000.

Simon, Marcel, *Versus Israel: A Study of the Relations Between Christians and Jews in the Roman Empire (AD 135–425)*, Littman Library, 1996.

Smallwood, E. Mary, *The Jews Under Roman Rule: From Pompey to Diocletian: A Study in Political Relations*, Prometheus Books, 2001.

Chapter 22

Jews in Babylonia

Timeline:

Early 3rd century	Rise of the Babylonian scholar class. *Exilarch* encourages the creation of academies
Second half of 3rd century	Development of rabbinic Judaism in Babylonia
4th century	Major scholars include Abbaye and Rava
Middle 4th century	Redaction of the Palestinian *Talmud*
c. 455–475	Persecution of Jews
c. 500	Re-establishment of Jewish institutions. Redaction of the Babylonian *Talmud*
6th century	Babylonian sages add comments and notes to the text of the Babylonian *Talmud*
589	Beginning of *Geonic* period

From the sixth century BCE when Nebuchadnezzar deported Jews from their native land, Babylonia had become an important centre of Jewish life. By the second century CE, the Persian king who had become overlord of Mesopotamia recognized an *exilarch* (in Aramaic *resh galuta* meaning 'head of the exiles') as leader of the Jewish community in Babylonia. This figure (who claimed descent from kings of Judah taken in captivity by Nebuchadnezzar) collected taxes, appointed judges, supervised the judiciary and represented the Jewish population in the Persian royal court. By the middle of this century rabbinic Judaism spread eastwards and some **Palestinian** scholars temporarily settled in Babylonia during the **Bar Kochba** revolt and Hadrian's persecutions. Subsequently a number of Babylonian Jews went to the centres of learning in Galilee to study under the leading sages in the Holy Land.

The codification of the *Mishnah* further intensified such interchange. In this context the *exilarch* encouraged the emergence of a Babylonian class of scholars from whom he appointed administrators and judges. While post-*Mishnaic* scholars in Israel engaged in learned debate about the application of Jewish law, the same development was taking place in Babylonia.

The great third century teacher Rav (Abba bar Aivu, a student of Judah ha-Nasi) founded an academy at Sura in central Mesopotamia; his contemporary Samuel was simultaneously head of another Babylonian academy at Nehardea. After Nehardea was destroyed in an invasion in 259 CE, the school at Pumbeditha also became a dominant Babylonian academy of Jewish learning.

Some years previously the Arsacid dynasty in Parthia was overthrown by the Sassanians who developed a more centralized administration in the Persian empire and authorized greater government supervision. In addition they promised a revised form of Zoroastrianism as the established religion of the empire with a hierarchical priestly structure. This priestly class attempted to pressurize Jews and others to adopt their religion during the reign of Ardashir (226–240 CE), the first Sassanian monarch. After his death, his successor Shapur I (241–270 CE) permitted religious freedom for non-Zoroastrians and officially recognized the Jewish exilarchate in Babylonia. Jewish leaders were compelled to accept the authority of Persian state law. Such an arrangement was enshrined in the Jewish sage Samuel's formula: 'Dina de-malkhut dina' ('The law of the government is the law'). In Israel there had never been an equivalent recognition of Roman law, but

Samuel's formula provided a basis for allowing Jewish law to be superseded by non-Jewish civil law as long as it did not touch on Jewish religious rituals and ceremonies.

The Babylonian Jews under the Sassanian dynasty encountered a number of new religious sects (such as the Manichaeans), but they remained faithful to the religion of their fathers. Their religious leaders were revered for their mastery of the tradition, and the **academies** they founded became major centres of Jewish learning. The Babylonian sages carried on and developed the Galilean tradition of disputation, and the fourth century produced two of the most distinguished scholars of the Amoraic period: Abbaye (278–338 CE) and Rava (229–352 CE), who both taught at Pumbeditha. With the decline of Jewish institutions in Israel, Babylonia became the most important centre of Jewish scholarship.

When Christianity became the official religion of the Roman empire, Christians rather than Jews were subject to persecution by the Sassanian dynasty, since Rome was perceived as its main military enemy. In the fourth and fifth centuries clergy, monks and lay Christians were attacked and martyred. Only during a short period in the fifth century (445–475 CE) did repression flare up against the Jewish population; the **exilarchate** was suspended, synagogues and academies were closed and the Torah was banned. But by the sixth century a new period of prosperity had begun, and Babylonian scholars completed the redaction of the *Talmud*, an editorial task begun by Ravi Ashi (335–427 CE) at Sura.

This massive work parallels the Palestinian *Talmud* and is largely a summary of the Amoraic discussions that took place in the Babylonian academies. Both *Talmuds* are essentially elaborations of the *Mishnah* though neither commentary contains material on every *Mishnah* passage. The Palestinian *Talmud* treats thirty-nine Mishnaic tractates whereas the Babylonian deals with slightly fewer, but the Babylonian *Talmud* is nearly four times the size of the Palestinian *Talmud*. The text itself consists largely of summaries of rabbinic discussion: a phrase of *Mishnah* is interpreted, discrepancies are resolved and redundancies are explained.

Figure 22 Adam and Eve and scene from the *Talmud*, compilation of Hebrew laws, Italy, 1438, Canon Or 79, folio 8v. Copyright The Art Archive/Bodleian Library Oxford/The Bodleian Library.

In this compilation conflicting opinions of the earlier sages are contrasted, unusual words are explained and anonymous opinions are identified. Frequently, individual teachers cite specific cases to support their views and hypothetical eventualities are examined to reach a solution to the discussion. Debates between outstanding scholars in one generation are often cited, as are differences of opinion between contemporary members of an academy or a teacher and his students. The range of Talmudic exploration is much broader than that of the Mishnah itself and includes a wide range of rabbinic teachings about such subjects as theology, philosophy and ethics; this aggadic (non-legal) material is usually presented as digressions and comprises about one-third of the Babylonian *Talmud*.

SOURCES

Jewish Learning in Palestine

Despite the loss of the Temple, the great Pharisaic tradition of learning and interpretation was preserved in the academy at Yavneh:

Simon the Righteous used to say: The world stands on three things – on the Torah, on the Temple service, and on acts of kindness. (*Mishnah, Sayings of the Fathers*, I, in SRJ, p. 63)

But his successor, Rabbi Simeon, son of Gamaliel, could say: The world stands upon three things: upon justice, upon truth and upon peace. (*Mishnah, Sayings of the Fathers*, I, in SRJ, p. 63)

Within a generation, the Sanhedrin, the *Nasi* and the *Av Bet Din* were re-established under Rabban Gamaliel II and Rabbi Joshua:

When the *nasi* comes in, all the people stand; they do not sit until he has told them to do so. When the *Av Bet Din* comes in, they stand on either side to make a passageway for him until he has come and taken his place. (*Talmud, Sanhedrin*, II, SRJ, p. 64)

The Sanhedrin was arranged in half circle so that everyone might see each other. The *nasi* sat in the middle with the elders on his right and his left sides. R. Eleazar, the son of Zadok said: When Rabban Gamaliel sat at Yavneh, my father and one other sat on his right and the other elders sat on his left. (*Talmud, Sanhedrin*, VIII, in SRJ, p. 64)

Bar Kochba

The history of the Bar Kochba Revolt is recorded in Dio Cassius' *History of Rome*:

The Emperor Hadrian founded a city named Aelia Capitolina in place of Jerusalem which had been burnt to the ground. On the site of the temple of the god, he built a new temple to Jupiter. This led to a war of no small importance or short duration, for the Jewish people thought it intolerable that foreigners should be settled in their city and the worship of foreign gods to be held there . . . Five hundred and eighty thousand men were killed in the various skirmishes and battles and there is no knowing how many died through famine, disease and fire. Thus, nearly the whole of Judea was made desolate.
(Dio Cassius, *History of Rome*, LXIX, in SRJ, pp. 64–65)

Letters of Bar Kochba have survived. He appears to have been dictatorial in approach:

Simeon Bar Kochba to Jonathan of Masabal . . . all the men from Tekoa and the other places who are with you must be sent to me immediately. If you will not send them, be assured that you will be punished.
(*Bar Kochba Letters*, in SRJ, p. 65)

Bar Kochba seems to have been religiously observant. The following letter refers to the celebration of *Sukkot*:

Simeon to Judah bar Menashe to Kiriath Araboya. I have sent you two donkeys. You will send two men with them to Jonathan bar Be'ayan and Masabala so that they pack up and send to the camp palm branches and citrons. From your place you must send others who will bring you myrtles and willows. See that they are set in order and send them on to the camp.
(*Bar Kochba Letters*, in SRJ, p. 65)

Mishnah

The *Mishnah* is a legal code compiled in the second century CE by Judah Ha-Nasi. This passage concerns the settlement of conflicting claims of ownership:

Two men are holding a cloak: This one says, 'I found it' and the other one says: 'I found it'. If this one says: 'It is all mine' and the other one says: 'It is all mine' – then this one must swear that he does not own less than a half and the other one must swear that he does not own less than a half and they divide it. If this one says: 'It is all mine' and the other one says: 'Half of it is mine' – then the one who says 'It is all mine' must swear that he does not own less than three quarters and the one who says: 'Half of it is mine' must swear that he does not own less than a quarter and this one takes three quarters and this one takes one quarter . . .

If two men were riding on an animal and one was riding and one was leading the animal: This one says: 'It is all mine' and the other one says: 'It is all mine' – then this one must swear that he does not own less than a half and the other one must swear that he does not own less than a half and they divide it. If they both agree or they both have witnesses they divide it without an oath . . .

A man said to two others: I know that I have stolen a *maneh* (one hundred *zuz*) from one of you but I do not know from which one of you. Or he says: The father of one of you deposited a *maneh* with me but

I do not know to which of you it belongs. He must give a *maneh* to this one and a *maneh* to the other one since he himself had admitted it . . .

If two men deposited some money with a third man, one of them depositing a *maneh* and the other two hundred *zuz*: This one says: 'The two hundred *zuz* are mine' and the other one says: 'The two hundred *zuz* are mine' – then he must give each one a *maneh* and the remainder should be left until Elijah comes. Rabbi Jose said: In that case what does the fraudulent one lose? But all the money should be left until Elijah comes . . .

The same applies to two vessels, one worth a *maneh* and the other worth a thousand *zuz*. This one says: 'The valuable vessel belongs to me' and the other one says: 'The valuable one belongs to me' – then he must give the less valuable vessel to one of them and from the purchase price of the more valuable he must give the value of the lesser to the other and the remainder should be left until Elijah comes. Rabbi Jose said: In that case what does the fraudulent one lose? But the whole should be left until Elijah comes.

(*Mishnah*, *Bava Metzia*, Chapters 1:1–2; 2:3–5 in JL, pp. 33–38)

The Academies

The sages maintained that the academies in which the oral law was debated originated in Biblical times:

R. Hama b. Hanina said: Our ancestors were never left without the Scholars' Council. In Egypt they had the Scholars' Council, as it is said: Go and gather the elders of Israel together (Exodus 3:16); in the desert they had the Scholars' Council, as it is said: Gather

for me seventy men of the elders of Israel (Numbers 11:16); our father Abraham was an elder and a member of the Scholars' Council.

(*Talmud*, *Yoma*, XXVIII, in SRJ, p. 70)

Many stories were told of the academies in the days of Hillel and Shammai before the Destruction of the Temple:

Our rabbis taught: The house of Shammai and the house of Hillel were in dispute for two and a half years. The house of Shammai insisted that it would have been better if man had never been created while the House of Hillel maintained that it was better that he was created than he never had been made. They finally took a vote.

(*Talmud*, *Erubin*, XIII, in SRJ, p. 71)

After the destruction, when the Sanhedrin had been re-established, other scholars founded their own academies throughout the land of Israel and beyond:

Follow the scholars to their academies: R. Eliezer to Lydda, R. Johanan b. Zakkai to Beror Hail, R. Joshua to Pekiin, Rabban Gamaliel to Yavneh, R. Akiva to Benai Berak, R. Jose to Sepphoris, R. Judah b. Bathyra to Nisibis, R. Joshua to the Exile, Rabbi to Beth Shearim.

(*Talmud*, *Sanhedrin*, XXXII, in SRJ, p. 71)

The purpose of the academies was to instruct students in Torah and to interpret the oral law:

There will come a time when a man will look for one of the laws of the Torah and will not find it, or one of the laws of the rabbis, and will not find it . . . Then they will say, 'Let us start with Hillel and Shammai.'

(*Tosefta*, *Eduyot*, I, in SRJ, p. 71)

The Sanhedrin in Palestine, presided over by the *Nasi*, held the greatest authority:

Once Rabban Gamaliel went to have his authority confirmed by the governor of Syria and it was a long time before he returned. So they declared the year a leap year, conditional on the approval of Rabban Gamaliel. When he did return, he said, 'I approve', so the year was counted as a leap year.

(*Mishnah*, *Eduyot*, 7:7, in SRJ, p. 71)

After the *Mishnah* was completed by Judah Ha-Nasi, its interpreters in the academies were known collectively as the *Amoraim*:

How are we to explain the phrase 'the weighing up of opinions?' R. Papa answered: If two *Tannaim* and two *Amoraim* are on opposing sides, and it is not stated explicitly whose side is correct, if a ruling is made in accordance with one set of opinions, but the general practice follows the other – this is a case of the erroneous weighing of opinions.

(*Talmud*, *Sanhedrin*, XXXIII, in SRJ, p. 71)

At the end of rabbinic discussion, a vote of all the scholars was taken:

Where one permits and one prohibits, where one declares levitically unclean and one declares clean and where all say: We have not heard a tradition concerning this. In these cases a vote is taken.

(*Tosefta*, *Sanhedrin*, VII, in SRJ, p. 72)

The Head of each academy was a *Rosh Yeshivah*:

R. Joseph was 'Sinai' (encyclopedic in his knowledge of the Torah) while Rabbah was an 'uprooter of mountains' (skilful in argument). When the time came that one should be *Rosh Yeshivah* (Head of the *Yeshivah*), they sent to ask: Who should be preferred, Sinai or the Uprooter of Mountains. The answer came back: Sinai, because everyone needs to know the authentic traditions.

(*Talmud*, *Berakot*, LXIV, in SRJ, p. 72)

Outside Palestine, the academies associated with Rav at Sura and Samuel at Nehardia were famous:

'Our rabbis in Babylon' refer to Rav and Samuel.
(*Talmud, Sanhedrin*, XVIII, in SRJ, p. 72)

The *Exilarch*

The day-to-day affairs of the Jewish community in Babylonia were in the hands of the *Exilarch*, a government-appointed official:

Our teacher (R. Judah Ha-Nasi) was very modest and he used to say: . . . If Huna, the *Resh Galuta* (the *Exilarch*) were to come to this place, I would stand up for him, for he is descended from Judah whereas I am descended from Benjamin. He is descended on the male side and I on the female side.
(*Genesis Rabba*, XXXIII, in SRJ, p. 72)

The heads of the Babylonian academies were initially subordinate to the *Exilarch*, but they later asserted their independence. At the end of the third century CE, the academy at Pumbedita was founded as a successor to Nehardia:

Rabina said: I visited Meremar at Sura. When the deputy of the congregation went down and recited it (the *kiddush* prayer) in the manner of the elders of Pumbedita, everyone tried to silence him, but he said to them, 'Leave him alone; the Law is declared by the elders of Pumbedita'.
(*Talmud, Pesahim*, CXVII, in SRJ, p. 73)

DISCUSSION

1. What was the nature of Jewish scholarship in Babylonia during the post-*Mishnaic* period?

2. Discuss the role of the *exilarch* and the heads of the Babylonian academies.

FURTHER READING

Brody, Robert, *The Geonim of Babylonia and the Shaping of Medieval Jewish Culture*, Yale University Press, 1998.

Neusner, Jacob, *A History of the Jews in Babylonia: From Shapur I to Shapur II*, Brill, 1997.

Neusner, Jacob, *A History of the Jews in Babylonia: The Age of Shapur II*, Brill, 1997.

Neusner, Jacob, *A History of the Jews in Babylonia: Early Sasanian Period*, Brill, 1997.

Neusner, Jacob, *A History of the Jews in Babylonia I: The Parthian Period*, Society of Biblical Literature, 1984.

Neusner, Jacob, *A History of the Jews in Babylonia: Later Sasanian*, Brill, 1997.

Neusner, Jacob (ed.), *History of Jews in Babylonia V*, University Press of America, 2000.

Neusner, Jacob, *Israel and Iran in Talmudic Times: A Political History*, University Press of America, 1987.

CHAPTER 23

Rabbinic Scriptural Interpretation

Timeline:

c. 100 BCE–200 CE *Tannaitic* period

c. 200–600 CE *Amoraic* period

During the *Tannaitic* period – between the first century BCE and the second century CE – and the *Amoraic* period – between the second and sixth centuries CE – scholars, referred to as *Tannaim* and *Amoraim*, actively engaged in the interpretation of Scripture. According to Pharisaic tradition, both the Written Torah and its interpretation (Oral Torah) were given by God to Moses on Mt Sinai. This belief implies that God is the direct source of all laws recorded in the Pentateuch and is also indirectly responsible for the authoritative legal judgements of the rabbis, and serves as the justification for the rabbinic exposition of Scriptural ordinances. Alongside this exegesis of the Jewish law (*halakhah*), scholars also produced interpretations of Scripture in which new meanings of the text were expounded (*aggadah*) in rabbinic commentaries (*midrashim*) and in the **Talmud**. Within the aggadic texts is found a wealth of theological speculation about such topics as the nature of God, divine justice, the coming of the Messiah and the hereafter. In addition, ethical considerations were of considerable importance in the discussions of these teachers of the faith.

The exegesis found in rabbinic literature of the *Tannaitic* and *Amoraic* periods is largely of two types: direct and explicit exegesis where the Biblical text is commented upon or accompanied by a remark, and indirect exegesis where a Scriptural text is cited to support an assertion. As an example of the first type, it was common practice among the sages to clear up a

Figure 23 The word when He created, from the *Talmud*, compilation of Jewish laws, Germany, early 1300s. (Arch Selden A5 folio 2v). Copyright The Art Archive/Bodleian Library Oxford/The Bodleian Library.

possible confusion about the meaning of a Biblical verse. In a *midrash* on Psalms, for example, R. Simlai (third century CE) explained that the fact that Psalm 50 begins with the words, 'The Mighty One, God the Lord speaks' does not signify that God has a trinitarian nature. Rather 'all three descriptions are only one name, even as one man can be called workman, builder, architect. The psalmist mentions these three names to teach you that God created the world with three names, corresponding with the three good attributes by which the world was created.'

The rabbis frequently reinforced their exhortations by a Biblical sentence that expressed their sentiments. Such a homiletical use of Scripture was illustrated in the first century CE by Simeon ben Shetach, who declared in a *midrash* on Deuteronomy:

> When you are judging, and there come before you two men, of whom one is rich and the other poor, do not say, 'The poor man's words are to be believed, but not the rich man's.' But just as you listen to the words of the poor man, so listen to the words of the rich man, for it is said, 'Ye shall not be partial in judgement.'
>
> (Deuteronomy 1:17)

It was also a usual custom in rabbinic circles to cite a text and then draw out its meaning. For example, in a *midrash* on Deuteronomy the verse 'Thou shalt open wide your hand to your brother' (Deuteronomy 15:11) is explained as meaning that one should give according to particular needs: 'To him for whom bread is suitable, give bread; to him who needs dough, give dough; to him for whom money is required, give money; to him for whom it is fitting to put food in his mouth, put it in.'

It was also a principle that a word should be understood in its strictest sense. For example, in the *Talmud* R. Meir (second century CE) said: 'Where is the resurrection derived from the Torah? As it is said, "Then will Moses and then will the children of Israel sing this song unto the Lord." (Exodus 15:1). It is not said "sang", but "will sing".' Hence, he argued, the resurrection is deducible from the Torah. In the same passage R. Joshua b. Levi (third century CE) asked the same question, and quoting Psalm 84 pointed out that it is not stated, 'They will have praised Thee', but 'will

be praising Thee'. Thus, he believed, the doctrine of resurrection is grounded in the Torah.

Turning to the method of indirect exegesis, it was a frequent practice in rabbinic literature to draw deductions from Scriptural texts by a means of a number of formal hermeneutical rules. Hillel the elder who flourished about a century before the destruction of the Second Temple, is reported to have been the first to lay down these principles. Hillel's seven rules were expanded in the second century CE by R. Ishmael ben Elisha into thirteen. The first rule – the inference from minor to major – states that if a certain restriction applies to a matter of minor importance, we may infer that the same restriction is applicable to a matter of major importance. Conversely, if a certain allowance is applicable to a thing of major importance, we may infer that the same allowance pertains to that which is of comparatively minor importance. In the *Mishnah*, for example, we read that the Sabbath is in some respects regarded as being of more importance than a common holiday. If therefore a certain kind of work is permitted on the Sabbath, we may infer that such work is more permissible on a common holiday; conversely, if a certain work is forbidden on a common holiday, it must be all the more forbidden on the Sabbath.

Another rule of indirect exegesis (rule six) was intended to solve a problem by means of a comparison with another passage in Scripture. For example, in the *Talmud* the question why Moses had to hold up his hands during the battle with Amalek (Exodus 17:11) is answered by referring to Numbers 21:8. There the text states that in order to be cured from snakebite the Israelites were to look at the fiery serpent raised up in the wilderness. The hands of Moses could no more bring victory than could the brass serpent cure those who had been bitten. But the point is that just as in the case of the fiery serpent, it was necessary for the Israelites to lift up their hearts to God in order to be saved.

A final example of indirect exegesis concerns the reconciliation of conflicting passages. Rabbi Ishmael's thirteenth rule states that if two passages contradict one another they are to be reconciled by a third if possible. Thus Exodus 13:6 ('Seven days you shall eat unleavened bread'), and Deuteronomy 16:8 ('For six days you shall eat unleavened bread') are an example of contradictory passages, but in a *midrash* on Exodus this conflict is resolved by referring to Leviticus 23:14 where the law enjoins that no use whatsoever was allowed to be made of the new corn until the offering of the first produce of the barley harvest had taken place on the morning after the first day of *Pesach* (Passover). Hence unleavened bread prepared of the new corn was to be eaten only during the six remaining days of that festival. Referring to this circumstance the passage in Deuteronomy 16:8 speaks of six days while the passage in Exodus 13:6 refers to the unleavened bread prepared of the produce of the former year's harvest which might be eaten during seven days.

These various methods of exegesis were based on the conviction that the Bible is sacred, that it is susceptible of interpretation and that, properly understood, it guides the life of the worthy. By means of this process of explanation of God's revelation, the rabbinic authorities were able to infuse the tradition with new meaning and renewed relevance. The literary outpouring of the first few centuries of Pharisaic Judaism bears witness to the fervent conviction that God's eternal word can have a living message for each generation of Jewry.

SOURCES

Talmud

The Babylonian *Talmud* was compiled in the sixth century CE. Here the passage concerns the laws of telling the truth when one does not want to hurt people:

Our rabbis taught: How should one sing praises in front of the bride? The School of Shammai says: 'A bride as she is'. But the School of Hillel says: 'A beautiful and graceful bride'. Said the School of Shammai to the School of Hillel: Supposing she was lame or blind is it right to say of her that she is beautiful and graceful since the Torah says: 'Keep far from falsehood' (Exod. 23:7)? Said the School of Hillel to the School of Shammai: Consider your own words. If a man buys something inferior in the market place should people praise it or disparage it? Surely they should praise it. From this the sages derived the rule that a man should always conduct himself toward others in a pleasant manner . . .

When Rav Dimi came (from Palestine to Babylon) he said: This is how they sing in front of the bride in the West (Palestine, which is to the West of Babylon): No eye shadow, no rouge, and no lipstick and yet a graceful gazelle. When the rabbis ordained Rabbi Zera they sang for him: No eye shadow, no rouge and no lipstick and yet a graceful gazelle . . .

When the rabbis ordained Rabbi Ammi and Rabbi Assi they sang for them: Like these, only like these, ordain for us. Do not ordain for us the confused thinkers or the ragged thinkers. Others say (that the rabbis said): No second-rate scholars and no third-rate scholars . . .

When Rabbi Abbahu came from the college to Caesar's house the maidservants of Caesar's house came out to meet him and sang to him: Head of his people and leader of his nation, candelabra of light, let thy coming be in peace . . .

They said regarding Rabbi Judah son of Illai that he used to take a twig of myrtle and dance in front of the bride saying: A beautiful and graceful bride. Rav Samuel son of Rav Isaac used to dance (in front of the bride) juggling with three twigs. Rabbi Zera said: The old man is causing us embarrassment. When he died a pillar of fire came down to act as a barrier between him and the people and we have a tradition that this only happens to one in a generation or to two in a generation. Rabbi Zera said: His twig helped the old man. Others say (that Rabbi Zera said): His attitude helped the old man. Others say (Rabbi Zera said): His folly helped the old man.

(Babylonian *Talmud*, *Tractate Ketuvot* 16b–17a in JL, pp. 85–88)

DISCUSSION

1. How did the belief in *Torah MiSinai* affect the Jewish exegesis of Scripture?

2. What is the distinction between the direct and indirect exegesis of the Biblical text?

FURTHER READING

Avery-Peck, Alan J., Neusner, Jacob (eds), *New Perspectives on Ancient Judaism: The Literature of Early Rabbinic Judaism: Issues in Talmudic Reduction and Interpretation*, University Press of America, 1989.

Hauptman, Judith, *Rereading the Rabbis: A Woman's Voice*, Westview Press, 1999.

Hasan-Rokem, Galit, *Web of Life: Folklore and Midrash in Rabbinic Literature*, Stanford University Press, 2000.

Ilan, Tal, *Mine and Yours Are Hers: Retrieving Women's History from Rabbinic Literature*, Brill, 1997.

Neusner, Jacob, *From Literature to Theology in Formative Judaism*, University Press of America, 1989.

Neusner, Jacob, *Judaism's Story of Creation: Scripture, Halakhah, Aggadah*, Brill, 2000.

Neusner, Jacob, *Rabbinic Political Theory: Religion and Politics in the Mishnah*, University of Chicago Press, 1991.

Neusner, Jacob, *The Hermeneutics of Rabbinic Category Formation*, University Press of America, 2001.

Neusner, Jacob, *The Unity of Rabbinic Discourse: Aggadah in the Halakhah*, University Press of America, 2001.

Neusner, Jacob, *Vanquished Nation, Broken Spirit: The Virtues of the Heart in Formative Judaism*, Cambridge University Press, 1987.

Strack, Herman L., Sternberger, Gunter, Bockmuehl, Markus, *Introduction to the Talmud and Midrash*, Fortress Press, 1992.

CHAPTER 24

Rabbinic Theology

Timeline:

c. 200 CE *Mishnah* compiled

c. 5th century CE Palestinian *Talmud* compiled

c. 6th century CE Babylonian *Talmud* compiled

Unlike the *Mishnah*, which consists of legislation presented without explicit reference to a Scriptural text, rabbinic *aggadah* focuses on the contemporary relevance of specific Biblical texts. The early halakhic *midrashim* consist of *Tannaitic* commentaries on the legal verse of the Bible such as the *Mekhilta* on Exodus, the *Sifra* on Leviticus, and the *Sifrei* on Numbers and Deuteronomy. Narrative *midrashim*, on the other hand, derive from sermons given by the *Amoraim* in synagogues and academies and include such texts as *Midrash Rabbah* (a series of commentaries on the Pentateuch and the Hagiographa – the Song of Songs, Ruth, Lamentations, Ecclesiastes and Esther). Though the sages were not speculative philosophers, they nevertheless expressed their theological views in these works and attempted to apply this teaching to daily life. This midrashic literature along with the aggadic sections of the *Talmud* serve as the basis for reconstructing the theology of early rabbinic Judaism.

Within these texts the rabbis expressed their theological views by means of stories, legends, parables and maxims based on Scripture. According to the sages of the *midrashim* and the *Talmud*, God's unity was of paramount importance; repeatedly they pointed out that though God has many differing Hebrew names in the Bible, he is always the same. Thus in the third century CE R. Abba ben Memel declared in a *midrash* on Exodus: 'God said to Moses, "Thou desirest to know my name. I am called according to my deeds. When I judge my creatures, I am called *Elohim*; when

I wage war against the wicked, I am called *Sabbaoth*; when I suspend judgement for a man's sins, I am called *El Shaddai*; but when I have compassion upon my world, I am called Yahweh".' The sages also stressed that God alone is the source of the universe and directs it according to a preordained plan. To illustrate this notion, scholars utilized such parables as a ship and its captain: just as it is impossible for a ship to reach its destination without a captain, so the government of the cosmos is inconceivable without a directing force.

The view of *Tannaitic* and *Amoraic* scholars regarding God's omniscience and human free will was summarized in a statement by R. Akiva in the second century CE: 'All is foreseen but freedom of choice is given; and the world is judged with goodness, and all is in accordance with thy works'. Here it is asserted that although God knows all things, human beings have nevertheless been accorded free will and as a consequence they will be judged on the basis of their actions. But such judgement is tempered by mercy as a *midrash* on Leviticus records: 'In the hour when the Israelites take up their ram's horns, and blow them before God, he gets up from the throne of judgement and sits down upon the throne of mercy and he is filled with compassion for them, and he turns the attribute of Judgement into the attribute of Mercy.'

For the rabbis God is concerned with all mankind but the Jewish people play a special role in the divine plan. Israel's love of God is reciprocated by God's tender loving concern. In the words of R. Simeon bar

Yohai (second century CE): 'Like a king who entrusted his son to a tutor, and kept asking him, "Does my son eat, does he drink, has he gone to school, has he come back from school?" So God yearns to make mention of the Israelites at every hour. It is out of this love that God has entrusted his chosen people with the Torah; the purpose of Israel's election is to sanctify God's name and be a holy people dedicated to his service. As one *midrash* explains: 'It says in Leviticus 11:45, "For I am the Lord who brought you out of Egypt to be your God: you shall therefore be holy, for I am holy". That means, I brought you out of Egypt on the condition that you should receive the yoke of the commandments.'

In some rabbinic sources the Torah is described as pre-existent. It is the instrument with which the world was created. Thus a *midrash* on Genesis proclaims: 'God created the world by the Torah: the Torah was his handmaid and his tool by the aid of which he set bounds to the deep, assigned the functions to sun and moon, and formed all nature.' As the word of God, every letter is sacrosanct and the study and doing of Torah is the Jew's most sacred task. As Ben Bag Bag recommends: 'Turn it and turn it over again, for everything is in it, and contemplate it, and wax grey and old over it, and stir not from it, for thou can have no better rule than this.' Beneath the literal meaning of the text, the rabbis asserted, it is possible to discover layers of meaning in which the divine mysteries are revealed.

The Torah also played a central role in the rabbinic depiction of the afterlife. This conception was a significant development from Biblical Judaism in which there was no explicit doctrine of eternal salvation. According to rabbinic sources, the world to come is divided into several stages. First there is the period of messianic redemption which is to take place on earth after a period of decline and calamity and will result in the complete fulfilment of every human aspiration. Peace will reign throughout nature; Jerusalem will be rebuilt; and at the close of this era the dead will be resurrected and rejoined with their souls and final judgement will come upon all humankind. Those Jews who have fulfilled the precepts of the law and are thereby judged righteous will enter into Heaven (*Gan Eden*) as well as gentiles who have lived in accord with the **Noachide Laws** (the laws which Noah and his descendants took upon themselves).

Figure 24 Detail of Hell from *The Garden of Earthly Delights*, Triptych before 1593. Artist: Bosch, Hieronymus: 1450–1516: Flemish. Copyright The Art Archive/Museo del Prado Madrid/Album/Joseph Martin.

In rabbinic sources the heavenly realm is depicted in various ways; in one *midrash* the inner chamber is built of precious stones, gold and silver and surrounded by myrrh and aloes. In front of the chamber runs the river Gihon on whose banks are planted flowers giving off perfume and aromatic incense. There are also ounces of gold and silver and fine drapery. There are also extensive descriptions of Hell (*Gehinnom*) in rabbinic literature. Confinement to Hell is a result of disobeying God's Torah as is illustrated by a *midrash* which describes Moses' visit there:

> When Moses and the Angel of Hell entered Hell together they saw men being tortured by the Angels of Destruction. Some sinners were suspended by their eyelids, some by their ears, and some by their hands, and some by their tongues. In addition, women were suspended by their hair and their breasts by chains of fire. Such

punishments were inflicted on the basis of the sins that were committed.

These central themes within rabbinic theology do not exhaust the scope of rabbinic speculation. In addition, early rabbinic authorities discussed a wide variety of religious issues including martyrdom, prayer, charity, atonement, forgiveness, repentance and peace. Within aggadic sources, the rabbis expressed their profound reflections on human life and God's nature and activity in the world. Unlike the legal precepts of the Torah and the rabbinic expansion of these Scriptural ordinances, these theological opinions were not binding on the Jewish community. They were formulated instead to educate, inspire and edify those to whom they were addressed. Study of the Torah was a labour of love which had no end, a task whose goal was to serve the will of God.

SOURCES

Noachide Laws

According to the rabbis, Noah was given seven commands, referred to as the *Noachide Laws*:

The sons of Noah were given seven commands: in respect of (1) idolatry, (2) incest, (3) shedding of blood, (4) profanation of the Name of God, (5) justice, (6) robbery, (7) cutting off flesh or limb from a living animal. R. Hanina said: Also about taking blood from a living animal. R. Elazar said: Also about 'diverse kinds' and 'mixtures' (Lev. 19:19). R. Simeon said:

Also about witchcraft. R. Jonanan b. Baroka said: Also about castration (of animals). R. Assi said: Everything forbidden in Deut. 18:10–11 was also forbidden to the sons of Noah, because it says, 'Whoever does these things is an abomination unto the Lord.'

(*Gen. R., Noah*, 34, 8, in RA, p. 556)

DISCUSSION

1. Discuss the concept of authority in relation to rabbinic theology.

2. Is rabbinic theology unsystematic in character?

FURTHER READING

Belkin, Samuel, *In His Image: The Jewish Philosophy of Man as Expressed in Rabbinic Tradition*, Greenwood, 1979.

Cohen, Abraham, Neusner, Jacob, *Everyman's Talmud: The Major Teachings of the Rabbinic Sages*, Schocken, 1995.

Jacobs, Louis, *The Book of Jewish Belief*, Behrman House, 1984.

Jacobs, Louis, *A Jewish Theology*, Behrman House, 1973.

Kraemer, David Charles, *Responses to Suffering in Classical Rabbinic Literature*, Oxford University Press, 1995.

Neusner, Jacob, *Handbook of Rabbinic Theology: Language, System, Structure*, Brill, 2002.

Neusner, Jacob, *Rabbinic Judaism, The Theological System*, Prometheus Books, 2002.

Neusner, Jacob, *The Theology of Rabbinic Judaism*, University Press of America, 1997.

Pearl, Chaim, *Theology in Rabbinic Stories*, Hendrickson Publishers, 1997.

Schechter, Solomon, *Aspects of Rabbinic Theology: Major Concepts of the Talmud*, Hendrickson Publishers, 1998.

Chapter 25

Judaism under Islamic Rule

Timeline:

622 CE Muhammad's flight from Mecca to Medina

632 CE Death of Muhammad

630s–640s CE Arab conquest of Syria, Palestine, Egypt and Persia

661 CE Consolidation of the Ummayad dynasty

711 CE Muslim conquest of Spain

740 CE Conversion to Judaism of the Khazars on the Volga River

750 CE Abbasid dynasty

756 CE Independent Ummayad caliphate in Spain

Mid-8th century CE Jewish messianic movements in the Middle East

The Arabs of the Arabian peninsula in the sixth and seventh centuries were polytheists living in nomadic tribes or settled in urban centres. At the beginning of the seventh century **Muhammad**, a caravan merchant from Mecca, denounced such paganism as a perversion of God's will. Claiming to have received a revelation from the one true God, he proclaimed a doctrine of divine reward and punishment. In the first phase of his preaching he stressed that Biblical figures such as Abraham and Moses had been sent by God to warn humankind to abandon idolatry. Those who rejected this message were destroyed except for Jews and Christians who had transmitted the revelations given them in the Torah and the Gospels. According to Muhammad, these earlier revelations were superseded by a new revelation from God which was passed on to them through his prophecy.

Initially Muhammad hoped to convert Jews to this new faith, but the Jewish community refused to recognize him as a true prophet. This rejection led Muhammad to denounce the Jewish nation: 'Now that a Book confirming their Scriptures has been revealed to them by Allah, they deny it, although they know it to be the truth and have long prayed for help against the unbelievers. May Allah's curse be upon the infidels!' According to Muhammad, the Jews distorted

Allah's message, and their Scripture contains false-hoods; a number of Biblical stories for example diverge from the *Qur'an* (the record of God's communication to Muhammad). Muhammad's view was that the *Qur'an* confirms and corrects the Torah. Islam is thus superior to Judaism, and Muhammad is the last and decisive apostle of God. Judaism is therefore a legitimate but incomplete religious system.

By 626 – only six years before Muhammad's death – two Jewish tribes had been expelled from Medina and a third had been exterminated, except for women and children, who were enslaved. In 628 Muslims conquered the Jewish oasis of Khaybar to the north; there Jews were subsequently permitted to remain if they gave half their produce as a tribute to the Muslims. By 644 Syria, Israel, Egypt, Iraq and Persia were occupied by Muslim soldiers. The eastern frontier of the Byzantine empire was pushed back to Asia Minor, and the Persian state was destroyed. In the next sixteen years the Ummayad dynasty of caliphs had consolidated their control of the Islamic empire, and Muslim armies continued their campaign. At the beginning of the eighth century a mixed army of Arabs and Muslim Berbers crossed the straits of Gibraltar to conquer the Iberian peninsula, thereby bringing Islam to continental Europe. The Arab empire in this first century of its existence was plagued by unrest over the right of leadership, and in 750 the Ummayads were overthrown and replaced by the Abbasid dynasty of caliphs who moved the capital from Damascus to Baghdad.

During the following century the Abbasid caliphate was at its height – the Islamic post-Scriptural oral tradition was formed, and Muslim jurisprudence, philosophy, theology and science flourished. At first widespread conversion to Islam was not encouraged; Jews were guaranteed religious toleration, judicial autonomy and exemption from the military. In turn they were required to accept the supremacy of the Islamic state. Such an arrangement was formally codified by the **Pact of Omar** dating from 800 CE. According to this treaty, Jews were restricted in a number of spheres: they were not allowed to build new houses of worship, make converts, carry weapons or ride horses. In addition, they were required to wear distinctive clothing and pay a yearly poll tax. Jewish farmers were also obligated to pay a land tax consisting of a portion of their produce. Nevertheless, under these conditions Jewish life prospered. In various urban centres many Jews were employed in crafts such as tanning, dyeing, weaving, silk manufacture and metal work; other Jews participated in interregional trade and established networks of agents and representatives.

This political and economic framework enabled Jews to migrate from Babylonia, which was held by the Arabs, to other parts of the diaspora. Some Jews created new centres of Jewish life and even went outside the Islamic empire to conduct trade. It was just such merchants who during this period converted to Judaism the kings of a Turkish people on the Volga, the Khazars. Jews in the former Byzantine provinces welcomed the Muslim regime. Instead of enduring oppression at the hands of the Christian community, they had a defined legal standing as protected subjects of the state. The political status of Jews under Islam resembled the position of Jews of Sassanian Persia in the third century CE when rabbis adapted Jewish law to the diaspora environment.

During the first two centuries of Islamic rule under the Ummayad and Abbasid caliphates, Muslim leaders confirmed the authority of traditional Babylonian Jewish institutions. When the Arabs conquered Babylonia, they officially recognized the position of the *exilarch* who for centuries had been the ruler of Babylonian Jewry. The *exilarch* represented Jews in the caliphal court, collected the poll tax, and supervised Jewish juridical and charitable institutions. By the Abbasid period, the *exilarch* shared his power with the heads of the rabbinic academies, which in Babylonia had for centuries been the major centres of rabbinic learning, with their rulings based on the interpretation of talmudic precedent widely accepted. The head of each academy was known as the *gaon* (excellency) who delivered lectures as well as learned opinions (*responsa*) on halakhic inquiries. These religious leaders were largely drawn from a small number of families who dominated Jewish life in Babylonia. In the eighth century the *exilarch* was supreme over the academies and appointed their heads, but soon the *geonim* became more independent and claimed the right to appoint the *exilarch*. Gradually the influence of the *exilarch* declined in relation to the *geonim*, and by the tenth century the academies moved from Sura and Pumbeditha to Baghdad. By the eleventh century the *exilarch*'s position became honorific and the academy of Pumbeditha-Baghdad gained pre-eminence over the Sura-Babylonia academy, thereby reversing their relationship in the earlier Muslim period.

SOURCES

Muhammad

In the seventh century CE Muhammad claimed to have received a revelation from Allah, the one true God, which superseded the messages given to Abraham and Moses:

You people of the book, why do you dispute so about Abraham, since the Torah and the Gospels were given after his time? Why don't you use your reason? You are always prepared to discuss things that you understand, why do you insist on arguing about matters of which you know nothing? Knowledge belongs to God – you do not have it. Abraham was not a Jew, nor was he a Christian. He was a true worshipper and a Muslim . . .

It is said that you must be a Jew or a Christian to be rightly guided. Instead you should say, 'The community of Abraham is ours. He was not a polytheist, he was a true worshipper'. Say, 'We believe in God and what he has revealed to us, and what he revealed to Abraham, Ishmael, Isaac, Jacob and the tribes, as well as what was shown to Moses, to Jesus and to the prophets from their Lord. We do not distinguish between any of them and we make submission only to God.' If they believe this faith of yours, then they are rightly guided but if they turn away, then they are clearly in schism. God the all-hearing and all-knowing will guide you in your dealings with them.

(*Qur'an, Sura* 2,3, in SRJ, pp. 78–79)

Initially Muhammad seems to have hoped that the Jews would join his movement:

Asishah reported: The Jews came to the Prophet (may the blessings and peace of Allah be upon him) and said, 'May death overtake you!' Asishah retorted, 'And you too! And may Allah curse you and may Allah's fury come down upon you!' But the Prophet said, 'Gently Asishah! Be courteous and keep away from harshness!'

(*Hadith, Bukhari* 78, in SRJ, p. 79)

When it became clear that the Jews were not going to accept Islam, Muhammad's attitude became more negative:

Long ago we made a covenant with the people of Israel and we sent messages to them. Each time a messenger came with a message that they did not like, they would say some of the messengers were liars and they would murder others. They imagined that nothing evil would come out of it and in this way they grew deaf and blind.

(*Qur'an, Sura* 5, in SRJ, p. 79)

Figure 25 Turkish Book Painting. 'Muhammad leading Moslems at Prayer at Kabah attacked by pagan Qorashi Abu Jahl.' Copyright The Art Archive/Topkapi Museum Istanbul/HarperCollins Publishers.

Pact of Omar

The *Pact of Omar* is a treaty listing privileges and limitations entered into between conquering Muslims and non-Muslims who had been vanquished. Although this treaty was made between Muslims and Christians, its provisions applied to Jews as well:

In the name of God, the Merciful, and the Compassionate! This is a writing to Omar from the Christians of such and such a city. When you (Muslims) marched against us (Christians), we asked of you protection for ourselves, our posterity, our possessions, and our co-religionists; and we made this stipulation with you, that we will not erect in our city or the suburbs any new monastery, church, cell or hermitage; that we will not repair any of such buildings that may fall into ruins, or renew those that may be situated in the Muslim quarters of the town; that we will not refuse the Muslims entry into our churches either by night or by day; that we will open the gates wide to passengers and travellers; that we will receive any Muslim traveller into our houses and give him food and lodging for three nights; that we will not harbour any spy in our churches or houses, or conceal any enemy of the Muslims.

That we will not teach our children the *Qur'an*; that we will not make a show of the Christian religion nor invite any one to embrace it; that we will not prevent any of our kinsmen from embracing Islam, if they so desire. That we will honour the Muslims and rise up in our assemblies when they wish to take their seats; that we will not imitate them in our dress, either in the cap, turban, sandals, or parting of the hair; that we will not make use of their expressions of speech, nor adopt their surnames; that we will not ride on saddles, or gird on swords, or take to ourselves arms or wear them, or engrave Arabic inscriptions on our rings; that we will not sell wine; that we will shave the front of our heads; that we will keep to our own style of dress, wherever we may be; that we will wear girdles round our waists.

That we will not display the cross upon our churches or display our crosses or our sacred books in the streets of the Muslims, or in their market-places; that we will strike the clappers in our churches lightly; that we will not recite our services in a loud voice when a Muslim is present; that we will not carry palmbranches or our images in procession in the streets; that at the burial of our dead we will not chant loudly or carry lighted candles in the streets of the Muslims or their market-places; that we will not take any slaves that have already been in the possession of Muslims; nor spy into their houses; and that we will not strike any Muslim.

(*Pact of Omar*, in JMedW, pp. 13–14)

DISCUSSION

1. What was Muhammad's attitude toward the Jewish community?

2. How were Jews treated in Muslim lands during the first centuries of Islamic rule?

FURTHER READING

Brann, Ross, *Power in the Portrayal: Representations of Jews and Muslims in Eleventh- and Twelfth-Century Islamic Spain*, Princeton University Press, 2002.

Cohen, Mark R., *Under Crescent and Cross: The Jews in the Middle Ages*, Princeton University Press, 1995.

Corrigan, John, Denny, Frederick M., Eire, Carlos M.N., Jaffee, Martin S. (eds), *Jews, Christians, Muslims: A Comparative Introduction to Monotheistic Religions*, Prentice Hall, 1997.

Courbage, Youssef, Fargues, Philippe, *Christianity and Jews Under Islam*, I.B. Tauris, 1997.

Fischel, Walters, *Jews in the Economic and Political Life of Medieval Islam*, KTAV, 1969.

Frank, D. (ed.), *The Jews of Medieval Islam: Community, Society, and Identity: Proceedings of an International Conference held by the Institute of Jewish Studies*, Brill, 1995.

Gubay, Lucien, *Sunlight and Shadow: The Jewish Experience of Islam*, Other Press, 2000.

Lecker, Michael, *Muslims, Jews and Pagans: Studies in Early Medina*, Brill, 1995.

Lewis, Bernard, *The Jews of Islam*, Princeton University Press, 1987.

Masters, Bruce Alan, *Christians and Jews in the Ottoman Arab World: The Roots of Sectarianism*, Cambridge University Press, 2001.

Nettler, Ronald, *Past Trials and Present Tribulations: A Muslim Fundamentalist's View of the Jews*, Pergammon Press, 1987.

Rubin, Uri, Wasserstein, David (eds), *Israel Oriental Studies: Dhimmis and Others: Jews and Christians and the World of Classical Islam*, Eisenbrauns, 2001.

Wasserstrom, Steven M., *Between Muslim and Jew*, Princeton University Press, 1995.

Ye'Or, Bat, *The Dhimmi: Jews and Christians Under Islam*, Associated University Press, 1985.

CHAPTER 26

Karaism

Timeline:

762–767 CE Anan ben David's break with rabbinic Judaism. Beginning of the Karaite movement

c. 757–761 CE Yehudah *gaon* of Sura

882–941 CE Saadiah Gaon

During the eighth century messianic movements appeared in the Persian Jewish community which led to armed uprisings against Muslim authorities. Such revolts were quickly crushed, but an even more serious threat to traditional Jewish life was posed later in the century by the emergence of an anti-rabbinic sect, the **Karaites**. This group was founded in Babylonia in the 760s CE by **Anan ben David**, who had earlier been passed over as *exilarch*, and traced its origin to the time of Jeroboam in the eighth century BCE. According to some scholars, Anan's movement absorbed elements of an extra-talmudic tradition and took over doctrines from Islam. The guiding interpretative principle formulated by Anan, 'Search thoroughly in Scripture and do not rely on my opinion', was intended to point to Scripture itself as the sole source of law. Jewish observances, the Karaites insisted, must conform to Biblical legislation rather than rabbinic ordinances. Anan however was not lenient concerning legal matters. He did not, for example, recognize the minimum quantities of forbidden foods fixed by the rabbis; in addition, he introduced more complicated regulations for circumcision, added to the number of fast days, interpreted the prohibition of work on the Sabbath in stricter terms than the rabbis, and extended the prohibited degrees of marriage. In short, he made the yoke of the law more burdensome.

After the death of the founder, new parties within the Karaite movement soon emerged. The adherents of Anan were referred to as the 'Ananites' and remained few in number. In the first half of the ninth century the Ukbarite sect was established by Ishmael of Ukbara (near Baghdad); some years later another sect was formed in the same town by Mishawayh Al-Ukbari. Another group was formed by a contemporary of Mishawayh, Abu Imran Al-Tiflisi. In Israel, yet another sect was established by Malik Al-Ramli. By the end of the ninth century Karaism had become a conglomerate of groups advocating different anti-rabbinic positions, but these sects were short-lived and in time the Karaites consolidated into a uniform movement. The central representative of mainstream Karaism was Benjamin ben Moses Nahawendi who advocated a policy of free and independent study of Scripture which became the dominant ideology of later Karaism. By the tenth century a number of Karaite communities were established in Israel, Iraq and Persia. These groups rejected rabbinic law and devised their own legislation, which led eventually to the foundation of a Karaite rabbinical academy in Jerusalem; the Karaite community there produced some of the most distinguished scholars of the period who composed legal handbooks, wrote Biblical commentaries, expounded on Hebrew philology and engaged in philosophical and theological reflection.

The growth of Karaism provoked the rabbis to attack it as a heretical movement. The first prominent

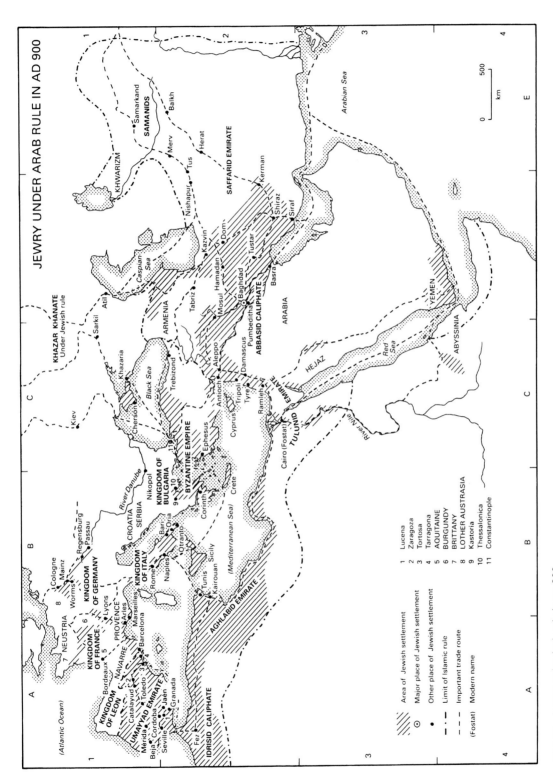

Map 27 Jewry under Arab rule in AD 900

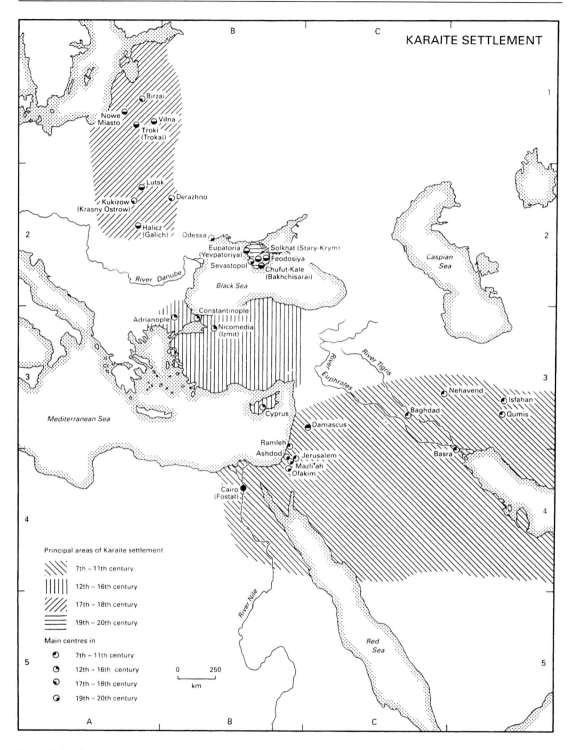

KARAITE SETTLEMENT

Birzai

Nowe
Miasto Vilna
Troki
(Trokai)

Lutsk
Kukizow Derazhno
(Krasny Ostrow)

Halicz   Odessa
(Galich) Eupatoria   Solkhat (Stary-Krym)
(Yevpatoriya) Feodosiya
Sevastopol   Chufut-Kale
(Bakhchisarai)

River Danube

Black Sea   *Caspian
Sea*

Constantinople
Adrianople
Nicomedia
(Izmit)

River Tigris

Nehavend

River Euphrates   Isfahan
Baghdad
Qumis

Cyprus

Mediterranean Sea   Damascus

Ramleh   Basra
Ashdod
Jerusalem
Mazli'ah
Ofakim

Cairo
(Fostat)

River Nile

*Red
Sea*

Principal areas of Karaite settlement

7th – 11th century

12th – 16th century

17th – 18th century

19th – 20th century

Main centres in

7th – 11th century
12th – 16th century   0   250
17th – 18th century   km
19th – 20th century

Map 28 Karaite settlement

authority to engage in anti-Karaite debate was **Saadiah Gaon** who in the first half of the ninth century wrote a book attacking Anan; this polemic was followed by other anti-Karaite tracts by eminent rabbinic authorities. After the Jerusalem Jewish community was devastated by the First Crusade, Karaite scholarly activity shifted to the Byzantine empire, and from there Jews founded communities in the Crimea, Poland and Lithuania. In Egypt the Karaite community continued to flourish, but after the eleventh century the movement diminished in influence, and in the centuries that followed Karaism survived only as a tiny minority within Jewry.

SOURCES

Anan ben David

Different accounts are given of the origin of Anan ben David. According to Saadiah Gaon:

Anan had a younger brother called Hananiah. Although Anan was older in age and had a greater understanding of the Torah, the sages of that time were unwilling to elect him as *exilarch* because of his persistent unruliness and irreverence which were an inherent part of his character. So the sages chose Hananiah his brother, who was exceedingly modest and shy and who feared God greatly, and made him *exilarch*. Then Anan was furious together with every scoundrel who still held the Sadducean and Boethusian opinion and he decided to cause a schism because he was frightened of the government of the time. These heretics appointed Anan as their *exilarch*.

(Saadiah Gaon, *The Refutation of Anan*, in SRJ, pp. 81–82)

Another account was given by a Karaite scholar writing in the eighteenth century:

Anan the Pious had been appointed Judge and *exilarch* of all the Jews in the Arab empire, by the agreement of the Arab king and the Jewish people. He wrapped himself in a cloak of zeal and was very jealous for the Lord of Hosts, the God of Israel, and for his true and perfect Torah which had for so many years been in the possession of the Pharisees. He wanted to restore the crown of the Law to its former glory so he began to preach in public and to argue against the *Mishnah*, the oral law, and to deny it and to reject it utterly. When the whole congregation of Pharisees saw and heard all this, these accursed villains met together and rebelled against him and plotted to murder him.

(Isaac Luzki, *The Path of the Righteous*, in SRJ, p. 81)

Karaites

The Karaites who first emerged in the eighth century CE rejected the oral law:

We are not compelled to follow the customs of our forefathers in every respect, but we must think about their ways and compare their behaviour and their laws with the words of the Torah. If we find that the teachings of our forefathers do correspond exactly to Scripture, then we must accept them and listen to them. We must follow them; we must not change them. But if their teachings are different from those of Scripture, we must reject them and must look for ourselves and investigate and ponder the commandments of the Torah for ourselves. What is written down in the Law of Moses (peace be unto him) about the commandments and other matters does not need any sign or witness to demonstrate its truth; but what is handed down from our forefathers needs both proof and a responsible witness.

(Sahl ben Mazliah, *An Open Rebuke*, in SRJ, p. 81)

Figure 26 Exterior of the great Karaite synagogue in El-Abassieh quarter, Cairo, Egypt, 1979. The synagogue was built in the early twentieth century. Photo: Micha Bar-Am, Israel. Copyright the Beth Hatefutsoth Photo Archive.

Since there was an emphasis in Karaite theology on individual opinion, there were many different groups of Karaites:

The rabbis believe that their laws and rulings have been passed down by the prophets; if this is so, there should exist no differences of opinion among them and the fact that there are such differences shows that their arrogant belief is false. We, however, reach our views through reason and reason can lead to a variety of conclusions.

(Jacob al-Kirkisani, *Book of Lights*, in SRJ, p. 82)

Karaite communities were established in Egypt, North Africa, Persia and Israel. The Karaites who settled in Israel were particularly famous for their Biblical scholarship:

With the Karaites, the correct understanding of the book of God increased. People came from the east and from the west and commitment to religion and the desire for knowledge grew ever greater. They wanted to live in Jerusalem so they left the comfort of their homes and lived in the world as ascetics . . . They are the lilies, and the pious who have clung to the teaching of the book will be numbered among them.

(Salman b. Jeruhim, *Explanation of Psalm 69* in SRJ, p. 82)

Concerning the Jews, both the Asma'ath (Rabbanites), who are the vast majority, and the Ananites (Karaites) who believe in righteousness and the one God, in their interpretation of the Hebrew books, the Torah, the Prophets and the Psalms (which make up the twenty-four books) and in their translations into Arabic, rely on a number of Jews who are greatly respected and most of whom we have met personally.

(al-Masudi, *Library of Arab Geography*, in SRJ, p. 82)

Among the most famous of the Karaite Biblical scholars was Ben Asher in the ninth century, of whose Biblical manuscript Moses Maimonides the philosopher wrote:

> Everyone relies on this book because it was corrected and its details were fixed by Ben Asher over a period of many years. It is said that he corrected it many times and I have relied on it.
>
> (Moses Maimonides, *Mishneh Torah*, in SRJ, p. 82)

Karaite Attack on Rabbinic Tradition

This attack on the rabbinic establishment was composed at the end of the tenth century:

Know, my Jewish brethren, that every one is responsible for himself, and God will not hearken to the words of him who tries to justify himself, saying: 'Well, my teachers taught me to do this', any more than he listened to the excuse of Adam who said (Gen. 3:12–13): 'The woman whom Thou gavest to be with me, she gave me of the tree, and I did eat'. Nor will God accept the excuse of the man who says: 'The sages fooled me', any more than he tolerated the excuse of Eve when she said: 'The serpent beguiled me, and I did eat'.

And just as He gave to each his due, and exercised his judgment on each one of them, so will He do to any one who argues in that manner, as it is written (Zech. 10:3): 'Mine anger is kindled against the shepherds, and I will punish the he-goats' are those who are led. Realize, therefore, that he who attempts to justify himself, saying: 'I walked in the ways of my fathers', will find that this excuse will not help him at all. Did not our God, blessed be He, answer (Zech. 1:4): 'Be ye not as your fathers'? And did He not further say (Psalm 78:8): 'They shall not be as their fathers, a stubborn and rebellious generation'.

This is to tell us that we are not bound to follow in the ways of our fathers in every respect, but we must reflect on their ways and compare their actions and their laws to the words of the Torah. If we see that the teachings of our fathers are exactly like the words of the Bible, then we must accept them and pay attention to them. We must follow them and dare not change them. But if the teachings of our fathers are different from the Bible, we must cast them out, and we must ourselves seek and investigate and think about the commands of the Torah. That which is written in the Torah of Moses – peace be unto him – about the commandments and other things does not require any sign or witness to show us whether or not it is true; but that which our fathers have told us requires proof and a responsible witness so that one may determine if it is true or not, and only that law which is proved to us will we perform, for thus it is written (Hosea 10:12): 'sow to yourselves according to righteousness, reap according to mercy'.

(*Karaite Attack on Rabbinic Tradition*, in JMedW, pp. 238–239)

Saadiah Gaon and the *Exilarch*

One of the most famous of the heads of the Babylonian academies was Saadiah Gaon. After becoming gaon at Sura, he engaged in a bitter controversy with the *exilarch*:

It was not long before a quarrel broke out between the *exilarch* and Saadiah, and Bagdad was divided into two parties. All the wealthy of Bagdad, the scholars of the academies and the prominent people of the city sided with Saadiah, ready to help him by means of their money and their influence with the king, his princes and advisers.

There was, however, a very influential man in Bagdad, Caleb ibn Sargado by name, who was a supporter of the *exilarch*. He gave 60,000 *zuz* of his fortune – for he was a rich man – to remove Saadiah from office, but he did not succeed, for the sons of Netira and all the wealthy of Bagdad were with Saadiah. The fact is that this Caleb was jealous of Saadiah, for though Caleb was eloquent and very learned and knew an answer or two for every question, Saadiah knew ten times more, and for this reason Caleb envied him.

The roots of the quarrel between Saadiah and the *exilarch* were some property that belonged to some men who were within the jurisdiction of the *exilarch*, and a large sum of money which fell to them through inheritance and which they desired to divide. They quarrelled about it until they voluntarily agreed to give to the *exilarch* ten percent of all that fell to them by inheritance, in order to remove all complaints against themselves and to settle the case. This ten percent which they gave to the *exilarch* as his share

amounted to seven hundred goldpieces, so he issued the documents for them, sealed them, and ordered them to go to the heads of the academies who would confirm them.

When the documents reached Saadiah he examined them and saw things in them that did not seem right to him. Nevertheless he spoke to the men courteously: 'Go to Kohen Zedek, the head of the Pumbedita academy, and let him sign this document first; then I will do so'. Now he only said this in order to cover up the unseemly thing which was obvious to him but which he did not wish to make public. They did as he commanded them and went to Kohen Zedek, the head of the Pumbedita academy, and he put his seal on them.

After Kohen Zedek had done this, they came back to Saadiah to have him also sign and confirm them. 'Why do you want my signature?' asked Saadiah of them. 'You already have the signatures of the *exilarch* and of Kohen Zedek, the head of the Pumbedita academy. You don't need my signature.' 'Why don't you sign?' they countered. 'I don't know', he answered, and refused to reveal the reason to them, until they adjured him many times to tell them what he found wrong in their documents.

(*Saadiah Gaon and the Exilarch*, in JMedW, pp. 288–289)

DISCUSSION

1. Why did Anan ben David separate from the rabbinic establishment?

2. What were the principles governing the Karaite exegesis of the Scripture?

FURTHER READING

Ankori, Zvi, *Karaites in Byzantium: The Formative Years, 970–1100*, AMS Press, 1971.

El-Kodsi, Mourad, Fox, Leonard, Gamzon, Marcy (eds), *Karaite Jews of Egypt 1882–1986*, Mourad El-Kodsi, 1987.

El-Kodsi, Mourad, *The Karaites of Poland, Lithuania, Russia and Ukraine*, Mourad El-Kodsi, 1993.

Freund, Roman, *Karaites and Dejudaization: A Historical Review of an Endogenous and Exogenous Paradigm*, Coronet, 1991.

Lutski, Joseph Solomon, Miller, Philip E., *Karaite Separatism in Nineteenth-Century Russia: Joseph Solomon Lutski's Epistle of Israel's Deliverance*, Hebrew Union College Press, 1993.

Schur, Nathan, *History of the Karaites*, Peter Lang, 1992.

Schur, Nathan, *The Karaite Encyclopedia*, Peter Lang, 1995.

Yaron, Yoseif (ed.), *Karaite Passover Haggadah*, Karaite Jews of America, 2001.

CHAPTER 27

Jews in Muslim Spain and Other Islamic Lands

Timeline:

750 CE Abbasid dynasty

756 CE Independent Ummayad caliphate in Spain

786–809 CE Harun al-Rashid Abbasid caliph

915–970 CE Hisdai ibn Shaprut

968–1006 CE Sherira ben Hanina *gaon* of Pumbeditha

993–1056 CE Samuel ibn Nagrela

1004–1038 CE Hai ben Sherira

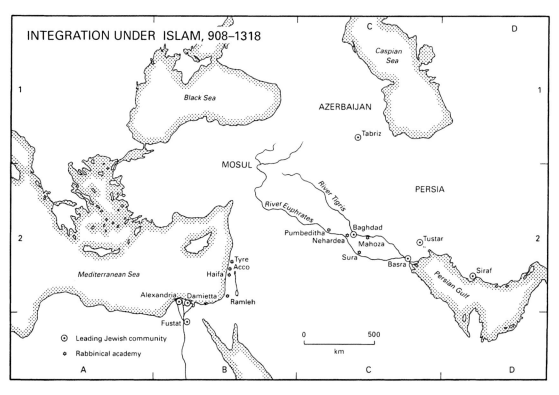

Map 29 Integration under Islam, 908–1318

As early as the eighth century the Muslim empire began to undergo a process of disintegration. When Abbasid caliphs conquered the Ummayads in 750 CE, Spain remained independent under a Ummayad ruler. As the century progressed, the Abbasids began to lose control of the outlying territories. After 850 CE, Turkish troops managed to gain control over the Abbasids and the caliph became essentially a figurehead behind which Turkish generals exerted power. In 909 CE Shi'ite Muslims (followers of Ali, Muhammad's son-in-law), the Fatimids, took control over North Africa; in 969 CE they conquered Egypt and Israel. By the end of the tenth century CE the Islamic world was divided into a number of separate states pitted against one another.

The disappearance of the political unity of the Islamic empire was accompanied by a decentralization of rabbinic Judaism. The rabbinic academies of Babylonia began to lose their hold on the Jewish scholarly world. In many places rabbinic academies (*yeshivot*) were re-established in which rabbinic sources were studied. The growth of these local centres of learning enabled individual teachers to exert their influence on Jewish learning independently of the academies of Sura and Pumbeditha. The locality in which the local rabbinate asserted itself was the Holy Land. Tiberius was the location of the rabbinical academy there as well as the centre of the Masoretic scholars, such as the families of Ben Asher and Ben Naphtali, who produced the standard tradition (*masorah*) of the Bible by adding vowels and punctuation to the Hebrew text. By the ninth century the rabbinic academy moved to Ramleh and then to Jerusalem; this institution was supported by the Jewish communities of Egypt, Yemen and Syria, but due to Turkish and Christian invasions its influence waned in the eleventh century CE.

Egyptian Jewry also underwent a transformation during this period. Under the Fatimids, Jewish life prospered in Egypt, and by the end of the tenth century a *yeshivah* had been established in Cairo. Kairouan had also become a centre of scholarship. At this time academies were established by distinguished talmudists and affluent Jewish families who supported Jewish scientists and philosophers. The city of Fez also reached a degree of eminence, producing one of the most important rabbinic scholars of the period, Isaac Alfasi (1013–1103 CE), who compiled an important code of

Figure 27 Book Painting. 'The Archangel Gabriel inspires Muhammad'. Copyright The Art Archive/Turkish and Islamic Art Museum, Istanbul.

Jewish law. But it was in Spain that the Jewish community attained the greatest level of achievement. In the tenth-century Spanish royal court the Ummayad caliphs Abd Al-Rahman III (912–961 CE) and Hakah II (961–972 CE) employed the Jewish statesman Hisdai Ibn Shaprut (915–970 CE) as court physician, administrator and diplomat. In addition, he acted as head of the Jewish community and patron of Jewish scholarship. Cordova, the capital of the Ummayad caliphate, became a vibrant centre of Jewish civilization, attracting poets, grammarians and *yeshivah* students from throughout the diaspora.

As the Ummayad caliphate began to disintegrate in the eleventh century CE, small Muslim principalities were often at odds with one another. Several of the rulers of these states used Jewish courtiers, such as Samuel Ibn Nagrela of Granada (**Samuel Ha-Nagid**: 993–1056 CE), in their adminstrations. This figure was knowledgeable about mathematics and philosophy, wrote in Hebrew and Arabic, and served as vizier of Granada for thirty years. In commemoration of his own military victories, he composed Hebrew poetry and wrote an introduction to the *Talmud.* Other scholars of the period lived in Seville, Saragossa, Toledo, Calatayud and Lucena.

In 1086 CE the life of Spanish Jewry was shaken when the Almoravides from North Africa were invited to Spain to lead an attack on Christian communities in the north and persecuted the Jewish population as well. Soon, however, Jews were restored to their former secure position and the next generation saw outstanding poets, philosophers, Biblical commentators, theologians and rabbinic authorities. But in the middle of the twelfth century the golden age of Spanish Jewry came to an end. Fearing Christian conquest, the Almohades – a Berber dynasty from Morocco – came to defend the country and simultaneously persecuted the Jewish community. Jews were forced to convert to Islam, and academies and synagogues were closed. Some Jews practised Judaism in secret; others escaped to the Middle East or migrated to Christian Spain. At the beginning of the thirteenth century the dominance of the Almohades came to an end when Christian kingdoms managed to seize control of most of the former Muslim territories in Spain.

In other parts of the Muslim empire, Jews faced changing circumstances during these centuries. In the mid-twelfth century, during the Almohade persecution, some Spanish Jews migrated to Egypt, including the Jewish philosopher Moses Maimonides. In Israel a small Jewish community survived during the Crusades, and was augmented by Jewish pilgrims who went to the Holy Land. Babylonian Jewry continued after the death of the last important *gaon*, Hai bar Sherira, in 1038 CE, but the Mongol invasions in the middle of the thirteenth century had devastating consequences for the region. In western North Africa Jewish communities were able to practise their faith as before when the Almohades were removed and many Jews prospered. Some North African Jewish merchants participated in the Saharan gold trade, maintaining links with the kingdom of Aragon in Spain.

SOURCES

Samuel Ha-Nagid

Samuel Ha-Nagid was a courtier rabbi and author of *Sefer Seder ha-Kabbalah*. His accomplishments were made possible by his service to Spanish Muslim rulers. Here the twelfth century Jewish philosopher Abraham ibn Daud of Toledo describes his activities:

Rabbi Samuel ha-Levi was appointed Prince in the year 4787 (1027 CE), and he conferred great benefits on Israel in Spain, in north-western and north-central Africa, in the land of Egypt, in Sicily, even as far as the Babylonian academy, and the Holy City, Jerusalem. All the students who lived in those lands benefited by his generosity, for he bought numerous copies of the Holy Scriptures, the *Mishnah*, and the *Talmud* – these, too, being holy writings . . .

To every one – in all the land of Spain and in all the lands that we have mentioned – who wanted to make the study of the Torah his profession, he would give of his money. He had scribes who used to copy *Mishnahs* and *Talmuds*, and he would give them as a gift to students, in the academies of Spain or in the lands we have mentioned, who were not able to buy them with their own means . . . Besides this, he furnished olive oil every year for the lamps of the synagogues in Jerusalem. He spread the knowledge of the Torah very widely and died an old man at a ripe age.

(In JMedW, pp. 299–300)

DISCUSSION

1. Why did Babylonian scholarship lose its hold on the Jewish scholarly world?

2. Discuss the efflorescence of Jewish life in medieval Spain.

FURTHER READING

Ashtor, Eliyahu, Wasserstein, David, *Jews of Moslem Spain*, Vols 1–3, Jewish Publication Society, 1993.

Brann, Ross, *Power in the Portrayal: Representations of Jews and Muslims in Eleventh- and Twelfth-Century Islamic Spain*, Princeton University Press, 2002.

Deshen, Shlomo, Zenner, Walter P. (eds), *Jews Among Muslims: Communities in the Precolonial Middle East*, New York University Press, 1996.

Gerber, Jane, *The Jews of Spain: A History of the Sephardic Experience*, Free Press, 1994.

Ginio, Alisa Meyuhas (ed.), *Jews, Christians and Muslims in the Mediterranean World after 1492*, Frank Cass, 2002.

Lecker, Michael, *Muslims, Jews and Pagans: Studies on Early Islamic Medina*, Brill, 1995.

Lewis, Bernard, *Cultures in Conflict: Christians, Muslims, and Jews in the Age of Discovery*, Oxford University Press, 1996.

Mann, Vivian B., Glick, Thomas F. (eds), *Convivencia: Jews, Muslims, and Christians in Medieval Spain*, George Braziller, 1992.

Mas, Paloma Diaz, Zocker, George K. (eds), *Sephardim: The Jews from Spain*, University of Chicago Press, 1993.

Menocal, Maria Rosa, Bloom, Harold, *The Ornament of the World: How Muslims, Jews, and Christians Created a Culture of Tolerance in Medieval Spain*, Little, Brown and Co, 2002.

Meyerson, Mark, English, Edward, *Christians, Muslims, and Jews in Medieval and Early Modern Spain: Interaction and Cultural Change*, University of Notre Dame Press, 2000.

Neuman, Abraham A., *The Jews in Spain: The Social, Political and Cultural Life During the Middle Ages*, Octagon, 1970.

Roth, Norman, *Jews, Visigoths and Muslims in Medieval Spain: Cooperation and Conflict*, Brill, 1994.

CHAPTER 28

Jewry in Christian Europe in the Middle Ages

Timeline:

c. 960–1028 Gershom ben Judah of Mainz

1040–1105 Rashi

1006 Jews settle in England

1096 Massacre of Jews in the Rhineland

c. 1100–1171 Jacob Tam

c. 1125–1198 Abraham ben David of Posquières

c. 1160–1235 Issaac the Blind

1144 Ritual murder charge at Norwich

1171 Blood libel at Blois

1182–1198 Expulsion of Jews from France by Philip II

1190 Massacre at York

1215–1293 Meir of Rothenberg

1240 Disputation of Paris

1242 Burning of *Talmud* in Paris

1288 Blood libel of Troyes

1290 Expulsion of Jews from England

1306 Philip IV expels Jews from France

1315 Jews recalled to France

1348–1349 Black Death

The Muslims did not manage to conquer all of Europe in their campaigns in the seventh century – many countries remained under Christian rule as did much of the Byzantine empire. The early Jewish communities in western Europe lived in small, self-contained enclaves and engaged in local trades. The Jews in each town constituted a separate unit since there was no equivalent of an *exilarch* (as in Muslim lands) to serve as the official leader of the Jewish population. Each community (*kahal*) established its own rules (*takkanot*) and administered local courts, in a form of self-government which was the Ashkenazic adaptation to the feudal structure of medieval Christian Europe. In this environment Jewish study took place in a number of important centres such as Mainz and Worms in the Rhineland and Troyes and Sens in northern France and produced such leading scholars as the legal expert Rabbenu Gershom of Mainz (960–1028) and the greatest commentator of the medieval period, Solomon ben Isaac of Troyes (known as **Rashi**: 1040–1105). In subsequent generations, the study of the *Talmud* reached great heights: in Germany and northern France scholars known as the *tosafists* (which included some of Rashi's family) utilized new methods of Talmudic interpretation. In addition, Ashkenazic Jews of this period composed religious poetry modelled on the liturgical compositions (*piyyutim*) of fifth- and sixth-century Israel.

Despite this efflorescence of Jewish learning, Jews in Christian countries were subject to frequent outbursts of anti-Jewish sentiment. In 1095 Pope Urban II proclaimed the First **Crusade** – an act which stimulated mobs in the Rhineland in 1096 to attack Jews in towns such as Worms and Mainz. Jews in these communities willingly martyred themselves as an act of sanctification rather than convert to the Christian faith. These massacres at the end of the century were not officially authorized by the state, and Jews who had

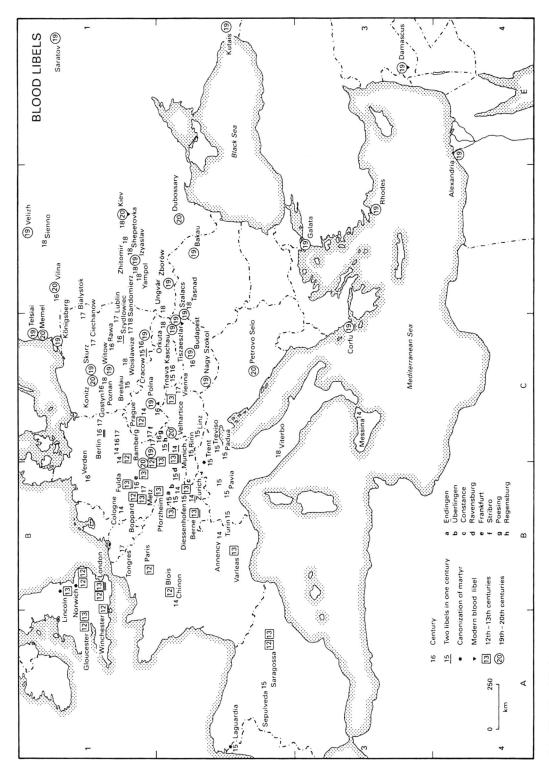

BLOOD LIBELS

Saratov ⑲

Velizh ⑲

18 Sienno

16 ⑳ Vilna

⑲ Telsiai

⑳ Memel

Königsberg

17 Ciechanow

17 Bialystok

Zhitomir 18 18 ⑳ Kiev

18 Shepetovka

18 ⑲ Yampol Izyaslav

⑳ Dubossary

⑲ Velizh

Kutais ⑲

Black Sea

Damascus ⑲

Alexandria ⑲

Rhodes

⑳

⑲ Bakau

Zborów

Ungvár 18

18 ⑲

⑲ Galata

Verden
16

Konitz ⑳ ⑲ Skurz

Gostyn 16 18

Poznan ⑲ Witow

Breslau 18

Prague 15 Cracow 15 16 ⑲

Szydlowiec

16 S. Lublin

16 Rawa

17 18 Sandomierz

Berlin 16 17

14 14 16 17

Cologne 14

Fulda ⑫ 16

⑬ 17

Metz ⑬ ⑲ Polna

14 16

Bamberg 14

⑫⑲① ⑬ ⑳

⑬ 15 d 15 d

Orkuta 18 18

⑲ Trnava Kaschau ⑲

17 ⑲ ⑲ Szalacs

16 ⑲ Budapest

Nagy Szokol

18 Tasnad

Tiszaeszlar ⑲

Corfu ⑲

Petrovo Selo ⑳

Boppard ⑫ 16 e

Pforzheim ⑬ ⑬ 17

⑬ 15 a b

Diessenhofen 15 15 c ⑬ c

Berne ⑬ 14 Zurich

Munich

Velhartice 15 Linz

15 Rinn

15 Trent

15 Treviso

15 Padua

15 Pavia

Annency 14 Turin 15

Varleas ⑬

Blois ⑫

14 Chinon

Tongres 17

Paris ⑫

London ⑫

Winchester ⑫

Gloucester ⑫ ⑬

Norwich ⑬

Lincoln ⑬

Messina 14

18 Viterbo

Mediterranean Sea

Laguardia 15

Sepulveda 15

Saragossa ⑫⑬

16	Century
15	Two libels in one century
✴	Canonization of martyr
▼	Modern blood libel
⑬	12th–13th centuries
⑳	19th–20th centuries

a	Endingen
b	Überlingen
c	Constance
d	Ravensburg
e	Frankfurt
f	Stribro
g	Poesing
h	Regensburg

km
0   250

Map 30 Blood libels

Figure 28 Crusaders winning battle against Moors, folio 92R of Canticles of Saint Mary, thirteenth-century manuscript by Alfonso X the Wise, 1221–84 King of Castile and Leon. Copyright The Art Archive/Real biblioteca de lo Escorial/Dagli Orti.

converted under duress were subsequently allowed to return to the Jewish tradition.

In the following two centuries the Jewish community of Christian Europe became increasingly more involved in moneylending as the Christian guilds forced Jews out of trade. The practice of usury intensified anti-Semitism especially by those who were unable to pay back loans. Added to this economic motive, Christians in the Middle Ages persecuted the Jews on religious grounds: the Jew was stereotyped as a demonic Christ-killer and murderer. As early as 1144 in Norwich, England, the Jewish community was accused of killing Christian children at Passover to use their blood in the preparation of unleavened bread. Later the same accusation was made in Blois, France, in 1171, and in Lincoln, England, in 1255. Another frequent charge against the Jews was that they **profaned the host** in order to torture Jesus' body. Further, Jews were also regarded with enmity since they obtained Church property through defaulted loans. Such factors led the Fourth Lateran Council in 1215 to strengthen the Church's restrictions regarding the Jewish people: 'It is decreed that henceforth Jews of both sexes will be distinguished from other people by their garments, as moreover has been prescribed to them by Moses. They will not show

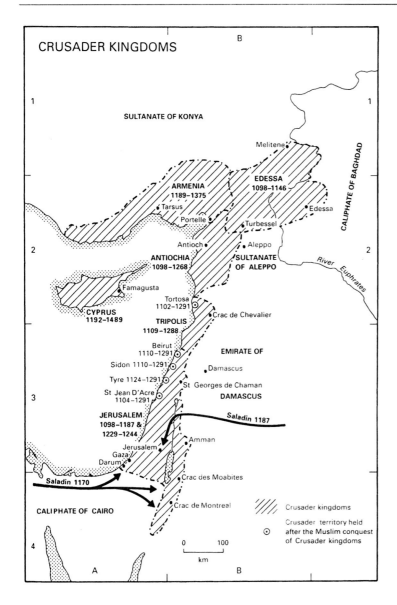

CRUSADER KINGDOMS

SULTANATE OF KONYA

Melitene

CALIPHATE OF BAGHDAD

ARMENIA
1189–1375

EDESSA
1098–1146

Tarsus

Edessa

Portelle

Turbessel

Antioch

Aleppo

ANTIOCHIA
1098–1268

SULTANATE
OF ALEPPO

Famagusta

River Euphrates

CYPRUS
1192–1489

Tortosa
1102–1291

Crac de Chevalier

TRIPOLIS
1109–1288

Beirut
1110–1291

EMIRATE OF

Sidon 1110–1291

Damascus

Tyre 1124–1291

St Georges de Chaman

St Jean D'Acre
1104–1291

DAMASCUS

Saladin 1187

JERUSALEM
1098–1187 &
1229–1244

Amman

Jerusalem
Gaza
Darum

Crac des Moabites

Saladin 1170

CALIPHATE OF CAIRO

Crac de Montreal

0   100
km

Crusader kingdoms

⊙ Crusader territory held
after the Muslim conquest
of Crusader kingdoms

Map 31 Crusader kingdoms

themselves in public during Holy Week, for some among them on these days wear their finest garments and mock the Christians clad in mourning. Trespassers will be duly punished by the secular powers, in order that they no longer dare flout Christ in the presence of Christians'.

In the same century Dominican priests were active against the Jewish community. In 1240 they participated in a **disputation about the Talmud** in Paris with leading Jewish scholars. Among the points raised were the following queries: Was it true that in the first century after the fall of Jerusalem Rabbi Simeon bar Yochai proclaimed: 'Seize the best of the *goyim* and kill them'? Does the *Talmud* claim that Jesus was in illegitimate child? Is it the *Talmud*'s view that Jesus will suffer the torment of boiling mud in Hell? In reply, the Jewish authorities stressed that many commandments prescribe an equal charity toward Jews and non-Jews. Yet, as a result of this debate the *Talmud* was condemned and all copies were burned.

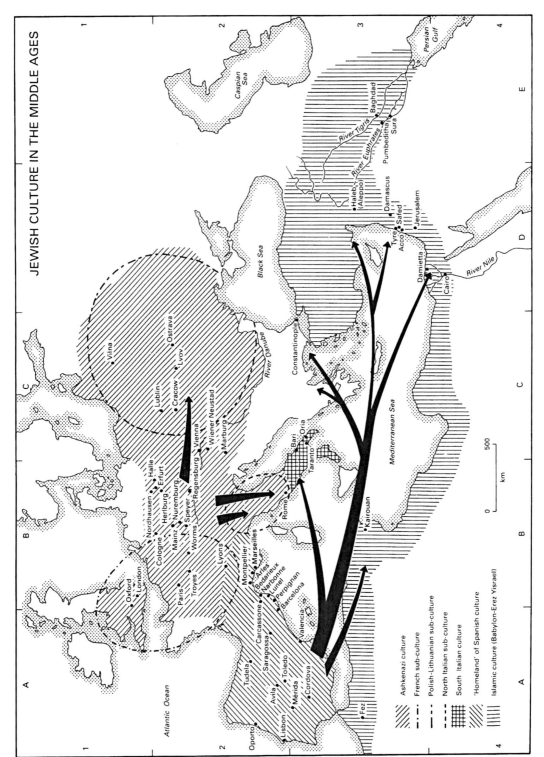

JEWISH CULTURE IN THE MIDDLE AGES

Caspian Sea

River Tigris

Baghdad

River Euphrates

Pumbeditha
Sura

Persian Gulf

Haleb (Aleppo)

Damascus

Safed
Tyre
Acco
Jerusalem

Damietta

Cairo

River Nile

Black Sea

River Danube

Vilna

Ostrava
Lvov
Cracow
Lublin

Wiener Neustad
Vienna
Marburg
Regensburg

Constantinople

Nordhausen
Halle
Erfurt
Cologne
Herlburg
Mainz
Nuremberg
Worms
Speyer

London
Oxford

Paris
Troyes

Lyons

Montpellier
Marseilles
Arles
Beziers
Narbonne
Lunel
Perpignan

Barcelona

Valencia

Bari
Oria
Taranto
Rome

Mediterranean Sea

Kairouan

Tudela
Saragossa
Toledo
Avila
Merida
Cordova

Lisbon
Oporto

Fez

Atlantic Ocean

500
km
0

Ashkenazi culture

French sub-culture

Polish-Lithuanian sub-culture

North Italian sub-culture

South Italian culture

'Homeland' of Spanish culture

Islamic culture (Babylon-Erez Yisrael)

Map 32 Jewish culture in the Middle Ages

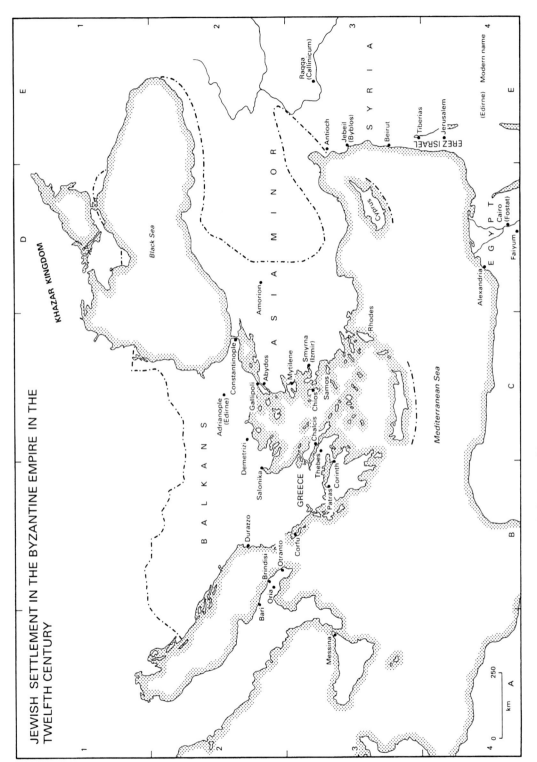

JEWISH SETTLEMENT IN THE BYZANTINE EMPIRE IN THE
TWELFTH CENTURY

KHAZAR KINGDOM

Black Sea

BALKANS

ASIA MINOR

SYRIA

GREECE

Mediterranean Sea

Cyprus

EREZ ISRAEL

EGYPT

Adrianople
(Edirne)
Constantinople
Gallipoli
Abydos
Mytilene
Smyrna
(Izmir)
Chios
Samos
Rhodes
Amorion
Demetrizi
Salonika
Thebes
Chalcis
Patras
Corinth
Durazzo
Corfu
Otranto
Brindisi
Oria
Bari
Messina

Antioch
Jebeil
(Byblos)
Berrut
Tiberias
Jerusalem
Raqqa
(Callinicum)
Alexandria
Cairo
(Fostat)
Faiyum

(Edirne) Modern name

km A
4 0   250

Map 33 Jewish settlement in the Byzantine empire in the twelfth century

Expulsion of the Jews from countries in which they lived also became a dominant policy of Christian Europe. In 1182 the king of France, Philip Augustus, expelled all Jews from the royal domains near Paris, cancelled nearly all Christian debts to Jewish money-lenders, and confiscated Jewish property. Though the Jews were recalled in 1198, they were burdened with an additional royal tax and in the next century they increasingly became the property of the king. In thirteenth-century England the Jews were continuously taxed and the entire Jewish population was expelled in 1290, as was that in France by Philip IV some years later. At the end of the thirteenth century in Germany, the Jewish community suffered violent attacks. In 1286 the most eminent scholar of the period, R. Meir of Rothenberg (1220–1293), was taken prisoner and died in custody. Twelve years later mobs rampaged the country destroying about 140 Jewish communities. In the next century Jews were blamed for bringing about the **Black Death** by poisoning the wells of Europe, and from 1348 to 1349 Jews in France, Switzerland, Germany and Belgium suffered at the hands of their neighbours. In the following two centuries, Jewish massacre and expulsion became a frequent occurrence.

SOURCES

Rashi

Pre-eminent among rabbinic scholars in northern France was Rabbi Solomon ben Isaac of Troyes (Rashi) who produced commentaries on all the books of the Bible and all the tractates of the *Talmud*:

Leviticus 19:18: 'Thou shalt not take vengeance, nor bear any grudge against the children of thy people, but thou shalt love thy neighbour as thyself: I am the Lord.'

Thou shalt not take vengeance: A person says: 'Lend me your sickle', and the other fellow answers: 'No'. On the following day the other fellow says: 'Lend me your axe', and the person answers: 'I won't lend you, just as you didn't lend me'. This is vengeance. But how then would you define a grudge? A person says: 'Lend me your axe'. The other fellow answers, 'No'. But the very next day the other fellow says: 'Lend me your sickle' and the man answers: 'Surely, here it is. I'm not like you who wouldn't lend me your axe.' Now this is a grudge, because this man was treasuring up hatred in his heart, even though he didn't take vengeance.

(*Solomon ben Isaac's Exegesis of Torah*,
in BRJ, pp. 121–122)

In addition to Exegesis, Rashi produced *responsa* concerning various issues:

Herewith do I, the undersigned, answer him who has questioned me concerning the marriage of a certain girl who was married at a time when she and the groom, as well as the witnesses to the ceremony, had already been forced by gentiles to disavow the Jewish religion.

I am of the opinion that this woman requires a bill of divorcement before she can marry another man. The marriage of a Jew who has even voluntarily become an apostate and then marries is legal (according to Jewish law). For it is said (Joshua 7:11): 'Israel has sinned', meaning (B. San. 44a) that even though he has sinned he is still an Israelite. How much the more is this true in the case of all these forced converts who are still loyal to God. Notice in this particular case how their final conduct reflects their original attitude, for as soon as they were able to find some form of escape they returned to Judaism. And even though the witnesses may have led a loose life while living among the non-Jews and may be suspected of the iniquities of the Gentiles, nevertheless their testimony to the marriage does not thereby become invalid.

(*Solomon ben Isaac on Forced Conversion*,
in BRJ, pp. 114–115)

Crusades

In the Rhineland where Jewish communities were the most numerous in Europe, the most horrendous massacres were inflicted on the Jewish community. A first massacre took place at Speyer; when news of this event reached Worms the Jewish community took refuge in their own homes and in the palace of the Bishop. Yet there was no way they could escape slaughter and death. These terrible events were recorded by the Jewish chronicler Solomon ben Simeon:

They fulfilled the words of the prophet: 'The mothers are laid upon their children, and fathers fell upon their sons.' This one killed his brother, that one his parents, his wife, and his children; the betrothed killed each other, even as the mothers killed the children. All accepted with a full heart the divine verdict . . . The enemies stripped them naked and dragged them off, granting quarter to none, save those few who accepted baptism.

(Massacre of Worms Jewish Community,
in CJ, p. 40)

Several days later the Jews of Mainz were attacked and attempted to defend themselves. The Christian chronicler Albert of Aix described these horrific events:

Having broken the locks and knocked on the doors, they seized and killed seven hundred who vainly sought to defend themselves against forces far superior to their own; the women were also massacred, and the young children, whatever their sex, were put to the sword. The Jews, seeing the Christians rise as enemies against them and their children, with no respect for the weakness of age, took arms in turn against their co-religionists, against their wives, their children, their mothers, and their sisters, and massacred their own. A horrible thing to tell of – the mothers seized the sword, cut the throats of their children at their breast, choosing to destroy themselves with their own hands rather than to succumb to the blows of the uncircumcised.

(Massacre at Mainz Jewish Community,
in CJ, p. 40)

Profanation of the Host

Throughout the Middle Ages, Jews were accused of profaning the Host. As the twelfth century chronicler of Liège, Jean d'Outremeuse stated:

In this year, it happened at Cologne that the son of a converted Jew went on Easter Day to church, in order to receive the body of God. Along with others he took it into his mouth and quickly bore it to his house; but when he returned from the church, he grew afraid and in his distress made a hole in the ground and buried the Host within it; but a priest came along, opened the hole, and in it found the shape of a child, which he intended to bear to the church. But there came from the sky a great light, the child was raised out of the priest's hands and borne up to heaven.

(In HA, Vol. I, p. 59)

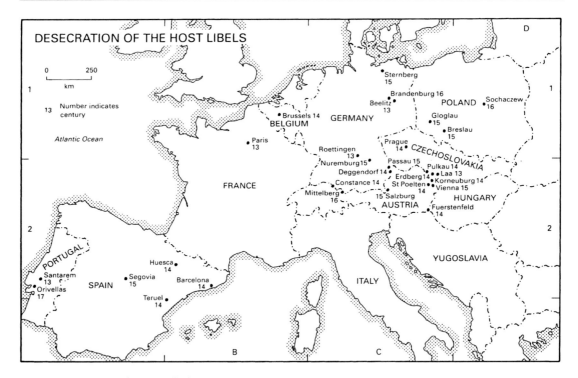

Map 34 Desecration of the host libels

Disputation about the *Talmud*

In the Paris Disputation, which took place in 1240, Christian adversaries argued that the *Talmud* should be destroyed since it serves as a rival to Scripture. It also contains attacks on the Christian faith. The Christian side was led by Nicholas Donin, a converted Jew who was opposed to the rabbinic tradition. On the Jewish side Rabbi Yehiel ben Joseph of Paris was joined by three other rabbis. According to the Jewish account of this disputation, Donin argued that the *Talmud* contains various blasphemies against Jesus; in response Yehiel declared that the Jesus referred to is a different Jesus:

> This Jesus mentioned here by the *Talmud* is another Jesus, not the one whom Christians worship. This was a certain Jesus who mocked the words of the sages, and believed only in the written Scripture like you. You can tell this, because he is not called 'Jesus of Nazareth', but simply 'Jesus'.
>
> (In JT, p. 156)

Undeterred by Yehiel's arguments, Donin turned to passages in the *Talmud* which discriminate against gentiles:

> The *Talmud* contains many passages directed against gentiles, saying (a) a gentile may be left to die though not actually killed; (b) a Jew who kills a gentile is not liable to the death penalty, whereas a gentile who kills a Jew is liable; (c) it is permitted to steal the money of a gentile; (d) a Jew must not drink wine touched by a gentile; (e) one may mock gentile religion; (f) gentiles are presumed to be habituated to adultery, bestiality and homo-sexuality; (g) it is forbidden to help a gentile woman to give birth or to suckle her child; (h) it is forbidden to praise the beauty of a gentile.
>
> (In JOF, pp. 49–50)

Black Death

From 1347 to 1350 the Back Death destroyed one-third of Europe's population. According to Boccaccio's account:

In the cities, men fell sick by thousands, and lacking care and aid, almost all died. In the morning their bodies were found at the doors of the houses where no further account was taken of a dying man than is today taken of the merest cattle. Nor were the villages spared. Lacking the succour of a physician, without the aid of any servant, the poor and wretched farmers perished with their families by day, by night, on the farms, and in their isolated houses, on the roads, and even in the fields. Then they abandoned their customs, even as the city dwellers: they no longer took any concern for their affairs nor for themselves; all, expecting to die from one day to the next, thought neither of working nor of putting by the fruits of their past labours, but sought rather to consume what they had before them.

(In HA, Vol. I, pp. 107–108)

Throughout Europe, the Jews were blamed for causing the Black Death. Nonetheless, some chroniclers maintained that this view was mistaken. As the chronicler Conrad von Meganberg reported:

In many wells, bags filled with poison were found, and a countless number of Jews were massacred in the Rhineland, in Franconia, and in all the German countries. In truth, I do not know whether certain Jews had done this. Had it been thus, assuredly the evil would have been worse. But I know, on the other hand, that no German city had so many Jews as Vienna, and so many of them there succumbed to the plague that they were obliged to enlarge their cemetery greatly and to buy more buildings. They would have been very stupid to poison themselves.

(In HA, Vol. I, p. 113)

DISCUSSION

1. What were the central differences between Jewish life in Christian Europe and Muslim lands?

2. Discuss the nature of Christian anti-Semitism in the Middle Ages.

FURTHER READING

Bachrach, Bernard, *Early Medieval Jewish Policy in Western Europe*, University of Minnesota Press, 1977.

Chazan, Robert, *Medieval Stereotypes and Modern Anti-Semitism*, University of California Press, 1997.

Cohen, Jeremy, *The Friars and the Jews: Evolution of Medieval Anti-Judaism*, Cornell University Press, 1984.

Edwards, John, *The Jews in Christian Europe, 1400–1700*, Routledge, 1991.

Friedlander, Saul (ed.), *The Jews in European History: Seven Lectures*, Hebrew Union College Press, 1997.

Hay, Malcolm, *Europe and the Jews: The Pressure of Christendom on the People of Israel for 1900 Years*, Academy Chicago Publishing, 1992.

Linder, Amnon, *The Jews in the Legal Sources of the*

Early Middle Ages, Wayne State University Press, 1998.

Rubin, Miri, *Gentile Tales: The Narrative Assault on Late Medieval Jews*, Yale University Press, 1999.

Schreckenberg, Heinz, *The Jews in Christian Art: An Illustrated History*, Continuum, 1997.

Signer, Michael Alan, Van Engen, John H. (eds), *Jews and Christians in Twelfth Century Europe*, University of Notre Dame Press, 2001.

Stow, Kenneth, *Alienated Minority, The Jews of Medieval Latin Europe*, Harvard University Press, 1984.

CHAPTER 29

The Jews in Christian Spain

Timeline:

1391 Massacres and conversions in Castile and Aragon

1413–1414 Disputation of Tortosa

1492 Jews expelled from Spain

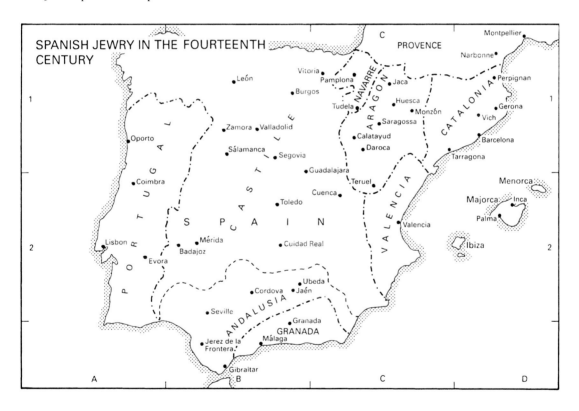

Map 35 Spanish Jewry in the fourteenth century

After the Christians had conquered most of the Iberian peninsula in the thirteenth century, Sephardic Jews in Spain combined many features of their life in Muslim lands with aspects of Jewish existence in Christian feudal countries. The Jewish population was employed in a wide range of occupations, including shopkeeping, artisan crafts, medicine and moneylending. The community was stratified into a broad range of social classes: many Jews were poor but a small minority participated in the administration of the country as royal councillors and financial experts.

Legally there were important similarities between the communities of Spanish Jews and their counterparts in northern Europe. Each corporate body (*aljama*) was granted a charter guaranteeing the economic rights of its members as well as their freedom to live according to the Jewish tradition. As a consequence each community was able to regulate its own social services, bureaucratic institutions and judicial system. As under Islamic rule, a number of Spanish Jews studied humanistic and scientific subjects and made notable contributions to a variety of disciplines: the thirteenth century witnessed a flowering of Jewish scholarly activity in fields of mysticism, theology and legal studies. Throughout the century Jews were generally more secure relative to the plight of their co-religionists in other European lands.

At the end of the fourteenth century, however, political instability led to the massacre of many Jewish communities in Castile and Aragon. Fearing for their lives, thousands of Jews converted to Christianity in 1391. Two decades later, in 1412, Spanish rulers introduced Castilian laws which attempted to segregate Jews from their Christian neighbours. In the following year a public **disputation was held in Tortosa** about the doctrine of the Messiah; as a result, pressure was applied to the Jewish population to convert. Those who became Christian apostates (*conversos*) found life much easier and some reached high positions in the government and the Church. But as the *conversos* were achieving social acceptance and recognition, those who had remained loyal to their faith attempted to rebuild Jewish life. *Aljamas* were reconstituted and new communities were established in towns in northern Castile.

By the fifteenth century anti-Jewish feelings had again become a major problem. Initially Jew-hatred was directed against *conversos* who had become tax-collectors. These attacks were justified on the grounds that these former Jews had not acted in good faith, and the term '*marrano*' was applied to those who were suspected of practising Judaism in secret. In 1480 Ferdinand and Queen Isabella established the **Inquisition** to determine if such charges were valid. As

a result, thousands of Jewish converts were convicted and punished, and those who refused to repent were burned at the stake. In the late 1480s inquisitors used torture to extract confessions regarding a blood libel case (alleging that *marranos* crucified a Christian boy to use his heart for witchcraft).

Under King Ferdinand and Queen Isabella the Inquisition came into full force, seeking to purge *conversos* who were suspected of practising Jewish customs. In 1478 a papal bull was promulgated which established the Castilian Inquisition; four years later the first tribunal came into operation in Seville. Once the Inquisition was instituted, the tribunal requested that heretics give themselves up – this 'Edict of Grace' lasted for thirty days. Those who came forward to admit that they observed Jewish rites were obliged to denounce all other Judaizers. In compensation, they were spared torture and imprisonment. Their sins were atoned for by flagellation, by wearing the *sambenito*, and by the confiscation of their belongings.

The next stage of the Inquisitional process involved the naming of suspects. An edict was issued which outlined various ways that such individuals could be recognized. Judaizers, it explained, celebrated Jewish festivals, kept dietary laws, consumed meat during Lent, omitted the phrase 'Glory be to the Father, and to the Son, and to the Holy Ghost' at the end of psalms, and cooked with oil. Once suspects were identified, the Inquisitors attempted to extract a confession. To achieve this end, various tortures were used, interspersed with kind words such as, 'I pity you, when I see you so abused and with a lost soul . . . So do not assume the sin of others . . . admit the truth to me, for, as you see, I already know everything . . . In order that I may be able to pardon you and free you soon, tell me who led you to this error.'

Those who confessed their sins were spared – those who persisted in denying the accusations made against them were burned at the stake. In this quest to root out Christian heresy, there were even some who praised the execution of innocent victims. In the sixteenth century, for example, Francesco Pegna declared that such persons died as martyrs of the faith. Even though thousands of Jews died in this way, the majority of those who appeared before the Inquisition sought to be reconciled to the Church and were sentenced to imprisonment after having their property taken away and undergoing various humiliations. In addition, their children and grandchildren were forbidden from wearing gold or silver or holding public as well as ecclesiastic offices.

In Seville, where the first tribunal took place, the majority of *conversos* hoped to placate the Inquisitors through acts of dedication to the faith as well as offerings and gifts. The rich *converso*, Mesa, for example, had the central place of atonement decorated with statues of the prophets. Nonetheless, for seven years the Inquisition purged five thousand individuals who were punished and accepted reconciliation with the Church. Seven hundred others were branded as heretics and burned at the stake. In 1483 Tomas de Torquemada became Inquisitor for all Spain, and tribunals were set up throughout the country. In Aragon, popular uprisings against the Inquisition occurred; in Saragossa an attempt was made to assassinate the Inquisitor Pedro de Arbues. From 1486 to 1490 some 4,850 *conversos* were reconciled to the Church, and less than 200 burned.

In this Christian onslaught, Jews who had never undergone baptism were often caught up in this conflict. The Inquisitors imposed a duty of identifying Judaizing *conversos*, and charges were frequently brought against those who sought to convince baptized kinsmen to keep Jewish practices. Further, those who supported the return of the *conversos* to Judaism were indicted. Jews were also accused of acting with *conversos* in committing ritual murder. Thus, in 1490 six Jews and five *conversos* of La Guardia were charged with attempting to bring about the destruction of Christendom though black magic.

In Spain and later in Portugal, the judicial sentence of the Inquisitors following such torture occurred in public in the presence of dignitaries and crowds. At these ceremonies, known as *autos da fé*, sermons were preached – the earliest took place in 1481, In all, the total of those who appeared to have been charged numbered hundreds of thousands. Over thirty thousand suffered the death penalty. However, the burning of heretics did not occur during the *autos da fé* – those

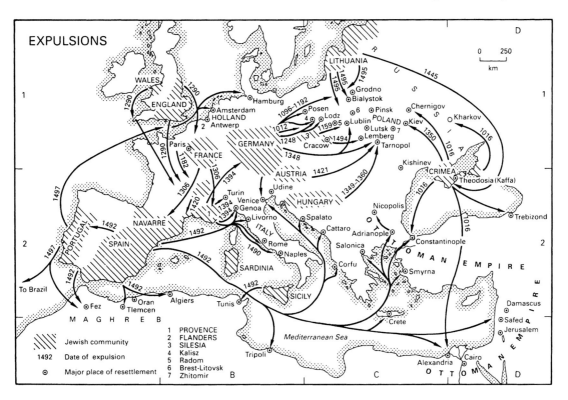

Map 36 Expulsions

found guilty were handed over to the secular authorities who were responsible for their execution.

Such treatment of the Jewish community ended with **expulsion**. On 31 March 1492, Ferdinand and Isabella signed the Edict of Expulsion which sealed the fate of Spanish Jewry. Once this decree was promulgated, Jews were given four months to liquidate their businesses and sell their property, but they were forbidden to export money or precious metals. Although the Jewish community sought to have this edict overturned, their attempts were unsuccessful. Only a last-minute baptism would save them, and during the weeks preceding the mass exodus Spanish clergy embarked on a missionary campaign.

SOURCES

Disputation of Tortosa

The most important disputation of the Middle Ages was held in Tortosa, presided over by Pope Benedict XIII. In this confrontation the main Christian spokesman was the Jewish convert Geronimo de Santa Fé (Joshua Halorki). According to Astruk Halevi, one of the leading Jewish figures in the disputation, this confrontation caused great hardship:

> We are away from our homes; our resources are diminished and are almost entirely destroyed; huge damage is resulting in our communities from our wives and children; we have inadequate maintenance here and even lack of food and are put to extra-ordinary expenses. Why should people suffering such woes be held accountable for their arguments?
>
> (In JT, p. 84)

The Hebrew account of this event begins with an explanation of the origin of this disputation:

> A shoot that went forth from us and thought to destroy us, and bring low down to the earth our religion of truth – is it not Joshua Halorki? He made plans to pervert us, to show that he was a true Christian and faithful to his new religion, and he asked the Pope to command the leading Jewish scholars to come before him for he wished to prove from their own *Talmud* that the Messiah had come; and he said to the Pope that when he proved this, it would be fitting to force them to adopt the Christian religion, when he showed true proofs before his high Holiness.
>
> (In JT, p. 168)

Inquisition

Torture during the Inquisition was designed to extract confessions from the guilty. When this end was achieved the Inquisitors were satisfied. An example of such torture is reflected in a report on Elvira del Campo who was accused of not eating pork and wearing clean clothes on the Sabbath:

She was carried to the torture chamber and told to tell the truth when she said that she had nothing to say. She was ordered to be stripped and again admonished, but was silent. When stripped, she said '*Señores*, I have done all that is said of me, and I bear false witness against myself, for I do not want to see myself in such trouble; please God, I have done nothing.' She was told not to bring false testimony against herself but to tell the truth. The tying of the arms was commenced. She said, 'I have told the truth; what have I to tell?' She was told to tell the truth and replied, 'I have told the truth and have nothing to tell.' One cord was applied to the arms and twisted, and she was admonished to tell the truth but said she had nothing to tell. Then she screamed and said, 'I have done all they say.'

(In HA, Vol. 2, p. 207)

Figure 29 Members of the Inquisition, from Auto da fé presidio por Santo Domingo de Guzman (Auto da fé presided over by Saint Dominic or Domingo Guzman of Castile, 1170–1221, who founded the Dominican order) (detail). Artist: Berruguete, Pedro: 1450–1504: Spanish. Copyright The Art Archive/Museo del Prado Madrid/Dagli Orti.

Expulsion from Spain

In 1492 King Ferdinand and Queen Isabella signed the Edict of Expulsion of the Jews of Spain.

We have been informed by the Inquisitors, and other persons, that the mingling of Jews with Christians leads to the worst evils. The Jews try their best to seduce the (New) Christians, and their children, bringing them books of Jewish prayers, telling them of the days of Jewish holidays, procuring unleavened bread for them at Passover, instructing them on the dietary prohibitions, and persuading them to follow the Law of Moses. In consequence, our holy Catholic faith is debased and humbled. We have thus arrived at the conclusion that the only efficacious means to put an end to these evils consists in the definitive breaking of all relations between Jews and Christians, and this can only be obtained by their expulsion from our kingdom.

(*Expulsion of the Jews from* Spain, in CJ, p. 88)

DISCUSSION

1. What was the purpose of the medieval disputations between Jewish and Christian scholars?

2. Discuss the nature of the Spanish Inquisition.

FURTHER READING

Altabe, David, *Spanish and Portuguese Jewry Before and After 1492*, Sepher-Hermon Press, 1993.

Baer, Yitzkak, Schoffman, Louis, *A History of the Jews in Christian Spain: From the Fourteenth Century to the Expulsion*, Jewish Publication Society, 1993.

Beinart, Haim, *The Expulsion of the Jews from Spain*, International Specialized Book Service, 2002.

Kedourie, Elie (ed.), *Spain and the Jews: The Sephardi Experience, 1492 and After*, Thames and Hudson, 1992.

Lazar, Moshe, Haliczer, Stephen, *The Jews of Spain and the Expulsion of 1492*, Labyrinthos, 1997.

Netanyahu, Benjamin, *The Origins of the Inquisition in Fifteenth Century Spain*, New York Review of Books, 2001.

Paris, Erna, *The End of Days: A Story of Tolerance, Tyranny, and the Expulsion of the Jews from Spain*, Prometheus, 1995.

Porter, Ruth, Harel-Hoshen, Sarah, *Odyssey of Exiles: The Sephardi Jews 1492–1992*, Ministry of Defence, 1997.

Raphael, Chaim, *The Sephardi Story: A Celebration of Jewish History*, Vallentine Mitchell, 1991.

Singerman, Robert, *Spanish and Portuguese Jewry: A Classified Bibliography*, Greenwood, 1993.

CHAPTER 30

The Dispersion of the *Marranos*

Timeline:

1492 Jews baptized or expelled from Spain   1536 Inquisition introduced in Portugal

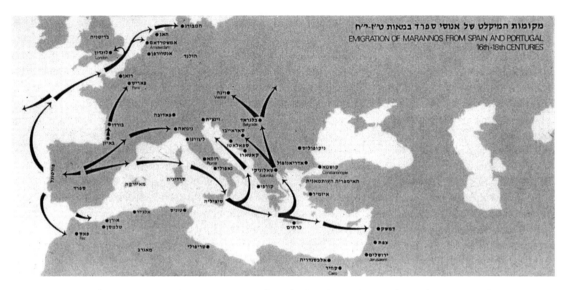

Figure 30 Map of places where Marranos sought refuge in the sixteenth to eighteenth centuries. Copyright Beth Hatefusoth, Permanent Exhibition.

When the Inquisition intensified its efforts to root out Christian heresy in Spain, *Marranos* fled to other countries for safety. Many of these *Marranos* settled in Portugal. These crypto-Jews, unlike their Spanish counterparts, imitated the Christian way of life and complied with all Catholic rites including attending mass and confession. Nonetheless, they selectively observed various Jewish rituals such as *Yom Kippur* and the Fast of Esther. In addition, they found solace in Apocryphal texts such as the *Prayer of Esther* which became a central prayer of the *Marranos*.

Marrano insecurity frequently manifested itself in various messianic movements. In the early sixteenth century, for example, the adventurer David Reubeni presented himself to the court of Pope Clement VII as a representative of a Jewish kingdom of the East. The Pope referred him to the king of Portugal where he sailed in a ship flying a Jewish flag. *Marranos* there were jubilant; their frenzy led them to attack the inquisitorial prison of Badajoz. One of them, Diego Pires, became a Jew taking the name Solomon Molcho and joined Reubeni. Together they travelled throughout Europe encouraging messianic expectations. They were received by Charles V but finally were delivered to the Inquisitor and burned at the stake.

The Inquisition was established in Portugal in 1536.

Yet it was recognized that the New Christians constituted an important part of the population regardless of their religious beliefs and practices.

Thus King John III informed the Pope that they greatly contributed to commerce and industry. They had served him well, he stated, and there was no reason to hate them. Nevertheless, the Inquisition operated with fervour, tracking down *Marranos* in cities, villages, forests and mountains. As in Spain, Jewish martyrs went to their deaths with bravery. During this onslaught a number of *Marranos* fled abroad, but many remained behind to practise Judaism in secret. However, among these individuals knowledge of Judaism seriously declined.

The expulsion of Jews from Spain in 1492 also drove thousands of Jews from Spain into Barbary, Turkey and the few Christian territories where they were allowed to settle. In the following two centuries *Marranos* continued to find homes abroad. In most cases these departures were facilitated through financial transactions, but in other instances they were the result of clandestine emigration. Thus in 1609–14 a number of Portuguese crypto-Jews and Spanish *conversos* joined the Moriscos who had been expelled and crossed the Pyrenees.

In Turkey the *Marranos* were well received, since efforts had been made to attract them from the Iberian Peninsula ever since the conquest of Constaninople. As a result many Jews fled to Constantinople, and by the middle of the sixteenth century a sizeable community had been established there. Salonica also constituted

a *Marrano* refuge in the sixteenth century. The rabbis there encouraged them to become observant, yet among ordinary Jews they were often regarded with disapproval. Their ambiguous status led to considerable confusion: many *Marranos* did not know who they were and vacillated between Judaism and Christianity. There were even those who returned to Judaism, and then out of longing for Christianity embraced the Christian faith. Others adopted Islam and served in the military under the Sultan.

Marranos settled in new countries for a variety of reasons. Some went to places where they could live freely as Jews; others were attracted by commercial and economic advantages. Aware of the financial contributions these newcomers could make, a number of Christian governments granted them special privileges. Yet wherever they went the *Marranos* remained Spanish in character and used Castilian written in Latin characters or Hebrew script to communicate with one another or for publishing their writings.

Social cohesion among the *Marrano* community meant that even when returning to Judaism, they retained their former cultural characteristics. Such attitudes frequently led to criticism. Others, however, viewed these displaced Jews in a more favourable light. The *Marranos* thus evoked differing responses from those among whom they lived. Spanish by origin, outwardly Christian, yet Jewish by inclination, they despised their co-religionists. Not surprisingly these contradictions frequently provoked profound crises of personal identity and loyalty.

SOURCES

Marranos

Marrano, term of opprobium used to denigrate the New Christians of Spain and Portugal. Various origins for the term have been suggested. These include the Hebrew *marit ayin* ('the appearance of the eye'), referring to the fact that the Marranos were ostensibly Christian but actually Judaizers; *mohoram attah* ('you are excommunicated'); the Aramaic-Hebrew *Mar Anus* ('Mr. forced convert'); the Hebrew *mumar* ('apostate') with the Spanish ending *ano*; the Arabic *mura'in* ('hypocrite'); and the second word of the ecclesiastical imprecation *anathema maranatha*. However, all such derivations are unlikely. The most

probable . . . is from the Spanish word meaning 'swine', a word already in use in the early Middle Ages . . . the term probably did not originally refer to the Judaizers' reluctance to eat pork, as some scholars hold. From its earliest use, it was intended to impart the sense of loathing conveyed by the word in other languages. Although romanticized and regarded by later Jewry as a badge of honour, the term was not as widely used, especially in official circles, as is often believed.

(In EJ, Vol. 11, p. 1018)

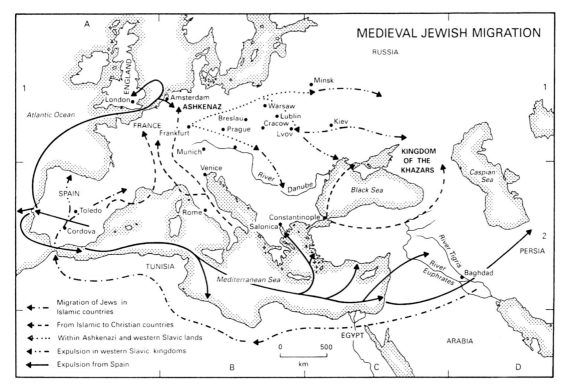

Map 37 Medieval Jewish migration

DISCUSSION

1. What was the nature of the *Marrano* community in Spain and Portugal?

2. Discuss the crises of personal identity faced by *Marranos* in attempting to reconcile Jewish sensitivities with a Christian life-style.

FURTHER READING

Faur, Jose, *In the Shadow of History: Jews and Conversos at the Dawn of Modernity*, State University of New York Press, 1992.

Gitlitz, David, *Secrecy and Deceit: The Religion of the Crypto-Jews*, Jewish Publication Society, 1997.

Jacobs, Janet Liebman, *Hidden Heritage: The Legacy of the Crypto-Jews*, University of California Press, 2002.

Kaplan, Gregory, *The Evolution of Converso Literature: The Writings of the Converted Jews of Medieval Spain*, University Press of Florida, 2002.

Netanyahu, B., *Toward the Inquisition: Essays on Jewish and Converso History in Late Medieval Spain*, Cornell University Press, 1998.

Netanyahu, B., *The Marranos of Spain: From the Late 14th to the Early 16th Century, According to*

Contemporary Hebrew Sources, Cornell University Press, 1999.

Roth, Cecil, *A History of the Marranos*, Schocken, 1975.

Roth, Norman, *Conversos, Inquisition and the Expulsion of the Jews from Spain*, University of Wisconsin, 1995.

CHAPTER 31

Early Medieval Thought

Timeline:

882–941 Saadiah Gaon

c. 1020–1057 Solomon ibn Gabirol

c. 1055–1135 Moses ibn Ezra

1075–1141 Judah Halevi

1089–1164 Abraham ibn Ezra

c. 1110–1180 Abraham ibn Daud

1135–1204 Moses Maimonides

1194–1270 Moses ben Nahman

In the Hellenistic period the Jewish philosopher **Philo** sought to integrate Greek philosophy and Jewish teaching into a unified whole. By applying the allegorical method of interpretation to Scripture, he explained the God of Judaism in philosophical categories and reshaped Jewish notions about God, human beings and the world. Philo was the precursor of medieval Jewish philosophy which also attempted to combine alternative philosophical systems with the received Biblical tradition.

The beginnings of this philosophical development took place in ninth century Babylonia during the height of the Abbasid caliphate when rabbinic Judaism was challenged by Karaite scholars who criticized the anthropomorphic views of God in midrashic and Talmudic sources. Added to this internal threat was the Islamic contention that Muhammad's revelation in the *Qur'an* superseded the Jewish faith. In addition, Zoroastrians and Manichaeans attacked monotheism as a viable religious system. Finally some gentile philosophers argued that the Greek scientific and philosophical world view could account for the origin of the cosmos without reference to an external Deity.

Figure 31 Solomon ibn Gabirol, statue by Read Armstrong, put up by the Municipal Council of Malaga, Spain. Copyright Judaica Photo Archive courtesy of Beth Hatefutsoth Photo Archive.

In combating these challenges, Jewish writers were influenced by the teachings of Muslim schools of theology (*kalam*) of the eighth to the eleventh centuries; in particular the contributions of one school of Muslim thought (the *Mutazilite kalam*) had a profound effect on the development of Jewish thought. These Islamic scholars maintained that rational argument was vital in matters of religious belief and that Greek philosophy could serve as the handmaiden of religious faith. In their attempt to defend Judaism from internal and external assault, rabbinic authorities frequently adapted the *Mutazilite kalam* as an important line of defence and as time passed also employed other aspects of Graeco-Arabic thought in their expositions of the Jewish faith.

The earliest philosopher of the medieval period, Saadiah ben Joseph al-Fayyumi (882–942) was Egyptian by origin and became a central spokesman against the Karaite movement. As *gaon* of one of the Babylonian academies, he wrote treatises on a wide range of subjects – Hebrew philology, Jewish liturgy and *halakhah* – and produced the first major Jewish theological treatise of the Middle Ages: *The Book of Beliefs and Opinions.* In this study Saadiah attempted to refute the religious claims of Christians, Muslims and Zoroastrians.

Basing his approach on the teachings of the *kalam*, he argued that there are four sources of knowledge: sense experience, intuition of self-evident truths, logical inference and reliable tradition. This fourth category, derived from the first three, is the mainstay of civilization; it was given by God to man to provide guidance and protection against uncertainty since the vast majority of humanity is incapable of engaging in philosophical speculation.

Adapting the teaching of the *Mutazilites*, Saadiah argued that religious faith and reason are fully compatible. On this basis he attempted to demonstrate that God exists since the universe must have had a starting point. Time, he believed, is rational only if it has a beginning because it is impossible to pass from an infinite past to the present. The Divine Creator, he believed, is a single, incorporeal Being who created the universe out of nothing.

In connection with God's unity, Saadiah, like the *Mutaziliate* philosophers, assumed that God has a plurality of attributes. This implies he must be composite in nature. Thus he argued, such terms as 'life', 'omnipotence' and 'omniscience' should be understood as implications of the concept of God as Creator rather than attributes of the Deity. The reason we are forced to describe God by means of these descriptions is because of the limitations of language, but they do not in any way involve plurality in God. In this light Saadiah argued that the anthropomorphic expressions in the Bible must not be taken literally since this would imply that God is a plurality. Hence when we read in the Bible that God has a head, eye, ear, mouth, face or hand, these terms should be understood figuratively. Similarly, when human activity is attributed to God or when He appears in a theophany such depictions should not be interpreted in a literal way.

After the eleventh century the *Mutazilite kalam* ceased to play a central role in Jewish philosophical thought. In Islam the *Mutazilites* were replaced by the more orthodox *Asharyites* who attempted to provide a rational basis for unquestioning traditionalism. These Muslim scholars argued, for example, that everything happens because it is God's will. Further, they maintained that all existing things are composed of elements of time and space directly created by God. Such doctrines were less attractive to Jewish theologians than the systems of neo-Platonism and Aristotelianism advocated by a number of Muslim philosophers.

The first Spanish Jewish philosopher to produce a work in the neo-Platonic tradition was Solomon ben Joseph ibn Gabirol (1020–57) from Malaga. In the *Fountain of Life* ibn Gabirol argued that God and matter are not opposed as two ultimate principles – instead matter is identified with God. It emanates from the essence of the Creator forming the basis of all subsequent emanations. For ibn Gabirol the universe consists of cosmic existences flowing out of the superabundant light and goodness of the Creator; it is a reflection of God though God remains in Himself and does not enter His creation with His essence. In a religious poem **Kingly Crown**, ibn Gabirol uses neo-Platonic images to describe God's activity.

Another important Spanish writer of this period, Bahya ben Joseph ibn Pakuda (1050–1120) from Saragossa, drew on neo-Platonic ideas in the composition of his ethical work, *Duties of the Heart.* The aim of this study was to correct what he saw as the overemphasis on ritualism within rabbinic Judaism. According to ibn Pakuda, human obligations are of two types. First there are duties involving action such as ritual and ethical observances commanded by the Torah. The second category consists of responsibilities related to the inner life. Like works of Islamic mysticism, this treatise attempts to lead Jews through various ascending stages of man's inner life toward spiritual perfection and communion with God. In accordance with neo-Platonism, ibn Pakuda maintained that man's soul is celestial in origin and is placed in the body by God. But with the aid of reason and revealed law the soul can triumph over the evil inclination. The ten chapters of this book deal with various aspects of this spiritual quest including divine worship, trust in God, sincerity of purpose, humility, repentance, self-examination and asceticism.

Another important philosopher of this period was Abraham ben David Halevi ibn Daud (1110–80) from Cordova. In his major philosophical writing, *The Exalted Faith*, ibn Daud utilized Aristotelian categories in attempting to harmonize the Bible with rational thought. Following Islamic Aristotelians, ibn Daud deduced God's absolute unity from His necessary existence. For ibn Daud this concept of divine oneness precludes the possibility of any positive attributes of God. Regarding the afterlife, ibn Daud believed that the human soul is able to continue after death without the body because the activities of the intellect are not dependent on bodily existence. The most radical feature of this treatise concerns ibn Daud's view of free will and divine omniscience. Unlike other Jewish philosophers, he argued that since human beings have free will, God does not know beforehand the undecided outcome of human decisions.

In opposition to such rationalistic formulations of Jewish belief, the contemporary Spanish theologian Judah Halevi (1075–1141) composed a treatise, *The Book of the Khazars*, to demonstrate that Judaism cannot be understood by the intellect alone. This work consists of a dialogue between a king of the Khazars and a Jewish sage who defends the Jewish faith against Aristotelian philosophy, Christianity and Islam. Though Halevi counters Christianity and the Karaites, his criticisms are directed primarily at Aristotelian philosophy which he considered the greatest threat to Judaism. For Halevi Biblical revelation rather than philosophy offers the true guide to the spiritual life. Despite its claims Aristotelianism is not scientific; its conclusions are ultimately inadequate. The God of the philosophers is unconcerned with human affairs – He is not attentive to prayer, nor does He guide history. The Torah, however, is based on divine encounter, and the God of the Jewish faith is concerned with human existence and is near to those who call upon Him.

Aristotelian philosophers maintain that the highest human attainment is knowledge of the most elevated type; but according to Halevi the Torah proclaims that the highest human ideal is the experience of God in prophecy. For Halevi, prophetic activity is not an actualization of the intellect, but rather a gift from God. Such prophetic inspiration is given to a few individuals and can only take place in the land of Israel. Since most Jews live in exile, no prophets have appeared since the Biblical period. Only when the messianic redemption takes place will prophetic activity again be actualized. Regarding Biblical law, Halevi stressed suprarational features. Reason can attain a conception of morality, but ritual ordinances transcend rational explanation.

Despite these criticisms of a rational understanding of God, prophecy and ritual, Halevi believed that science originated among Jews. The Jewish faith, he argued, does not conflict with the study of the natural world, nor does the Torah disagree with the conclusions of reason. Yet faith is not explained by the intellect. In propounding this position, Halevi offered a serious challenge to the rationalism of medieval Jewish philosophy that preceded him and was to flourish in subsequent centuries.

SOURCES

Philo

The Jewish philosopher Philo was the first Jew to formulate the central principles of the Jewish faith:

By his account of the creation of the world of which we have spoken, Moses teaches us among many other things five that are fairest and best of all. Firstly that the Deity is and has been from eternity. This with a view to atheists, some of whom have hesitated and have been of two minds about his eternal existence, while the bolder sort have carried their audacity to the point of declaring that the Deity does not exist at all, but that it is a mere assertion of men obscuring the truth with myth and fiction. Secondly, that God is one. This with a view to the propounders of polytheism, who do not blush to transfer from earth to heaven mob rule, that worst of evil policies. Thirdly, as I have said already, that the world came into being. This because of those who think that it is without beginning and eternal, who thus assign to God no superiority at all. Fourthly, that the world too is one as well as its maker, who made his world like himself in its uniqueness, who used up for the creation of the whole all the material that exists; for it would not have been a whole had it not been formed and consisted of parts that were wholes. For there are those who suppose that there are more worlds than one, while some think that they are infinite in number. Such men are themselves in every deed lacking in knowledge of things which it is good to know. Fifthly, that God also exercises forethought on the world's behalf. For that the Maker should care for the thing made is required by the laws and ordinances of nature, and it is in accordance with these that parents take thought beforehand for children. He that has begun by learning these things with his understanding rather than with his hearing, and has stamped on his soul impressions of truth so marvellous and priceless, both that God is and is from eternity, and that He that really is is one, and that He has made the world and has made it one world, unique as himself is unique, and that He never exercises forethought for his creation, will lead a life of bliss and blessedness, because he has a character moulded by the truths that piety and holiness enforce.

(Philo, *De Opifico Mundi*, LXI, in PJF, pp. 8–9)

Mishnah

Although the *Mishnah* does not explicitly isolate the fundamental beliefs of Judaism, it specifies those who will be excluded from the world to come:

> All Israelites have a share in the world to come . . . And these are they who have no share in the world to come: he that says there is no resurrection of the dead in the Torah; and he that says that the Torah is not from Heaven; and the Epicurean. R. Akiba says: 'Also he that reads the external books, or that utters a charm over a wound and says: "I will put none of the diseases upon thee which I have put upon the Egyptians: for I am the Lord that healeth thee" (Ex. 15:26)'. Abba Saul says: 'Also he that pronounces the Name with its proper letters'.
>
> (*Mishnah, Sanhedrin*, 10:I, in PJF, p. 11)

Kingly Crown

The end of the first part of this poem by the eleventh century Jewish theologian Solomon ibn Gabirol concludes with a series of statements about the topics dealt with in the *Fountain of Life*: God and his wisdom; the will; matter and form; and the combination of the two which forms all creation.

> Thou art wise; and wisdom, the fountain of life, flows from Thee, and every man is too
>   brutish to know Thy wisdom.
> Thou art wise, pre-existent to all pre-existence, and wisdom was with Thee at nurseling.
> Thou art wise, and Thou didst not learn from any other than Thyself, nor acquire
>   wisdom from another.

Thou art wise, and from Thy wisdom Thou didst send forth a predestined Will, and
made it as an artisan and a craftsman,
To draw the stream of being from the nothingness as the light is drawn that comes
from the eye.
To take from the source of light without a vessel, and to make all without a tool and cut
and hew and cleanse and purify.
That Will called to the nothingness and it was cleft asunder, to existence and it was set
up, to the universe and it was spread out.
It measured the heavens with a span, and its hand coupled the pavilion of the spheres,
And linked the curtains of all creatures with loops of potency; and its strength reaches
as far as the last and lowest creature – 'the uttermost edge of the curtain in the
coupling'.

(Solomon ibn Gabirol, *The Kingly Crown*, in KC, pp. 32–33)

DISCUSSION

1. In what ways did Islamic thinkers influence the development of medieval Jewish philosophy?

2. What were the major theological issues facing Jewish medieval philosophers?

FURTHER READING

Cohn-Sherbok Dan, *Modern Jewish Philosophy: An Introduction*, Routledge, Curzon, 1997.

Effros, Israel Isaac, *Studies in Medieval Jewish Philosophy*, Columbia University Press, 1974.

Frank, Daniel H., Leaman, Oliver (eds), *The Cambridge Companion to Medieval Jewish Philosophy*, Cambridge University Press, 2004.

Goodman, Lenn Evan, *Jewish and Islamic Philosophy*, Rutgers University Press, 1999.

Husik, Isaac, *A History of Medieval Jewish Philosophy*, Dover, 2002.

Hyman, Arther, Walsh, James, *Philosophy in the Middle Ages: The Christian, Islamic and Jewish Traditions*, Hackett, 1983.

Kreisel, Howard T., *Prophecy: The History of an Idea in Medieval Jewish Philosophy*, Kluwer Academic Publishers, 2001.

Rudavsky, Tamar M., *Time Matters: Time, Creation, and Cosmology in Medieval Jewish Philosophy*, State University of New York, 2000.

Sirat, Colette, *A History of Jewish Philosophy in the Middle Ages*, Cambridge University Press, 1990.

Twersky, Isadore, Harris, Jay M. (eds), *Studies in Medieval Jewish History and Literature*, Harvard University Press, 2001.

Wolfson, Harry Austryn, *Repercussions of the Kalam in Jewish Philosophy*, Harvard University Press, 1979.

CHAPTER 32

The Philosophy of Maimonides

Timeline:

1135–1204 Moses Maimonides

Figure 32 Statue of Maimonides, erected in 1964 in his birthplace, Cordova, and located near to the Jewish Synagogue which was built in 1315 on Calle de los Judios. Copyright *Jewish Chronicle*, London.

Moses Maimonides (1135–1204), the greatest philosopher of the twelfth century, was born in Cordova but when the Almohades came to power he and his family were forced to emigrate. After travelling through Spain and North Africa, Maimonides eventually settled in Cairo where he wrote numerous studies ranging from *halakhah* to philosophy. In his major philosophical treatise, *The Guide for the Perplexed,* he relied on the great Muslim expositors of Aristotle such as Avicenna and al-Farabi. For Maimonides reason and faith are harmoniously interrelated, and in this study he criticized various aspects of *Mutazilite* and *Asharyite* philosophy and attempted to reconcile the Torah with a number of central tenets of Aristotelianism.

The Guide for the Perplexed was deliberately written for the intellectual elite. In the introduction Maimonides explains that his book was intended only for those whose study of logic, mathematics, natural science and metaphysics had led them to a state of perplexity about seeming contradictions between the Torah and human reason. The first part of this work begins with a discussion of the anthropomorphic terms in the Bible. A literal reading of these passages implies that God is a corporeal being but according to Maimonides this is a mistake: such depictions must be understood figuratively. In this connection, he argued as did ibn Daud that no positive attributes can be predicated of God since the Divine is an absolute unity. Thus when God is described positively in the Bible, such ascriptions must refer to his activity. The only true attributes, he contended, are negative ones – they lead to a knowledge of God because in negation no plurality is involved. Each negative attribute excludes from God's essence some imperfection. Thus when one says God is incorporeal, this means He has no body. Such negation, Maimonides believed, brings one nearer to the knowledge of the Godhead.

Turning from God's nature to prophecy, Maimonides pointed out that most people believe that God chooses any person He desires and inspires him with the prophetic spirit. Such a view is opposed by the philosophers who contend that prophecy is a human gift requiring ability and study. Rejecting both these positions, Maimonides stated that prophecy is an inspiration from God which passes through the mediation of the Active Intellect and then to the faculty of imagination. It requires perfection in theoretical

wisdom, morality and development of the imagination. On the basis of this conception, Maimonides asserted that human beings can be divided into three classes according to the development of their reasoning capabilities. First there are those whose rational faculties are highly developed and receive influences from the Active Intellect but whose imagination is defective. These are wise men and philosophers. The second group consists of those where the imagination alone is in good condition, but the intellect is defective. These are statesmen, lawgivers and politicians. Thirdly there are the prophets – those whose imagination is constitutionally perfect and whose Active Intellect is well developed.

Maimonides insisted that God withholds prophetic inspiration from certain individuals but those whom he has selected teach speculative truth and adherence to the Torah. Unlike the other prophets who only intermittently received prophecy, Moses prophesied continuously and was the only one to give legislation. The purpose of the body of Mosaic law is to regulate society and provide for spiritual well-being and perfection. As far as ceremonial law is concerned, Maimonides argued that the purpose of a number of ritual commandments was to prevent Israel from participating in pagan cultic practices which could lead to idolatry. Sacrifice, he suggested, was a concession to the popular mentality of the ancient Israelites since the nation could not conceive of worship without sacrificial offerings.

The problem of evil is also a central theological issue in the *Guide.* Maimonides contended that evil does not exist as an independent entity; rather it is a privation of good. What appears evil, such as human immorality, is frequently the fault of human beings and can be corrected through good government. Similarly, personal suffering is often the result of vice. Physical calamities – earthquakes, floods and disease – are not the result of human failing but are part of the natural order. To complain that there is more evil than good in the world results from an anthropomorphic conception of the place of human beings in the universe: God's final purpose cannot be known.

Unlike Aristotelian philosophers, Maimonides conceived of God's providence as concerned with each person. For him such providential care is proportional to the degree that an individual has activated his

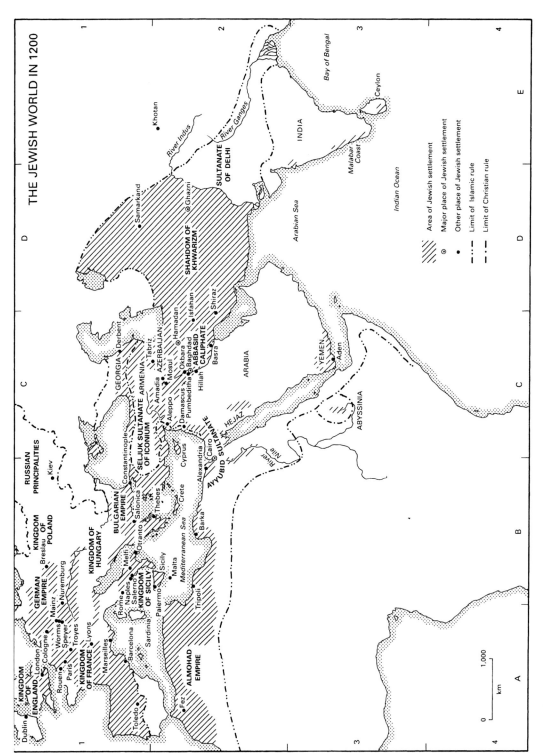

Map 38 The Jewish world in 1200

intellect. In this regard, Maimonides argued that the ideal of human perfection involves reason and ethical action. To illustrate his view, he used a parable about a king's palace. Those who are outside the walls have no doctrinal belief; those within the city but with their backs to the palace hold incorrect positions; others wishing to enter the palace not knowing how to do so are traditionalists who lack philosophical sophistication. But those who have entered the palace have speculated about the fundamental principles of religion. Only the person who has achieved the highest level of intellectual attainment can be near the throne of God.

Such intellectual attainment, however, is not in itself sufficient. To be perfect a person must go beyond communion with God to a higher state. Just as God is merciful, just and righteous, so the perfected individual should emulate God's actions in his daily life. Here then is a synthesis of the Aristotelian emphasis on intellectualism and Jewish insistence on the moral life. Such a philosophical exposition of the Jewish faith not only influenced later Jewish writers, but also had an impact on medieval Christian scholars such as Albertus Magnus and Thomas Aquinas.

SOURCES

Moses Maimonides

In his commentary to the *Mishnah*, the twelfth century Jewish philosopher, Maimonides, formulated Thirteen Articles of the Faith:

(1) Belief in the existence of God.
(2) Belief in God's unity.
(3) Belief in God's incorporeality.
(4) Belief in God's eternity.
(5) Belief that God alone is to be worshipped.
(6) Belief in prophecy.
(7) Belief in Moses as the greatest of the prophets.
(8) Belief that the Torah was given by God to Moses.
(9) Belief that the Torah is immutable.
(10) Belief that God knows the thoughts and deeds of men.
(11) Belief that God rewards and punishes.
(12) Belief in the advent of the Messiah.
(13) Belief in the resurrection of the dead.

(In PJF, p. 14)

Maimonides concludes his statement of these central beliefs with the reflection:

When all these principles are in the safe keeping of man, and his conviction of them is well established, he then enters 'into the general body of Israel', and it is incumbent upon us to love him, to care for him, and to do for him all that God commanded us to do for one another in the way of affection and brotherly sympathy. And this, even though he were to be guilty of every transgression possible, by reason of the power of desire or the mastery of the base natural passions. He will receive punishment according to the measure of his perversity, but he will have a portion in the world to come, even though he be of the 'transgressors in Israel'. When, however, a man breaks away from any of these fundamental principles of belief, then of him it is said that 'he has gone out of the general body of Israel' and 'he denies the root truth of Judaism'. And he is then termed 'heretic' and 'unbeliever' and 'hewer of the small plants' (*Talmud, Hag.* 14b), and it is obligatory upon us to hate him and cause him to perish, and it is concerning him that the Scriptural verse says: ' Shall I not hate those who hate thee, O Lord?' (Ps. 139:21).

(In PJF, pp. 14–15)

DISCUSSION

1. Discuss Maimonides' concept of negative and positive attributes.

2. Critically evaluate Maimonides' understanding of Biblical prophecy.

FURTHER READING

Arbel, Ilil, *Maimonides: A Spiritual Biography*, Crossroad, 2001.

Benor, Ehud, *Worship of the Heart: A Study of Maimonides' Philosophy of Religion*, State University of New York, 1995.

Buijs, Joseph, *Maimonides: A Collection of Critical Essays*, University of Notre Dame Press, 1988.

Hartman, David, Pines, Shlomo, *Maimonides: Torah and Philosophic Quest*, Jewish Pubication Society, 1977.

Heschel, Abraham Joshua, Heschel, Sylvia, Neugroschel, Joachim, *Maimonides*, Noonday, 1982.

Leaman, Oliver, *Moses Maimonides*, Routledge, 1990.

Leibowitz, Yeshayahu, *The Faith of Maimonides*, Lambda Publishers, 1987.

Seeskin, Kenneth (ed.), *The Cambridge Companion to Maimonides*, Cambridge University Press, 2004 [seen in typescript].

Seeskin, Kenneth, *Searching for a Distant God: The Legacy of Maimonides*, Oxford University Press, 2000.

Strauss, Leo, *Philosophy and Law: Contributions to the Understanding of Maimonides and His Predecessors*, State University of New York Press, 1995.

Twersky, Isadore, (ed.) *Studies in Maimonides*, Harvard University Press, 1992.

Twersky, Isadore (ed.), *Maimonides Reader*, Behrman House, 1989.

Weiss, Raymond, *Maimonides' Ethics: The Encounter of Philosophic and Religious Morality*, University of Chicago Press, 1991.

CHAPTER 33

Jewish Philosophy after Maimonides

Timeline:

1194–1270 Nahmanides

1235–1310 Solomon ibn Adret

1263 Disputation of Barcelona

1288–1344 Gersonides

c. 1340–1414 Hasdai Crescas

c. 1360–1444 Joseph Albo

1437–1508 Isaac Abrabanel

In the thirteenth century most of the important philosophical texts had been translated into Hebrew by Jews living in southern France. Judah ibn Tibbon (1120–90) who emigrated from Muslim Spain to Provence translated such works as ibn Pakudah's *Duties of the Heart*, **Halevi's** *Kuzari*, and Saadiah Gaon's *Book of Beliefs and Opinions*. His son, Samuel (1150–1230) translated Maimonides' *The Guide for the Perplexed*. Furthermore, the writings of Plato and Aristotle as well as commentaries on Aristotle by such Islamic scholars as Averroes were translated into Hebrew as well.

As a consequence of this scholarly activity, Jews in Spain, Provence and Italy produced philosophical and scientific writings including commentaries on Maimonides' *Guide*. Though Maimonides was admired as a halakhic authority, some Jewish scholars were troubled by his views. In particular they were dismayed that he appeared not to believe in resurrection; that he viewed prophecy, providence and immortality as dependent on intellectual attainment; that he regarded the doctrine of divine incorporeality as a fundamental tenet of the Jewish faith; and that he felt that knowledge of God should be based on Aristotelian principles.

For these sages Maimonides' theology was seen as a threat to Judaism and rabbinic learning. In 1230 some of those opposed to the Maimonidean philosophical system attempted to prevent the study of the *Guide* as

well as the philosophical sections of Maimonides' legal code, the *Mishneh Torah*. The bitter antagonism between Maimonideans and anti-Maimonideans came quickly to an end when Dominican inquisitors in France burned copies of Maimonides' writings. Both sides were appalled by such an action, yet opposition to Maimonides continued throughout the century. In 1300 anti-Maimonideans issued a ban against studying Greek philosophy before the age of twenty-five, but the conflict subsided when many Jews were expelled from France in 1306.

The most prominent Jewish philosopher after Maimonides who was attracted to Aristotelianism was Levi ben Gershom, known as Gersonides (1288–1344). Originally from Provence, he wrote works on a wide range of topics including mathematics, astronomy, law and philosophy. In his philosophical treatise, *The Wars of the Lord*, he discussed a variety of theological issues. Like medieval Christian thinkers, he first surveyed the main Aristotelian authorities on each subject and then offered his own views. As opposed to Maimonides, Gersonides maintained that God only knows human events if they are determined by heavenly bodies; He does not know them insofar as they are dependent upon individual choice. This limitation to divine knowledge, Gersonides believed, is entirely consonant with Scripture and it is also coherent with the concept of freedom of the will. Regarding providence, Gersonides' view was similar to

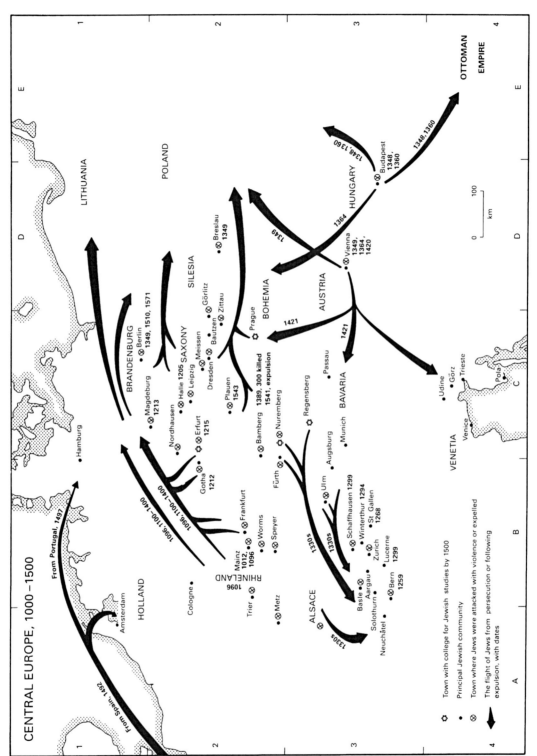

Map 39 Central Europe, 1000–1500

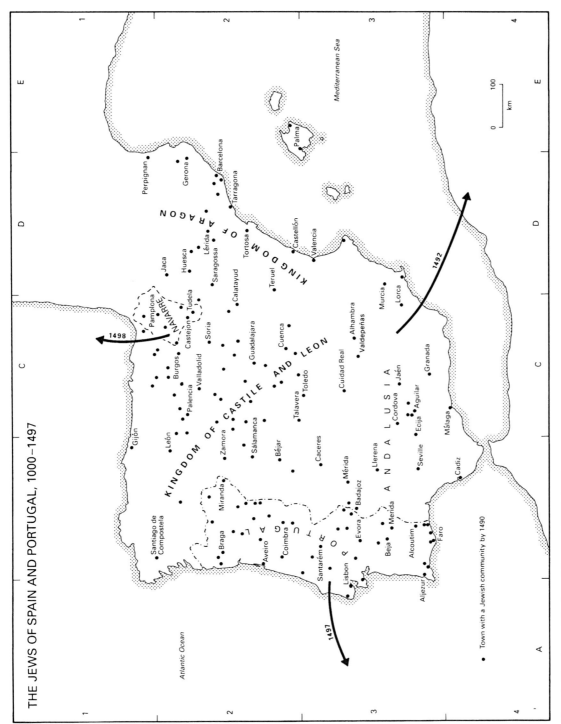

THE JEWS OF SPAIN AND PORTUGAL, 1000–1497

Atlantic Ocean

Santiago de
Compostela
Gijón

León
Zamora
Braga
Miranda
Coimbra
Aveiro
Santarém
Lisbon
Beja
Mérida
Alcoutim
Faro
Aljezur

Burgos
Palencia
Valladolid
Salamanca
Béjar
Cáceres
Mérida
Badajoz
Évora
Llerena
Seville
Cádiz

Pamplona
Castejón
Tudela
Soria
Guadalajara
Cuenca
Talavera
Toledo
Cuidad Real
Córdova
Ecija
Aguilar
Málaga
Granada
Jaén
Alhambra
Valdepeñas
Murcia
Lorca

NAVARRE

KINGDOM OF CASTILE AND LEON

ANDALUSIA

Jaca
Huesca
Lérida
Saragossa
Calatayud
Teruel
Tortosa
Castellón
Valencia
Tarragona
Barcelona
Gerona
Perpignan

KINGDOM OF ARAGON

PORTUGAL

Palma

Mediterranean Sea

1492

1498

1497

0   100
km

A   B   C   D   E

● Town with a Jewish community by 1490

Map 40 The Jews of Spain and Portugal, 1000–1497

ספר
מלחמות השם

Figure 33 Title page from *Milhamot ha-Shem* [*Wars of the Lord*], by Gersonides. Riva da Trento, 1560. Shelfmark 1933.f.9. Copyright British Library.

that of Maimonides: the nearer a person is to the Active Intellect the more he receives God's care. When a person's intellectual faculties are activated, God gives him knowledge through dreams, divination or prophecy.

The last major philosopher of Spanish Jewry was **Hasdai Crescas** (*c.*1340–1414) from Barcelona. After the Barcelona riots of 1391 Crescas settled in Saragossa, where he composed his philosophical treatise, *The Light of the Lord*. The purpose of this study was to offer an alternative account of the basic principles of the Jewish faith in opposition to Maimonides' thirteen principles. According to Crescas, there are several categories of belief in relation to the Torah. First there are the logical presuppositions of the law – the belief in the existence and nature of God. Added to these are the fundamental principles of the

Torah, concerning providence, omniscience, prophecy, omnipotence, freewill, the purpose of the law and human life. The third category consists of the logical consequences of belief in the Torah – creation, immortality, resurrection, the eternity of the Torah, the superiority of Moses and the coming of the Messiah.

In this work Crescas attempted to refute Aristotelianism by criticizing a number of doctrines found in the writings of Aristotle and Maimonides. In opposition to these thinkers Crescas argued that there is an infinite void outside the universe. Hence there may be many worlds. By positing the existence of the infinite, Crescas also called into question the Aristotelian concept of an unmoved mover which was based upon the impossibility of a regress to infinity. Similarly, Crescas argued that Maimonides' proofs of the existence, unity and incorporeality of God are invalid because they are based on the concept of finitude. In addition, Crescas disagreed with Maimonides' opinion that no positive attributes can be applied to God. According to Crescas, we cannot avoid making a comparison with human beings when we apply the terms 'cause' and 'attribute of action' to God. Maimonides was simply mistaken in thinking that such ascriptions do not imply a relationship between God and human beings.

Regarding divine providence, Crescas held that God acts either directly or through intermediate agents such as angels and prophets. Intellectual perfection, he insisted, is not the criterion of divine providence nor the basis for reward and punishment. In his discussion of prophecy Crescas also adopted an anti-intellectual position. Unlike Maimonides Crescas accepted the traditional understanding of the prophet as a person chosen by God because of his moral virtues rather than intellectual attainment. Throughout his treatment of the central beliefs of the Jewish tradition, Crescas presented a view of Judaism based on the spiritual and emotional sides of human beings' nature rather than intellectual and speculative capacities. In this respect he shared the same view as Judah Halevi who was equally critical of a rational presentation of the faith.

After Crescas, the philosophical approach to religion lost its appeal for most Jewish thinkers in Spain. Though some thinkers were still attracted to the Maimonidean system, Aristotelianism ceased to be the dominant philosophy in the Jewish world. Instead of philosophizing about Judaism a number of subsequent Jewish writers directed their attention to defining the basic doctrines of the Jewish faith. Such Spanish thinkers as **Simon ben Zema Duran** (1361–1444), **Joseph Albo** (*c.* 1360–1444) and Isaac Arama (1420–94) devoted their writings to critiques of Maimonides' formulation of the thirteen principles of the Jewish religion.

Another Spanish Jewish philosopher, **Isaac Abrabanel** (1437–1508), on the other hand, attempted to defend Maimonides against his critics and offered an examination of the concept of the principles of faith. Yet paradoxically Abrabanel argued that since every part of the Torah is of equal value, it is not possible to formulate an underlying list of central beliefs. According to Abrabanel, the impetus to isolate the principles of the Jewish faith is based on an analogy between religion and science. Such an approach is misguided since science requires first principles, but this is not the case for Judaism. It is a mistake, he believed, to think that one part of the Torah is superior to any other part. By the end of the fifteenth century the impulse to rationalize the Jewish tradition in the light of Greek philosophy had come to an end, and succeeding generations of Jews turned to the mystical tradition as a basis for speculation about God's nature and his creation.

SOURCES

Judah Halevi

In the *Kuzari* the twelfth century Jewish theologian Judah Halevi describes the conversion to rabbinic Judaism of the king of the Khazars. The book opens with an exposition of different religious views and ideologies: philosophical, Christian, Muslim and Jewish. Questioned by the king, the rabbi who represents Judaism affirms his faith in God:

I believe in the God of Abraham, Isaac and Israel, who brought the children of Israel out of Egypt by means of signs and miracles, took care of them in the wilderness, and gave them the land of Canaan after crossing the sea and the Jordan by means of miracles. He sent Moses with his religious law by means of promises to whoever observed it and threats to whoever transgressed it.

(Judah Halevi, *Kuzari*, in BK, p. 11)

The *Kuzari* concludes with the Jewish sage's decision to leave the land of the Khazars in order to travel to Jerusalem. Such dedication to the Holy Land is reflected in Halevi's other works where he glorifies Zion. In one of his poems, he extols Jerusalem in the most glowing terms. These sentiments help to explain Halevi's determination to go to *Eretz Israel* near the end of his life.

If only I could roam through those places where God was revealed to your prophets and heralds! Who will give me wings, so that I may wander far away? I would carry the pieces of my broken heart over the rugged mountains. I would bow down, my face on your ground; I would love your stones; your dust would move me to pity. I would weep, as I stood by my ancestors' graves, I would grieve, in Hebron, over the choicest of burial places! I would walk in your forests and meadows, stop in Gilead, marvel at Mount Abarim . . . The air of your land is the very life of the soul, the grains of your dust are flowing myrrh, your rivers are honey from the comb. It would delight my heart to walk naked and barefoot among the desolate ruins where your shrines once stood; where your Ark was hidden away.

(In PBHV, pp. 348–349)

Hasdai Crescas

Although Maimonides' Principles of the Jewish Faith were widely accepted in the Middle Ages, not all Jewish philosophers agreed that these were the central tenets of Judaism. The fourteenth century Jewish philosopher Hasdai Crescas, for example, argued that there is one central belief in God, that he exists, is one and is incorporeal. In addition to this basic belief, he stated that there are five fundamental beliefs without which Judaism is inconceivable:

1. Providence
2. Divine power
3. Prophecy
4. Freewill
5. The Torah is humanity's true hope

Added to these tenets are beliefs which Crescas termed 'true opinions' which can be divided into two types. The first are beliefs which are independent of any precept:

1. Creation
2. Immortality of the soul
3. Reward and punishment
4. Resurrection
5. The immutability of the Torah
6. Moses
7. The High Priest had the oracle of the *Urim* and *Thumim*
8. Messiah

The second type consists of beliefs dependent on particular precepts:

1. Beliefs implied in prayer and blessing of the high priest
2. Beliefs implied in repentance
3. Beliefs implied in the Day of Atonement and other festivals

According to Crescas, any individual who denies one of these fundamental beliefs or true opinions is an unbeliever. However, there is another category of beliefs which are not religiously obligatory:

1. Is the world eternal?
2. Are there many worlds?
3. Are the spheres living creatures?
4. Do the stars have an influence over human destiny?
5. Is there any efficacy to charms and amulets?
6. Do demons exist?
7. Is the doctrine of metempsychosis true?
8. Is the soul of an infant immortal?
9. Do Heaven and Hell exist?
10. Are the doctrines of 'Works of Creation' and the 'Works of the heavenly chariot' identified with 'physics' and 'metaphysics'?
11. What is the nature of comprehension?
12. Is there a First Cause?
13. Can the nature of God be comprehended?

(Hasdai Crescas, *Light of the Lord*, in FJ, pp. 40–41)

Simon ben Zemah Duran

Another formulation of the central principles of the Jewish faith was propounded by the fifteenth-century Jewish theologian Simon ben Zemah Duran. According to Duran there are three central principles of the Jewish faith:

1. The existence of God
2. The divine origin of the Torah
3. Reward and punishment

These principles, Duran argued, are explicitly denoted in the *Mishnah* which refers to three persons who are denied a share in the World-to-Come. For Duran the denial of these central beliefs implicitly involves the denial of the other basic beliefs:

The foundation of faith is to believe in God, blessed be He, that He is one, that He is eternal, that He is incorporeal and that it is fitting to worship him alone. All these are included in the term *epiquoros*. Next, one must believe in the predictions of the prophets and of Moses, in the Torah and that it is eternal. These are included in the term 'Torah from Heaven'. Next, one must believe in reward and punishment and their offshoots, which is included in the term 'the resurrection of the dead'.

(In FJ, p. 41)

Joseph Albo

Another formulation of the central beliefs of Judaism was proposed by the fitheenth-century Jewish theologian Joseph Albo. Critical of Maimonides, Albo argued that an unbeliever should be defined as one who knows the Torah lays down a principle but denies its truth:

When he undertakes to investigate these matters with his reason and scrutinizes the texts is misled by his speculation and interprets a given principle otherwise than it is taken to mean at first sight; or denies the principle because he thinks that it does not represent a sound theory which the Torah obliges us to believe; or which however he believes as he believes the other dogmas of the Torah which are not fundamental principles; or entertains a certain notion in relation to one of the miracles of the Torah because he thinks that he is not thereby denying any of the doctrines which is obligatory upon us to believe by the authority of the Torah – a person of this sort is not an unbeliever; his sin is due to error and requires atonement.

(Joseph Albo, *Book of Principles*, in FJ, p. 42)

In Albo's view, there are three basic tenets of the Jewish faith:

1. Belief in God
2. Belief in revelation
3. Belief in reward and punishment

Like Duran, he subdivided these principles into subordinate beliefs. In Albo's view, the three benedictions incorporated in the additional service for New Year represent these principles. In conclusion, Albo stated that the number of fundamental principles derived from them is eleven:

1. The existence of God
2. Unity
3. Incorporeality
4. God's independence from time
5. Freedom from defect
6. Prophecy
7. Authenticity of prophecy
8. Revelation
9. God's knowledge
10. Providence
11. Reward and punishment

In addition, Albo stated that there are six dogmas which everyone who professes Mosaic law is obliged to accept – whoever denies them is a heretic who has no share in the World-to-Come:

1. *Creatio ex nihilo*
2. The superiority of Moses' prophecy
3. The immutability of the Torah
4. Human perfection can be attained by fulfilling even one of the commandments of the Torah
5. Resurrection of the dead
6. The Messiah

(In FJ, p. 43)

Isaac Abrabanel

In the fifteenth century the philosopher Isaac Abrabenel discussed Maimonides' formulation of the principles of Judaism. Although he defended Maimonides from criticism, he argued that since every part of the Torah is of divine origin, the attempt to formulate principles of the Jewish faith is misguided:

I am convinced that it is improper to postulate principles or foundations with regard to the Torah and we are not permitted to doubt the smallest matter therein that it should be necessary to prove its truth by reference to principles or root ideas. For whoever denies or doubts any matter, small or great, of the beliefs or narratives contained in the Torah is a heretic and an unbeliever. Since the Torah is true no single belief or narrative in it can be superior to any other.

(Isaac Abrabanel, *Pinnacle of Faith*, in FJ, p. 44)

DISCUSSION

1. Why was Maimonides' theology perceived as a threat to Judaism?

2. Discuss Gersonides' concept of divine omniscience.

FURTHER READING

Cohn-Sherbok, Dan, *Medieval Jewish Philosophy: An Introduction*, Curzon, 1996.

Frank, Daniel H., *Maimonides and Medieval Jewish Philosophy*, Westview Press, 2001.

Frank, Daniel H., Leaman, Oliver (eds), *History of Jewish Philosophy*, Routledge, 1997.

Husik, Isaac, *A History of Medieval Jewish Philosophy*, Dover, 2002.

Kassim, Husain, *Aristotle and Aristotelianism in Medieval Muslim, Jewish, and Christian Philosophy*, Austin and Winfield, 1998.

Leaman, Oliver, Frank, Daniel H., Manekin, Charles Harry (eds), *The Jewish Philosophy Reader*, Routledge, 2000.

Leaman, Oliver, *Evil and Suffering in Jewish Philosophy*, Cambridge University Press, 1997.

Samuelson, Norbert, *Jewish Philosophy*, Continuum, 2003.

Sirat, Colette, *A History of Jewish Philosophy in the Middle Ages*, Cambridge University Press, 1990.

CHAPTER 34

Rabbinic Mysticism

Timeline:

c. 2nd century *Sefer Yetsirah*

c. 6th century Redaction of the Babylonian *Talmud*

Medieval Jewish mysticism is based on earlier rabbinic speculation. Within aggadic sources the rabbis engaged in mystical reflection concerning the Biblical text. These doctrines were frequently of a secret nature; in a *midrash* on Genesis it is reported that these mystical traditions were repeated in a whisper so they would not be overheard by those for whom they were not intended. In their mystical reflections, the first chapter of **Ezekiel** played an important role in early rabbinic mysticism. In the Biblical text the divine chariot (*Merkavah*) is described in detail, and this Scriptural source served as the basis for **mystical teaching** about the nature of the Deity. It was the aim of the mystic to be a '*Merkavah* Rider' so that he would be able to penetrate the heavenly mysteries. Within this contemplative system, the rabbis believed that the pious would free themselves from the fetters of bodily existence and enter paradise.

A further dimension of this theory is that certain pious individuals can temporarily ascend into the unseen realm and having learnt the deepest secrets may return to earth. These mystics were able to attain a state of ecstasy, to behold visions and hear voices. As students of the *Merkavah* they were the ones able to attain the highest degree of spiritual insight. A description of the experiences of these Merkavah mystics is contained in **Hekhalot** (heavenly hall) literature from the later Geonic period (from the seventh to the eleventh centuries CE). In order to make their **heavenly ascent**, these mystics followed strict ascetic disciplines, including fasting, ablutions and the invocation of God's name. After reaching a state of ecstasy, the mystic was able to enter the seven heavenly halls and attain a vision of the divine chariot.

Closely associated with this form of speculation were mystical theories about creation (*Maaseh Bereshit*). Within aggadic sources the rabbis discussed the hidden meanings of the Genesis narrative. The most important early treatise, possibly from the second century CE, which describes the process of creation is The Book of Creation (**Sefer Yetsirah**). According to this cosmological text God created the universe by thirty-two mysterious paths consisting of twenty-two letters of the **Hebrew alphabet** together with ten emanations (*sefirot*).

These letters are of three types: mothers, doubles and singles. The mothers (*shin, mem, aleph*) symbolize the three primordial elements of all existing things: water (the first letter of which is *mem* in Hebrew) is symbolized by *mem*; fire (of which *shin* is the most prominent sound) is represented by *shin*; air (the first letter of which in Hebrew is *aleph*) is designated by *aleph*. These three mothers represent in the microcosm (the human form) the head, the belly and the chest. The head is from fire; the belly from water, and the chest from the air that lies in between.

In addition to these three mother letters, there are seven double letters (*beth, gimel, daleth, caph, peh, resh, tau*) which signify the contraries in the universe (forces which serve two mutually opposed ends). These letters were formed, designed, created and combined into the stars of the universe, the days of the week, and the orifices of perception in human beings: two eyes, two ears, two nostrils and a mouth. Finally, there are twelve simple letters (*he, vav, zayin, chet, tet, yod, lamed, nun, samek, ayin, tsade, kof*) which correspond to the chief activities: sight, hearing, smell, speech, desire for food, the sexual appetite, movement, anger, mirth, thought, sleep and work. The letters are also emblematic of the twelve signs of the zodiac in the heavenly sphere, the twelve months, and the chief limbs of the body. In this way, human beings, world and time are linked to one another through the process of creation by means of the Hebrew alphabet.

These recondite doctrines are supplemented by a theory of divine emanation through the ten divine emanations (*sefirot*). The first of the *sefirot* is the spirit of the living God; air is the second of the *sefirot* and is derived from the first – on it are hewn the twenty-two letters. The third *sefirah* is the water that comes from the air. The fourth of the *sefirot* is the fire which comes from water through which God made the heavenly wheels, the seraphim and the ministering angels. The remaining six *sefirot* are the six dimensions of space – north, south, east, west, height and depth.

These ten *sefirot* are the moulds into which all created things were originally cast. They constitute form rather than matter. The twenty-two letters, on the other hand, are the prime cause of matter: everything that exists is due to the creative force of the Hebrew letters, but they receive their form from the *sefirot*. According to this cosmological doctrine, God transcends the universe; nothing exists outside of Him. The visible world is the result of the emanation of the divine: God is the cause of the form and matter of the cosmos. By combining emanation and creation in this manner, the *Sefer Yetsirah* attempts to harmonize the concept of divine immanence and transcendence. God is immanent in that the *sefirot* are an outpouring of his spirit, and He is transcendent in that the matter which was shaped into the forms is the product of his creative action. Such speculation served as the basis for later mystical reflection of the medieval period.

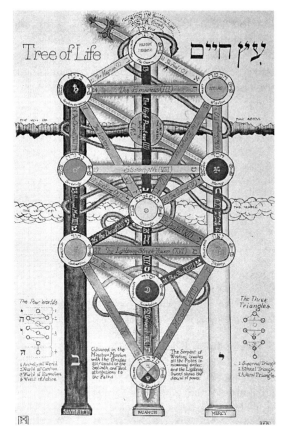

Figure 34 Mark Penney Maddocks Tree of Life showing the ten spheres. Copyright The Art Archive/Eileen Tweedy.

SOURCES

Ezekiel

The post-exilic prophets encouraged the people not to give hope. This message of consolation was revealed to the prophet Ezekiel in a vision of the divine chariot (*Merkavah*). As Ezekiel gazed over the plain, he saw what appeared to be an approaching storm with thunder, lightning and black clouds. Then he made out the figures of four angelic creatures standing wing-tip to wing-tip. At the centre a fire glowed and above under the blue vault of Heaven was the Lord in human form circled by a rainbow:

In the thirteenth year, in the fourth month, on the fifth day of the month, as I was among the exiles by the river Chebar, the heavens were opened, and I saw visions of God . . . As I looked, behold a storm wind came out of the north, and a great cloud, with the brightness round about it, and fire flashing forth continually, and in the midst of the fire, as it were gleaming bronze. And from the midst of it came the likeness of four living creatures.

And this was their appearance: they had the form of men, but each had four faces, and each of them had four wings. Their legs were straight, and the soles of their feet were like the sole of a calf's foot; and they sparkled like burnished bronze. Under their wings on their four sides they had human hands. And the four had their faces and their wings thus: their wings touched one another; they went every one straight forward, without turning as they went.

As for the likeness of their faces, each had the face of a man in front; the four had the face of a lion on the right side, the four had the face of an ox on the left side, and the four had the face of an eagle at the back. Such were their faces. And their wings were spread out above; each creature had two wings, each of which touched the wing of another, while two covered their bodies. And each went straight forward; wherever the spirit would go, they went, without turning as they went . . .

Now as I looked at the living creatures, I saw a wheel upon the earth beside the living creatures, one for each of the four of them. As for the appearance of the wheels and their construction: their appearance was like the gleaming of a chrysolite; and the four had the same likeness, their construction being as it were a wheel within a wheel. When they went, they went in any of the four directions without turning as they went . . .

And above the firmament over their heads there was the likeness of a throne, in appearance like sapphire, and seated above the likeness of a throne was a likeness as it were of a human form. And upwards from what had the appearance of his loins I saw as it were gleaming bronze, like the appearance of fire enclosed round about; and downwards from what had the appearance of his loins I saw as it were the appearance of fire, and there was brightness round about him. Like the appearance of the brightness round about. Such was the appearance of the likeness of the glory of the Lord.

(Ezekiel 1:1–28)

Mystical Teaching

The mystical interpretation of Scripture was reserved for only a few. According to *Midrash Bereshit Rabbah*, such interpretations should be repeated in a whisper so that no one else would hear them.

Simeon, son of Jehozedek, asked Samuel, son of Nahman, and said to him, 'Seeing I have heard you are an expert in the *aggadah* (scriptural interpretation), tell me from where the light was created'. He replied that the *aggadah* tells us that the Holy One, blessed be He, wrapped himself in a garment and the brightness of his splendour lit up the universe.

Samuel, son of Nahman, said this in a whisper, seeing that it is taught in Psalm 104:2, 'Who coverest thyself with light as with a garment'. 'Just as I myself had this whispered to me,' he said, 'even so have I whispered it to you.'

(*Bereshit Rabbah* on Genesis 3, in JM, 67)

According to the rabbis, the attainment of knowledge of the *Merkavah* was an exceedingly difficult task beset with obstacles. The *Talmud* relates that even learned scholars were not immune from the hazards of fire.

Johanan ben Zakkai was once riding on an ass, and Eliezer ben Arach was on an ass behind him. Eliezer ben Arach said to Johanan ben Zakkai, 'O master! Teach me a chapter of the *Merkavah* mysteries'. 'No!' replied the master, 'Did I not already tell you that the *Merkavah* may not be taught to anyone unless he is a sage and has an original turn of mind?' 'Very well, then!' replied Eliezer ben Arach. 'Will you give me permission to tell you a thing which you taught me?' 'Yes!' replied Johanan ben Zakkai, 'Say it!' Immediately the master dismounted from his donkey, wrapped himself in a garment, and sat on a stone beneath an olive tree. 'Why, O master, have you dismounted from your ass?' asked the disciple. 'Is it possible,' he replied, 'that I will ride on my donkey at the moment when you are expounding the mysteries of the *Merkavah*, and the *Shekhinah* is with us, and the ministering angels are accompanying us?' Then Eliezer ben Arach began his discourse on the mysteries of the *Merkavah*. No sooner had he begun, than fire came down from heaven and encompassed all the trees of the field which with one accord burst into song.

(*Talmud*, *Haggigah* 14b, in JM, p. 68)

According to rabbinic tradition, only certain individuals should engage in mystical reflection – the insistence on moral and religious fitness was essential. According to the *Talmud*, Judah said in the name of the third century sage Rab that the use of God's name should be entrusted only to specific persons.

> The name of forty-two letters can only be entrusted by us to a person who is modest and meek, in the midway of life, not easily provoked to anger, temperate, and free from vengeful feelings. Whoever understands it, is cautious with it, keeps it in purity, is loved above and is liked here below. He is revered by his fellows; he is heir to two worlds – this world and the world to come.
>
> (*Talmud*, *Kiddushin* 71a, in JM, p. 67)

Heavenly Ascent

According to rabbinic sources, certain pious individuals were able to ascend the heavenly heights through mystical reflection. After living spiritual lives, these sages were able to attain a state of ecstasy and behold visions as well as voices that brought them into contact with the Divine. Yet the *Talmud* relates that such mystical ascent was dangerous, even for such as Ben Azzai, Ben Zoma, Akiva and Aher.

Our rabbis taught that four entered an orchard. These are they: Ben Azzai, Ben Zoma, Aher and Akiva. Akiva said to them, 'When you reach the stones of pure marble, do not say, "Water, water!" For it is said, "He who speaks falsehood shall not be established before my eyes".' Ben Azzai gazed and died. Concerning him, Scripture says, 'Precious in the sight of the Lord is the death of his saints'. Ben Zoma gazed and was stricken. Concerning him, Scripture says, 'Have you found honey? Eat as much as is sufficient for you, lest you be filled therewith, and vomit it'. Aher cut down the shoots. Akiva departed in peace.

(*Talmud*, *Haggigah* 14b, in JM, p. 69)

Sefer Yetsirah

The *Sefer Yetsirah* provides a detailed explanation of the process of creation. According to this anonymous work dating from the second century CE, God created the universe through a process of emanation:

There are ten intangible *sefirot*: ten and not nine; ten and not eleven. Understand with wisdom, and be wise with understanding; test them and explore them . . . Understand the matter fully, and set the creator in his place. Only He is the former and creator. There is none other. His attributes are ten and infinite. There are ten intangible *sefirot* whose measure is ten without end . . . Ten intangible *sefirot* whose appearance is like lightning, whose limits are infinite. His word is in them in their backward and forward movement, and they run at his decree like the whirlwind, and they bow down before his throne. There are ten intangible *sefirot* whose end is fixed in their beginning, just as a flame is bound to coal.

One: spirit of living *Elohim* (God), blessed and blest is the name of him who lives forever . . . His beginning has no beginning; his end has no end.

Two: spiritual air from spirit. He engraved and hewed out in it twenty-two letters as a foundation: three mothers, seven doubles, and twelve simples. They are of one spirit.

Three: spiritual water from spiritual air. He engraved and hewed out in it chaos and disorder, mud and mire. He engraved it like a type of furrow. He raised it like a type of wall. He surrounded it like a type of ceiling. He poured snow over them and it became earth, as it is said, 'For he said to the snow, be earth' (Job 37:6).

Four: spiritual fire from spiritual water. He engraved and hewed out in it the Throne of Glory, *seraphim* and *ophanim* and *hayyot* (living creatures), and ministering angels. From the three of them he established his dwelling place, as it is said, 'Who makes winds his messengers, the flaming fire his ministers' (Psalm 104:4).

He chose three of the simple letters, sealed them with spirit and set them into his great name, YHV, and sealed through them six extremities. Five: he sealed height; he turned upwards and sealed it with YHV. Six: he sealed abyss; he turned downwards, and sealed it with YHV. Seven: he sealed east; he turned forwards and sealed it with HYV. Eight: he sealed west; he turned backwards and sealed it with HYV. Nine: he sealed south; he turned right and sealed it with VYH. Ten: he sealed north: he turned left and sealed it with VHY.

These ten intangible *sefirot* are One – spirit of living *Elohim*; spiritual air from spirit; spiritual water from spiritual air; spiritual fire from spiritual water, height, abyss, east, west, north and south.

(*Sefer Yetsirah* 1:4–14, in JM, pp. 61–62)

Hebrew Letters

In addition to the ten *sefirot*, the *Sefer Yetsirah* depicts the process of creation as taking place through the Hebrew letters. These twenty-two letters are divided into three groups, beginning with the mother letters which symbolize the elements air, fire and water:

Three mothers: *aleph, mem, shin*. A great secret, wonderful and hidden. He seals them with six rings. From them go out: air, fire and water. From them the fathers are born. From the fathers, the progeny.

Three mothers: *aleph, mem, shin*. He engraved them. He hewed them. He combined them. He weighed them. He set them at opposites. He formed through them: three mothers – *aleph, mem, shin* in the universe; three mothers – *aleph, mem and shin* in the year; three mothers – *aleph, mem and shin* in the body of male and female.

Three mothers: *aleph, mem, shin*. The product of fire is heaven; the product of air is air; the product of water is earth. Fire is above; water is below; air tips the balance between them. From them, the fathers were generated, and from them, everything is created.

Three mothers: *aleph, mem, shin* are in the universe – air, water and fire. Heaven was created first from fire; earth from water; air from air.

Three mothers: *aleph, mem* and *shin* are in the year – cold, heat and temperate-state. Heat was created from fire; cold from water; temperate-state from air.

Three mothers: *aleph, mem, shin* are in the body of male and female – head, belly and chest. Head was created from fire; belly from water; chest from air.

He caused the letter *aleph* to reign over air . . . He combined them with one another. He formed through them: air in the universe, the temperate-state in the year, the chest in the body of male with *aleph, mem, shin* and female with *aleph, mem, shin*.

He caused the letter *mem* to reign over water. He combined them with one another. He formed through them: earth in the universe; cold in the year; the belly in the body of male with *mem, aleph, shin*, and female with *shin, mem, aleph*.

He caused the letter *shin* to reign over fire. He combined them with one another. He formed through them: heaven in the universe; heat in the year; head in the body of male with *shin, aleph, mem*, and female with *shin, mem, aleph*.

(*Sefer Yetsirah* 3:2–10, in JM, pp. 62–63)

Hekhalot Literature

An early *Hekhalot* (heavenly hall) source, *Hekhalot Rabbati* contains a detailed explanation of the experiences of the Riders of the Chariot:

When one is on a higher level, he can enter. He is brought in and led to the heavenly chambers where he is permitted to stand before the Throne of Glory. He then knows what will happen in the future, who will be raised up, who will be lowered, who will be made strong, who will be cut off, who will be made poor, who will be made rich, who will die, who will live, who will have his inheritance taken away from him, who will have it given to him, who will be invested with the Torah, and who will be given wisdom. When one is on a higher level, he can see all the secret deeds of man . . . When one is on a higher level, he knows all kinds of sorcery . . . when one is on a higher level, whoever speaks against him maliciously is taken and cast down . . . When one is on a higher level, he is separated from all men, and distinguished from all humanity by his traits. He is honoured by those on earth and by those on high.

(*Hekhalot Rabbati* 1, in JM, p. 76)

DISCUSSION

1. What are the major differences between medieval Jewish philosophy and Jewish mysticism?

2. Can one reconcile the cosmology of early mystical texts with a scientific understanding of creation?

FURTHER READING

Ariel, David, *The Mystic Quest: An Introduction to Jewish Mysticism*, Schocken, 1992.

Bokser, Ben Zion, *The Jewish Mystical Tradition*, Jason Aronson, 1994.

Cohn-Sherbok, *Jewish and Christian Mysticism: An Introduction*, Gracewing, 1994.

Cohn-Sherbok, Dan, *Jewish Mysticism: An Anthology*, Oneworld, 1995.

Dan, Joseph, *Jewish Mysticism and Jewish Ethics*, University of Washington Press, 1986.

Dan, Joseph, *The Ancient Jewish Mysticism*, Geten Books, 1990.

Dan, Joseph, *Jewish Mysticism: Late Antiquity*, Vol. 1, Jason Aronson, 1998.

Dan, Joseph, *Jewish Mysticism in the Middle Ages*, Vol. 2, Jason Aronson, 1998.

Dan, Joseph, *Jewish Mysticism: General Characteristics and Comparative Studies*, Vol. 4, Jason Aronson, 1999.

Dan, Joseph, *The Heart and the Fountain: An Anthology of Jewish Mystical Experiences*, Oxford University Press, 2002.

Feldman, Ron H., *Fundamentals of Jewish Mysticism and Kabbalah*, Crossing Press, 1999.

Glotzer, Leonard R., *Fundamentals of Jewish Mysticism*, Kuperard, 1995.

Jacobs, Louis (ed.), *The Jewish Mystics*, Kyle Cathie, 1990.

Jacobs, Louis, *Jewish Mystical Testimonies*, Schocken, 1977.

Kaplan, Aryeh, *Meditation and Kabbalah*, Jason Aronson, 1998.

Matt, Daniel C., *The Essential Kabbalah: The Heart of Jewish Mysticism*, HarperCollins, 1996.

Wexelman, David M., *Kabbalah: The Splendor of Judaism*, Jason Aronson, 2001

CHAPTER 35

The *Hasidei Ashkenaz*

Timeline:

1096 Massacre of the Rhineland mystics

1150–1217 Judah ben Samuel of Regensburg

1165–1230 Eleazar ben Judah of Worms

Contemporaneous with the development of Jewish philosophy and theology, Jewish thinkers of the

Figure 35 The Sefirotic Tree showing the number ten as the foundation of the world system, after the Book of Jezirah. Holzschnitt woodcut. From Paulus Ricius, *Portae Lucis*, Augsburg 1516. Copyright AKG, London.

Middle Ages elaborated a complex system of mystical thought. Drawing on the traditions of early rabbinic Judaism, these thinkers expanded and elaborated many of the mystical doctrines found in midrashic and Talmudic literature as well as in mystical tracts such as the *Sefer Yetsirah*. In their writings these mystics saw themselves as the transmitters of a secret tradition which describes a supernatural world to which all human beings are linked. One strand of this heritage focused on the nature of the spiritual world and its relationship with the terrestrial plane; the other more practical side attempted to utilize energies from the spiritual world to bring about miracle-working effects. According to these mystics, all of creation is in a struggle for redemption and liberation from evil, and their goal was to restore world harmony so that universal salvation would be attained through the coming of the Messiah and the establishment of the Kingdom of God.

The mystical texts of early rabbinic Judaism were initially studied by Jewish settlers in the Rhineland from approximately the ninth century. During the twelfth and thirteenth centuries these authorities – the *Hasidei Ashkenaz* – delved into *Hekhalot* literature, the *Sefer Yetsirah*, as well as the philosophical works of such scholars as Saadiah Gaon and various Spanish and Italian Jewish neo-Platonists. Among the greatest figures of this period were the twelfth-century Samuel ben Kalonymus of Speyer, his son Judah ben Samuel of Regensburg (1150–1217) who wrote the *Book of the*

Pious, and Eleazer ben Judah of Worms (1165–1230) who composed the treatise, *The Secret of Secrets*. Though the writings of these and other mystics were not systematic in character, their works do display a number of common characteristics.

In their writings these mystics were preoccupied with the mystery of divine unity. God Himself, they believed, cannot be known by human reason. Thus all anthropomorphic depictions of God in Scripture should be understood as referring to God's glory which was formed out of divine fire. This divine glory – *kavod* – was revealed by God to the prophets and is made manifest to mystics in different ways through the ages. The aim of German mysticism was to attain a vision of God's glory through the cultivation of the life of **pietism** (*hasiduth*) – which embraced devotion, saintliness and contemplation. *Hasiduth* made the highest demands on the devotee in terms of humility and altruism. The ultimate sacrifice for these *Hasidim* was martyrdom (*Kiddush Hashem*), and during this period there were ample opportunities for Jews to die in this way in the face of Christian persecution. Allied to such a manifestation of selfless love of God was the *Hasidic* emphasis on a profound sense of God's presence in the world; for these sages God's glory permeates all things.

Within this theological framework the concept of the *Hasid* (the pious one) was of paramount importance. To be a *Hasid* was a religious ideal which transcended all intellectual accomplishments. The *Hasid* was remarkable, not because of any scholarly qualities, but through his spiritual attainments. According to these scholars, the *Hasid* must reject and overcome every temptation of ordinary life; insults and shame must be endured. In addition, he should renounce worldly goods, mortify the flesh and make penance for any sins. Such an ascetic way of life against all obstacles would lead the devotee to the heights of true fear and love of God. In its most sublime form, such fear was conceived as identical with love and devotion, enabling joy to enter the soul. In the earlier *Merkavah* tradition the mystic was the keeper of holy mysteries, but for these German sages humility and self-abnegation were the hallmarks of the authentic religious life. Allied with these personal characteristics, the *Hasid* was perceived as capable of mastering magical powers. In the writings of Eleazar of Worms, for example, are found tracts on

magic and the effectiveness of God's secret names as well as recipes for creating the *golem* (an artificial man) through letter manipulation.

Another feature of this movement concerned prayer mysticism. In the literature of the Pietists attention was given to the techniques of mystical speculation based on the calculation of the words in prayers, benedictions and hymns. The number of words in a prayer as well as the numerical value were linked to Biblical passages of equal numerical value as well as with designations of God and angels. Here prominence was given to the techniques of *gematria* (the calculation of the numerical value of Hebrew words and the search for connections with other words of equal value) and *notarikon* (the interpretation of the letters of a word as abbreviations of whole sentences). According to these German *Hasidim*, prayer is like Jacob's ladder extended from earth to Heaven; it is a process of mystical ascent. It was in this milieu that the famous *Hymn of Glory* was composed – a prayer which subsequently gained a central place in the Ashkenazi liturgy. Here the unknowability of God is suffused with a longing for intimacy with the Divine:

> Sweet hymns and songs will I recite
> To sing to Thee by day and night
> Of Thee who art my soul's delight.
>
> How doth my soul within me yearn
> Beneath Thy shadow to return,
> The Secret mysteries to learn.
>
> Thy glory shall my discourse be,
> In images I picture Thee,
> Although myself I cannot see.
>
> In mystic utterances alone,
> By prophet and by seer made known,
> Hast Thou Thy radiant glory shown.
>
> My meditation day and night,
> May it be pleasant in Thy sight,
> For Thou art my soul's delight.

For the *Hasidei Ashkenaz*, such prayers as well as mystical practices and beliefs provided a means of consolation and escape from the miseries that beset the Rhineland communities during the twelfth and thirteenth centuries.

SOURCES

Life of Piety

The mystical texts of early rabbinic Judaism were studied by Jewish settlers in the Rhineland from approximately the ninth century. During the twelfth and thirteenth centuries these authorities – the *Hasidei Ashkenaz* – delved into the *Sefer Yetsirah* and *Hekhalot* literature. Among the greatest figures of this period was Eleazar ben Judah of Worms who described the fear and love of God in *The Book of Raziel*. In his view, the life of piety is a necessary stage in the quest for enlightenment through the study of the *Merkavah*:

'Let a person always be subtle in the fear of God'. This means that a person should reflect on the subtleties and the glories of the world: how, for example, a mortal king commands his soldiers to engage in battle. Even though they know they may be killed, they are afraid of him and obey him even though they know that the fear of him is not ever-lasting, because he will eventually die and perish and they can escape to another country. How much more so, therefore, should men fear the king of the king of Kings, the Holy One, blessed be He, and walk in his ways, since He is everywhere and gazes at the wicked as well as the good.

(Eleazer ben Judah, *The Book of Raziel*, 96, in JM, 90)

DISCUSSION

1. Discuss the ways in which the *Hasidei Ashkenaz* sought to cultive a life of pietism.

2. What was the nature of prayer mysticism among the *Hasidei Ashkenaz*?

FURTHER READING

Ariel, David, *The Mystic Quest: An Introduction to Jewish Mysticism*, Schocken, 1992.

Besserman, Perle, Epstein, Perle, *Kabbalah: The Way of the Jewish Mystic*, Shambhala, 2001.

Dan, Joseph, *The Ancient Jewish Mysticism*, Geten Books, 1990.

Dan, Joseph, *Jewish Mysticism: Late Antiquity*, Vol. 1, Jason Aronson, 1998.

Dan, Joseph, *Jewish Mysticism in the Middle Ages*, Vol. 2, Jason Aronson, 1998.

Dan, Joseph, *Jewish Mysticism, Vol. 3: The Modern Period*, Jason Aronson, 1998.

Dan, Joseph, *Jewish Mysticism: General Characteristics and Comparative Studies*, Vol. 4, Jason Aronson, 1999.

Dan, Joseph, *The Heart and the Fountain: An Anthology of Jewish Mystical Experience*, Oxford University Press, 2002.

Elior, Rachel, *Jewish Mysticism*, Littman Library, 2003.

Feldman, Ron H., *Fundamentals of Jewish Mysticism and Kabbalah*, Crossing Press, 1999.

Idel, Moseh, Ostow, Mortimer, Marcus, Ivan G. (eds), *Jewish Mystical Leaders and Leadership in the 13th Century*, Jason Aronson, 1998.

Ivry, Alfred L., Wolfson, Elliot, Arkush, Alan (eds), *Perspectives on Jewish Thought and Mysticism*, Routledge, 1997.

Matt, Daniel, *The Essential Kabbalah: The Heart of Jewish Mysticism*, HarperCollins, 1996.

Scholem, Gershom, *Major Trends in Jewish Mysticism*, Schocken, 1995.

Spector, Shelia, *Jewish Mysticism: An Annotated*

Bibliography on Kabbalah in English, Garland, 1984.

Wexelman, David M., *Kabbalah: The Splendor of Judaism*, Jason Aronson, 2001.

Wolfson, Elliot R., *Lexicon of Jewish Mysticism*, Brill, 2000.

CHAPTER 36

The Emergence of *Kabbalah*

Timeline:

1160–1235 Isaac the Blind

1194–1270 Nahmanides

1240–1271 Abraham Abulafia

1250–1305 Moses de Leon

Parallel with these developments in Germany, Jewish mystics in southern France engaged in mystical speculation about the nature of God, the soul, the existence of evil, and the religious life. In twelfth century Provence the earliest kabbalistic text, the *Bahir*, re-interpreted the concept of the *sefirot* as depicted in the *Sefer Yetsirah*. According to the *Bahir*, the *sefirot* are conceived as vessels, crowns or words that constitute the structure of the divine realm.

Basing themselves on this anonymous work, various Jewish sages of Provence engaged in similar mystical reflection. Isaac the Blind (1160–1235), the son of Abraham ben David of Posquières, for example, conceived of the *sefirot* as emanations of a hidden dimension of the Godhead. Utilizing neo-Platonic ideas, he argued that out of the infinite (*Ayn Sof*) emanated the first supernal essence, the Divine Thought, from which came the remaining *sefirot*. Beings in the world beneath, he believed, are materializations of the *sefirot* at lower degrees of reality. The purpose of mystical activity is to ascend the ladder of emanations to unite with Divine Thought.

In Gerona the traditions from Isaac the Blind were broadly disseminated. One of the most important of these Geronese kabbalists was Azriel ben Menahem who replaced the Divine Thought with the Divine Will as the first emanation of the *Ayn Sof*. The most famous figure of this circle was Nahmanides, who helped this mystical school gain general acceptance. His involvement in kabbalistic speculation combined with his halakhic authority persuaded many Jews that mystical teachings were compatible with rabbinic Judaism. In his commentary on the Torah he frequently referred to kabbalistic notions to explain the true meaning of the text.

During the time that these Geronese mystics were propounding their kabbalistic theories, different mystical schools of thought developed in other parts of Spain. Influenced by the *Hasidei Ashkenaz* and the Sufi traditions of Islam, Abraham ben Samuel Abulafia (1240–71) wrote meditative texts concerning the technique of combining the letters of the alphabet as a means of realizing human aspirations toward prophecy. As an admirer of Maimonides, he believed his system was a continuation and elaboration of the teaching of *The Guide for the Perplexed*. Another Spanish kabbalist, Isaac ibn Latif, also attempted to elaborate ideas found in Maimonides' *Guide*. For ibn Latif, the Primeval Will is the source of all emanation.

Adopting neo-Platonic conceptions, he argued that from the first created thing emanated all the other stages, referred to symbolically as light, fire, ether and water. Each of these, he believed, is the subject of a branch of wisdom: mysticism, metaphysics, astronomy and physics. According to ibn Latif, *kabbalah* is superior to philosophy – the highest intellectual understanding reaches only the 'back' of the Divine whereas the 'face' is disclosed only in supra-intellectual ecstasy. True prayer leads to communion with the Active Intellect, and then to union of the Active Intellect with the first created thing. Beyond this union is the union through thought which is intended to reach the Prime Will and ultimately to stand before God Himself.

Other Spanish kabbalists were more attracted to

Gnostic ideas. Isaac ha-Kohen, for example, elaborated the theory of a demonic emanation whose ten *sefirot* are counterparts of the holy *sefirot*. The mingling of such Gnostic teaching with the *kabbalah* of Gerona resulted in the publication of the major mystical work of Spanish Jewry, the *Zohar*, composed by Moses ben Shem Tov de Leon (1250–1305) in Guadalajara. Although the author places the work in a second century CE setting, focusing on Rabbi Simeon bar Yochai and his disciples after the Bar Kochba uprising, the doctrines of the *Zohar* are of a much later origin. Written in Aramaic, the text is largely a *midrash* in which the Torah is given a mystical or ethical interpretation.

According to these various kabbalistic systems, God in Himself lies beyond any speculative comprehension. To express the unknowable aspect of the Divine, early kabbalists of Provence and Spain referred to the Divine Infinite as *Ayn Sof* – the absolute perfection in which there is no distinction or plurality. The *Ayn Sof* does not reveal itself; it is beyond all thought and at times is identified with the Aristotelian First Cause. In kabbalistic teaching, creation is bound up with the manifestation of the hidden God and His outward movement. According to the *Zohar*, the *sefirot* emanate out of the hidden depths of the Godhead like a flame.

These *sefirot* emanate successively from above to below, each one revealing a stage in the process. The common order of the *sefirot* and the names most generally used are: (l) supreme crown; (2) wisdom; (3) intelligence; (4) greatness; (5) power (or judgement); (6) beauty (or compassion); (7) endurance; (8) majesty; (9) foundation (or righteous one); (10) kingdom. These ten *sefirot* are formally arranged in threes. The first triad consists of the first three *sefirot* and constitutes the intellectual realm of the inner structure of the Divine. The second triad is composed of the next three *sefirot* from the psychic or moral level of the Godhead. Finally *sefirot* seven, eight and nine represent the archetypes of certain forces in nature. The remaining *sefirah*, kingdom, constitutes the channel between the higher and the lower worlds. The ten *sefirot* together demonstrate how an infinite, undivided and unknowable God is the cause of all the modes of existence in the finite plane.

In their totality these *sefirot* are frequently represented as a cosmic tree of emanation. It grows from its root – the first *sefirah* – and spreads downwards in the direction of the lower worlds to those *sefirot* which constitute its trunk and its main branches. Another depiction of the *sefirot* is in the form of a man (Adam Kadmon): the first *sefirah* represents the head; the next three *sefirot* the cavities of the brain, the fourth and fifth *sefirot* the arms; the sixth the torso; the seventh and eighth the legs; the ninth the sexual organ; and the tenth the all-embracing totality of this image. In kabbalistic literature this heavenly man is also divided into two parts – the left column is made up of the female *sefirot* and the right column of the male. Another arrangement presents the *sefirot* as ten concentric circles, a depiction related to medieval cosmology in which the universe is understood as made up of ten spheres.

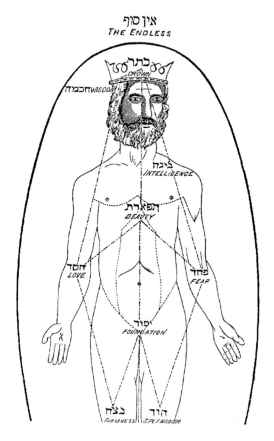

Figure 36 Adam Kadmon illustration, reproduced from the frontispiece of Isaac Myer's *Kabbalah*, 1888.

For the kabbalists the *sefirot* are dynamically structured; through them divine energy flows from its source and separates into individual channels, reuniting in the lowest *sefirah*. These *sefirot* were also understood as divine substances as well as containers of His essence; often they are portrayed as flames of fire. Yet despite their individuality, they are unified with the *Ayn Sof* in the moment of creation. According to the *Zohar*, all existences are emanations from the Deity: He is revealed in all things because He is immanent in them. To reconcile this process of emanation with the doctrine of creation *ex nihilo*, some kabbalists argued that the *Ayn Sof* should be seen as *Ayin* (nothingness); thus the manifestation of the Divine through the *sefirot* is a self-creation out of divine nothingness. Other kabbalists, however, maintained that creation does not occur within the Godhead. It takes place at a lower level where created beings are formed independent of God's essence.

For the mystic, deeds of *tikkun* (cosmic repair) sustain the world, activate nature to praise God, and bring about the coupling of the tenth and the sixth *sefirot*. Such repair is accomplished by keeping the commandments which were conceived as vessels for establishing contact with the Godhead and for ensuring divine mercy. Such a religious life provided the kabbalist with a means of integrating into the divine hierarchy of creation. The supreme rank attainable by the soul at the end of its sojourn is the mystical cleaving to God

(*devekut*). The early kabbalists of Provence defined *devekut* as the goal of the mystic way. For Nahmanides *devekut* is a state of mind in which one constantly remembers God and his love. In his view, the true *Hasid* is able to attain such a spiritual state. *Devekut* does not completely eliminate the distance between God and human beings; it denotes instead a state of beatitude and intimate union between the soul and its source.

In ascending the higher worlds, the path of prayer paralleled the observance of God's commandments. Yet, unlike the *mitzvot*, prayer is independent of action and can become a process of meditation. Mystical prayer, accompanied by meditative *kavvanot* (intention) focusing on each prayer's kabbalistic content, was a feature of the various systems of *kabbalah*. For the kabbalists prayer was seen as the ascent of human beings into the higher realms where the soul could integrate with the higher spheres. By using the traditional liturgy in a symbolic fashion, prayer repeats the hidden processes of the cosmos. In addition to mystical meditation, the kabbalists made use of the letters of the Hebrew alphabet and of the names of God for the purposes of meditative training. By engaging in the combination of letters and names, the mystic was able to empty his mind so as to concentrate on divine matters. Through such experiences the kabbalists believed they could attempt to conduct the soul to a state of the highest rapture in which divine reality was disclosed.

SOURCES

Azriel of Gerona

In the *Gate of Kavvanah* Azriel of Gerona depicted the meditative methods used by the Provence school. Here kabbalistic meditation is based on light in which one elevates the mind from one light to a higher one:

> Imagine that you yourself are light, and that all of your surroundings on every side, are also light. Above this throne is a light called *nogah* (glow). Facing this is another throne. Above the second throne is a light called *tov* (good). You are standing between the two. If you wish to take revenge, turn to the *nogah*; if you wish to seek mercy, turn to the *tov*. The words that you speak should be directed towards this light. Now turn yourself to the right of it, and there you will find another light. This is a light that is called *bahir* (brilliant). To its left you will find a light. This is a light called *zohar* (radiant). Above these two, directly between them, is a light called *kavod* (glory). Around it is a light called *chaim* (life). Above it is the crown. This is the light that crowns the desires of the mind and illuminates the paths of the imagination, enhancing the radiance of the vision. This light has no end, and it cannot be fathomed. From the glory of its perfection issues desire, blessing, peace, life and all good to those who keep the way of its unification.
>
> (Azriel of Gerona, *Gate of Kavvanah* in JM, p. 104)

Abraham Abulafia

Advancing a theory of prophetic mysticism, Abraham Abulafia believed that through the technique of combining letters of the various divine names one could receive an outpouring of the Holy Spirit and thereby become a prophet:

> Prophecy is a mode of the intellect. It is the expression of the love of the Lord our God, the Lord is one . . . Here is the strong foundation which I deliver to you that you should know it and engrave it upon your heart: the Holy Name, the whole of the Torah, the sacred Scriptures and all the prophetic books; these are all full of divine names and tremendous things. Join one to the other. Depict them to yourself. Test them, try them, combine them . . . First begin by combining the letters of the name YHVH. Gaze at all its combinations. Elevate it. Turn in over like a wheel that goes round and round, backwards and forwards like a scroll. Do not set it aside except when you observe that it is becoming too much for you because of the confused movements in your imagination.
>
> (Abraham Abulafia, *The Book of the Sign*, in JM, p. 105)

Zohar

According to the *Zohar*, the *Ayn Sof* is beyond all comprehension; it encompasses all worlds, but cannot be encompassed:

Master of the worlds, you are the cause of causes, the first cause who waters the tree with a spring; this spring is like the soul to the body, since it is like the life of the body. In you there is no image, nor likeness of what is within, nor of what is without.

You created the heaven and earth, and you have produced from them sun and moon and stars and plants, and in the earth, trees and grasses and the Garden of Eden and wild beasts and fish and men so that through them the upper realms might be known, as well as how the upper and lower realms are governed and how the upper and lower realms might be distinguished.

There is none that knows anything of you, and besides you there is no singleness or unity in the upper or the lower worlds. You are acknowledged as Lord over all. As for all the *sefirot*, each one has a known name and you are the perfect completion of them all. When you remove yourself from them, all the names are left like a body without a soul.

(*Zohar* in JM, p. 119)

DISCUSSION

1. What is the nature of *Ayn Sof* according to medieval mysticism?

2. Discuss the origins and role of the *sefirot* according to medieval kabbalists.

FURTHER READING

Drob, Sanford, *Symbols of the Kabbalah*, Jason Aronson, 2000.

Drob, Sanford, *Kabbalistic Metaphors*, Jason Aronson, 2000.

Halevi, Zev Ben Shimon, *Kabbalah*, Thames and Hudson, 1979.

Halevi, Zev Ben Shimon, *Astrology and Kabbalah*, Urania Trust, 2000.

Idel, Moshe, *Kabbalah: New Perspectives*, Yale University Press, 1990.

Idel, Moshe, *Absorbing Perfections: Kabbalah and Interpretation*, Yale University Press, 2002.

Matt, Daniel, *The Essential Kabbalah*, Harper Collins, 1996.

Matt, Daniel, *Zohan: The Book of Enlightenment*, Paulist Press, 1983.

Scholem, Gershom, *Kabbalah*, Plume, 1978.

Scholem, Gershom, *Origins of the Kabbalah*, Princeton University Press, 1987.

Scholem, Gershom, *Major Trends of Jewish Mysticism*, Schocken, 1995.

Scholem, Gershom, *Zohar: The Book of Splendor: Basic Readings from the Kabbalah*, Schocken, 1995.

Scholem, Gershom, *On the Kabbalah and its Symbolism*, Schocken, 1996.

Sheinkin, David, *Path of the Kabbalah*, Continuum, 1986.

CHAPTER 37

Jews in the Ottoman Empire

Timeline:

1488–1575 Joseph Caro

1510–1569 Dona Gracia

1522–1570 Moses Cordovero

1524–1579 Joseph Nasi

1534–1572 Isaac Luria

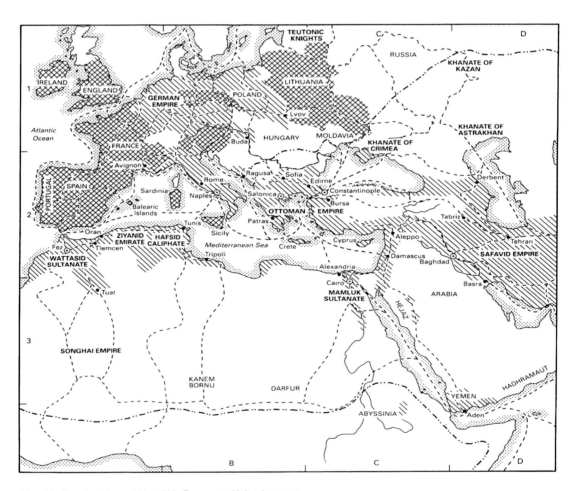

Map 41 The Jewish world in 1500: Europe and Islamic states

In the centuries following the medieval period the majority of Jews lived in Eastern Europe and in the lands of the Ottoman empire. By the fifteenth century the Ottoman Turks had become a major world power and many Ashkenazic Jews settled in Ottoman lands. In the next century the population was supplemented by large numbers of Jewish *Marranos* fleeing from the Spanish and Portuguese inquisitions. The Jewish population was further increased when many Spanish Jews sought refuge after the expulsion of Jews from Spain in 1492. In various parts of the empire – such as the Balkans, Greece, Cairo, Damascus and Constantinople – Jewish communities flourished into the sixteenth century.

Some of these Sephardic immigrants prospered and became part of the Ottoman court, such as Dona Gracia (1510–69) who resided in Constantinople and served as leader as well as patron of the Jewish community. Her nephew Joseph Nasi (1524–79) was also an important figure in the Ottoman court and sponsored the establishment of a Jewish settlement of textile workers in Tiberias. This project was partly inspired by messianic longing and laid the foundations for later spiritual and social activity in Israel. This influx of Jews into the Ottoman empire revitalized Jewish religious life as well, and rabbinic academies were founded in several important centres such as Cairo, Constantinople and Salonika.

Prominent among the rabbinic scholars of this period was **Joseph Caro** (1488–1575) who emigrated

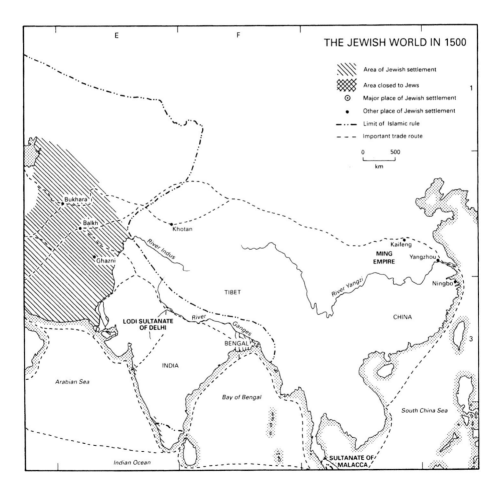

Map 42 The Jewish world in 1500: the East

Figure 37 The Caliph of Baghdad receives in his palace the two heads of the Jewish Community – Rabbi Sa'adia Gaon and the *exilarch* David Ben Zakkai, Baghdad, tenth century. Diorama. Copyright the Beth Hatefutsoth Permanent Exhibition (see also Chapter 31 for Saadiah Gaon).

from Spain to the Balkans. In the 1520s Caro commenced a vast study of Jewish law, the *House of Joseph*, based on a number of previous codes by such scholars as Maimonides, Isaac ben Jacob Alfasi of Lucena (1013–1103), Asher ben Yechiel (1250–1327) and Jacob ben Asher (1270–1340). Caro's study was a detailed commentary to Jacob ben Asher's code, the *Sefer Ha-Turim.*

Relying on previous legal codes, Caro asserted as binding the majority decisions of the earlier scholars he regarded as most authoritative: Alfasi, Maimonides and Asher ben Yechiel. Though the *House of Joseph* was regarded as a monumental contribution to halakhic learning, Caro compiled a shorter work, the **Shulkhan Arukh**, which listed only the binding rulings of the *halakhah.* This collection, which appeared in 1564, became the authoritative code of law in the Jewish world. While working on the *Shulkhan Arukh* Caro

emigrated to Safed in Israel which had become a major focus of Jewish religious life. In the sixteenth century this small community had become a centre for the manufacture of cloth and had grown to a population of over 10,000 Jews. Here Talmudic academies were established and small groups engaged in the study of kabbalistic literature as they piously awaited the coming of the Messiah.

Heightened by the expulsion of Jews from Spain and Portugal, such messianic expectation became a prevalent theme of religious poetry written in Safed during this period. The hymn composed by Solomon ha-Levy Alkabetz, *Come, My Beloved,* for instance, speaks of the Holy City as an abode for the Sabbath bride and the Davidic king. In this town mystics also participated in various ascetic practices such as fasting, public confessions of sins, wearing sackcloth and ashes, and praying at the graves of venerable sages. Such self-

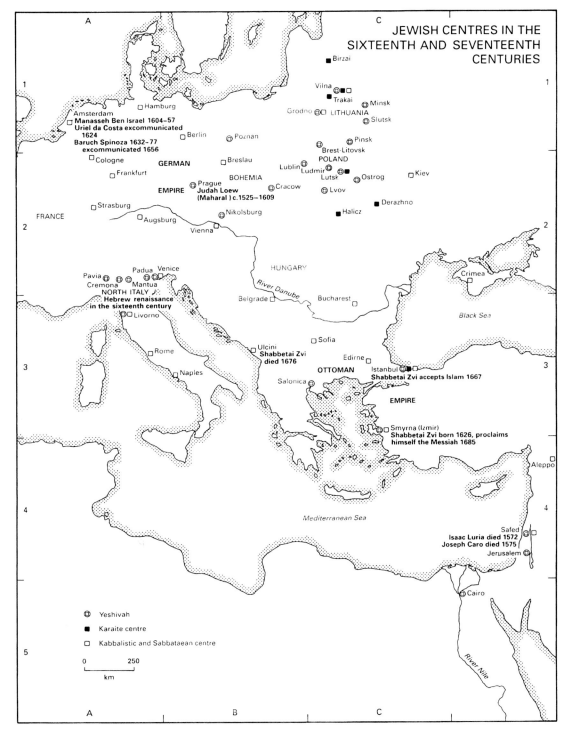

Map 43 Jewish centres in the sixteenth and seventeenth centuries

mortification was carried to an extreme by Abraham ha-Levi Beruchim who wandered through the streets of Safed calling on people to repent; he then led those he attracted to the synagogue, climbed into a sack, and ordered these individuals to throw stones at him.

In this centre of kabbalistic activity, one of the greatest mystics of Safed, **Moses Cordovero** (1522–70) collected, organized and interpreted the teachings of earlier mystical authors. His work constitutes a systematic summary of the *kabbalah* up to his time, and in his most important treatise, *Pardes*, he outlined the Zoharic concepts of the Godhead, the *sefirot*, the celestial powers and the earthly processes. Later in the sixteenth century kabbalistic speculation was transformed by the greatest mystic of Safed, **Isaac Luria** (1534–72). Originally brought up in Egypt where he studied the *Talmud* and engaged in business, Luria withdrew to an island on the Nile where he meditated on the *Zohar* for seven years.

In 1569 he arrived in Safed and died two years later after having passed on his teaching to a small group of disciples. Of primary importance in the Lurianic system is the mystery of creation. In the literature of early kabbalists creation was understood as a positive act: the will to create was awakened within the Godhead and this resulted in a long process of emanation. For Luria, however, creation was a negative event. The *Ayn Sof* had to bring into being an empty space in which creation could occur since divine light was everywhere leaving no room for creation to take place. This was accomplished by the process of *tzimtzum* – the contraction of the Godhead into itself. Thus the first act was not positive, but rather one that demanded withdrawal. God had to go into exile from the empty space (*tehiru*) so that the process of creation could be initiated. *Tzimtzum* therefore postulates divine exile as the first step of creation.

After this act of withdrawal, a line of light flowed from the Godhead into the *tehiru* and took on the shape of the *sefirot* in the form of *Adam Kadmon*. In this process divine lights created the vessels – the external shapes of the *sefirot* – which gave specific characteristics to each divine emanation. Yet these vessels were not strong enough to contain such pure light and they shattered. This breaking of the vessels (*shevirat ha-keilim*) brought disaster and upheaval to the emerging emanations: the lower vessels broke down and fell, the three highest emanations were damaged; and the empty space was divided into two parts. The first part consisted of the broken vessels with many divine sparks clinging to them; the second part was the upper realm where the pure light of God escaped to preserve its purity.

In explaining the purpose of the *tzimtzum*, Luria pointed out that the *Ayn Sof* before creation was not completely unified. There were elements in it that were potentially different from the rest of the Godhead. The *tzimtzum* separated these different elements from one another. After this contraction occurred a residue was left behind (*reshimu*) like the water clinging to a bucket after it was emptied. This residue included different elements that were part of the Godhead, and after the withdrawal, they were emptied into the empty space. Thus the separation of different elements from the Godhead was accomplished. The reason for the emanation of the divine powers and the formation of primordial man was the attempt to integrate these now separate elements into the scheme of creation and thereby transform them into co-operative forces. Their task was to create the vessels of the *sefirot* into which the divine light would flow. But the breaking of the vessels was a rebellion of these different elements, a refusal to participate in the process of creation. And by this rebellious act they were able to attain a realm of their own in the lower part of the *tehiru*, after the breaking of the vessels, these elements expressed themselves as the powers of evil.

Following the shattering of the vessels the cosmos was divided into two parts – the kingdom of evil in the lower part and the realm of divine light in the upper part. For Luria evil was understood as opposed to existence, therefore it was not able to exist by its own power. Instead it had to derive spiritual force from the divine light. This was accomplished by keeping captive the sparks of the divine light that fell with them when the vessels were broken and subsequently gave sustenance to the satanic domain. Divine attempts to bring unity to all existence now had to focus on the struggle to overcome the evil forces. This was achieved by a continuing process of divine emanation which at first created the *sefirot*, the sky, the earth, the Garden of Eden and human beings.

Rather than relying on the action of one person, God chose the people of Israel to vanquish evil and raise up the captive sparks. The Torah was given to symbolize the Jews' acceptance of this allotted task. When the ancient Israelites undertook to keep the law, redemption seemed imminent. Yet the people of Israel then created the golden calf, a sin parallel to Adam's disobedience. Again divine sparks fell and the forces of evil were renewed. For Luria, history is a record of attempts by the powers of goodness to rescue these sparks and unite the divine and earthly spheres. Luria and his disciples believed they were living in the final stages of this last attempt to overcome evil in which the coming of the Messiah would signify the end of the struggle.

SOURCES

Joseph Caro

Joseph Caro, who is primarily remembered for his legal code, the *Shulkhan Arukh*, was also a noted mystic. Believing himself to be the recipient of a heavenly mentor (*maggid*), he identified this *maggid* with the soul of the *Mishnah* and the *Shekhinah* (Divine Presence) in *The Heavenly Mentor*.

> Then slumber came upon me and I slept for about half an hour. I was in distress since he (the *maggid*) did not converse with me at length as previously. I began once more to rehearse the *Mishnah* and before I had completed two chapters, the voice of my beloved began to knock in my mouth saying: Although you imagined I had forsaken you and left you, do not think I really will leave you before I have fulfilled my promise not to withhold good from your mouth. You must cleave to me and to the fear of me, as I have said, and then you will be elevated, lifted up and made high before all the members of the heavenly academy, all of whom send you greetings because you busy yourself all the time with the *Talmud* and the codes and combine the two.
>
> (Joseph Caro, *The Heavenly Mentor*, in SRJ, pp. 108–10)

According to Solomon Alkabetz, one of Caro's disciples, the revelations of this *maggid* form the utterances through which Caro spoke to the circle of mystics:

> No sooner had we studied two tractates of the *Mishnah* than our Creator smote us so that we heard a voice speaking out of the mouth of the saint, may his light shine. It was a loud voice with letters clearly pronounced. All the companions heard the voice but were incapable of understanding what was said. It was an exceedingly pleasant voice that became increasingly strong. We all fell on our faces and none of us had any spirit left in him because of our great fear and awe. The voice began addressing us, 'Friends, choicest of the choice peace to you, beloved companions. Happy are you and happy those who bore you. Happy are you in this world and happy in the next that you resolve to adorn me on this night. For these many years had my head fallen with no one to comfort me. I was cast down to the ground to embrace the dunghills but now you have restored the crown to its former place . . . Behold I am the *Mishnah*, the mother who chastises her children and I have come to converse with you.'
>
> (Solomon Alkabetz, letter in JM, p. 144)

Shulkhan Arukh

The *Shulkhan Arukh*, *The Code of Jewish Law*, was compiled in the sixteenth century by Joseph Caro. This work has served as the basis for traditional Jewish life from that time to the present. This section concerns the rules of decency:

A person should accustom himself to respond to the call of nature once in the evening and once in the morning; such a habit is conducive to alertness and cleanliness. If he is unable to ease himself, he should walk a distance of four cubits (six feet), repeating it several times if need be; or he should divert his attention from other matters. He who defers easing himself, is guilty of violating a Biblical command (Lev. 11:43): 'Ye shall not make yourselves detestable;' and he who defers urination, is guilty of violating the Divine Promise (Deut. 7:14): 'There shall not be male or female barren among you.'

A man must exercise modesty when in the lavatory; he should not expose himself before he sits down, and should not expose his body more than is actually necessary. One should not ease oneself in the presence of other people; but one may urinate in the presence of other people even in the daytime, because there is danger involved in this restraint. Nevertheless, even in the latter case, one should at least turn aside.

One should not ease himself while standing, nor should one overstrain oneself, lest one ruptures the glands of the rectum; nor should one leave the lavatory too soon before one is certain that one is no longer in need of it. When one urinates while standing, one should take care not to splash any urine on one's shoes or clothes, and one should be extremely careful to hold the membrum.

While in the lavatory it is forbidden to think of sacred matters; it is, therefore, best to concentrate there upon one's business affairs and accounts, so that one may not be led to think either of holy matters, or, God forbid, indulge in sinful thoughts. On the Sabbath, when it is forbidden to think of business, one should think of some interesting things that one has either seen or heard, or something similar to that.

One should be careful to wipe oneself thoroughly, for should even a trace of faeces cling to the body, one is not permitted to utter a holy word. One should not clean himself with the right hand, for with this hand one puts on the *tefillin*. A left-handed person should clean himself with his right hand, which is like everybody else's left hand.

After each defecation or urination, even of one drop, one must wash one's hands and say the benediction, *Asher yatzar*. If one has forgotten to say the benediction, and after having responded to the call of nature again, one became aware of one's neglect, one need not say the benediction more than once. If one takes a laxative and knows that one will have to ease oneself several times, one should say the benediction only after surmising that this would be the last call.

(*Shulkhan Arukh*, Vol. I, 4 in CJL, pp. 7–8)

Moses Cordovero

Moses Cordovero, a student of Joseph Caro, was one of the most important kabbalists of sixteenth-century Safed. A member of an ascetic circle of mystics, Cordovero composed several important mystical treatises. In his *Pardes Rimonim* (*The Orchard of Pomegranates*), he advocated a system of meditation whereby one can bind oneself to the *sefirot* (divine emanations). Such a technique, he believed, is enhanced when colours are used:

In many places in *kabbalistic* texts and in the *Zohar*, we find various colours parallel the *sefirot*. One should be extremely careful and not imagine this is to be taken literally. Colour is something physical

used to describe the physical world, and the *sefirot*, which are spiritual, should not be depicted with physical properties. If a person believes these are literally the colours of the *sefirot*, he destroys the entire system and oversteps the boundaries fixed by the ancients. One who looks into this should be very careful not to assume that anything physical is implied; rather these colours allude to the results that are transmitted from the highest roots. For example, *Gevurah* (strength) is responsible for victory in war. Because this involves bloodshed (where blood is spilt), it is suitable to ascribe the colour red to this *sefirah*. The colour red likewise expresses hatred, anger and fury.

We therefore ascribe red to the place of judgement. Moreover, everything that is red is derived from the power of this root . . . Likewise the colour white indicates mercy and peace. This is because people with white hair are usually merciful . . . There is no question that things that are white emanate from the power of this root . . . This then is the proper interpretation of the relationship between the colours and the *sefirot*. The colours are used allegorically to allude to their functions and results . . . There is no question that the colours can thus serve as a door to the dynamics of the *sefirot*.

(Moses Cordovero, *Pardes Rimonim* in JM, pp. 146–147)

According to Cordovero, an individual should seek to unify the *sefirot*.

If one is pure and upright in deed, and if he grasps the cords of love existing in the holy roots of his soul, he will be able to ascend to every level in all the supernal universes . . . When a person is upright and righteous, he can meditate with suitable thoughts and thereby ascend through the levels of the transcendental. He must unify the levels of his soul, joining one part to another, drawing the different levels of his soul to vest themselves in one another. It thereby becomes like a single candelabrum made up of different parts joined together.

The individual must then unify the *sefirot*, bringing them to bind themselves together with a strong knot. He and his soul thus become a channel through which the *sefirot* can exert influence. All of them, from the highest to the lowest, act together through the powerful cord that unites them.

(Moses Cordovero, in JM, pp. 147–148)

Isaac Luria

In the sixteenth century, kabbalistic speculation was transformed by the greatest mystic of Safed, Isaac Luria. In 1569 he settled in Safed and died two years later after having passed on his teachings to a small group of disciples. According to Hayyim Vital, Luria was able to penetrate the deepest secrets. In *Etz Hayyim*, Vital praised his teacher's accomplishments:

The Ari (Isaac Luria) was overflowing with Torah. He was thoroughly expert in the Bible, *Mishnah*, *Talmud*, *pilpul* (talmudic interpretation), *midrash* (rabbinic commentary), *aggadah* (Biblical commentary), the workings of creation and the workings of the *merkavah* (divine chariot). He was adept in the conversation of trees, the conversation of birds and the speech of angels. He could also read faces in the manner outlined in the *Zohar*. He could discern everything that any individual had done, and could see what they would do in the future. He was able to read people's thoughts frequently before they even entered the individual's mind. He knew future events, and was conscious of everything happening here on earth as well as what was decreed in heaven.

In addition, he knew the mysteries of reincarnation: who had been born previously and who was here for the first time. He could look at a person and explain how he was connected to the Supernal Man and how he was related to Adam. He could read wondrous things in the light of a candle or the flame of a fire. With his eyes he gazed and could see the souls of the righteous, those who had died recently or those who had lived in ancient times. With these he studied the true mysteries that were lying in his bosom, ready to be used whenever he desired. He did not have to meditate to seek them out . . . None of this came through the practical *kabbalah* . . . Instead it came automatically as a result of his piety and asceticism after many years of study, in both the ancient and newer kabbalistic texts. He then increased his piety, asceticism, purity and holiness until he reached a level whereby Elijah would constantly reveal himself to him, speaking to him 'mouth to mouth' and teaching him these mysteries.

(Hayyim Vital, *Etz Hayyim*, in JM, p. 151)

Of primary importance in the Lurianic system is the mystery of creation. In Luria's view, the *Ayn Sof* had to bring into being an empty space in which creation could occur. This was accomplished by the process of *tzimtzum*, the contraction of the Godhead into itself. As Hayyim Vital explained in *Etz Hayyim*:

Know that before the emanations emerged and the creatures created, the simple supernal light of the *Ayn Sof* filled all these, and there was no empty area at all, namely, an empty atmosphere and a vacuum. All was filled with that infinite light. It had neither beginning nor end. All was simple light in total sameness . . . When in his simple will it was resolved to create worlds and send out the emanations, to bring to objective existence the perfection of his deeds, and his names and his appellations, which was the reason for the creation of the worlds, then he contracted himself in the middle point in himself, in the very centre. He contracted that light; it was withdrawn to the sides around the middle point. Then there was left an empty space, an atmosphere, and a vacuum extending from the precise point of the centre.

The contraction was equally distributed around that middle empty point in order that the vacuum was circular on all sides equally. It was not in the shape of a square with fixed angles because the *Ayn Sof* also contracted himself in a circular fashion in equal proportions on all sides. The reason for this was because the light of the *Ayn Sof* is equally pervasive. It was thus necessary that it contract itself in equal measure on all sides . . . There was another reason for this. It was for the sake of the emanations that were due to be sent out thereafter in that vacuum . . . By being in the form of circles, the emanations could all be equally close and attached to the *Ayn Sof*. They could all receive in equal measure the light and the influences they needed from the *Ayn Sof* . . . The purpose of this contraction was to bring to light the source of judgement to act in the worlds. After this contraction . . . when a vacuum was left, an empty atmosphere through the meditation of the light of the *Ayn Sof*, blessed be he, there was now available an area in which there could be the emanations, the beings created, formed and made.

(Hayyim Vital, *Etz Hayyim*, in JM, pp. 152–153)

DISCUSSION

1. What is the nature of the *Shulkhan Arukh*?

2. How did Isaac Luria transform the mystical teaching of the *Zohar*?

FURTHER READING

Corrigan, John *et al.*, *Jews, Christians, Muslims*, Prentice Hall, 1997.

Courbage, Youssef, Fargues, Philippe, *Christians and Jews under Islam*, I. B. Tauris, 1998.

Frank, Daniel (ed.), *The Jews of Medieval Islam: Community, Society and Identity*, Brill, 1995.

Gubbay, Lucien, *Sulight and Shadow: The Jewish Experience of Islam*, Other Press, 2000.

Lewis, Bernard (ed.), *Christians and Jews in the Ottoman Empire: The Functioning of a Plural Society*, Vol. 2, Holmes and Meier, 1982.

Lewis, Bernard, *The Jews of Islam*, Princeton University Press, 1992.

Masters, Bruce, *Christians and Jews in the Ottoman Arab World*, Cambridge University Press, 2001.

Randall, Albert B., *Theologies of War and Peace Among Jews, Christians and Muslims*, Edwin Mellen Press, 1998.

Shaw, Stanford, J., *Jews of the Ottoman Empire and the Turkish Republic*, Macmillan, 1991.

CHAPTER 38

The Shabbatean Movement

Timeline:

1626–1676 Shabbatai Zevi

1726–1791 Jacob Frank

Figure 38 The Jewish mystic and messiah, Shabbatai Zevi (1626–76) who was born in Smyrna (now Izmir), Turkey, and who proclaimed himself the Messiah in 1665 and convinced the entire Jewish world from England to Persia, Germany to Morocco, Poland to the Yemen.

By the beginning of the seventeenth century, Lurianic mysticism had made a major impact on Sephardic Jewry, and messianic expectations had also become a central feature of Jewish life. In this milieu the arrival of a self-proclaimed messianic king, **Shabbatai Zevi** (1626–76) brought about a transformation of Jewish life and thought. Born in Smyrna into a wealthy family, Shabbatai had received a traditional Jewish education and later engaged in study of the *Zohar*. After leaving Smyrna in the 1650s he spent ten years in various cities in Greece as well as in Istanbul and Jerusalem. Eventually he became part of a kabbalistic group in Cairo and travelled to Gaza where he encountered Abraham-Nathan Ashkenazi (1644–80) who believed Shabbatai was the Messiah. In 1665 his Messiahship was proclaimed, and Nathan sent letters to Jews in the diaspora asking them to repent and recognize Shabbatai Zevi as their redeemer. Shabbatai, he announced, would take the Sultan's crown, bring back the lost tribes, and inaugurate the period of messianic redemption.

After a brief sojourn in Jerusalem, Shabbatai went to Smyrna where he encountered strong opposition on the part of some local rabbis. In response he denounced the disbelievers and declared that he was the Anointed of the God of Jacob. This action evoked a hysterical response -- a number of Jews fell into trances and had visions of him on a royal throne crowned as king of Israel. In 1666 he journeyed to Istanbul, but on the order of the grand vizier he was arrested and put into prison. Within a short time the prison quarters became a messianic court; pilgrims from all over the world made their way to Istanbul to join in messianic rituals and ascetic activities. In addition hymns were written in his honour and new festivals were introduced. According to Nathan, who remained in Gaza, the alteration in Shabbatai's moods from illumination to withdrawal symbolized his soul's struggle with demonic powers. At times he was imprisoned by the powers of evil (*kelippot*) but at other moments he prevailed against them.

This same year Shabbatai spent three days with the Polish kabbalist, Nehemiah ha-Kohen, who later denounced him to the Turkish authorities. Shabbatai was brought to court and given the choice between conversion and death. In the face of this alternative, he converted to Islam and took on the name Mehemet Effendi. Such an act of apostasy scandalized most of his followers, but he defended himself by asserting that he had become a Muslim in obeisance to God's commands. Many of his followers accepted this explanation and refused to give up their belief. Some thought it was not Shabbatai who had become a Muslim, but rather a phantom who had taken on his appearance; the Messiah himself had ascended to Heaven. Others cited Biblical and rabbinic sources to justify Shabbatai's action. Nathan explained that the messianic task involved taking on the humiliation of being portrayed as a traitor to his people. Furthermore, he argued on the basis of Lurianic *kabbalah* that there were two kinds of divine light – a creative light and another light opposed to the existence of anything other than the *Ayn Sof*. While creative light formed structures of creation in the empty space, the other light became after the *tzimtzum* the power of evil. According to Nathan, the soul of the Messiah had been struggling against the power of evil from the beginning; his purpose was to allow divine light to penetrate this domain and bring about repair (*tikkun*). In order to do this, the soul of the Messiah was not obligated to keep the law, but was free to descend into the abyss

to liberate sparks and thereby conquer evil. In this light Shabbatai's conversion to Islam was explicable.

After Shabbatai's act of apostasy, Nathan visited him in the Balkans and then travelled to Rome where he performed secret rites to bring about the end of the Papacy. Shabbatai remained in Adrianople and Constantinople where he lived as both Muslim and Jew. In 1672 he was deported to Albania where he disclosed his own kabbalistic teaching to his supporters. After he died in 1676, Nathan declared that Shabbatai had ascended to the supernal world. Eventually a number of groups continued in their belief that Shabbatai was the Messiah including a sect, the Dissidents (*Doenmeh*), which professed Islam publicly but nevertheless adhered to their own traditions. Marrying among themselves, they eventually evolved into antinomian sub-groups which violated Jewish sexual laws and asserted the divinity of Shabbatai and their leader, Baruchiah Russo. In Italy several Shabbatean groups also emerged and propagated their views.

In the eighteenth century the most important Shabbatean sect was led by Jacob Frank (1726–91) who was influenced by the *Doenmeh* in Turkey. Believing himself to be the incarnation of Shabbatai, Frank announced that he was the second person of the Trinity and gathered together a circle of disciples who indulged in licentious orgies. In the 1750s disputations took place between traditional Jews and Frankists; subsequently Frank expressed his willingness to become a Christian but he wished to maintain his own group. This request was refused by Church leaders, yet Frank and his disciples were baptized. The clergy however became aware that Frank's trinitarian beliefs were not consonant with Christian doctrine, and he was imprisoned in 1760 for thirteen years. Frank then settled in Germany where he continued to subscribe to a variant of the Shabbatean kabbalistic tradition.

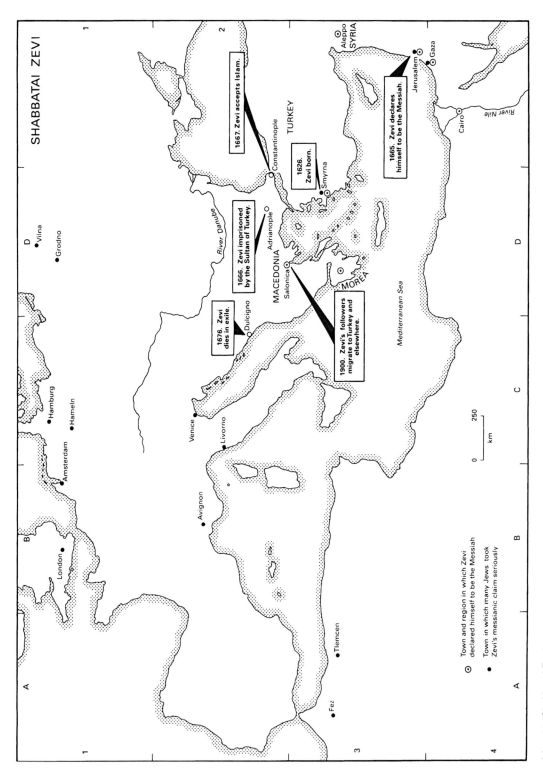

SHABBATAI ZEVI

1667. Zevi accepts Islam.

1626. Zevi born.

1665. Zevi declares himself to be the Messiah.

1666. Zevi imprisoned by the Sultan of Turkey.

1676. Zevi dies in exile.

1900. Zevi's followers migrate to Turkey and elsewhere.

⊙ Town and region in which Zevi declared himself to be the Messiah

● Town in which many Jews took Zevi's messianic claim seriously

Aleppo
SYRIA
Gaza
Jerusalem
River Nile
Cairo
Constantinople
TURKEY
Smyrna
Adrianople
MACEDONIA
Salonica
MOREA
Mediterranean Sea
River Danube
Vilna
Grodno
Hamburg
Hameln
Amsterdam
London
Venice
Livorno
Dulcigno
Avignon
Tlemcen
Fez

0   250
km

Map 44 Shabbatai Zevi

SOURCES

Shabbatai Zevi

Shabbatai Zevi was seen by many throughout the Jewish world as the Messiah. The following contemporary account gives an idea of the excitement he inspired. According to Sir Paul Rycaut in *History of the Turkish Empire*:

According to the predictions of several Christian writers, especially of such who comment upon the Apocalypse or Revelations, this year of 1666 was to prove a year of wonders, of strange revolutions in the world, and particularly, of blessing to the Jews . . .

In this manner millions of people were possessed when Shabbetai Zevi first appeared at Smyrna, and published himself to the Jews for their Messiah, relating the greatness of their approaching kingdom, the strong hand whereby God was about to deliver them from bondage, and gather them from all parts of the world. It was strange to see how this fancy took and how fast the report of Shabbetai and his doctrine flew through all parts where Jews inhabited and so deeply possessed them with a belief of their new kingdom and riches, and many of them with promotion to offices of government, renown and greatness; that in all places from Constantinople to Budu (to which it was my fortune this year to travel), I perceived a strange transport in the Jews, none of them attending to any business, unless to wind up former negotiations and to prepare themselves and their families for a journey to Jerusalem. All their discourses, their dreams and disposal of their affairs tended to no other design but a re-establishment in the Land of Promise, to greatness and glory, wisdom and doctrine of the Messiah . . .

An example of which is most observable in the Jews of Thessalonica, who now, full of assurance that the restoration of their kingdom and the accomplishment of the times for the coming of the Messiah was at hand . . . applied themselves immediately to fastings; and some in that manner beyond the abilities of nature, that having for the space of seven days taken no sustenance, were famished. Others buried themselves in their gardens, covering their naked bodies with earth, their hands only excepted, remained in those beds of dirt until their bodies were stiffened with cold and moisture. Others would endure to have melted wax dropped upon their shoulders; others to roll themselves in snow and throw their bodies in the coldest season of the winter into the sea or frozen waters. But the most common manner of mortification was first to prick their backs and sides with thorns and then to give themselves thirty-nine lashes. All business was laid aside.

(Paul Rycaut, *History of the Turkish Empire*, in SRJ, pp. 110–111)

When Shabbatai converted to Islam, the community was deeply disillusioned. As Sir Paul Rycaut explained in *History of the Turkish Empire*:

The news that Shabbetai had become a Turk and that the Messiah was now a Muslim spread throughout Turkey. The Jews were astounded and were very embarrassed by their own credulity and by the arguments they had used to persuade others and the converts they had made within their own families. Further afield they were generally mocked in all the towns in which they lived. Street urchins jeered after them, producing a new nickname . . . which they all would shout with contempt and scorn, pointing their fingers whenever they saw a Jew. So for a long time these deceived people remained confused and silent and they were profoundly depressed in their spirits.

(Paul Rycaut, *History of the Turkish Empire*, in SRJ, p. 116)

DISCUSSION

1. How did Nathan of Gaza use mystical categories to rationalize Shabbatai's Zevi's conversion to Islam?

2. Discuss the teachings of Jacob Frank.

FURTHER READING

Eskinazi, Salamon, *The Reluctant Messiah*, Jason Aronson, 2002.

Carlebach, Elisheva, *Pursuit of Heresy: Rabbi Moses Hagiz and the Sabbatian Controversy*, Columbia University Press, 1990.

Cohn-Sherbok, Dan, *The Jewish Messiah*, T. and T. Clark, 1997.

Evelyn, John, *The History of Sabatai Sevi, the Supposed Messiah of the Jews*, Ams Press, 2000.

Fine, Lawrence (ed.), *Judaism in Practice: From the Middle Ages Through the Early Modern Period*, Princeton University Press, 2001.

Freely, John, *The Lost Messiah: In Search of the Mystical Rabbi Shabbatai Sevi*, Overlook Press, 2003.

Lenowitz, Harris, *The Jewish Messiahs: From the Galilee to Crown Heights*, Oxford University Press, 1999.

Liebes, Yehuda, Stein, Batya, *Studies in Jewish Myth and Messianism*, State University of New York, 1992.

Patai, Raphael, *Messiah Texts*, Wayne State University Press, 1979.

Saperstein, Marc (ed.), *Essential Papers on Messianic Movements and Personalities in Jewish History*, New York University Press, 1992.

Scholem, Gershom, *Sabbatai Sevi; The Mystical Messiah 1626–1676*, Princeton University Press, 1973.

Scholem, Gershom, *The Messiah Idea in Judaism*, Random House, 1995.

CHAPTER 39

Jewry in Eastern and Western Europe

Timeline:

1264 Charter of Prince of Kalisz

1334, 1364, 1367 Casimir III, King of Poland, confirms and extends the Charter of 1264

1453 Casimir IV ratifies the Charter of Casimir III

1483–1546 Martin Luther

1511–1578 Azariah dei Rossi

1527–1592 Leone de'Sommo

1553 *Talmud* burned in Italy

1555 Pope Paul IV orders Jews of Rome into a ghetto

1590 *Marranos* arrive in Amsterdam

1648–1649 Cossack uprising under Bugdan Chmielnicki

1655–1667 Russian and Swedish invasions of Poland

1720–1791 Vilna Gaon

1768 *Haidemak* attack on Jews in the Ukraine

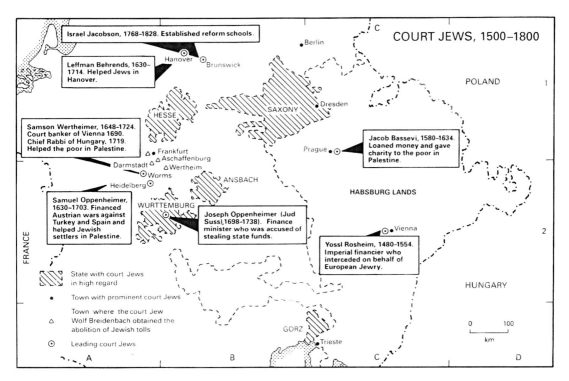

Map 45 Court Jews, 1500–1800

During the medieval period Ashkenazic Jewry in Poland was increased by migration from the Crimea, the Russian steppes, the Middle East and Spain. In 1264 the Prince of Kalisz issued a charter to the Jews granting them legal protection; this was followed in the next century by a series of decrees by King Casimir III which expanded their charter to include the entire Polish kingdom. In 1388 the Grand Duke of Lithuania granted similar rights to the Jews, which were renewed in the middle of the fifteenth century by Casimir IV Jagiello. By these decrees Polish and Lithuanian rulers provided a relatively secure basis for Jewish communal existence. In this environment Polish Jews became fiscal agents, tax collectors, and managers of noblemen's estates. In addition, some Jews leased lands and supervised various agricultural activities such as farming, harvesting, manufacture and export. Yet despite such prosperity, the Polish Jewish community was subject to various forms of discrimination: Jews were forced to wear garments different from other members of society; they were the victims of outbursts of anti-Jewish persecution; and occasionally Jews were accused of desecrating the host and using the blood of Christians for ritual purposes.

By the beginning of the fifteenth century the Polish Jewish community numbered 10–15,000 Jews, and in the next century the population grew to over 150,000. In the sixteenth and seventeenth centuries the Polish nobility, who owned large tracts of land in the Ukraine, employed Jews on their estates; there they collected taxes, fees, tolls and produce from the serfs. Noblemen also established private cities in which they welcomed Jews as employees in their houses, where they undertook business activities. Within this milieu Polish Jewry was regulated along the lines of communal self-government. Each local community (*kehillah*) engaged a Board of Trustees that collected taxes for the government and provided educational and other necessary facilities for Jewish life. In the larger cities, the *kehillot* were supervised by paid officials including rabbis who were usually employed for three-year periods to serve as authorities in matters of Jewish law as well as heads of Talmudic academies.

As a result of this efflorescence of Jewish life, Poland became a great centre of scholarship. In the rabbinical academies the method of *hilluk* (the differentiation and reconciliation of rabbinic opinions) generated considerable activity in the study of Talmudic law. Moreover, a number of scholars collected together the legal interpretations of previous *halakhists*, and commentaries were written on the *Shulkhan Arukh*. To regulate Jewish life in the country at large, Polish Jews established regional federations that administered Jewish affairs from the mid-sixteenth to the mid-eighteenth centuries. Further, a Council of the Four Lands composed of the most eminent rabbinical and lay leaders met twice a year to allocate taxes to the synods and *kehillot*, select and finance Jewish representatives to the Polish court, and issue ordinances regarding a wide range of Jewish interests and activities.

In the midst of this general prosperity, the Polish Jewish community was subject to a series of massacres in the seventeenth century carried out by Cossacks of the Ukraine as well as Crimean Tartars and Ukrainian peasants who rebelled against the Polish nobility. In 1648 **Bogdan Chmielnicki** was elected *hetman* of the Cossacks and thereupon instigated an insurrection against the Polish gentry which had previously oppressed the Cossack population. As administrators of noblemen's estates, Jews were slaughtered in these revolts. Estates and manor houses were destroyed and victims were flayed, burned alive and mutilated. Infants were murdered and cast into wells; women were cut open and sewn up again with live cats thrust into their wounds. In these massacres thousands of Jews died in towns east of the Dnieper and elsewhere.

As the Cossacks advanced, the Polish king died and was succeeded by John Casimir who attempted to negotiate with the Cossacks, who demanded an independent Ukrainian state. After several more years of battle, Chmielnicki appealed to the Russian allies who invaded north-eastern Poland and the Ukraine. In 1655 the Swedes advanced into western Poland, but by the following year a Polish partisan movement drove back these foreign invaders. Finally in 1667 Russia and Poland signed the Treaty of Adrusovo which distributed the western Ukraine to Poland, and the eastern Ukraine and the Smolensk region to Russia. During these years of war the Jewish population was decimated by the various opposing forces: the Cossacks and Ukrainian peasants regarded Jews as representatives of the Polish aristocracy; the Russians, who did not allow Jews to settle in the lands, joined the Cossack hordes in this slaughter; and the Polish partisans saw

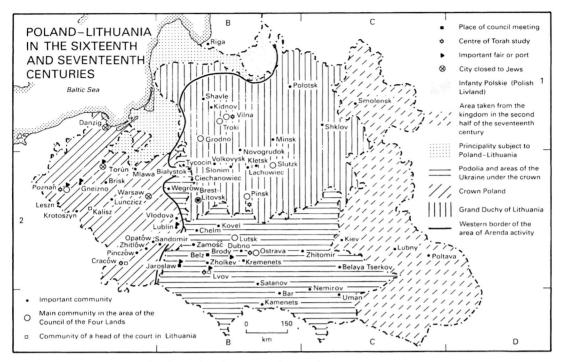

Map 46 Poland–Lithuania in the sixteenth and seventeenth centuries

Map 47 Jewish communities in Poland and Lithuania under the Council of the Four Lands and the Council of Lithuania

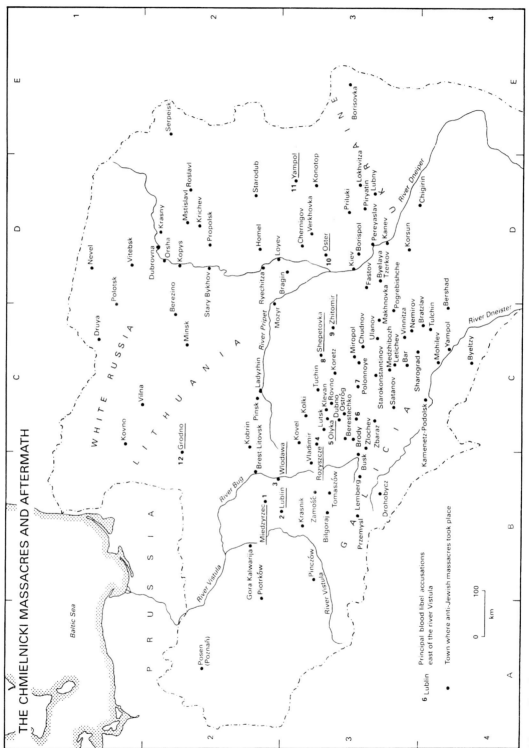

Map 48   The Chmielnicki massacres and aftermath

Jews as allied with the Swedes. Approximately a quarter of the entire Jewish community died in this onslaught, and thousands were ransomed from the Tartars in the slave markets in Constantinople.

As the century progressed, Jewish life in Poland became increasingly insecure due to political instability; nevertheless the Jewish community considerably increased in size during the eighteenth century. Approximately a third of Polish Jewry lived in the countryside in small groups where they were subject to repeated blood libel accusations. In the 1730s and 1740s Cossacks, known as *Haidemaks*, invaded the Ukraine robbing and murdering Jewish inhabitants, and finally butchering the Jewish community of Uman in 1768. Throughout the period the Polish *kehillot* were heavily taxed, and at times claims were made that the leaders of the Jewish community placed most of the tax burdens on the poor.

In Lithuania, on the other hand, Jewish life flourished, and Vilna became an important centre of rabbinic scholarship. Here Elijah ben Solomon Zalman (1720–91), referred to as the **Vilna Gaon**, lectured to disciples on a wide range of subjects and composed commentaries on the Bible, *Mishnah, Talmud, midrashim*, the *Sefer Yetsirah, Zohar* and the *Shulkhan Arukh*. Unlike earlier eastern European sages, he rejected the method of *hilluk* and focused on the simple meaning of the text. In addition, his interests extended to secular fields such as algebra, geometry, astronomy and geography. As a symbol of rabbinic learning, he stood out against the excesses of religious piety which began to make an impact on Polish Jewry in the latter half of the eighteenth century.

In the medieval period Spain and Provence played leading roles in the development of Jewish philosophy and mysticism. Yet by the fourteenth century these communities had lost their influence as a result of increased persecution, and many Jews were attracted to northern Italian states to act as moneylenders for the middle classes. In 1500 Jewish communities existed in such cities as Ferrara, Mantua, Venice, Padua, Florence and Rome. During the Renaissance, some Jews emulated the lifestyle of the Italian aristocracy and contacts were established with Italian humanists. The *Zohar* in particular exerted a strong influence on these Italian thinkers and resulted in the outpouring of Christian kabbalistic writing. On the Jewish side, the study of classical sources in the Renaissance made a significant impression on Jewish scholars and preachers. In addition, Italy became a major centre for Jewish printing; synagogue music was written in Italy in the Renaissance style, and a Jewish theatre was established by Leone de'Sommo (1527–92) for the production of Hebrew drama. Among Jewish scholars influenced by the Renaissance, Azariah dei Rossi (1511–78) applied the writings of classical antiquity to the understanding of rabbinic sources.

Despite this positive contact between humanists and Jews, Christian persecution and expulsion occurred repeatedly. In the sixteenth century the Counter-Reformation Church attempted to isolate the Jewish community. The *Talmud* was burned in 1553, and two years later Pope Paul IV reinstated the segregationist edict of the Fourth Lateran Council forcing Jews to live in ghettos and barring them from most areas of economic life. In addition, *marranos* who took up the Jewish tradition were burned at the stake and Jews were expelled from most Church domains. As a result of these measures Italian Jewry retreated to the more secure world of traditional rabbinic study and kabbalistic speculation.

In Germany the growth of Protestantism frequently led to adverse conditions for the Jewish population. Though **Martin Luther** was initially well disposed to the Jews, he soon came to realize that the Jewish community was intent on remaining true to its faith. As a consequence he composed a virulent attack on the Jews. At the beginning of the early modern period German Jews lived primarily in villages where they were oppressed by discriminatory legislation, but by the middle of the sixteenth century they were freed from the restrictions against living in cities. As a result a new class of court Jews (*hofjuden*) offered their services to German princes. These Jews utilized their connections with co-religionists in North Atlantic countries, in Poland and Lithuania as well as in Mediterranean states to the commercial advantage of their employers. They were engaged in providing military equipment, arranging loans, managing mints, providing the court with clothes and jewellery and founding industries. In return these court Jews were released from many Jewish disabilities and were free to settle in restricted areas. A number of these favoured individuals were appointed by the rulers as chief elders

of the Jewish community, and they acted as spokesmen and defenders of German Jewry.

In Holland some Jews had also attained an important influence on trade and finance. By the mid-seventeenth century both *marranos* and Ashkenazic Jews came to Amsterdam and established themselves in various areas of economic activity. By the end of the century there were nearly 10,000 Jews in Amsterdam; there the Jewish community was employed on the stock exchange, in the sugar, tobacco and diamond trades, and in insurance, manufacturing, printing and banking. In this milieu Jewish cultural activity flourished: Jewish writers published works of drama, theology, and mystical lore. Though Jews in Holland were not granted full rights as citizens, they nevertheless enjoyed religious freedom, personal protection and the liberty of participating in a wide range of economic affairs.

Figure 39 Martin Luther (1483–1546). German priest, *c.* 1529. Artist: Cranach, Lucas the elder: 1472–1553: German. Copyright The Art Archive/Galleria degli Uffizi Florence/Dagli Orti.

SOURCES

Chmielnicki Massacre

From the thirteenth century Jews were protected in Poland and Lithuania. Here the community benefited from a system of communal authority, the Council of the Four Lands, which regulated all Jewish affairs. Yet, against this background of prosperity and security, the Chmielnicki massacres in Poland during the seventeenth century were an enormous shock. As Nathan Hannover explained in *The Miry Depth*:

The oppressor Chmielnicki, may his name be blotted out, heard that many Jews were gathered together in the fortress of Nemirov and that they had a great deal of gold and silver with them . . . Accordingly he sent an enemy of the Jews to lead six hundred swordsmen against this holy congregation. He also wrote to the city magistrates that this band should be given every assistance. The citizens agreed to help them with all their resources – not because they liked the Cossacks, but because they hated the Jews

. . . As soon as the fortress gates were opened, the Cossacks rushed in with drawn swords and the townspeople followed them with swords, lances, scythes and even clubs. They killed a huge number of Jews, they raped the women and the young girls, although some of the women jumped into the moat near the fortress and were drowned. Many men who could swim also jumped into the water in order to swim away and escape from the slaughter. But the Russians swam after them and killed them in the water with their swords and scythes. Also some of the enemy kept shooting into the moat with their guns so that the water flowed red with blood . . . The number of those drowned and murdered in this holy congregation of Nemirov was about six thousand people. As has been described, they met all kinds of appalling deaths. May God avenge their blood!

(Nathan Hannover, *The Miry Depth*, in SRJ, p. 115)

Vilna Gaon

Born in Selets in the eighteenth century, Elijah ben Solomon Zalman – known as the Vilna Gaon – was the most important rabbinic scholar of his age. In addition to traditional rabbinic studies, he was adept at kabbalistic study. According to Hayyim of Volozhin (18th–19th century), he was unique in his learning:

There are few only who can study the sources of our exoteric Torah . . . the Babylonian and Palestinian *Talmud* . . . let alone the innermost mysteries of the Torah . . . and the writings of the Ari (Isaac Luria) . . . For even the saintly disciples of the Ari could not penetrate the innermost depths of the meaning of this holy one of the most high, the Ari, except Rabbi Hayyim Vital . . . Until he, for his righteousness's sake, to magnify the law and make it honourable and to show us marvellous things from his law, made his merciful kindness exceedingly great over us; behold one like the son of man came with the clouds of heaven, to him glory was given, unique was this great man, none had been like him for a previous generation . . . all the ways and paths of exoteric and esoteric wisdom were clear to him . . . this is the *gaon* (eminence) of the world, the *Hasid* (pious) and saint, our great and holy master . . . and with a mighty and marvellous adhesion to God, and a wonderful purity, until he was granted permission to penetrate the full understanding of things.

(In JM, pp. 180–181)

Martin Luther

In 1542 Martin Luther published his pamphlet *Against the Jews and their Lies*. In this work, he attacked both Judaism and the Jewish people:

No one wants them. The countryside and the roads are open to them; they may return to their country when they wish; we shall gladly give them presents to get rid of them, for they are a heavy burden on us, a scourge, a pestilence and misfortune in our country. This is proved by the fact that they have often been expelled by force: from France, where they had a downy nest; recently from Spain, their chosen roots, and even this year from Bohemia, where in Prague they had another cherished nest; finally, in my own lifetime, from Ratisbon, Magdeburg, and from many other places . . .

Know, O adored Christ, and make no mistake, that aside from the Devil, you have no enemy more venomous, more desperate, more bitter, than a true Jew who truly seeks to be a Jew. Now whoever wishes to accept venomous serpents, desperate enemies of the Lord, and to honour them to let himself be robbed, pillaged, corrupted, and cursed by them, need only turn to the Jews . . .

First, their synagogues should be set on fire, and whatever does not burn up should be covered or spread over with dirt, so that no one may ever be able to see a cinder or stone of it. And this ought to be done for the honour of God and of Christianity in order that God may see that we are Christians, and that we have not wittingly tolerated or approved of such public lying, cursing and blaspheming of his Son and his Christians . . . Secondly, their homes should likewise be broken down and destroyed. For they perpetuate the same things there that they do in their synagogues . . . Thirdly, they should be deprived of their prayerbooks and *Talmuds* in which such idolatry, lies, cursing and blasphemy are taught.

Fourthly, their rabbis must be forbidden under threat of death to teach any more . . . Fifthly, passport and travelling privileges should be absolutely forbidden to the Jews . . . Sixthly, they ought to be stopped from usury . . . Seventhly, let the young and strong Jews and Jewesses be given the flail, the axe, the hoe, the spade, the distaff, and spindle, and let them earn their bread by the sweat of their noses . . . To sum up, dear princes and nobles who have Jews in your domains, if this advice of mine does not suit you, then find a better one so that you may all be free of this insufferable devilish burden – the Jews.

(Martin Luther, *Against the Jews and their Lies*, in CJ, pp. 72–73)

DISCUSSION

1. What was the nature of the Chmielnicki massacre?

2. Discuss the anti-Jewish attitudes of Martin Luther.

FURTHER READING

Blom, J.H.C., Fuks-Mansfeld, Renate G., Schoffer, I. (eds), *The History of the Jews in the Netherlands*, Littman Library, 2002.

Dawidowicz, Lucy S. (ed.), *The Golden Tradition: Jewish Life and Thought in Eastern Europe*, Syracuse University Press, 1996.

Edwards, Joan, *The Jews in Western Europe*, Manchester University Press, 1994.

Elon, Amos, *The Pity of It All: A History of the Jews in Germany, 1743–1933*, Metropolitan, 2002.

Gidal, Nachum T., *The Jews in Germany*, Konemann, 1998.

Hay, Malcolm, *Europe and the Jews*, Academy Chicago Publications, 1992.

Kaplan, Yosef, *An Alternative Path to Modernity: The Sephardi Diaspora in Western Europe*, Brill, 2000.

Pogonowski, Iwo Cyprian, *Jews in Poland: A Documentary History*, Hippocrene, 1993.

Polonsky, Antony, *The Jews in Poland and Russia: A History from 1750 to the Present Day*, Littman Library, 2003.

Roth, Joseph, Hofmann, Michael, *The Wandering Jews*, Granta, 2001.

CHAPTER 40

The Rise of the Hasidic Movement

Timeline:

1700–1760 Baal Shem Tov

1710–1772 Dov Baer

1740–1810 Levi Yitzhak of Berdichev

1747–1812 Shneur Zalman of Lyady

1772 Denunciation of the *Hasidim* by their opponents in Vilna

1780 Jacob Joseph of Polonnoye publishes *Toldot Yaakov Yosef*

1781 Excommunication of *Hasidim* by *Mitnaggedim*

By the middle of the eighteenth century, the Jewish community had suffered numerous waves of persecution and was deeply dispirited by the conversion of Shabbatai Zevi. Following the massacres of the previous century, many Polish Jews became disenchanted with rabbinic Judaism and through Hasidism sought individual salvation by means of religious pietism. The founder of this new movement was Israel ben Eleazar (1700–60), known as the **Baal Shem Tov** or Besht. According to tradition, Israel ben Eleazar was born in southern Poland and in his twenties journeyed with his wife to the Carpathian mountains. In the 1730s he travelled to Mezibozh where he performed various miracles and instructed his disciples in kabbalistic lore. By the 1740s he had attracted a considerable number of disciples who passed on his teaching. After his death in 1760, **Dov Baer** (1710–72) became the leader of this sect and Hasidism spread to southern Poland, the Ukraine and Lithuania.

The growth of this movement engendered considerable hostility on the part of rabbinic authorities. In particular the rabbinic leadership of Vilna issued an edict of **excommunication**; the *Hasidim* were charged with permissiveness in their observance of the commandments, laxity in the study of the Torah, excess in prayer, and preference for the Lurianic rather

than the Ashkenazic prayerbook. In subsequent years the **Hasidim** and their opponents (*mitnaggedim*) bitterly denounced one another. Relations deteriorated further when Jacob Joseph of Polonnoye published a book critical of the rabbinate; his work was burned and in 1781 the *mitnaggedim* ordered that all relations with the *Hasidim* cease.

By the end of the century the Jewish religious establishment of Vilna denounced the *Hasidim* to the Russian government, an act which resulted in the imprisonment of several leaders. Despite such condemnation the Hasidic movement was eventually recognized by the Russian and Austrian governments; in the ensuing years the movement divided into a number of separate groups under different leaders who passed on positions of authority to their descendants.

Hasidim initiated a profound change in Jewish religious pietism. In the medieval period, the *Hasidei Ashkenaz* attempted to achieve perfection through various mystical activities. This tradition was carried on by Lurianic kabbalists who engaged in various forms of self-mortification. In opposition to such ascetic practices, the Besht and his followers emphasized the omnipresence of God rather than the shattering of the vessels and the imprisonment of divine sparks by the powers of evil. For Hasidic Judaism there is

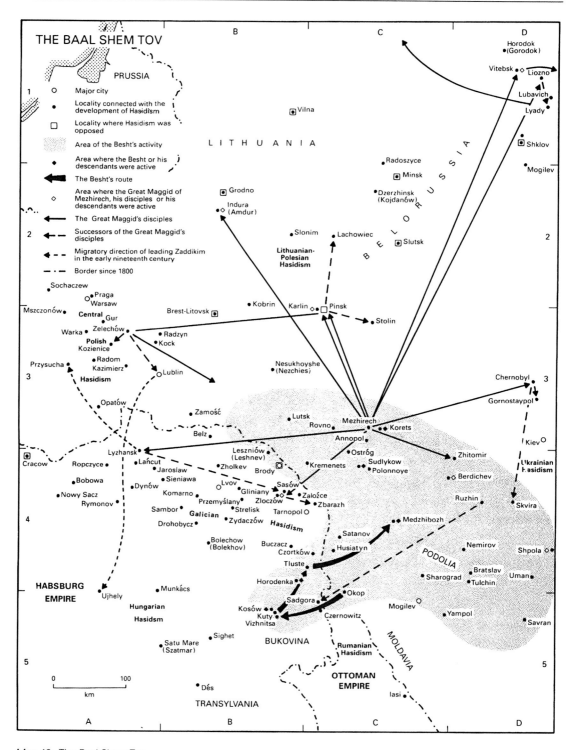

THE BAAL SHEM TOV

○	Major city
●	Locality connected with the development of Hasidism
□	Locality where Hasidism was opposed
(shaded)	Area of the Besht's activity
◆	Area where the Besht or his descendants were active
◀━	The Besht's route
◇	Area where the Great Maggid of Mezhirech, his disciples or his descendants were active
◀───	The Great Maggid's disciples
◀──	Successors of the Great Maggid's disciples
◀- - -	Migratory direction of leading Zaddikim in the early nineteenth century
─·─·─	Border since 1800

PRUSSIA

LITHUANIA

● Vilna

Horodok
●(Gorodok)

Vitebsk ◇ ◇ Liozno

Lubavich

Lyady

● Radoszyce

⊡ Minsk

⊡ Shklov

● Mogilev

⊡ Grodno

Indura
●◇ (Amdur)

● Slonim   ● Lachowiec

Lithuanian-Polesian Hasidism

●Dzerzhinsk
(Kojdanów)

⊡ Slutsk

B
E
L
O
R
U
S
S
I
A

Sochaczew
○ ●Praga
Warsaw

Mszczonów●

Brest-Litovsk ⊡

● Kobrin   Karlin ◇   □ Pinsk

● Stolin

Central   Gur

Warka ● ●Zelechów

Polish
Kozienice

●Radzyn
●Kock

Przysucha ●
●Radom
Kazimierz ●
○Lublin

Hasidism

Nesukhoyshe
●(Nezchies)

Chernobyl ●

Gornostaypol ●

● Opatów

● Zamość

Belz ●

● Lutsk
Rovno ●   Mezhirech ● ◇●Korets

Lyzhansk ●

Ropczyce ●

⊡ Cracow

●Łańcut

Jaroslaw ●
● Sieniawa

Annopol ●

Leszniów
(Leshnev) ●   Ostróg ●
⊙ Brody   Kremenets ●   Sudlykow ●
Polonnoye ●

Zhitomir ●

Kiev ○

Ukrainian Hasidism

● Berdichev

Bobowa ●

● Dynów

Komarno ●
○ Lvov
Gliniany ●   ● Sasów   Załoźce ●

Ruzhin ●

● Nowy Sacz
Rymonov ●

Przemyślany ●
Zloczów ●   Zbarazh ●

Skvira ●

Sambor ●   ●Strelisk
Drohobycz ●   Zydaczów ●   Tarnopol ○

Galician
Hasidism

Medzhibozh ●

Satanov ●

Nemirov ●

Shpola ◇

● Bolechow
(Bolekhov)   Buczacz ●
Czortków ●   Husiatyn ●

PODOLIA

Bratslav ●
Sharograd ●   ●Tulchin

Uman ●

Tluste ●

Horodenka ●

HABSBURG
EMPIRE   Ujhely ●

● Munkács

Hungarian
Hasidsm

Sadgora ●   ●Okop

Kosów ●●
Kuty ●   Vizhnitsa   Czernowitz

Mogilev ○

● Yampol

Savran ●

Satu Mare ●
(Szatmar)   ● Sighet

BUKOVINA

MOLDAVIA

Rumanian
Hasidism

OTTOMAN
EMPIRE

0   100
km

● Dés

TRANSYLVANIA

Iasi ●

Map 49 The Baal Shem Tov

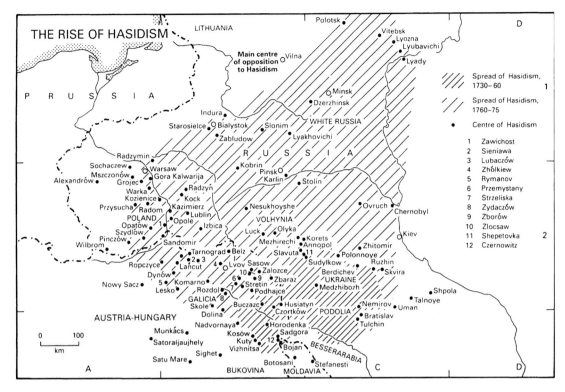

THE RISE OF HASIDISM

Main centre of opposition to Hasidism

///// Spread of Hasidism, 1730–60

///// Spread of Hasidism, 1760–75

• Centre of Hasidism

1 Zawichost
2 Sieniawa
3 Lubaczów
4 Zhólkiew
5 Rymanov
6 Przemystany
7 Strzeliska
8 Zydaczów
9 Zborów
10 Zlocsaw
11 Shepetovka
12 Czernowitz

Map 50   The rise of Hasidism

no place where God is absent; the doctrine of the *tzimtzum* was interpreted by Hasidic sages as only an apparent withdrawal of the divine light. Divine light, they believed, is everywhere. As the Besht explained: in every one of a person's troubles, physical and spiritual, even in that trouble God Himself is there.

For some *Hasidim* cleaving to God (*devekut*) in prayer was understood as the annihilation of selfhood and the ascent of the soul to divine light. In this context joy, humility, gratitude and spontaneity were seen as essential features of Hasidic worship. The central obstacles to concentration in prayer are distracting thoughts; according to Hasidism such sinful intentions contain a divine spark which can be released. In this regard, the traditional kabbalistic stress on theological speculation was replaced by a preoccupation with mystical psychology in which inner bliss was conceived as the highest aim rather than repair (*tikkun*) of the cosmos. For the Beshtian *Hasidim* it was also possible to achieve *devekut* in daily activities including eating,

drinking, business affairs and sex. Such ordinary acts became religious if in performing them one cleaves to God, and *devekut* is thus attainable by all Jews rather than a scholarly elite. Unlike the earlier mystical tradition, Hasidism provided a means by which ordinary Jews could reach a state of spiritual ecstasy. Hasidic worship embraced singing, dancing and joyful devotion in anticipation of the period of messianic redemption.

Another central feature of this new movement was the institution of the **tzaddik** (or *rebbe*) which gave expression to a widespread disillusionment with rabbinic leadership. According to Hasidism, the *tzaddikim* are spiritually superior individuals who have attained the highest level of *devekut*. The goal of the *tzaddik* was to elevate the souls of his flock to the divine light; his tasks included pleading to God for his people, immersing himself in their everyday affairs, and counselling and strengthening them. As an authoritarian figure the *tzaddik* was seen by his followers as possessing miraculous power to ascend to the divine realm. In this context *devekut* to God involved cleaving to the *tzaddik*. Given this emphasis on the role of the *rebbe*, Hasidic literature included summaries of the spiritual and kabbalistic teachings of various famous *tzaddikim* as well as stories about their miraculous deeds. Foremost among these **leading figures** was Zusya of Hanipol (eighteenth century), Shneur Zalman of Liady (1747–1812), Levi Yitzhak of Berdichev (1740–1810), and Nahman of Bratslav (1772–1811). These various leaders developed their own customs, doctrines and music and gathered around themselves disciples who made pilgrimages to their courts in the Ukraine and in Polish Galicia. In central Poland Hasidism emphasized the centrality of faith and Talmudic study; Lubavich *Hasidim* in Lithuania, on the other hand, combined kabbalistic speculation and rabbinic scholarship.

SOURCES

Baal Shem Tov

The founder of the Hasidic movement was Israel ben Eliezer (1700–60), known as the Baal Shem Tov ('Master of the Good Name') or Besht. There are many legends about him:

After his father's death, when the Besht was growing up, the Jews of his community were good to him because they had dearly loved his father. They sent him to a teacher for his education and he was an excellent student and made speedy progress. However, after studying for a few days, he regularly used to run away from school. They used to search for him and would find him sitting by himself in the forest. They thought he behaved like this because he had no one to look after him and was an orphan and had to make his own way. They used to bring him back to his teacher, but the same thing would happen again. He ran away to the woods to be by himself. Eventually they all gave up. They lost interest and no longer sent him to the teacher. So the boy grew up in very unusual circumstances . . .

This is how he earned his living. Two or three times a week his wife used to bring a horse and waggon to him and he dug out clay for bricks. She would take it to the city and this is how she worked for him. The Besht used not to eat anything for long periods of time. When he did want to eat, he would dig a hole in the ground and put a little flour and water into the hole. This would cook in the heat of the sun. That was all he ate after fasting and he spent all his time by himself. After seven years of living like this among the mountains, the time came for him to reveal himself . . . He decided to live in the area of Galicia and he taught there. He could not always

Figure 40 Photograph of a painted portrait of Israel Baal Shem Tov (1700–1760), founder of the Hassidic movement. Copyright Beth Hatefusoth Photo Archive, courtesy of Rachel Yodfat, Israel.

gather together ten men for a service in his house, but he invited a smaller number and prayed with them. He wore the very coarsest clothes and, in his poverty, his toes stuck out of the holes of his shoes. Nonetheless, he always had a ritual bath before he prayed, even on the coldest winter day, and he prayed with such concentration that sweat fell from him in great beads. Although those who were ill often visited him, he would not receive them at first. Then one day they brought a madman (or it may have been a woman) to see him and he would not meet him. That night it was shown to him that he had passed his thirty-sixth year. He checked in the morning and found that this was correct. Then he saw the mad person and healed him . . . From then on people journeyed to see him from far and wide.

(*Praises of the Besht*, in SRJ, pp. 116–117)

The Baal Shem Tov taught that sincere devotion to God was to be valued above traditional rabbinic learning:

> The Besht used to say: No child is born except as the result of joy and pleasure. In the same way, if a man wants his prayers to be heard, he must offer them up with joy and pleasure.
>
> The Besht used to say: Do not laugh at a man who gestures as he prays fervently. He gestures in order to keep himself from distracting thoughts which intrude upon him and threaten to drown his prayer. You would not laugh at a drowning man who gestures in the water in order to save himself.
>
> The Besht used to say: Sometimes a man becomes intoxicated with ecstasy when rejoicing over the law. He feels the love of God burning within him and the words of prayer come rushing out of his mouth. He must pray quickly to keep pace with them all.
>
> (Aaron of Apt, *Kether Shem Tov*, in SRJ, p. 117)

Dov Baer

The followers of the Baal Shem Tov were known as the *Hasidim*. After his death the movement spread throughout eastern Europe and beyond. Famous early Hasidic leaders included Dov Baer:

> Dov Baer used to say: A father was playing with his small son and hid himself for fun. The boy looked for him and finally found him. This increased his father's love for him. In the same way, God sometimes hides himself and when, after looking for him, we eventually find him, God loves us all the more . . .
>
> Dov Baer used to say: When a king is at a celebration, he is more approachable to many people who would otherwise not be allowed into the palace. Similarly when we approach God with joy, He is more approachable.
>
> (S.A. Horodetzky, *The Teaching of the Preacher of Mezeritz*, in SRJ, p. 117)

> Dov Baer used to say: When a child wants something from his father, the father rejoices when he can grant his son's wish. Similarly when a good man wants something, God rejoices in granting his prayer.
>
> (*Letter from Rabbi Baruch of Medziboz*, in SRJ, p. 117)

Hasidic Leaders

The next generation of Hasidic leaders included Levi Yitzhak of Berdichev, Shneur Zalman of Lyady and Elimelech of Lyzhansk:

> Levi Yitzhak of Berdichev used to say: Do not despair if you preach and see no result. You can be sure that the seed you have planted will blossom in the heart of one listener.
>
> (Pinchas of Koretz, *Midrash Pinchas*, in SRJ, p. 118)

> Shneur Zalman used to say: You can recognize a really great man by watching how he talks to ordinary people. It requires real wisdom for a learned man to talk with an ordinary man and hold his attention.
>
> (J.K.K. Rokotz, *Siach Sarfei Kodesh*, in SRJ, p. 118)

> Elimelech of Lyzhansk used to offer the following prayer: O Lord, guard us from selfishness and from pride when we do your will. Guard us from anger and resentment, from tale-bearing and from every other evil. May no jealousy enter our hearts or the hearts of our fellowmen. Give us the power within our hearts to see no evil, but only virtue within our companions.
>
> (Y.A. Kamelhar, *Dor Deah*, in SRJ, p. 118)

Tzaddik

Central to the philosophy of Hasidism is the doctrine of the *tzaddik*, or righteous man. For the *Hasidim*, their *tzaddik* is their spiritual ruler or mentor:

> A Hasidic follower asked Hayim Halberstam of Lublin whether the miracles ascribed to the *tzaddikim* in such books as *Stories of the Tzaddikim* really occurred. He replied: I cannot guarantee that what is written down is true, but I am convinced that a real *tzaddik* can accomplish whatever he wants provided it is in accord with the will of God.
>
> (I. Berger, *Esser Tzachtzochoth*, in SRJ, p. 118)

> A *tzaddik* fell ill and the Baal Shem Tov was asked by his followers to pray for him to be restored to health, but the Baal Shem Tov refused. A few days later, a group of brigands who had planned to raid the town were surprised and arrested by the police. The same day the *tzaddik* recovered from his illness. The Baal Shem Tov explained that the *tzaddik*'s pain had caused the brigands' raid to be deferred until the police could discover them. The sufferings of a *tzaddik* act like a shield.
>
> (Aaron of Apt, *Kether Shem Tov*, in SRJ, p. 118)

> Dov Baer used to explain that the *tzaddik* is like the seed of the world. When a seed is planted, it draws nourishment from the earth and brings forth fruit. Similarly the *tzaddik* draws forth the holy sparks from every soul and brings them heavenwards as an offering to the Creator.
>
> (*Letter from Rabbi Baruch of Medziboz*, in SRJ, p. 119)

Just as the *tzaddik* goes down to the doors of Hell to rescue the souls of the wicked who have retained the thought of repentance because of him, so every day, in this world, the *tzaddik* goes down from his rung in order to join himself with those on a lower level . . . When he again climbs up to his rung, he brings them up with him.

(Jacob Joseph of Polonnoye, *Toledot Ya'akov Yosef*, in SRJ, p. 119)

Ban of Excommunication

An edict of excommunication was issued by the *mitnaggedim* against the *Hasidim*:

As a result of our sins, wicked and worthless men known as the *Hasidim* have left the Jewish fold and have set up their own places of worship. As everyone knows, they conduct their services in a mad and unseemly fashion, following different rituals which do not conform to the teachings of our holy Law . . . The exaggerations and miracle tales which are described in their books are clear and obvious lies and . . . there is even a move to disregard the obligations of the Law of Moses . . . The following are the protective measures agreed at our meeting:

1. We order a fast and public prayer to be kept on 25 *Tevet* of this year . . .
2. Every effort should be made to end the prayer meetings of the heretics.

3. Careful watch should be kept to ensure that no one studies their literature . . .
4. The validity of the ordinances proclaimed in Brody and Vilna are confirmed . . .
5. The animals killed by their ritual slaughters may not be eaten. It is to be regarded as carrion . . .
6. No one is to shelter any member of the *Hasidim* . . .
7. No member of the *Hasidim* may bring a suit in a Jewish court, nor hold a position as Cantor, Rabbi or, as goes without saying, as teacher of children . . .
8. All information, both good and bad, about the *Hasidim* must be brought to the attention of the court.

(*Decree of the Shklov Community*, 1786, in SRJ, p. 122)

Hasidic Authorities

In 1772 under the Vilna Gaon's influence, the Jews of Vilna issued edicts against the *Hasidim*. According to the *Hasidim*, the Hasidic leaders showed great forbearance:

When conflict broke out between the *Hasidim* and the *mitnaggedim*, Rabbi Elijah of Vilna did not argue the matter out. He issued a decree of expulsion against those who followed the Hasidic way and put them all under a ban of excommunication. When Rabbi Dov Baer heard this, he quoted the Law to his disciples: Our enemies follow the commandment, 'You shall remove evil from your midst' (Deut. 21:21). We will follow another commandment: 'You shall not take revenge or bear malice' (Leviticus 19:18).

Rabbi Dov Baer summarized the teachings of the *Hasidim* in the two maxims: Love God and love man. He forbade his followers from indulging in bitter arguments. When eventually, in despair, they issued their own ban against their oppressors, the rabbi was so upset that he fell seriously ill. He did not live to see the full conflict.

(Chaim Bloch, *Gemeinde der Chassidim*, in SRJ, p. 121)

DISCUSSION

1. What were the causes of the Hasidic rebellion against the rabbinic establishment?

2. How did Hasidism alter Jewish religious pietism?

FURTHER READING

Buber, Martin, *The Way of Man: According to the Teaching of Hasidism*, Citadel Press, 1983.

Buber, Martin, *The Origins and Meaning of Hasidism*, Humanity, 1988.

Buber, Martin, *Tales of the Hasidim*, Schocken, 1991.

Goldstein, Niles Eliot, *Forests of the Night: The Fear of God in Early Hasidic Thought*, Jason Aronson, 1996.

Guary, Natan, *Chasidism: Its Development, Theology and Practice*, Jason Aronson, 1997.

Heilman, Samuel, *Defenders of the Faith: Inside Ultra-Orthodox Jewry*, Schocken, 1993.

Jacobson, Yoram, *Hasidic Thought*, Jewish Lights, 1999.

Klein, Eliahu, *Meetings with Remarkable Souls: Legends of the Baal Shem Tov*, Kuperard, 1995.

Lamm, Norman (ed.), *The Religious Thought of Hasidism: Text and Commentary*, KTAV, 1999.

Rabinowicz, Tzvi, *Lithuanian Hasidim*, Vallentine Mitchell, 1970.

Rabinowicz, Tzvi, *World of Hasidism*, Vallentine Mitchell, 1970.

Rabinowicz, Tzvi, *Encyclopedia of Hasidism*, Jason Aronson, 1996.

Rabinowicz, Tzvi, Sacks, Jonathan, *Hasidism in Israel: A History of the Hasidic Movement and Its Masters in the Holy Land*, Jason Aronson, 2000.

Raz, Simcha, *Hasidic Wisdom: Sayings from the Jewish Sages*, Jason Aronson, 1997.

Zinberg, Israel, *Hasidim and Enlightenment*, KTAV, 1975.

CHAPTER 41

The Status of Jewry in Europe

Timeline:

1781 Wilhelm Christian Dohm publishes *Concerning the Amelioration of the Civil Status of the Jews*

1782 Joseph II issues Edict of Toleration

1783 Moses Mendelssohn publishes *Jerusalem*. Beginning of Berlin *Haskalah*

1791 Emancipation of French Jewry

1796 Emancipation of Jews in the Batavian Republic

1797–1799 Emancipation in areas of Italy by French Revolutionary Army

1799 Napoleon becomes First Consul of France

1804 Napoleon crowned Emperor of France

1807 Napoleon summons Sanhedrin in Paris

1814–1815 Congress of Vienna

1848 Revolutions in France and Central Europe

1871 Unification of Germany

In many respects the medieval period extended into the eighteenth century for the Jewish community. Despite the numerous changes taking place in European society, monarchs continued to rule by divine right. In addition the aristocracy was exempt from taxation and enjoyed special privileges; the established Church retained control over religious matters; and merchants and artisans closed ranks against outsiders. At the other end of the social scale peasants continued to be burdened with obligations to feudal masters, and in eastern and central Europe serfs were enslaved and exploited. By 1770 nearly 2 million Jews lived in this environment in Christian Europe. In some countries such as England and Holland they were relatively free from economic and social restrictions. The English and Dutch governments, for example, did not interfere with the private affairs and religious life of the Jewish population. Central European Jewry, however, was subject to a wide range of oppressive legal restrictions, and Jews were confined to special areas of residence. Furthermore, Jews were forced to sew signs on their cloaks or wear special hats to distinguish them from their non-Jewish neighbours.

By the 1770s and the 1780s the treatment of Jews in central Europe was greatly improved due to the influence of such polemicists as Wilhelm Christian Dohm (1751–1820). In an influential tract, *Concerning the Amelioration of the Civil Status of the Jews*, Dohm argued that Jews did not pose any threat and could become valuable and patriotic citizens. A wise and benevolent society, he stressed, should abolish restrictions which prevent the Jewish population from having close contact with Christians and acquiring secular knowledge. All occupations, he argued, should be open to Jews and educational opportunities should be provided. The Holy Roman Emperor Joseph II (1741–90) echoed such sentiments. In 1781 he abolished the Jewish badge as well as taxes imposed on Jewish travellers; in the following year he issued an edict of toleration which granted Jews of Vienna a freedom in trade and industry and the right of residence outside Jewish quarters. Moreover, regulations prohibiting Jews from leaving their homes before noon on Sunday and attending places of public amusement were abolished. Jews were also permitted to send their children to state schools or set up their own educational institutions. In 1784 Jewish judicial autonomy was abolished and three years later some Jews were inducted into the Habsburg army.

As in Germany, reforms in France during the 1770s and 1780s ameliorated the situation of the Jewish population. Though Sephardic Jews in Paris and in the south and south-west lived in comfort and security, the Ashkenazic Jews of Alsace and Lorraine had a traditional Jewish lifestyle and were subject to a variety of disabilities. In 1789 the National Assembly issued a declaration proclaiming that all human beings are born and remain free and equal in rights and that no person should be persecuted for his opinions as long as they do not subvert civil law. In 1790 the Sephardim of south-west France and Jews from Papal Avignon were granted citizenship. This decree was followed in September 1791 by a resolution which granted citizenship rights to all Jews. This change in Jewish status occurred elsewhere in Europe as well – in 1796 the Dutch Jews of the Batavian republic were also granted full citizenship rights and in 1797 the ghettos of Padua and Rome were abolished.

In 1799 Napoleon became the First Consul of France and five years later he was proclaimed Emperor. Napoleon's code of Civil Law propounded in 1804 established the right of all inhabitants to follow any trade and declared equality for all. After 1806 a number of German principalities were united in the French kingdom of Westphalia where Jews were granted the same rights. Despite these advances the situation of Jews did not undergo a complete transformation, and Napoleon still desired to regulate Jewish affairs. In July 1806 he convened an Assembly of Jewish Notables to consider a number of issues: do Jewish marriage and divorce procedures conflict with French civil law? Are Jews allowed to marry Christians? Do French Jews consider Frenchmen their compatriots and is France their country?

In reply the Assembly decreed that Jewish law is compatible with French civil law; Jewish divorce and marriage are not binding unless preceded by a civil act; mixed marriage is legal but cannot be sanctioned by the Jewish faith; France is the homeland of French Jews and Frenchmen should be seen as their kin. In the next year Napoleon summoned a Grand Sanhedrin consisting of rabbis and laymen to confirm the views of the Assembly. This body pledged its allegiance to the Emperor and nullified any features of the Jewish tradition that conflicted with the particular requirements of citizenship. In 1808 Napoleon issued two edicts regarding the Jewish community. In the first he set up a system of district boards of rabbis and laymen (consistories) to regulate Jewish affairs under the supervision of a central body in Paris. These consistories were responsible for maintaining synagogues and religious institutions, enforcing laws of conscription, overseeing changes in occupations ordered by the government and acting as a local police force. Napoleon's second decree postponed, reduced or abrogated all debts owed to Jews, regulated Jewish trade and residence rights and prohibited Jewish army conscripts from hiring substitutes.

After Napoleon's defeat and abdication, the map of Europe was redrawn by the Congress of Vienna between 1814 and 1815 and in addition the diplomats at the Congress issued a resolution that instructed the German confederation to ameliorate the status of the Jews. Yet despite this decree the German governments disowned the rights of equality that had previously been granted to Jews by the French and instead imposed restrictions on residence and occupation. In place of the spirit of emancipation unleashed by the French Revolution, Germany became increasingly patriotic and xenophobic. Various academies maintained that the Jews were 'Asiatic aliens' and insisted that they could not enter into German-Christian culture without converting to Christianity. In 1819 German Jewry was attacked in cities and the countryside during the Hep Hep riots. After 1830 however a more liberal attitude prevailed and various writers advocated a more tolerant approach. The most important Jewish exponent of emancipation, Gabriel Riesser (1806–63), argued that the Jews were not a separate nation and were capable of loving Germany as their homeland. Jewish converts to Christianity such as Heinrich Heine (1797–1856) also defended the rights of Jews during this period.

The French Revolution of 1848 which led to outbreaks in Prussia, Austria, Hungary, Italy and Bohemia forced rulers to grant constitutions which guaranteed freedom of speech, assembly and religion. In Germany a National Assembly was convened to draft a constitution which included a bill of rights designating civil, political and religious liberty for all Germans.

Although this constitution did not come into effect because the revolution was suppressed, the 1850s and 1860s witnessed economic and industrial expansion in Germany in which liberal politicians advocated a policy of civil equality. In 1869 the parliament of the North German Federation proclaimed Jewish emancipation for all its constituents, and in 1871, when all of Germany, excluding Austria, became the German Reich under the Hohenzollern dynasty, Jewish emancipation was complete. All restrictions concerning professions, marriage, real estate and the right to vote were eliminated.

SOURCES

Wilhelm Christian Dohm

By the late eighteenth century, some Christian writers such as Wilhelm Christian Dohm were advocating tolerance for the Jewish population in the face of widespread prejudice:

Only common people believe that it is permissible to deceive a Jew or accuse him of being permitted by his law to deceive non-Jews. It is only bigoted clergy, who have collected tales of the prejudices of the Jews which are used to reinforce their own prejudices . . . Jews have wisdom; they are intelligent and hard-working and dogged. They are capable of finding their own way in every situation . . . Although . . . they have a strong tendency to be on the lookout for every sort of gain and they love usury . . . These defects are made worse in many of them by their self-imposed isolation which is based on their religious laws and on rabbinic sophistry . . . If our arguments are correct, we shall find the oppression under which they suffer and the trade restrictions imposed on them are the real reason for their shortcomings. Therefore it follows that we have also discovered the means by which their faults may be cured and by which they will become both better human beings and more useful citizens.

(Wilhelm Christian Dohm, *Concerning the Amelioration of the Civil Status of Jews*, in SRJ, p. 127)

Edict of Toleration

The Holy Roman Emperor Joseph II issued an edict of toleration in 1781:

In order to make the Jews more useful, discriminatory Jewish clothing which has been worn in the past is now abolished. Within two years the Jews must abandon their own language; from now on all their contracts, bonds, wills, accounts. ledgers, certificates and any legally binding document must be drawn up in German . . . Jews may continue to use their own language during religious services . . . Jews who do not have the opportunity of sending their children to Jewish schools must send them to Christian ones to learn reading, writing, arithmetic and other subjects . . . Jews will also be permitted to attend the imperial universities . . . Leaders of local communities must rationally instruct their people that the Jews may be treated like any other fellow human being. There must be an end to the prejudice and contempt which some subjects, particularly the less intelligent, have shown towards the Jewish people.

(Edict of Joseph II, SRJ, p. 128)

Assembly of Jewish Notables

In 1806 the Emperor Napoleon of France convened an Assembly of Jewish Notables. The question at issue was whether Jews could be full citizens of the host countries:

Do Jews born in France and treated by the law as French citizens, acknowledge France as their country? Do they feel obliged to defend it? Must they keep its laws and follow all the provisions of the Civil Code?

Answer of the Assembly: Men who have adopted a country and who have lived there for many generations and who, even when certain of the country's laws have curtailed their civil rights, are so attached to it that they prefer the misfortune of civil disability to that of leaving, must be seen in France as Frenchmen. Jews regard the obligation of defending France as both an honourable and a precious duty. Jeremiah 29 strongly recommends the Jews to see Babylon as their country, even though they were only to stay there for seventy years. He tells them to cultivate the fields, to build houses, to sow and to plant. The Jews followed his advice to such an extent that, according to Ezra 2, when Cyrus allowed them to return to Jerusalem to rebuild the Temple, only forty-two thousand, three hundred and sixty of them left Babylon. Mostly it was the poor people who went; the rich stayed in Babylon.

Love of one's country is an entirely natural and lively sentiment among the Jews. It is completely in harmony with their religious beliefs that a French Jew in England feels himself to be a stranger, even in the company of English Jews. English Jews feel the same in France. Their patriotism is so great that in the last war French Jews could be found fighting against Jews of other countries with which France was at war. Many of them were honourably wounded and others won on the field of battle fervent testimonies to their valour.

(*Record of the Assembly of Jewish Notables, 1806*, in SRJ, p. 128)

Figure 41 First Great Sanhedrin (supreme court and legislative body of the Jewish people) of French Jews in Paris, 9 February 1807, engraving. Copyright The Art Archive/Fondation Thiers Paris/Dagli Orti.

Napoleon's Sanhedrin

As a result of the Assembly of Jewish Notables, Napoleon revived the institution of the Sanhedrin. Not all reactions were favourable. In 1807 the Holy Synod of the Russian Orthodox Church ordered the following proclamation to be read in all its churches:

> In order to complete the degradation of the Church, (Napoleon) has convened the Jewish synagogues of France, restored the dignity of the rabbis and laid the foundation of a new Hebrew Sanhedrin, the same notorious tribunal which dared to condemn Our Lord and Saviour Jesus Christ to the cross. He now has the audacity to gather together all of the Jews whom God, in his anger, had scattered over the face of the earth, and launch all of them into the destruction of Christ's Church. O unspeakable presumption! Greater than any appalling crime that they should proclaim Napoleon as the Messiah!
>
> (*Edict of the Russian Church, 1807*, in SRJ, p. 129)

Hep Hep Riots

Outbreaks against Jews began in August 1819 in Würzburg and spread throughout German towns and the countryside. The populace was aroused by travelling rioters whose cry was Hep! Hep! In response the Christian mob armed with axes and iron bars proceeded to the Jewish quarter and demolished the synagogue. In Berlin a contemporary account recorded:

> The excesses which have been committed against the Jews in several towns in Germany have given rise to fear amongst the Israelites in this capital; there have been been some small scenes here already. A few of the Jews' enemies paid a fair number of ne'er-do-wells to cry Hep! Hep! under the windows of the country house of a banker of that nation. An old Israelite pedlar of ribbons and pencils was chased by delinquents in the street which echoed with the ominous cry; he made the best of it like a man with a sense of humour and continued on his way laughing and even shouting Hep! Hep! incessantly himself, but having taken it into his head to peer into a shop and shout inside, a woman who happened to be on the threshold dealt him a violent box on the ears, to which he immediately replied with another. A police employee, who was within call, took him under his protection and, to get him out of reach of the ill-treatment to which he was still exposed, conducted him to the police station.
>
> (Leon Poliakov, *History of Anti-Semitism*, in CJ, p. 150)

Heinrich Heine

After Napoleon's defeat at Waterloo in 1815 there was an attempt to turn the clock back. There were serious anti-Jewish riots in Germany, but increasingly, liberal views began to prevail. Heinrich Heine, who was himself a baptized Jew, correctly read the signs of the times:

What is the great question of the age? It is Emancipation! Not just the emancipation of the Irish, the Greeks, the Jews of Frankfurt, the Negroes of the West Indies or of other oppressed groups, but the emancipation of the whole world . . . which even now is pulling away from the leading strings of the aristocracy and the privileged classes.

(Heinrich Heine, *Germany*, in SRJ, p. 129)

DISCUSSION

1. How did the Enlightenment alter the nature of Jewish life in Europe?

2. What were Napoleon's motives in summoning the Sanhedrin?

FURTHER READING

Breuer, Edward, *The Limits of the Enlightenment*, Harvard University Press, 1996.

Cohn-Sherbok, Dan, *Anti-Semitism*, Sutton, 2002.

Eisenbach, Artur, *The Emancipation of the Jews in Poland 1780–1870*, Blackwell, 1991.

Greenberg, Louis, *Jews in Russia: The Struggle for Emancipation*, Schocken, 1988.

Hertzberg, Arthur, *French Enlightenment and the Jews*, Columbia, 1990.

Hess, Jonathan, *Germans, Jews and the Claims of Modernity*, Yale University Press, 2002.

Mahler, Raphael, *Hasidism and the Jewish Enlightenment*, Jewish Publication Society, 1984.

Reinharz, Jehuda, Schatzberg, Walter, *The Jewish Response to German Culture: From the Enlightenment to the Second World War*, Brandeis University Press, 1985.

Schwarzfuchs, Simon, *Napoleon, The Jews and the Sanhedrin*, Routledge, 1979.

Sorkin, David, *Moses Mendelssohn and the Religious Enlightenment*, Peter Halban, 1996.

CHAPTER 42

Jews in Eastern Europe

Timeline:

1791 Jewish merchants prohibited from central Russia, but allowed to settle in Odessa

1804 Statute of Alexander I regularizing the Pale of Settlement

1825–1855 Nicholas I

1824 Russian attempts to deport Jews from the villages

1827 Nicholas I orders Jewish boys to be inducted into the army

1835 Revised Russian code of laws concerning the Jews

1840 Damascus Blood Libel

1840s *Haskalah* spreads to Russia

1844 Government schools established for Jews

1855–1881 Alexander II

1859 Beginning of the easing of restrictions on Jews living outside the Pale of Settlement

1864 Jews admitted to the Russian legal profession

Compared with the west, the social and political conditions of eastern European Jewry were less conducive to emancipation. After the partitions of Poland in the latter half of the eighteenth century and the decision of the Congress of Vienna to place the Duchy of Warsaw under Alexander I, most of Polish Jewry was under Russian rule. At the beginning of the nineteenth century Russia preserved its previous social order: social classes were legally segregated; the aristocracy maintained its privileges; the peasantry lived as serfs; and the Church was under state control. In many towns and villages during this period Jews were in the majority and engaged in a wide range of occupations. In the countryside they worked as leaseholders of estates, mills, forests, distilleries and inns, but increasingly many of these village Jews migrated to larger urban centres where they laboured as members of the working class. Despite this influx into the cities, the Jewish population retained its traditional religious and ethnic distinctiveness.

Initially Catherine the Great exhibited tolerance toward her Jewish subjects, but in 1791 Jewish merchants were prohibited from settling in central Russia. Only in the southern Ukraine were Jews allowed to establish a community; this exception was followed several years later by the granting of permission for Jews to live in other areas such as Kiev. In 1804 Alexander I (1801–25) specified territory in western Russia as an area in which Jews would be allowed to reside, and this was known as the Pale of Settlement. After several attempts to expel Jews from the countryside, the czar in 1817 initiated a new policy of integrating the Jewish community into the population by founding a society of Israelite Christians which extended legal and financial concessions to baptized Jews. In 1824 the deportation of Jews from villages began; in the same year Alexander I died and was succeeded by Nicholas I (1825–55) who adopted a severe attitude to the Jewish community. In 1827 he initiated a policy of inducting Jewish boys into the

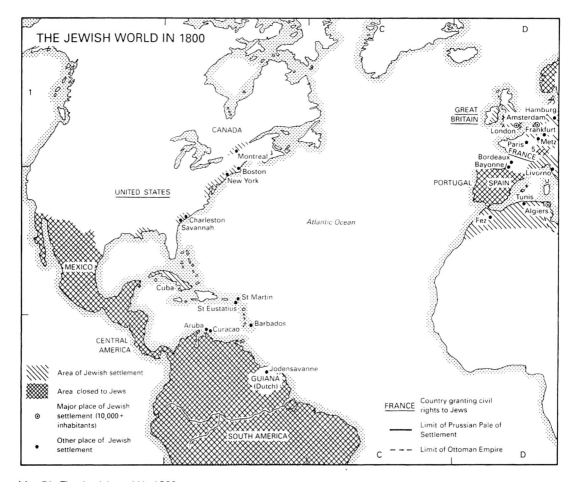

THE JEWISH WORLD IN 1800

	Area of Jewish settlement
	Area closed to Jews
⊙	Major place of Jewish settlement (10,000 + inhabitants)
•	Other place of Jewish settlement

FRANCE — Country granting civil rights to Jews

⎯⎯⎯ Limit of Prussian Pale of Settlement

– – – Limit of Ottoman Empire

Map 51 The Jewish world in 1800

Russian army for a twenty-five-year period in order to increase the number of converts to Christianity. Nicholas I also deported Jews from villages in certain areas; in 1827 they were expelled from Kiev and three years later from the surrounding province. In 1835 the Russian government propagated a revised code of laws to regulate Jewish settlement in the western border. In order to reduce Jewish isolation the government set out to reform education in 1841; a young Jewish educator, Max Lilienthal (1815–82), was asked to establish a number of reformed Jewish schools in the Pale of Settlement which incorporated western educational methods and a secular curriculum. Initially Lilienthal attempted to persuade Jewish leaders that by supporting this project the Jewish community could

improve their lot, but when he discovered that the intention of the czar was to undermine the *Talmud* he left the country. These new schools were established in 1844 but they attracted a small enrolment and the Russian government eventually abandoned its plans to eliminate traditional Jewish education.

In the same year Nicholas I abolished the *kehillot* and put Jewry under the authority of the police as well as municipal government. Despite this policy it was impossible for the Russian administration to carry out the functions of the *kehillot*, and it was recognized that a Jewish body was needed to recruit students for state military schools and to collect taxes. Between 1850 and 1851 the government attempted to forbid Jewish dress, men's sidecurls, and the ritual of shaving women's hair.

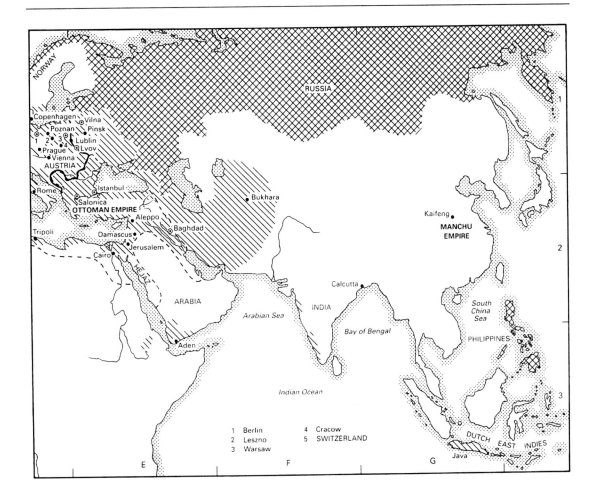

1   Berlin   4   Cracow
2   Leszno   5   SWITZERLAND
3   Warsaw

In 1851 a plan was initiated to categorize all Jews in the country along economic lines. Those who were considered useful subjects included craftsmen, farmers, and wealthy merchants, whereas the vast majority of Jews were liable to further restrictions. After the Crimean War of 1853–6, Alexander II (1855–81) emancipated the serfs, modernized the judiciary and established a system of local self-government. In addition he allowed certain groups, including wealthy merchants, university graduates, certified artisans,

discharged soldiers and all holders of diplomas, to reside outside the Pale of Settlement. As a result Jewish communities appeared in St Petersburg and Moscow. Furthermore, a limited number of Jews were allowed to enter the legal profession and participate in district councils. Government-sponsored Jewish schools also attracted more Jewish students, and in the 1860s and 1870s emancipated Jews began to take an active role in the professions and in Russian economic life.

ALEXANDER I.

Emperor of all the Russias —

From an original Drawing taken in London during his Visit in 1814

Leeds Published by Edwd Baines Sepr 2.1814

Figure 42 Czar Alexander I (1777–1825), engraving by H. Meyer at the time of his visit to England in 1814. Copyright the Mary Evans Picture Library, London.

SOURCES

Delineation of the Pale of Settlement

Under Nicholas I the Pale of Settlement was created, which included fifteen provinces in Western Russia and ten provinces of the former Kingdom of Poland.

A permanent residence is permitted to the Jews: (a) In the provinces: Grodno, Vilna, Volhynia Podolia, Minsk, Ekaterinoslav. (b) In the districts: Bessarabia, Bialystok.

Jews who have gone abroad without a legal exit permit are deprived of Russian citizenship and not permitted to return to Russia.

Within the general area of settlement and in every place where the Jews are permitted permanent residence, they are allowed not only to move from place to place and to settle in accordance with the general regulations, but also to acquire real estate of all kinds, with the exception of inhabited estates, the ownership of which is strictly forbidden to Jews.

(In JMW, p. 379)

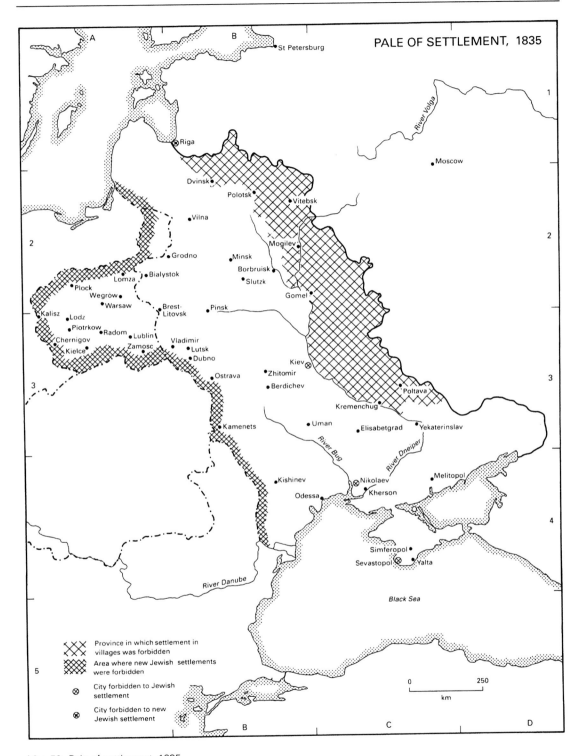

PALE OF SETTLEMENT, 1835

St Petersburg

River Volga

Moscow

Riga

Dvinsk

Polotsk

Vitebsk

Vilna

Mogilev

Minsk

Grodno

Borbruisk

Lomza

Bialystok

Slutzk

Plock

Wegrów

Warsaw

Brest-Litovsk

Gomel

Pinsk

Kalisz

Lodz

Piotrkow

Radom

Lublin

Vladimir

Chernigov

Zamosc

Lutsk

Kielce

Dubno

Ostrava

Kiev

Zhitomir

Poltava

Berdichev

Kremenchug

Kamenets

Uman

Elisabetgrad

Yekaterinslav

River Bug

River Dnieper

Kishinev

Nikolaev

Melitopol

Odessa

Kherson

Simferopol

Sevastopol

Yalta

River Danube

Black Sea

Province in which settlement in villages was forbidden

Area where new Jewish settlements were forbidden

City forbidden to Jewish settlement

City forbidden to new Jewish settlement

0   250
km

Map 52   Pale of settlement, 1835

DISCUSSION

1. Compare and contrast Jewish life in western and eastern Europe during the nineteenth century.

2. Discuss the nature of Russian anti-Semitism in the nineteenth century.

FURTHER READING

Dawidowicz, Lucy G. (ed.), *The Golden Tradition: Jewish Life and Thought in Eastern Europe*, Syracuse University Press, 1996.

Gruber, Ruth Ellen, *Upon the Doorposts of Thy House: Jewish Life in East-Central Europe, Yesterday and Today*, John Wiley and Sons, 1994.

Hay, Malcolm, *Europe and the Jews*, Academy Chicago Publications, 1992.

Haumann, Heiko, *A History of East European Jews*, Central European University Press, 2002.

Heschel, Abraham Joshua, *The Earth is the Lord's: The Inner World of the Jew in Eastern Europe*, Jewish Lights, 1995.

Meltzer, Milton, *World of Our Fathers: The Jews of Eastern Europe*, Farrar Straus and Giroux, 1974.

Pogonowski, Iwo Cyprian, *Jews in Poland: A Documentary History*, Hippocrene, 1993.

Polonsky, Antony, *The Jews in Poland and Russia: A History from 1750 to the Present Day*, Littman Library, 2003.

Zipperstein, Steven J., *The Jews of Odessa: A Cultural History, 1794–1881*, Stanford University Press, 1985.

Zipperstein, Steven J., *Imagining Russian Jewry: Memory, History, Identity*, University of Washington Press, 1999.

CHAPTER 43

The Emergence of Jewish Thought in the Enlightenment

Timeline:

1632–1677 Baruch Spinoza

1729–1786 Moses Mendelssohn

1729–1781 Gotthold Ephraim Lessing

1783 Mendelssohn publishes *Jerusalem*

1783 Production of the first Jewish literary magazine, *The Gatherer*

1820s Spread of *Haskalah* to Austrian Galicia

1821–1832 Publication of *First Fruits of the Times*

1833–1856 Publication of *Vineyard of Delight*

1863 Establishment of the Society for the Promotion of Culture Among the Jews of Russia

The roots of Jewish thought during the Enlightenment go back to seventeenth-century Holland where a number of Jewish thinkers attempted to view the Jewish tradition in the light of the new scientific conception of the world. Uriel Acosta (1590–1640), for example, argued that the Torah was probably not of divine origin since it contained many features contrary to natural law. The greatest of these Dutch Jewish thinkers was Baruch Spinoza (1632–77) who published a treatise, *Tractatus Theologico-Politicus*, in which he rejected the medieval synthesis of faith and reason. In the first section of this work Spinoza maintained that the prophets possessed moral insight rather than theoretical truth. Rejecting the Maimonidean belief that the Bible contains a hidden esoteric meaning, Spinoza argued that the Hebrew Scriptures were intended for the masses. As far as the Torah is concerned, it was not composed in its entirety by Moses – the historical books were compilations assembled by many generations.

For Spinoza the function of religion was to provide a framework for ethical action. Philosophy, on the other hand, is concerned with truth, and philosophers should be free to engage in philosophical speculation unconstrained by religious opinions. It is a usurpation of the social contract and a violation of human rights

to legislate belief. On the basis of this view, Spinoza propounded a metaphysical system based on a pantheistic conception of nature. Beginning with the belief in an infinite, unlimited, self-caused Substance which he conceived as God or nature, Spinoza maintained that Substance possesses a theoretical infinity of attributes, only two of which – extension and thought – are apprehended by human beings. God or nature can also be seen as a whole made up of finite, individual entities. In this way God exists in all things as their universal essence; they exist in God as modifications.

Spinoza's rational reflections on theological matters provided the background to the philosophical enquiries of the greatest Jewish thinker of the Jewish Enlightenment, **Moses Mendelssohn** (1729–86). Born in Dessau, Mendelssohn travelled to Berlin as a young student where he pursued secular as well as religious studies and befriended leading figures of the German Enlightenment, such as Gotthold Ephraim Lessing (1729–81). Under Lessing's influence, Mendelssohn published a number of theological studies in which he argued for the existence of God and creation, and he propounded the view that human reason is able to discover the reality of God, divine providence, and the immortality of the soul. When challenged by a Christian apologist to explain why he remained loyal

Figure 43 Moses Mendelssohn (1729–86), considered to be the father of the Jewish Enlightenment. Copyright the *Jewish Chronicle*, London.

to the Jewish faith, Mendelssohn published a defence of the Jewish religion, *Jerusalem*, or *On Religious Power and Judaism*, in 1783. In this study Mendelssohn contended that no religious institution should use coercion; neither the Church nor the state, he believed, has the right to impose its religious views on the individual. Addressing the question as to whether the Mosaic law sanctions such coercion, Mendelssohn stressed that Judaism does not coerce the mind through dogma. Rather, he stated that the Israelites possess a divine legislation – laws, commandments, statutes, rules of conduct, instruction in God's will and in what they are to do to attain temporal and eternal salvation. In his view, Moses revealed to them these laws and commandments, but not dogmas.

The distinction Mendelssohn drew between natural religion and the Jewish faith was based on three types of truth: logically necessary truth, contingent truths such as the laws of nature, and temporal truths that occur in history. All human beings, he argued, have the innate capacity to discover the existence of God, providence, and the hereafter. But Judaism is uniquely different from other religions in that it contains a revealed law. The Jewish people did not hear God proclaim that He is an eternal, necessary, omnipotent and

omniscient being who rewards and punishes humankind. Instead divine commandments were revealed to God's chosen people. The purpose of this legal code was to make Israel into a priestly people.

For Mendelssohn Jewish law does not give power to the authorities to persecute individuals for holding false doctrines. Yet Jews, he argued, should not absolve themselves from following God's law. Thus, despite Mendelssohn's recognition of the common links between Judaism and other faiths, he followed the traditions of his ancestors and advocated the retention of the distinctive features of the Jewish faith. By combining philosophical theism and Jewish traditionalism, Mendelssohn sought to transcend the constrictions of ghetto life and enter the mainstream of western European culture as an observant Jew.

To bring about the modernization of Jewish life, Mendelssohn also translated the Pentateuch into German so that Jews would be able to learn the language of the country in which they lived, and he spearheaded a commentary on Scripture (the *Biur*) which combined Jewish scholarship with secular thought. Following Mendelssohn's example, a number of Prussian followers known as the *maskilim* fostered a Jewish Enlightenment – the *Haskalah* – which encouraged Jews to abandon medieval patterns of life and thought. The *maskilim* also attempted to reform Jewish education by widening the curriculum to include secular subjects; to further this end they wrote textbooks in Hebrew and established Jewish schools. The *maskilim* also produced the first Jewish literary magazine, *The Gatherer*, in 1783. Contributors to this publication wrote poems and fables in the classical style of Biblical Hebrew and produced studies of Biblical exegesis, Hebrew linguistics and Jewish history.

By the 1820s the centre of this movement had shifted to the Austrian empire. A new journal, *First Fruits of the Times*, was published in Vienna between 1821 and 1832 and was followed between 1833 and 1856 by a Hebrew journal, *Vineyard of Delight*, devoted to modern Jewish scholarship. In the 1840s the *Haskalah* spread to Russia where writers made important contributions to Hebrew literature and translated textbooks and European fiction into Hebrew. During the reign of Alexander II, Hebrew weeklies appeared and the Society for the Promotion of Culture Among the Jews of Russia was established in 1863. In

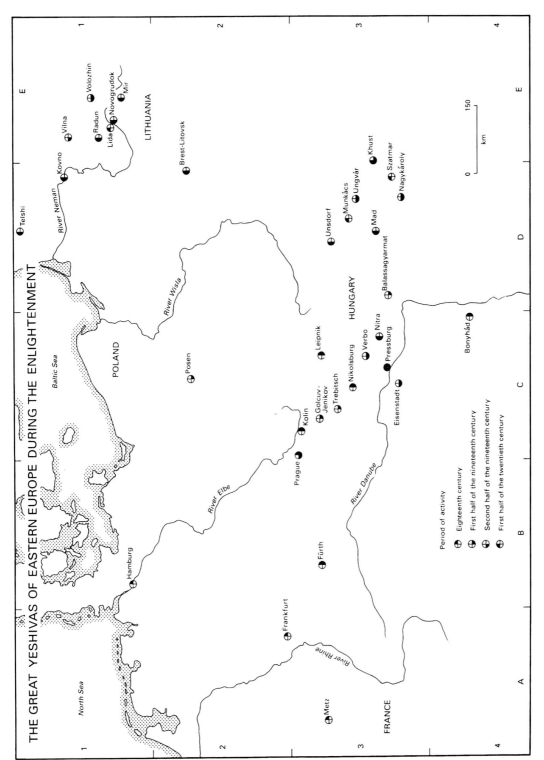

THE GREAT YESHIVAS OF EASTERN EUROPE DURING THE ENLIGHTENMENT

North Sea

Baltic Sea

LITHUANIA

Telshi

Kovno
Vilna
Radun
Lida
Novogrudok
Mir
Volozhin

River Neman

Brest-Litovsk

POLAND

River Wisla

Posen

Hamburg

River Elbe

Prague
Kolin

Golcuv-
Jenikov
Trebitsch

Leipnik

Nikolsburg
Verbo
Nitra
Pressburg

Unsdorf

Munkács
Ungvár
Mad

HUNGARY

Khust
Szatmar
Nagykároly

Balassagyarmat

Eisenstadt

Bonyhád

Fürth

River Danube

Frankfurt

River Rhine

Metz

FRANCE

Period of activity

Eighteenth century

First half of the nineteenth century

Second half of the nineteenth century

First half of the twentieth century

0   150
km

Map 53 The great yeshivas of eastern Europe during the Enlightenment

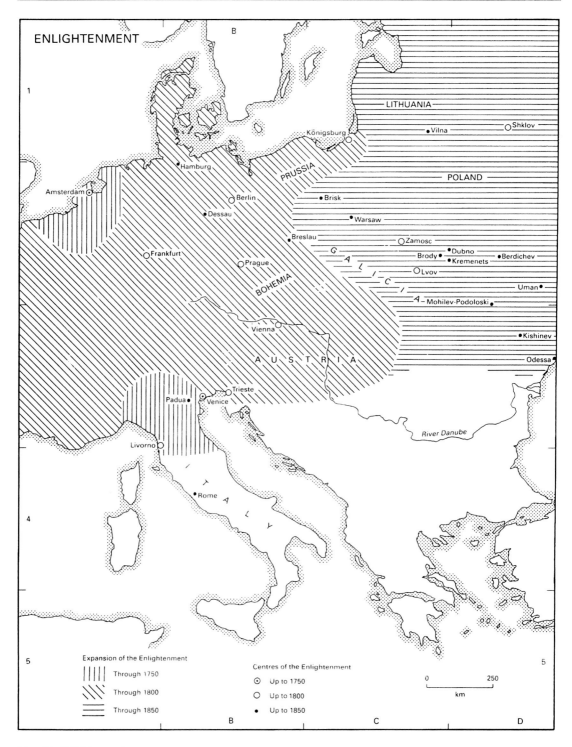

ENLIGHTENMENT

LITHUANIA

●Vilna   ○Shklov

Königsburg

Hamburg

PRUSSIA

Amsterdam

POLAND

Berlin   ●Brisk

Dessau   ●Warsaw

Breslau   ○Zamosc

Frankfurt   Brody● ●Dubno ●Berdichev
Prague   ●Kremenets

BOHEMIA   ○Lvov

Uman●

Mohilev-Podoloski●

Vienna

AUSTRIA   ●Kishinev

Odessa

Trieste

Padua● ○Venice   River Danube

Livorno○

ITALY

●Rome

Expansion of the Enlightenment

||||| Through 1750

\\\\\ Through 1800

≡≡≡ Through 1850

Centres of the Enlightenment

⊙ Up to 1750

○ Up to 1800

● Up to 1850

0   250
km

B   C   D

Map 54 Enlightenment

the next two decades *maskilim* produced works of social and literary criticism. These thinkers, however, were not typical of the Jewish masses. Many lived isolated lives because of their support of the Austrian and Russian governments' efforts to reform Jewish life.

In addition, they were virulently critical of traditional rabbinic Judaism and so were regarded with suspicion and hostility by the religious establishment which endeavoured to perpetuate the faith of their fathers.

SOURCES

Moses Mendelssohn

Moses Mendelssohn was the most important thinker of the *Haskalah*; he worked tirelessly for freedom of conscience of religion. Not only did he translate the Pentateuch into German, he also encouraged the modernization of Jewish education to include the teaching of secular culture. He advised other Jews:

> Adopt the customs and constitution of the country in which you live, but also be careful to follow the religion of your fathers. As well as you can you must carry both burdens. It is not easy because, on the one hand, people make it hard for you to carry the burden of civil life because of your faithfulness to your religion and, on the other hand, the climate of the times makes keeping religious law harder than it need be in some respects. Nevertheless you must try. Stand fast in the place you have been allocated by Providence and submit to everything that happens to you as you were commanded long ago by your law giver. Indeed, I do not understand how those who are part of the household of Jacob can with a good conscience not fully observe the Jewish law.
>
> (Moses Mendelssohn, *Jerusalem*, in SRJ, p. 130)

According to Mendelssohn, Judaism does not contain dogma; instead, it is based on divine legislation which is obligatory on all Jews:

> I believe that Judaism knows of no revealed religion in the sense in which Christians understand this term. The Israelites possess a divine legislation – laws, commandments, ordinances, rules of life, instruction in the will of God as to how they should conduct themselves in order to attain temporal and eternal felicity. Propositions and prescriptions of this kind were revealed to them by Moses in a miraculous and supernatural manner, but no doctrinal opinions, no saving truths, no universal propositions of reason. These the Eternal reveals to us and to all other men, at all times, through nature and thing, but never through word and script.
>
> (Moses Mendelssohn, *Jeruslem*, in JMW, pp. 97–98)

DISCUSSION

1. In what ways did Moses Mendelssohn bring about a transformation of Jewish life and thought?

2. Discuss the reaction of the Jewish religious establishment to the activities of the *maskilim*.

FURTHER READING

Altmann, Alexander, *Moses Mendelssohn*, Routledge 1973.

Arkush, Allan, *Moses Mendelssohn and the Enlightenment*, State University of New York Press, 1994.

Birnbaum, Pierre, Katznelsohn, Ira (eds), *Paths of Emancipation: Jews, States and Citizenship*, Princeton University Press, 1995.

Frankel, Jonathan, Zipperstein, Steven J. (eds), *Assimilation and Community: The Jews in Nineteenth-Century Europe*, Cambridge University Press, 1992.

Katz, Jacob, *Out of the Ghetto: The Social Background of Jewish Emancipation, 1770–1870*, Harvard University Press, 1979.

Katz, Jacob (ed.), *Toward Modernity: The European Jewish Model*, Transaction Publ., 1987.

Malino, Frances, Sorkin, David (eds), *From East and West: Jews in a Changing Europe, 1780–1870*, Blackwell, 1991.

Mendes-Flohr, Paul R. and Reinharz, Jehuda (eds), *The Jew in the Modern World: A Documentary History*, Oxford University Press, 1995.

Meyer, Michael A., *The Origins of the Modern Jew: Jewish Identity and European Culture in Germany, 1749–1824*, Wayne State University Press, 1967.

Sorkin, David, *Moses Mendelssohn and the Religious Enlightenment*, Peter Haldau, 1996.

CHAPTER 44

The Origins of Reform

Timeline:

1768–1828 Israel Jacobson

1794–1886 Leopold Zunz

1801 Israel Jacobson establishes a boarding school for boys in Seesen, Westphalia

1801–1875 Zacharias Frankel

1818 Hamburg Temple established

1819–1900 Isaac Mayer Wise

1823 Publication of Leopold Zunz's *Sermons of the Jews*

1830s German-Jewish immigration to the United States

1836 Samson Raphael Hirsch publishes *The Nineteen Letters on Judaism*

1838 Abraham Geiger appointed rabbi of Breslau

1842 Society of the Friends of Reform established

1844–1846 Reform synods in Germany

1853 Publication of Heinrich Graetz's *History of the Jews*

1854 Breslau Seminary opened

1872 Reform rabbinic seminary founded in Berlin

1873 Union of American Hebrew Congregations for Reform synagogues founded

1875 Hebrew Union College for Reform rabbis opened in Cincinnati, Ohio

1885 Pittsburgh Platform

1887 Jewish Theological Seminary established in New York

The Enlightenment brought about major changes in Jewish life. No longer were Jews insulated from non-Jewish currents of culture and thought, and this transformation of Jewish existence led many Jews to seek a modernization of Jewish worship. At the beginning of the nineteenth century the Jewish financier and communal leader **Israel Jacobson** (1768–1828) initiated a programme of reform. He founded a boarding school for boys in Seesen, Westphalia in 1801, and subsequently established other schools throughout the kingdom. In these new foundations general subjects were taught by Christian teachers while a Jewish instructor gave lessons about Judaism. The consistory under Jacobson's leadership also introduced external reforms to the Jewish worship service including choral singing, hymns and addresses, and prayers in German. In 1810 Jacobson built the first Reform temple next to the school which was dedicated in the presence of Christian clergy and dignitaries.

After Napoleon's defeat Jacobson moved to Berlin where he sought to put these principles into practice by founding the Berlin Temple. In **Hamburg** in 1818 a Reform Temple was opened in which a number of innovations were made to the liturgy including prayers and sermons in German as well as choral singing and organ music. The central aim of these early reformers was to adapt Jewish worship to contemporary aesthetic standards. For these innovators, the informality of the traditional worship service seemed foreign and undignified, and they therefore insisted on greater

Figure 44 Israel Jacobson (1768–1828), a lay leader, who began a structured programme of reforming synagogue practice in the nineteenth century.

decorum, more unison in prayer, a choir, hymns and music responses as well as alterations in prayers and the length of the service. Yet for some Jews influenced by the Romantic movement these modifications were insufficient. Two of Moses Mendelssohn's daughters, for example, became Christian converts as did Henriette Herz (1764–1847) and Rahel Varnhagen (1771–1883) whose literary salons in Berlin were attended by leading German intellectuals. These women longed for a faith which would provide sublime devotion and mystical bliss.

Such Romantic concern also generated a new intellectual development within post-Enlightenment Jewry: the establishment of a Society for the Culture and Academic Study of Judaism. This discipline encouraged the systematic study of history and a respect for historical fact. The purpose of this new approach to the past was to gain a true understanding of the origins of the Jewish tradition in the history of

western civilization, and in this quest the philosophy of Hegel had a profound impact. In 1824, however, the society collapsed and several of its members such as the poet Henrich Heine and the historian of law Eduard Gans converted to Christianity to advance their careers.

In response to these developments a number of Orthodox Jews asserted that any alteration to the tradition was a violation of the Jewish heritage. For these traditionalists the written and oral Torah constituted an infallible chain of divinely revealed truth. The most prominent of these scholars was **Samson Raphael Hirsch** (1808–88) who was educated at a German gymnasium and the University of Bonn. At the age of twenty-two Hirsch was appointed as Chief Rabbi of the Duchy of Oldenburg. In 1836 he published *The Nineteen Letters on Judaism*, a defence of Orthodoxy in the form of essays by a young rabbi to a friend who questioned the importance of remaining a Jew.

According to Hirsch, the purpose of life is not to attain personal happiness and perfection; rather, humans should strive to serve God by obeying His will. To serve as an example of such devotion, the Jewish people was formed so that through its way of life all people would come to know that true happiness lies in obeying God. Thus the people of Israel were given the Promised Land in order to be able to keep God's law. When the Jewish nation was exiled, they were able to fulfil this mission by remaining loyal to God and to the Torah despite constant persecution and suffering. According to Hirsch, the purpose of God's commands is not to repress physical gratification or material prosperity. Rather the aim of observing God's law is to lead a religious life thereby bearing witness to the messianic ideal of universal brotherhood. In this light, Reform Judaism was castigated for abandoning this sacred duty. For Hirsch citizenship rights are of minor importance since Jewry is united by a bond of obedience to God's laws.

Despite Hirsch's criticisms of reforming tendencies, a number of German rabbis who had been influenced by the Enlightenment began to re-evaluate the Jewish tradition. In this undertaking the achievements of Jewish scholars such as **Leopold Zunz** (1794–1886), who engaged in the scientific study of Judaism, had a profound impact. As this new movement began to grow, **Orthodox** authorities vigorously attacked its leadership and ideals. In 1838, for example, when Abraham Geiger was appointed as second rabbi of Breslau, the Chief Rabbi of the city, Solomon Tiktin, denounced him as a radical. According to Tiktin, anyone who does not subscribe to the inviolable and absolute truth of tradition could not serve with him. Tiktin's allies joined in this protest and declared Geiger unfit for the position. In 1842 Tiktin published a tract in which he insisted on the validity of Jewish law and the authority of the rabbinic tradition. In response Geiger's supporters produced a defence of religious reform.

During this period Reform Judaism spread to other countries, but it was in Frankfurt that Reform became most radical. In 1842 the Society of the Friends of Reform was founded and published a proclamation justifying their innovative approach to tradition. In the declaration of their principles, the society declared that they recognized the possibility of unlimited progress in the Jewish faith and rejected the authority of the legal code as well as the belief in messianic redemption. Furthermore, members of the society considered circumcision a barbaric rite which should be eliminated from Judaism. A similar group, the Association for the Reform of Judaism was founded in Berlin in 1844 and under the leadership of Samuel Holdheim (1806–60) called for major changes in the Jewish tradition.

In 1844 the first Reform synod took place at Brunswick in which the participants advocated the formulation of a Jewish creed and the modification of Sabbath and dietary laws as well as the traditional liturgy. This consultation was followed by another conference in 1845 in Frankfurt which recommended that petitions for the return to Israel and the restoration of the Jewish state be omitted from the prayerbook. At this meeting one of the more conservative rabbis, Zacharias Frankel of Dresden (1801–75), expressed his dissatisfaction with the decision of the synod to regard the use of Hebrew in worship as advisable rather than necessary and resigned from the Assembly. Subsequently Frankel became head of a Jewish theological seminary in Breslau which was based on free enquiry combined with a commitment to the Jewish tradition. In 1846 a third synod took place at Breslau and discussed Sabbath observance. Though these reformers

upheld the rabbinic ordinances against work on the Sabbath, they stated that the *Talmudic* injunctions regarding the boundary for walking on the Sabbath were no longer binding. Further, they stipulated that the second day observance of festivals should be eliminated.

The revolution of 1848 and its aftermath brought about the cessation of these conferences, and nearly a generation passed before reformers met again to formulate a common policy. In 1868 twenty-four rabbis assembled at Cassel to lay the foundations for a synodal conference of rabbis, scholars and communal leaders. In the following year over eighty congregations were represented when this gathering met at Leipzig. Two years later another synod took place in Augsburg which dealt with pressing theological and practical problems.

The first signs of Reform appeared in the United States in 1824 when a small group of congregants in Charleston, South Carolina, attempted to introduce some of the reforms of Germany's Hamburg Temple into synagogue worship. In the period preceding and following the revolution of 1848, there was an outpouring of Jews including some reformers from Germany to the United States; many of these immigrants settled in New York. By 1842 there were three German congregations in New York City, and three years later Congregation Emanuel was organized and introduced various reforms in worship. Among these German newcomers were several Reform rabbis who had taken part in the early European Reform synods and were anxious to initiate a policy of Reform in the New World.

Prominent among these early reformers were David Einhorn of Har Sinai Congregation in Baltimore and Samuel Adler and Gustave Gottheil of Temple Emanuel in New York, but it was not until Isaac Mayer Wise (1819–1900) exercised his leadership and organizing skills that Reform Judaism in America reached maturity. Settling in Cincinnati, Ohio, he published a new Reform prayerbook as well as several Jewish newspapers. Wise also directed his energies to convening an American synod. After several abortive attempts at rabbinic union, the first Conference of American Reform Rabbis took place in Philadelphia in 1869; this was followed in 1873 by the founding of the Union of American Hebrew Congregations.

Two years later Wise established the Hebrew Union College, the first Reform rabbinical seminary on American soil. But the principles of American Reform Judaism were not explicitly set out until 1885 when a gathering of Reform rabbis met in Pittsburgh. Their deliberations resulted in the adoption of a formal set of principles, the Pittsburgh Platform.

Simultaneously, another non-Orthodox branch of Judaism – Conservative Judaism – underwent significant development in the United States. As we noted, in 1845 **Zacharias Frankel** broke ranks with other reformers and subsequently became the head of the Jewish Theological Seminary in Breslau. In the United States a number of like-minded adherents of the positive-historical approach to Judaism estab-lished the Jewish Theological Seminary in 1887 in New York, which was later headed by the Cambridge scholar Solomon Schechter. It was Schechter's desire to combine Jewish traditionalism with a commitment to the scientific study of Judaism so as to build a school of learning, which would embrace all the departments of Jewish thought. Disdainfully, Schechter rejected both Reform and Orthodoxy; instead, he emphasized the importance of traditional rituals, customs and observances, as well as belief, while simultaneously stressing the need for a historical perspective. As a champion of such an evolutionary understanding of Jewish civilization, Schechter pressed for the estab-lishment of a union of congregations sympathetic to Conservatism.

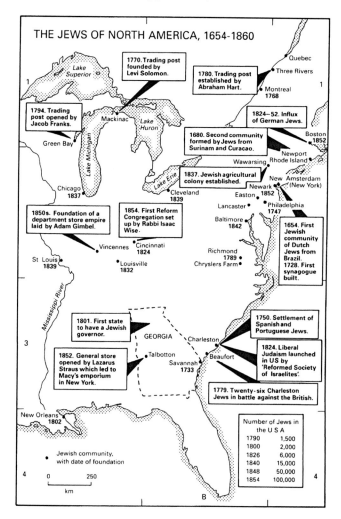

THE JEWS OF NORTH AMERICA, 1654-1860

1770. Trading post founded by Levi Solomon.

1780. Trading post established by Abraham Hart.

1794. Trading post opened by Jacob Franks.

1824–52. Influx of German Jews.

1680. Second community formed by Jews from Surinam and Curacao.

1837. Jewish agricultural colony established.

1850s. Foundation of a department store empire laid by Adam Gimbel.

1854. First Reform Congregation set up by Rabbi Isaac Wise.

1654. First Jewish community of Dutch Jews from Brazil. 1728. First synagogue built.

1801. First state to have a Jewish governor.

1750. Settlement of Spanish and Portuguese Jews.

1852. General store opened by Lazarus Straus which led to Macy's emporium in New York.

1824. Liberal Judaism launched in US by 'Reformed Society of Israelites'.

1779. Twenty-six Charleston Jews in battle against the British.

Quebec
Three Rivers
Montreal 1768
Boston 1852
Newport Rhode Island
Wawarsing
New Amsterdam (New York)
Newark 1852
Easton 1852
Lancaster
Philadelphia 1747
Baltimore 1842
Richmond 1789
Chryslers Farm
GEORGIA
Charleston
Talbotton
Savannah 1733
Beaufort

Lake Superior
Lake Huron
Mackinac
Green Bay
Lake Michigan
Chicago 1837
Lake Erie
Cleveland 1839
Vincennes
Cincinnati 1824
St Louis 1839
Louisville 1832
Mississippi River
New Orleans 1802

• Jewish community, with date of foundation

0   250
km

Number of Jews in the U S A	
1790	1,500
1800	2,000
1826	6,000
1840	15,000
1848	50,000
1854	100,000

Map 55 The Jews of North America, 1654–1860

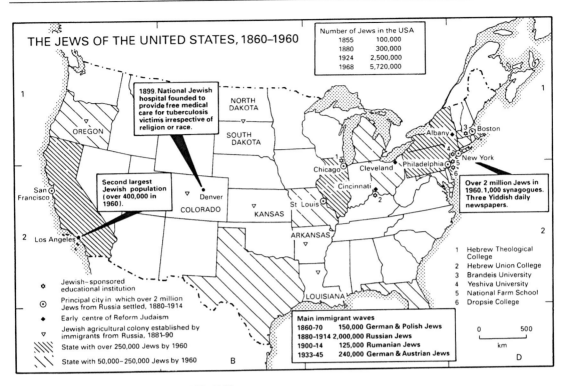

Map 56 Jews of the United States, 1860–1960

SOURCES

Israel Jacobson

As a result of the *Haskalah*, Jews were no longer insulated from the currents of European civilization. At the beginning of the nineteenth century a programme of religious reform was initiated and the first Reform Temple was opened in Seesen, Westphalia in 1810. In his address, the founder, Israel Jacobson, emphasized the need for such religious change:

> Let me be frank, my brothers, our ritual is weighed down with religious customs, which are offensive both to reason and to our Christian friends. The sacredness of our religion is desecrated and the reasonable man dishonoured if too much emphasis is put upon such customs. On the other hand, a man is greatly respected if he encourages himself and his friends to dispense with them . . . And you, my other greatly honoured friends, who do not share some aspects of my faith and identify yourselves by a different name, I hope I have full agreement of your sympathetic hearts for the principles behind this Temple building and for our hopes for a happier future for my co-religionists. Our intentions in no way contradict the principles of pure religion, the demands of reason, general morality or your own humanitarian attitude. Therefore I am sure that you will receive my brothers warmly, that you will not reject them, as too often your ancestors did, but instead that you will lovingly accept them into your business and social circles.
>
> (Israel Jacobson, *Dedication Address*, in SRJ, pp. 131–132)

Hamburg Reform Temple

Another Reform Temple was founded in Hamburg in 1818 where the congregation issued its own prayerbook:

> Public worship has for some time been neglected by too many because there is less and less knowledge of the language in which it is traditionally conducted and also because many other corruptions have crept in over the years. Because of this, the undersigned, convinced of the necessity of restoring pubic worship to its proper place and dignity, have combined to follow the example of several Israelitish congregations, particularly the one in Berlin. They plan to arrange in this city, together with others of a like mind, a dignified and orderly ritual according to which services will be conducted on the Sabbath, on the holy days, and on other solemn occasions. They will be conducted in their own Temple, especially built for this purpose.
>
> (*Constitution of the Hamburg Temple*, in SRJ, p. 132)

Orthodox Critique of Reform

Responding to the reforms made to Jewish worship, the Orthodox were vehemently critical:

> It is forbidden to change anything in the order of prayer as it was handed down to us from earliest times.
>
> It is forbidden in the synagogue to pray in any language except the holy language, as has been used in all Israel.
>
> It is forbidden to play on any musical instruments in the synagogue either on Sabbath or on holidays, even if the player is not a Jew.
>
> (*These are the Words of the Covenant*, in SRJ, p. 132)

Samson Raphael Hirsch

The most eloquent critic of Reform Judaism, Samson Raphael Hirsch was the founder of Neo-Orthodoxy in the middle of the nineteenth century:

It was not the 'Orthodox' Jews who introduced the word 'orthodoxy' into Jewish discussion. It was the modern 'progressive' Jews who first applied this name to 'old', 'backward' Jews as a derogatory term. This name was at first resented by 'old' Jews. And rightly so. 'Orthodox' Judaism does not know any varieties of Judaism. It conceives Judaism as one and indivisible. It does not know a Mosaic, prophetic and rabbinic Judaism, nor Orthodox and Liberal Judaism. It only knows Judaism and non-Judaism. It does not know Orthodox and Liberal Jews. It does indeed know conscientious and indifferent Jews, good Jews, bad Jews or baptised Jews; all, nevertheless, Jews with a mission which they cannot cast off. They are only distinguished accordingly as they fulfil or reject their mission.

(Samson Raphael Hirsch, *Religion Allied to Progress*, in JMW, p. 198)

According to Samson Raphael Hirsch, traditional Judaism should be combined with a recognition of the importance of modern life:

Judaism never remained aloof from true civilization and progress; in almost every era its adherents were fully abreast of contemporary learning and very often excelled their contemporaries. If in recent centuries German Jews remained more or less aloof from European civilization the fault lay not in their religion but in the tyranny which confined them by force within the walls of their ghettoes and denied them intercourse with the outside world . . .

Our aims also include the conscientious promotion of education and culture, and we have clearly expressed this in the motto of our Congregation: An excellent thing is the study of the Torah combined with the ways of the world (*Yafeh talmud torah im derekh erez*) – thereby building on the same foundations as those which were laid by our sages of old.

(Samson Raphael Hirsch, *Religion Allied to Progress*, in JMW, p. 200)

Leopold Zunz

Leopold Zunz pursued research into Jewish history as a private scholar. Modern Jewish studies are indebted to his pioneering efforts. In this essay published in 1818, he presents a programme for the scientific study of Judaism:

The development of our science in a grand style is a duty, one whose weight increases because of the fact that the complex problem of the fate of the Jew may derive a solution, if only in part, from this science . . .

How is it possible, one may ask, that at a time when all science and all of man's doings have been illumined in brilliant rays, when the most remote corners of the earth have been reached, the most obscure languages studied and nothing seems too insignificant to assist in the construction of wisdom, how is it possible that our science (i.e., the academic study of rabbinic literature) alone lies neglected? What hinders us from fully knowing the contents of rabbinic literature, from understanding it, from properly interpreting it, from estimating its proper worth, from surveying it at ease? (We who have no fear of being misunderstood in this matter. The entire literature of the Jews, in its widest scope, is presented here as the object of scholarly research; in this context it is not at all our concern whether the context of this entire literature should, or could, also be the norm for our own judgment.)

(Leopold Zunz, *On Rabbinic Literature*, in JMW, p. 222)

Figure 45 Leopold Zunz (1794–1886), one of the founders of the 'scientific investigation of Judaism' and a leading advocate of Jewish reform. Portrait, 1875, Ölauf Leinwand, 44 × 33 cm, Israel Museum, Jerusalem. Photo copyright Jens Ziehe, Berlin.

Zacharias Frankel

Zacharias Frankel left the Reform Synod at Frankfurt because of the radical stance adopted by its participants; in his view, a less revolutionary approach should be adopted by reformers:

> Maintaining the integrity of Judaism simultaneously with progress, this is the essential problem of the present. Can we deny the difficulty of a satisfactory solution? Where is the point where the two apparent contraries can meet? . . . In order to have a conception of what changes should and can be introduced, we must ask ourselves the question – does Judaism allow any changes in any of its religious forms? Does it consider all of them immutable, or can they be altered? Without entering into the citation of authorities pro and con, we may point out that Judaism does indeed allow changes. The early teachers, by interpretation, changed the literal meaning of the Scriptures; later scholars that of the *Mishnah*, and the post-*talmudic* scholars that of the *Talmud*. All these interpretations were not intended as speculation. They addressed themselves to life precepts . . .
>
> We have, then, reached a decisive point in regard to moderate changes, namely, that they must come from the people and that the will of the entire community must decide. Still, this rule alone may accomplish little. The whole community is a heavy unharmonious body and its will is difficult to recognize. It comes to expression only after many years. We must find a way to carry on such changes in the proper manner, and this can be done by the help of the scholars . . .
>
> The scholars thus have an important duty in order to make their work effective. It is to guard the sense of piety of the people and to raise their spirit to the height of the great ideas. For this they need the confidence of the people. Opposition to the views of the people, such as some reformers display, is unholy and fruitless. The teacher thereby loses the power to make the essence of faith effective, for in place of that confidence which is the basis in correct relations between teacher and community there comes mistrust and unwillingness to follow. The truths of faith must be brought nearer to the people so that they may learn to understand the divine content within them and thus come to understand the spiritual nature and inner worth of the forms which embody these truths.
>
> (Zacharias Frankel, *On Changes in Judaism*, in JMW, pp. 194–196)

Isaac Mayer Wise

The leader of American Reform Judaism in the United States in the nineteenth century, Isaac Mayer Wise was the founder of the major institutions of Reform Judaism. In 1854, he stressed the need for an American rabbinical college:

> We ought to be American Israelites, i.e. Americans as men and citizens and Israelites in our religion . . . If this truth was acknowledged we would be united at one; and if our ministers were thoroughly Americanized the fact would successfully be urged upon the people. Let us educate our ministers here, in our own college, and we will soon have American ministers, American congregations, and an Amercian Union of Israelites for religious and charitable purposes.
>
> (Isaac Mayer Wise, *Appeal*, 1854, in SRJ, p. 134)

Pittsburgh Platform

The principles of Reform Judaism in the United States were established at the Pittsburgh Conference in 1885. These came to be known as the Pittsburgh Platform:

First . . . We hold that Judaism presents the highest conception of the God-idea as taught in our holy scriptures and developed and spiritualized by the Jewish teachers in accordance with the moral and philosophical progress of their respective ages . . .

Second . . . We hold that the modern discoveries of scientific researches in the domains of nature and history are not antagonistic to the doctrines of Judaism, the Bible reflecting the primitive ideas of its own age and at times clothing its conception of divine providence and justice dealing with man in miraculous narratives.

Third . . . Today we accept as binding only the moral laws and maintain only such ceremonies as elevate and sanctify our lives, but reject all such as are not adapted to the views and habits of modern civilization.

Fourth . . . We hold that all such Mosaic and rabbinical laws as regulate diet, priestly purity and dress originated in ages and under the influence of ideas altogether foreign to our present mental and spiritual state . . . Their observance in our day is apt rather to obstruct than to further modern spiritual elevation.

Fifth . . . We consider ourselves no longer a nation but a religious community, and therefore expect neither a return to Palestine, nor a sacrificial worship under the administration of the sons of Aaron, nor the restoration of any of the laws concerning the Jewish state.

Sixth . . . We recognize in Judaism a progressive religion, ever striving to be in accord with the postulates of reason . . . We acknowledge that the spirit of broad humanity of our age is our ally in the fulfilment of our mission, and therefore we extend the hand of fellowship to all who co-operate with us in the establishment of the reign of truth and righteousness among men.

Seventh . . . We reassert the doctrine of Judaism, that the soul of man is immortal . . . We reject as ideas not rooted in Judaism the belief both in bodily resurrection and in *Ghenna* (Hell) and Eden, as abodes for everlasting punishment or reward.

Eighth . . . In full accord with the spirit of Mosaic legislation, which strives to regulate the relations between rich and poor, we deem it our duty to participate in the great task of modern times, to solve on the basis of justice and righteousness the problems presented by the contrasts and evils of the present organization of society.

(*Pittsburgh Platform*, in SRJ, pp. 135–136)

DISCUSSION

1. What were the main criticisms levelled by the Orthodox against the Reformers?

2. How did the Pittsburgh Platform of Reform principles differ from Maimonides' principles of the Jewish faith?

FURTHER READING

Davis, Moshe, *The Emergence of Conservative Judaism: The Historical School in Nineteenth Century America*, Greenwood, 1977.

Geiger, Abraham, *Judaism and Its History*, University Press of America, 1985.

Gillman, Neil, *Conservative Judaism: The New Century*, Behrman, 1993.

Kaplan, Dana Evan, *Contemporary Debates in American Reform Judaism: Conflicting Visions*, Routledge, 2000.

Kershen, Anne J. (ed.), *150 Years of Progressive Judaism in Britain 1840–1990*, London Museum of Jewish Life, 1990.

Marcus, Jacob R., *Israel Jacobson: The Founder of the Reform Movement in Judaism*, Caddylak, 1972.

Marmur, Dow (ed.), *Reform Judaism: Essays on Reform Judaism in Britain*, RSGB, 1973.

Mendes-Flohr, Paul R., Reinharz, Jehuda (eds), *The Jew in the Modern World: A Documentary History*, Oxford University Press, 1995.

Meyer, Michael, A., *Response to Modernity: A History of the Reform Movement in Judaism*, Oxford University Press, 1990.

Petuchowski, Jacob J., *Prayerbook Reform in Europe: The Liturgy of European Liberal and Reform Judaism*, Union of American Hebrew Congregations, 1969.

Philipson, David, *The Reform Movement in Judaism*, KTAV, 1967.

Plaut, W. Gunther (ed.), *The Growth of Reform Judaism: American and European Sources until 1948*, World Union for Progressive Judaism, 1965.

Plaut, W. Gunther (ed.), *The Rise of Reform Judaism: A Sourcebook of its European Origins*, World Union for Progressive Judaism, 1965.

Raphael, M.L., *Profiles in American Judaism*, HarperCollins, 1988.

Rubinstein, Hilary L., Cohn-Sherbok, Dan, Edelheit, Abraham J., Rubenstein, William, *The Jews in the Modern World: A History since 1750*, Edward Arnold, 2002.

Sachar, Howard Morley, *The Course of Modern Jewish History*, Vintage, 1990.

CHAPTER 45

Jewish Thought in the Age of Reform

Timeline:

1789–1866 Solomon Ludwig Steinheim

1801–1889 Solomon Formstecher

1810–1874 Abraham Geiger

1815–1889 Samuel Hirsch

1817–1891 Heinrich Graetz

In the mid-1800s a number of German thinkers who were influenced by the cause of Reform sought to re-evaluate the course of Jewish history. One of the most important of these reformers was **Abraham Geiger** who combined a commitment to the scientific study of Judaism with a rabbinical career. Born in Frankfurt, Geiger studied at the universities of Heidelberg and Bonn. In 1832 he served as rabbi in Wiesbaden where he edited the *Scientific Journal for Jewish Theology*. Later in 1838 he was appointed rabbi in Breslau where he published studies on a variety of Jewish subjects as well as a book on the ancient text and translations of the Bible. In this work Geiger maintained that post-Biblical movements shaped the canonized version of Scripture. Even though Geiger did not write a systematic Jewish theology, his approach was based on a programme to reformulate Judaism to achieve theological clarity according to the scientific spirit of the time.

For Geiger religion was rooted in the human recognition of finitude and the quest for the infinite. Judaism, he believed, is a faith founded on the trust in one who guides the universe and in the task imposed upon Jews to practise justice and mercy. Unlike the Greeks, who believed in fate, the Jewish faith conceives spiritual perfection as the ultimate aim of human striving. According to Geiger, this vision reached its climax in the prophetic tradition; it should be distinguished from earlier, more primitive religious practices such as animal sacrifice which had been discarded in

the course of Jewish history. Similarly, he argued that the Biblical concept of nationhood is not needed in the modern world.

For Geiger, the evolution of Jewish history divided into four stages of development. First, in the age of revelation the idea of Judaism was understood as a moral, spiritual concept capable of continual development. In the second stage of Jewish history – the age of tradition – the Bible was continually reshaped and reinterpreted. The third stage – the age of legalism – which occurred after the completion of the *Talmud*, formalized the tradition so as to ensure its continuance. Finally, in the age of critical study, legalism was transcended through historical research. Yet, though the *halakhah* was not considered binding in the fourth stage, this does not imply that Judaism is cut off from the past; on the contrary, historical studies can revitalize the heritage. Those aspects of the Jewish tradition which are to be eliminated should be regarded as medieval abnormalities resulting from restraints. They are not connected to the core of the Jewish faith.

In Geiger's view, anti-Jewish sentiment was the result of the Church's belief that Judaism had been superseded by Christianity. But for Geiger Christianity was seen as the inferior religion since the doctrine of the Incarnation compromised the original purity of the Jewish concept of God. Further, Geiger asserted that the concept of original sin undermines the Biblical view that human beings are capable of moral improvement. Geiger also pointed out that the validity of

Judaism does not rest on a historical figure like Jesus, nor does the Jewish faith denigrate earthly life as does Christianity. Finally, Geiger emphasized that Judaism does not contain fixed dogmas which constrain free enquiry. For these reasons Geiger believed that Judaism rather than the Christian faith is the ideal religious system for the modern age. Within this framework emancipation was of vital consequence since it was only in an age of scientific investigation that Judaism could find its true character. Historical knowledge would provide a basis for determining what is anachronistic in the tradition and what should be discarded.

Heinrich Graetz (1817–91) was another major thinker concerned with the scientific study of Judaism. In the 1840s Graetz espoused Zacharias Frankel's approach to Jewish civilization: in an essay written in 1846 he asserted that the essence of Judaism resided not only in a theoretical conception of the Jewish faith but also in the features of Jewish existence that reformers had rejected. Adapting Hegelian notions, Graetz believed that all aspects of the Jewish tradition are the result of the unfolding of Judaism as a religious system. For Graetz this was not a logical but rather a historical process, and in his investigations he attempted to illustrate how Jewish beliefs and practices evolved throughout history.

Judaism, Graetz argued, cannot be reduced to an abstract definition. Rather, the Jewish tradition is historically based and can be divided into three stages. The first period began with the conquest of the land and ended with the destruction of the first Temple in 586 BCE. The second stage took place after the Babylonian exile and lasted until the destruction of the second Temple in 70 CE. During this cycle of history the struggle against Greek paganism culminated in the emergence of the Pharisees who introduced doctrines concerning the afterlife into Jewish thought. For Graetz the third stage was the diaspora period in which Jews attempted to attain intellectual self-perfection and rationalize their religious faith. This scheme of Jewish history was elaborated in Graetz's *History of the Jews* published between 1853 and 1876.

Just as Geiger and Graetz had been influenced by German philosophy, so other Jewish writers sought to integrate German philosophical thought into their conceptions of Judaism. In 1841 the Reform rabbi,

Solomon Formstecher (1801–89), published *The Religion of the Spirit*. In this study, which was influenced by the work of the philosopher Freidrich Wilhelm Joseph von Schelling, Formstecher argued that ultimate reality is the Divine World Soul, a cosmic unity manifesting itself both in nature and in spirit. For Formstecher nature is an organic hierarchy of events and forces which reaches self-consciousness in the realm of spirit. As the highest form of consciousness spirit can be known through its various manifestations, but Formstecher was anxious to point out that such conceptions are symbols and do not describe God's essence. The Divine Soul as it is in itself is unknowable.

On the basis of this metaphysical system Formstecher distinguished between the religion of nature and the religion of spirit. The religion of nature refers to paganism which deifies nature; the religion of spirit identifies God not only with nature but also with the ethical good. In the history of religion, Judaism was the first religion of spirit, but within the tradition there has been a gradual development. In the early stages of Jewish history, truth was understood through the medium of statehood, and then by a theocracy of religious law. But once emancipation had taken place, it became possible for Jews to realize their mission of establishing a universal ethical religion of spirit for all people.

Like Formstecher, the Reform rabbi Samuel Hirsch (1815–89) utilized German idealism in the presentation of his conception of the Jewish heritage. In *The Religious Philosophy of the Jews*, published in 1842. Hirsch adopted Hegel's view that human beings become free by seeing themselves as distinct persons, but he rejected the Hebrew notion that sin can be overcome through rational self-determination. For Hirsch, sin is a moral rather than an intellectual state; it can only be eliminated through ethical action. Thus, the essential feature of religion is not the eventual self-realization of God, but the actualization of moral freedom in which natural sensuality is subordinated to ethical duty. In this light Hirsch conceived of religion as either passive or active. In passive religions such as paganism, believers are dominated by their sensual side, and nature is understood as a divine force. But in active religions, the devout can attain self-chosen freedom. During the patriarchal period Judaism possessed the insight of active religion; miracles and prophecies were necessary to eliminate paganism from the faith. Yet the need for such miraculous occurrences has ceased; the only miracle is the survival of the Jewish nation. On this basis, Hirsch believed that there is no evolution of truth in Judaism though development does take place in the ethical sphere. The purpose of education is to encourage Jews to choose virtue rather than sinfulness and to act as God's suffering servants so as to demonstrate the impotence of evil.

Similar to these Reform rabbis, Solomon Ludwig Steinheim (1789–1866), who was a physician and poet, published *Revelation and the Doctrine of the Synagogue* in the mid-nineteenth century. According to Steinheim, Judaism should not be confused with philosophical reflection. Not only did Steinheim criticize Formstecher and Hirsch for their reliance on German philosophy, he also disagreed with Mendelssohn's conviction that natural religion is the source of theoretical truth. For Steinheim the Bible contains beliefs contrary to ancient Greek philosophy as well as modern thought. Adopting Kant's belief that things-in-themselves cannot be known through human knowledge, Steinheim argued that reason is limited in its scope and must be supplemented by revelation. In propounding this thesis, Steinheim advanced the view that natural religion is based on the assumption that everything has a cause as well as the belief that nothing can come from nothing. These concepts, he argued, are incompatible. The only way out of this dilemma is through the Biblical view that the creation of the universe was due to God's will. Belief in such a creative act qualifies determinism and provides a basis for moral freedom. For Steinheim, the mission of the Jews in the past was to refute natural religion; in contemporary society philosophical rationalism must be overcome as well. Steinheim's anti-rationalism thus reverses the direction of Jewish philosophical thought in a post-Maimonidean age.

SOURCES

Abraham Geiger

Abraham Geiger was one of the leaders of Reform Judaism. In this letter to the French Jewish educator Joseph Naphtali Derenbourg, he argues that religious reform must be based on critical scholarship:

The *Talmud*, and the Bible, too, that collection of books, most of them so splendid and uplifting, perhaps the most exalting of the literature of human authorship, can no longer be viewed as of Divine origin. Of course, all this will not come to pass today, or even tomorrow, but it should be our goal, and will continue to be so, and in this fashion we are working closely with every true endeavour and movement of our day, and we will accomplish more by study than we could by means of a hundred sermons and widespread religious instruction. For the love of Heaven, how much longer can we continue this deceit, to expound the stories of the Bible from the pulpits over and over again as actual historical happenings, to accept as supernatural events of world import stories which we ourselves have relegated to the realm of legend, and to derive our teachings from them or, at least, to use them as the basis for sermons and texts. How much longer will we continue to pervert the spirit of the child with these tales that distort the natural good sense of tender youth.

(Abraham Geiger, *Jewish Scholarship and Religious Reform*, in JMW, p. 233)

DISCUSSION

1. How did Reform thinkers view Jewish history?

2. In what ways did the Reform conception of the development of Judaism serve as a basis for reforming the faith?

FURTHER READING

Borowitz, Eugene B., Patz, Naomi, *Explaining Reform Judaism*, Behrman House, 1985.

Borowitz, Eugene B., *Reform Jewish Ethics and the Halakhah: An Experiment in Decision Making*, Behrman House, 1995.

Freehof, Solomon B., *Reform Responsa for Our Time*, Behrman House, 1977.

Jacob, Walter, Zemer, Moshe (eds), *Re-Examining Progressive Halakhah*, Berghahn Books, 2002.

Kaplan, Dana Evan (ed.), *Contemporary Debates in Reform Judaism*, Routledge, 2001.

Kaplan, Dana Evan, Umansky, Ellen (eds), *Platforms and Prayer Books: Theological and Liturgical Perspectives on Reform Judaism*, Rowman and Littlefield, 2002.

Meyer, Michael A., *Response to Modernity: A History of the Reform Movement in Judaism*, Oxford University Press, 1990.

Meyer, Michael A., Plaut, W. Gunther (eds), *The Reform Judaism Reader: North American Documents*, UAHC Press, 2000.

Olitzky, Kerry M., Sussman, Lance J., Stern, Malcolm H. (eds), *Reform Judaism in America: A Bibliographical Dictionary and Sourcebook*, Greenwood, 1993.

Petuchowski, Jakob J., *Prayerbook Reform in Europe: The Liturgy of European Liberal and Reform Judaism*, UAHC Press, 1969.

Raphael, Mark, *Profiles in American Judaism*, Harper-Collins, 1988.

Temkin, Sefton D., *Creating American Reform Judaism*, Littman Library, 1998.

Zemer, Moshe, *Evolving Halakhah: A Progressive Approach to Traditional Jewish Law*, Jewish Lights, 1999.

CHAPTER 46

The Rise of Anti-Semitism

Timeline:

1860–1905 Theodor Herzl

1878 Adolf Stoecker establishes the Christian Social Party

1879–1881 Anti-Semitic movement in Germany

1881 Alexander II assassinated

1881 Russian pogroms

1881 Beginning of mass immigration of Eastern European Jews to the United States

1884 Kattowicz Conference of the Lovers of Zion

1887 Quotas on Jews in general Russian schools and universities

1891 Expulsion of Jews from Moscow

1893 Anti-Semitic parties gain 250,000 votes in Germany

1894–1899 Dreyfus Affair in France

1895 Karl Lueger uses anti-Semitic slogans. Elected mayor of Vienna

1899 Houston Stewart Chamberlain publishes *The Foundations of the Nineteenth Century*

1903 Pogrom against Jews in Kishinev

1905 Publication of the *Protocols of the Elders of Zion*

1905–1907 Pogroms in Russia

1911–1913 Beilis blood libel case

By the last decades of the nineteenth century the European Jewish community had attained a high degree of emancipation. Nevertheless, political conditions in Europe after 1870 brought about considerable disruption: several proud and independent nations emerged and fought against indigenous minority groups which threatened their homogeneity. Living in such conditions Jews were viewed as aliens and unassimilable. Symptomatic of such attitudes was the invention of the term 'anti-Semitism' by the German journalist **Wilhelm Marr** in the 1870s. Previously Jewish persecution was based largely on religious grounds but Marr's concept of anti-Semitism focused on biological descent. Anti-Semitism was thus a racial doctrine which significantly differed from previous dislike of Jews and Judaism. According to Marr, the Jews had corrupted all standards, banned idealism from society, dominated commerce, and ruled cultural

life. In Marr's opinion there is a continuous struggle in modern society between these Semitic aliens and native Teutonic stock.

Anti-Jewish attitudes intensified in the 1870s in Germany as a result of economic and cultural upheaval. The political liberalism of previous decades had enabled Jews to benefit from economic activities, and in reaction conservatives blamed the Jewish community for the ills besetting society. In 1878 Adolf Stoecker founded a Christian Social Party on the basis of an anti-Semitic platform. By accusing the press and the financial institutions of being controlled by Jewish interests, many artisans, shopkeepers, clerks and professionals were attracted to his political movement.

Such allegations were also supported by German nationalists who emphasized that Jews would need to assimilate to German life before they could be accepted as Germans. Other nationalists adopted a more radical position; in 1881 for example **Eugen Dühring** argued that the Jewish type constitutes a biological threat to the German nation. In the same year anti-Semites presented a petition of 225,000 signatures to stop all Jewish immigration; this was followed in 1882 by an international anti-Semitic congress. In the next decade anti-Semitic parties elected sixteen deputies to the German Reichstag. At the end of the century anti-Semitism was utilized by Karl Lueger to foster the creation of the first political party in Europe which obtained power on the basis of anti-Jewish feeling.

During this period French anti-Semitism was also used by the monarchy and clergy who were unhappy with the liberal ideas of the French Revolution. Such anti-Semitism reached a climax with the Dreyfus Affair. Accused of treason, Alfred Dreyfus was banished from the army and sentenced to life imprisonment in 1894. Subsequently, however, it was discovered that forged evidence had been used to implicate Dreyfus and a scandal ensued which divided public opinion. Those opposed to Dreyfus believed that he was part of a Jewish conspiracy to undermine the military and discredit France; his supporters viewed the court martial of Dreyfus as an injustice which threatened the stability of French life. Eventually Dreyfus was pardoned, but for many Jews this episode illustrated that despite the forces of emancipation, anti-Semitism was deeply rooted in European society. In a tract written after the Dreyfus affair, Theodor Herzl (1860–1905) came to the conclusion that Jews would never be accepted in the countries where they lived. According to Herzl, even though Jews seek to integrate into those societies where they live, they will never be accepted as equals: the only solution to the Jewish problem is for Jews to have their own homeland.

In Russia anti-Semitism became an official policy of the state. After Alexander II was assassinated in 1881, a succession of pogroms against the Jewish population took place in the southern Ukraine. Jewish property was looted and destroyed, and in 1882 the minister of the interior decreed a series of laws which curtailed Jewish residence in the Pale of Settlement. In the later 1880s quotas were imposed on the admittance of Jews to Russian schools, universities and professions. In addition more than 20,000 Jews were expelled from Moscow in 1891–2. In 1903 a violent pogrom was unleashed on the Jews of Kishinev. In the next year

Figure 46 Alfred Dreyfus (1859–1935), French army officer, before the war council, December 1894 engraving from French publication *Le Petit Journal*. Copyright The Art Archive/Dagli Orti.

Jews were accused of helping the enemy in the war against Japan and armed gangs attacked Jews in various towns and cities. Though these outbursts ceased in 1907 a right-wing political party, the Union of the Russian People, initiated a campaign of anti-Semitic propaganda. In 1911 Mendel Beilis, a Jew from Kiev, was accused of ritual murder but was exonerated in 1913.

Such manifestations of anti-Jewish sentiment were based on the belief that the Jewish people constitute a dangerous racial group. Ideologues argued that the Semitic mentality is egoistic, materialistic, economic-minded, cowardly and culturally degenerate. In this context a number of writers propagated racist theories. In *The Foundations of the Nineteenth Century*, published at the turn of the century, Houston Stewart Chamberlain maintained that the antiquity and the mobility of the Jewish nation illustrates that the confrontation between superior Aryans and parasitic Semites is the central theme of history. Earlier, in the 1880s, the *Protocols of the Elders of Zion* were believed to be the minutes of a clandestine world government. In this document the elders were depicted as attempting to strengthen their hold over the European economy, the press, and the parties opposed to the Tsar as well as other autocratic regimes.

SOURCES

Wilhelm Marr

Wilhelm Marr was a racial anti-Semite whose pamphlet, *The Victory of Judaism over Germandom: Regarded from a Non-Denominational Point of View* compared the Jew with the German:

> Jewry's control of society and politics, as well as its practical domination of religious and ecclesiastical thought, is still in the prime of its development . . .
>
> By now, a sudden reversal of this process is fundamentally impossible, for if it were, the entire social structure, which has been so thoroughly Judaized, would collapse, and there is no viable alternative to this social structure which could take its place . . . We were vanquished and it is entirely proper that the victor shouts '*Vae Victis*!'
>
> German culture has proved itself ineffective and powerless against this foreign power. This is a fact; a brute inexorable fact. State, Church, Catholicism, Protestantism, Creed and Dogma, all are brought low before the Jewish tribunal . . .
>
> The Jews were late in their assault on Germany, but once they started there was no stopping them . . .
>
> (Wilhelm Marr, *The Victory of Judaism over Germandom*, in JMW, pp. 331–332)

Eugen Dühring

An economist and philosopher, Eugen Dühring was an earlier proponent of modern racial anti-Semitism:

A Jewish question would still exist, even if every Jew were to turn his back on his religion and join one of our major churches. Yes, I maintain that in that case, the struggle between us and the Jews would make itself felt as ever more urgent – although the struggle certainly is felt now even when the Jews have yet to convert (in large numbers). It is precisely the baptized Jews who infiltrate furthest, unhindered in all sectors of society and political life. It is as though they have provided themselves with an unrestricted passport, advancing their stock to those places where members of the Jewish religion are unable to follow. Furthermore, several doors are closed to members of the Jewish religion by our legislation, and more particularly, by the principles of our administration. Through these portals the racial Jew, who has forsaken his religion, can enter unhindered . . . I return therefore to the hypothesis that the Jews are to be defined solely on the basis of race, and not on the basis of religion.

(Eugen Dühring, *The Question of the Jew is a Question of Race*, in JMW, pp. 333–334)

Houston Stewart Chamberlain

British by origin, Houston Stewart Chamberlain espoused racial anti-Semitism in *The Foundations of the Nineteenth Century*:

We live today in a 'Jewish age'; we may think what we like about the past history of the Jews; their present history actually takes up so much room in our own history that we cannot possible refuse to notice them. Herder in spite of his outspoken humanism had expressed the opinion that 'the Jewish people is and remains in Europe an Asiatic people alien to our part of the world, bound to that old law which it received in a distant climate, and which according to its own confession it cannot do away with'. Quite correct. But this alien people, everlastingly alien, because – as Herder well remarks – it is indissolubly bound to an alien law that is hostile to all other peoples – this alien people has become precisely in the course of the nineteenth century a disproportionately important and in many spheres actually dominant constituent of our life. Even a hundred years ago that same witness had sadly to confess that the 'ruder nations of Europe' were 'willingly slaves of Jewish usury'; today he could say the same of by far the greatest part of the civilized world. The possession of money in itself is, however, of least account; our governments, our law, our science, our commerce, our literature, our art . . . partically all branches of our life have become more or less willing slaves of the Jews.

(Houston Stewart Chamberlain, *The Foundations of the Nineteenth Century*, in JMW, pp. 358–359)

DISCUSSION

1. How did modern anti-Semitism differ from anti-Semitism of previous centuries?

2. Critically evaluate the theories of racism propounded by nineteenth century thinkers.

FURTHER READING

Almog, Shmuel (ed.), *Antisemitism Through the Ages*, Butterworth-Heinemann, 1988.

Berger, David (ed.), *History and Hate: The Dimensions of Anti-Semitism*, Jewish Publication Society, 1995.

Cohn-Sherbok, Dan, *Anti-Semitism*, Sutton, 2002.

Ettinger, Shmuel, *Nationalism and Antisemitism in Modern Europe, 1815–1945*, Butterworth-Heinemann, 1990.

Gilman, Sander, Katz, Stephen T. (eds), *Anti-Semitism in Times of Crisis*, New York University Press, 1991.

Langmuir, Gavin, *History, Religion and Antisemitism*, University of California Press, 1990.

Levy, Richard S., *Antisemitism in the Modern World: An Anthology of Texts*, D.C. Heath, 1999.

Littell, Franklin H., *The Crucifixion of the Jews*, Mercer University Press, 1975.

Litvinoff, Barnet, *The Burning Bush: Antisemitism and World Jewry*, Fontana, 1989.

Parkes, James, *Antisemitism*, Times Books, 1963.

Poliakov, Leon, *A History of Antisemitism*, Vols 1–4, Littman Library, 1974–85.

Praeger, Dennis, Telushkin, Joseph, *Why the Jews? The Reasons for Antisemitism*, Touchstone, 1985.

Reinharz, Jehuda (ed.), *Living with Antisemitism: Modern Jewish Responses*, Brandeis University Press, 1987.

Rubenstein, Richard L., Roth, John K., *Approaches to Auschwitz: The Holocaust and its Legacy*, Westminster John Knox Press, 1997.

Rubinstein, William D., Rubinstein, Hilary L., *Philosemitism: Administration and Support in the English-speaking World for Jews, 1840–1939*, Palgrave Macmillan 1999.

Weinberg, Meyer, *Because They Were Jews: A History of Anti-Semitism*, Greenwood, 1986.

Wistrich, Robert S., *Antisemitism: The Longest Hatred*, Schocken, 1991.

CHAPTER 47

The Zionist Movement

Timeline:

1840s Judah Hai Alkalai publishes Zionist pamphlets and books

1856–1927 Ahad Ha-Am

1858–1922 Ben Yehudah

1881 Beginning of the First *Aliyah*

1882 Publication of Leon Pinsker's *Autoemancipation*

1880s–1890s Establishment of Jewish farming villages in Palestine

1886–1973 David Ben Gurion

1889 Ahad Ha-Am publishes essays

1896 Theodor Herzl publishes *The Jewish State*

1897 First Zionist Congress at Basle, Switzerland

1903 Sixth Zionist Congress. Uganda controversy

1904–1914 Second *Aliyah*

1909 Tel Aviv founded

1910 Establishment of Deganyah, the first kibbutz

1917 British troops occupy Palestine. Balfour Declaration

The pogroms of 1881–2 forced many Jews to emigrate; most went to the United States, but a sizeable number were drawn to Palestine. In the Pale of Settlement nationalist zealots organized Zionist groups (Lovers of Zion) which collected money and organized courses in Hebrew and Jewish history. In 1882 several thousand Jews left for Palestine where they worked as shopkeepers and artisans; other Jewish immigrants, known as *Bilu* (from the Hebrew 'house of Jacob, let us go') combined Marxist ideals with Jewish nationalist fervour and worked as farmers and labourers. During this period **Leon Pinsker** (1821–91), an eminent Russian physician, published an influential tract, *Autoemancipation*, in which he argued that the liberation of Jewry could only be secured by the establishment of a Jewish homeland. Nations, he wrote, live side by side in a state of relative peace, which is based chiefly on fundamental equality between them. But it is different with the people of Israel. This people is not counted among the nations, because when it was exiled from its land it lost the essential attributes of nation-

ality by which one nation is distinguished from another.

In the 1890s the idea of Jewish nationalism had spread to other countries in Europe. Foremost among its proponents was **Theodor Herzl** – profoundly affected by the **Dreyfus affair** – who made contact with the Lovers of Zion. In 1897 the first **Zionist Congress** took place in Basle which called for a national home for Jews based on international law. At this congress Herzl stated that emancipation of the Jews had been an illusion: Jews were everywhere objects of contempt and hatred. The only solution to the Jewish problem, he argued, was the re-establishment of a Jewish homeland in Palestine. In the same year the Zionist Organization was created with branches in Europe and America. After establishing these basic institutions of the Zionist movement, Herzl embarked on diplomatic negotiations. In 1898 he met with Kaiser Wilhelm II who promised he would take up the matter with the Sultan. When nothing came of this, Herzl himself attempted to arrange an interview, and in 1901 a meeting with

Figure 47 Theodor Herzl (1860–1904), who convened the first Zionist congress in Basle, Switzerland, in 1897: 204 people from 17 countries attended to lay the groundwork for the creation of a legal homeland for the Jewish people. The Basle Programme, which resulted, created the World Zionist Movement with Herzl as President. Six Zionist congresses were held before his death in 1904. A later photograph of Herzl hangs behind Ben Gurion as he declares the independence of the state of Israel in 1948 (see Figure 51). Copyright the *Jewish Chronicle*, London.

the Sultan took place. In return for a charter of Jewish settlement in Palestine, Herzl suggested that wealthy Jewish bankers might be willing to pay off the Turkish debt. In the following year the Sultan agreed to approve a plan of Jewish settlement throughout the Ottoman empire, but not a corporate Jewish homeland in Palestine.

Unwilling to abandon a diplomatic approach, Herzl sought to cultivate contacts in England such as Lord Nathan Rothschild (1840–1915) who arranged an interview for him with Joseph Chamberlain, the Secretary of State for Colonial Affairs. During their

conversation Herzl suggested that El Arish in the Sinai Peninsula might be a feasible area of settlement. Though this plan was discussed at the highest political levels, it never reached fruition. In 1903 Herzl was summoned to London for a second talk with Chamberlain after his return from Africa. Chamberlain explained that he had seen a country which might be suitable: **Uganda**. Aware of increasing persecution in Russia, Herzl was uncertain whether to wait for Palestine and asked for time to consider the offer.

After a trip to the Pale of Settlement where he encountered poverty and deprivation, Herzl reluctantly agreed to Chamberlain's proposal in August 1903 for a place of temporary asylum. At the next Zionist conference in Basle this plan was presented for ratification. When Chamberlain's scheme was explained, it was emphasized that Uganda was not meant to serve as a permanent solution, but rather as a temporary residence. When the resolution was passed by a small margin, the delegates from eastern Europe walked out of the auditorium. During the next few days the Zionist movement was threatened by schism; at the end of the proceedings the Russian Jews set off for Kharkov where they convened their own conference committing themselves to the idea of Palestine.

In England public opinion was opposed to the transference of Uganda to the Jews, and the offer was eventually withdrawn. In the following year, Herzl died, and the Zionist movement was led by a new President, David Wolffsohn (1856–1914), who attempted to heal the rifts between competing factions. Under his leadership Orthodox Jews joined the Zionist Organization as members of the *Mizrachi* Party; socialist Jews also became members through the Labour Zionist Party. In the 1907 congress during Wolffsohn's presidency a resolution was passed which pledged the movement to the quest for a charter, the physical settlement of Palestine and the revival of the Hebrew language.

During the next decade the major developments in the Zionist movement took place in Israel, and by the beginning of the twentieth century a sizeable number of Jews had migrated to Palestine. Most of these pioneers lived in cities but a small minority worked on farm colonies under the control of the Palestine Jewish Colonization Association. In 1904 when a second wave of immigrants departed for the Holy Land, most of these settlers were determined to become farmers. Prominent among these newcomers was Aaron David Gordon (1856–1922) who urged Jews to cultivate the land. Socialist ideas were espoused by men such as Nachman Syrkin (1867–1924), who founded the *Poale Zion* Party, and Ber Borochov (1881–1917), the founder of the radical *Hapoel Hatzair* Party. Both of these leaders maintained that Zionism and socialism were compatible ideologies.

Among those who were attracted to such socialist policies was David Ben Gurion (1886–1973) who later became Prime Minister of Israel. Those who came in this second wave organized trade unions, edited their own newspapers and attempted to establish their own collective settlements. In addition these settlers were determined to create Hebraic culture for the country: they put their children in Hebrew language schools and used Hebrew in their daily life. The philologist Ben Yehuda (1858–1922) produced a Hebrew dictionary and such writers as Ahad Ha'Am (1856–1927), Reuben Brainin (1862–1939) and Hayyim Nahman Bialik (1873–1934) contributed to the development of Hebrew literature. By 1917 the Jewish community numbered approximately 90,000.

SOURCES

The Dreyfus Affair

Anti-Semitism was prevalent in France in the late nineteenth century. It was the Dreyfus case of 1894 which brought the issue into the national arena:

> There are forty thousand military officers in France. Captain Dreyfus is merely one of this forty thousand . . . If he had been a Catholic or a free-thinker, he would have been classified as an isolated, extraordinary case, which recur throughout history. The next day the public would have been interested in other matters . . . However, now everybody in France is speaking of only one man and of his treason and that is because that man is a Jew.
>
> (Emmanuel Bucheron, article in *Figaro*, in SRJ, p. 141)

In 1897, the real traitor was identified. In January 1898 the novelist Emil Zola addressed an open letter to the president of the Republic:

> These, Monsieur le President, are the facts. This is how the judicial error can be explained. The moral proofs, the position of Dreyfus as a wealthy man, the absence of motive, the continual cry of innocence, complete the demonstration that Dreyfus is a victim of the extraordinary fantasies of Major du Paty de Calm, of his clerical surroundings and of the victimization of the 'filthy Jews', which is a disgrace to our era.
>
> (Emile Zola, 'J'accuse' in *L'Aurore*, in SRJ, p. 141)

Theodor Herzl

The father of Zionism, Theodor Herzl was the founder of the World Zionist Organization. In his writing, he argued that the Jewish problem can only be solved by the establishment of a Jewish homeland:

I therefore address my first words to those Jews who are strong and free of spirit. They shall form my earliest audience, and they will one day, I hope, become my friends. I am introducing no new idea; on the contrary, it is a very old one. It is a universal idea – and therein lies its power – old as the people, which never, even in the time of bitterest calamity, ceased to cherish it. This is the restoration of the Jewish state.

It is remarkable that we Jews should have dreamt this kingly dream all through the long night of our history. Now day is dawning. We need only rub the sleep out of our eyes, stretch our limbs, and convert the dream into a reality. Though neither prophet, nor visionary, I confess I cherish the hope and belief that the Jewish people will one day be fired by a splendid enthusiasm . . .

We who are the first to inaugurate this movement, will scarcely live to see its glorious close; but the inauguration of it is enough to bring a noble kind of happiness into our lives. We shall plant for our children in the same way as our fathers preserved the tradition for us. Our lives represent but a moment in the permanent duration of our people . . .

We have honestly striven everywhere to merge ourselves in the social life of surrounding communities, and to preserve only the faith of our faiths. It has not been permitted to us. In vain are we loyal patriots, in some places, our loyalty running to extremes; in vain do we make the same sacrifices of life and property as our fellow-citizens; in vain do we strive to increase the fame of our native land in science and art, or her wealth by trade and commerce. In countries where we have lived for centuries we are still cried down as strangers; and often by those whose ancestors were not yet domiciled in the land where Jews had already made experience of suffering . . .

Distress binds us together, and thus united, we suddenly discover our strength. Yes, we are strong enough to form a state, and a model state. We possess all human and material resources necessary for the purpose.

(Theodor Herzl, *A Solution to the Jewish Question*, in JMW, pp. 553–554)

Leon Pinsker

Leon Pinsker initially espoused the ideals of the Enlightenment, but after the pogroms of 1881 he became determined to create a Jewish homeland. In 1882 he published *Autoemancipation* in which he argued that the Jewish problem could only be resolved by creating a Jewish commonwealth since Jews have always been seen as aliens:

> For the living, the Jew is a dead man; for the natives, an alien and a vagrant; for property holders, a beggar; for the poor, an exploiter and millionaire; for patriots, a man without a country; for all classes, a hated rival.
>
> (Leon Pinsker, *Autoemancipation*, in ZI, p. 188)

In recent times, he argued, there has been a growing awareness of the need for a Jewish homeland:

> Nowadays, when in a small part of the earth our brethren have caught their breath and can feel more deeply for the sufferings of their brothers; nowadays, when a number of other dependent and oppressed nationalities have been allowed to regain their independence, we, too, must not sit even one moment longer with folded hands; we must not admit that we are doomed to play on in the future the hopeless role of the 'wandering Jew' . . . it is our bounden duty to devote all our remaining moral force to re-establish ourselves as a living nation, so that we may finally assume a more fitting and dignified role.
>
> (Leon Pinsker, *Autoemancipation*, in ZI, p. 191)

According to Pinsker, what is required is simply a secure land for the Jewish nation:

> We need nothing but a large piece of land for our poor brothers; a piece of land which shall remain our property, from which no foreign master can expel us . . . Perhaps the Holy Land will again become ours. If so, all the better, but first of all, we must determine . . . what country is accessible to us, and at the same time adapted to offer the Jews of all lands who must leave their homes a secure and unquestioned refuge which is capable of being made productive.
>
> (Leon Pinsker, *Autoemancipation*, in ZI, p. 194)

Zionist Congress

The First Zionist Congress took place in Basle in 1897 and adopted a series of objectives:

> The aim of Zionism is to create for the Jewish people a home in Palestine secured by public law. The Congress contemplates the following means to the attainment of this end:
>
> 1. The promotion, on suitable lines, of the colonization of Palestine by Jewish agricultural and industrial workers.
> 2. The organization and binding together of the whole Jewry by means of appropriate institutions, local and international in accordance with the laws of each country.
> 3. The strengthening and fostering of Jewish national sentiment and consciousness.
> 4. Preparatory steps towards obtaining government consent, where necessary, to the attainment of the aim of Zionism.
>
> (*The Basle Programme*, in JMW, p. 540)

Uganda Plan

In 1905 the Seventh Zionist Congress meeting in Basle officially rejected the Uganda Plan:

The Seventh Zionist Congress declares:

The Zionist organisation stands firmly by the fundamental principle of the Basle programme, namely: 'The establishment of a legally-secured, publicly recognised home for the Jewish people in Palestine', and it rejects either as an end or as a means all colonising activity outside Palestine and its adjacent lands.

The Congress resolves to thank the British Government for its offer of a territory in British East Africa, for the purpose of establishing there a Jewish settlement with autonomous rights. A Commission having been sent out to examine the territory, and having reported thereon, the Congress resolves that the Zionist organisation shall not engage further with the proposal. The Congress records with satisfaction the recognition accorded by the British Government to the Zionist organisation in its desire to bring about a solution of the Jewish problem, and expresses the sincere hope that it may be accorded the further good offices of the British Government where available in any matter it may undertake in accordance with the Basle programme.

(*Anti-Uganda Resolution*, in JMW, p. 548)

DISCUSSION

1. Why did Zionists believe that the creation of a Jewish state would be a solution to the problem of anti-Semitism?
2. Discuss the conflicts that existed in the Zionist movement prior to the establishment of Israel in 1948.

FURTHER READING

Avineri, Shlomo, *The Making of Modern Zionism: Intellectual Origins of the Jewish State*, Basic Books, 1981.

Cohn-Sherbok, Dan, El-Alami, Dawoud S., *The Palestine-Israeli Conflict: A Beginner's Guide*, Oneworld, 2002.

Edelheit, Abraham J., *The Yishuv in the Shadow of the Holocaust: Zionist Politics and Rescue Aliyah, 1933–1939*, Westview, 1996.

Gilbert, Martin, *Israel: A History*, William Morrow & Co., 1998.

Herzog, Chaim, *The Arab-Israeli Wars: War and Peace in the Middle East from the War of Independence through Lebanon*, Random House, 1984.

Hertzberg, Arthur (ed.), *The Zionist Idea: A Historical Analysis and Reader*, Jewish Publication Society, 1976.

Karsh, Efraim (ed.), *Israel: The First Hundred Years*, Vol. 1, International Specialized Book Service, 2000.

Laqueur, Walter, *A History of Zionism*, Fine Communications, 1997.

Laqueur, Walter, Rubin, Barry (eds), *The Israel-Arab Reader: A Documentary History of the Middle East Conflict*, Penguin, 2001.

O'Brien, Conor Cruise, *The Siege: The Saga of Israel and Zionism*, Simon and Schuster, 1986.

Sokolow, Nahum, *History of Zionism 1600–1918*, Longman, 1949.

Vital, David, *The Origins of Zionism*, Oxford University Press, 1975.

CHAPTER 48

Jewry in the United States, Palestine, Africa and Asia

Timeline:

1879–1881 Anti-Semitism in Germany

1881 Assassination of Alexander II

1881–1882 Pogroms in Russia

1894–1899 Dreyfus Affair

1902 Jewish Theological Seminary in New York reorganized with Solomon Schechter as president

1906 Founding of the American Jewish Committee

1906–1907 Mass immigration to America

1913 Establishment of the Anti-Defamation League

1914–1918 First World War

1917 Balfour Declaration

1919 Peace Treaty of Versailles

1921 Arab riots in Palestine

1922 League of Nations approves British Mandate in Palestine and the Jewish National Home

1928 Birobidzhan project in Russia to settle Jews in eastern Siberia

1929 Arab riots in Jerusalem and other cities in Palestine

1930 British impose restrictions on Jewish immigration to Palestine

1935 Congress of Zionist Revisionists

1936 Arab strike in Palestine and attacks on the *yishuv*

1937 Peel Commission recommends partition of Palestine

By 1880 there were about 250,000 Jews in the United States; after the pogroms of 1881–2 the Jewish community increased enormously. Approximately 2,750,000 eastern European Jews emigrated between 1881 and 1914: about 350,000 settled in continental Europe; 200,000 went to England; 40,000 emigrated to South Africa; 115,000 to Argentina; 100,000 to Canada; and nearly 2,000,000 to the United States. This massive influx strongly affected the composition of American Jewry. Initially Sephardic Jews dominated Jewish life in the coastal towns of the New World. Jews of German origin who emigrated in the nineteenth century settled throughout the country. Many worked as businessmen in midwestern, southern and west coast cities. These German Jews quickly assimilated and Americanized their religious traditions.

The majority of eastern European Jews who arrived at the end of the century settled in the north-east. In the lower East Side of New York City settlers engaged in various manual trades such as the garment industry. Crowded together in tenements these newcomers worked in unhealthy surroundings, but after 1900 trade unions brought about enormous improvements in working conditions. In this milieu these immigrants created a wide range of societies which supported synagogues, provided insurance for sickness and burial, and supported educational programmes. In this environment Yiddish flourished, resulting in the efflorescence of Yiddish language, theatre and journalism. Yet despite the vibrancy of this immigrant community, many Jews who prospered fled to middle-class neighbourhoods.

Between 1881 and 1914 the American Jewish population was divided between native-born Jews of German origin and eastern European immigrants.

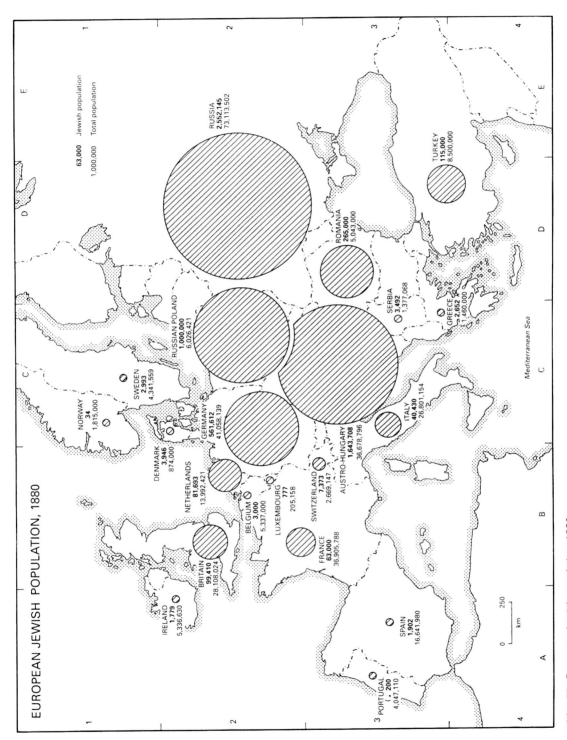

EUROPEAN JEWISH POPULATION, 1880

63,000 Jewish population
1,000,000 Total population

RUSSIA
2,552,145
73,113,502

TURKEY
115,000
8,500,000

ROMANIA
265,000
5,043,000

RUSSIAN POLAND
1,000,000
6,026,421

SERBIA
3,492
1,377,068

GREECE
2,652
1,460,000

NORWAY
34
1,815,000

SWEDEN
2,993
4,341,559

DENMARK
3,946
874,000

GERMANY
561,612
41,058,139

ITALY
40,430
26,801,154

NETHERLANDS
81,693
13,992,421

AUSTRO-HUNGARY
1,643,708
36,678,796

BELGIUM
3,000
5,337,000

LUXEMBOURG
777
205,158

SWITZERLAND
7,373
2,669,147

IRELAND
1,779
5,336,630

BRITAIN
99,410
28,108,024

FRANCE
63,000
36,905,788

SPAIN
1,902
16,641,980

PORTUGAL
200
4,047,110

Mediterranean Sea

0   250
km

Map 57 European Jewish population, 1880

Those German Jews who had already settled in the new country found their eastern European co-religionists too remote and unworldly. As a result a number of acculturated German Jews attempted to defend Jewish interests and advance the process of assimilation. In 1902 they revived the Jewish Theological Seminary in New York in order to train modern rabbis in line with the modernized traditional stance of Zacharias Frankel. Under the leadership of Solomon Schechter this rabbinical seminary became the centre for Conservative Judaism which advocated a scientific approach to the Jewish faith as well as an adherence to the Jewish heritage. This movement had considerable appeal for many eastern European Jews who desired to combine dedication to the Jewish faith with an openness to their new surroundings.

German Jews also founded settlements for immigrants as well as a number of Jewish charities. In 1906 German Jews also established the American Jewish Committee in order to influence the government on behalf of persecuted Jews who lived in foreign countries. The German Jewish community was also instrumental in the creation of the Anti-Defamation League under the auspices of the *B'nai B'rith* to counter anti-Semitism in the United States. German Jews were also active in encouraging Zionist initiatives which attracted native-born advocates such as Louis Brandeis who maintained that a dedication to Zionist ideals could be combined with loyalty to one's own country.

The development of Jewish life in the United States was interrupted by the First World War. During the war Jews fought on the side of the Allies and the Central Powers. In Russia the Tsar was overthrown in March 1917 after two years of fighting, and the provisional government abolished all legal discrimination against the Jewish community. In November the military and political situation deteriorated and a second revolution was carried out by the Bolsheviks. Lenin sued for peace, and in March 1918 a treaty was signed with Germany that gave the Germans control over Estonia, Latvia, Lithuania, Poland and the Ukraine. After America entered the war an armistice was declared on 11 November 1918; in the east, however, fighting continued. When the Germans withdrew from the Ukraine, a number of groups fought for control. In this situation the Red Army attempted to eliminate anti-Jewish feeling in its ranks, but other troops massacred the Jewish population. By 1920 when the the fighting ceased, between 100,000 and 150,000 Jews had been killed.

After the war Jewish immigration to the United States increased but was curtailed by restrictive laws passed in 1921 and 1924. Other western countries also followed similar policies. This cessation of Jewish immigration led to the decline of the Jewish working class and the erosion of Yiddish culture. The Jewish community became increasingly middle-class and prosperous and a number of Jews attained positions of importance in politics, the arts, music, science and literature.

The First World War also profoundly altered European centres of Jewish population: over 3,000,000 Jews lived in reconstituted Poland; 445,000 in Hungary; 850,000 in expanded Romania; 95,000 in Latvia; 115,000 in Lithuania; 375,000 in Czechoslovakia; 191,000 in Austria; 68,000 in Yugoslavia; 48,000 in Bulgaria; and 73,000 in Greece. In these countries the war had taken a significant toll: property was destroyed, large markets were replaced by small economic units and high protective tariffs were introduced. In all these cases governments were anxious to foster middle-class interests at the expense of minority groups.

In this situation Jews were unable to find political allies and became increasingly vulnerable. In 1919 Jewish delegates attended the Paris peace talks to ensure that political treaties would guarantee the rights of minority groups, but their efforts were largely unsuccessful. In Lithuania, Poland, Czechoslovakia, Hungary and Romania most Jews steadfastly adhered to the Jewish faith and were regarded as outsiders. In universities and the professions quotas were strictly applied; Jews were excluded from state bureaucracies; and anti-Semitic policies were advocated by various political parties. Yet despite such anti-Jewish sentiment Jewish life flourished and Jewish political parties founded Hebrew and Yiddish schools competing with one another for support. Eastern European Jewry was also enriched by such institutions as the Yivo Institute of Jewish Research founded in Vilna in 1925 as well as the establishment of the Jewish youth movements and *yeshivot*.

In post-revolutionary Russia Jewish organizations, except for synagogue committees, were eliminated and poor Jews living in villages were deprived of their civil

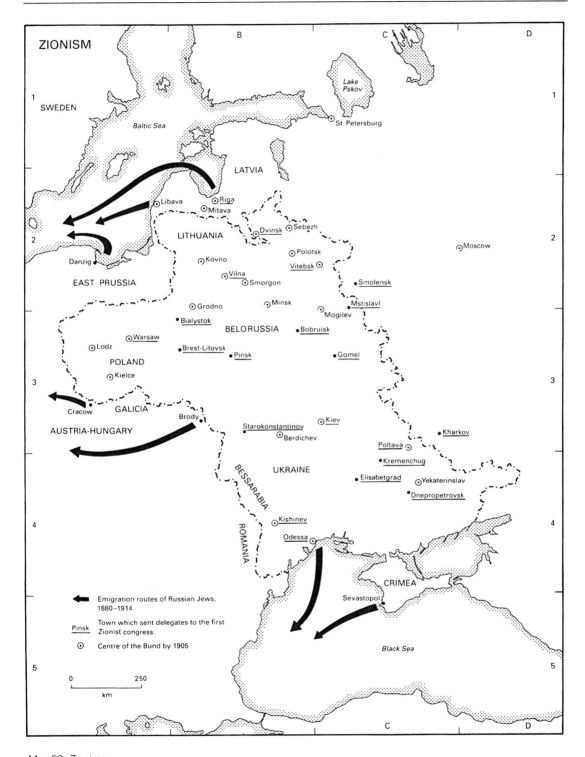

Map 58 Zionism

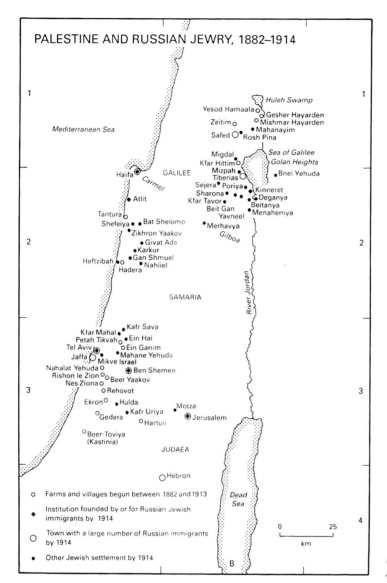

PALESTINE AND RUSSIAN JEWRY, 1882–1914

Mediterranean Sea

Huleh Swamp

Yesod Hamaala ○◐ Gesher Hayarden
Zeitim ○ ○ Mishmar Hayarden
● Mahanayim
Safed ○● Rosh Pina

Migdal ●
Kfar Hittim ○
Mizpah ●
Tiberias ○
Sejera ● Poriya ●
Sharona ●
Kfar Tavor ●
Beit Gan ●
Yavneel
● Merhavya
Gilboa

Haifa ◉
Carmel
GALILEE
● Atlit

Tantura ○
Shefeiya ● ● Bat Shelomo
● Zikhron Yaakov
● Givat Ada
● Karkur
Heftzibah ● ○ ● Gan Shmuel
Hadera ○ ● Nahliel

Sea of Galilee
Golan Heights
● Bnei Yehuda
● Kinneret
● Deganya
● Beitanya
● Menahemya

SAMARIA

River Jordan

Kfar Mahal ● ● Kafr Sava
Petah Tikvah ○ ● Ein Hai
Tel Aviv ◉ ○ Ein Ganim
Jaffa ○● ● Mahane Yehuda
● Mikve Israel
Nahalat Yehuda ○
Rishon le Zion ○ ○ Beer Yaakov
Nes Ziona ○ ◉ Ben Shemen
○ Rehovot
Ekron ○ ● Hulda
○ ● Kafr Uriya ● Motza
Gedera ○ Hartuv ◉ Jerusalem
○ Beer-Toviya
(Kastinia)

JUDAEA

○ Hebron

○ Farms and villages begun between 1882 and 1913

◆ Institution founded by or for Russian Jewish
   immigrants by 1914

○ Town with a large number of Russian immigrants
   by 1914

● Other Jewish settlement by 1914

*Dead
Sea*

0   25
         km

B

*Map 59 Palestine and Russian
Jewry, 1882–1914*

rights. In the 1920s all *yeshivot* were closed and the printing of religious books ceased. Such anti-Semitism however did not hinder Jews from settling in Russian cities where they worked as managers and bureaucrats. A significant number attended institutions of higher education in order to obtain professional qualifications, and in 1921 the New Economic Policy encouraged Jews to establish farming villages in various parts of the Soviet Union; in the 1920s Birobidzhan was set aside for Jewish colonization. But in 1928 this

policy was revoked, and as a result of industrialization many Jews worked instead as labourers, technicians, scientists and engineers. During this period the communist government established Yiddish-speaking workers' councils, schools, scholarly institutes, publishing houses and theatres. In such a climate anti-Semitism was officially prohibited. Yet in subsequent years Jewish institutions and cultural programmes were dismantled and Jews were removed from the party and governmental positions.

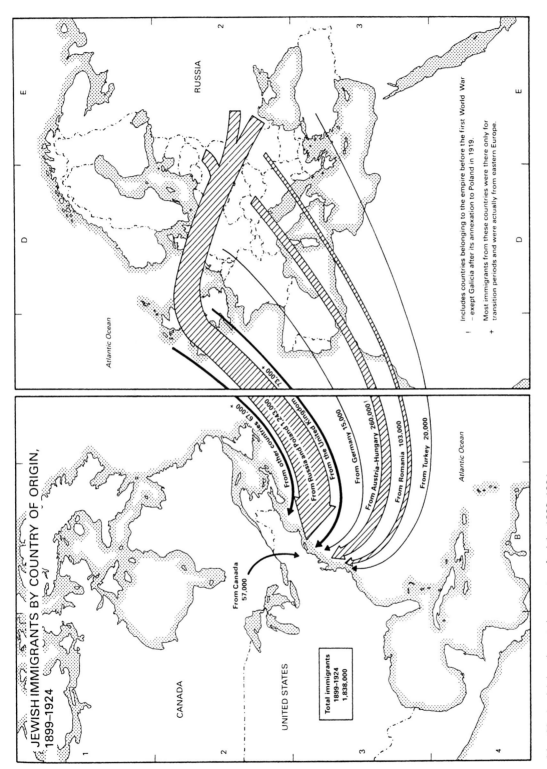

JEWISH IMMIGRANTS BY COUNTRY OF ORIGIN, 1899–1924

CANADA

UNITED STATES

From Canada 57,000

Total immigrants 1899–1924 1,838,000

From Other Countries 67,000 *

From Russia and Poland 1,243,000 *

From the United Kingdom

From Germany 15,000

From Austria–Hungary 260,000 !

From Romania 103,000

From Turkey 20,000

Atlantic Ocean

RUSSIA

73,000 *

Atlantic Ocean

! Includes countries belonging to the empire before the first World War – exept Galicia after its annexation to Poland in 1919.

+ Most immigrants from these countries were there only for transition periods and were actually from eastern Europe.

Map 60 Jewish immigrants by country of origin, 1899–1924

After the First World War, Jews in Palestine organized a National Assembly and an Executive Council. By 1929 the Jewish community (*yishuv*) numbered 160,000 with 110 agricultural settlements; in the next ten years the community increased to 500,000 with 233 agricultural communities. About a quarter of this population lived in co-operatives. Tel Aviv had 150,000 settlers, Jerusalem 90,000 and Haifa 60,000. Industrialization was initiated by the Palestinian Electric Corporation and developed by the *Histadrut*. In 1925 the Hebrew University was opened. During this period Palestine was only 160 miles long and 70 miles wide; this territory contained about one million Arabs consisting of peasants (*fellahin*) and a number of landowners in addition to the Jewish population. In 1929 the Arab community rioted following a dispute concerning Jewish access to the Western Wall of the ancient Temple. This conflict caused the British to curtail Jewish immigration as well as the purchase of Arab land.

By the late 1920s Labour Zionism had become a dominant force in Palestinian Jewish life. In 1930 various socialist and Labour groups joined together in the Israel Labour Party. Within the Zionist movement a right-wing segment criticized the President of the World Zionist Congress, **Chaim Weizmann** (1874–1952), who was committed to co-operating with the British. **Vladimir Jabotinsky** (1880–1940), leader of the Union of Zionist Revisionists, stressed that the central aim of Zionism was the establishment of an independent state in the whole of Palestine.

After several Zionist congresses, the Revisionist movement formed its own organization and withdrew from the militia of the *yishuv* (*Haganah*) to form its own military force. In 1936 the Arabs, supported by Syria, Iraq and Egypt, commenced an offensive against Jews, the British and moderate Arabs. In 1937 a British Royal Commission proposed that Palestine be partitioned into a Jewish and Arab state with a British zone. This recommendation was accepted by the Zionists but rejected by the Arabs. Eventually the British government published a White Paper in 1939 which rejected the concept of partition, limited Jewish immigration to 75,000 and decreed that Palestine would become independent in ten years.

While these events were taking place in Palestine, Jews in North Africa flourished as a result of French influence. In the 1860s the Alliance Israelite began to establish modern French-language schools for these communities and such progressive attitudes continued into the twentieth century. In India the long-established Jewish communities continued until the modern period. Modern Jewry was active in Alexandria and Cairo under British rule. The Jews of Iraq also prospered and played an important role in educational and economic life. At the beginning of the nineteenth century Jews in the Caucasus, Georgia and Bukhara were incorporated into the Russian empire and continued their religious traditions. In Turkey Sephardic Jews developed a distinctive culture based on Ladino, a Jewish Spanish dialect. The Jews of Persia lived under oppressive conditions throughout the nineteenth century, but a revival of Judaeo-Persian literature took place at the end of the century. In the 1920s Persia was modernized and the Jewish community began to establish cultural and educational institutions.

SOURCES

David Ben-Gurion

David Ben-Gurion, who became Prime Minister of Israel, presented evidence to the Royal Commission following the 1936 Arab riots, defending Jewish intentions:

We do not intend to create in Palestine the same intolerable position for the Jews as in all other countries. It means a radical change for the Jewish people; otherwise, there is no need for a National Home. It is not to give the Jews equal rights in Palestine. It is to change their position as a people. I want to say one word on why we are here in Palestine. It is not because we once conquered Palestine. Many people have conquered a country and lost it, and they have no claim to that country, but

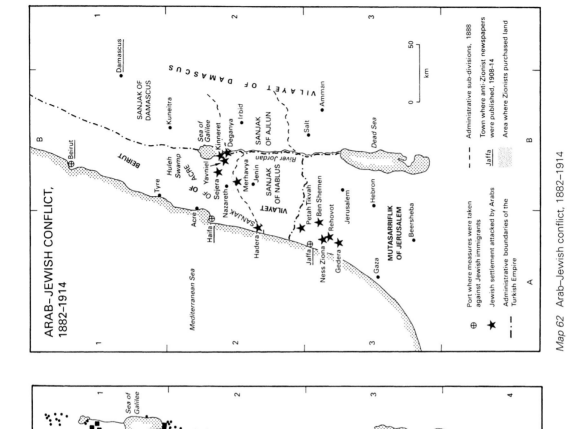

JEWISH SETTLEMENT IN PALESTINE

□ Jewish settlement to 1881
■ Jewish settlement to 1941
• Jewish settlement to 1948

0 ____ 25
km

Mediterranean Sea

Acre
Haifa
Tel Aviv
Jaffa
Gaza

Safed
Tiberias
Sea of Galilee

Nablus (Shechem)
Jerusalem
Hebron

River Jordan

Dead Sea

Map 61 Jewish settlement in Palestine

ARAB–JEWISH CONFLICT, 1882–1914

⊕ Port where measures were taken against Jewish immigrants
★ Jewish settlement attacked by Arabs
━·━ Administrative boundaries of the Turkish Empire

——— Administrative sub-divisions, 1888
– – – Town where anti-Zionist newspapers were published, 1908–14
Jaffa
▒ Area where Zionists purchased land

Mediterranean Sea

• Damascus

SANJAK OF DAMASCUS

VILAYET OF DAMASCUS

Beirut ⊕
Tyre
Acre
Haifa

Huleh Swamp
Sea of Galilee
Kinneret
Deganya
Yavniel
Sejera
Nazareth
Merhavya
Jenin
Kuneitra
Irbid
SANJAK OF ACRE
SANJAK OF AJLUN
Salt
Amman

VILAYET OF BEIRUT

SANJAK OF NABLUS
River Jordan

Hadera
Petah Tikvah
Ben Shemen
Jaffa
Ness Ziona
Rehovot
Gedera
Jerusalem
Hebron
Gaza
Beersheba

MUTASARRIFLIK OF JERUSALEM

Dead Sea

0 ____ 50
km

Map 62 Arab–Jewish conflict, 1882–1914

here we are for two reasons unprecedented in history. The first is this – Palestine is the only country in the world that the Jews, not as individuals but as a nation, as a race, can regard as their own country, as their historic homeland, and the second reason is there is no other nation – I do not say population, I do not say sections of a people – there is no other race or nation as a whole which regards this country as their only homeland. All the inhabitants of Palestine are children of this country and have full rights in this country, not only as citizens but as children of this homeland, but they have it in their capacity as inhabitants of this country. We have it as Jews, as children of the Jewish people, whether we are here already or whether we are not here yet. When the Balfour Declaration was made, there were 60,000 Jews here. It was not only the right of those 60,000. Now we are 400,000, and it is not only the right of these 400,000. It is because we are the children of the Jewish people and it is the only homeland of the Jewish people that we have rights in this country.

(David Ben-Gurion, *On the Arab Question*, in JMW, pp. 603–604)

Figure 48 Chaim Weizmann, first Prime Minister of the State of Israel, is sworn into office on 14 May 1948. Copyright AKG, London.

Ahad Ha-Am

Though dedicated to the creation of a Jewish state, the Russian essayist Ahad Ha-Am was aware of ignoring the Arab presence and trampling on their rights. After visiting settlements in Palestine at the end of the nineteenth century, he stressed that Palestine was not devoid of a native population:

We tend to believe abroad that Palestine is nowadays almost completely deserted, a non-cultivated wilderness, and anyone can come there and buy as much land as his heart desires. But in reality this is not the case. It is difficult to find anywhere in the country Arab land which lies fallow.

(Ahad Ha-Am, *Truth from the Land of Palestine*, in MMZ, p. 122)

In his view, what is required is a sense of realism. Jews should not regard themselves as superior to their Arab neighbours:

We tend to believe abroad that all Arabs are desert barbarians, an asinine people who do not see or understand what is going on around them. This is a cardinal mistake . . . The Arabs, and especially the city dwellers, understand very well what we want and what we do in the country; but they behave as if they do not notice it because at present they do not see any danger for themselves or their future in what we are doing and are therefore trying to turn to their benefit these new guests . . . But when the day will come in which the life of our people in the land of Israel will develop to such a degree that they will push aside the local population by little or much, then it will not easily give up its place.

(Ahad Ha-Am, *The Truth from the Land of Israel*, in MMZ, p. 123)

Hayyim Nahman Bialik

The poet Hayyim Nahman Bialik had an important impact on the development of early modern Hebrew poetry. In *The City of Slaughter* he criticized those Jews who failed to rise against the Russian mobs that besieged them:

> Come, now, and I will bring thee to their lairs
> The privies, jakes and pigpens where the heirs
> Of Hasmoneans lay, with trembling knees,
> Concealed and cowering – the sons of the Maccabees!
> The seed of saints, the scions of the lions!
> Who, crammed by scores in all the sanctuaries of their shame,
> So sanctified My name!
> It was the flight of mice they fled,
> The scurrying of roaches was their flight;
> They died like dogs, and they were dead.
>
> (Chaim Nahman Bialik, *The City of Slaughter*, in JMW, p. 411)

Vladimir Jabotinsky

Vladimir Jabotinksy was born in Russia in 1880, and later became the leader of the Revisionists. In 1923 he resigned from the Zionist Executive, and spearheaded a radical approach to Zionism. In 1926 he explained the aims of this new movement:

> The first aim of Zionism is the creation of a Jewish majority on both sides of the Jordan river. This is not the ultimate goal of the Zionist movement, which aspires to more-far-reaching ideals, such as the solution of the question of Jewish suffering throughout the entire world and the creation of a new Jewish culture. The pre-condition for the attainment of these noble aims, however, is a country in which the Jews constitute a majority. It is only after this majority is attained that Palestine can undergo a normal political development on the basis of democratic, parliamentary principles without thereby endangering the Jewish national character of the country . . .
>
> It is too late to preach 'a modified Zionism', for the Arabs have already read Herzl's *The Jewish State* as well as an even more 'dangerous' Zionist manifesto – the Bible. Furthermore, the concealment, and particularly the negation of our aims is politically dangerous. It can only lead to the sanction of all preventive measures against Jewish immigration, which, in fact, is what has already happened . . .
>
> In order to create a solid Jewish majority within twenty-five years in western Palestine we need an average yearly immigration of 40,000 Jews. If we take the area east of the Jordan into consideration, then we will need from 50,000 to 60,000 Jewish immigrants annually . . .
>
> It follows from this that the creation of a Jewish majority in Palestine requires special measures in order to provide economic opportunities for the new settlers. Our enthusiasm, our national funds, our energy and willingness to sacrifice, as great as they (all) may be, are not sufficient for this. The problem of the orderly absorption of such a large annual influx of people necessitates the direct intervention of governmental authority, that is to say, a whole series of administrative and legislative measures which only a government is in a position to execute.
>
> (Vladimir Jabotinsky, *What the Zionist-Revisionists Want*, in JMW, pp. 594–595)

DISCUSSION

1. What was the nature of immigrant Jewish life in the United States at the beginning of the twentieth century?

2. Discuss the nature of Jewish life in Palestine during the late nineteenth and early twentieth century.

FURTHER READING

Edelheit, Abraham, *The Yishuv in the Shadow of the Holocaust: Zionist Politics and Rescue Aliyah, 1933–1939*, Westview, 1996.

Feingold, Henry L. (ed.), *The Jewish People in America*, Vols 1–5, Johns Hopkins University Press, 1992.

Gilbert, Martin, *Israel: A History*, William Morrow & Co., 1998.

Grose, Peter, *Israel in the Mind of America*, Schocken, 1988.

Hertzberg, Arthur, *The Jews in America: Four Centuries of an Uneasy Encounter – A History*, Simon and Schuster, 1989.

Hertzberg, Arthur (ed.), *The Zionist Idea: A Historical Analysis and Reader*, Kuperord, 1995.

Marcus, Jacob Rader, *The Jew in the American World: A Source Book*, Wayne State University Press, 1995.

Sachar, Howard, *A History of the Jews in America*, Random House, 1995.

Sarna, Jonathan D., *The American Jewish Experience*, Holmes and Meier, 1986.

Vital, David, *The Origins of Zionism*, Oxford University Press, 1975.

Vital, David, *Zionism: The Formative Years*, Clarendon, 1982.

CHAPTER 49

The Nazi Regime

Timeline:

1933 Hitler appointed Chancellor. Nazi boycott of Jewish businesses

1935 Nuremberg Laws

1938 Kristallnacht

1939 Invasion of Poland

1940 Ghettos established in eastern Europe

1941 Invasion of Russia

1942 Wannsee Conference

1942–1944 Extermination camps established

After the First World War Germany flourished as a federal republic, but the depression of 1930–32 brought about massive unemployment. As a consequence extremist parties gained considerable support forcing the government to rule by presidential decree. After several unsuccessful conservative coalitions, the president, Field Marshal Paul von Hindenburg, appointed the leader of the National Socialist Workers' Party (the Nazi Party), **Adolf Hitler** (1889–1945) as chancellor. The ideology of the Nazi party was based on German nationalism, anti-capitalism and anti-Semitism. According to Hitler, the Jews were responsible for Germany's defeat in the war as well as the economic and cultural decline of the post-war period. In addition the Bolshevik victory in Russia was portrayed as part of a Jewish plot for world domination. To combat the plans of international Jewry, Hitler believed it was necessary for Germany to gain control over a vast empire in which Ayran supremacy could be ensured.

Once the Nazis gained control of the government, they pursued these racist objectives by curtailing civil liberties. In 1933 all political parties were eliminated; strikes were forbidden; and trade unions were dissolved. The arrest of dissident scholars and scientists was followed by a purge of the party's radicals. During the next few years Jews were eliminated from the civil service, the legal and medical professions, and cultural and educational institutions. In September 1935 the Nuremberg Laws made Jews into second-class inhabitants, and all marriage and sexual liaisons were described as crimes against the state. In 1938 Jewish communal bodies were put under the control of the Gestapo, and Jews were forced to register their property. Later in the year the Nazi party organized an onslaught against the Jewish population in which Jews were murdered and Jewish property was destroyed. This event, known as **Kristallnacht**, was a prelude to the Holocaust which brought about a new stage of modern Jewish history.

With the first phase of war, pressure on Jews in Germany increased. From September 1939 Jews had to be off the streets by 8.00 p.m.; their movements were restricted; they were banned from various types of transport and deprived of the use of the telephone. From December 1939 Jewish rations were cut and Jews were restricted to specific shopping hours. The Nazis' plan for the elimination of the Jews proceeded in stages. Initially thousands of Jews were deported or put into forced labour camps which frequently led to their death. But in 1941 when the invasion of Russia was imminent, rumours began to circulate that Hitler had entrusted Reinhard Heydrich with the preparation of a Final Solution to the Jewish problem. On 30 July 1940 Hermann Göring, who was in charge of the

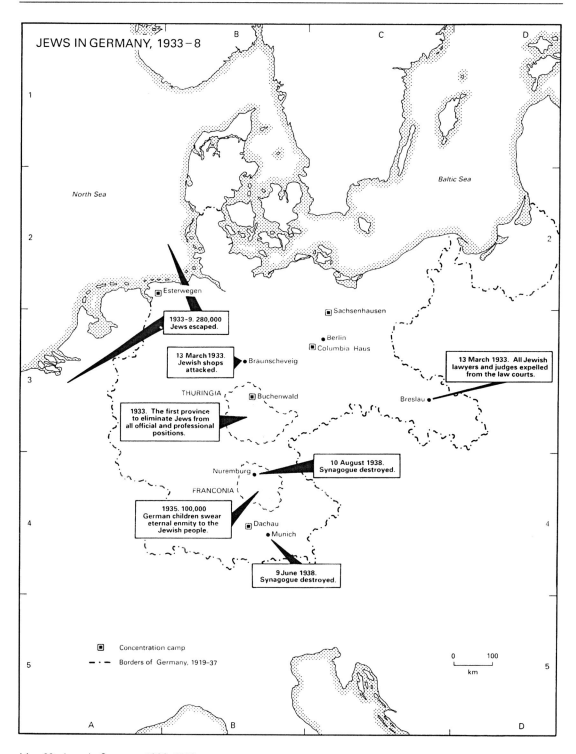

JEWS IN GERMANY, 1933–8

North Sea

Baltic Sea

■ Esterwegen

■ Sachsenhausen

1933–9. 280,000
Jews escaped.

● Berlin
■ Columbia Haus

13 March 1933.
Jewish shops
attacked.

● Braunscheveig

13 March 1933. All Jewish
lawyers and judges expelled
from the law courts.

THURINGIA

■ Buchenwald

1933. The first province
to eliminate Jews from
all official and professional
positions.

Breslau ●

10 August 1938.
Synagogue destroyed.

Nuremburg ●

FRANCONIA

1935. 100,000
German children swear
eternal enmity to the
Jewish people.

■ Dachau
● Munich

9 June 1938.
Synagogue destroyed.

■ Concentration camp

— · — Borders of Germany, 1919–37

0   100
km

Map 63 Jews in Germany, 1933–1938

German economy, had ordered Reinhard Heydrich to take all preparatory measures required for the final solution of the Jewish question in the European territories under German influence. Heydrich himself revealed the Final Solution to staff members at the Wannsee conference on 20 January 1942 in the office of the International Criminal Police Commission outside Berlin. The war with Russia, he explained, made the plan of deporting all Jews an impossibility. The only alternative was extermination.

The first stage of the Nazis' plan for European Jewry had already begun with the invasion of Poland. In September 1939 Hitler decided to incorporate much of Poland into Germany, and move more than 600,000 Jews into a central area ('General Government'). When the Jewish population was **ghettoized** into what Hitler referred to as a huge Polish labour camp, a massive work programme was initiated. Here Jews worked all day, seven days a week, dressed in rags and fed on bread, soup and potatoes. This slave-labour operation was a form of murder; the phrase 'destruction through work' was used repeatedly in discussions between Georg Thierack, Joseph Goebbels, and Heinrich Himmler in September 1942.

According to Rudolf Hess, the commandant at Auschwitz, by the end of 1944 about 400,000 slaves worked in the German armaments industry. These workers had no names, only numbers tattooed on their bodies; if one died a replacement was sought without any inquest into the cause of death. Yet working Jews to their graves was not sufficient for the Nazi regime; what was needed was a plan of mass extermination which began with the **invasion of Russia** in 1941. This was designed to destroy the centre of what was described by the Nazis as the 'Jewish-Bolshevik conspiracy'.

At first mobile killing battalions of 500–900 men (the *Einsatzgruppen*) under the supervision of Heydrich began the slaughter of Russian Jewry. Of the 4,500,000 Jews who resided in Soviet territory, more than half fled before the German invasion; those who remained were concentrated in large cities making it easier for Heydrich's troops to carry out their task. Throughout the country the *Einsatzgruppen* moved into Russian towns, sought out the rabbi or Jewish council and obtained a list of all Jewish inhabitants. The Jews were then rounded up in market places, crowded into trains, buses and trucks and taken to the woods where mass graves had been dug. They were then machine-gunned to death. In this slaughter some Jews attempted to escape the onslaught by hiding under floorboards and cellars, but they were buried alive or blasted out with grenades. A few girls offered themselves to stay alive; they were used during the night but killed the next morning. In the initial sweep between October and December 1941, these troops killed over 300,000 Jews; in a second stage that lasted throughout 1942 over 900,000 were murdered.

SOURCES

Hitler and the Jews

In *Mein Kampf*, Hitler described his growing awareness of Jewry once he lived in Vienna:

> Once, as I was strolling through the inner city, I suddenly encountered an apparition in a black caftan and black hair locks. Is this a Jew? was my first thought. For, to be sure, they had not looked like that in Linz. I observed this man furtively and cautiously, but the longer I stared at this foreign face, scrutinizing feature for feature, the more my first question assumed a new form: Is this a German?
>
> (Adolf Hitler, *Mein Kampf*, in UH, p. 29)

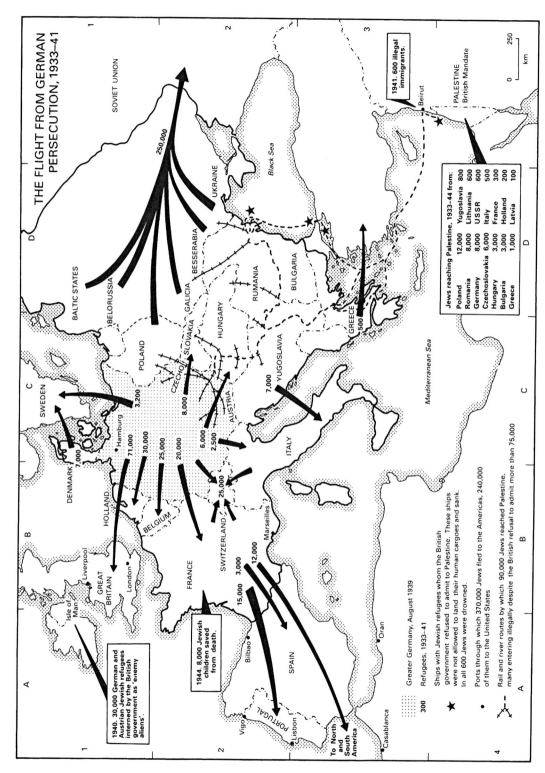

THE FLIGHT FROM GERMAN
PERSECUTION, 1933–41

1941. 600 illegal immigrants.

1940. 30,000 German and
Austrian Jewish refugees
interned by the British
government as 'enemy
aliens'.

1944. 8,000 Jewish
children saved
from death.

Jews reaching Palestine, 1933–44 from:			
Poland	12,000	Yugoslavia	800
Romania	8,000	Lithuania	600
Germany	8,000	USSR	600
Czechoslovakia	6,000	Italy	500
Hungary	3,000	France	300
Bulgaria	3,000	Holland	200
Greece	1,000	Latvia	100

Greater Germany, August 1939

300   Refugees, 1933–41

Ships with Jewish refugees whom the British
government refused to admit to Palestine. These ships
were not allowed to land their human cargoes and sank.
In all 600 Jews were drowned.

Ports through which 370,000 Jews fled to the Americas, 240,000
of them to the United States.

Rail and river routes by which 90,000 Jews reached Palestine,
many entering illegally despite the British refusal to admit more than 75,000

Map 64   The flight from German persecution, 1933–1941

For Hitler the Jew could never become a German because he was racially and religiously distinct. The difference between Jews and Germans was so vast as to make them inherently aliens. Jews, he asserted, were:

> not Germans of a special religion, but a people in themselves; for since I had begun to concern myself with this question and to take cognizance of the Jews, Vienna appeared to me in a different light than before. Wherever I went, I began to see Jews, and the more I saw, the more sharply they became distinguished in my eyes from the rest of humanity.
>
> (Adolf Hitler, *Mein Kampf*, in UH, p. 30)

Comparing Jews with vermin, he wrote:

> Was there any form of filth or profligacy, particularly in cultural life, without at least one Jew involved in it? If you cut even cautiously into such an abscess you found, like a maggot in a rotting body, often dazzled by the sudden light – a *kike*!
>
> (Adolf Hitler, *Mein Kamp*, in UH, p. 30)

Figure 49 Anti-semitic cartoon from a German schoolbook. Copyright Imperial War Museum, London.

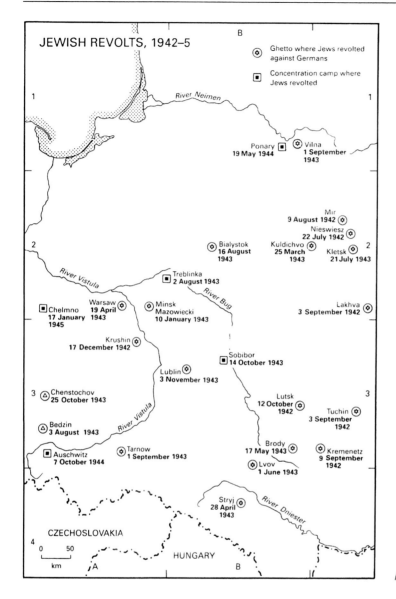

JEWISH REVOLTS, 1942–5

⊕ Ghetto where Jews revolted against Germans

■ Concentration camp where Jews revolted

River Neimen

Ponary ■
19 May 1944

⊕ Vilna
1 September
1943

Mir
9 August 1942 ⊕

Nieswiesz ⊕
22 July 1942

⊕ Bialystok
16 August
1943

Kuldichvo ⊕
25 March
1943

Kletsk ⊕
21 July 1943

River Vistula

■ Treblinka
2 August 1943

River Bug

Warsaw ⊕
■ Chelmno   19 April
17 January   1943
1945

⊕ Minsk
Mazowiecki
10 January 1943

Lakhva ⊕
3 September 1942

Krushin ⊕
17 December 1942

Sobibor
■ 14 October 1943

Lublin ⊕
3 November 1943

River Vistula

Lutsk
12 October
1942 ⊕

Tuchin ⊕
3 September
1942

3 ⊕ Chenstochov
25 October 1943

⊕ Bedzin
3 August 1943

■ Auschwitz
7 October 1944

⊕ Tarnow
1 September 1943

Brody
17 May 1943 ⊕

⊕ Kremenetz
9 September
1942

⊕ Lvov
1 June 1943

Stryj ⊕
28 April
1943

River Dniester

CZECHOSLOVAKIA

0   50

km

HUNGARY

Map 65 Jewish revolts, 1942–1945

The SS

In the creation of the Third Reich, the SS played an increasingly important role. Eventually it became a party police force, a regular army within the army. Infiltrating every aspect of German life, it spread its tentacles throughout the nation. The principles of selection to the SS embodied the values espoused by the Nazi regime, as Heinrich Himmler explained in a speech delivered in 1935:

> The first principle for us was and is the recognition of the values of blood and selection
> . . . We went about it like a seedsman who, wanting to improve the strain of a good old

variety which has become crossbred and lost its vigour, goes through the fields to pick up the best plants . . . The nature of the selection process was to concentrate on the choice of those who came physically closest to the ideal of the Nordic man . . . The second principle and virtue which we tried to instil in the SS and to give it an indelible characteristic for the future is the will to freedom and a fighting spirit . . . The third principle and virtue are the concepts of loyalty and honour . . . The fourth principle and virtue that is valid for us is obedience, which does not hesitate for a moment but unconditionally follows every order which comes from the Führer or is legitimately given by a superior.

(Heinrich Himmler, *Speech at the Reich Peasant Congress*, in UH, p. 66)

Kristallnacht

On 10 November 1938 anti-Jewish demonstrations took place throughout Germany during which Jewish shops were demolished and synagogues set on fire. A witness to this assault in Leipzig was the American Consul David Buffum who described this attack on the Jewish community:

The shattering of shop windows, looting of stores and dwellings of Jews which began in the early hours of 10 November 1938 was hailed subsequently in the Nazi press as a 'spontaneous wave of righteous indignation throughout Germany, as a result of the cowardly Jewish murder of Third Secretary von Rath in the German Embassy at Paris.' . . . At 3 a.m. on 10 November 1938 was unleashed a barrage of Nazi ferocity as had no equal hitherto in Germany, or very likely anywhere else in the world since savagery began. Jewish buildings were smashed into and contents demolished or looted. In one of the Jewish sections an 18–year-old boy was hurled from a third-storey window to land with both legs broken on a street littered with burning beds and other household furniture and effects from his family and apartments.

(David Buffum, *Nuremburg Document*, in UH, p. 97)

The Ghetto

The largest ghetto created by the Nazis was in Warsaw. One of those who visited the Warsaw ghetto provided a chilling account of its residents:

The majority are nightmare figures, ghosts of former human beings, miserable destitutes, pathetic remnants of former humanity. One is most affected by the characteristic change which one sees in their faces: as a result of misery, poor nourishment, the lack of vitamins, fresh air and exercise, the numerous cares, worries, anticipated misfortunes, suffering and sickness, their faces have taken on a skeletal appearance. The prominent bones around their eye sockets, the yellow facial colour, the slack pendulous skin, the alarming emaciation and sickliness. And, in addition, this miserable frightened, restless, apathetic and resigned expression, like that of a hunted animal. I pass my closest friends without recognizing them and guessing their fate. Many of them recognize me, come up to me and ask curiously how things are 'over there' behind the walls – where there is enough fresh air, freedom to move around, and above all freedom . . .

On the streets children are crying in vain, children who are dying of hunger. They howl, beg, sing, moan, shiver with cold, without underwear, without clothing, without shoes, in

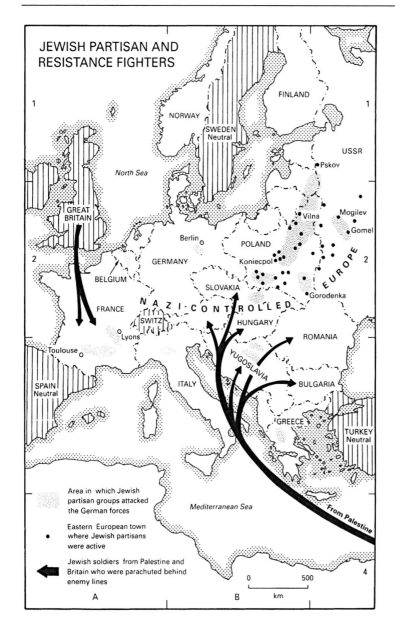

Map 66 Jewish partisan and resistance fighters

rags, sacks, flannel which are bound in strips round the emaciated skeletons, children swollen with hunger, disfigured, half conscious, already completely grown-up at the age of five, gloomy and weary of life. They are like old people and are only conscious of one thing: 'I'm cold', 'I'm hungry'. They have become aware of the most important things in life that quickly. Through their innocent sacrifice and their frightening helplessness the thousands upon thousands of these little beggars level the main accusation against the proud civilization today.

(Stanislav Rozycki, *Description of the Warsaw Ghetto*, UH, pp. 127–128)

The Assault Against Russia

A typical example of the horror that took place throughout Russia occurred in the city of Lvov shortly after the German invasion. At the beginning of the German occupation, Ukrainian mobs murdered Jews wherever they were found. A witness to this onslaught recalled the scene in the yard of a police station where more than 5,000 Jews had been gathered:

Thousands of men were lying here in rows. They lay on their bellies, their faces buried in the sand. Around the perimeter of the field searchlights and machine guns had been set up. Among them I caught sight of German officers standing about. We were ordered to lie flat like the others. We were pushed and shoved brutally, this way and that. My father was separated from me, and I heard him calling out in despair: 'Let me stay with my son! I want to die with my son!' Nobody took any notice of him.

Now that we were all lying still, there was a hush that lasted for a moment or two. Then the 'game' started. We could hear the sound of a man, clearly one of us, stumbling awkwardly around, chased and beaten by another as he went. At last the pursued collapsed out of sheer exhaustion. He was told to rise. Blows were rained down upon him until he dragged himself to his feet again and tried to run forward. He fell to the ground again and tried to run forward. He fell to the ground again and hadn't the strength to get up. When the pursuers were at last satisfied that the incessant blows had rendered him unable to stir, let alone run, they called a halt and left him there. Now it was the turn of the second victim. He received the same treatment . . .

Thoughts raced in disorder and confusion through my mind. I was so exhausted that I fell asleep. Not even the agonizing screams, the sound of savage blows, or the continual trampling on our bodies could prevent me any longer from sinking into oblivion . . .

The welcome state of unconsciousness passed all too quickly. I came to, and was startled by a painful stab of dazzling light. Powerful searchlights were focused on us. We sat up, one beside the other, so close that we could not stir. Directly in front of me sat two men with shattered skulls. Through the mess of bone and hair I could see the very brains. We whispered to them. We nudged them. But they did not stir. They just sat there, propped up, bulging eyes staring ahead. They were quite dead.

(Leon Weliczker Wells, *Eichmann Trial*, in UH, pp. 140–141)

DISCUSSION

1. What was the nature of Jewish life in Germany once Hitler became Chancellor?

2. Discuss the racist ideology of the Nazi state and its effect on Jewry.

FURTHER READING

Bullock, Alan, *Hitler: A Study in Tyranny*, Konecky and Konecky, 1999.

Bullock, Alan, *Hitler and Stalin: Parallel Lives*, Fontana, 1998.

Burleigh, Michael, Wippermann, Wolfgang, *The Racial State: Germany 1933–45*, Cambridge University Press, 1991.

Cohn-Sherbok, Dan, *Understanding the Holocaust: An Introduction*, Cassell, 2000.

Dawidowicz, Lucy S., *The War Against the Jews 1933–1945*, Bantam Doubleday Dell, 1991.

Gilbert, Martin, *The Holocaust*, HarperCollins, 1987.

Kershaw, Ian, *Hitler, 1889–1936: Hubris*, W.W. Norton, 1999.

Kershaw, Ian, *Hitler, 1936–1945: Nemesis*, W.W. Norton, 2000.

Landau, Connie S., *The Nazi Holocaust*, I.B. Tauris, 1992.

Lifton, Robert Jay, *The Nazi Doctors: Medical Killing and the Psychology of Genocide*, Basic Books, 2000.

Lipstadt, Deborah E., *Denying the Holocaust: The Growing Assault on Truth and Memory*, Free Press, 1993.

Noakes, Jeremy, Pridham, Geoffrey, (eds), *Nazism 1919–1945*, Exeter University Press, 1998.

Rhodes, James M., *The Hitler Movement: A Modern Millenarian Revolution*, Hoover Institute Press, 1980.

Shirer, William L., *The Rise and Fall of the Third Reich: A History of Nazi Germany*, Touchstone, 1981.

Sofsky, W., *The Order of Terror: The Concentration Camp*, Princeton University Press, 1997.

Wistrich, Robert, *Who's Who in Nazi Germany*, Routledge, 1995.

CHAPTER 50

The Death Camps

Timeline:

1942 Wannsee Conference

1942–1944 Extermination camps established in Chelmno, Auschwitz, Belzec, Sobibor, Majdanek, Treblinka

1943 Warsaw ghetto uprising

Figure 50 Door to the gas chamber at the Majdanek concentration camp. Copyright Imperial War Museum, London.

Other methods were also employed by the Nazis. Mobile gas vans were sent to each battalion of the *Einsatzgruppen*. Meanwhile these mobile killing operations were being supplemented by the use of fixed centres, the death camps. Six of these were at Chelmno and Auschwitz in the Polish territories, and at Treblinka, Sobibor, Majdanek and Belzec in the Polish 'General Government'. Construction of this mass-murder industry began in 1941. Two civilians from Hamburg went to Auschwitz to teach the staff how to use Zyklon-B gas. In September 1941 the first gassing took place in Auschwitz Block II; then work began on Birkenau, the central killing centre in Auschwitz. The first death camp to be completed was Chelmno near Lodz which started functioning in December 1941. Subsequently Belzec became operational and the building of Sobibor began in March 1942. At the same time Majdanek and Treblinka were transformed into death centres.

The eradication of the Jews in western Europe (as opposed to the destruction of Polish and Russian Jewry) was the private preserve of Adolf Eichmann. In 1942 he decided to send 100,000 Jews from the Greater Reich (Germany, Austria and Czechoslovakia) to Poland where they were gassed at Belzec and Majdanek. By the end of 1943 the majority of Jews from the Greater Reich were killed: 180,000 from Germany; 60,000 from Austria; and 243,000 from Czechoslovakia. The **deportation** of Jews in countries west and south of Poland was on an equally massive scale. Out of a population of 140,000 Dutch Jews, 110,000 were deported to Auschwitz and Sobibor to be exterminated between 1941 and 1942. During this period 25,000 Belgian Jews, 50,000 Yugoslav Jews and 80,000 Greek Jews perished in the death camps.

Until the summer of 1942 Jewish deportees from central and western Europe were divided equally between Auschwitz and the other **death camps**, but in August 1942 Himmler decided that Auschwitz should become the central extermination centre for western Europe. At its fullest capacity it held 140,000 inmates and its five crematoria could burn 10,000 bodies each day. Those who escaped the gassing engaged in forced labour for twelve to fourteen hours a day surviving on a watery turnip soup until they became living corpses.

Though nearly all of European Jewry had no other option but to succumb to Nazi terror without resistance, there were some Jews who revolted against the Germans. In the summer of 1942 a young Zionist, Mordecai Anielewicz, persuaded the Jewish leaders of the Warsaw ghetto that resistance offered the only possibility of survival. Underground shelters and bunkers were constructed; money was raised from Jewish capitalists; revolvers and grenades were purchased. By the autumn of 1942 the Jewish resistance had become a powerful force.

By January of the next year Himmler visited the Warsaw ghetto and issued the order for a final eradication of the remaining Jews; in April SS Major-General Jürgen Stroop arrived to put this operation into effect. When the 2,000 SS troops moved into position, they were attacked from rooftops. In response the Nazis bombarded buildings and systematically levelled the places where Jews were hiding. In the sewers and shelters the Jews continued their resistance. Jewish patrols disguised in German uniforms ventured out to capture arms and rations; grenades and molotov cocktails were tossed at German troops and tanks. The SS retaliated with dynamite and gas shells, flooded the sewers and released police dogs.

In the face of such a powerful enemy the Jewish community in Europe was doomed to mass destruction. Nearly 9 million Jews were resident in European countries under German control. Of those it is estimated that the Nazis killed about 6 million. In Poland more than 90 per cent were killed. The same percentage of the Jewish population died in the Baltic States, Germany and Austria. More than 70 per cent were murdered in the Bohemian protectorate, Slovakia, Greece and the Netherlands. More than 50 per cent were killed in White Russia, the Ukraine, Belgium, Yugoslavia, Romania and Norway. The six major death camps constituted the main areas of killing: over 2,000,000 died at Auschwitz; 1,380,000 at Majdanek; 800,000 at Treblinka; 600,000 at Belzec; 340,000 at Chelmno; and 250,000 at Sobibor.

SOURCES

The Wannsee Conference

The Wannsee Conference of 20 January 1942 in a villa outside Berlin discussed the Final Solution to the Jewish problem. In his trial in 1960 Adolf Eichmann described this event:

What I know is that the gentlemen sat together, and then in very blunt terms – not in the language that I had to use in the minutes, but in very blunt terms – they talked abut the matter without any circumlocution. I certainly could not have remembered that if I had not recalled saying to myself at the time: look, just look at Stuckart, who was always regarded as a legal pedant, punctilious and fussy, and now what a different tone! The language being used here was very unlegalistic. I should say that this is the only thing from all this that has still stuck clearly in my mind . . . The talk was of killing, elimination, and annihilation.

(Adolf Eichmann, *The Wannsee Conference*, in UH, p. 149)

Deportation

As deportations took place throughout Europe, rumours constantly circulated about what fate awaited those who travelled eastward. An observer of this events noted:

There is great unhappiness and fear among the Jews. From everywhere comes the news about the incredible violence against the Jews. They are bringing trainloads of Jews from Czechoslovakia, Germany and even from Belgium. They are also resettling the Jews from various towns and villages and taking them somewhere towards Belzec. Today I heard a story about what they did to the Jews in Lublin. It is difficult to believe it's true. Today they deported Jews from Izbica – they were also taken to Belzec where there is supposed to be some monstrous camp . . .

On the way to Belzec people can see horrifying scenes – especially the railwaymen – because the Jews know very well why they are being taken there, and on the journey they are given neither food nor water. On the station in Szczebrzeszyn the railwaymen could see with their own eyes, and hear with their own ears Jews offering 150 *zlotys* for a kilo of bread, and a Jewess took off a gold ring from her finger and offered it in exchange for a glass of water for her dying child.

(Zygmunt Klukowski, *Description of the Deportations*, in UH, pp. 156–157)

Arrival at the Camps

When trains arrived at the camps, terrible scenes took place. According to one of the deportees from Lvov to Belzec, the entire area of the camp was occupied by the SS:

The train entered a yard which measured about one kilometre by one kilometre and was surrounded by barbed wire and fencing about two metres high, which was not electrified. Entry to the yard was through a wooden gate covered with barbed wire. Next to the gate there was a guard house with a telephone and standing in front of the guard house were several SS men with dogs. When the train entered the yard the SS men closed the gate and went into the guard house. At that moment, dozens of SS men opened the doors of the waggons shouting 'Out!' They pushed people out with their

Map 67 Concentration camps

whips and rifles. The doors of the waggons were about one metre from the ground. The people hurried along with blows from whips, were forced to jump down, old and young alike, it made no difference.

They broke arms and legs, but they had to obey the orders of the SS men.

(Rudolf Reder, *Belzec* in UH, p. 159)

Once Jews had arrived at Belzec, they were told that they were going to the bath house and then would be sent to work. Fearing the worst, they were filled with hope:

The women went about 200 metres farther on – to a large barrack hut which measured about 30 metres by 15 metres. There they had their heads shaved, both women and girls. They entered, not knowing what for. There was silence and calm. Later, I knew that only a few minutes after entering, they were asked to sit on wooden stools across the barrack hut, and Jewish barbers, like automatons, as silent as the grave, came forward to shave their heads. Then they understood the whole truth, none of them could have

any doubts any more. All of them – everyone – except a few chosen craftsmen – were going to die.

The girls with long hair went to be shaved, those who had short hair went with the men – straight into the gas chambers. Suddenly there were cries and tears, a lot of women had hysterics. Many of them went cold-bloodedly to their deaths, especially the young girls . . .

(Rudolf Reder, *Description of the Arrival at Belzec*, in UH, p. 160)

Burial

Members of the *Sonderkommando* of about 500 Jews who were selected from previous transports were responsible for burying the dead at Belzec:

We dug huge mass graves and dragged bodies. We used spades, but there was also a mechanical excavator which dug up the sand and piled it into mounds and later covered over the graves already full of bodies. About 450 of us worked at the graves. It took a week to dig one pit.

The most horrible thing for me was that there was an order to pile the bodies up to a level one metre

above the edge of the graves, and then cover them with a layer of sand, while thick, black blood flowed out and flooded the ground like a lake. We had to walk along the ledges from one pit to the next, and our feet were soaked with our brothers' blood. We walked over their bodies and that was even worse.

(Rudolf Reder, *Description of Graves*, in UH, p. 160)

SS Doctors

In their quest to carry out the Final Solution, SS doctors played a central role in the functioning of the camps. When deportees arrived after their long journeys it was the doctors who were instrumental in implementing the process of selection. In addition, such individuals carried out a ruthless and barbaric programme of medical experimentation in line with Nazi racial theory:

We arrived at night . . . Because you arrived at night, you saw miles of lights – and the fire from the . . . crematoria. And then screaming and the whistles and the 'Out, out!', and the uniformed men and the SS with the dogs, and the stripped prisoners . . . They separated you and then lined up everybody in

fives . . . and there were two men standing . . . On one side, was the doctor, one was Mengele . . . and on the other side was the . . . *Arbeitsführer*, which was the . . . man in charge of the work *Kommando*.

(Robert Jay Lifton, *The Nazi Doctors*, in UH, p. 188)

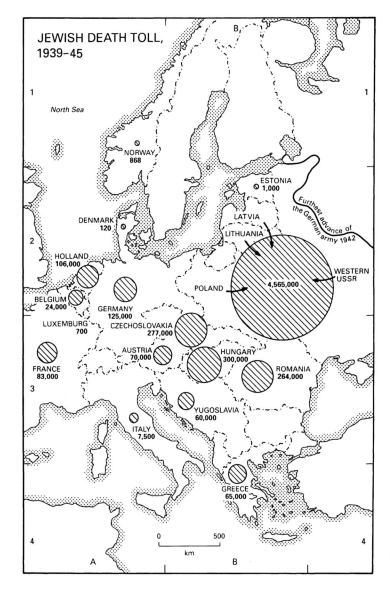

JEWISH DEATH TOLL,
1939–45

North Sea

NORWAY
868

ESTONIA
1,000

DENMARK
120

LATVIA

LITHUANIA

HOLLAND
106,000

WESTERN
USSR

POLAND

4,565,000

Furthest advance of
the German army 1942

BELGIUM
24,000

GERMANY
125,000

LUXEMBURG
700

CZECHOSLOVAKIA
277,000

AUSTRIA
70,000

HUNGARY
300,000

ROMANIA
264,000

FRANCE
83,000

YUGOSLAVIA
60,000

ITALY
7,500

GREECE
65,000

0   500
km

A   B

Map 68 Jewish death toll,
1939–1945

DISCUSSION

1. Discuss life in the ghettos and concentration camps under Nazi rule.

2. In what ways did the Wannsee Conference determine the fate of European Jewry?

FURTHER READING

Botwinick, Rita Steinhardt, *A History of the Holocaust: From Ideology to Annihilation*, Prentice Hall, 1997.

Burleigh, Michael, Wippermann, Wolfgang, *The Racial State: Germany 1933–45*, Cambridge University Press, 1996.

Dawidowicz, Lucy C., *The War Against the Jews 1933–1945*, Weidenfeld and Nicolson, 1975.

Fischer, Klaus P., *Nazi Germany*, Constable, 1996.

Fischer, Klaus P., *The History of an Obsession*, Constable, 1998.

Friedlander, Saul, *Nazi Germany and the Jews*, Weidenfeld and Nicolson, 1997.

Gilbert, M., *The Holocaust*, HarperCollins, 1987.

Hilberg, Raul, *The Destruction of the European Jews*, 3 Vols, Yale University Press, 2002.

Landau, Ronnie S., *The Nazi Holocaust*, I.B. Tauris, 1992.

Marrus, Michael R., *The Holocaust in History*, Key Porter, 2000.

Reitlinger, Gerald, *The Final Solution: The Attempt to Exterminate the Jews of Europe*, Vallentine Mitchell, 1953.

Rubenstein, William D., *The Myth of Rescue: Why the Democracies Could Not Save More Jews from the Nazis*, Routledge, 1997.

Sofsky, W., *The Order of Terror: The Concentration Camp*, Princeton University Press, 1997.

Yahil, Leni, *The Holocaust: The Fate of European Jewry*, Oxford University Press, 1990.

CHAPTER 51

The State of Israel

Timeline:

1945–1947 Jewish–British conflict in Palestine

1947 General Assembly of the United Nations votes in favour of partition

1948 British leave Palestine. Declaration of Independence of Israel. Arab attack on Israel

1949 Ceasefire between Israel and Arabs

1949 Mass immigration of Jews from Displaced Persons camps in Europe and other countries

1956 Sinai campaign

1967 Six Day War

1969–1970 Egypt launches attack along the Suez Canal

1973 *Yom Kippur* War

1977 President Sadat visits Israel

1982 Israeli invasion of Lebanon

1985 Palestinian *intifada* begins

1991 Gulf War

1995 Yitzhak Rabin assassinated

1996 Benjamin Netanyahu elected Prime Minister

1999 Ehud Barak elected Prime Minister

2001 Ariel Sharon elected Prime Minsiter

The Holocaust and the establishment of the State of Israel were organically related events – the death of millions of Jews in the Second World War profoundly affected Jewry throughout the world. Some traditional Jews believed that the Holocaust was a punishment upon the community because of its sins but would be followed by the founding of a Jewish state; others thought the creation of Israel was the consequence of Jewish suffering. Whatever the cause, Hitler's policy unintentionally assisted the Jewish community in Palestine: 60,000 Jews initially left Germany for Israel and contributed substantially to the growth and development of the homeland. In addition, from the beginning of the war in 1939, the creation of a Jewish state became the primary aim of Zionists. In order to achieve this objective the Jewish community had to persuade the allies of the virtues of their plan. As far as the British were concerned, though the **Balfour Declaration** of 1917 supported the establishment of a

Jewish homeland in Palestine, the 1939 White Paper effectively rejected this proposal and projected a future in which there would be no predominantly Jewish presence.

During the war and afterwards, the British steadfastly maintained this policy and prevented illegal immigrants from entering the Holy Land. In the Jews' struggle against the British, Menachem Begin, the leader of the Revisionists' military arm (the *Irgun*), played an important role. Similarly an extremist group called the Stern Gang, which broke away from the *Irgun*, carried on a campaign against British domination.

On 6 November 1944 the Stern Gang murdered Lord Moyne, the British Minister for Middle East Affairs. The official Zionist military force, the *Haganah*, was appalled by this action and launched an offensive against the Sternists and the *Irgun*. Yet despite this internal conflict these various Jewish factions

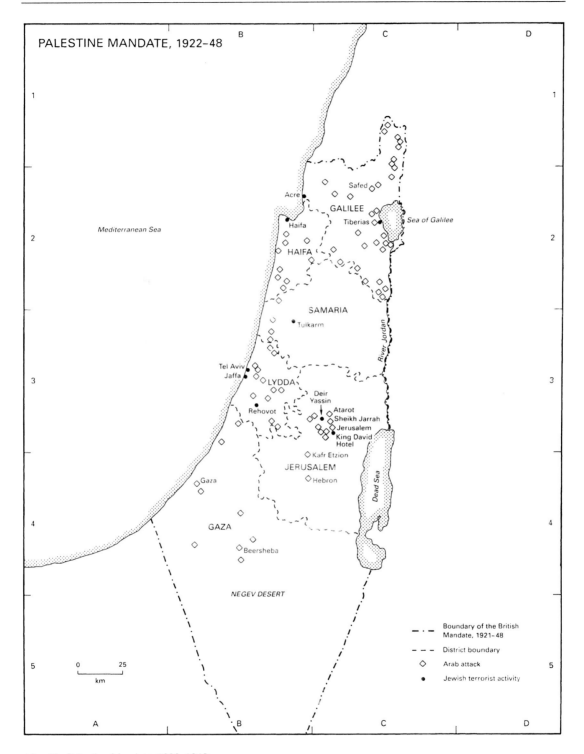

Map 69 Palestine Mandate, 1922–1948

eventually joined forces in forming a united resistance movement.

In this struggle two episodes involving Menachem Begin were instrumental in forcing Britain to capitulate. On 29 June 1946 the British arrested over 2,000 Jewish activists. In response Begin convinced the *Haganah* to blow up the King David Hotel in Jerusalem where part of the British administration was housed. At the end of July an explosion took place killing twenty-eight British, forty-one Arabs and seventeen Jews plus five others. Subsequently the British government proposed a tripartite division of Palestine, but both Arabs and Jews rejected this scheme. On 14 February the British Foreign Secretary Ernest Bevin handed over the Palestinian problem to the United Nations though Britain did not immediately withdraw from the country. In April 1947 three members of the *Irgun* were arrested and hanged for attacking the prison in Acre and freeing 251 soldiers. In response anti-Jewish riots took place in various English cities, which helped to persuade the British to leave Palestine as soon as possible.

Once the British announced their intention, President Harry Truman argued for the creation of a Jewish state. In May 1947 the United Nations discussed the Palestinian problem. Two reports were issued by a special committee: a minority recommended a federated bi-national state; the majority advocated a new plan of partition in which there would be a Jewish and an Arab state as well as an international zone in Jerusalem. This latter proposal was endorsed by the General Assembly of the United Nations on 29 November 1947. Once the UN plan for partition was endorsed, the Arabs began to attack Jewish settlements. By March 1948 over 1,000 Jews had been killed, but in the next month David Ben-Gurion ordered the *Haganah* to link up all the Jewish enclaves and consolidate the territory given to Israel under the UN partition plan. On 14 May 1948 Ben-Gurion read out the **Scroll of Independence**.

Immediately a government was formed, Egyptian air raids began. A truce lasting a month was formalized on 11 June during which time the Arabs reinforced their armies. When the fighting began again on 9 July, the Israelis appeared to be in control – they took Lydda, Ramleh and Nazareth as well as large territories beyond the partition borders. Though the Arabs agreed

to a truce, there were outbursts of violence, and in October the Israelis launched an offensive which resulted in the capture of Beersheba. On 12 January 1949 armistice talks were held and later signed with Egypt, the Lebanon, Transjordan and Syria. During this period more than 650,000 Arab inhabitants of Palestine escaped from Israeli-held territory: 280,000 to the West Bank; 70,000 to Transjordan; 100,000 to Lebanon; 4,000 to Iraq; 75,000 to Syria; 7,000 to Egypt; and 190,000 to the Gaza Strip.

Because of these Palestinian refugees the Arabs regarded the armistice as merely a temporary truce. Under President Nasser of Egypt, a plan for the elimination of the Jewish state was put into operation. From 1956 President Gamal Abdel Nasser refused Israeli ships access to the Gulf of Aqaba; in April he signed a pact with Saudi Arabia and Yemen; in July he seized the Suez Canal; in October he formed a military command with Jordan and Syria. In response Israel launched a strike on 29 October conquering Sinai and opening the sea route to Aqaba. In an agreement which ended the fighting, Israel undertook to withdraw from Sinai provided that Egypt did not remilitarize it and UN forces constituted a *cordon sanitaire*. This arrangement existed for a decade though armed struggle between both sides continued.

In 1967 Nasser began another offensive against Israel. On 15 May he moved 100,000 troops into the Sinai and ordered the UN forces to leave. He then blockaded Aqaba by closing the Tiran Straits to Israeli shipping, and signed a military agreement with King Hussein of Jordan. On 5 June the Israelis launched a preemptive strike devastating the Egyptian air force on the ground. Jordan and Syria then entered the war on Egypt's side. Two days later Israel captured the Old City of Jerusalem and on the following day the West Bank. During the next two days Israel attacked the Golan Heights and reoccupied Sinai.

The Six Day War was a major victory for the Israelis but did not bring security to the Jewish state. In July 1972 President Anwar Sadat of Egypt expelled Egypt's Soviet advisers, dispensed with Nasser's alliances with other Arab states, and on *Yom Kippur*, 6 October 1973, he attacked Israel. The Egyptian and Syrian forces broke through Israeli lines and serious losses were inflicted on Israeli planes and armour. On 9 October the Syrian advance was halted, and the next day the

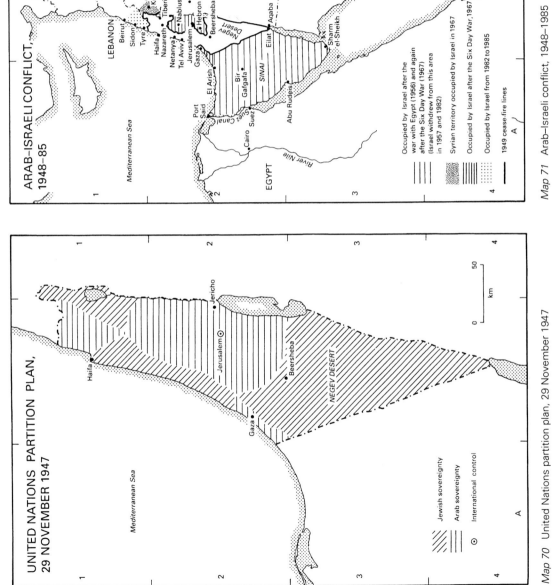

UNITED NATIONS PARTITION PLAN, 29 NOVEMBER 1947

Mediterranean Sea

Haifa

Jericho

Jerusalem ⊙

Gaza

Beersheba

NEGEV DESERT

Jewish sovereignty

Arab sovereignty

⊙ International control

km
0   50

ARAB–ISRAELI CONFLICT, 1948–85

Mediterranean Sea

SYRIA

LEBANON

Beirut
Sidon
Tyre

Damascus
Golan Heights
Kuneitra
Tiberias

IRAQ

JORDAN

SAUDI ARABIA

Haifa
Nazareth
Netanya
Tel Aviv
Jerusalem
Gaza
El Arish

Nablus
Amman
Hebron
Beersheba

Negev
Desert

Port
Said
Suez Canal
Cairo
Suez

Bir
Gafgafa

SINAI

Abu Rudeis

EGYPT

River Nile

Aqaba
Eilat

Sharm
el-Sheikh

Occupied by Israel after the
war with Egypt (1956) and again
after the Six Day War (1967)
(Israel withdrew from this area
in 1957 and 1982)

Syrian territory occupied by Israel in 1967

Occupied by Israel after the Six Day War, 1967

Occupied by Israel from 1982 to 1985

1949 cease-fire lines

km
0   100

Map 70 United Nations partition plan, 29 November 1947

Map 71 Arab–Israeli conflict, 1948–1985

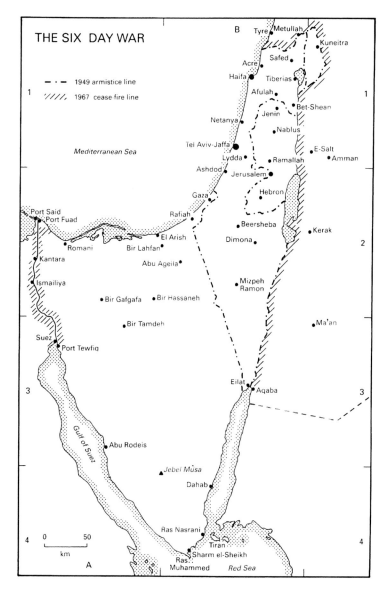

THE SIX DAY WAR

- · — 1949 armistice line
- ///// 1967 cease-fire line

Map 72 The Six Day War

American President Richard Nixon began an airlift of weapons. Two days later the Israelis mounted a counter-attack on Egypt – this was a turning point in the conflict and a ceasefire came into force on 24 October 1973.

During this period and for the next few years, the Israeli government was led by a Labour-dominated coalition, but in May 1977 the *Likud* Party led by Menachem Begin came to power. On 9 November 1977 President Sadat offered to negotiate peace terms

with Israel which were formalized at Camp David on 5 September 1978. Under the terms of this agreement, Egypt recognized Israel's right to exist, and provided guarantees for Israel's southern border; in return, Israel gave back Sinai, undertook to negotiate away much of the West Bank, and made concessions over Jerusalem in exchange for a complementary treaty with the Palestinians and other Arab peoples. These latter terms, however, were not realized since the plan was rejected by the Palestinian Arabs.

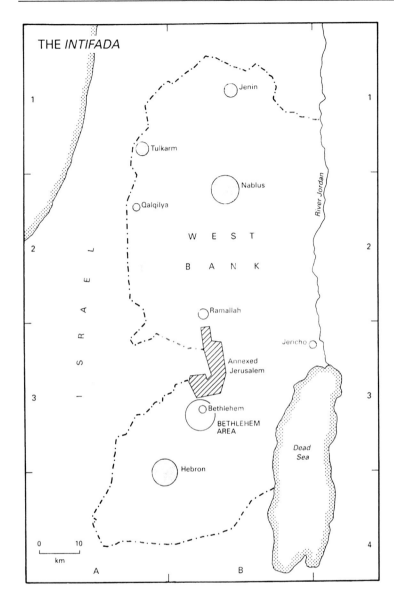

THE *INTIFADA*

Jenin

Tulkarm

Nablus

Qalqilya

W E S T

B A N K

Ramallah

Jericho

Annexed
Jerusalem

Bethlehem

BETHLEHEM
AREA

Dead
Sea

Hebron

River Jordan

I S R A E L

0   10
km

A   B

Map 73 The *intifada*

In the 1980s Israel attempted to combat the menace of the Palestine Liberation Organization which continually threatened Israeli security. From 6 June 1982 the Israel Defence Forces launched an offensive against the PLO in southern Lebanon; this occupation involved heavy bombing which resulted in massive Arab casualties. In addition, Muslim refugees were slaughtered by Christian Falangist Arabs in the Sabra and Shatilla refugee camps on 16 September 1982. Both the invasion of Lebanon and this massacre provoked discord between Israel and her allies as well as controversy in Israel.

By 1987 the Palestinians in the occupied territories were largely young educated people who had benefited from formal education. Yet despite such educational advances, they suffered from limited job expectations and this situation led to political radicalism. As hostilities increased, the *intifada* (resistance) demonstrated that occupying the West Bank and the Gaza Strip would be a perpetual problem. From the Israeli side, the Israeli Defence Forces viewed the *intifada* in the context of Israel's relationship with its Palestinian neighbours and the world in general. Repeatedly both Israel and the Palestinians sought a formal agreement, yet such an attempt to reach an accomodation between both sides has been thwarted by various factions within the State of Israel and in the Arab world.

SOURCES

Balfour Declaration

The Balfour Declaration which was written by James Balfour on 2 November 1917 stated that Britain supported the creation of a national home for the Jewish people in Palestine:

> His Majesty's Government view with favour the establishment in Palestine of a national home for the Jewish people, and will use their best endeavours to facilitate the achievement of this object, it being clearly understood that nothing shall be done which may prejudice the civil and religious rights of existing non-Jewish communities in Palestine, or the rights and political status enjoyed by Jews in any other country.
>
> (*Balfour Declaration*, in JMW, p. 582)

Figure 51 Ben-Gurion reading the Declaration of Independence for the newly formed State of Israel, 14 May 1948, in the City Museum. Copyright AKG, London.

Declaration of the State of Israel

On 14 May 1948 the Scroll of Independence was read by David Ben-Gurion:

The Land of Israel was the birthplace of the Jewish people. Here their spiritual, religious and national identity was formed. Here they achieved independence and created a culture of national and universal significance. Here they wrote and gave their Bible to the world.

Exiled from Palestine, the Jewish people remained faithful to it in all the countries of their dispersion, never ceasing to pray and hope for their return and the restoration of their national freedom.

Impelled by this historic association, Jews strove throughout the centuries to go back to the land of their fathers and regain their Statehood. In recent decades they returned in their masses. They reclaimed the wilderness, revived their language, built cities and villages and established a vigorous and evergrowing community, with its own economic and cultural life. They sought peace yet were prepared to defend themselves. They brought the blessings of progress to all inhabitants of the country.

In the year 1897 the First Zionist Congress, inspired by Theodor Herzl's vision of the Jewish State, proclaimed the right of the Jewish people to national revival in their own country.

This right was acknowledged by the Balfour Declaration of 2 November 1917, and reaffirmed by the Mandate of the League of Nations, which gave explicit international recognition to the historic connection of the Jewish people with Palestine and their right to reconstitute their national home.

The Nazi holocaust, which engulfed millions of Jews in Europe, proved anew the urgency of the reestablishment of the Jewish State, which would solve the problem of Jewish homelessness by opening the gates to all Jews and lifting the Jewish people to equality in the family of nations . . .

On 29 November 1947 the General Assembly of the United Nations adopted a Resolution for the establishment of an independent Jewish State in Palestine, and called upon inhabitants of the country to take such steps as may be necessary on their part to put the plan into effect.

This recognition by the United Nations of the right of the Jewish people to establish their independent state may not be revoked. It is, moreover, the self-evident right of the Jewish people to be a nation, like all other nations, in its own sovereign state.

Accordingly, we, the members of the National Council, representing the Jewish people in Palestine and the Zionist movement of the world, met together in solemn assembly today, the day of the termination of the British Mandate for Palestine and by virtue of the national and historic right of the Jewish people and of the resolution of the General Assembly of the United Nations, hereby proclaim the establishment of the Jewish State in Palestine, to be called Israel.

(*Proclamation of the State of Israel*, in JMW, p. 629)

DISCUSSION

1. Discuss the early conflict between Zionists and Arabs in Palestine.

2. Critically evaluate the claims of Israelis and Palestinians regarding the creation of a Jewish state.

FURTHER READING

Bauer, Yehuda, *From Diplomacy to Resistance: A History of Jewish Palestine*, 1939–1945, Atheneum, 1973.

Bethel, Nicholas, *The Palestine Triangle*, Futura, 1980.

Cohn-Sherbok, Dan, *Israel: The History of an Idea*, SPCK, 1992.

Eban, Abba, *Heritage, Civilization and the Jews*, Weidenfeld and Nicolson, 1984.

Frankel, William, *Israel Observed, An Anatomy of the State*, Thames and Hudson, 1982.

Gilbert, Martin, *Israel: A History*, Black Swan, 1999.

Goldberg, David, *To the Promised Land, A History of Zionist Thought from Its Origin to the Modern State of Israel*, Penguin, 1996.

Hertzberg, Arthur (ed.), *The Zionist Idea: A Historical Analysis and Reader*, Atheneum, 1959.

Hiro, Dilip, *Sharing the Promised Land, An Interwoven Tale of Israelis and Palestinians*, Hodder and Stoughton, 1996.

Laqueur. Walter, *A History of Zionism*, Weidenfeld and Nicolson, 1972.

O'Brien, Conor Cruise, *The Siege*, Weidenfeld and Nicolson, 1986.

Vital, David, *Origins of Zionism*, Clarendon Press, 1975.

Vital, David, *The Formative Years*, Oxford University Press, 1982.

CHAPTER 52

Jewry After the Holocaust

Timeline:

1950 Korean War

1953 West Germany signs reparations agreement with Israel

1953 Arrest of prominent Jews in Russia accused of planning to murder government officials

1954–1968 French Jewry increased by immigration of Jews from North Africa

1961 Eichmann Trial

1965 Formal diplomatic relations between West Germany and Israel

1967 Six Day War

1968 Anti-Zionist campaigns in USSR and Poland. Immigration of Polish Jews

1969–1970 Egypt launches war of attrition along the Suez Canal

1970s Illegal Jewish activity in the USSR. Russian Jewish emigration to Israel and the West

1973 Yom Kippur War

1977 Menachem Begin Prime Minister of Israel. Anwar Sadat visits Israel

1978 Meetings between Sadat and Begin

The Holocaust significantly changed the nature of Jewry in the modern world. By the beginning of the twenty-first century the Jewish community had not recovered from the losses of the Nazi period. Out of a total of 15,000,000 Jews, approximately 4,500,000 live in Israel, but the largest Jewish community is in America: about 6,888,757 live in North or South America. The next largest community is in the former Soviet Union, 1,450,000. Some eastern European countries also have a sizeable number of Jews such as Hungary with 100,000 and Romania with 14,000. In western Europe there is a sizeable population: 600,000 in France, 285,000 in Great Britain, 67,000 in Germany; 30,000 in Belgium, 35,000 in Italy, 25,000 in Holland and 17,500 in Switzerland. On the African continent, 90,000 Jews reside in South Africa, 10,000 in Morocco and about 1,000 in Ethiopia. In Asia there are 25,000 Jews in Iran and 25,000 in Turkey. The Australian and New Zealand communities consist of about 110,000.

These various Jewish populations have had a complex history since the war. In many cases Jewry was reduced to only a fraction of its size before the Holocaust. The Jewish community of Salonika, for example, was 60,000 in 1939 but had only l,500 in the 1980s; Vienna shrank from 200,000 to less than 8,000; Berlin Jewry fell from approximately 175,000 to about 6,000; the Jews in Poland dwindled from 3,300,000 to about 5,000. Yet in other parts of the world Jewish numbers have increased as a result of immigration. In France Sephardic immigrants from the Muslim world swelled the Jewish population and intensified Jewish identification. Britain also welcomed a large number of newcomers after the war which increased the community and added to its cultural development. But it was in the United States particularly that the Jewish community grew in size and importance.

Before the war the American Jewish population was diverse and vibrant, and refugees from Nazi Europe increased its dynamism. These immigrants included

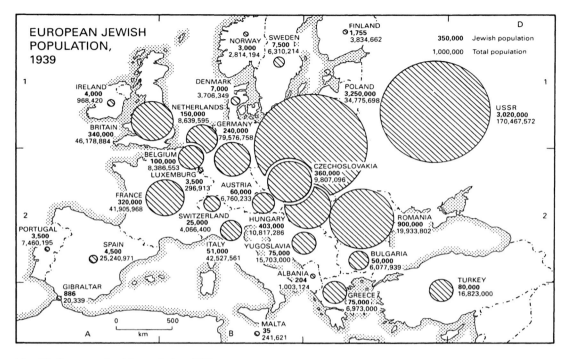

Map 74 European Jewish population, 1939

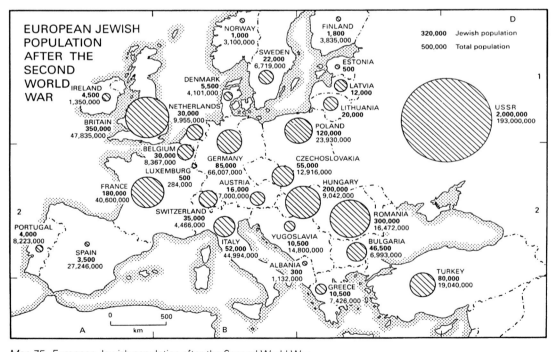

Map 75 European Jewish population after the Second World War

Figure 52 Jewish refugee children, aged between 5 and 16, arriving in New York from Hamburg, Germany, on the liner *President Harding* on 3 June 1939. Copyright Associated Press.

adherents of more developed forms of European liberalism as well as *Hasidim* with strong folk traditions. As Jewish numbers increased, earlier religious groupings gained strength and influence. On the left of the religious spectrum the **Reform movement** gradually became more favourable to Zionism and once the State of Israel became a reality previous Reform antipathy to a Jewish homeland largely disappeared. In the latter half of the twentieth century the Jewish Institute of Religion founded by Stephen Wise in 1922 merged with the Hebrew Union College and campuses were established in California and Jerusalem. In matters of ritual as well as belief Reform Judaism has moved towards a more traditional stance, though recently reformers took the radical step of ordaining women to the rabbinate, redefined **Jewish identity** to include children of Jewish fathers, and regarded **homosexuality** as morally acceptable.

In the Conservative movement tension between liberals and traditionalists was expressed in the 1960s and 1970s concerning the ordination of women which has now become official policy. In addition it was from the ranks of Conservative Jews that Reconstructionist

Judaism emerged; this new branch was founded by Mordecai Kaplan who adopted a radical approach to the tradition which envisaged Judaism as a civilization. Rejecting belief in a personal God, Kaplan argued that the Jewish heritage should be perpetuated with the synagogue as the centre of Jewish life. A more radical approach to contemporary Judaism emerged in the 1960s under the leadership of Rabbi Sherwin Wine who was originally ordained as a Reform rabbi: Humanistic Judaism is a non-theistic interpretation of Judaism based on humanistic values.

Within the Orthodox fold internal divisions have also been evident. Yeshivah University in New York and the Hebrew Theological College of Chicago produced rabbinical graduates who belonged mainly to the Rabbinical Council of America, whereas Orthodox rabbis of a more traditional orientation were generally members of the *Aggudas Ha-Rabbonim* founded by Yiddish-speaking immigrant rabbis at the turn of the century. The divisions within the Orthodox camp reflect differing attitudes to Americanization and co-operation with other Jews, yet despite this diversity the majority of American Orthodox Jewry are unified today in their commitment to the State of Israel.

In contrast with Jewish life in the United States, Jewish activities in the Soviet Union were officially curtailed by the government. During the war anti-Semitism existed in the Red Army, and as the war ended many Jews were removed from government departments. In September 1948 an article in *Pravda* denounced Israel as a bourgeois tool of American capitalism; the Jewish anti-Fascist committee was eliminated; and Yiddish schools were closed. This was followed by an attack on Jewish writers, painters, musicians and intellectuals. The campaign extended to Czechoslovakia, and on 20 November 1952 the Czech Communist Party General Secretary as well as other communist leaders, including eleven Jews, were accused of a Trotskyite-Titoist-Zionist conspiracy and executed. In 1953 nine doctors, including six Jews, were accused of plotting to poison Joseph Stalin in conjunction with British, American and Zionist agents. This trial was to have been a prelude to the deportation of Jews to Siberia but Stalin died before the doctors were tried. Stalin's successor, Nikita Khrushchev, changed the orientation of anti-Jewish propaganda from spying to economic criminality. Many Jews were convicted and sentenced to death. Furthermore, during Khrushchev's reign the number of synagogues was reduced from 450 to 60 and he permitted the publication of the anti-Semitic tract, *Judaism Without Embellishment*. After Krushchev's fall there was a brief respite, but following the Six Day War in 1967 the campaign against Jews was resumed. In 1971 Leonid Brezhnev decided to allow a large number of Jews to leave the Soviet Union, and during the next decade 250,000 Jews emigrated. But accompanying this large-scale exodus there was an increase in trials of Jews and the procedure for obtaining an exit visa became more complicated. In the 1980s even fewer visas were granted as the Soviet campaign against Zionism intensified. During the Gorbachev years, chauvinist anti-Semitism flourished, particularly within *Pamyat*, which spearheaded the Movement for the Restoration of Monuments of Russian Culture and the Russian Republic Culture Fund. Other organizations with similar views promoted anti-Jewish hostility. Advocating patriotism and traditional values, supporters of these groups have attacked what they believe to be the destructive influences of Western cosmopolitanism. Thus the paradox

of *glasnost* is that it unleashed fury against the Jewish population.

Parallel with Soviet anti-Semitism was the propaganda disseminated in the Arab World. Arab polemics against Jews were based in part on the **Protocols of the Elders of Zion** which circulated widely in Arab countries. Extracts and summaries from this anti-Semitic work were used in Arab school textbooks and in training manuals for the Arab military forces. In addition, blood-libel material appeared in 1962 as a government publication of the United Arab Republic entitled *Talmudic Human Sacrifice*. In Iran Ayatollah Khomeini portrayed Zionism as an emanation of Satan. Such anti-Jewish material from the Soviet bloc and the Arab states contributed to the United Nations' decision to condemn Zionism. More recently, **Arab hostility** to Jewry was unleashed in the aftermath of the 11 September 2002 assault on the United States: throughout the Arab world virulent hostility against Israel and world Jewry has been unleashed by Osama bin Laden and the defenders of Islam. Thus the spectre of anti-Semitism, which led to the destruction of six million Jews in the Holocaust, has again emerged in modern society.

SOURCES

Reform Judaism and Zionism

In the nineteenth century the Reform movement was highly critical of Zionism. However, in a post-Holocaust world, Reform Jews have embraced Israel as essential to Jewish survival:

In 1885 the framers of the Pittsburgh Platform of Reform Judaism declared that they no longer expected Jews to return to a national homeland in Palestine. The Platform's authors proclaimed: 'We consider ourselves no longer a nation, but a religious community, and, therefore, expect neither a return to Palestine . . . nor the restoration of any of the laws concerning the Jewish state.'

By 1937 the CCAR (Central Conference of American Rabbis) had reversed its stand on Jewish peoplehood, and declared in its Columbus Platform that 'Judaism is the soul of which Israel (the people) is the body'. . . . The CCAR returned again to the question of Zionism in 1976, asserting in its Centenary Perspective: 'We are bound to . . . the

newly reborn State of Israel by innumerable religious and ethnic ties'.

The CCAR affirms through this Platform those principles which will guide Reform Judaism into the twenty-first century.

The restoration of *Am Yisrael* to its ancestral homeland after nearly two thousand years of statelessness and powerlessness represents an historic triumph of the Jewish people, providing a physical refuge, the possibility of religious and cultural renewal on its own soil, and the realization of God's promise to Abraham: 'to your offspring I assign this land'. From that distant moment until today, the intense love between *Am Yisrael* and *Eretz Yisrael* has not subsided.

We believe that the eternal covenant established at Sinai ordained a unique religious purpose for *Am Yisrael. Medinat Yisrael*, the Jewish State, is therefore unlike all other states. Its obligation is to strive towards the attainment of the Jewish people's highest moral ideals to be a *mamlechet kohanim* (a kingdom of priests), a *goy kadosh* (a holy people), and *l'or goyim* (a light unto the nations).

(Reform Judaism and Zionism: A Centenary Platform, in www.ccarnet.org/miami.html)

Jewish Identity

In the past the Reform movement regarded individuals born of Jewish mothers as well as converts as Jews. However, in 1983 Reform Judaism embraced patrilineal as well as matrilineal descent:

> One of the most pressing human issues for the North American Jewish community is mixed marriage, with all its attendant implications . . . This issue was . . . addressed . . . in the 1961 edition of the *Rabbi's Manual*:
>
> Jewish law recognizes a person as Jewish if his mother was Jewish, even though the father was not a Jew. One born of such mixed parentage may be admitted to membership in the synagogue and enter into a marital relationship with a Jew, provided he has not been reared in or formally admitted into some other faith. The child of a Jewish father and a non-Jewish mother, according to traditional law, is a Gentile; such a person would have to be formally converted in order to marry a Jew or become a synagogue member.
>
> Reform Judaism, however, accepts such a child as Jewish without a formal conversion, if he attends a Jewish school and follows a course of studies leading to Confirmation. Such procedure is regarded as sufficient evidence that the parents and the child himself intend that he shall live as a Jew.
>
> We face today an unprecedented situation due to the changed conditions in which decisions concerning the status of the child of a mixed marriage are to be made.
>
> There are tens of thousands of mixed marriages. In a vast majority of these cases the non-Jewish extended family is a functioning part of the child's world, and may be decisive in shaping the life of the child. It can no longer be assumed a priori, therefore, that the child of a Jewish mother will be Jewish any more than that the child of a non-Jewish mother will not be.
>
> This leads us to the conclusion that the same requirements must be applied to establish the status of a child of a mixed marriage, regardless of whether the mother or the father is Jewish.
>
> Therefore, the Central Conference of American Rabbis declares that the child of one Jewish parent is under the presumption of Jewish descent. This presumption of the Jewish status of the offspring of a mixed marriage is to be established through appropriate and timely public and formal acts of identification with the Jewish faith and people. The performance of these *mitzvot* serves to commit those who participate in them, both parent and child, to Jewish life.
>
> Depending on circumstances, *mitzvot* leading toward a positive and exclusive Jewish identity will include entry into the covenant, acquisition of a Hebrew name, Torah study, *Bar/Bat Mitzvah*, and *Kabbalat Torah* (Confirmation). For those beyond childhood claiming Jewish identity, other public acts or declarations may be added or substituted after consultation with their rabbi.
>
> (Reform Movement's Resolution on Patrilineal Descent, in www.us-israel.org/jsource/Judaism/patrilineal1.html)

Homosexuality

The Religious Action Centre is the Washington Office of the Union of American Hebrew Congregations and the Central Conference of American Rabbis representing over a million Jews in the United States. In a statement of its principles, Rabbi Marc Israel, Director of Congregational Relations, spoke out on behalf of tolerance and respect for gays and lesbians in Judaism:

> I stand here today on behalf of the Union of American Hebrew Congregations and the Central Conference of American Rabbis, representing 1.5 million American Reform Jews, to say that we fervently believe in God and the Torah, and also to state that there is no room for discrimination against gays, lesbians, or bisexuals in our synagogues, in our communities, or in our nation.
>
> The Family Research Council is correct when it asserts that the Bible and the Torah 'present clear and definitive principles'. Among the most important of these is the fundamental Jewish principle that we are all created *b'tselem elohim*, in the divine image. We are all welcome in God's eyes, whether heterosexual or gay or lesbian, married or single, parents or childless, female or male, Black or white. We are all equal recipients of God's love.
>
> We agree that religious views should not be excluded from the public square. In that dialogue we will certainly have areas on which we respectfully disagree. But we condemn any and all campaigns by those who, in the name of God and under the guise of religion, preach intolerance, hatred and bigotry.
>
> (*Statement of Reform Judaism on Gays*, in
> www.uahc.org/reform'rac/news/081298.html)

Arab Anti-Semitism

In the modern world virulent anti-Semitism has been expressed in the Arab world largely due to the political conflict in the Middle East. In 1983, for example, the Libyan representative of the United Nations declared:

> It is high time for the United Nations and the United States, in particular, to realize that the Jewish Zionists here in the United States attempt to destroy Americans. Look around New York. Who are the owners of pornographic film operations and houses? Is it not the Jews who are exploiting the American people and trying to debase them? If we succeed in eliminating that entity, we shall by the same token save the American and European peoples.
>
> (In I, p. 174)

In December 1984 the President of the World Muslim Congress, Dr Ma'ruf al-Dawalibi, claimed to quote the *Talmud* at the UN Centre for Human Rights' Seminar alleging that it is necessary for Jews to drink the blood of non-Jews:

> If a Jew does not drink every year the blood of a non-Jewish man, then he will be damned for all eternity.
>
> (In A, p. 342)

In an interview given to Al-Jazeera Arab television in 1998, the Arab terrorist Osama bin Laden chillingly castigated America and the Jewish community and encouraged Muslims to wage a holy war against the enemies of Islam:

'Our duty is to wage a holy war against the enemies of Islam and their allies . . . With the grace of God we have established (common cause) with a large number of our brothers in the International Islamic Front to confront Jews and the Crusaders. We believe that the affairs of many of those are moving in the right direction and have the ability to move widely. We pray to God to grant them victory and revenge on the Jews and Americans.

(In A, p. vii)

DISCUSSION

1. How has the Holocaust affected Jewish life and thought in the modern world?

2. Compare the different religious movements in the Jewish community.

FURTHER READING

Alderman, Geoffrey, *Modern British Jewry*, Oxford University Press, 1998.

Brym, Robert, Shaffir, William, Weinfeld, Morton, *The Jews in Canada*, Oxford University Press, 1993.

Cohn-Sherbok, Dan, *Anti-Semitism*, Sutton, 2002.

Cohn-Sherbok, Dan, *Issues in Contemporary Judaism*, Macmillan, 1991.

Cohn-Sherbok, Dan, *Modern Judaism*, Macmillan, 1996.

Elazar, Daniel, *Jewish Communities in Frontier Societies: Argentina, Australia and South Africa*, Holmes and Meir, 1983.

Hertzberg, Arthur, *The Jews in America: Four Centuries of an Uneasy Encounter – A History*, Columbia University Press, 1998.

Levine, Stephen, *The New Zealand Jewish Community*, 1999.

Rubenstein, W.D., *The History of the Jews in the English-Speaking World*, Palgrave, 1995.

Rubenstein, W.D., Rubinstein, Hilary, *Chosen: The Jews in Australia*, Allen and Unwin, 1987.

Rubinstein, Hilary, Cohn-Sherbok, Dan, Rubenstein, W.D., Edelheit, Abraham, *The Jews in the Modern World*, Arnold, 2002.

Sachar, Howard, *A History of the Jews in America*, Random House, 1993.

Sachar, Howard, *Diaspora: An Inquiry into the Contemporary Jewish World*, HarperCollins, 1985.

Webber, Jonathan (ed.), *Jewish Identities in the New Europe*, Littman Library, 1994.

CHAPTER 53

Modern Jewish Thought

Timeline:

1842–1918 Hermann Cohen

1856–1922 Aaron David Gordon

1865–1935 Abraham Isaac Kook

1873–1956 Leo Baeck

1878–1965 Martin Buber

1881–1983 Mordecai Kaplan

1886–1929 Franz Rosenzweig

1907–1972 Abraham Joshua Heschel

1917– Emil Fackenheim

1924– Richard Rubenstein

Figure 53 Parade of gay and lesbian Jews in New York, USA, 1989. Copyright Richard Stern, Amsterdam. Beth Hatefutsoth Photo Archive, courtesy Richard Stern, Amsterdam.

At the beginning of the twentieth century the German liberal rabbi, **Leo Baeck** (1873–1956) exerted an important influence on Jewish theology. In *The Essence of Judaism*, he argued that Judaism represents a classical type of religion, embodying ethical optimism and a commitment to human freedom. In other writings Baeck stated that certain forms of Christianity influenced by Paul emphasize faith at the expense of works; this attitude, he maintained, leads to a passive indifference to the struggle against evil. Judaism, however, focuses on the ethical life as a response to divine mystery. In apprehending God's commandments, the Jew becomes aware that he is obligated to create a better world.

Another Jewish thinker of this period, **Aaron David Gordon** (1856–1922), visualized a means of Jewish redemption in the agricultural settlements of the Holy Land. For Gordon authentic religiosity is expressed through a bond between human beings and nature; in this fashion Jews are able to experience moral rebirth in Palestine which makes the Jewish people an 'incarnation' of ideal humanity. A similar mystical outlook was expressed by another settler in Palestine, Chief Rabbi **Abraham Isaac Kook** (1865–1935) who argued that there is no segregation between religious and secular life. Drawing on the *kabbalah*, Kook maintained that Jews have the task of transmuting earthly aspects of existence to a higher realm. For Kook Israel has the capacity to reach a state of holiness. The renewal of Jewish life in the land of Israel, he believed, was a crucial stage in humanity's spiritual progress.

Another seminal thinker of the early twentieth century was the German philosopher Hermann Cohen (1842–1918) who attempted to harmonize certain aspects of Jewish belief with Kantian idealism in presenting a defence of Jewish ethical monotheism. In *Religion of Reason Out of the Sources of Judaism* Cohen argued that God is the source of everything in the phenomenal world; in Kantian terms this means that the idea of God is the precondition of causality. For Cohen the universe is eternal rather than created at a single point in time – thus there is renewal in the world as the Jewish prayerbook proclaims. Revelation also is not tied to a particular historical occurrence. According to Cohen, revelation refers to the human capacity to reason. In this regard, Cohen asserted that the spirit of holiness denotes the moral quality shared by God and

human beings. God's holiness is the archetype of ethical action.

Another European theologian of this period, **Franz Rosenzweig** (1886–1929) explored in *The Star of Redemption* the ways in which theology complements philosophy. In this work Rosenzweig contended that in revelation God confronts human beings. What is revealed is God's presence, and through the experience of divine love human beings are commanded to love in return. In propounding this view Rosenzweig distinguished between commandments, which are directed to individuals, and laws for humanity – revelation results in commandments rather than laws. This relationship between God and human beings is supplemented by creation which relates the individual to the world. Creation, Rosenzweig argued, establishes the dependence that all creatures have on God's power. A third relationship is provided by redemption which links human beings and the world. For Rosenzweig, through redemption it is possible to overcome isolation because of God's command to love one's neighbour. Rosenzweig was also concerned with the relationship between Christianity and Judaism. In his view, both traditions represent authentic communities of love through which the Divine manifests His presence in the world.

A contemporary of Rosenzweig, the German theologian **Martin Buber** (1878–1965), exerted an important influence on Jewish thought with the publication of *I and Thou*. In this work, Buber stated that there are two primary attitudes that individuals can take in relation to the world. The I–It relationship is based on a detachment of the self from the others in which knowledge is objectified. But in the posture of I–Thou there is an encounter between two subjects in which each stands over against the other. Such an attitude is characterized by total presentness: the I addresses the Thou spontaneously and intensely. In a relationship of I–It, however, there is predetermination and control. In presenting this thesis, Buber stressed that he can offer no description of the I–Thou posture; it can only be pointed to. The attitude of I–Thou is a basic dimension of human existence in the world and a key to the concept of relation; it has the character of a dialogue and can only be properly understood through personal experience.

Turning to the work of Jewish theologians in

America, the writings of **Mordecai Kaplan** (1881–1983) have had a significant impact. In *Judaism as a Civilization*, Kaplan argued that Jews in the past believed in a supernatural God who revealed Himself to the Jewish people and provided a means for salvation. Today, however, this religious view has disintegrated. According to Kaplan, it is no longer possible to believe in a transcendent God who acts in history. Yet he remained convinced that a non-supernatural orientation to religion can provide the basis for spiritual life. The Jewish faith, he believed, is a civilization which is manifest in *sancta* (holy acts) which commemorate what the Jewish people hold most sacred.

Another Jewish theologian of importance was Abraham Joshua Heschel (1907–72) who in various writings was concerned with faith and its antecedents – the experiences, insights, emotions, attitudes and acts out of which faith arises. According to Heschel, certain experiences and acts that are commonly regarded as aspects of faith are also antecedents of faith. Wonder before the sublime mystery of nature, for example, is not in itself an aspect of the Jewish faith. Such wonder may occur prior to the emergence of faith. Realities through which God is revealed, like nature and tradition, may be considered sources of faith even prior to the perception of God's presence insofar as they occasion the perception and response to God.

More recently, a number of Jewish theologians have grappled with the question of whether it is possible to believe in God after the Holocaust. In various writings the Jewish philosopher Emil Fackenheim argued that in the death camps God manifested his will that His chosen people survive. In Fackenheim's view, God revealed Himself to Israel out of the furnaces and through the ashes of the victims of Auschwitz. Through the Holocaust, he believed, God issued the 614th commandment: 'Jews are forbidden to grant a posthumous victory to Hitler'. According to Fackenheim, the commitment of faith is not called

into question by any event of history, including the Holocaust. Thus Fackenheim urged Jews to hold fast to the traditional covenant God who is present in and the Lord of history.

Arguing along different lines, the Orthodox scholar Eliezer Berkovits maintained that the events of the Holocaust should be understood as part of God's inscrutable plan. In *Faith after the Holocaust*, Berkovits wrote that the modern Jewish response to the destruction of six million Jews should be modelled on Job's example. Further, he stressed that the solution to the problem of the Holocaust can be solved by appealing to the free will argument. If God did not respect human freedom, not only would morality be abolished, but men and women would cease to be human. In this light, the Holocaust must be seen as an expression of human evil, a tragedy inflicted by the Nazis on the Jewish people. God did not intervene to save the Jewish nation because He had bestowed free will on humanity at creation.

Other writers, however, have been unable to accept such a conclusion. In *After Auschwitz* the radical Jewish theologian Richard Rubenstein contended that the Holocaust is the utter and decisive refutation of the traditional affirmation of a providential God who acts in history and watches over the Jewish people whom he has selected from all nations. In Rubenstein's opinion the Auschwitz experience has resulted in a rejection of the traditional theology of history which must be replaced by a positive affirmation of the value of human life in and for itself. According to Rubenstein, God is the ultimate Nothing, and it is to this divine nothing that human beings and the world are ultimately to return. There is no hope of salvation for humanity. In this context Auschwitz fits into the archaic religious consciousness and observance of the universal cycle of death and rebirth. The mass slaughter of European Jewry was followed by a rebirth of the Jewish people in the land of Israel.

SOURCES

Leo Baeck

Leo Baeck was the President of the *Reichsvertretung,* the representative body of German Jews during the Holocaust in addition to his activities as a teacher and theologian. Determined to stand firm against Nazi attack on German Jewry he turned to God in faithfulness to the tradition:

The great task of dark days, and the greater one of bright hours, was to keep faith with the expectation. Man waits for God, and God waits for man. The promise and the demand speak here, both in one: the grace of the commandment and the commandment of grace. Both are one in the One God. Around the One God there is the concealment. He does not reveal himself, but he reveals the commandment and the grace. And he, the Eternal One, has given mortal man freedom of will and has shown him a goal for his will. But the ultimate remains concealed from man. Thus the prophet announced the word of God. For my thoughts are not your thoughts, neither are your ways my ways, saith he-who-is (Is. 55:8). The great reverence was exalted in this, and it always clung to this, even when men dared the supposition that their ways were God's ways. The mystery surrounds God. He is not the revealed God, but he is the revealing God. Wherever the great reverence lives in a man and the great readiness for God rises out of it, there and then, man is near to God . . .

(Leo Baeck, *This People Israel* in HT, p. 82)

Aaron David Gordon

Born in a village in Podolia, Aaron David Gordon emigrated to Palestine where he worked as a farmer in the vineyards and wineries of *Petah Tikva*. Later he worked in Galilee. In his writings, he stressed the importance of working the land:

And when, O Man, you will return to Nature – on that day your eyes will open, you will gaze straight into the eyes of Nature, and in its mirror you will see your own image. You will know that you have returned to yourself, that when you hid from Nature, you hid from yourself. When you return you will see that from you, from your hands and from your feet, from your body and from your soul, heavy, hard, oppressive fragments will fall and you will begin to stand erect. You will understand that these were fragments of the shell into which you had shrunk in the bewilderment of your heart and out of which you had finally emerged. On that day you will know that your former life did not befit you, that you must renew all things: your food and your drink, your dress and your home, your manner of work and your mode of study – everything!

On that day, O Man, deep in your heart you will know that you had been wandering until you returned to Nature. For you did not know life. A different life, a life not ready-made, a life to be experienced in preparation and creation – that life you did not know. Therefore your life was cut in two – a very small shred of existence and a huge experience of nonexistence, of work, of labour, of busyness – 'Sabbath' and the 'Eve of the Sabbath'. You did not think, and it did not occur to you, that there is no life in a life ready-made.

(Aaron David Gordon, *Logic for the Future*, in ZI, pp. 371–372)

Abraham Isaac Kook

Born in Latvia in 1865, Abraham Isaac Kook emigrated to Palestine and became Ashkenazi Chief Rabbi. In his writings, he transformed religious messianic anticipation into the basis for collaboration with the aspirations of modern Zionism:

Deep in the heart of every Jew, in its purest and holiest recesses, there blazes the fire of Israel. There can be no mistaking its demands for an organic and indivisible bond between life and all of God's commandments; for the pouring of the spirit of the Lord, the spirit of Israel which completely permeates the soul of the Jew, into all the vessels which were created for this particular purpose; and for expressing the word of Israel fully and precisely in the realms of action and idea.

In the hearts of our saints, this fire is constantly blazing up with tongues of holy flame. Like the fire on the altar of the Temple, it is burning unceasingly, with a steady flame, in the collective heart of our people. Hidden away in the deepest recesses of their souls, it exists even among the backsliders and sinners of Israel. Within the Jewish people as a whole, this is the living source of its desire for freedom, of its longing for a life worthy of the name for man and community, of its hope for redemption – of the striving toward a full, uncontradictory, and unbounded Jewish life.

This is the meaning of the Jew's undying love for *Eretz Israel* – the Land of Holiness, the Land of God – in which all of the Divine commandments are realized in their perfect form. This urge to unfold to the world the nature of God, to raise one's head in His Name in order to proclaim His greatness in its real dimension, affects all souls, for all desire to become as one with Him and to partake of the bliss of His life. This yearning for a true life, for one that is fashioned by all the commandments of the Torah and illumined by all its uplifting splendour, is the source of the courage which moves the Jew to affirm, before all the world, his loyalty to the heritage of his people, to the preservation of its identity and values, and to the upholding of its faith and vision.

An outsider may wonder: How can seeming unbelievers be moved by this life force, not merely to nearness to the universal God but even toward authentic Jewish life – to expressing the divine commandments concretely in image and idea, in song and deed. But this is no mystery to anyone whose heart is deeply at one with the soul of the Jewish people and who knows its marvellous nature. The source of this Power is in the Power of God, in the everlasting glory of life.

(Abraham Isaac Kook, *The Land of Israel*, in ZI, pp. 421–422)

Franz Rosenzweig

Born in Kassel, Germany, in 1886, Franz Rosenzweig studied medicine at the universities of Göttingen, Munich and Freiburg and later philosophy, theology, art, literature, and classical languages at the universities of Berlin and Freiburg. In 1912 he completed his doctoral dissertation on Hegel's political philosophy. His major work was *The Star of Redemption* in which he presented his own interpretation of the Jewish religion. Although he considered converting to the Christian faith, he decided not to do so. In *Jewish Learning and the Return to Judaism* he discusses the predicament of the modern Jew:

What is new is not so much the collapse of the outer barriers, even previously; while the ghetto had certainly sheltered the Jew, it had not shut him off. He moved beyond its bounds, and what the ghetto gave him was only peace, home, a home for his spirit. What is new is not that the Jew's feet could now take him farther than ever before – in the Middle Ages the Jew was not an especially sedentary, but rather a comparatively mobile element of medieval society. The new feature is that the wanderer no longer returns at dusk. The gates of the ghetto no longer close behind him, allowing him to spend the night in solitary learning. To abandon the figure of speech – he finds his spiritual and intellectual home outside the Jewish world . . .

There is no one today who is not alienated, or who does not contain within himself some small fraction of alienation. All of us to whom Judaism, to whom being a Jew, has again become the pivot of our lives – and I know that in saying this here I am not speaking for myself alone – we all know that in being Jews we must not give up anything, not renounce anything, but lead everything back to Judaism. From the periphery back to the centre, from the outside, in . . .

It is not a matter of apologetics, but rather of finding the way back into the heart of life. And of being confident that this heart is a Jewish heart. For we are Jews.

(Franz Rosenzweig, *Jewish Learning and the Return to Judaism*,
in JMW, pp. 282–283)

Martin Buber

Born in Vienna in 1878, Martin Buber grew up as a child in Lemberg; later he studied at the universities of Vienna, Leipzig, Zurich and Berlin. After emigrating to Palestine, be became a professor at the Hebrew University. In *I and Thou* he outlines his religious philosophy of dialogue:

Every particular Thou is a glimpse through to the eternal Thou: by means of every particular Thou the primary word addresses the eternal Thou. Through this mediation of the Thou of all beings fulfilment, and non-fulfilment, of relations comes to them: the inborn Thou is realized in each relation and consummated in none. It is consummated only in the direct relation with the Thou that by its nature cannot become It.

(Martin Buber, *I and Thou*, in FJT, p. 26)

Another important dimension of Buber's writings is the relationship between Judaism and Christianity:

What joins Jews and Christians together is their common knowledge about one uniqueness . . . Every authentic sanctuary can acknowledge the mystery of every other authentic sanctuary. The mystery of the other one is internal to the latter and cannot be perceived from without. No one outside Israel can understand the mystery of Israel. And no one outside Christendom can understand the mental difference and impart to each other with unreserved confidence our knowledge of the unity of this house, a unity which we hope will one day surround us without divisions. We will serve until the day when we may be united in common service . . .

(Martin Buber, *Die Stunde und die Erkenntnis*,
in FJT, pp. 26–27)

Notwithstanding such reservations, Buber explored various aspects of Christianity. In his view, Jews and Christians should strive to find common ground between their two traditions:

It behoves both you (Christian) and us (Jews) to hold inviolably fast to our own true faith, that is to our deepest relationship to truth. It behooves both of us to show a religious respect for the true faith of others. This is not what is called 'tolerance'; our task is not to tolerate each other's waywardness but to acknowledge the real relationship in which both stand to the truth. Whenever we both, Christian and Jew, care more for God Himself than for our images of God, we are united in the feeling that our Father's house is differently constructed than our human models take it to be.

(Martin Buber, *Israel and the World*,
in FJT, p. 27)

Mordecai Kaplan

Born in Lithuania in 1881, Mordecai Kaplan emigrated from Vilna to the United States and served as a professor at the Jewish Theological Seminary. In his seminal work *Judaism as a Civilization*, and elsewhere, he argued that Jews must abandon their belief in a supernatural Deity and reconstruct Judaism on new lines:

In getting to work upon a programme for the reconstruction of Judaism we must take care not to miscalculate the magnitude of the task before us. Unless we are prepared to go to the root of the spiritual ills in Jewish life, we had better not begin at all. We must not be like physicians who are content to treat the symptoms of a disease rather than attack the cause, and who, instead of suggesting a real remedy, recommend some patent medicine or incantation. The real issue is not how to render our ritual in keeping with the requirements of modern life, but how to get our people sufficiently interested in religion to want a ritual. If we are not prepared to do much more for Judaism than revise the prayerbook, we should leave the prayerbook alone. We are faced with a problem no less than that of transforming the very mind and heart of the Jewish people. Unless its mythological ideas about God give way to the conception of divinity immanent in the workings of the human spirit, unless its static view of authority gives way to the dynamic without succumbing to individualistic lawlessness, and unless it is capable of developing a sense of history without, at the same time, being a slave to the past, the Jewish people have nothing further to contribute to civilization.

(Mordecai Kaplan, *A Program for the Reconstruction of Judaism* in JMW, p. 500)

DISCUSSION

1. Trace the development of modern Jewish thought from the early twentieth century until today.

2. Discuss the views of Holocaust theologians concerning the presence and activity of God in Jewish history.

FURTHER READING

Bergman, S.H., *Faith and Reason: An Introduction to Modern Jewish Thought*, Schocken, 1963.

Berkovits, Eliezer, *Major Themes in Modern Philosophies of Judaism*, KTAV, 1974.

Borowitz, Eugene, *Choices in Modern Jewish Thought*, Behrman House, 1983.

Cohn-Sherbok, Dan, *Fifty Key Jewish Thinkers*, Routledge, 1997.

Guttman, Julius, *Philosophies of Judaism: The History of Jewish Philosophy from Biblical Times to Franz Rosenzweig*, Holt, Rinehart and Winston, 1964.

Kaplan, Mordecai, *Judaism as a Civilization*, Schocken, 1967.

Katz, Steven, *Post-Holocaust Dialogues*, New York University Press, 1983.

Kaufman, Walter, *Contemporary Jewish Philosophies*, Behrman House, 1976.

Martin, Bernard (ed.), *Great Twentieth-Century Jewish Philosophers: Sheshtov, Rosenzweig, Buber, with Selections from Their Writings*, Macmillan, 1970.

Mendes-Flohr, Paul, Reinharz, Jehuda (eds), *The Jew in the Modern World*, Oxford University Press, 1995.

Noveck, Simon (ed.), *Great Jewish Thinkers of the Twentieth Century*, B'nai Brith, 1963.

Sachar, Howard, *The Course of Modern Jewish History*, Random House, 1990.

Seltzer, Robert, *Jewish People, Jewish Thought: The Jewish Experience in History*, Macmillan, 1980.

CHAPTER 54

The Future of Judaism

Figure 54 Will Judaism burn bright in an ever-darkening world? Copyright Getty images.

In the modern world Judaism has undergone a profound transformation. No longer is the Jewish faith a unified structure embracing different interpretations of the same tradition. Rather the modern period has witnessed the fragmentation of the Jewish community into a variety of sub-groups ranging from ultra-Orthodox Hasidism to progressive Reform Judaism. In addition, the events of the last century – including the Holocaust, the emergence of the State of Israel, the persecution of Jews in the Soviet Union and Arab lands, and the continuing conflict in the Middle East – have intensified the complications regarding the future of Judaism and the Jewish people. After nearly 4,000 years of history, the Jewish nation today faces new difficulties.

First, and arguably most importantly, Jews ask themselves what they should make of the greatest tragedy of modern Jewish history – the destruction of six million of their number by the Nazis. If the God of Israel is an all-powerful, omniscient, benevolent father who loves His children, how could He have allowed such an event to take place? If there is a divine providential scheme, what is the purpose of this slaughter of the chosen people? These haunting questions will not disappear, and even if some theologians wish to suspend judgement about the horrific experiences of the death camps, individual Jews will not find it so easy to escape from this religious dilemma.

Some Jews in contemporary society have simply abandoned their belief in God; others have substituted the State of Israel as the source of salvation. Yet whatever the response there is a vitally important theological task to be undertaken if the Jewish faith is to continue as a vibrant force. Within the Biblical and rabbinic heritage, the belief in a merciful and compassionate Deity is of fundamental significance. The Holocaust challenges such a religious commitment: Jewish theologians must grapple with the religious perplexities of the death camps if Judaism is to survive as a coherent religious tradition.

Related to the problem of religious belief is the dilemma of halakhic observance. Today Orthodoxy claims the largest number of adherents. Yet many of those who profess allegiance to Orthodox Judaism do not live by the code of Jewish law. Instead all Jews feel free to write their own *Shulkhan Arukh*. This is so also within the other branches of Judaism. For most Jews the halakhic tradition has lost its hold on Jewish consciousness – the bulk of rituals and observances appear anachronistic and burdensome. As we have seen, in previous centuries this was not the case. Despite the divisions within the Jewish world – between Sadducees and Pharisees, rabbinates and *Karaites, Hasidim* and *mitnaggedim* – all Jews accepted the binding authority of the law in the Torah. The 613 Biblical commandments were universally viewed as given by God to Moses on Mt Sinai and understood as binding for all time.

Throughout Jewish history the validity of the written Torah was never questioned. In contemporary society, however, most Jews of all religious positions have ceased to regard the legal heritage in this light. Instead individual Jews, including those of the Orthodox persuasion, feel at liberty to choose which laws have a personal spiritual significance. Such an anarchic approach to the halakhic tradition highlights the fact that Jewish law no longer serves as a cohesive force for contemporary Jewry. In short, many modern Jews no longer believe in the doctrine of *Torah MiSinai* which previously served as a cardinal principle of the Jewish faith. Instead, they subscribe only to a limited number of legal precepts which for one reason or another they find meaningful. Such a lack of uniformity of Jewish practice means that there is a vast gulf between the requirements of halakhic observance and the actual lifestyle of the majority of Jews both in Israel and the diaspora.

In this connection there is also considerable confusion about the status of the Five Books of Moses. According to Orthodox belief, the Torah was revealed to Moses on Mt Sinai. This act of revelation provided the basis for the legal system as well as Jewish theology. Many modern Orthodox adherents pay lip-service to this conviction, but in their daily lives illustrate that such a belief has little if any relevance. They fail to live up to the halakhic requirements as prescribed in Scripture and are agnostic about the nature and activity of God. The gap between traditional belief and contemporary views of the Torah is even greater in the non-Orthodox branches of Judaism. Here there is a general acceptance of the findings of Biblical scholarship. The Five Books of Moses are perceived as divinely inspired but at the same time the product of human reflection. Thus the Torah is viewed as a unified text, combining centuries of tradition, in which a variety of individual sources were woven together by a number of editors.

Such a non-fundamentalistic approach, which takes account of recent scholarly developments in the field of Biblical studies, rules out the traditional belief in the infallibility of Scripture and in this way provides a rationale for halakhic change. Thus in contemporary society many Orthodox Jews who express allegiance to the Torah do not live according to the tenets of the tradition while non-Orthodox Jews are uncertain which aspects of Scripture should be revered. In both cases the Torah has for most Jews ceased to be, in the words of the psalmist 'A tree of life to those who hold fast to it'.

Not only is there uncertainty in the Jewish world about practice and belief; there is also a great deal of confusion about Jewish identity. Are the Jews a nation, a civilization or a religious community? In the past it was relatively easy to answer this question – Jewry was united by a common heritage and way of life. Jews constituted an identifiable religious grouping sharing ancient customs. No longer is this the case. Contemporary Jewish existence is pluralistic and most Jews are secularized and assimilated. This disordered situation is further complicated by the fact that the Reform movement has altered the sociological definition of Jewish status. Previously all branches of Judaism held that view that a person was Jewish if that individual had a Jewish mother; in other words, Jewishness was seen as dependent on maternal descent. However, in 1983 the Central Conference of American Rabbis decreed that children of either a Jewish mother or a Jewish father should be regarded as Jewish as long as they observed religious timely acts. By expanding the determination of Jewishness to include children of both matrilineal and patrilineal descent the Reform movement defined as Jews individuals whom the other branches of Judaism regard as gentiles. This means that neither those persons nor their descendants can be accepted as Jews by the non-Reform religious establishment.

A similar situation applies to Reform converts and their offspring who, according to Orthodox Judaism, are non-Jews. The Orthodox movement has debarred such individuals from access to Jewish privileges and has exerted pressure on the government of Israel not to allow Reform converts the right to return to the Holy Land as Jewish citizens. A final complication concerning Jewish status concerns the remarriage of female Jews who, though civilly divorced, have failed to obtain a Jewish bill of divorce (*get*). Orthodoxy does not recognize their divorces as valid and any subsequent liaison, even when accompanied by a non-Orthodox

Jewish marriage ceremony or civil marriage, is regarded as adulterous. Further, the children of such unions are stigmatized as *mamzerim* and barred from marrying other Jews unless they are also *mamzerim*. These problems, produced by deviations from traditional Jewish practice, present contemporary Jewry with enormous perplexities and highlight the fissures separating the various Jewish religious groupings.

All of these dilemmas about the nature of contemporary Judaism are in varying degrees related to the fundamental issue of assimilation. Prior to the Enlightenment Jews did not have full citizenship rights of the countries in which they lived. Nevertheless, they were able to regulate their own affairs through an organized structure of self-government. Within such a context Jewish law served as the basis of communal life, and rabbis were able to exert power and authority in the community. But as a result of political emancipation, Jews entered the mainstreams of modern life taking on all the responsibilities of citizenship. The rabbinical establishment thereby lost its status and control, and the halakhic system became voluntary. In addition, Jews took advantage of widening social advantages: they were free to choose where to live, whom to marry, and what career to follow. By gaining access to secular educational institutions, the influence of the surrounding culture also pervaded all aspects of Jewish life. As a consequence Jewry in modern society is fragmented and secularized, and intermarriage is on the increase. As Jews stand on the threshold of the twenty-first century, answers must urgently be found to the perplexing problems now facing the Jewish people.

SOURCES

The Future

Some commentators believe that there is no long-term future for the Jewish religion. The birth-rate among diaspora Jews is too low, they say, and the attractions of assimilation are too great; there will be no more pious Jewish generations. Admittedly the State of Israel probably enjoys a greater measure of security than at any time since its creation, but despite Orthodox control over matters of personal status, Israel is a secular state. The vast majority of Israelis understand their Jewishness as a national rather than as a religious identity. Thus in Israel, as in the diaspora, this theory maintains, the Jewish faith will survive among the strictly Orthodox who, despite their many children, will remain an eccentric minority, following their ancient customs, keeping within their own communities, and living lives completely out of tune with manners and mores of the twenty-first century. They will become like the modern Karaites or Samaritans within Judaism, or like the Amish or Mennonites within Christianity – interesting subjects for anthropological theses, but irrelevant to mainstream culture. The more secular-minded of their co-religionists will intermarry with their gentile neighbours, and in common with the Spanish Marranos, they will have dim memories of a Jewish past, but like the Ten Lost Tribes of old, they will ultimately disappear from history.

Other prognoses are not so gloomy, pointing out that Judaism has always adapted itself to changing times and circumstances. The heroes of Masada believed that they were the last of their people, but the scholars of Janvneh managed to shake off the trauma of the destruction of the Temple in Jerusalem and to forge a new religious system centred on the synagogue and Torah. Through the mechanism of debate and scholarship, Jewish law adapted itself to changing circumstances. There have been successful communities throughout Europe, America and Asia; they have all had their own individual characteristics, but ultimately they have all accepted the yoke of the covenant. There have always been differences of opinion; the Sadducees quarrelled with the Pharisees, the Rabbanites with the Karaites, the Maimonideans with the anti-Maimonideans, the Shabbeteans with the sceptics and the Hasidim with the Mitnaggedim. But those who support this prognosis emphasize that Judaism has survived, and there is no reason to suppose that things will be any different in the future. Although in each generation some Jews will fall away, enough will remain faithful to Torah and synagogue for the system to survive.

(In SHJ, pp. 133–134)

DISCUSSION

1. Is a belief in an interventionist concept of God essential for the continuation of Judaism as a religious system?

2. Does the erosion of commitment to the Jewish legal tradition threaten Jewish survival?

FURTHER READING

Agus, Jacob, *The Evolution of Jewish Thought*, Arno, 1973.

Ben-Sasson, Hayim, *A History of The Jewish People*, Harvard University Press, 1985.

Blumenthal, David, *The Banality of Good and Evil: Moral Lessons from the Shoah and Jewish Tradition*, Georgetown University Press, 1999.

Cohn-Sherbok, Dan, *Holocaust Theology: A Reader*, Exeter University Press, 2002.

Cohn-Sherbok, Dan, *The Future of Judaism*, T. and T. Clark, 1994.

De Lange, Nicholas, *Judaism*, Oxford University Press, 1986.

Fackenheim, Emil, *God's Presence in History: Jewish Affirmations and Philosophical Reflections*, Harper and Row, 1972.

Friedlander, Albert (ed.), *Out of the Whirlwind*, Schocken, 1988.

Goldberg, Michael, *Why Should Jews Survive?*, Oxford University Press, 1995.

Greenberg, Irving, *On the Third Era in Jewish History*, National Jewish Resource Centre, 1980.

Jacobs, Steven, *Rethinking Jewish Faith*, State University of New York Press, 1994.

Kaufman, Walter, *Contemporary Jewish Philosophies*, Behrman House, 1976.

Marmur, Dov, *Beyond Survival*, Darton, Longman and Todd, 1982.

Plaskow, Judith, *Again at Sinai: Judaism from a Feminist Perspective*, HarperCollins, 1990.

Rubenstein, Richard, Roth, John, *Approaches to Auschwitz*, SCM, 1987.

Seltzer, Robert, *Jewish People, Jewish Thought*, Macmillan, 1980.

Sacks, Jonathan, *The Dignity of Difference*, Continuum, 2002.

Solomon, Norman, *Judaism and World Religion*, Macmillan, 1991.

Trepp, Leo, *A History of the Jewish Experience: Eternal Faith, Eternal People*, Behrman House, 1973.

Vital, David, *The Future of the Jews*, Harvard University Press, 1990.

Wyschogrod, Michael, *The Body of Faith*, Seabury Press, 1983.

PART II BELIEF AND PRACTICE

Discussing such issues as the nature of God, creation, divine providence, revelation, Torah and mitzvah, sin and repentance, the chosen people, the Promised Land, the Messiah, the afterlife, worship and festivals, and life cycle events, this survey of Jewish belief and practice explores Judaism both as a religion and way of life, providing essential information on Jewish family and community customs as well as on the beliefs and traditions that have shaped the Jewish faith throughout nearly four thousand years of history.

CHAPTER 55

The Unity of God

In the Hebrew Scriptures the Israelites experienced God as the Lord of history. The most uncompromising expression of his unity is the *Shema* Prayer: 'Hear, O Israel, the Lord, our God, the Lord is One'. (Deuteronomy 6:4). According to the Hebrew Bible, the universe owes its existence to the one God, the creator of heaven and earth, and since all human beings are created in his image, all men and women are brothers and sisters. Thus the belief in one God implies for the Jewish faith that there is one humanity and one world. Jewish Biblical teaching emphasizes that God alone is to be worshipped. As the sixth century BCE prophet Isaiah declared:

> I am the Lord, and there is no other,
> besides me there is no God; . . .
> I form light and create darkness,
> I make weal and create woe,
> I am the Lord, who do all these things.
>
> (Isa. 45:5,7)

Within the Bible the struggle against polytheism was a dominant motif, continuing into the rabbinic period. Combating the dualistic doctrine that there are two gods in heaven, the rabbis commented on Deuteronomy 32:39 ('See now that I, even I, am he, and there is no God beside me'): 'If anyone says that there are two powers in Heaven the retort is given to him: "There is God with me"' (*Sifre* to Deuteronomy 32:39). In a passage in the *Mekhilta* (*midrash* on Exodus), dualism is rejected since when God said: 'I am the Lord your God' (Exodus 20:2) no one protested (*Mekhilta, Ba-Hodesh* 5). Again, the *Mishnah* states that if a person says in his prayers, 'We acknowledge Thee, we acknowledge Thee', implying belief in two gods, he is to be silenced (Ber. 5:3; Meg. 4:9). Although dualistic tendencies are reflected in the doctrines of Satan and *Metatron*, and in kabbalistic theories

about the demonic realm (*Sitra Ahra*), Jewish monotheism became the central tenet of traditional Judaism.

In the early rabbinic period Jewish sages were troubled by the Christian doctrine of the Incarnation, which they viewed as dualistic in character. In third century Caesarea, for example, R. Abahu commented on the verse, 'God is not man, that he should lie, or a son of man, that he should repent. Has he said, and will he not do it? Or has he spoken, and will he not fulfil it? (Num. 23:19). According to R. Abahu, the last

Figure 55 Samuel persuades Israelites against gods Baal and Ashtaroths for deliverance from Philistines. Fresco 13th century AD. Copyright The Art Archive/Anagni Cathedral Italy/Dagli Orti.

part of this verse refers to man rather than God. Thus he declared: 'If a man says to you, "I am god", he is lying: "I am the Son of Man", he will end up being sorry for it; "I am going up to heaven", he will not fulfil what he has said' (*Jer. Talmud Taan* 2:1). Again, in *Exodus Rabbah* (*midrash* on Exodus), R. Abahu states: '"I am the first" for I have no father; "and I am the last", for I have no brother; "and besides me there is no God", for I have no son.' (*Exodus, Rabbah* 29:5)

In the Middle Ages the Christian doctrine of the Trinity was frequently attacked by Jewish scholars since it appeared to undermine pure monotheism. In contrast to Christian exegetes who interpreted the *Shema* with its three references to God as denoting the Trinity, Jewish scholars maintained that the *Shema* implies that there is only one God, rather than three persons of the Godhead. For medieval Jewish theology the belief in divine unity was a fundamental principle of Judaism. For a number of Jewish theologians the concept of God's unity implies that there can be no multiplicity in his being. Thus the tenth century philosopher **Saadiah Gaon** insisted in The *Book of Beliefs and Opinions* that the Divine creator is a single, incorporeal Being who created the universe out of nothing. Like the Islamic *Mutazilite* theologians, he asserted that if God has a plurality of attributes, He must be composite in nature. Thus, such terms as 'life', 'omnipotence' and 'omniscience' should be understood as implications of the concept of God as creator rather than attributes of the Deity. According to Saadiah, the reason why we are forced to describe God by means of these descriptions is because of the limitations of language, but they do not in any way involve a plurality in God. In this light Saadiah argued that the anthropomorphic expressions in the Bible must not be taken literally, since this would imply that God is a plurality.

Another thinker of this period, **Solomon ibn Gabirol** (eleventh century), argued that God and matter are not opposed as two ultimate principles – instead matter is identical with God. It emanates from the essence of the creator, forming the basis of all subsequent emanations. For ibn Gabirol the universe consists of cosmic existences flowing out of the superabundant light and goodness of the creator; it is a reflection of God, though God remains in himself and does not enter his creation with his essence. In a poem,

Religious Crown, ibn Gabirol uses neo-Platonic images to describe God's activity:

Thou art One, the beginning of all computation,
the base of all construction,
Thou art One, and in the mystery of thy
Oneness the wise of heart are astonished,
for they know not what it is.
Thou art One, and thy Oneness neither
    diminishes
nor increases, neither lacks nor exceeds.
Thou art One, but not as the one that is counted
or owned, for number and chance cannot
reach thee, nor attribute, nor form.

This insistence on God's unity was a theme of the twelfth century Jewish philosopher **Abraham ibn Daud**, who in *The Exalted Faith* derives God's absolute unity from his necessary existence. For ibn Daud this concept of divine oneness precludes the possibility of any positive attributes of God. Similarly, Moses Maimonides in the same century argued in *The Guide for the Perplexed* that no positive attributes can be predicated of God since the Divine is an absolute unity. Thus when God is described positively in the Bible, such ascriptions refer to his activity. The only true attributes are negative ones; they lead to a knowledge of God because in negation no plurality is involved. Each negative attribute excludes from God's essence some imperfection.

In the Middle Ages kabbalistic belief in divine unity was also a central doctrine. As we previously noted, the kabbalists substituted the concept of a dynamically structured Godhead for the static concept of self-contained Deity. According to the kabbalists, there are ten *sefirot* (divine emanations): (1) *Keter* (Crown), the divine will to create; (2) *Hokhmah* (Wisdom), in which is found God's potential power to create; (3) *Binah* (Understanding), in which is located the divine plan of creation; (4) *Hesed* (Lovingkindness), the outpouring of divine goodness; (5) *Gevurah* (Power), divine judgement which curtails the flow of lovingkindness so that creatures can enjoy the splendour of divine grace; (6) *Tiferet* (Beauty), the harmonizing principle which controls the balance between *Hesed* and *Gevurah*; (7) *Netzah* (Victory); (8) *Hod* (Splendour); (9) *Yesod* (Foundation), the principle of generation;

and (10) *Malkhut* (Kingdom), the principle of divine rule over creation. By means of these ten emanations, the Deity manifests himself, emerging from his concealment so that human beings can share in his goodness.

According to the kabbalists, *Keter* as the link between *Ayn Sof* and the *sefirotic* realm is too elevated for human beings to comprehend. An aspect of such remoteness also applies to the *sefirot* of *Hokhmah* and *Binah*. Thus the *Zohar* relates that regarding *Binah* one can ask what it is yet expect no answer, whereas it is not even possible to raise the question regarding *Hokhmah*. The seven lower *sefirot*, ranging from *Hesed* to *Malkhut*, on the other hand, can be objects of contemplation. By their actions, human beings can influence the higher worlds and bring down the flow of divine grace; when this occurs, there is harmony in the sefirotic realm. If this does not take place, the *Shekhinah* (divine presence) is in exile.

Not surprisingly, critics of the kabbalistic system were anxious to stress that such doctrines concerning division within the Godhead were heretical in character. It was even alleged that the kabbalistic doctrine of the ten *sefirot* who constitute a divine unity is an even more serious heresy than the Christian conception of the Trinity. In response, the kabbalists argued that the *sefirot* are united with *Ayn Sof*, and that when kabbalistic prayer is directed to the *sefirot* it is in fact the *Ayn Sof* to whom such prayers are offered. Further, they stressed that it is a mistake to believe that any of the *sefirot* can be separated from the others.

Turning to the development of these medieval doctrines in the teaching of Isaac Luria, it was previously noted that after Divine contraction occurred (*tzimtzum*) an empty space was left. Into this domain a ray of light emerged from the *Ayn Sof*. From this emanation *Adam Kadmon* (Primal Man) was generated. Subtle lights then came forth from the 'ear', 'nose', and 'mouth' of *Adam Kadmon*: these produced *in potentia* the vessels which were to contain the divine light of the *sefirot* which were to be formed. Light then proceeded from the 'eyes' of *Adam Kadmon* while the vessels of the highest *sefirot* – *Keter, Hokhmah* and *Binah* – were able to contain these lights, yet the vessels of the lower *sefirot* were unable to do so. This resulted in the catastrophe of the 'shattering of the vessels'. This was necessary for the *sitra ahra* to emerge so that

human beings would be able to choose good from evil. As a consequence of the shattering of the vessels the light of the *Ayn Sof* was fragmented: holy sparks from the Infinite light were scattered to form the power to sustain the sefirotic realm as well as the worlds beneath it. Yet, this calamity also resulted in cosmic disarray which can only be repaired by human action reclaiming the holy sparks and restoring them to the divine source. This process is known as cosmic repair: *tikkun*. When this aim is attained, there will be redemption of Israel, humanity and the cosmos.

In modern times the various mainstream branches of Judaism have continued to embrace the belief in divine unity. Yet, among Reconstructionist Jews the concept of God has been radically modified. In the 1930s Mordecai Kaplan, Professor at the Jewish Theological Seminary, advanced a reinterpretation of the Jewish tradition. In his view, it is a mistake for modern Jews to believe in an external Deity. Rather, he argued that God is not a supernatural being, but the power that makes for salvation. God, he stated, is the sum of all the animating, organizing forces and relationships which are forever making a cosmos out of chaos. In his view, the idea of God must be understood fundamentally in terms of its effect. Thus, God is a transcendence which does not infringe on the laws of nature. Even though he did not redefine the concept of divine unity, he nonetheless formulated a notion of God which is far removed from the Biblical and rabbinic understanding of God as the creator and sustainer of the universe who chose the Jewish people and guides them to their final ultimate destiny.

A more extreme theological position has been adopted by Humanistic Jews who reject the belief in God altogether. In the 1960s the Reform rabbi Sherwin Wine founded a new movement, Humanistic Judaism, which denies any form of supernaturalism. Intent on abandoning any form of theistic belief, Humanistic Jews categorically reject any notion of divine reality and have removed any references to God in their worship services. For Humanistic Jews, Scripture as well as the rabbinic sources are perceived as human in origin: thus they must be submitted to critical evaluation. Viewed in this light, the Torah is regarded as an unreliable guide to the history of the Jewish people. Adopting a secular perspective, Humanistic Jews contend that the true nature of

Jewish history can be discovered through scientific investigation.

Despite such a radical vision of Judaism, Humanistic Jews are intent on preserving a Jewish lifestyle. In their view, the Jewish holidays are of religious significance in so far as they promote humanistic values. The same applies to life-cycle events; they too are reinterpreted so as to stress their humanistic features. Humanistic Judaism thus offers an option for those who wish to identify with the Jewish community despite their rejection of of the traditional understanding of God. Here, then, is a radical departure from the conviction about the unity of God despite the commitment of Humanistic Jews to the continuation of the Jewish heritage.

SOURCES

Saadiah Gaon

Born in 882 in Egypt, Saadiah Gaon served as *gaon* of Sura. In *The Book of Doctrines and Beliefs*, he describes the nature of God and the creation of the world – a work based on Islamic *Mutazilite* theology. Concerning God's unity, Saadiah asserted:

> Our Lord (be He exalted and glorified) has informed us through the words of his prophets that He is One, Living, Powerful and Wise, and that nothing can be compared to him or unto his works. They established this by signs and miracles and we accepted it immediately. Later, speculation led us to the same result. In regard to his unity, it is said, 'Hear of Israel, the Lord our God, the Lord is One' (Deut. 6:4); furthermore, 'See now that I, even I, am He, and that there is no god with me' (Deut. 32:39), and also, 'The Lord alone did lead him, and there was no strange god with him' (Deut. 32:12).
>
> (Saadiah Gaon, *The Book of Doctrines and Beliefs*, in HJPMA, p. 25)

Turning from the doctrine of God's unity, Saadiah advanced several arguments to demonstrate that God created the world at a given moment:

> (1) the world being limited in space, if the force moving it were the world itself, it would also be limited; since the world moves perpetually, a force other than that of the world must be the mover of the world.
>
> (2) The world is made up of parts that are sometimes joined and sometimes separate: neither the separation nor the union are part of their essence; one must therefore admit that an external force joins or separates them in order to form bodies, small like plants, or large like the spheres; this force is God the creator.
>
> (3) The third proof is based on accidents: everything in this world is composed of necessary substance and of accidents (like the form of an object, its colour, its warmth, its movement); as no thing is without its accidents, which succeed each other in the same body and change continually, it must be God who produces these changes.
>
> (4) The fourth proof depends on time, which is finite; for if the succession of instants were infinite, it could not be retraced in thought: only a succession with a temporal beginning could explain the existence of the world at the present time.
>
> (Saadiah Gaon, *The Book of Doctrines and Beliefs*, in HJPMA, pp. 23–24)

Solomon ibn Gabirol

Born in *c.* 1021 most likely in Malaga, Solomon ibn Gabirol lived in Saragossa. Influenced by Neoplatonism, he discusses the process of creation in *The Fountain of Life*. Here he argues that universal matter is one and subsists by itself:

If all things have only one universal matter, this necessarily has the following properties: that of being, that of subsisting by itself, that of having only one essence, that of bearing diversity and that of giving to all things its essence and its name. We accord to it the property of being, for non-being cannot be the matter of what is; that of subsisting by itself, for reasoning would go on *ad infinitum* if matter existed by something else; that of being one,

for we require an unique matter for all things; that of bearing diversity, because diversity is reached through forms and the forms do not subsist by themselves; finally that of giving to all things its essence and its name, because, sustaining all things, it must be in all things and, being in all things, it must give to all things its essence and its name.
(Solomon ibn Gabirol, *The Fountain of Life*, in HJPMA, p. 74)

Nonetheless, ibn Gabirol insists that matter cannot subsist without form; universal matter cannot subsist by itself except potentially. In his view, universal matter and universal form cannot subsist without each other:

The substance of matter cannot be without form for a single instant, nor can the substance of form exist without matter. And in this there is a strong proof that the existence of each of them is of necessary existence only by the necessary existence of the other. Consider now the properties of unity, and you will find them attached to the form: it is unity that produces multiplicity and keeps it, it gives it its being, comprehends it and exists in all its parts, it is born

by what is its substratum and it is more dignified than its substratum. In consequence, these properties are in form, because it is form which constitutes the essence of that within which it is, it gives it its being; comprehends it, retains it, is in all its parts, it is born in the matter which is its substratum, and it is superior to it, and matter is below it.
(Solomon ibn Gabirol, *The Fountain of Life*, in HJPMA, p. 74)

Abraham ibn Daud

Living in Spain between 1110 and 1180, Abraham ibn Daud discusses the nature of divine unity in *The Exalted Faith*. Like Maimonides, he perceives the seeming contradiction between science and religion. In his view, Biblical passages should be understood in their rational sense:

The first (reason) is that the Torah and philosophy are in flagrant contradiction when they attempt to describe the divine essence; for the philosophers, the incorporeal God is in no way capable of alteration; the Torah, on the contrary, narrates God's movements, his feelings . . . Given that philosophy and the Torah are in opposition on this subject, we are in the situation of a man with two masters, one great and the other small; he cannot please the first without opposing the opinion of the second, and in consequence, if we find a method of making them agree, we shall be very happy with it . . .

The second imperious necessity arises from the Torah itself. If we reject the opinion of the philosophers as a whole, even if it is firmly based on demonstrations and is of an elevated level, if we cast doubt on their proofs, have scant respect for their eminence, and depend on what necessarily results from the revealed text, then we shall see that the texts themselves contradict one another and really agree only on the principle that we shall enunciate in this chapter (that is to say, the divine incorporeality).
(Abraham ibn Daud, *Exalted Faith*, in HJPMA, pp. 143–4)

Nonetheless, in his view, religion and philosophy are in agreement:

Indeed, in our times, it sometimes happens that one who investigates the sciences but slightly, lacks the strength to grasp two lamps with his two hands: with his right hand the lamp of his religion and with his left hand the lamp of his science. For when he lights the lamp of science, the lamp of religion goes out . . . When someone is just beginning his study of the sciences, he is perplexed about what he knows from the point of view of the traditional knowledge because he has not attained in science the degree where he could state the Truth in the questions which are not clear. Accordingly, this book will be very useful to him for it will acquaint him with many points of science which we have built on the principles of religion.

(Abraham ibn Daud, *Exalted Faith*, in HJPMA, p. 143)

DISCUSSION

1. Does the doctrine of the *sefirot* undermine the concept of divine unity?

2. Discuss the rabbinic view that the doctrine of the Trinity conflicts with the belief in God's unity.

FURTHER READING

Blumenthal, David, *Facing the Abusing God: A Theology of Protest*, Westminster John Knox, 1993.

Braiterman, Zachary, *(God) after Auschwitz: Tradition and Change in Post-Holocaust Jewish Thought*, Princeton University Press, 1998.

Buber, Martin, *I and Thou*, Scribner, 2000.

Cohn-Sherbok, Dan, *Holocaust Theology: A Reader*, Exeter University Press, 2002.

Gordis, Daniel, *God Was Not in the Fire: The Search for a Spiritual Judaism*, Touchstone, 1997.

Heschel, Abraham Joshua, *Interpretation of Judaism from the Writings of Abraham Joshua Heschel*, Free Press, 1997.

Hoffman, Joshua, Rosenkrantz, Cory, *The Divine Attributes*, Blackwell, 2002.

Jacobs, Louis, *Principles of the Jewish Faith*, Vallentine Mitchell, 1964.

Jacobs, Louis, *A Jewish Theology*, Behrman House, 1973.

Koltach, Alfred (ed.), *What Jews Say about God*, Jonathan David, 1999.

Lang, Bernhard, *The Hebrew God*, Yale, 2002.

Seeskin, Kenneth, *No Other Gods: The Continuing Struggle Against Idolatry*, Behrman House, 1995.

CHAPTER 56

Divine Transcendence and Immanence

Figure 56 God creating the waters, from Genesis, creation of the world, folio 4v of late twelfth century Souvigny Bible (detail). Copyright The Art Archive/Bibliothèque Municipale Moulins/Dagli Orti.

For Jews, God is conceived as the transcendent creator of the universe. Thus in Genesis 1:1–2 he is described as forming heaven and earth:

> In the beginning God created the heavens and the earth. The earth was without form and void, and darkness was upon the face of the deep; and the Spirit of God was moving over the face of the waters.

Throughout Scripture this theme of divine transcendence is repeatedly affirmed. Thus the sixth century BCE prophet Isaiah proclaimed:

> Have you not known? Have you not heard? Has it not been told you from the beginning? Have you not understood from the foundations of the earth? It is he who sits above the circle of the earth, and its inhabitants are like grasshoppers; who stretches out the heavens like a curtain and spreads them like a tent to dwell in (Isa. 40:21–22)

Later in same book Isaiah declared that God is beyond human comprehension:

> For my thoughts are not your thoughts neither are your ways my ways, says the Lord. for as the heavens are higher than the earth, so are my ways higher than your ways and my thoughts than your thoughts (Isa. 55:8–9)

In the book of Job the same idea is repeated – God's purposes transcend human understanding:

> Can you find out the deep things of God?
> Can you find out the limit of the Almighty?
> It is higher than heaven – what can you do?
> Deeper than *Sheol* – what can you know?
> Its measure is longer than the earth, and broader than the sea. (Job 11:7–9)

According to the author of Ecclesiastes, God is in heaven whereas human beings are confined to earth. Thus the wise person should recognize the limitations of his knowledge:

> Be not rash with your mouth, nor let your heart be hasty to utter a word before God, for God is in

heaven, and you upon earth; therefore let your words be few. (Eccles. 5:2)

Despite this view of God's remoteness from his creation, He is also viewed as actively involved in the cosmos. In the Bible his omnipresence is repeatedly stressed. Thus the Psalmist rhetorically asked:

> Whither shall I go from thy Spirit?
> Or whither shall I flee from thy presence?
> If I ascend into heaven, thou art there! . . .
> If I take the wings of the morning
> and dwell in the uttermost parts of the sea,
> even there thy hand shall lead me. (Ps. 139:7–10)

In the rabbinic period Jewish scholars formulated the doctrine of the **Shekhinah** to denote the divine presence. As the in-dwelling presence of God, the *Shekhinah* is compared to light. Thus the *midrash* paraphrases Numbers 6:25 ('The Lord make His face to shine upon you and be gracious to you'): 'May he give thee of the light of the *Shekhinah*' (divine presence). In another *midrash* the 'shining' of the *Shekhinah* in the Tent of Meeting is compared to a cave by the sea. When the sea rushes in to fill the cave, it suffers no diminution of its waters. Likewise the divine presence filled the Tent of Meeting, but simultaneously filled the world. In the third century the Babylonian scholar Rab said: 'In the world to come there is no eating nor drinking nor propagation nor business nor jealousy nor hatred nor competition, but the righteous sit with their crowns on their heads and enjoy the brightness of the *Shekhinah*' (*Ber.* 17a). Again, the *Talmud* states: 'Come and see how beloved Israel is before God' for wherever they went into exile the *Shekhinah* went with them; in Babylon, the *Shekhinah* was with them and in the future, when Israel will be redeemed, the *Shekhinah* will be with them' (*Meg.* 29a).

In the medieval period the doctrine of the *Shekhinah* was further elaborated by Jewish scholars. According to **Saadiah Gaon** the *Shekhinah* is identical with the glory of God, which serves as an intermediary between God and human beings during the prophetic encounter. For Saadiah the 'Glory of God' is a Biblical term whereas the *Shekhinah* is a rabbinic concept which refers to the created splendour of light which acts as an intermediary between God and human beings. At times this manifestation takes on human form. Thus when Moses asked to see God's glory, he was shown the *Shekhinah*. Similarly when the prophets in their visions saw God in human form, what they actually perceived was the *Shekhinah*. Such a view avoids compromising God's unity and incorporeality.

Following Saadiah, **Judah Halevi** argued in the *Kuzari* that it is the *Shekhinah* rather than God himself who appears to the prophets. However, unlike Saadiah he did not describe the *Shekhinah* as a created light. Rather, he identified the *Shekhinah* with the divine influence. For Halevi the *Shekhinah* initially dwelt in the Tabernacle; subsequently it was manifest in the Temple. With the cessation of prophecy it ceased to appear, but will return with the Messiah. In his discussion Halevi distinguished between the visible *Shekhinah* which dwelt in the Temple and appeared to the prophets, and the invisible *Shekhinah* which is with every born Israelite who leads a virtuous life, is pure of heart, and has an upright mind.

In his *Guide*, **Maimonides** embraced Saadiah's belief that the *Shekhinah* is a created light, identified with glory. In addition, he associated the *Shekhinah* with prophecy. According to Maimonides, prophecy is an overflow from God which passes through the mediation of the Active Intellect and then to the faculty of imagination. It requires perfection in theoretical wisdom, morality and development of the imagination. On the basis of this conception, Maimonides asserted that human beings can be divided into three classes according to the development of their reasoning capabilities.

First, there are those whose rational faculties are highly developed and receive influences from the Active Intellect, but whose imagination is defective. These are wise men and philosophers. The second group consists of those where the imagination alone is in good condition, but the intellect is defective – these are statesmen, lawgivers and politicians. Thirdly, there are the prophets – those whose imagination is consistently perfect and whose Active Intellect is fully developed.

In kabbalistic teaching the *Shekhinah* also played an important role. In early kabbalistic thought the *Shekhinah* was identified as the feminine principle in the world of the *sefirot*. Later the *Shekhinah* was understood as the last in the hierarchy of the *sefirot*, representing the female principle. Like the moon, this *sefirah* has no light of her own, but instead receives the divine light from the other *sefirot*. The symbolism describing the *Shekhinah* refers to her relationship with the other *sefirot* (such as her acceptance of the divine light, her relationship to them as an inferior aspect of themselves, and her coming close to the masculine element in the divine sphere). In addition, other symbols depict the *Shekhinah* as the battleground between the divine powers of good and evil.

As the divine power closest to the created world, she is the medium through which the divine light passes. Further, in kabbalistic thought the *Shekhinah* is the divine principle of the Jewish people. Everything that happens to Israel is reflected upon the *Shekhinah* which grows stronger or is weakened with every meritorious act or sinful act of each Jew and of the people as a whole. Finally, the *Shekhinah* is viewed as the goal of the mystic who attempts to achieve communion with the divine powers.

In the early modern period the traditional belief in God's transcendence and immanence was attacked by the seventeenth-century Jewish philosopher Baruch Spinoza. In *Tractatus Theologico-Politicus* Spinoza propounded a metaphysical system based on a pantheistic conception of nature. Beginning with the belief in an infinite, unlimited, self-caused Substance which he conceived as God or nature, Spinoza maintained that Substance possessed a theoretical infinity of attributes, only two of which – extension and thought – are apprehended by human beings. God or nature can also be seen as a whole made up of finite, individual entities. In this way God exists in all things as their universal essence. They exist in God as modifications.

With the rise of science in the eighteenth century, the traditional belief in divine immanence became more difficult to sustain. Nonetheless Jewish thinkers continued to insist on the validity of the Biblical and rabbinic view of God's involvement with the universe. Pre-eminent among those who championed the traditional view was Schneur Zalman, the founder of the *Habad* movement of Hasidism. In the *Tanya* he wrote:

> Here lies the answer to the heretics and here is uncovered the root of their error, in which they deny God's providence over particular things and

the miracles and wonders recorded in Scripture. Their false imagination leads them into error, for they compare the work of the Lord, creator of heaven and earth, to the works of man and his artifices. These stupid folk compare the work of heaven and earth to the vessel which comes from the hands of a craftsman. Once the vessel has been fashioned it requires its maker no longer. Even when the maker has completed his task and goes about his own business, the vessel retains the form and appearance it had when fashioned. Their eyes are too blind to notice the important distinction between the works of man and his artifices – in which 'something' is made from 'something', the form alone being changed from a piece of silver into an ornament – and the creation of heaven and earth, which is the creation of 'something' out of 'nothing' . . . It follows *a fortiori* that with regard to creation *ex nihilo* . . . it is certain that the creature would revert to the state of nothingness and negation, God forfend, if the creator's power over it were removed. It is essential, therefore, for the power of the worker to be in his work constantly if that work is to be kept in existence. (*Tanya, Shaar Ha-Yihud Ve-Ha-Emunah*, Chapter 2, pp. 153–154)

Such an argument has been echoed across the modern Jewish religious spectrum. Religious believers from within the Orthodox, Reform and Conservative movements have continued to affirm the Biblical and rabbinic doctrine of God's transcendence and immanence. Although some thinkers have argued that God limited his own intervention in the world by allowing human beings to exercise free will, there has been a firm rejection of deistic ideas in which the Deity is perceived as an absentee God. Instead, Jews from these main groupings have universally affirmed that the transcendent God is immanent in the universe he has created. The song of the Hasidic master, Levi Yithzak of Berditchev, is characteristic of Jewish belief through the ages to the present:

> Where I wander – You!
> Where I ponder – You!
> Only you. You again, always You!
> You! You! You!

When I am gladdened – You!
When I am saddened – You!
Only You. You again. always You!
You! You! You!

Within the various branches of contemporary Judaism – from Orthodoxy to Reform Judaism – there has been a universal acceptance of the doctrine of divine transcendence and immanence. In the various liturgies of these movements, the belief that God transcends the world and is active in human experience is continually asserted. Yet, within the Jewish community, voices have been raised critical of this view. Obviously, Reconstructionist and Humanistic Jews who reject the belief in any form of supernaturalism have been insistent that such an understanding of divine reality is misguided. In their view, it makes no sense to conceive of God as an active agent in human history. Instead they subscribe to a naturalistic understanding of the origin of the universe and the course of human history.

Such a rejection of the traditional understanding of God is echoed in the writings of a number of leading Jewish thinkers. The Conservative rabbi and death-of-God theologian, **Richard Rubenstein**, in an influential book published in the 1960s, *After Auschwitz*, asserted that in light of the events of the Holocaust, it makes no sense to believe in a God who intervenes in human affairs. According to Rubenstein, it is no longer possible to believe in a supernatural Deity who controls human history. Rather, the Holocaust has demonstrated that such a belief has no foundation. Jews today, he contends, live in the time of the death of God.

Other Jewish thinkers contend that it is a mistake to believe that God intervenes in history. In *Faith After the Holocaust*, the Orthodox Jewish theologian Eliezer Berkovits asserts that if God did not respect human freedom, then men and women would cease to be human. Freedom and responsibility are the preconditions of human life. Hence, the Holocaust should be understood as a manifestation of evil, a tragedy inflicted by the Germans on the Jewish people. God did not intervene because he had bestowed free will on human beings at the time of creation.

Arguing along similar lines, the Reform rabbi Steven Jacobs writes in *Rethinking Jewish Faith* that traditional Jewish theology is inadequate to solve the problems presented by the events of the Nazi era. What is now needed, he believes, is a thorough re-evaluation of the religious tenets of the Jewish faith. In his view, it is no longer possible to believe in a God who intervenes in the world. This concept must be replaced by the notion of a God who is compatible with the reality of radical evil which admits of human freedom for good or evil.

Hence, in the modern world there is a growing awareness of the limitations of traditional Jewish theology. Even though the belief in the immanence and transcendence of God served as a bulwark of the faith in previous centuries, many Jews today find it increasingly difficult if not impossible to subscribe to such an understanding of divine activity. Influenced by scientific discovery and overwhelmed by the terrible events of the Nazi era, they are unable to embrace the theological beliefs of the past which sustained the Jewish people through centuries of persecution and suffering.

SOURCES

Shekhinah

For the rabbis God's presence in the universe was represented by the *Shekhinah*. Based on such Biblical passages as 'And let them make me a sanctuary that I may dwell among them' (Exodus 15:18), rabbinic sages maintained that the divine Spirit is continually in the midst of Israel. As the *Mishnah* explains:

> Rabbi Halafta, the son of Dosa, of the village of Hananya said, 'When ten people sit together and occupy themselves with the Torah, the *Shekhinah* abides among them, as it is said, "God stands in the congregation of the godly" (Psalms 82:I). And whence can it be shown that the same applies to five? Because it is said, "He has founded his band

upon the earth" (Amos 9:6). And whence can it be shown that the same applies to three. Because it is said, "He judges among the judges" (Psalms 82:l). And whence can it be shown that the same applies to two? Because it is said, "Then they that feared the Lord spake one with the other; and the Lord hearkened, and heard" (Malachi 3:16). And whence can it be shown that the same applies even to one? Because it is said, "In every place where I cause my name to be remembered, I will come unto you and I will bless you" (Exodus 20:24).'

(*Mishnah*, 3:6, in JM, p. 60)

Saadiah Gaon

Born in Egypt, Saadiah Gaon settled in Babylonia. In 928 he became *gaon* of Sura. In *The Book of Doctrines and Belief*, he argues that God manifests himself in the world; yet he insists that God is utterly transcendent as well. Here he propounds a series of arguments for *creatio ex nihilo*:

Having made it perfectly clear to myself that all things are created, I considered the question whether it was possible that they had created themselves, or whether the only possible assumption is that they were created by someone external to them. In my view it is impossible that they should have created themselves for a number of reasons of which I shall mention three. The first reason is this: Let us assume that an existing body has produced itself. It stands to reason that after having brought itself into existence that particular body should be stronger and more capable of producing its like than before. For if it was able to produce itself when it was in a relatively weak state, it should all the more be able to produce its like now that it is relatively strong. But seeing that it is incapable of creating its like now when it is relatively strong, it is absurd to think that it created itself when it was relatively weak. The second reason is: If we imagine that a thing has created itself, we shall find that the question of the time when it did so presents an insuperable difficulty. For if we say that

the thing created itself before it came into being, then we assume that it was non-existent at the time when it created itself, and obviously something non-existent cannot create a thing. If, on the other hand, we say that it created itself after it had come into being, the obvious comment is that after a thing has come into existence there is no need for it to create itself. There is no third instant between 'before' and 'after' except the present which, however, has no duration in which an action can take place. The third reason is: If we assume that a body is able to create itself, we must necessarily admit that at the same time it is likewise capable of abstaining from the act of self-creation. Under this assumption we shall find that the body is both existent and non-existent at the same time.,.Obviously, to attribute existence and non-existence to the same thing at the same time is utterly absurd.

(Saadiah Gaon, *The Book of Doctrines and Beliefs*, TJP, pp. 58–59)

Judah Halevi

Born in Toledo the eleventh century Jewish philosopher Judah Halevi defended the Jewish faith in the *Kuzari*. In explaining God's action in the world, he stressed that those things which are capable of receiving divine influence are not under human control:

It is impossible for him to gauge their quantity or quality; and even if their essence were known, yet

neither their time, place, constitution, nor preparation are revealed. For this an instruction is required, inspired by God, detailed through sublime evidence. He who has been thus inspired and who obeys the order with all its determinations and conditions with a pure mind, is the true believer. But an unbeliever is he who strives by speculation and deduction to influence conditions for the reception of this (divine) power, as revealed in the writings of astrologers, who try to call down supernatural beings, or who manufacture talismans. He brings offerings and burns incense in accordance with his own analogic deductions and conjectures, being in reality ignorant of that which we should do, how much, in which way, by what means, in which place, by whom, in which manner, and many other details, the enumeration of which would lead us too far. He is like an ignorant man who enters the surgery of a physician famous for the curative power of his medicines. The physician is not at home, but people come for medicines. the ignorant man dispenses them out of the jars, knowing nothing of the contents, nor how much should be given to each person. Thus he kills with the very medicine which should have cured them. Should he by chance have effected a cure with one of the drugs, the people will turn to him and say that it helped them – till they discover that he deceived them; or they note the accidental success of another drug and turn to it. They do not notice that the real cure was effected by the skill of the learned physician who prepared the medicines and explained the proper manner in which they were to be administered, and also taught the patients what food and drink, exercise and rest, sleep, ventilation and kind of bed, etc., was necessary. Men before the time of Moses, with few exceptions, were like these patients. They were deceived by astrological and physical doctrines; they turned from doctrine to doctrine, from god to god, or adopted a plurality (of doctrines and gods) at the same time; they forgot the guide and master of those powers and regarded the latter as helpful factors, whereas they are in reality mostly harmful factors, by reason of their construction and arrangement. Profitable on its own account is the divine influence, and harmful on its own account, the absence thereof.

(Judah Halevi, *Kuzari*, Book I, 79, in TJP, pp. 40–41)

Moses Maimonides

In *The Guide for the Perplexed*, the twelfth century Jewish philosopher Moses Maimonides discussed the nature of God's influence on the prophets:

The opinions of people concerning prophecy are like their opinions concerning the eternity of the world or its creation in time. I mean by this that just as the people to whose mind the existence of the Deity is firmly established, have, as we have set forth, three opinions concerning the eternity of the world or its creation in time, so are there also three opinions concerning prophecy.

The first opinion – that of the multitude of those among the pagans who considered prophecy as true and also believed by some of the common people professing our Law – is that God, may He be exalted, chooses whom He wishes from among men, turns him into a prophet, and sends him with a mission. According to them it makes no difference whether this individual is a man of knowledge or ignorant, aged or young . . .

The second opinion is that of the philosophers. It affirms that prophecy is a certain perfection in the nature of man. This perfection is not achieved in any individual from among men except after a training that makes that which exists in the potentiality of the species pass into actuality, provided an obstacle due to temperament or to some external cause does not hinder this, as is the case with regard to every perfection whose existence is possible in a certain species . . .

According to this opinion, it is not possible that an ignoramus should turn into a prophet; nor can a man not be a prophet on a certain evening and be a prophet on the following morning, as though he had made some find. Things are rather as follows: When, in the case of a superior individual who is perfect with respect to his rational and moral qualities, his imaginative faculty is in its most perfect state and when he has been prepared in the way that you will hear, he will necessarily become a prophet . . .

The third opinion is the opinion of our Law and the foundation of our doctrine. It is identical with the philosophic opinion except in one thing. For we believe that it may happen that one who is fit for prophecy and prepared for it should not become a prophet, namely, on account of the divine will . . .

Know that the true reality and quiddity of prophecy consist in its being an overflowing from God, may He be cherished and honoured, through the intermediation of the Active Intellect, toward the rational faculty in the first place and thereafter toward the imaginative faculty.

(Moses Maimonides, *The Guide for the Perplexed*, III, 32, 36, in GP, pp. 360–369)

Richard Rubenstein

Amongst radical theologians, the conception of God as active in history has been widely criticized. In *After Auschwitz*, the Conservative rabbi Richard Rubenstein argued that the traditional concept of God must be rejected in the light of the events of the Holocaust:

No man can really say that God is dead. How can we know that? Nevertheless, I am compelled to say that we live in the time of the 'death of God'. This is more a statement about man and his culture than about God. The death of God is a cultural fact. Buber felt this. He spoke of the eclipse of God. I can understand his reluctance to use the more explicitly Christian terminology. I am compelled to utilize it because of my conviction that the time when Nietzsche's madman said was too far off has come upon us. There is no way around Nietzsche. Had I lived in another time

or another culture, I might have found some other vocabulary to express my meanings. I am, however, a religious existentialist after Nietzsche and after Auschwitz. When I say we live in the time of the death of God, I mean that the thread uniting God and man, heaven and earth, has been broken. We stand in a cold, silent, unfeeling cosmos, unaided by any purposeful power beyond our own resources. After Auschwitz, what else can a Jew say about God?

(Richard Rubenstein, *After Auschwitz*, in HT, p. 42)

DISCUSSION

1. Discuss Maimonides' belief that the prophecy is an overflow from God which passes through the mediation of the Active Intellect and then to the faculty of imagination. Is such a view consistent with Scripture?

2. In what ways does science undermine the traditional Jewish belief in God's immanence?

FURTHER READING

Berkovits, Eliezer, *Faith After the Holocaust*, KTAV, 1973.

Cohen, Arthur, *Tremendum: A Theological Interpretation of the Holocaust*, Crossroad, 1981.

Fackenheim, Emil, *The Jewish Bible after the Holocaust: A Re-Reading*, Indiana University Press, 1991.

Isaacson, Sara, *Principles of Jewish Spirituality*, Thorsons, 1999.

Kushner, Harold, *When Bad Things Happen to Good People*, Schocken, 2001.

Maybaum, Ignaz, *The Face of God after Auschwitz*, Polak and Van Gennep, 1965.

Maza, Bernard, *With Fury Poured Out*, KTAV, 1986.

Unterman, Alan, *Jews: Their Religious Beliefs and Practices*, Sussex Academic Press, 1996.

Waskow, Arthur, *Godwrestling, Round 2: Ancient Wisdom, Future Paths*, Jewish Lights, 1998.

Wine, Sherwin, *Judaism Beyond God*, Society for Humanistic Judaism, 1985.

Wyschogrod, Michael, *The Body of Faith: God in the People Israel*, HarperCollins, 1989.

CHAPTER 57

Eternity

Figure 57 Jews praying in a synagogue in Richmond, London. Copyright David Rose.

Throughout Scripture God is described as having neither beginning nor end. Thus the Psalmist declared:

> Before the mountains were brought forth,
> or ever thou hadst formed the earth and the
>   world,
> from everlasting to everlasting thou art God.

In Psalm 90:4 the Psalmist states that all generations pass before God:

> For a thousand years in Thy sight
> Are but as yesterday when it is past.
>   (Ps. 90:2)

Further, the Psalmist proclaims that God will remain when everything has perished:

They shall perish but Thou shalt endure;
Yes, all of them shall wax old like a garment;
As a vesture shalt Thou change them, and they
    shall pass away;
But Thou art the selfsame,
And Thy years shall have no end.
(Psalm 102:26–27)

Again the sixth century BCE prophet Isaiah proclaimed:

Thus says the Lord, the King of Israel,
and his Redeemer, the Lord of hosts:
'I am the first and I am the last;
besides me there is no God'. (Isa. 44:6)

In the Bible the term *olam* is most frequently used
to denote the concept of God's eternity. In Genesis
21:33 He is described as the eternal God; He lives for
ever (Deut. 32:40), and reigns for ever (Exod. 15:18;
Ps. 10:16). He is the living God and everlasting King
(Jer. 10:10); His counsel endures for ever (Ps. 33:11)
as does his mercy (Ps. 106:1). For the Biblical writers,
God's eternal existence is different from the rest of
creation – He exists permanently without beginning
or end.

Another term used in Scripture to denote eternity
is *netzah* (everlastingness). According to the Book of
Samuel, God is *netzah yisrael* (the Eternal One of
Israel) (1 Sam. 15:29). Further the word *netzah* is used
to express the idea of permanence in Amos 1:11; Ps.
49:20; Job 20:7. The term *netzah* is also understood
as an attribute of God together with other attributes
in 1 Chron. 29:11. The Psalmist asserts that at God's
right hand is bliss for evermore (*netzah*) (Ps. 16:11);
that He will not forsake the needy for ever (*la-netzah*)
(Ps. 9:19); that his mercy will not be withheld for ever
(*la-netzah*) (Ps. 77:9); that He will not contend for ever
(Ps. 103:9); and that He will banish death for ever
(Is. 25:8).

This Biblical teaching was later elaborated by the
rabbis. According to the *Talmud* there is an un-
bridgeable gap between God and human beings:
'Come and see! The measure of the Holy One, blessed
be He, is unlike the measure of flesh and blood. The
things fashioned by a creature of flesh and blood

outlast him; the Holy One, blessed be He, outlasts the
things he has fashioned (Ber. 9a).

In midrashic literature God's eternal reign is similarly affirmed. Thus, when Pharaoh was told by Moses
and Aaron in the name of God to let the people go,
Pharaoh declared that God's name is not found in the
list of gods. In reply Moses and Aaron declared: 'O
fool! The dead can be sought among the living but how
can the living be sought among the dead. Our God
lives, but those you mention are dead. Our God is "the
living God, and everlasting King"' (Jer. 10:10). In
response Pharaoh asked whether this God is young or
old, how old he is, how many cities he has conquered,
how many provinces he has subdued, and how long he
has been king. In reply they proclaimed: 'The power
and might of our God fill the world. He was before the
world was created and He will be when all the world
comes to an end and He has created thee and gave thee
the spirit of life.' (Ex. R. 5:14)

Again, in the *Talmud* it is reported that when the
first century CE sage Rabban Johanan ben Zakkai was
about to die, he wept. When his pupils asked why he
cried, he said:

If I were being taken before a king of flesh and
blood who is here today and tomorrow in the
grave, whose anger does not last for ever, who
cannot imprison me for ever, who cannot kill me
for ever even if he sentences me to death, and
whom I can persuade and bribe to reconsider his
judgement, even so I would weep. Now that I am
being taken before the supreme King of kings, the
Holy One, blessed be He, who lives and endures
for ever and ever, whose anger, if he is angry
with me, is everlasting, who if he imprisons me,
the imprisonment is for ever, who if he puts me
to death, puts me to death for ever, and whom I
cannot persuade or bribe . . . shall I not weep?
(Ber. 28b)

Even though the rabbis were convinced that God
would endure for ever, they discouraged speculation
about the nature of eternity. Such reluctance is
reflected in the Mishnah's dictum: 'Whoever reflects
on four things, it were better for him that he had not
come into the world: What is above? What is beneath?
What is before? What is after?' (Hag. 2:1). Yet, despite

such teaching, in the Middle Ages Jewish theologians debated this issue. In *The Guide for the Perplexed* the twelfth-century philosopher **Moses Maimonides** argues that time itself was part of creation. Therefore when God is described as existing before the creation of the universe, the notion of time should not be understood in its normal sense:

> In the beginning God alone existed and nothing else; neither angels nor spheres, nor the things that are contained within the spheres existed. He then produced from nothing all existing things such as they are, by his will and desire. Even time itself is among the things created; for time depends on motion, i.e. on an accident in things which move, and the things upon whose motion time depends are themselves created beings, which have passed from non-existence into existence. We say that God existed before the creation of the Universe, although the verb existed appears to imply the notion of time; we also believe that He existed in an infinite space of time before the Universe was created; but in these cases we do not mean time in its true sense. We only use the term to signify something analogous or similar to time . . . We consider time a thing created; it comes into existence in the same manner as other accidents, and the substances which form the substratum for the accidents. For this reason, viz., because time belongs to the things created, it cannot be said that God produced the Universe in the beginning. (*The Guide for the Perplexed* 2:13)

The concept of time as part of creation was later developed by the fifteenth-century Jewish philosopher Joseph Albo. In his *Ikkarim* he maintains that the concepts of priority and perpetuity can only be applied to God in a negative sense. That is, when God is described as being 'before' or 'after' some period, this only means He was not non-existent before or after that time. However, these terms indicating a time span cannot be applied to God himself. Following Maimonides, Albo asserted that there are two types of time: measured time which depends on motion, and time in the abstract. This second type of time has no origin – this is the infinite space of time before the universe

was created. Although it is difficult to conceive of God existing in such a duration, it is likewise difficult to imagine God outside space. For this reason, Albo argues, the rabbis state that one should not ask what is above, what is below, what is before and what is behind.

According to other Jewish thinkers God is outside time altogether: He is in the 'Eternal Now'. Such a view is paralleled in Christian thought. Thus the sixth-century Christian Neo-Platonic theologian Boethius wrote in *The Consolation of Philosophy*:

> Since God lives in the eternal present, His knowledge transcends all movement of time and abides in the simplicity of its immediate present. It encompasses the infinite sweep of past and future, and regards all things in its simple comprehen-sion as if they were not taking place. Thus, if you think about the foreknowledge by which God distinguishes all things, you will rightly consider it to be not a foreknowledge of future events but knowledge of a never changing present. (*The Consolation of Philosophy*, Book 5, 6, p. 116)

Within the Jewish tradition similar views were expressed. Thus the thirteenth-century theologian Bahya Ibn Asher in his commentary on the Pentateuch discussed the verse, 'The Lord will reign for ever and ever' (Exod. 15:18): 'All times, past and future, are in the present so far as God is concerned, for He was before time and is not encompassed by it' (*Commentary to the Pentateuch*, Vol. 2, p. 134). Likewise the sixteenth-century scholar Moses Almosnino commented on 'For now I know' (Gen. 22:12). According to Almosnino, God is in the 'Eternal Now' and he uses this notion to explain how God's foreknowledge is not incompatible with human free will. In the eighteenth century the Hasidic teacher Nahman of Bratslav wrote in *Likkute Maharan, Tinyana*:

> God, as is well-known, is above all time. This is a truly marvellous notion, utterly incomprehensible, impossible for the human mind to grasp. You must appreciate, however, that basically time is the product of ignorance, that is to say, time

only appears real to us because our intellect is so puny. The greater the mind the smaller and less significant does time become for it. Take, for instance, a dream, in which the mind is dormant and the imaginative faculty takes over. In the dream it is possible for a seventy year span to pass by in a quarter of an hour . . . On awakening, the dreamer senses that the whole seventy year period of the dream occupied in a reality only a fraction of time. This is because man's intellectual capacity has been restored to him in his waking life and so far as his mind is concerned the whole seventy year period of the dream is no more than a quarter of an hour . . . There is a Mind so elevated that for It the whole of time is counted as naught, for so great is that Mind that for It the whole time span is as nothing whatever. Just as, so far as we are concerned, the seventy years which pass by in the dream are no more than a quarter of an hour in reality, as we have seen, so it is with regard to that Mind, which is so far above anything we know as mind for It time has no existence at all. (*Likkute Maharan, Tinyana*, No. 61, p. 29)

According to this view, God is outside time. He does not live in the present, have a past, or look forward to the future. He lives in the Eternal Now. Such a notion is very difficult to understand since it is totally outside the sphere of our experience. God is thus experiencing every moment in the past and future history of the created world simultaneously and eternally. What for us are fleeting moments rushing by, bringing one experience after another, are a huge static tapestry for God, of which He sees every part continually. An analogous experience is that of a cinema. When we go to a film, we see shown on the screen the experiences of other people. Almost invariably they are portrayed in the order in which they occurred. But if after the

film, we go into the room where the film was projected, we would be able to look at the film roll itself composed of a series of small pictures. When we look at it, we can perhaps have some experience of God's timelessness. We see all these photographs simultaneously which we had previously experienced in a temporal sequence. Such an experience is akin to God's eternal timelessness.

This conception of God's eternity – that He is outside time – and the alternative view that God exists in infinite duration before creation, constitute the two central Jewish interpretations of the Deity's relation to time. Yet for most Jews God's eternal existence is an impenetrable mystery. Nonetheless, the doctrine of God's eternity is a major feature of the Jewish faith. Through the centuries Jews have been convinced that God was, is, and will be forever. Hence in Maimonides' formulation of the thirteen central principles of the Jewish faith, the belief that God is eternal is the fourth tenet: 'This means', he wrote, 'that the unity whom we have described is first in the absolute sense. No existent thing outside him is primary in relation to him. The proofs of this in the Scriptures are numerous. The fourth principle is indicated by the phrase: "The eternal God is a refuge" (Deut. 33:27)'. In the *Ani Maamin* (I believe) prayer the fourth principle is formulated as follows: 'I believe with perfect faith that the creator, blessed be his name, is the first and the last.' And at the conclusion of the synagogue services in all branches of Judaism, the faithful voice their commitment that God is eternal in time in the *Adon Olam* prayer:

He is the Lord of the universe,
Who reigned ere any creature yet was formed,
At the time when all things shall have had an end,
He alone, the awsome one, shall reign:
Who was, who is, and who will be in glory.

SOURCES

Philo

According to the first century philosopher Philo, the eternal God is everywhere and fills all things:

> God fills all things; He contains but is not contained. To be everywhere and nowhere is his property and his alone. He is nowhere, because He himself created space and place and coincidentally with material things, and it is against all right principles to say that the maker is contained in anything that He has made. He is everywhere, because He has made his powers extend through earth and water, air and heaven, and left no part of the universe without his presence, and uniting all with all has bound them fast with invisible bonds, that they should never be loosed.
>
> (Philo, *The Confusion of Tongues*, 136–137, in TJP, pp. 27–28)

Saadiah Gaon

According to Saadiah Gaon in *The Book of Beliefs and Opinions*, it is a mistake to think that the eternal God emanated into the world:

> The third theory is held by those who maintain that the creator of the physical universe created it from his own substance. These, it seems to me, are people who found it impossible to deny the existence of the maker, but whose reason would not allow them to believe that something can come out of nothing. And since there existed nothing except the creator, they believe that He created the things out of himself. These people are more foolish than those first mentioned. I will now proceed to expose their foolishness by thirteen arguments. Four of these are identical with those advanced against the adherents of the doctrine of incorporeal substances; then there are four proofs for creation; then there are four more proofs for the *creatio ex nihilo*. The four methods of refuting those who assume the eternity of incorporeal substances do not, however, apply to the adherents of this theory, and therefore we substitute for them five methods which do apply to them and each of which disproves this view.
>
> (1) Reason rejects the idea that the nature of the eternal being, to whom is not attached any form, quality, quantity, limit, space and time, should be transformed in such a way that part of his being becomes a body to which is attached form, quantity, quality, space, time, and all other general characteristics of existent things. One cannot consider this but as in the highest degree improbable.
>
> (2) Reason rejects the idea that the wise whom no suffering can befall, whom no influence can affect and whom no perception can perceive, should make part of himself into a body so that he can be perceived by the senses and affected by external influence; that He should become ignorant after having been wise, suffer pain after having been at ease, endure hunger, thirst sadness and fatigue, and be exposed to all the other evils from which He had been free from all eternity. He did not require them for any useful purpose, nor is it possible to suppose that He could have attained his purpose through them.
>
> (Saadiah Gaon, *The Book of Beliefs and Opinions*, in TJP, pp. 66–67)

Bahya ibn Pakuda

In *The Book of Directions of the Duties of the Heart*, the eleventh-century Jewish philosopher Bahya Ibn Pakuda discusses the implications of the claim that God is one:

> Three premises are needed in order to prove that the world has indeed been created from nothingness by a single creator:
>
> 1 Nothing can make itself.
> 2 Causes are limited in number and there must be a first cause that is unpreceded by any other.
> 3 Everything that is composite is a thing created.
>
> If these three suppositions are correct, everyone who can apply and combine them will see that the world has indeed been created from nothingness by a single creator, as will be explained in the following, if God so wishes.
>
> The proof of the validity of these three propositions is as follows: Everything that comes into a state of being after having been a nonbeing cannot escape one of the two possiblities – either it made itself, or something else has brought it into being. And everything we imagine to have made itself cannot escape one of two possibilities – either it made itself before it existed, or after. Both these propositions are impossible.
>
> They are impossible because if it made itself after it already existed, it did nothing, because there was no need for it to make itself after it was already in being. If it made itself before its existence, it must have made itself while it was in a state of nonbeing, and a nonbeing can neither act nor can it refrain from action. It can do nothing at all. Thus we see that it is impossible for a thing to make itself in any way. This is the verificaton of the first presupposition.
>
> The proof of the validity of the second is as follows: Everything that has an end also has a beginning, for if it has no beginning, neither can it have an end. One cannot reach the limit of something without a starting point. When we reach the end of something we may conclude that it has only a beginning unpreceded by any other beginning – a first and only cause. When we find an end to one of the elementary causes of creation, we may indeed conclude that there was a beginning not preceded by any other – a first and only cause. There can be no beginning without an end.
>
> (Bahya ibn Pakuda, *The Book of Directions to the Duties of the Heart*,
> in BDDH, pp. 116–117)

Moses Maimonides

In *The Guide for the Perplexed*, Maimonides argues that Exodus 3:14 implies God's necessary existence:

Accordingly when God, may He be held sublime and magnified, revealed himself to Moses our master and ordered him to address a call to people and to convey to them his prophetic mission, Moses said: the first thing that they will ask of me is that I should make them acquire true knowledge that there exists a God with reference to the world; after that I shall make the claim that He has sent me. For at that time all the people except a few were not aware of the existence of the Deity, and the utmost limits of their speculation did not transcend the sphere, its faculties, and its actions, for they did not separate themselves from things perceived by the senses and had not attained intellectual perfection. Accordingly God made known to Moses the knowledge that he was to convey to them and through which they would acquire a true notion of the existence of God, this knowledge being: I am that I am. This is a name deriving form the verb to be (*hayah*), which signifies existence, for *hayah* indicates the notion: he was. And in Hebrew, there is no difference between your saying: he was and he existed. The whole secret consists in the repetition in a predicative position of the very word indicative of existence. For the word 'that' requires the mention of an attribute immediately connected with it. For it is a deficient word requiring a connection with something else; it has the same meaning as *alladhi* and *allati*, the male and female relative pronouns in Arabic. Accordingly, the first word is 'I am' considered as a term to which a predicate is attached; the second word that is predicated of the first is also 'I am', that is, identical with the first. Accordingly Scripture makes, as it were, a clear statement that the subject is identical with the predicate. This makes it clear that He is existent not through existence. This notion may be summarized and interpreted in the following way: the existent that is the existent, or the necessarily existent. This is what demonstration necessarily leads to: namely, to the view that there is a necessarily existent thing that has never been, or ever will be, nonexistent.

(Moses Maimonides, *The Guide for the Perplexed*, in GP, pp. 154–155)

Judah Halevi

The twelfth-century Jewish philosopher Judah Halevi in the *Kuzari* discusses the attributes of God, emphasizing that they do not in any way imply that God is a multiplicity or that He is bound by time:

In the same way we take the term 'one', viz. to controvert plurality, not to establish unity as we understand it; for we call a thing 'one', when the component parts are coherent and of the same materials, e.g., one bone, one sinew, one water, one air; in a similar way we speak of time, in comparison with a compact body (saying) 'one day, one year'. The divine essence is not subject to complexity or divisibility, and 'one' only stands as the negation of plurality. In the same way, 'first' in order to exclude the notion of later origin, but not to assert that He has a beginning; thus also 'last' stands to negate the idea of finality, but not to fix a term for him. None of these attributes touch on the divine essence, nor do they imply multiplicity in connection with it.

(Judah Halevi, *Kuzari*, in TJP, p. 62)

DISCUSSION

1. Discuss the belief that God is outside time.

2. If God knows the future, could human beings have free will?

FURTHER READING

Brenner, Reeve Robert, *The Faith and Doubt of Holocaust Survivors*, Jason Aronson, 1997.

Cohen, Jack, *Major Philosophies of Jewish Prayer in the Twentieth Century*, Fordham University Press, 2000.

Friedlander, Albert (ed.), *Out of the Whirlwind*, Schocken, 1999.

Heschel, Abraham Joshua *et al.*, *Israel: An Echo of Eternity*, Jewish Lights, 1997.

Hoffman, Roald, Schmidt, Shira Leibowitz, *Old Wine New Flasks: Reflections on Science and Jewish Tradition*, W.H. Freeman and Co., 1997.

Jacobs, Louis, *Principles of the Jewish Faith*, Vallentine Mitchell, 1974.

Jacobs, Louis, *A Jewish Theology*, Behrman House, 1973.

Novak, David, Samuelson, Norbert (eds), *Creation and the End of Days*, University Press of America, 1987.

Ochs, Peter, Borowitz, Eugene (eds), *Renewing the Covenant: Eugene B. Borowitz and the Postmodern Renewal of Jewish Theology*, State University of New York Press, 2000.

Radavsky, Tamar, *Time Matters: Time, Creation and Cosmology in Medieval Jewish Philosophy*, State University of New York Press, 2000.

Samuelson, Norbert, *Judaism and the Doctrine of Creation*, Cambridge University Press, 1994.

Unterman, Alan, *Jews: Their Beliefs and Practices*, Sussex University Press, 1996.

CHAPTER 58

Omnipotence and Omniscience

Figure 58 The Hospitality of Abraham and his wife Sarah to the three angels. Greek icon, seventeenth century. Artist unknown. Copyright The Art Archive/Byzantine Museum Athens/Dagli Orti.

From Biblical times the belief in God's omnipotence has been a central feature of Judaism. Thus in the Book of Genesis when Sarah expressed astonishment at the suggestion she should have a child at the age of ninety, she was criticized: 'The Lord said to Abraham, "Why did Sarah laugh, and say 'Shall I indeed bear a child now that I am old?' Is anything too hard for the Lord?"' (Genesis 18:13–14). Similarly, in the Book of Jeremiah when the city was threatened by the Chaldeans, God declared: 'Behold I am the Lord the God of all flesh: is anything too hard for me?' (Jer. 32:27). On such a view there is nothing God cannot do: what appears impossible is within his power.

For the Biblical writers as well as the **rabbis**, this conviction was a central feature of their faith. However, in the Middle Ages, Jewish thinkers wrestled with the philosophical perplexities connected with this notion. Pre-eminent among their concerns was the question whether God can do absolutely everything. According to the tenth century Jewish philosopher **Saadiah Gaon** in *The Book of Beliefs and Opinions*, the soul will not praise God for causing five to be more than ten without further addition, nor for being able to put the world through the hollow of a signet ring without making the world narrower and the ring wider, nor for bringing back the day which has passed in its original state. These, he argued, would be absurd acts. 'Of course,' he wrote, 'certain heretics ask us about such matters, and we do indeed answer them that God is able to do everything. This thing, however, that they ask of him is not anything because it is absurd, and the absurd is nothing. It is therefore, as though they were to ask: "Is God capable of doing what is nothing?"' (*The Book of Beliefs and Opinions*, II, 13, p. 134).

Subsequently, the fifteenth-century Jewish philosopher Joseph Albo discussed the same problem. In his view there are two kinds of impossibility: some things are intrinsically impossible so that even God cannot make them possible. We cannot imagine, for example, that God can make a part equal to the whole, a diagonal of a square equal to one of its sides, or the angle of a triangle equal to more than two right angles. Further, it is not possible for God to make two contradictory propositions true at the same time, or the affirmative and negative true simultaneously. Similarly, it is impossible to believe that God could create another being like himself. In all these cases, the human mind cannot conceive of such a state of affairs. The other type of impossibility is that which contradicts the law of nature, such as the resurrection of the dead. In these instances, it is possible to imagine such an occurrence; therefore, Albo argued, God can bring about such events since they are not inherently impossible. Thus, logical impossibilities are impossible for God, but not physical impossibilities.

Arguing along similar lines the twelfth-century Jewish philosopher **Moses Maimonides** in *The Guide for the Perplexed* explored the notion of God's omnipotence. According to Maimonides, although God is all-powerful, there are certain actions which He cannot perform because they are logically impossible:

> That which is impossible has a permanent and constant property, which is not the result of some agent, and cannot in any way change, and consequently we do not ascribe to God the power of doing what is impossible . . . it is impossible to produce a square with a diagonal equal to one of its sides, or a solid angle that includes four right angles, or similar things . . . We have thus shown that according to each one of the different theories there are things which are impossible, whose existence cannot be admitted, and whose creation is excluded from the power of God. (*The Guide for the Perplexed*, in JF, p. 48)

Again, in the thirteenth century Ezra ben Solomon similarly wrote:

> The fact that God is unable to bring about what is logically absurd, e.g. creating a square the diagonal of which is equal in length to one of its sides, or asserting and denying the same proportion, does not indicate any deficiency in God's power. Just as this does not indicate any deficiency in his power, so the fact that God cannot cause an emanation of something from nothing does not indicate that God is deficient in any way. This, also, would be logically absurd. (*Commentary on the Song of Songs*, in JF, p. 48)

Such theological reflection was paralleled within medieval Christianity. In the thirteenth century Thomas Aquinas in his *Summa Theologica* cautioned against assuming that God can do everything:

> When you say that God has the power for everything, you are most correctly interpreted as meaning this: that since power is relative to what is possible, divine power can do everything that is possible, and on this account is God called omnipotent . . . Now it is incompatible with the meaning of absolute possibility that anything involving the contradiction of simultaneously being and not being should be conceived as divine omnipotence . . . Whatever does not involve a contradiction is in that realm of the possible with respect to which God is called omnipotent. Whatever involves a contradiction is not held by omnipotence, for it just cannot possibly make sense of being possible. (*Summa Theologica*, in JF, p. 48)

Such medieval reflections were not intended to impose restrictions on God's power; rather these theologians were preoccupied with defining those acts which are logically incoherent. Since they are inherently absurd, they argued, it is impossible to believe that God could perform them. In the modern world a number of non-Jewish theologians have advanced the doctrine of a limited or finite God. Following such Christian writers as Charles Hartshorne, Jewish thinkers such as the Reform rabbi Levi Olan have conceived of God as limited by His own nature. This has been propounded to account for the existence of evil: if God is limited in power, He should not be held responsible for human suffering.

Such a conception of God has been formulated in different ways by a range of contemporary thinkers who have wrestled with the religious dilemmas of the events of the Nazi era. Some theologians argue that God intentionally limited himself when he bestowed free will on human beings. Thus, the Othodox rabbi and Jewish philosopher Eliezer Berkovits argued in *Faith after the Holocaust*, that if God did not respect human freedom, not only would morality be abolished but men and women would cease to be human. God did not intervene to save the Jewish nation because He had bestowed free will on humanity at creation. Arguing along similar lines, the Jewish scholar André Neher contended that human beings rather than God are responsible for human suffering:

> In creating man free, God introduced into the universe an element of extreme incertitude, which no divine or divinatory wisdom, no mathematic calculation, nor prayer even, could foresee or anticipate or incorporate into a pre-determined design. Free man is improvisation of flesh and history; he is the absolutely unforeseeable; he is the limit which the directive forces of the creative plan encounter, and no one is able to foretell whether this limit may be crossed. ('*The Exile of the Word: From the Silence of the Bible to the Silence of Auschwitz*' in HT, p. 161)

In *God and Evil*, the Orthodox scholar David Birnbaum similarly maintained that human beings must accept that God is 'Holy Potential', allowing through the process of contradiction space for the exercise of personal freedom. In his view, human beings are able to attain spiritual maturity in the exercise of such liberty and thereby attain their fullest possible potential. This view serves as the basis for reconciling the horrors of the Holocaust with the traditional understanding of God's nature.

Other Jewish theologians stress that the concept of God needs to be reformulated in the light of the events of the Nazi regime. The Reform rabbi Steven Jacobs, for example, argues in *Rethinking Jewish Faith*, that the concept of God in the Bible and rabbinic Judaism must be altered in the post-Holocaust world:

> What is now demanded in the realm of theological integrity is a notion of a Deity compatible with the reality of radical evil at work and at play in our world, a notion which, also, admits of human freedom for good or evil because He or She could not act. To continue to affirm the historically traditional notions of faith in God as presented by both Biblical and rabbinic traditions is to ignore those who, like myself, continue to feel the pain of family loss, yet want to remain committed to Jewish survival. (*Rethinking Jewish Faith*, in HT, p. 258)

According to the Jewish feminist theologian Melissa Raphael the patriarchal image of God in the Bible and rabbinic sources must be abandoned in a post-Holocaust world. The patriarchal model of God, she stated, was the God who failed Israel during the Holocaust. Drawing on the records of women's experiences during the Nazi period, she offers a post-Holocaust theology of relation that affirms the redemptive presence of God at Auschwitz. 'The feminist historiography of women's experiences in the death and concentration camps', she wrote, 'provides a methodological and substantive groundwork on which a feminist theology might build' (*When God Beheld God*, in HT, p. 246).

Paralleling the doctrine of God's omnipotence, Jews throughout the ages have affirmed that God is all-knowing. In the Bible the Psalmist declared:

> The Lord looks down from Heaven,
> He sees all the sons of men . . .
> He who fashions the hearts of them all,
> and observes all their deeds. (Ps. 33:13,15)

Again in Psalm 139 we read:

> Thou knowest when I sit down and when I
>   rise up;
> thou discernest my thoughts from afar.
> Thou searchest out my path and my lying down,
> and art acquainted with all my ways.
> (Ps. 139:2–3)

Following the Biblical view, rabbinic Judaism asserted that God's knowledge is not limited by space and time. Rather, nothing is hidden from him. Further, the rabbis declared that God's foreknowledge of events does not deprive human beings of free will. As the second century CE sage Rabbi Akiva declared: 'All is foreseen, but freedom of choice is given' (*Sayings of the Fathers*, 3:16).

In *The Guide for the Perplexed*, Maimonides claimed that God knows all things before they occur. Nonetheless, human beings are unable to comprehend the nature of God's knowledge because it is of a different order from that of human beings. On this account it is similarly not possible to understand how divine foreknowledge is compatible with human freedom.

Other medieval thinkers, however, were unconvinced by such an explanation. In *The Wars of the Lord*, the fourteenth-century philosopher Gersonides argued that God only knows things in general. The world is therefore constituted so that a range of possibilities is open to human beings. Since human beings are able to exercise free will, these are possibilities, rather than certainties (which they would be if God knew them in advance). Thus although God knows all it is possible to know, his knowledge is not all-embracing. He does not know how individuals will respond to the possibilities open to them since they are only possibilities.

According to Gersonides, such a view does not undermine God's providential plan. Even though God does not know all future events, He is cognisant of the outcome of the whole process. In the same century the Jewish theologian Hasdai Crescas, however, held a radically different position in *The Light of the Lord*. For Crescas human beings only appear to be free, but in reality all their deeds are determined by virtue of God's foreknowledge. Thus rather than attempting to reconcile free will and omniscience, he asserted that God's knowlege is absolute and free will is an illusion.

In the modern period the devout have been less concerned about such philosophical issues. Instead, there has been a general reaffirmation of the traditional belief that God knows past, present and future and that human beings have freedom of choice. Thus in his explanation of the Jewish faith, *The Jewish Religion*, the twentieth-century Jewish writer, Michael Friedlander, declared with regard to divine foreknowledge:

His knowledge is not limited, like the knowledge of mortal beings by space and time. The entire past and future lies unrolled before his eyes, and nothing is hidden from him. Although we may form a faint idea of the knowledge of God by considering that faculty of man that enables him within a limited space of time, to look backward and forward, and to unroll before him the past and the future, as if the events that have happened and those that will come to pass were going on in the present moment, yet the true nature of God's knowlege no man can conceive. 'God considereth all the deeds of man', without depriving him of his free will; he may in this respect be compared to a person who observes and notices the actions and the conduct of his fellow-men, without interfering with them. It is the will of God that man should have free will and should be responsible for his actions; and his foresight does not necessarily include predeterminaton. In some cases the fate of nations or of individual men is predetermined; we may even say that the ultimate fate or development of mankind is part of the design of Creation. But as the actual design in the Creation is concealed from man's searching eye, so is also the extent of the predetermination a mystery to him. To solve this problem is beyond the intellectual powers of short-sighted mortals; it is one of 'the hidden things that belong to the Lord our God'. (The *Jewish Religion*, in JF, pp. 50–51)

SOURCES

The Rabbis and Divine Omnipotence

According to the *midrash*, God is capable of doing everything, including doing everything simultaneously:

> 'God spoke all these things, saying' (Ex. 20:1). God can do everything simultaneously. He kills and makes alive at one and the same moment; He strikes and heals; the prayer of the woman in travail, of them who are upon the sea, or in the desert, or who are bound in the prison; He hears them all at once; whether men are in the east or west, north or south, He hearkens to all at once.
>
> (*Ex. R., Yitro*, 28, 4 in RA, p. 31)

Saadiah Gaon

In *The Book of Doctrines and Beliefs*, Saadiah Gaon discusses the nature of divine foreknowledge:

Perhaps, someone will ask further: 'If God knows that which is going to be before it comes into being, He knows in advance if a certain person will disobey him; now that person must by necessity disobey God, for otherwise God's foreknowledge would not prove to be correct.' The fallacy underlying this question is even more evident than that underlying the previous one. It is this: He who makes this assertion has no proof that the knowledge of the creator concerning things is the cause of their existence. He merely imagines this to be so, or chooses to believe it. The fallacy of this assumption becomes quite clear when we consider that, if God's knowledge of things were the cause of their existence, they would have existed from eternity, since God's knowledge of them is eternal. We do, however, believe that God knows things as they exist in reality, i.e. of those things which He creates.

He knows in advance that He is going to create them, and of those things which are subject to man's free will He knows in advance that man is going to choose them. Should one object, If God knows that a certain person will speak, is it possible for that person to be silent?' we answer quite simply that if that person were to keep silent instead of speaking we should have said in our original statement that God knew that this man would be silent, and we were not entitled to state that God knew that this person would speak. For God knows man's ultimate action such as it will be whether sooner or later after all his planning; it is exactly the thing God knows, as it is said, 'The Lord knoweth the thoughts of man' (Ps. 94:11).

(Saadiah Gaon, *The Book of Doctrines and Beliefs*, in TJP, pp. 122–123)

Moses Maimonides

In *The Guide for the Perplexed*, the twelfth-century Jewish philosopher Moses Maimonides discusses the nature of God's omnipotence:

That God should bring into existence someone like himself, or should annihilate himself, or should become a body, or should change – all of these belong to the class of the impossible; and the power to do any of these things cannot be attributed to God. Regarding the question whether He is able to bring into existence an accident that exists alone, not in a substance, a group among the men of speculation, namely, the *Mu'tazila*, have imagined this and held that it was possible, whereas others have asserted that it was impossible. It is true that those who assert that an accident may exist without a substratum are not led to this affirmation by speculation alone, but wished to safeguard thereby certain doctrines of the law that are violently rebutted by speculation; thus the assertion in question was a way out for them. Similarly, the bringing into being of a corporeal thing out of no matter whatever, belongs – according to us – to the class of the possible, and to the class of

the impossible – according to the philosophers. The philosophers say similarly that to bring into being a square whose diagonal is equal to one of its sides or a corporeal angle encompassed by four plane right angles and other similar things belong all of them to the class of the impossible; and some of those who are ignorant of mathematics and, concerning these matters, know only the words by themselves and do not conceive their notion, think that they are possible . . .

It has then become clear that, according to every opinion and school, there are impossible things whose existence cannot be admitted. Power to bring them about cannot be ascribed to the deity. The fact that He does not change them signifies neither inability nor deficiency of power on his part.

(Moses Maimonides, *The Guide for the Perplexed*, in GP, pp. 460–461)

DISCUSSION

1. If God is omnipotent, are there actions which He is unable to perform?

2. Discuss the view that God is limited and therefore should not be held responsible for human suffering.

FURTHER READING

Birnbaum, David, *God and Evil*, KTAV, 1989.

Blumenthal, David, *Facing the Abusing God: A Theology of Protest*, Westminster John Knox Press, 1993.

Brenner, Reeve Robert, *The Faith and Doubt of Holocaust Survivors*, Jason Aronson, 1997.

Cohen, Arthur, *Tremendum: A Theological Interpretation of the Holocaust*, Crossroad, 1981.

Friedlander, Albert, *Out of the Whirlwind*, Schocken, 1988.

Isaacs, Ronald, *Miracles: A Jewish Perspective*, Jason Aronson, 1998.

Jacobs, Louis, *A Jewish Theology*, Behrman House, 1973.

Kamenetz, Rodger, *The Jew in the Lotus: A Poet's Rediscovery of Jewish Identity in Buddhist India*, Harper San Francisco, 1995.

Kushner, Harold, *When Bad Things Happen to Good People*, Schocken, 2001.

Learner, Michael, *Jewish Renewal: A Path to Healing and Transformation*, HarperCollins, 1995.

Levin, Edward, *I Will Be Sanctified: Religious Responses to the Holocaust*, Jason Aronson, 1998.

Maza, Bernard, *With Fury Poured Out*, KTAV, 1986.

Patterson, David, *Sun Turned to Darkness: Memory and Recovery in the Holocaust Memoir*, Syracuse University Press, 1998.

Raphael, Melissa, *The Female Face of God at Auschwitz: A Jewish Feminist Theology of the Holocaust*, Routledge, 2003.

CHAPTER 59

Creation

Figure 59 Creation of the animals, sixteenth-century fresco. Artist unknown. Copyright The Art Archive/Sucevita Monastery Moldavia, Romania/Dagli Orti.

According to Genesis 1, God created Heaven and Earth:

> In the beginning God created the Heaven and the Earth. The Earth was without form and void, and darkness was upon the face of the deep; and the Spirit of God was hovering on the face of the waters. And God said, 'Let there be light!'; and there was light. And God saw that the light was good; and God separated the light from the darkness. God called the light Day and the darkness he called Night. And there was evening and there was morning, one day. And God said, 'Let there be a firmament in the midst of the waters, and let it separate the waters from the waters.' And God made the firmament and separated the waters which were under the firmament from the waters which were above the firmament. And it was so. And God called the firmament Heaven. And there was evening and there was morning, a second day. And God said, 'Let the waters under the heavens be gathered together into one place, and let the dry land appear.' And it was so. God called the dry land Earth. (Genesis 1:1–10)

This belief has become a central feature of the synagogue service – in the synagogue hymn before the reading from the **Psalms**, for example, God is depicted as the creator of everything:

> Blessed be He who spoke, and the world existed:
> Blessed be He;
> Blessed be He who was the Master of the world
>   in the beginning.

In another synagogue hymn the same view is expressed:

> You are the same before the world was created;
> You have been the same since the world was
>   created.

In the *Ani Maamin* (I believe) prayer, the first principle of the Jewish faith is formulated as follows:

> I believe with perfect faith that
> the creator, blessed be His name is
> the Author and Guide of everything
> that has been created, and that He alone
> has made, does make, and will make all things.

In rabbinic literature scholars speculated about the nature of the creative process. In *Genesis Rabbah* (*midrash* on Genesis), for example, the idea of the world as a pattern in the mind of God is expressed in relation to the belief that God looked into the Torah and created the world. Here the Torah is conceived as a type of blueprint. With respect to the order of creation, the School of Shammai stated: 'The heavens were created first and then the earth' (following Genesis 1:1). The School of Hillel, in contrast, argued Heaven and Earth were created simultaneously (*Gen. R.* 1:9).

In the same text a philosopher said to the first-century CE sage Rabban Gamaliel: 'Your God is a great craftsman, but He found good materials to help him in the work of creation, namely *tohu* and *vohu*, darkness, spirit, water and the deep.' Rabban Gamaliel, however, cited other verses which illustrate that these materials were created by God. (*Gen. R.* 1:9) In the third century R. Johanan argued that God took two coils, one of fire and the other of snow, wove them into each other, and created the world (*Gen. R.* 10:3). According to another rabbinic source, all things were formed at the same time on the first day of creation, but appeared at the other six days just as figs are gathered simultaneously in one basket but each selected individually (*Gen. R.* 12:4). Again, in *Genesis Rabbah* the sages stressed that God created several worlds, but destroyed them before creating this one (*Gen. R.* 9:2). The goal of creation is summed up in the rabbinic claim that whatever the Holy One, blessed be He, created in his world, He created for his glory (**Sayings of the Fathers**, 6:11).

In the Middle Ages, a number of Jewish theologians believed that God created the universe *ex nihilo*. The kabbalists, however, interpreted the doctrine of *ex nihilo* in a special sense. God, they maintained, should be understood as the Divine Nothing because as He is in and of himself, nothing can be predicated. The Divine is beyond human understanding. Creation *ex nihilo* thus refers to the creation of the universe out of God, the Divine Nothing. This occurred, they argued, through a series of divine emanations. For the kabbalists the first verse of Genesis alludes to the process within the Godhead prior to the creation of the universe. In Lurianic kabbalah the notion of God creating and destroying worlds before the creation of this world is viewed as referring to spiritual worlds. Thus *tohu* (void) in Genesis denotes the stage of God's self-revelation known as *olam ha-tohu* (world of the void) which precedes *olam ha-tikkun* (world of perfection). In later kabbalistic thought the nineteenth-century kabbalist Kalonymous Kalman of Cracow in his *Maor Va-Shemesh* maintained that the void in Genesis is the primordial void remaining after God's withdrawal to make room for the universe. On this reading, God's decree 'Let there be light' (Gen. 1:3) means that God caused his light to be emanated into the void in order to provide sustaining power required for the worlds which were later to be formed.

Regarding the question whether in the process of creating the cosmos, God also created intelligent beings on other planets, the Bible offers no information. Although rabbinic sources attest to the creation of other worlds, they similarly contain no reference to the existence of other sentient creatures. In the nineteenth century, however, Phineas Elijah ben Meir Hurwitz of Vilna discussed this issue on the basis of Isaiah 45:18: 'For thus says the Lord who created the Heavens (He is God!), who formed the Earth and made it (He established it; He did not create it a chaos, He formed it to be inhabited!): "I am the Lord; and there is no other"'. In this connection he referred to the passage in the *Talmud* in which *Meroz* (Judg. 5:32) is a star. Since it is cursed, Hurwitz concluded that it is inhabited. He alleged that creatures on other planets may have intelligence, yet he did not think they would have free will since only human beings have such capacity. 'Consequently', he wrote, 'there is only room for Torah and worship in this world, for neither Torah nor worship has any meaning where there is no free will' (*Sefer Ha-Berit*, Part I, *Maamar* 3, Chapters 2–4, pp. 30–32).

The belief in extraterrestrial beings raises problems for both Judaism and Christianity. In *The Fall and Rise of Man*, the modern writer Jerome Eckstein explored the religious implications of such a possibility:

> Let our imaginations roam, and let us speculate about the possible conflicts between future discoveries of space exploration and our old religious beliefs, if these religious beliefs are understood as offering knowledge of the kind given by science. Suppose a strangely figured race of creatures with

the approximate intelligence of humans and a culture and ethics radically different from ours was discovered on some distant star, would this not pose serious problems to the dogmatic and authoritarian interpretations of the Judaeo-Christian religions? Would these creatures, who obviously were not descended from Adam and Eve, be tainted with original sin? Would they too have souls? Would they be in need of grace and salvation? Did Jesus absorb their sins? Would they be in need of the Messiah? Would they be subject to the laws and traditions of these earth-centred religions? Would they be eligible to life in the hereafter? ('The Fall and Rise of Man', *Journal for the Scientific Study of Religion*, Vol. V, 1, 1965, p. 80)

Discussing the impact that the discovery of other creatures would have on the Jewish faith, the Reform rabbi W. Gunther Plaut in *Judaism and the Scientific Spirit* asked:

Will the possibility that there are intelligent creatures on other planets impose any strain on our beliefs? . . . The modern Jew will answer this question with a firm 'No'. An earlier generation, rooted in beliefs in an earth-centred universe, might have had some theological difficulties, but we have them no longer . . . Just as a father may love many children with equal love, so surely may our Father on high spread his pinions over the vastness of creation. (*Judaism and the Scientific Spirit*, 1962, pp. 36–39)

An alternative Jewish view has been advanced by the Orthodox rabbi Norman Lamm in *The Religious Implication of Extraterrestrial Life*. There are, he believed, three major challenges confronting Judaism. The existence of extraterrestrial beings undermines the conviction that human beings are the ultimate purpose of God's creation. The second challenge relates to the generation of life. If life is generated by natural processes on other planets, how is one to understand the doctrine of God as creator? The final challenge concerns the temptation to view God in non-personal terms given this new vision of the universe. Lamm believed that Judaism is able to resolve these difficulties. He concluded that human beings are not alone.

We may yet learn that, as rational, sentient, and self-conscious creatures, we are not alone, he wrote. But then again, he insisted, we never felt before nor need we feel today or in the future that we are alone, 'For Thou art with me'.

In his *A Jewish Theology*, the modern Jewish scholar Louis Jacobs pointed out that the challenges Lamm mentioned are not the crucial ones. The most serious difficulty is the question of the uniqueness of the Torah: 'Lamm's arguments', he wrote, 'centre around what the Torah means in the light of the new possible situation. But if this possibility is real, the far more difficult and radical question to be faced is that there are whole worlds for which the Torah, given to humans, can have no meaning. In asking what Judaism has to say about extraterrestrial life, Lamm begs the question whether Judaism has any relevance in this context' (*A Jewish Theology*, 1973, pp. 106–107).

Regarding creatures other than human beings, the twelfth century Jewish philosopher Moses Maimonides in *The Guide for the Perplexed* argued that it is a mistake to believe that the sole purpose of all creation is for the benefit of human beings. Yet on such an account how is one to explain the suffering of animals? In the *Kuzari*, the twelfth century Jewish theologian Judah Halevi declared that if the wisdom of the creator is truly wise, then human beings must accept in faith that nature is not contrary to the ways of an all-benevolent creator. As far as the human treatment of animals is concerned, the tradition is strictly opposed to inflicting pain on animals unless it is for the purpose of satisfying urgent human needs. Turning to angels that are referred to frequently in the Bible and rabbinic sources: they are immortal and have no evil inclination. Often they serve as God's messengers and at times they offer moral objections to God's conduct of the world.

In the Middle Ages a number of Jewish theologians interpreted such figures in spiritual and rationalistic terms. According to Maimonides, they are creatures who possess form without matter – they are pure spirits. When the prophets depict angels as fire or as possessing wings, they are simply using figurative language. The higher the angel, the greater his perception of God. With regard to demons, the *Talmud* contains numerous accounts of their activities. Even though some Jewish philosophers such as Maimonides disputed such doctrines, the belief in the demonic realm was an important feature of the Jewish faith through the ages.

In the modern period, however, Jews have largely abandoned belief in angels and demons; yet the conviction that God created the universe still remains a central feature of the religion. The belief that God is the source of all continues to animate religious sensibilities. With the exception of Reconstructionist and Humanistic Jews who have eschewed any form of supernaturalism, Maimonides' formulation of this principle in the beginning of his *Code* expresses what has remained the central feature of the Jewish religious system: 'The foundation of all foundations and the pillar of wisdom is to know that there is a First Being. He it is who brought all things into being and all the beings in Heaven and Earth and in between only enjoy existence by virtue of his true being' (*Mishneh Torah, Yesod Ha-Torah*, 1:1–3).

SOURCES

Psalms

The Book of Psalms repeatedly affirms the divine creation. Psalm 19, for example, depicts the glories of the Lord as manifest in the world:

The heavens are telling the glory of God;
and the firmament proclaims his handiwork.
Day to day pours forth speech,
and night to night declares knowledge.
There is no speech, nor are there words;
their voice is not heard;
yet their voice goes out through all the earth,
and their words to the end of the world.

In them He has set a tent for the sun,
which comes forth like a bridegroom leaving his
  chamber,
and like a strong man runs its course with joy.
Its rising is from the end of the heavens,
and its circuit to the end of them;
and there is nothing hid from its heat.

(Psalm 19:1–6)

Sayings of the Fathers

According to the *Sayings of the Fathers*, God created the universe for his glory:

> All that God created in his world, he created only for his glory, as it is said, 'All that is called by my name, for my glory I created and fashioned and made it' (Is. 43:7).
> (*Sayings of the Fathers*, 6:11, in RA, p. 36)

Solomon Ibn Gabirol

In *The Kingly Crown*, the twelfth-century Neoplatonic Jewish philosopher Solomon ibn Gabirol describes the process whereby divine creation occurs:

> Thou art wise; and wisdom, the fountain of life, flows from thee, and every man is too brutish to know thy wisdom.

> Thou art wise, pre-existent to all pre-existence, and wisdom was with thee as nurseling.

> Thou art wise, and thou didst not learn from any other than thyself, nor acquire wisdom from another.

Thou art wise, and from thy wisdom thou didst send forth a predestined will, and made it as an artisan and a craftsman,

To draw the stream of being from the nothingness as the light is drawn that comes from the eye,

To take from the source of light without a vessel, and to make all without a tool and cut and hew and cleanse and purify.

That will called to the nothingness and it was cleft asunder, to existence and it was set up, to the universe and it was spread out.

It measured the heavens with a span, and its hand coupled the pavilion of the spheres,

And linked the curtains of all creatures with loops of potency; and its strength reaches as far as the last and lowest creatures – 'the uttermost edge of the curtain in the coupling'.

(Solomon ibn Gabirol, *Kingly Crown*, in HJPMA, pp. 70–71)

Prayer Book

A central feature of the Jewish liturgy is that God created the universe. In the traditional prayer book, this belief is repeatedly affirmed as is illustrated by the prayers preceding the recitation of the *Shema*:

Blessed art Thou, O Lord our God, king of the universe, who formest light and createst darkness, who makest peace and createst all things:

Who in mercy givest light to the earth and to them that dwell thereon, and in thy goodness renewest the creation every day continually. How manifold are thy works, O Lord! In wisdom hast Thou made them all: the earth is full of thy creatures. O King, who alone wast exalted from aforetime, praised, glorified and extolled from days of old; O everlasting God, in thine abundant mercies, have mercy upon us, Lord of our strength, Rock of our stronghold, Shield of our salvation, Thou stronghold of ours!

The blessed God, great in knowledge, designed and formed the rays of the sun: it was a boon he produced as a glory to his name: He set the luminaries round about his strength. The chiefs of his hosts are holy beings that exalt the Almighty, and continually declare the glory of God and his holiness. Be thou blessed, O Lord our God, for the excellency of thy handiwork, and for the bright luminaries which thou hast made: they shall glorify thee for ever.

(In DPB, p. 111)

DISCUSSION

1. Is the Biblical view of creation in conflict with a scientific understanding of the origin of the universe?

2. If intelligent life is discovered on other planets, does this undermine the Biblical account of creation?

FURTHER READING

Alter, Michael (ed.), *What is the Purpose of Creation: A Jewish Anthology*, Jason Aronson, 1991.

Duchrow, Ulrich, *Shalom: Biblical Perspectives on Creation, Justice and Peace*, CCBI, 1989.

Goldfinger, Andrew, *Thinking About Creation: Eternal Torah and Modern Physics*, Jason Aronson, 1998.

Kaplan, Aryeh, *Sefer Yetzirah – the Book of Creation*, Samuel Weiser, 1993.

Klein, Eliahu, *Kabbalah of Creation: Isaac Luria's Earlier Mysticism*, Jason Aronson, 2000.

Levenson, Jon, *Creation and the Persistence of Evil*, Princeton University Press, 1994.

Maybaum, Ignaz, *Creation and Guilt*, Vallentine Mitchell, 1969.

Reventlow, Henning Graf, Hoffman, Yair (eds), *Creation in Jewish and Christian Tradition*, Continuum, 2000.

Samuelson, Norbert, *Judaism and the Doctrine of Creation*, Cambridge University Press, 1994.

Schroeder, Gerald, *Genesis and the Big Bang: The Discovery of Harmony Between Modern Science and the Bible*, Bantam, 1991.

Wexelman, David, *The Jewish Concept of Reincarnation and Creation: Based on the Writings of Rabbi Chaim Vital*, Jason Aronson, 1998.

CHAPTER 60

Providence

Figure 60 The Destruction of the Temple in Jerusalem 70 AD by Roman soldiers. Artist: Hayez, Francesco (1791–1882): Italian. Copyright The Art Archive/Galleria d'Arte Moderna Venice/Dagli Orti.

In the Bible the notion that God controls and guides the universe is an essential belief. The Hebrew term for such divine action is *hashgahah*, derived from Psalm 33:14: 'From where he sits enthroned he looks forth (*hishgiah*) on all the inhabitants of the earth.' Such a view implies that the dispensation of a wise and benevolent providence is found everywhere – all events are ultimately foreordained by God. According to the Biblical tradition, there are two types of providence: (1) general providence – God's provision for the world in general, and (2) special providence – God's care for each individual. In Scripture God's general providence was manifest in his freeing the ancient Israelites from Egyptian bondage and guiding them to the Promised Land. The belief in the unfolding of his plan for salvation is a further illustration of such providential care for his creatures. Linked to this concern for all is God's providential concern for every person. In the words of Jeremiah: 'I know, O Lord, that the way of man is not in himself, that it is not in man who walks to direct his steps' (Jer. 10:23).

Subsequently the doctrine of divine providence was developed in rabbinic literature. The *Mishnah* declares: 'Everything is foreseen.' In the *Talmud* we read: 'No man suffers so much as the injury of a finger when it has been decreed in heaven.' Such a conviction became a central feature of the *Rosh Hashanah* service. According to the New Year liturgy, God, the judge of the world, provides for the destiny of individuals as well as nations on the basis of their actions.

For the rabbis the doctrine that divine providence affects the lives of all creatures was of central significance. Thus the *Talmud* states that for the gazelle that seeks to cast its seed at the time of pregnancy from the top of the mountain, the Holy One prepares an eagle that catches it in its wings and places it before her. Were it to come a moment earlier or a moment later the offspring would immediately die (*Talmud, BB* 16a–b). Similarly, the Holy One sits and nourishes both the horns of the wild ox and the ova of lice (*Shabb.* 107b). Concerning human beings, it was said: 'No man bruises his finger on earth unless it is decreed in heaven' (*Hul.* 7b). Again, all is revealed and known before God, even the small talk of a man's conversation with his wife (*Lev. R.* 8:1; *Gen. R.* 68:4). Similarly, 'The Holy One sits and pairs couples – the daughter of so-and-so to so-and-so' (*Lev. R.* 8:1; *Gen. R.* 68:4).

Speculation about God's providential control of history extended to a consideration of what would take place at the end of days. Once the Temple had been destroyed and the Jewish nation driven out of their homeland, the nation was bereft. In their despair Jews longed for a kingly figure who would deliver them from exile and rebuild their holy city. Drawing on messianic ideas found in Scripture, the Apocrypha and Pseudepigrapha, they foresaw the coming of a future divine deliverance when all peoples would be converted to the worship of the one true God.

Such conceptions animated rabbinic speculation about the eschatological unfolding of history when God would intervene on behalf of Jewry. According to the early rabbinic sages, such a process of redemption would be brought about through charity, repentance and the observance of Jewish law. Nevertheless, prior to the coming of such messianic deliverance, the world would be subject to tribulations defined as 'the birth pangs of the Messiah'. These would be followed by the arrival of Elijah, the forerunner of the Messiah. Subsequently, a second figure, the Messiah ben Joseph, would engage in conflict with Gog and Magog, the enemies of the Israelites. Although he would be killed in battle, the King–Messiah (Messiah ben David) would eventually be victorious, and with his coming the dispersion of Israel would cease. All exiles would be returned to Zion and earthly life would be totally transformed. Finally, at the end of this messianic period all human beings would undergo judgement and either be rewarded with heavenly bliss or punished everlastingly.

During the medieval period, Jewish theologians continued to be preoccupied with the doctrine of providence. In *The Guide for the Perplexed* the twelfth-century Jewish philosopher **Moses Maimonides** defends both general and special providence. The latter, he argues extends only to human beings and is in proportion to a person's intellect and moral character. Such a view implies that God is concerned about each non-human species, but not with every individual. Only humans come under divine care as they rise to intellectual and moral stature.

In the fifteenth century Hasdai Crescas, however, maintained that God created human beings out of his love for them. Thus his providential care is not related to their personal characteristics. All persons enjoy God's special providence.

The kabbalists were also concerned with this subject. In his *Shomer Emunim*, for example, the eighteenth-century scholar Joseph Ergas explains that there are various types of providence:

> Nothing occurs by accident, without intention and divine providence, as it is written: 'Then will I also walk with you in chance' (Lev. 21:24). You see that even the state of 'chance' is attributed to God, for all proceeds from him by reason of special providence.

Nonetheless, Ergas limited special providence to human beings:

> However, the guardian angel has no power to provide for the special providence of non-human species; for example, whether this ox will live or die, whether this ant will be trodden on or saved, whether this spider will catch this fly and so forth. There is no special providence of this kind for animals, to say nothing of plants and minerals, since the purpose for which they were created is attained by means of the species alone, and there is no need for providence to be extended to individuals of the species. Consequently, all events which happen to individuals of these species are by pure chance and not by divine decree, except ... where it is relevant for the divine providence regarding mankind. (*Shomer Emunim*, Jer. 1965, pp. 31–33)

Such views caused offence to a number of *Hasidic* teachers – divine providence, they insisted, is exercised over all things. Thus Phineas of Koretz in the eighteenth century in his *Peer La-Yesharim* states: 'A man should believe that even a piece of straw that lies on the ground does so at the decree of God. He decrees that it should lie there with one end facing this way and the other end the other way' (*Peer La-Yesharim*, No. 38). Again, Hayyim of Sanz in his *Divre Hayim* to *Mikketz* contends: 'It is impossible for any creature to enjoy existence without the creator of all worlds sustaining it and keeping it in being, and it is all through divine providence. Although Maimonides has a different opinion in this matter the truth is that not even a bird is ensnared without providence from above.' (*Divre Hayim* to *Mikketz*, beg.)

In the Middle Ages Jewish theologians also wrestled with dilemmas concerning God's foreknowledge as it relates to human freedom. If God knows everything which will come to pass, how can human beings be free? As we have seen, Maimonides argued that human beings are free despite God's knowledge of future events. This is possible, he asserts, because God's knowledge is not our knowledge. In his *Code*, he writes:

> You may ask: God knows all that will happen. Before someone becomes a good or a bad man God either knows that this will happen or he does not know it. If he knows that the person will be good it is impossible for that person to be bad. You must know that the solution to this problem is larger than the earth and wider than the sea ... God does not 'know' with a knowledge that is apart from him, like human beings ... God's knowledge and his self are one and the same though no human being is capable of clearly comprehending this matter – it is beyond human capacity to comprehend or discover the creator's knowledge. It follows that we are incapable of comprehending how God knows all creatures and all deeds. But this we do know beyond any doubt, that man's deeds are in his own hands, God neither compelling him nor determining that he should behave in a certain way. (In PJF, p. 325)

Other scholars, such as the twelfth-century Jewish theologian Abraham Ibn Daud, disagreed. For Ibn Daud God's foreknowledge is not determinative or causative. Thus human beings are able to act freely: 'His knowledge is not in the nature of a compelling decree but can be compared to the knowledge of the astrologers who know, by virtue of some other power, how a certain person will behave.'

Some later scholars such as Yom Tobh Lippman Heller in the seventeenth century in his *Tos. Yom. Tobh* appealed to the concept of the Eternal Now to resolve this problem:

> When a man sees someone else doing something the fact that he sees it exercises no compulsion on the thing that is done. In exactly the same way the fact that God sees man doing the act exercises no compulsion over him to do it. For before God there is no early and late since he is not governed by time. (In Louis Jacobs, *Principles of the Jewish Faith*, Jason Aronson, 1988, p. 328)

In the modern world such theological issues have ceased to preoccupy Jewish thinkers. Rather, the rise of science has challenged the traditional understanding of God's providential activity. In place of the religious interpretation of the universe as controlled by the Deity, scientific investigation has revealed that nature is governed by complex laws. Thus it is no longer possible for most Jews to accept the Biblical and rabbinic conception of divine activity. As a result, many Jews have simply abandoned the belief in providence. Others, however, envisage God as working through natural causes: as creator of all, he established the laws which regulate the natural order.

Regarding special providence, many Jews would want to say that God is concerned with each individual even though he does not miraculously intervene in the course of human history. Divine providence should hence be understood as a mode of interaction in which God affects the consciousness of the individual without curtailing his free will. Knowing the innermost secrets of every human heart, He introduces into the conscious awareness of individuals aims consonant with his will. Viewed in this way, special providence involves a dynamic relationship between the human and the divine. Such a reinterpretation of the traditional doctrine of providence has enabled many contemporary Jews to affirm the ancient formulation of the *Ani Maamin* (I believe) prayer: 'I believe with perfect faith that the creator, blessed be his name, is the author and guide of everything that has been created, and that he alone has made, does make, and will make all things.'

SOURCES

Psalms

According to the Book of Psalms, God watches over the faithful and blots out the enemy:

> I will give thanks to the Lord with my whole heart;
> I will tell of all thy wonderful deeds.
> I will be glad and exult in thee,
> I will sing praise to thy name, O Most High.
>
> When my enemies turned back,
> they stumbled and perished before thee.
> For thou hast maintained my just cause;
> thou hast sat on the throne giving righteous judgment.
>
> Thou hast rebuked the nations, thou hast destroyed the wicked;
> thou hast blotted out their name for ever and ever.
> The enemy have vanished in everlasting ruins;
> their cities thou hast rooted out;
> the very memory of them has perished.
>
> (Psalm 9:1–6)

Midrash

According to tradition, God exercises providence over his creation and determines the fate of his people. Thus the *midrash* asserts that God loves Israel as a father loves his children:

> 'My beloved is mine and I am his' (Song of Songs 2:16). Israel says: He is my God and I
> am his people; He is my father, and I am his son; He is my shepherd, and I am his flock;
> He is my guardian, and I am his vineyard. R. Judah b. Ilai said: He sings of me, and I sing

of him; He praises me, and I praise him; He calls me 'My sister, my friend, my dove, my perfect one', and I say to him, 'He is my beloved, my friend'; He says to me, 'Thou art fair, my friend', and I say to him, 'Thou art fair, my beloved, and pleasant.' He says to me, 'Happy art thou, Israel, who is like unto thee?' And I say to him, 'Who is like unto thee, O Lord, among the gods?' He says to me, 'Who is like unto Israel, a unique people on the earth', and I confess the unity of his name twice every day.

(*Song of Songs Rabba* 2:16, 1 in RA, p. 66)

Moses Maimonides

In *The Guide for the Perplexed* the twelfth-century Jewish philosopher Moses Maimonides argues that God's providential care is determined by character:

That intellect which overflowed from him, may He be exalted, toward us is the bond between us and him. You have the choice: if you wish to strengthen and to fortify this bond, you can do so; if, however, you wish gradually to make it weaker and feebler until you cut it, you can also do that. You can only strengthen this bond by employing it in loving him and in progressing toward this, just as we have explained. And it is made weaker and feebler if you busy your thought with what is other than He. Know that even if you were the man who knew most the true reality of the divine science, you would cut that bond existing between you and God if you would empty your thought of God and busy yourself totally in eating the necessary or in occupying yourselves with the necessary. You would not be with him then, nor He with you.

(Moses Maimonides, *The Guide for the Perplexed*, in GP, p. 621)

Bernard Maza

In *With Fury Poured Out*, the Orthodox Jewish theologian Bernard Maza seeks to explain God's providence in relation to the Holocaust. In his view, God brought about the Holocaust in order to renew Torah Judaism:

It was the will of *Hashem* that the Jewish people, the bearers of the Torah, would not forsake the Torah. The present generation of the righteous would not be the last. The ambition of the coming generation to be like all the nations of the world would not be.

Hashem knew that the oppression of the Jewish people had to end or the sun of Torah would set. The Jewish people had to be redeemed and returned to the land of Israel. Only in the land of Israel would they find freedom from the suffering that was inevitably their lot in the lands of their exile.

When they would be returned to their land and the burden of oppression lifted from their backs, the heaviness would be removed from their hearts. When their hearts and minds would be free, they would seek and find themselves . . .

This was therefore the moment in the divine history of the Jewish people that *Hashem* judged to be the time for redemption from oppression.

The prophet Ezekiel had said:

'As I live', says the Lord, 'that only with a strong hand and outstretched arm, and with fury poured out will I be king over thee' . . .

The beginning of redemption was to be ushered in with all of its prophetic accompaniments. It meant the coming of the fury. It meant a holocaust.

(Bernard Maza, *With Fury Poured Out*, in HT, p. 95)

Steven Jacobs

Other Jewish Holocaust theologians, however, have rejected the concept of divine providence, In their view, it no longer makes sense to believe in divine intervention in the light of the Holocaust:

> Both the Bible and postbiblical or rabbinic Judaism . . . present their understanding of Deity as the God-who-acts-in-history, whose caring concern for Jews was ultimately expressed at Sinai . . . for reasons largely unknown to his human children. No longer acceptable or comforting, when juxtaposed to the Holocaust, is the midrashic . . . understanding of a Deity, who, sadly, went with his children into exile in Egypt and rejoiced, gladly, with them when they celebrated their liberation from slavery and bondage. No amount of rationalization can overcome the enormity of the loss of 6 million.
>
> (Steven Jacobs, *Rethinking Jewish Faith*, in HT, p. 257)

DISCUSSION

1. Does the belief in divine providence conflict with the Biblical view that human beings can act freely?

2. Does divine providence extend only to human beings or to other creatures as well?

FURTHER READING

Berkovits, Eliezer, *Faith after the Holocaust*, KTAV, 1973.

Birnbaum, David, *God and Evil*, KTAV, 1989.

Blumenthal, David, *The Banality of Good and Evil: Moral Lessons from the Shoah and Jewish Tradition*, Georgetown University Press, 1999.

Borowitz, Eugene, *Choices in Modern Jewish Thought*, Behrman House, 1983.

Braiterman, Zachary, *(God) After Auschwitz*, Princeton University Press, 1998.

Cohen, Arthur, *Tremendum: A Theological Interpretation of the Holocaust*, Crossroad, 1981.

Cohn-Sherbok, Dan, *Holocaust Theology: A Reader*, Exeter University Press, 2002.

Fackenheim, Emil, *God's Presence in History: Jewish Affirmations and Philosophical Reflections*, Harper and Row, 1972.

Friedlander, Albert (ed.), *Out of the Whirlwind*, Schocken, 1988.

Jacobs, Louis, *A Jewish Theology*, Behrman House, 1973.

Jacobs, Steven, *Rethinking Jewish Faith*, State University of New York Press, 1994.

Maza, Bernard, *With Fury Poured Out*, KTAV, 1986.

Raphael, Melissa, *The Female Face of God after Auschwitz*, Routledge, 2003.

Schulweis, Harold, *Evil and the Morality of God*, Hebrew Union College Press, 1994.

CHAPTER 61

Divine Goodness

Figure 61 Sephardic women praying during Passover at the Wailing Wall in Jerusalem, 1890. Photographer Frederick Vester. Copyright AKH London.

According to the Hebrew Bible, God is the all-good ruler of the universe. Thus in the Psalms He is described as good and upright (Ps. 25:8); his name is good (Ps. 54:8); He is good and does good (Ps. 118:68); He is good to all (Ps. 145:9). In rabbinic literature the same view prevails: God is the supremely beneficent creator who guides all things to their ultimate destiny.

In the unfolding of his plan, He has chosen Israel as his messenger to all peoples – as creator and redeemer, He is the father to all. Such affirmations about God's goodness have given rise to intense speculation about the mystery of evil. In Scripture the authors of Job and Ecclesiastes explored the question why the righteous suffer, and this quest continued into the rabbinic period. Yet, it was not until the Middle Ages that Jewish thinkers began to wrestle with the philosophical perplexities connected with the existence of evil.

In the twelfth century, for example, Abraham Ibn Daud argued that both human reason and the Jewish tradition teach that God cannot be the cause of evil. Reason demonstrates that this is so because God is wholly good; it would be self-contradictory for him to be the source of evil. Because God does not have a composite nature, it is logically impossible for him to bring about both good and evil. But why then does evil exist? Poverty, for example, is the absence of wealth; darkness the absence of light, and folly the absence of understanding. It is a mistake to think that God creates any of these things, just as it would be an error to assume that God made no elephants in Spain. Such a lack of elephants is not divinely willed. Similarly, evil is not divinely created. It occurs when goodness is not present. The absence of good is not inherently evil; instead imperfections in the world exist so that God can benefit a multitude of creatures of different forms.

In his *Guide*, the twelfth-century Jewish philosopher **Moses Maimonides** argued along similar lines. All evils, he asserts, are privations. For this reason, God is not responsible for evil – He is liable only for the privation of good.

This attempt to resolve the problem of evil is paralleled in early Christian thought. In the fifth century Augustine asked: 'For what is that which we call evil but the absence of good?' Continuing this argument, he asserts:

> In the bodies of animals, disease and wounds mean nothing but the absence of health; for when a cure is effected, that does not mean that the evils which were present – namely, the diseases and wounds – go away from the body and dwell elsewhere; they altogether cease to exist; for the wound or disease is not a substance, but a defect in the fleshy substance – the flesh itself being a substance, and therefore something good of which those evils – that is, privations of the good which we call health – are accidents. (Augustine, *Works*, IX, Edinburgh, T. and T. Clark, 1873, pp. 181–182)

By defining evil as a privation of good, Augustine, like Ibn Daud and Maimonides, was anxious to demon-strate how apparent evil could exist in a universe created by a wholly good and omnipotent God. Since evil does not in fact exist, it is incorrect to assume that God is responsible for its occurrence. For Augustine, evil is nothing but the corruption of natural measure, form or order. What is called an evil nature is a corrupt nature. If it were not corrupt, it would be good. But when it is corrupted, so far as it remains a natural thing, it is good. It is bad only so far as it is corrupted. Thus everything that exists is good, and those things which are now less good or no longer good at all have merely fallen away from their original state.

For the kabbalists, the existence of evil constituted a central problem for the Jewish faith. According to one tradition evil has no objective reality. Human beings are unable to receive all of the influx from the *sefirot*, and it is this inability which is the origin of evil. Created beings are therefore estranged from the source of emanation, and this results in the illusion that evil exists. Another view depicts the *sefirah* of power as an attribute whose name is evil. On the basis of such a teaching Isaac the Blind in the thirteenth century concluded that there must be a positive root of evil and death. During the process of differentiation of forces below the *sefirot* evil became concretized. This inter-pretation led to the doctrine that the source of evil was the supra-abundant growth of judgement. This was due to the separation and substitution of the attribute of judgement from its union with compassion. Pure judgement produced from within itself the *Sitra Ahra* (Other Side). The *Sitra Ahra* consists of the domain of emanations and demonic powers. Though it origi-nated from one of God's attributes, it is not part of the divine realm.

In the *Zohar* there is a detailed hierarchical structure of this emanation in which the *Sitra Ahra* is depicted as having ten *sefirot* of its own. The evil in the universe, the *Zohar* explains, has its origins in the leftovers of worlds that were destroyed. Another view in the *Zohar* is that the Tree of Life and the Tree of Knowledge were harmoniously bound together until Adam sepa-rated them, thereby bringing evil into the world. This event is referred to as 'the cutting of the shoots' and is the prototype of sins in the Bible. Evil thus originated through human action. Both these views concerning the origin of evil were reconciled in another passage where it is asserted that the disposition towards evil derives from the cosmic evil which is in the realm of the *Sitra Ahra*.

According to the *Zohar*, evil is like the bark of a tree of emanation; it is the husk or shell in which the lower dimensions of existing things are encased. As the *Zohar* explains: When King Solomon went into the nut garden, he took a nutshell and drew an analogy from its layers to these spirits which inspire sensual desires in human beings, as it is written, 'and the delights of the sons of men are from male and female demons' (Ecclesiasticus 2:8). This verse also indicates that the pleasures in which men indulge in the time of sleep give birth to multitudes of demons. In this context evil is understood as a waste product of an organic process – it is compared to bad blood, foul water, dross after gold has been refined and the dregs of wine. Yet despite this depiction, the *Zohar* asserts that there is holiness even in the *Sitra Ahra*, regardless of whether it is conceived as a result of the emanation of the last *sefirah* or a consequence of man's sin. The domains of good and evil are intermingled and it is man's duty to separate them.

In explaining this picture of divine creation, kabbalists adopted a neo-Platonic conception of a ladder of spiritual reality composed of four worlds in descending order. First, is the domain of *Atzilut* (emanation) consisting of the ten *sefirot* which form Adam Kadmon (primordial man). The second world is the realm of *Beriyah* (creation) which is made up of the throne of glory and the seven heavenly palaces. In the third world *Yetsirah* (formation) most of the angels dwell, presided over by the angel *Metatron*. His is the scene of the seven heavenly halls guarded by angels to which *Merkavah* (chariot) mystics attempt to gain admission. In the fourth world of *Asiyah* (making) are the lower order of angels – the *ophanim* who combat evil and receive prayers. This is the spiritual archetype of the material cosmos, heaven, and the earthly world. *Asiyah* is both the last link in the divine chain of being and the domain where the *Sitra Ahra* is manifest; in this realm the forces of good struggle with the demons.

In modern times philosophical theories about the existence of evil have ceased to attract attention within the Jewish community. Similarly, most Jews have ignored the mystic theories in the *Zohar* and their later development by Isaac Luria. Instead, a number of Jewish writers have grappled with the question whether it is possible to believe in God's goodness after the Holocaust. In *The Face of God after Auschwitz*, Ignaz Maybaum contends that Jews died in the concentration camps for the sins of humanity, as God's suffering servant. For Maybaum Jews suffer in order to bring about the rule of God over the world and its peoples – their God-appointed mission is to serve the course of historical progress and bring human beings into a new era.

Arguing along different lines, a number of Orthodox thinkers have attempted to make sense of the Holocaust in terms of God's aim for the Jewish nation. In '*Hester Panim* in the Holocaust versus the Manifest Miracles in our Generation', the Chief Rabbi of Haifa, Sha'ar Yashuv Cohen, maintains that it is a mistake to believe that the Holocaust is a punishment for sin. Rather, the murder of millions of Jews in the camps should be understood as part of God's plan. The suffering of Jewry, he argues, should be seen as the last phase of the birth pangs of the Messiah. Those who walked to the gas chambers singing 'I believe with perfect faith in the coming of the Messiah' were aware that they were living in the last days prior to divine deliverance.

An alternative approach to the Holocaust is to see in the death camps a manifestation of God's will that his chosen people survive. Such a view has been expressed in various writings by Emil Fackenheim who asserts that God revealed himself to Israel out of the furnaces and through the ashes of the victims of Auschwitz. Through the Holocaust, he believes, God issued an additional 614th commandment to the traditional 613:

Jews are forbidden to hand Hitler posthumous victories. They are commanded to survive as Jews lest the Jewish people perish. They are commanded to remember the victims of Auschwitz lest their memory perish. They are forbidden to despair of man and his world, and to escape into either cynicism or otherworldliness, lest they cooperate in delivering the world over to the forces of Auschwitz. Finally, they are forbidden to despair of the God of Israel, lest Judaism perish. (Emil Fackenheim, 'Jewish Faith and the Holocaust' in Michael Morgan (ed.), *The Jewish Thought of Emil Fackenheim*, Wayne State University Press, 1987, 176)

Another interpretation of the Holocaust focuses on free will. In the view of a number of thinkers, it is a mistake to hold God responsible for the tragedy of the Holocaust. In *Faith After the Holocaust*, for example, the Orthodox theologian Eliezer Berkovits asserts that if God did not respect human freedom, then men and women would cease to be human. Freedom and responsibility are the preconditions of human life. Hence, the Holocaust should be understood as a manifestation of evil, a tragedy inflicted by the Germans on the Jewish people. God did not intervene because He has bestowed free will on human beings at the time of creation.

Arguing along different lines, a number of Jewish thinkers have maintained that the concept of God must be modified in light of the evil of the Holocaust. According to Arthur A. Cohen, Jews must now re-evaluate the traditional understanding of God's providential concern for his people. In *Tremendum* he states that God is not an interruptive agent. Instead,

Jews should conceive of the Deity as transcendent. If God were to act in the world, the created order would simply be an extension of his will rather than an independent domain in which human beings would be able to act freely. Hence it is a mistake to blame God for the terrible events of the Nazi regime.

A radically different assessment of the religious implications of the Holocaust is formulated in *After Auschwitz* by Richard Rubenstein who, as we have seen, argues that it is no longer possible to believe in an all-good God. According to Rubenstein, Auschwitz is the utter and decisive refutation of the traditional affirmation of a providential God who acts in history and watches over the Jewish people whom He has selected from all nations. Although there are Jews who would agree with Rubenstein's assessment, most Jewish believers continue to affirm the traditional belief in a wholly good God. Despite the horrors of the concentration camps, they remain convinced that He rules the world in goodness, justice and truth.

SOURCES

Job

As the Book of Job opens, Job is portrayed as a person of integrity and faith. The scene then shifts to a discussion between God and Satan. Convinced that Job's piety was due to his prosperity, Satan sought to test him:

> Does Job fear God for naught? Hast thou not put a hedge about him and his house and all that he has, on every side? Thou has blessed the work of his hands, and his possessions have increased in the land. But put forth thy hand now, and touch all that he has, and he will curse thee to thy face.
>
> (Job 1:9–11)

Following Job's recitation of his woes, his friends sought to comfort him by stressing that God does not punish the righteous. Hence Job should recognize that his misfortune is due to his own sinfulness. In reply, Job rebuked his friends:

> Teach me, and I will be silent;
> make me understand how I have erred . . .
> But now, be pleased to look at me;
> for I will not lie to your face.
> Turn, I pray. Let no wrong be done.
> Turn now, my vindication is at stake.
> Is there any wrong on my tongue?
> Cannot my taste discern calamity?
>
> (Job 6:24, 28–30)

In Chapter 38 God replies to Job, emphasizing that he cannot understand his ways. In a series of rhetorical questions, He demonstrates that his wisdom exceeds human comprehension:

> Where were you when I laid the foundation of the earth?
> Tell me, if you have understanding.
> Who determined its measurements – surely you know!
> Or who stretched the line upon it?
> On what were its bases sunk,
> or who laid its cornerstone,
> when the morning stars sang together,
> and all the sons of God shouted for joy?
>
> (Job 38:4–7)

Later in the Book, Job accepts God's judgement:

> Then Job answered the Lord:
> 'I know that thou canst do all things,
> and that no purpose of thine can be thwarted.
> Who is this that hides counsel without knowledge?
> Therefore I have uttered what I did not understand,
> things too wonderful for me,
> which I did not know.
>
> (Job 42:1–3)

Ecclesiastes

The Book of Ecclesiastes was ascribed to King Solomon, but in all likelihood it was written at a much later period in the history of ancient Israel. The author proposes a pessimistic philosophy of life. Throughout he emphasizes that life is without meaning. Reflecting on life pursuits, Ecclesiastes advances a fatalistic philosophy:

> For everything there is a season, and a time for every matter under heaven:
> A time to be born, and a time to die;
> a time to plant, and a time to pluck up what is planted;
> a time to kill, and a time to heal;
> a time to break down, and a time to build up;
> a time to weep, and a time to laugh;
> a time to mourn, and a time to dance;
> a time to cast away stones, and a time to gather stones together;
> a time to embrace, and a time to refrain from embracing;
> a time to seek, and a time to lose;
> a time to keep, and a time to cast away;
> a time to rend, and a time to sew;
> a time to keep silence, and a time to speak;
> a time to love, and a time to hate;
> a time for war, and a time for peace. (Eccl. 3:1–8)

This cycle is fixed; all things are bound in an unceasing pattern. Both human beings and beasts go to the same place. There is no advantage for one over the other. Such pessimism is reflected in his assessment of the consequences of sin. Unlike the prophets, he was unable to detect divine justice in the fate of the righteous and the wicked:

> There are righteous men to whom it happens according to the deeds of the wicked, and there are wicked men to whom it happens according to the deeds of the righteous (Eccl. 8:4)

God's ways are inscrutable:

> When I applied my mind to know wisdom, and to see the business that is done on earth, how neither day nor night one's eyes see sleep; then I saw all the work of God, that man cannot find out the work that is done under the sun. However much many may toil in seeking, he will not find it out; even though a wise man claims to know, he cannot find it out. (Eccl. 8:16–17)

Prayer Book

According to the traditional Jewish Prayer Book, God guides and inspires his people to act with goodness:

And may it be thy will, O Lord our God and God of our fathers, to accustom us to walk in thy Torah, and to make us cleave to thy commandments. O lead us not into sin, or transgression, iniquity, temptation, or disgrace: let not the evil inclination have sway over us: keep us far from a bad man and a bad companion: make us cleave to the good inclination and to good works: subdue our inclination so that it may submit itself to thee: and let us obtain this day, and every day, grace, favour, and mercy in thine eyes, and in the eyes of all who behold us; and bestow loving-kindnesses upon thy people Israel.

May it be thy will, O Lord my God and God of my fathers to deliver me this day, and every day, from arrogant men and from arrogance, from a bad man, from a bad companion and from a bad neighbour, and from any mishap or evil hindrance; from a hard judgment, and from a hard opponent, be he a son of the covenant or be he not a son of the covenant.

(In DPB, pp. 25–27)

Saadiah Gaon

According to the tenth-century Jewish philosopher, Saadiah Gaon, God in his goodness rewards the righteous for their faithfulness and punishes the wicked:

God has further told us that during the time we stay in this World of Action, He observes every single deed of ours and reserves its reward for the Future World which is the World of Reward. That world He will call into being when the total number of men which He decided in his wisdom to create will be complete. There He will reward everyone according to his actions, as the wise king said, 'The righteous and the wicked God will judge' (Eccl. 3:17), and furthermore, 'God shall bring every work into the judgment concerning every hidden thing, whether it be good or whether it will be evil' (Eccl. 12:14).

Nevertheless, God by no means leaves his servants without reward for their merits, and punishment for their sins, even in this world, thus giving us a sign and a hint of all that is reserved for the time when the harvest of all human actions will be gathered in. For this reason we find that in the Torah He sets forth the blessings in the passage, 'If ye walk in my statutes' (Lev. 26:3–13; Deut. 28:1–14). Of such blessings it is said, 'Work in my behalf a sign for good' (Ps. 86:17). He also sets forth the curses in the passage, 'But if ye will not hearken unto me' (Lev. 26:14–45; Deut. 28:15–68).

With reference to this matter we say further that God in his wisdom has decided that He should requite his servants in this world only for that class of deeds (good or evil) which are in the minority in order that there may remain for the Future World the class of deeds which are in the majority. For it cannot be thought that God should shift their souls in the coming world from one rank to another seeing that each of the two classes of retribution is destined to last eternally, as it says, 'Some to everlasting life and some to reproaches and everlasting abhorrence' (Dan. 12:2). He has arranged the retribution for the class of deeds which are in the minority to be meted out in this world, in the way in which He has explained that the total sum of good deeds of a pious man is stored up for the Future World, whereas the few good deeds of an impious man are rewarded in this world.

(Saadiah Gaon, *The Book of Doctrines and Beliefs*, in TJP, pp. 134–135)

Moses Maimonides

According to the twelfth-century Jewish philosopher, Moses Maimonides, God is the source of all good; evil, in his view, should be understood as a privation:

In accord with this interpretation, the dictum of Isaiah – who forms the light and creates darkness, who makes peace and creates evil – has become clear. For darkness and evil are privations. Consider that he does not say, who makes darkness and who makes evil, for these are not existent things with which the word making could be connected. With regard to these two things, he simply uses the expression who creates. For this word has a connection with nonbeing in the Hebrew language. Thus it says: In the beginning God created, and so on; namely, out of nonbeing. And the relation between privation and the act of an agent is according to the manner that we have stated.

(Moses Maimonides, *The Guide for the Perplexed*, in GP, p. 438)

Zohar

In the *Zohar*, the *Sitra Ahra* (other side) is viewed as opposed to divine abundance and grace. It should be conceived as a counter-*sefirot*, a realm of dark, unclean powers opposed to holiness and goodness:

At the beginning of the night, when darkness falls, all the evil spirits and powers scatter abroad and roam about the world and the *Sitra Ahra* sets forth and enquires the way to the King from all the holy sides. As soon as the *Sitra Ahra* is roused to this activity here below, all human beings experience a foretaste of death in the midst of their sleep. As soon as the impure power separates itself from the realm above and descends to begin its rule here below, three groups of angels are created who praise the Holy One in three night watches – one following another, as the companions have pointed out. But while these sing hymns of praise to the Holy One, the *Sitra Ahra* . . . roam about here below, even into the uttermost parts of the earth. Until the *Sitra Ahra* has thus departed from the upper sphere, the angels of light cannot unite themselves with their Lord.

(*Zohar*, in JM, pp. 127–128)

DISCUSSION

1. Discuss the rabbinic view that God cannot be the cause of evil.

2. If God is all-good, how could He have allowed the Holocaust to take place?

FURTHER READING

Ariel, David, *What Do Jews Believe?: the Jewish Faith Examined*, Rider, 1996.

Birnbaum, David, *God and Evil*, KTAV, 1989.

Blumenthal, David, *The Banality of Good and Evil: Moral Lessons from the Shoah and Jewish Tradition*, Georgetown University Press, 1999.

Cohn-Sherbok, Dan, *Holocaust Theology: A Reader*, University of Exeter Press, 2002.

Eichenstein, Zevi Hirsch, Jacobs, Louis (eds), *Turn Aside from Evil and Do Good: An Introduction and a Way to the Tree of Life*, Littman Library, 1995.

Gillman, Neil, *Sacred Fragments: Recovery Theology for the Modern Jew*, Jewish Publication Society, 1992.

Gillman, Neil, *The Death of Death*, Jewish Lights, 1997.

Gillman, Neil, *The Way into Encountering God in Judaism*, Jewish Lights, 2001.

Hick, John, *Evil and the God of Love*, Macmillan, 1985.

Jacobs, Louis, *A Jewish Theology*, Behrman House, 1973.

Jacobs, Louis, *Principles of the Jewish Faith*, Valentine Mitchell, 1964.

Rosenberg, Shalom, *Good and Evil in Jewish Thought*, Mod Books, 1989.

Rowe, William (ed.), *God and the Problem of Evil*, Blackwell, 2001.

CHAPTER 62

Revelation

Figure 62 Rabbi Sylvia Rothchild at the Bromley Synagogue, London. Copyright David Rose.

According to tradition the entire Bible was communicated by God to the Jewish people. In the twelfth-century Jewish philosopher Moses Maimonides' formulation of the thirteen principles of the faith, this belief is the eighth tenet:

> The Torah was revealed from Heaven. This implies our belief that the whole of the Torah found in our hands this day is the Torah that was handed down by Moses, and that it is all of divine origin. By this I mean that the whole of the Torah came unto him from before God in a manner which is metaphorically called 'speaking'; but the real nature of that communication is unknown to everybody except to Moses (peace to him!) to whom it came. (Moses Maimonides, *Commentary to the Mishnah, Sanhedrin*, X, I)

In **rabbinic literature** a distinction is drawn between the revelation of the Five Books of Moses (Torah in the narrow sense) and the prophetic writings. This is frequently expressed by saying that the Torah was given directly by God, whereas the prophetic books were given by means of prophecy. The remaining books of the Bible (Hagiographa) were conveyed by means of the holy spirit rather than through prophecy. Nonetheless, all these writings constitute the canon of Scripture. The Hebrew term referring to the Bible as a whole is *Tanakh*. This word is made up of the first three letters of the three divisions of Scripture: Torah (Pentateuch); *Neviim* (Prophets); and *Ketuvim* (Writings). This is the Written Torah (*Torah She-Bi-Ketav*).

According to the rabbis, the expositions and elaborations of the Written Law were also revealed by God to Moses on Mount Sinai; subsequently they were passed from generation to generation, and through this process additional legislation was incorporated. This process was referred to as 'The Oral Torah' (*Torah She-Be-Al Peh*). Thus traditional Judaism affirms that God's revelation was two-fold and binding for all time. Committed to this belief, Jews pray in the synagogue that God will guide them to do his will as recorded in their sacred literature:

> O our Father, merciful Father, ever compassionate, have mercy upon us: O put it into our hearts

to understand and to discern, to mark, learn and teach, to heed, to do and fulfil in love all the words of instruction in thy Torah. Enlighten our eyes in thy Torah, and let our hearts cling to thy commandments, and make us single-hearted to love and fear thy name, so that we be never put to shame. (*Singer's Prayerbook*, p. 41)

In the Middle Ages, this traditional belief was continually affirmed. Like Maimonides, the thirteenth-century Jewish philosopher Nahmanides in his *Commentary to the Pentateuch* argued that Moses wrote the Five Books of Moses at God's dictation. It is likely, he observed, that Moses wrote Genesis and part of Exodus when he descended from Mount Sinai. At the end of the forty years in the wilderness he completed the rest of the Pentateuch. Nahmanides observes that this view follows the rabbinic tradition that the Torah was given scroll by scroll. For Nahmanides, Moses was like a scribe who copied an older work. Underlying this conception is the mystical idea of a primordial Torah which contains the words describing events long before they happened. This entire record was in Heaven before the creation of the world. In addition, Nahmanides maintains that the secrets of the Torah were revealed to Moses and are referred to in the Torah by the use of special letters, the numerical values of words and letters, and the adornment of Hebrew characters.

Paralleling Nahmanides' mystical interpretation of the Torah, the *Zohar* asserts that the Torah contains mysteries beyond human comprehension. As the *Zohar* explains:

> Said R. Simeon: 'Alas for the man who regards the Torah as a book of mere tales and everyday matters! If that were so, even we could compose a Torah dealing with everyday affairs, and of even greater excellence. Nay, even the princes of the world possess books of greater worth which we could use as a model for composing such Torah. The Torah, however, contains in all its words supernal truths and sublime mysteries . . . Thus, had the Torah not clothed herself in garments of this world, the world could not endure it. The stories of the Torah are thus only her outer garments, and whoever looks upon that garment

as being the Torah itself, woe to that man – such a one has no portion in the next world.' (*Zohar*, III, 152a)

In the modern period, however, it has become increasingly difficult to sustain the traditional concept of divine revelation in the light of scholarly investigation and discovery. As early as the ninth century, Hiwi Al-Balkhi offered two hundred objections to the doctrine of the divine origin of the Bible. In response Saadiah Gaon composed a refutation of Hiwi's views. In Jewish circles Hiwi was regarded as a heretic. Later the twelfth-century Jewish scholar Abraham Ibn Ezra expressed the opinion that there are post-Mosaic additions in the Pentateuch. For example, in his commentary to Deut. 1:2 he is troubled by Deut. 1:1: 'These are the words which Moses spoke unto all Israel beyond the Jordan'. In Moses' day the Israelites had not yet entered the Promised Land; thus the term 'beyond the Jordan' would not have been used to designate the side of the Jordan on which they were encamped.

Later in the sixteenth century, scholars pointed out that the Five Books of Moses appear to be composed of different sources. Subsequently Jean Astruc, a Catholic physician, was disturbed by the evidence of the composite nature of the Pentateuch. As a consequence, he put forward the theory that Moses used ancient documents as the sources for the Five Books of Moses. This theory was advanced by Astruc in his '*Conjectures sur les memoires originaux dont il paroit que Moyse se servit pour composer le livre de la Genèse* which was published in the middle of the eighteenth century. In advancing his theory Astruc noted that portions of Genesis use the name '*Elohim*' while other portions used the Tetragrammaton. This led Astruc to conclude that one of the documents used by Moses was the *Elohist*, the document describing the origins of the world where God is referred to as '*Elohim*'.

Other theories based on Astruc's hypothesis suggested that various fragments of documents could be detected in the Torah. Eventually two main documents were detected: one using the name '*Elohim*'; the other using the Tetragrammaton, referred to as 'J'. In 1805 another scholar, De Wette, published a dissertation entitled *Discourse on Deuteronomy* in which he argued that this book was a work compiled shortly before it was found in the days of Josiah. Thus there were three documents detected in the Torah: E, J and D. E was viewed as the main document, with J and D as additions. Each of these documents was regarded as having been compiled at different times.

In the middle of the nineteenth century sustained investigation by two German scholars, Karl Heinrich Graf and Julius Wellhausen, concluded that the Five Books of Moses are composed of four main documents which once existed separately but were later combined by a series of editors and redactors. The first document, 'J', dating from the ninth century BCE, attributes the most anthropomorphic character to God, referred to by the four Hebrew letters YHWH. The second source, 'E', stemming from the eighth century BCE, is less anthropomorphic and utilizes the divine name *Elohim*. In the seventh century BCE, the 'D' source was written, concentrating on religious purity and the priesthood. Finally, the 'P' source from the fifth century BCE, which has a more transcendent view of God, emphasizes the importance of the sacrificial cult.

By utilizing this framework, Graf and Wellhausen maintained that it is possible to account for the manifold problems and discrepancies in the Biblical text. According to Graf and Wellhausen, the following characteristics are found within these sources:

1. J

Anthropomorphisms and a simple style. Here the divine name is J. There is an occasional mention of angels. There is also an interest in the South of Palestine.

2. E

This source is less anthropomorphic and focuses on angels, and dreams. The divine name *Elohim* is used. There is a special interest in the North of Palestine.

3. D

Here there is an interest in purity of religion, and the role of the priests.

4. P

The P source is particularly concerned with the sacrificial system, and adopts a transcendental view of God. Only *kohanim* are allowed to offer sacrifices in the Temple. Tithes are to be given to priests and Levites.

The Graf–Wellhausen hypothesis was subsequently modified by other scholars. Some preferred not to speak of separate sources but of circles of tradition. On this view, J, E, D and P represent oral traditions rather than written documents. Further, these scholars stress that the separate traditions themselves contain early material; thus it is a mistake to think they originated in their entirety at particular periods. Other scholars reject the theory of separate sources altogether; they argue that oral traditions were modified throughout the history of ancient Israel and only eventually were compiled into a single narrative. Yet despite these different theories, there is a general recognition among modern Biblical critics – including Reform, Conservative, Reconstructionist and Humanistic Jews – that the Pentateuch was not written by Moses. Rather, it is seen as a collection of traditions originating at different times in ancient Israel.

In addition to the findings of Biblical scholarship, textual studies of ancient manuscripts highlight the improbability of the traditional Jewish view of Scripture. According to the Jewish heritage, the Hebrew text of the Five Books of Moses used in synagogues today (the *Masoretic* text) is the same as that given to Moses. Yet it is widely accept among scholars that the script of contemporary Torah scrolls is not the same as that which was current in ancient Israel from the time of the monarchy until the sixth century BCE. It was only later, possibly under Aramaic influence, that the square script was adopted as the standard for Hebrew writing. Furthermore, the fact that the ancient translations of the Hebrew Bible into languages such as Syriac and Greek contain variant readings from the *Masoretic* text suggests that the Hebrew text of the Pentateuch now in use is not entirely free from error.

A final aspect of modern studies which bears on the question of Mosaic authorship concerns the influence of the ancient Near East on the Bible. According to Orthodox Judaism, the Five Books of Moses were essentially created out of nothing. But as we have seen, there are strong parallels in the Jewish Bible to laws, stories and myths found throughout the ancient Near

East. It is unlikely that this is simply a coincidence – the similarities offer compelling evidence that the Pentateuch emerged in a specific social and cultural context. The authors of the Biblical period shared much of the same world view as their neighbours and no doubt transformed this framework to fit their own religious ideas. In this light, most modern Biblical scholars would find it impossible to reconcile the traditional conception of Mosaic authorship of the Five Books of Moses with the discoveries of modern Biblical criticism and scientific discovery.

For Orthodox Jews, however, such investigations are irrelevant. Orthodox Judaism remains committed to the view that the Written as well as the Oral Torah were imparted by God to Moses on Mount Sinai. This act of revelation serves as the basis for the entire legal system as well as doctrinal beliefs about God. Yet despite such an adherence to tradition, many modern Orthodox Jews pay only lip service to such

a conviction. The gap between traditional belief and contemporary views of the Torah is even greater in the non-Orthodox branches of Judaism. Here, among **Reform**, Conservative, Reconstructionist and **Humanistic** Jews, there is a general acceptance of the findings of Biblical scholarship. Such a non-fundamentalistic approach, which takes account of recent scholarly developments in the field of Biblical studies, rules out the traditional belief in the infallibility of Scripture and thereby provides a rationale for changing the law and reinterpreting the theology of the Hebrew Scriptures in the light of contemporary knowledge. In the modern period, therefore, there has been a shift away from the fundamentalism of the past – nonetheless non-Orthodox Jews join ranks with the Orthodox in continuing to regard the Jewish bible as fundamental to the faith. As the liturgy used in all synagogues proclaims: 'It is a tree of life to those who hold fast to it.'

SOURCES

Hebrew Bible

The Hebrew Bible consists of three sections: Torah (Five Books of Moses); *Neviim* (Prophets); and *Ketuvim* (Writings):

Torah

Genesis; Exodus; Leviticus; Numbers; Deuteronomy.

Prophets

Former Prophets: Joshua; Judges; I and 2 Samuel; I and 2 Kings.
Latter Prophets: Isaiah; Jeremiah: Ezekiel; Hosea; Joel; Amos; Obadiah; Jonah; Micah; Nahum; Habakkuk; Zephaniah; Haggai; Zechariah; Malachi.

Writings

Psalms; Proverbs; Job; Song of Songs; Ruth; Lamentations; Ecclesiastes; Esther; Daniel; Ezra; Nehemiah; I and 2 Chronicles.

Rabbinic Literature

According to the *midrash*, God gave the law to his people to sustain them:

The words of the Law are likened to a medicine of life. Like a king, who inflicted a big wound upon his son, and he put a plaster upon his wound. He said, 'My son, so long as this plaster is on your wound, eat and drink what you like, and wash in cold or warm water, and you will suffer no harm. But if you remove it, you will get a bad boil. So God said to the Israelites, 'I created within you the *evil yetzer* (evil inclination),

but I created the Law as a medicine. As long as you occupy yourselves with the Law, the *yetzer* will not rule over you. But if you do not occupy yourselves with the Torah, then you will be delivered into the power of the *yetzer*, and all its activity will be against you.'

(*Sefer Deuteronomy*, in RA, p. 125)

Judah Halevi

In the *Kuzari*, the twelfth-century Jewish philosopher Judah Halevi argues that God revealed himself to Adam, his descendants, and the Jewish people:

The first of these was Adam. He would never have known God, if He had not addressed, rewarded and punished him and created Eve from one of his ribs. By this he was convinced that He was the creator of the world, and he characterized him by words and attributes and called him 'the Lord'. Had it not been for this experience he would have been satisfied with the name God; he would not have perceived what God was, whether He is one or many, whether He knows individuals or not. Cain and Abel also perceived God, after having been taught by their father, through prophetic vision. Then Noah, Abraham, Isaac,

and Jacob, down to Moses and the later prophets called him 'the Lord' by reason of their visions; and so did the people, having been taught on their authority, and through their authority, in as far as God's influence and guidance is with man and in as far as the pick of mankind enters into connection with him, viewing him through intermediaries called 'Glory, *Shekhinah*, Dominion, fire, cloud, likeness, form, appearance of the rainbow', etc., all proving to them that He had spoken to them.

(Judah Halevi, *Kuzari*, in TJP, p. 114)

Reform Judaism

Although Reform Jews continue to believe in the doctrine of revelation, they have distanced themselves from the traditional understanding of God's disclosure. In the Columbus Platform of 1937, for example, reformers advanced the notion of progressive revelation to explain God's interaction with later generations:

God reveals himself not only in the majesty, beauty and orderliness of nature, but also in the vision of moral striving of the human spirit. Revelation is a continuous process, confined to no one group and to no one age. Yet the people of Israel, through its prophets and sages, achieved unique insight into the realm of religious truth. The Torah, both written and oral, enshrines Israel's ever-growing consciousness of God and of the moral law. It preserves the historical precedents, sanctions and norms of Jewish life, and seeks to mould it in the patterns of goodness and of holiness. Being products of historical processes, certain of its laws have lost their binding force with the passing of the conditions that called them forth. But as a depository of permanent spiritual ideals, the Torah remains the dynamic source of the life of Israel. Each age has the obligation to adapt the teachings of the Torah to its basic needs in consonance with the genius of Judaism.

(Columbus Platform, in FJ, p. 107)

Humanistic Judaism

For Humanistic Jews, the concept of revelation is no longer meaningful given the rejection of belief in God:

> We believe in the value of human reason and in the reality of the world which reason discloses. The natural universe stands on its own, requiring no supernatural intervention. We believe in the value of human existence and in the power of human beings to solve their problems both individually and collectively. Life should be directed to the satisfaction of human needs. Every person is entitled to life, dignity and freedom. We believe in the value of Jewish identity and in the survival of the Jewish people. Jewish history is a human story. Judaism, as the civilization of the Jews, is a human creation.

(Proclamation of Humanistic Judaism, in FJ, pp. 138–139)

DISCUSSION

1. Critically evaluate the doctrine that God revealed the Torah to Moses on Mt Sinai.

2. Discuss the doctrine of progressive revelation in the non-Orthodox branches of Judaism.

FURTHER READING

Buber, Martin, *The Revelation and the Covenant*, Humanities Press International, 1988.

Cohn-Sherbok, Dan (ed.), *Torah and Revelation*, Edwin Mellen Press, 1992.

Fishbane, Michael, *Judaism: Revelation and Traditions*, HarperCollins, 1986.

Halivni, David Weiss, *Revelation Restored*, Westview, 1997.

Jacobs, Louis, *God, Torah and Israel: Traditionalism Without Fundamentalism*, Hebrew Union College Press, 1997.

Jacobs, Louis, *Principles of the Jewish Faith*, Kuperard, 1995.

Kepnes, Steven, Ochs, Peter, Gibbs, Robert, *Reasoning After Revelation*, SCM, 2002.

Neusner, Jacob, Chilton, Bruce, *Revelation*, Trinity Press International, 1995.

Oppenheim, Michael, *What Does Revelation Mean for the Modern Jew?*, Edwin Mellen Press, 1985.

Samuelson, Norbert, *Revelation and the God of Israel*, Cambridge University Press, 2002.

CHAPTER 63

Torah and *Mitzvot*

Figure 63 Ner Tamid, the ever-burning light symbolizing God (J78.22). Copyright David Rose.

According to tradition, God revealed 613 commandments (*mitzvot*) to Moses on Mount Sinai; they are recorded in the Five Books of Moses. These prescriptions, which are to be observed as part of God's covenant with Israel, are classified in two major categories: (l) statutes concerned with ritual performances characterized as obligations between human beings and God; and (2) judgements consisting of ritual laws that would have been adopted by society even if they had not been decreed by God (such as laws regarding murder and theft). These 613 commandments consist of 365 negative (prohibited) and 248 positive (duties to be performed) prescriptions.

Traditional Judaism maintains that Moses received the Oral Torah in addition to the Written Law. This was passed down from generation to generation and was the subject of rabbinic debate. The first authoritative compilation of the Oral Law was the *Mishnah* composed by Judah Ha-Nasi in the second century CE. This work is the most important book of law after the Bible; its purpose is to supply teachers and judges with an authoritative guide to the Jewish legal tradition. It consists of six divisions:

1. *Zeraim* (Seeds). This contains regulations about agriculture and the contributions which must be set aside for the poor, the priests and levites. It is divided into tractates as follows:

   1. *Berakhot* (Benedictions). These are principally daily prayers.
   2. *Peah* (Corner). This is the part of the field which must be left for the poor.
   3. *Demai* (Uncertain). A discussion of crops of which it is doubtful whether or not tithes should be made.
   4. *Kilayim* (Mixtures). This deals with the crops, materials and animals which must not be crossed or mixed with one another.
   5. *Sheviit* (Seventh year). In this year all the fields have to be left fallow.
   6. *Terumot* (Heave offerings). Those which are due to the priests.
   7. *Maasrot* (Tithes). A tithe has to be made of the produce of the field to be given to the Levites.

8. *Maaser Sheni* (Second Tithe). The tithe which is to be made as an offering to the Temple.
9. *Hallah* (Dough). This must be given as an offering.
10. *Orlah* (Uncut). This refers to the fruits of a tree during the first three years after it was planted.
11. *Bikkurim* (First fruits). These must be brought to Jerusalem.

2. *Moed* (Appointed Time). This contains the regulations about the festivals and special days during the year.

1. *Shabbat.* The laws which apply to the Sabbath.
2. *Eruvin* (Mixtures). On the Sabbath it is permitted to travel or carry objects only within a certain distance. This concerns how these limitations can be extended.
3. *Pesahim* (Passovers). This discusses the regulations regarding Passover.
4. *Sheqalim* (Shekels). This is an agricultural measure which must be paid per head for Temple worship.
5. *Yoma* (Day). This is a discussion of the regulations for the Day of Atonement and Temple worship on that day.
6. *Sukkah* (Booth). Regulations concerning *Sukkot.*
7. *Betzah* (Egg). It discusses regulations about festivals.
8. *Rosh Hashanah* (New Year). The celebration of this day is discussed, as is the ascertaining of the new moon.
9. *Taanit* (Fast Day). This deals with fasting.
10. *Megillah* (Scroll). This discusses the reading of the Scroll of Esther and the festivities of *Purim.*
11. *Moed Katan* (Lesser Appointed Time). The rules related to the days between the feasts of Passover and *Sukkot.*
12. *Hagigah* (Celebration of a Festival). The celebration of the Pilgrim Festivals.

3. *Nashim* (Women). This concerns the laws about marriage, marriage rights and divorce.

1. *Yevamot* (Sisters-in-Law). This discusses levirate marriage and marriage practices which are forbidden.

2. *Ketubot* (Marriage Contracts). The Laws regarding the contract between bride and groom.
3. *Nedarim* (Vows). This discusses the difference between an oath, a promise, obligations to celibacy and their annulment.
4. *Nazir* (*Nazirite*). This laws concern the *Nazirite.*
5. *Gittin* (Bills of Divorce). The laws regarding divorce.
6. *Sotah* (Woman Suspected of Adultery). The regulations concerning a woman suspected of committing adultery.
7. *Kiddushin* (Betrothals). Laws concerning marriage.

4. *Neziqin* (Damages)

1. *Baba Kamma* (First Gate). Civil and criminal law.
2. *Baba Metzia* (Middle Gate). Civil and criminal law.
3. *Bava Batra* (Last Gate). Civil and criminal law.
4. *Sanhedrin* (Law Court). This discusses a judicial body.
5. *Makkot* (Blows). This deals with corporal punishment.
6. *Shavuot* (Oaths). Deals with legal matters.
7. *Eduyot* (Testimonies). This deals with various subjects connected with judicial matters.
8. *Avodah Zara* (Idolatry). Laws concerning idolatry.
9. *Avot* (Fathers). Sayings of the Fathers deals with ethical matters.
10. *Horayot* (Instructions). This discusses what must be done when a wrong decision has been made.

5. *Kodashim* (Holy Things). This discusses sacrificial laws and service for the Temple.

1. *Zevahim* (Sacrifices). This discusses sacrifices.
2. *Menahot* (Meal Offerings). Dealing with grain and bread.
3. *Hullin* (Non-Holy Things). Food laws concerning animals; that which makes them suitable to use.
4. *Bekhorot* (First-born). Concerning the first-born of cattle.
5. *Arakhin* (Valuations). Deals with the fulfilment of oaths.
6. *Temurah* (Exchange). Laws concerning sacrifices.

7. *Keritot* (Uprootings). Concerning the punishment of uprooting from the people.
8. *Meilah* (Sacrilege). Concerning the misuse of consecrated objects.
9. *Tamid* (Always). Laws regarding the daily offering.
10. *Middot* (Measurements). Laws regarding the Temple.
11. *Qinnim* (Birds' Nests). Deals with the offering of birds.

6. *Tohorot* (Cleannesses). Deals with ritual impurity.

1. *Kelim* (Things). Deals with ritual uncleanliness.
2. *Oholot* (Tents). Laws concerning the prohibition against remaining with a dead body under one roof.
3. *Negaim* (Plagues). Laws concerning leprosy.
4. *Parah* (Cow). Deals with the ashes of a red cow as a means of purification.
5. *Tohorot* (Cleannesses). Deals with ritual impurity.
6. *Miqvaot* (Ritual Baths). Discussion of the requirements of ritual baths.
7. *Niddah* (Object of Impurity). Deals with menstruating women.
8. *Makhshirin* (What Makes Things Capable of Defilement). Deals with liquids which make dry materials unclean.
9. *Zavim* (Persons with Fluxes). Deals with men who are unclean.
10. *Tevul Yom* (Immersion of the day). Laws concerning someone who bathed during the day but must wait until sunset for ritual purity to be complete.
11. *Yadayim* (Hands). Concerns the impurity of hands.
12. *Uqtzin* (Stalks). Discusses how fruits can become unclean through their stalks.

In subsequent centuries sages continued to discuss the content of Jewish law; their deliberations are recorded in the Palestinian and Babylonian *Talmuds* which are arranged according to the structure of the *Mishnah*. Both *Talmuds* incorporate the *Mishnah* and later rabbinic discussions known as the *Gamara*. The *Gamara* text preserves the proceedings of the academics in both Palestine and Babylonia, where scholars assembled to study the *Mishnah*. The central purpose of these deliberations was to elucidate the *Mishnah* text.

After the compilation of the *Talmuds* in the sixth century CE, outstanding **rabbinic authorities** continued the development of Jewish law by issuing answers to specific questions. These responses (known as '*responsa*') touched on all aspects of Jewish law and ensured a standardization of practice. In time various scholars felt the need to produce codes of Jewish law so that all members of the community would have access to the legal tradition. In the eleventh century, Isaac Alfasi produced a work that became the standard code for Sephardic Jewry. Two centuries later, Asher ben Jehiel wrote a code that became the code for Ashkenazi Jews. Moses Maimonides in the twelfth century also wrote an important code that had a wide influence, as did the code by Jacob ben Asher in the fourteenth century, the son of Asher ben Jehiel. In the sixteenth century Joseph Caro published the *Shulkhan Arukh*, which together with glosses by Moses Isserles has served as the standard **Code of Jewish law** for Orthodox Jewry until the present day. The *Shulkhan Arukh* is divided into four divisions: (1) *Orah Hayyim* dealing with everyday conduct, prayer, and festivals: (2) *Yoreh Deah* concerning dietary and ritual laws; (3) *Even Ha-Ezer* which deals with matters of personal status; and (4) *Hoshen Mishpat* dealing with courts, civil law and torts.

In kabbalistic thought the observance of the *mitzvot* takes on cosmic significance. For the mystic, deeds of *tikkun* (cosmic repair) sustain the world, activate nature to praise God, and bring about the coupling of the tenth and sixth *sefirot*. Such repair is accomplished by keeping the commandments which were conceived as vessels for establishing contact with the Godhead and for experiencing divine mercy. Such a religious life provided the kabbalist with a means of integrating into the divine hierarchy of creation – the *kabbalah* was able to guide the soul back to its infinite source.

The supreme rank attainable by the soul at the end of its sojourn is the mystical cleaving to God. The early kabbalists of Provence defined such cleaving as the ultimate goal. According to Isaac the Blind (in the twelfth to thirteenth century), the principal task of the mystics and of those who contemplate his name is, 'And you shall cleave to him' (Deut. 13:4); this is a central principle of the Torah and of prayer as well as blessings – to harmonize one's thought above, to conjoin God in his letters and to link the ten *sefirot* to him.

For Nahmanides in the thirteenth century, such cleaving is a state of mind in which one constantly remembers God and his love to the point that when that person speaks with someone else, his heart is not with them at all but is still before God. Whoever cleaves in this way to his creator, he stated, becomes eligible to receive the Holy Spirit. According to Nahmanides, the pious are able to attain such a spiritual state. Mystical cleaving does not completely eliminate the distance between God and human beings. It denotes instead a state of beatitude and intimate union between the soul and its source.

Within Lurianic *kabbalah*, these notions were elaborated. According to Isaac Luria in the sixteenth century, when the vessels were shattered, the cosmos was divided into two parts – the kingdom of evil in the lower part and the realm of divine light in the upper part. For Luria evil was seen as opposed to existence; therefore it was not able to exist by its own power. Instead it had to derive spiritual force from the divine light. This was accomplished by keeping captive the sparks of the divine light that fell with them when the vessels were broken and subsequently gave sustenance to the satanic domain.

Divine attempts to bring unity to all existence now had to focus on the struggle to overcome the evil forces. This was first achieved by a continuing process of divine emanation which at first created the *sefirot*, the sky, the earth, the Garden of Eden and human beings. Human beings were intended to serve as the battleground for this conflict between good and evil. In this regard Adam reflected symbolically the dualism in the cosmos – he possesses a sacred soul while his body represents the evil forces. God's intention was that Adam defeat the evil within himself and bring about Satan's downfall. But when Adam failed, a catastrophe occurred parallel to the breaking of the vessels; instead of divine sparks being saved and uplifted, many new divine lights fell and evil became stronger.

Rather than relying on the action of one person, God then chose the people of Israel to vanquish evil and raise up the captive sparks. The Torah was given to symbolize the Jews' acceptance of this allotted task.

When the ancient Israelites undertook to keep the law, redemption seemed imminent. Yet the people of Israel then created the golden calf, a sin parallel to Adam's disobedience. Again, divine sparks fell and the forces of evil were renewed. For Luria, history is a record of attempts by the powers of good to rescue these sparks and unite the divine and earthly spheres. Luria and his disciples believed they were living in the final stages of this last attempt to overcome evil, in which the coming of the Messiah would signify the end of the struggle.

Related to the contraction of God, the breaking of the vessels and the exiled sparks, was Luria's conception of *tikkun*. For Lurianic mystics, this concept refers to the mending of what was broken during the shattering of the vessels. After the catastrophe in the divine realm, the process of restoration began and every disaster was seen as a setback in this process. In this battle, keeping God's commandments was understood as contributing to repair – the divine sparks which fell down can be redeemed by ethical and religious deeds. According to Luria, a spark is attached to all prayers and moral acts; if the Jew keeps the ethical and religious law these sparks are redeemed and lifted up. When the process is complete evil will disappear, but every time a Jew sins a spark is captured and plunges into the satanic abyss. Every deed or misdeed thus has cosmic significance in the system of Lurianic *kabbalah*.

In the modern world such traditional and mystical ideas have lost their force except among the *Hasidim*. Today Orthodoxy claims the largest number of adherents. Yet the majority of those who profess allegiance to Orthodox Judaism do not always live by the code of Jewish law. This is also so within the other branches of Judaism. For most Jews the legal tradition has lost its hold on Jewish consciousness – the bulk of rituals and observances appear anachronistic and burdensome. In previous centuries this was not the case; despite the divisions within the Jewish world all Jews accepted the abiding authority of the law contained in the Torah. The 613 commandments were universally viewed as given by God to Moses on Mount Sinai and understood as binding for all time. Thus food regulations, stipulations regarding ritual purity, the moral code as well as other *mitzvot* served as the framework for an authentic Jewish way of life.

Throughout Jewish history the validity of the written Torah was never questioned. In contemporary society, however, most Jews of all religious positions have ceased to regard the legal heritage in this light. Instead individual Jews, including those of the Orthodox persuasion, feel at liberty to choose which *mitzvot* have a personal spiritual significance. Such an anarchic approach to the legal tradition highlights the fact that Jewish law no longer serves a cohesive force for contemporary Jewry. In short, many modern Jews no longer believe in the doctrine of Torah from Sinai, which previously served as a cardinal principle of the Jewish faith. Instead they subscribe only to a limited number of legal precepts which for one reason or another they find meaningful. Such a lack of uniformity of Jewish practice means that there is a vast gulf between the requirements of legal observance and the actual lifestyle of the majority of Jews, both in Israel and the diaspora.

SOURCES

Rabbis

According to the rabbis, both the Oral and the Written Torah were given by God to Moses on Mt Sinai. In their opinion it was the Oral Law that distinguished the Jewish people from other nations:

God gave the Israelites two Laws, the Written Law and the Oral Law. He gave them the Written Law with its 613 ordinances, to fill them with commandments, and to cause them to become virtuous, as it is said, 'The Lord was pleased for his righteousness' sake to increase the Law and make it glorious. And He gave them the Oral Law to make them distinguished from the other nations. It was not given in writing so that the nations should not falsify it, as they have done with the Written Law, and say that they are the true Israel. Therefore it says, "If I were to write for him the many things of my Law, they would be counted as strange"' (Hos. 8:12). The many things are the *Mishnah*, which is larger than the Law and God says, If I were to write for Israel the 'many things', they would be accounted as strange.

(*Num*. R., *Naso*, 14, 10, in RA, p. 159)

Code of Jewish Law

The *Code of Jewish Law* (*Shulkhan Arukh*) contains regulations regarding all aspects of Jewish life, such as restrictions concerning actions on the Sabbath:

There are certain things forbidden on the Sabbath although they neither have any resemblance to work, nor do they in any way lead to the performance of work. Why, then are they forbidden? Because it is written (Isaiah 58:13): 'If thou turn away thy foot because of the Sabbath, from pursuing thy business on my holy day; and thou shalt honour it, not doing thy wonted ways, nor pursuing thy business, nor speaking thereof . . .'

On the Sabbath, one is forbidden to walk to the end of the Sabbath boundary, or even a lesser distance, and wait there until dark, in order to complete his journey sooner at the conclusion of the Sabbath, for it is obvious that he has walked there principally for that purpose. This, however, is forbidden only if he goes there to do something which may not possibly be done on the *Shabbat*, as to hire workmen, or to pick fruit . . .

From the phrase, 'Nor speaking thereof', our rabbis, of blessed memory, have inferred that one's speech on the Sabbath should not be the same as on weekdays . . .

Inasmuch as it is written, 'Thy business', our rabbis, of blessed memory, have inferred that only personal business is forbidden, but religious affairs are permitted . . .

From the phrase, 'Nor speaking thereof', our rabbis, of blessed memory, have inferred that only speaking is forbidden, but thinking is permissible . . .

If one hires a Jewish workman to guard anything for him, the workman is forbidden to take any pay for the Sabbath by itself . . .

On the Sabbath, one is forbidden to make a gift to anyone, unless the recipient needs it on the Sabbath . . .

On the Sabbath, it is forbidden to peruse ordinary documents, such as bills, accounts, or personal letters . . .

It is forbidden to measure anything that we may need for the Sabbath, unless it is essential for the performance of a precept . . .

Whatever we ourselves are forbidden to do on the Sabbath, we may not tell a non-Jew to do it for us . . .

If a non-Jew, of his own accord, wishes to perform some work for us, we must prevent him from doing it . . .

It is forbidden to send a non-Jew outside the Sabbath boundary limit to summon the relatives of a dead man, or one to deliver a funeral oration . . .

If a non-Jew had bought some merchandise from a Jew, and he comes to take it on the Sabbath, he should be prevented from doing it, if possible.

(*Code of Jewish Law* in CJL, pp. 125–130)

Reform Judaism

Progressive Jews do not feel the same compulsion to observe the *mitzvot* as Orthodox Jews. In their view, the law needs to be modified in accordance with modern circumstances. In a discussion of modern *halakhah*, the British Liberal rabbi John Rayner argues that a new approach to law should be embraced by modern Jewry:

My thesis . . . is that we need to evolve a new modern *halakhah*. It will differ from the old *halakhah* in the following respects: (I) It will re-examine the sources of the traditional *halakhah* – Scripture, exegesis, tradition, custom and precedent – with respect but not with subservience. It will ascribe to it only a presumptive, never a conclusive, authority. (2) it will bring into play not only the traditional criteria, but also considerations drawn from general ethical principles inherent in the tradition as well as from modern thought, modern knowledge and modern realities. (3) It will therefore require the co-operation, not only of *halakhists*, but also of historians and theologians, and of experts in 'secular' disciplines such as medicine, psychology, sociology, jurisprudence, etc. (4) It will lay special emphasis on moral law, which is the most enduringly valid and the most universally relevant. But it will also concern itself with civil law, so that we may make our contribution both to the legislative processes of our 'host country' and to the development of Israeli law in the spirit of Judaism. And, of course, it will deal with ritual law. (5) It will not claim finality in any of these areas. Whatever it decides will be 'subject to alteration' by subsequent generations in the light of their own insights and judgements. (6) Wherever uniformity is not essential, for example in matters of personal and domestic observance, it will offer guidance rather than legislation. (7) Whenever there is a divergence of opinions it will state not only the majority view but all minority views as well, just as the Talmud did.

(8) In all cases, it will state not only the conclusion reached, but the thought processes which led to it.

(John Rayner, Towards a Modern Halakhah, in RJ, p. 127)

DISCUSSION

1. Explain how the observance of the *mitzvot* takes on cosmic significance in kabbalistic thought.

2. Discuss the role of Jewish law in the non-Orthodox branches of Judaism.

FURTHER READING

Caplan, Philip, *The Puzzle of the 613 Commandments and Why Bother?*, Jason Aronson, 1996.

Cardozo, Nathan, *The Written and Oral Torah, A Comprehensive Introduction*, Jason Aronson, 1997.

Carmel, Aryeh, *Masterplan: Judaism, Its Program, Meanings and Goals*, Feldheim, 1991.

Chill, Abraham, *The Mitzvot: The Commandments and Their Rationale*, Bloch, 1974.

Dosick, Wayne, *The Business Bible: 10 New Commandments for Bringing Spirituality and Ethical Values into the Workplace*, Jewish Lights, 2000.

Fenton, Anne Lobock, *Tikun Olam: Fixing the World*, Brookline, 1997.

Mikva, Rachel (ed.), *Broken Tablets: Restoring the Ten Commandments and Ourselves*, Jewish Lights, 2001.

Plaut, Gunther, *Torah: A Modern Commentary*, UAHC Press, 1981.

Speling, Abraham, *Reasons for Jewish Customs and Traditions*, Bloch, 1975.

Trepp, Leo, *A History of the Jewish Experience: Book One, Torah and History; Book Two, Torah, Mitzvot and Jewish Thought*, Behrman House, 2001.

CHAPTER 64

Commandments

Figure 64 Moses in the Sinai desert (with the tablets of the law). Artist: Letin, Jacques de: 1597–1661: French. Copyright The Art Archive/Musée des Beaux Arts Troyes/Dagli Orti.

According to tradition, God revealed the 613 commandments to Moses on Mount Sinai. This list follows Moses Maimonides' formulation; it contains the Biblical law followed by the rabbinic definition:

1. Gen 1:28   Marry and produce children
2. Gen 17:12   Circumcise eight-day-old boy
3. Gen 32:33   Do not eat sinew
4. Ex 12:2   Calculate and fix months of the year

5.	Ex 12:6	Sacrifice the Passover lamb on 14 *Nisan*
6.	Ex 12:8	Eat the Passover lamb on 15 *Nisan*
7.	Ex 12:9	Eat the Passover lamb roasted
8.	Ex 12:10	Do not leave the Passover lamb to the next day
9.	Ex 12:15	Remove leaven on 14 *Nisan*
10.	Ex 12:18	Eat unleavened bread on the first night of Passover
11.	Ex 12:19	Let no leaven be found throughout Passover
12.	Ex 12:20	Eat nothing containing leaven throughout Passover
13.	Ex 12:43	No apostate may eat the Passover lamb
14.	Ex 12:45	No non-Israelite may eat the Passover lamb
15.	Ex 12:46	Passover lamb should not be shared with others than the designated participants
16.	Ex 12:46	Break no bone of the Passover lamb
17.	Ex 12:48	No uncircumcised male may eat the Passover lamb
18.	Ex 13:2	Sanctify firstborn males of men and cattle
19.	Ex 13:3	Eat no leaven on Passover
20.	Ex 13:7	No leaven should be seen in your possession throughout Passover
21.	Ex 13:8	Recount the story of the Exodus on the eve of 15 *Nisan*
22.	Ex 13:13	Redeem firstborn male donkeys with a sheep
23.	Ex 13:13	If you fail to redeem the firstborn male donkey, break its neck
24.	Ex 16:29	Do not transgress the Sabbath boundary
25.	Ex 20:2	Believe that God exists
26.	Ex 20:3	Do not believe in other gods
27.	Ex 20:4	Do not make idols
28.	Ex 20:5	Do not bow down to idols
29.	Ex 20:5	Do not worship idols
30.	Ex 20:7	Do not take an empty oath
31.	Ex 20:8	Sanctify the Sabbath day
32.	Ex 20:10	Refrain from work on the Sabbath
33.	Ex 20:12	Honour your father and mother
34.	Ex 20:13	Do not murder
35.	Ex 20:13	Do not commit adultery
36.	Ex 20:13	Do not kidnap
37.	Ex 20:13	Do not give false testimony
38.	Ex 20:14	Do not covet that which is your neighbour's
39.	Ex 20:23	Do not make an image in human form even for decorative purposes
40.	Ex 20:25	Do not build an altar from hewn stones
41.	Ex 20:26	Do not ascend the altar by steps
42.	Ex 21:2f	Treat the Hebrew slave according to the law
43.	Ex 21:8,9	The master of a Hebrew slave girl should betroth her to himself or his son
44.	Ex 21:8	If he does not betroth her, he must redeem her
45.	Ex 21:8	A master may not sell a Hebrew slave girl
46.	Ex 21:9	A man must not withhold maintenance, clothing or conjugal rights of his wife or slave girl
47.	Ex 21:15	Do not strike your mother or father
48.	Ex 21:12	The court must carry out the penalty of death by strangulation in appropriate cases
49.	Ex 21:18	The court must judge cases of personal injury
50.	Ex 21:20	The court must execute by the sword murderers and the inhabitants of the wayward city

51.	Ex 21:28f	The court must implement the laws of the goring ox
52.	Ex 21:28	The flesh of the goring ox may not be eaten
53.	Ex 21:33f	The court must implement the laws of damage caused by the pit
54.	Ex 21:37	The court must implement the laws of theft
55.	Ex 22:4	The court must implement the laws of damage caused by an animal walking or eating
56.	Ex 22:5	The court must implement the laws of damage caused by fire
57.	Ex 22:6f	The court must implement the law of the unpaid bailee
58.	Ex 22:8	The court must implement the laws of plaintiff and defendant
59.	Ex 22:9f	The court must implement the laws of the hirer and the paid bailee
60.	Ex 22:13f	The court must implement the law of the borrower
61.	Ex 22:15f	The court must implement the law of seduction
62.	Ex 22:17	The court must not suffer a witch to live
63.	Ex 22:20	Do not oppress a proselyte with words
64.	Ex 22:20	Do not oppress a proselyte in money matters
65.	Ex 22:21	Do not oppress the widow or the orphan
66.	Ex 22:24	Lend money to the needy Israelite
67.	Ex 22:24	Do not reclaim a debt from one you know is unable to pay
68.	Ex 22:24	Do not be involved with the charging of interest
69.	Ex 22:27	Do not curse the judge
70.	Ex 22:27	Do not blaspheme
71.	Ex 22:27	Do not curse a prince or a king
72.	Ex 22:28	Do not settle tithes and priestly gifts in the wrong order
73.	Ex 22:30	Do not eat torn meat from an animal
74.	Ex 22:1	A judge must not hear a claim other than in the presence of the defendant
75.	Ex 23:1	Do not accept the testimony of a known sinner
76.	Ex 23:2	Capital cases cannot be resolved by a simple majority
77.	Ex 23:2	In capital cases a member of the court who has previously argued for the defence may not subsequently argue the prosecution
78.	Ex 23:2	A court must decide by majority vote
79.	Ex 23:3	A court should not decide in favour of the poor out of compassion
80.	Ex 23:5	Help remove the burden from a crouching beast
81.	Ex 23:6	The court should not decide against the defendant on account of previous convictions
82.	Ex 23:7	The court must not decide on the basis of conjecture
83.	Ex 23:8	A judge should not take a bribe
84.	Ex 23:10	During the Sabbatical Year, you should make your produce available to all
85.	Ex 23:12	Abstain from work on the Sabbath
86.	Ex 23:13	Do not swear by a false god
87.	Ex 23:13	Do not lead a city astray to idolatry
88.	Ex 23:14f	Celebrate three pilgrim festivals each year
89.	Ex 23:18	Do not slaughter the Passover lamb when leaven is in your possession
90.	Ex 23:18	Do not keep the inner parts of the Passover lamb until the morning
91.	Ex 23:19	Bring first-fruits to the Temple
92.	Ex 23:19	Do not cook meat and milk together
93.	Ex 23:32	Make no covenant with idolaters
94.	Ex 23:33	Do not permit idolaters to settle in the land of Israel
95.	Ex 25:8	Build a Temple

96.	Ex 25:15	Do not remove the staves from the Ark
97.	Ex 25:20	Priests should arrange Shewbread in the Temple
98.	Ex 27:20f	Priests should kindle the Temple candelabrum daily
99.	Ex 28:2	Priests must wear robes
100.	Ex.28:28	Breastplate must not be moved from the ephod
101.	Ex 28:32	Robes of priest must not be torn
102.	Ex 29:33	Priests must eat the flesh of the sin and guilt offerings
103.	Ex 29:33	No layman may eat these offerings
104.	Ex 30:7	Incense must be offered twice every day
105.	Ex 30:9	Offerings must not be made on the golden altar
106.	Ex 30:13	Every Israelite should contribute half a shekel annually for Temple offerings
107.	Ex 30:19	Priests must wash their hands and feet before service
108.	Ex 30:25	To make the oil of anointing
109.	Ex 30:32	Not to anoint with it other than those designated
110.	Ex 30:32	Not to prepare similar oil for nonsacred use
111.	Ex 30:37	Not to prepare similar incense for nonsacred use in accordance with the formula for sacred incense
112.	Ex 34:15	Do not partake of food offered to idols
113.	Ex 34:21	Abstain from agricultural work in the sabbatical year
114.	Ex 34:26	Do not eat meat boiled in milk
115.	Ex 35:3	The court may not punish on the Sabbath
116.	Lev 1:3f	Offer the burnt offering correctly
117.	Lev 2:1f	Offer the meal offering correctly
118.	Lev 2:11	No leaven or honey may be offered as a burnt offering
119.	Lev 2:13	Do not neglect to put salt on offerings
120.	Lev 2:13	Put salt on all offerings
121.	Lev 4:13f	If the Sanhedrin has unwittingly committed an error in judgement, it must bring a sacrifice
122.	Lev 4:27f	If an individual has unwittingly sinned, he must bring a sin offering
123.	Lev 5:1f	A witness must testify before the court
124.	Lev 5:11f	Certain categories of offenders must bring an offering that varies according to their means
125.	Lev 5:8	The head must not be separated from the body of a fowl killed as a sacrifice
126.	Lev 5:11	Do not put olive oil on the sinner's meal offering
127.	Lev 5:11	Do not put frankincense on the sinner's meal offering
128.	Lev 5:16	One who has used holy things for profane purposes must add a fifth in value to his restitution
129.	Lev 5:17f	One who is not sure whether he sinned should bring a guilt-offering
130.	Lev 5:23	The robber must restore what he has stolen
131.	Lev 5:25	The penitent robber must bring a guilt offering
132.	Lev 6:3	Ashes must be removed from the altar daily
133.	Lev 6:6	Priests must kindle fire daily on the altar
134.	Lev 6:6	Do not extinguish the altar fire
135.	Lev 6:9	Male priests must eat remains of the meal offerings
136.	Lev 6:10	Remains of the meal offerings must not be allowed to become leaven
137.	Lev 6:13f	High Priest must offer a 10th of an ephah of flour morning and evening
138.	Lev 6:16	Nothing may be eaten of a priest's meal offering

139. Lev 6:18f   Offer the sin offering correctly
140. Lev 6:23   The sin offerings of the inner sanctuary may not be eaten
141. Lev 7:1f   Offer the guilt offering correctly
142. Lev 7:11f   Offer the peace offering correctly
143. Lev 7:15   Do not leave offerings past their allotted time
144. Lev 7:17   Burn whatever is left over
145. Lev 7:18   Do not eat *piggul*, a sacrifice on which an essential service has been performed with the wrong intention as to the time at which it should be eaten or offered
146. Lev 7:19   Do not eat sacrificial flesh that has been defiled
147. Lev 7:19   Burn sacrificial flesh that has been defiled
148. Lev 7:22f   Do not eat those fats of cow, sheep and goat that would constitute part of the offering
149. Lev 7:26f   Do not consume the blood of beast or fowl
150. Lev 10:6   Priests must not enter the Temple or serve there with more than thirty days' growth of hair
151. Lev 10:6   Priests must not enter the Temple or serve there with torn garments
152. Lev 10:8f   Priests must not enter the Temple or serve there while drunk
153. Lev 10:7   A priest may not leave the Temple in the middle of performing a service
154. Lev 11:1f   Distinguish clean from unclean beasts
155. Lev 11:4f   Do not eat unclean beasts
156. Lev 11:9f   Distinguish clean from unclean fish
157. Lev 11:11   Do not eat unclean fish
158. Lev 11:13f   Do not eat unclean birds
159. Lev 11:22   Distinguish clean from unclean locusts
160. Lev 11:29f   Eight reptiles are subject to uncleanness
161. Lev 11:34   Implement the ritual purity laws of food and drink
162. Lev 11:39f   Animal carcasses are unclean and convey uncleanness
163. Lev 11:41   Do not eat creatures that crawl on the earth
164. Lev 11:42   Do not eat the worms and maggots in fruit and vegetables
165. Lev 11:43   Do not eat water creatures other than fish
166. Lev 11:44   Do not eat spontaneously generated creeping things
167. Lev 12:2f   Laws of purification following childbirth
168. Lev 12:4   One who is unclean may not eat sacred food
169. Lev 12:6   A woman who gives birth must bring sacrifice
170. Lev 13:2f   A leper is unclean and makes unclean
171. Lev 13:33   A leper must not shave the affected patch
172. Lev 13:45   A confirmed leper must rend his garments
173. Lev 13:47f   Law of garments affected by leprosy
174. Lev 14:2f   Procedure for purifying the confirmed leper on recovery
175. Lev 14:9   He should shave his hair on the seventh day of purification
176. Lev 14:10   He should bring a sacrifice on the eighth day
177. Lev 14:9   A person who is unclean must immerse completely in at least 40 *seah* of water
178. Lev 14:34   Law of houses affected by leprosy
179. Lev 15:2   Law of the *zav*, man with involuntary seminal discharge
180. Lev 15:14   On purification of the *zav*, he must bring a bird sacrifice
181. Lev 15:16f   Semen is unclean and renders unclean
182. Lev 15:19f   The menstruant is unclean and renders unclean
183. Lev 15:25f   A woman with an untimely menstrual flow is unclean and renders unclean

184. Lev 15:29   On purification she must bring a bird sacrifice
185. Lev 16:2   Restriction of times at which a high or ordinary priest may enter the Sanctuary
186. Lev 16:3   High priest must carry out the Day of Atonement ritual
187. Lev 17:3   Sacrifices must not be slaughtered outside the Temple courtyard
188. Lev 17:13   Cover the blood when you slaughter a bird or wild animal
189. Lev.18:6   Avoid close contact with those with whom sexual relations are forbidden
190. Lev 18:7   Do not engage in homosexual acts with your father
191. Lev 18:7   Do not have sexual intercourse with your mother
192. Lev 18:8   Do not have sexual intercourse with a wife of your father even if she is not your mother
193. Lev 18:9   Do not have sexual intercourse with your sister
194. Lev 18:10   Do not have sexual intercourse with your son's daughter
195. Lev 18:10   Do not have sexual intercourse with your daughter's daughter
196. Lev 18:11   Do not have sexual intercourse with your daughter
197. Lev 18:11   Do not have sexual intercourse with your sister from the same father
198. Lev 18:12   Do not have sexual intercourse with your father's sister
199. Lev 18:13   Do not have sexual intercourse with your mother's sister
200. Lev 18:14   Do not engage in homosexual acts with your father's brother
201. Lev 18:15   Do not have sexual intercourse with your father's brother's wife
202. Lev 18:16   Do not have sexual intercourse with your daughter-in-law
203. Lev 18:17   Do not have sexual intercourse with your brother's wife
204. Lev 18:17   Do not have sexual intercourse with a woman and her daughter
205. Lev 18:17   Do not have sexual intercourse with a woman and her son's daughter
206. Lev 18:17   Do not have sexual intercourse with a woman and her daughter's daughter
207. Lev 18:18   Do not have sexual intercourse with your wife's sister during your wife's lifetime
208. Lev 18:19   Do not have sexual intercourse with a menstruant woman
209. Lev 18:21   Do not 'give your seed to Molech'
210. Lev 18:22   Do not particpate in male homosexual acts
211. Lev 18:23   A man may not commit sexual acts with an animal
212. Lev 18:23   A woman may not commit sexual acts with an animal
213. Lev 19:3   Fear your mother and father
214. Lev 19:4   Do not turn to idols
215. Lev 19:4   Do not manufacture idols
216. Lev 19:6   Do not eat sacrificial meat after its due time
217. Lev 19:9   Do not completely reap the corners of your field
218. Lev 19:10   Leave the corners for the poor to harvest
219. Lev 19:9   Do not pick up fallen gleanings of your field
220. Lev 19:10   Leave the gleanings for the poor to pick up
221. Lev 19:10   Do not harvest the small bunches of grapes
222. Lev 19:10   Leave the small bunches for the poor
223. Lev 19:10   Do not pick up the grapes that fall as you harvest
224. Lev 19:10   Leave the fallen grapes for the poor
225. Lev 19:11   Do not steal
226. Lev 19:11   Do not deny holding other people's property
227. Lev 19:11   Do not support a denial by a false oath
228. Lev 19:12   Do not swear a false oath
229. Lev 19:13   Do not forcefully retain other people's property
230. Lev 19:13   Do not rob

231.	Lev 19:13	Do not delay payment of a hired worker
232.	Lev 19:14	Do not curse your fellow Israelite
233.	Lev 19:14	Do not mislead anyone
234.	Lev 19:15	Do not act unjustly
235.	Lev 19:15	Do not respect persons in judgment
236.	Lev 19:15	Mete out justice equitably
237.	Lev 19:16	Do not gossip or slander
238.	Lev 19:16	Do not refrain from saving people from danger
239.	Lev 19:17	Do not nurture hatred in your heart
240.	Lev 19:17	Reprove sinners
241.	Lev 19:17	Do not put anyone to shame
242.	Lev 19:18	Do not take vengeance on your fellow
243.	Lev 19:18	Do not bear a grudge against your fellow
244.	Lev 19:18	Love your neighbour as yourself
245.	Lev 19:19	Do not cross-breed animals or birds
246.	Lev 19:19	Do not sow mixed species of seeds together
247.	Lev 19:23	Do not eat fruit produced by a tree in its first three years
248.	Lev 19:24	The fruit of the fourth year is sacred and must be redeemed or eaten in Jerusalem
249.	Lev 19:26	Do not eat gluttonously
250.	Lev 19:26	Do not practise enchantments
251.	Lev 19:26	Do not prognosticate luck times, or conjure
252.	Lev 19:27	Do not shave the corners of your head
253.	Lev 19:27	Do not shave the corners of your beard
254.	Lev 19:28	Do not tattoo yourself
255.	Lev 19:30	Treat the Temple Sanctuary with awe
256.	Lev 19:31	Do not practise as a wizard
257.	Lev 19:31	Do not practise as a sorcerer
258.	Lev 19:32	Rise before the elderly and honour the wise
259.	Lev 19:35	Do not cheat with weights and measures
260.	Lev 19:36	Make sure your scales and measures are accurate
261.	Lev 20:9	Do not curse your father or your mother
262.	Lev 20:14	The court must carry out the sentence of burning those liable
263.	Lev 20:23	Do not follow the way of the nations
264.	Lev 21:1	A priest must not defile himself by contact with a corpse
265.	Lev 21:2,3	He must defile himself to bury close relatives
266.	Lev 21:6	A priest who has bathed to remove defilement may not serve until nightfall
267.	Lev 21:7	A priest may not marry a prostitute
268.	Lev 21:7	A priest may not marry a woman disqualified from the priesthood
269.	Lev 21:7	A priest may not marry a divorcee
270.	Lev 21:8	Pay respect to priests
271.	Lev 21:11	The high priest may not enter a tent where there is a corpse
272.	Lev 21:11	He may not defile himself to bury even his mother or father
273.	Lev 21:13	He must marry a virgin
274.	Lev 21:14	He must not marry a widow, divorcee, woman disqualified from the priesthood or a prostitute
275.	Lev 21:15	He must not have intercourse with a widow
276.	Lev 21:17	A priest with a permanent defect must not serve

277. Lev 21:18   A priest with a transient defect must not serve
278. Lev 21:23   A priest with a defect must not enter the sanctuary
279. Lev 22:3   An unclean priest must not serve
280. Lev 22:4   An unclean priest must not eat the heave-offering
281. Lev 22:10   A nonpriest must not eat the heave-offering
282. Lev 22:10   Even the priest's servant may not eat it
283. Lev 22:11   An uncircumcised priest must not eat the offerings
284. Lev 22:12   A woman disqualified from the priesthood may not eat the offerings
285. Lev 22:15   Do not eat untithed food
286. Lev 22:21   Every sacrifice must be free from blemish
287. Lev 22:22   Do not slaughter a blemished animal as a sacrifice
288. Lev 22:22   Do not cause a blemish to a sacrificial animal
289. Lev 22:24   Do not sprinkle its blood on the altar
290. Lev 22:25   Do not offer up its fat
291. Lev 22:24   Do not sprinkle its blood on the altar
292. Lev 22:24   Do not castrate any animal
293. Lev 22:25   Do not accept a blemished animal as a sacrifice from a non-Israelite
294. Lev 22:27   Do not offer an animal less than eight days old
295. Lev 22:28   Do not offer an animal and its offspring on one day
296. Lev 22:32   Do not act in such a way as to profane God's name
297. Lev 22:32   Sanctify God's name, even through martyrdom
298. Lev 23:7   Refrain from work on the first day of Passover
299. Lev 23:7   Do no work on the first day of Passover
300. Lev 23:8   Offer the Passover *Musaf*
301. Lev 23:8   Refrain from work on the seventh day of Passover
302. Lev 23:8   Do no work on the seventh day of Passover
303. Lev 23:10   Bring the *Omer* offering on 16 *Nisan*
304. Lev 23:14   Do not eat bread of the new harvest before the *Omer*
305. Lev 23:14   Do not eat roasted corn of the new harvest before the *Omer*
306. Lev 23:14   Do not eat fresh green ears of corn of the new harvest before the *Omer*
307. Lev 23:15   Count seven complete weeks from the day of the *Omer*
308. Lev 23:16f   Offer two loaves of bread on Pentecost
309. Lev 23:21   Refrain from work on Pentecost
310. Lev 23:21   Do no work on Pentecost
311. Lev 23:24   Refrain from work on 1 *Tishri*
312. Lev 23:25   Do no work on 1 *Tishri*
313. Lev 23:25   Offer *Musaf* on 1 *Tishri*
314. Lev 23:27   Afflict yourselves on 10 *Tishri*
315. Lev 23:29   Do not eat or drink on 10 *Tishri* (*Yom Kippur*)
316. Lev 23:31   Do no work on 10 *Tishri*
317. Lev 23:32   Refrain from work on 10 *Tishri*
318. Lev 23:27   Offer *Musaf* on 10 *Tishri*
319. Lev 23:35   Refrain from work on the first day of Tabernacles
320. Lev 23:35   Do no work on the first day of Tabernacles
321. Lev 23:36   Offer *Musaf* on all seven days of Tabernacles
322. Lev 23:36   Refrain from work on *Shemini Atzeret*
323. Lev 23:36   Do no work on *Shemini Atzeret*

324. Lev 23:36   Offer *Musaf* on *Shemini Atzeret*
325. Lev 23:40   Take the four species on Tabernacles
326. Lev 23:42   Dwell in booths throughout Tabernacles
327. Lev 25:4   Do not sow your fields in the sabbatical year
328. Lev 25:4   Do not prune your vines in the sabbatical year
329. Lev 25:5   Do not reap that which grows of its own accord in the sabbatical year
330. Lev 25:5   Do not harvest fruit in the sabbatical year
331. Lev 25:8   The court must count seven sabbatical year cycles to make up the Jubilee
332. Lev 25:9   Sound the *shofar* on the Day of Atonement in the Jubilee year
333. Lev 25:10   The High Court must sanctify the Jubilee year
334. Lev 25:11   Do not work on land or trees in the Jubilee year
335. Lev 25:11   Do not reap that which grows of its own accord in the Jubilee year
336. Lev 25:11   Do not harvest fruit in the Jubilee year
337. Lev 25:14   Conduct commercial transactions correctly
338. Lev 25:14   Do not wrong one another in commerce
339. Lev 25:17   Do not offend one another with words
340. Lev 25:23   Israelite inheritance must not be sold permanently
341. Lev 25:24   Land must be returned to its owner in the Jubilee year
342. Lev 25:29f   Implement the law of the houses of the walled city
343. Lev 25:34   No part of the Levitical towns may be sold
344. Lev 25:36   Do not lend money or goods to an Israelite on interest
345. Lev 25:42   Do not treat an Israelite slave in a humiliating manner
346. Lev 25:42   Do not sell him in the market
347. Lev 25:43   Do not force him to work arduously
348. Lev 25:53   Do not permit others to force him to work arduously
349. Lev 25:46   A heathen slave should be kept permanently
350. Lev 26:1   Do not make a figured stone on which to bow down
351. Lev 27:2f   Implement the law of valuation for vows of persons
352. Lev 27:10   If anyone dedicates an animal by vow as a sacrifice he must not substitute another for it
353. Lev 27:10   If he does substitute, both animals are holy
354. Lev 27:12f   Implement the law of valuation for vows of animals
355. Lev 27:14f   Implement the law of valuation for vows of houses
356. Lev 27:16f   Implement the law of valuation for vows of fields
357. Lev 27:26   Do not change the status of a dedicated animal
358. Lev 27:28f   Implement the law of dedicated things
359. Lev 27:28   Such things may not be sold by the priests
360. Lev 27:28   Nor may they be redeemed by their original owners
361. Lev 27:32   Take a tithe of cattle and sheep
362. Lev 27:33   Do not sell or redeem an animal designated as tithe
363. Num 5:2f   The unclean must be sent outside the camp
364. Num 5:3   An unclean person may not enter the sanctuary
365. Num 5:7   The sinner must repent and confess his or her sin to God
366. Num 5:12f   To implement the law of the suspected wife
367. Num 5:15   The meal offering of the suspected wife must not contain oil
368. Num 5:15   The meal offering of the suspected wife must not contain frankincense
369. Num 6:3   The *Nazirite* must eat nothing containing wine
370. Num 6:3   The *Nazirite* must not eat grapes

371. Num 6:3   The *Nazirite* must not eat raisins
372. Num 6:3   The *Nazirite* must not eat grape pips
373. Num 6:4   The *Nazirite* must not eat grape skins
374. Num 6:5   He must not cut his hair
375. Num 6:5   He must let his hair grow
376. Num 6:6   He must not enter a tent where there is a corpse
377. Num 6:7   He must not defile himself, even for close relatives
378. Num 6:9f   He must shave off his hair and bring sacrifice
379. Num 6:22f   The priests must bless the people with the triple blessing
380. Num 7:9   The priests must carry the Ark on their shoulders
381. Num 9:10f   If anyone was unable to offer the Passover lamb on the proper date on account of uncleanness or distance, he may offer it on 14 *Iyar*
382. Num 9:11   The second Passover should be eaten with *matzah* and bitter herbs
383. Num 9:12   None of it should be left over till morning
384. Num 9:12   No bone of it should be broken
385. Num 10:10   The *shofar* should be sounded over the sacrifices
386. Num 15:20   An offering for the priests must be separated from the dough
387. Num 15:38   Make fringes on the corners of your garments
388. Num 15:39   Do not go astray after your eyes or imagination
389. Num 18:3   Place guards around the Temple
390. Num 18:5   Do not fail to place guards around the Temple
391. Num 18:3   Levites and priests must not do each other's work
392. Num 18:4   Non-Aaronide priests may not serve in the Temple
393. Num 18:15   Israelites must redeem their firstborn sons
394. Num 18:17   Do not redeem the firstborn of clean animals
395. Num 18:23   Levites must serve in the Temple
396. Num 18:24   Give the first tithe to the Levites
397. Num 18:24   Levites must give a tithe of their tithe to the priests
398. Num 19   Carry out the cleansing procedure of the red heifer
399. Num 19:14   A corpse is unclean and renders unclean by touch or through being under the same roof
400. Num 19:19   The water containing ashes of the red heifer cleanses the unclean and defiles the clean
401. Num 27:8f   To operate the laws of inheritance
402. Num 28:3f   To offer a daily sacrifice morning and afternoon
403. Num 28:9f   To offer a *Musaf* sacrifice on Sabbaths
404. Num 28:11   To offer a *Musaf* sacrifice on New Moons
405. Num 28:27   To offer a *Musaf* sacrifice on Pentecost
406. Num 29:1   Hear the sound of the *shofar* on 1 *Tishri*
407. Num 30:2f   Implement laws on the annulment of vows
408. Num 30:3   Do not break a vow
409. Num 35:2   Set up towns for the Levites in the land of Israel
410. Num 35:12   Do not kill a murderer without due process of law
411. Num 35:25   An accidental homicide must be sent to the city of refuge
412. Num 35:30   A witness cannot act as a judge in capital cases
413. Num 35:31   Do not ransom a murderer who is sentenced to death
414. Num 35:32   Do not ransom an accidental homicide who is sentenced to flee to the city of refuge
415. Dt 1:17   Do not appoint as judge one who is unfit for office
416. Dt 1:17   The judge must not fear the litigants

417. Dt 5:18   Do not desire in your heart that which belongs to another
418. Dt 6:4   Proclaim and believe in the unity of God
419. Dt 6:5   Love God with all your heart, soul and strength
420. Dt 6:7   Learn Torah and teach it
421. Dt 6:7   Recite the *Shema* morning and evening
422. Dt 6:8   Wear *tefillin* on your arm
423. Dt 6:8   Wear *tefillin* on your head
424. Dt 6:98   Affix a *mezuzah* to your door
425. Dt 6:16   Do not test a prophet excessively
426. Dt 7:2   Destroy the seven nations
427. Dt 7:2   Do not pity idolaters in the land of Israel; do not permit them a foothold in the land
428. Dt 7:3   Do not intermarry with idolaters
429. Dt 7:25   Do not benefit from the overlay of idols
430. Dt 7:26   Do not benefit from idols or their accessories
431. Dt 8:10   Recite the grace after meals
432. Dt 10:19   Love the stranger
433. Dt 10:20   Fear God
434. Dt 10:20   Serve God through daily prayer
435. Dt 10:20   Cleave to the sages and their disciples
436. Dt 10:20   Swear truly by God's name
437. Dt 12:2   Destroy idols and their appurtenances
438. Dt 12:4   Do not destroy any holy thing or erase God's name
439. Dt 12:11   Bring sacrifices to the Temple
440. Dt 12:13   Do not make sacrifice outside the Temple courtyard
441. Dt 12:14   Offer your sacrifices only in the Temple
442. Dt 12:15   Redeem sacrificial animals which have suffered a blemish
443. Dt 12:17   Do not eat unredeemed Second Tithe grain outside Jerusalem
444. Dt 12:17   Do not drink unredeemed Second Tithe wine outside Jerusalem
445. Dt 12:17   Do not eat unredeemed Second Tithe oil outside Jerusalem
446. Dt 12:17   Priests may not eat unblemished firstborn lambs outside Jerusalem
447. Dt 12:17   Priests may not eat sin- or guilt-offerings outside the Temple precincts
448. Dt 12:17   Priests may not eat the flesh of burnt offerings
449. Dt 12:17   Priest may not eat the flesh of any offerings before the blood has been sprinkled
450. Dt 12:17   Priests may not eat firstfruits outside Jerusalem
451. Dt 12:19   Do not neglect the Levites
452. Dt 12:21   Practise animal slaughter as prescribed
453. Dt 12:23   Do not eat the limb torn from a living animal
454. Dt 12:26   Bring your sacrifices to the Temple even from abroad
455. Dt 13:1   Do not add to the commands of the Torah
456. Dt 13:1   Do not diminish from the commands of the Torah
457. Dt 13:4   Do not listen to one who prophesies in the name of an idol
458. Dt 13:7   Do not lead any Israelite astray to idolatry
459. Dt 13:9   Do not love the one who leads astray
460. Dt 13:9   Do not desist from hating him
461. Dt 13:9   Do not save him
462. Dt 13:9   Do not plead in his favour
463. Dt 13:9   Do not refrain from testifying against him

464.	Dt 13:15	The court must examine the evidence and question the witnesses thoroughly
465.	Dt 13:17	Burn the 'city that has strayed'
466.	Dt 13:17	Do not permit it to be rebuilt
467.	Dt 13:18	Do not benefit from it
468.	Dt 14:1	Do not make incisions in your flesh; whether for the dead or an idol; do not be divisive
469.	Dt 14:1	Do not pluck your hair out for the dead
470.	Dt 14:3	Do not eat the meat of invalidated sacrifices
471.	Dt 14:11	Examine fowl to know which are permitted
472.	Dt 14:19	Do not eat swarming, flying creatures
473.	Dt 14:21	Do not eat carrion
474.	Dt 14:22	Set aside Second Tithe after the first
475.	Dt 14:28	Set aside a tithe and give it to the poor
476.	Dt 15:2	Release debts at the end of the sabbatical year
477.	Dt 15:2	Do not claim a debt that has passed the sabbatical year
478.	Dt 15:3	Compel the non-Israelite to pay his debt
479.	Dt 15:7	Do not restrain yourself from helping your brother
480.	Dt 15:7	Give freely to needy Israelites and sojourners
481.	Dt 15:9	Do not be deterred by the sabbatical release of debts from lending to your brother Israelite
482.	Dt 15:13	Do not release a Hebrew slave without maintenance
483.	Dt 15:14	Give maintenance to the Hebrew slave you release
484.	Dt 15:19	Do not work an animal designed for sacrifice
485.	Dt 15:19	Do not shear an animal designed for sacrifice
486.	Dt 16:3	Do not eat leaven after midday on Passover eve
487.	Dt 16:4	Do not leave overnight meat of the festival offering which accompanies the Passover
488.	Dt 16:14	Rejoice in the Pilgrim festivals
489.	Dt 16:16	All males should appear before the Lord on the three Pilgrim festivals, bringing offerings
490.	Dt 16:16	They should not appear empty handed
491.	Dt 16:18	Appoint judges and officers to uphold and enforce the law
492.	Dt 16:21	Do not plant a tree within the Temple precinct
493.	Dt 16:22	Do not set up a pillar for worship
494.	Dt 17:1	Do not offer a blemished animal as a sacrifice
495.	Dt 17:10	Act in accordance with the decisions of the Sanhedrin
496.	Dt 17:11	Do not depart from their words
497.	Dt 17:15	Appoint a king
498.	Dt 17:15	Do not appoint a non-Israelite as king
499.	Dt 17:16	The king must not have too many horses
500.	Dt 17:17	He must not have more than 18 wives inclusive of concubines
501.	Dt 17:17	He must not have too much silver and gold
502.	Dt 17:18	He must write himself a Torah scroll in addition to the one he must write as a common Israelite
503.	Dt 17:16	Do not settle in Egypt
504.	Dt 18:1	Levites must not take a share of the spoils of war
505.	Dt 18:2	Levites are not allotted territory in the land of Israel
506.	Dt 18:3	When you slaughter an animal for meat, give the priests the shoulder, the two cheeks, and the maw

507.	Dt 18:4	Give priests' due from your grain, wine and oil
508.	Dt 18:4	Give the first fleece to the priests
509.	Dt 18:8	Priests' watches should share equally with festival offerings
510.	Dt 18:10	Do not practise sorcery
511.	Dt 18:10	Do not practise witchcraft
512.	Dt 18:10	Do not practise enchantment
513.	Dt 18:10	Do not consult a wizard
514.	Dt 18:11	Do not consult a sorcerer
515.	Dt 18:11	Do not consult the dead
516.	Dt 18:15	Obey a true prophet
517.	Dt 18:20	Do not prophesy falsely in God's name
518.	Dt 18:20	Do not prophesy in the name of an idol
519.	Dt 18:22	Do not fear to execute a false prophet
520.	Dt 19:2	Set up cities of refuge
521.	Dt 19:13	A judge should not pity the murderer
522.	Dt 19:14	Do not move boundary marks or infringe the proprietary rights of others
523.	Dt 19:15	The court may not make any determination on the testimony of a lone witness
524.	Dt 19:19	Witnesses whose falsity is established by testimony that they were absent from the scene of the crime must receive the punishment that they intended for the accused
525.	Dt 20:1	Do not fear or flee before the nations in war
526.	Dt 20:2	Appoint an anointed priest to address the army
527.	Dt 20:10	Make an offer of peace before commencing battle
528.	Dt 20:16	Leave none alive of the seven nations
529.	Dt 20:19	Do not destroy fruit trees when besieging
530.	Dt 21:4	The valley where the ceremony is carried out may be neither cultivated nor sown
532.	Dt 21:10f	Follow the law of the beautiful captive
533.	Dt 21:14	Release, do not sell her, if you do not want her as a wife
534.	Dt 21:22	Hang the blasphemer or idolater after execution
536.	Dt 21:23	Do not leave him hanging overnight
537.	Dt 21:23	Bury all convicts on the day of execution
538.	Dt 21:1	If you find a lost object, return it to its owner
539.	Dt 21:3	Do not pretend you have not seen it
540.	Dt 21:4	Help your brother Israelite to unload his beast
541.	Dt 21:4	Help him to load it
542.	Dt 21:5	A man must not wear women's clothing
543.	Dt 21:5	A woman must not wear men's clothing
544.	Dt 21:6	Do not take the mother bird with the young
545.	Dt 22:7	If you take the young, first send away the mother bird
546.	Dt 22:8	Make a parapet around your roof
547.	Dt 22:8	Remove all dangerous objects from your house
548.	Dt 22:9	Do not sow wheat and barley together in the vineyard
549.	Dt 22:9	Do not eat or otherwise benefit from crops thus sown
550.	Dt 22:10	Do not plow with an ox and ass together
551.	Dt 22:11	Do not wear garments in which wool and linen are woven together
552.	Dt 22:13	Marriage must take place through the *kiddushin* process
553.	Dt 22:19	If a man falsely alleges that his new wife is not a virgin, he forfeits the right to divorce her.

554.	Dt 22:19	He is forbidden to divorce her against her will
555.	Dt 22:24	Execute by stoning those liable to the penalty
556.	Dt 22:26	Do not punish one who trangresses under duress
557.	Dt 22:29	The rapist must marry his victim if she wishes
558.	Dt 22:29	He has no right to divorce her
559.	Dt 23:2	One with crushed testicles or maimed penis may not marry a native Israelitess
560.	Dt 23:3	A *mamzer* may not marry a native Israelitess
561.	Dt 23:4	An Ammonite or Moabite proselyte may not marry a native Israelitess
562.	Dt 23:7	Do not seek peace with Ammonites or Moabites
563.	Dt 23:8,9	A third-generation Edomite proselyte may marry a native Israelitess
564.	Dt 23:8,9	A third-generation Egyptian proselyte may marry a native Israelitess
565.	Dt 23:11	No unclean person may ascend the Temple mount
566.	Dt 23:13	In war, set aside latrines for the army
567.	Dt 23:14	Equip the latrines properly
568.	Dt 23:16	If a slave escapes from abroad, do not return him to his owner; he must be set free
569.	Dt 23:17	Do not taunt him verbally
570.	Dt 23:18	Do not have intercourse with a prostitute
571.	Dt 23:19	Animals received as the fee of a married prostitute or in exchange for a dog may not be sacrificed in the Temple
572.	Dt 23:20	Do not lend on interest to an Israelite
573.	Dt 23:21	Do not lend on interest to a non-Israelite
574.	Dt 23:22	Do not delay fulfilment of vows
575.	Dt 23:24	Fulfil your vows
576.	Dt 23:25	Allow your workers to eat from the crops among which they are working
577.	Dt 23:26	The worker should eat only when he has completed his job
578.	Dt 23:25	The worker should not take more than his own needs
579.	Dt 24:1	If a man divorces his wife, he should write a bill of divorce and place it in her hand
580.	Dt 24:4	A man may not remarry his divorced wife if she has since been married to another
581.	Dt 24:5	A bridegroom may not be enlisted in the army or for any public service
582.	Dt 24:5	He must be free for a year to make his wife happy
583.	Dt 24:6	Do not take as a pledge utensils needed for a living
584.	Dt 24:8	Do not evade the leprosy law by manually removing a symptom
585.	Dt 24:11	Do not forcefully enter the debtor's house to take a pledge
586.	Dt 24:12	Do not retain a pledge when it is needed by its owner
587.	Dt 24:13	Return a pledge if it is needed by its owner
588.	Dt 24:15	Pay a hired worker on the day he does the job
589.	Dt 24:16	The court must not accept testimony from relatives
590.	Dt 24:17	A judge must not bend the law in cases
591.	Dt 24:17	The widow's garment may not be taken as a pledge
592.	Dt 24:19	Do not go back to pick up a sheaf forgotten at harvest
593.	Dt 24:19	Leave the forgotten sheaf for the poor
594.	Dt 25:2	The officers of the court must inflict 39 stripes with a strap on condemned officers
595.	Dt 25:3	They must not exceed 39 stripes
596.	Dt 25:4	Do not prevent an animal eating while it is working
597.	Dt 25:5	A childless widow may not marry a stranger
598.	Dt 25:5	Her deceased husband's brother must marry her
599.	Dt 25:9	If he refuses, she must perform the ceremony of releasing the shoe

600.	Dt 25:12	If someone is about to kill another, you should save the victim even at the expense of the attacker's life
601.	Dt 25:12	Do not have pity on the attacker
602.	Dt 25:13f	Do not retain in your possession inaccurate weights and measures
603.	Dt 25:17	Remember and say what Amalek did to us
604.	Dt 25:19	Cut off the seed of Amalek
605.	Dt 25:19	Do not forget Amalek
606.	Dt 26:3	Make the firstfruits declaration
607.	Dt 26:13	Make confession over Second Tithe
608.	Dt 26:14	Do not eat Second Tithe when in mourning
609.	Dt 26:14	Do not eat Second Tithe when unclean
610.	Dt 26:14	Do not spend money for which Second Tithe has been redeemed on anything other than food, drink or unguents
611.	Dt 28:9	Emulate the ways of God
612.	Dt 28:12	Assemble men, women and children on the Feast of Tabernacles, following the sabbatical year, for the king to read Deuteronomy to them
613.	Dt 19	Every male Israelite must write a scroll of the Torah for himself

(In HDJ, pp. 433–456)

DISCUSSION

1. Critically evaluate the traditional Jewish view that the 613 commandments were given by God to Moses on Mt Sinai.

2. In what ways does the belief in *Torah MiSinai* serve as the basis of Jewish theology and law?

FURTHER READING

Biale, Rachel, *Women and Jewish Law: The Essential Texts, Their History, and the Relevance for Today*, Schocken, 1995.

Borowitz, Eugene, Schwartz, Frances Weinman, *The Jewish Moral Virtues*, Jewish Publication Society, 1999.

Casgin, Esther, *Mitzvot As Spiritual Practices: A Jewish Guidebook for the Jew*, Jason Aronson, 1997.

Chill, Abraham, *The Mitzvot: The Commandments and their Rationale*, Bloch, 1974.

Hoenig, Samuel, *The Essence of Talmudic Law and Thought*, Jason Aronson, 1993.

Isaacs, Ronald, *Every Person's Guide to Jewish Law*, Jason Aronson, 2000.

Jacob, Walter, Zemer, Moshe (eds), *Re-Examining Progressive Halakhah*, Berghahn, 2002.

Katz, Jacob, *The Shabbes Goy: A Study of Halakhic Flexibility*, Jewish Publication Society, 1992.

Leet, Leonora, *Renewing the Covenant: A Kabbalistic Guide to Jewish Spirituality*, Innter Traditions International, 1999.

Lewittes, Mendell, *Jewish Law: An Introduction*, Jason Aronson, 1993.

Rabinowitz, Abraham Hirsh, *The Study of the Talmud: Understanding the Halachic Mind*, Jason Aronson, 1996.

Sears, David (ed.), *Compassion for Humanity in the Jewish Tradition*, Jason Aronson, 1998.

Warshowfsky, Mark, *Jewish Living: A Guide to Contemporary Reform Practice*, UAHC Press, 2000.

Wolowelsky, Joel, *Women, Jewish Law and Modernity: New Opportunities in a Post-Feminist Age*, KTAV, 1997.

Zemer, Moshe, *Evolving Halakhah: A Progressive Approach to Traditional Jewish Law*, Jewish Lights, 1999.

CHAPTER 65

Sin and Repentance

Figure 65 Adam and Eve. Artist: Cranach, Lucas the Elder: 1472–1553: German. Copyright The Art Archive/National Museum of Prague/Dagli Orti.

In the Bible, sin is understood as a transgression of God's decree. In Biblical Hebrew the word *het* means 'to miss' or 'to fail'. Here sin is conceived as a failing, a lack of perfection in carrying out one's duty. The term *peshah* means a 'breach'; it indicates a broken relationship between human beings and God. The word *avon* expresses the idea of crookedness. Thus according to Biblical terminology, a sin is characterized by failure, waywardness, and illicit action. A sinner is one who has not fulfilled his obligations to God.

According to rabbinic Judaism, sins can be classified according to their gravity as indicated by the punishments prescribed by Biblical law. The more serious the punishment, the more serious the offence. A distinction is also drawn in rabbinic texts between sins against other human beings (*bain adam la-havero*) and offences against God alone (*bain adam la-Makom*). Sins against God can be atoned for by repentance, prayer, and giving charity. In cases of offence against others, however, such acts require restitution and placation as a condition of atonement.

Rabbinic literature teaches that there are two tendencies in every person: the good inclination (*yetzer ha-tov*), and the **evil inclination** (*yetzer ha-ra*). The former urges individuals to do what is right, whereas the latter encourages sinful acts. At all times, a person is to be on guard against assaults of the *yetzer ha-ra*. It is not possible to hide one's sins from God since the Omnipresent knows all things. In the words of the *Mishnah*, 'Know what is above thee – an eye that sees, an ear that hears, and all the deeds are written in a book.' (*Mishnah Avot*, 2:1) Thus, God is aware of all sinful deeds, yet through repentance and prayer it is possible to achieve reconciliation with him.

In rabbinic sources the *yetzer ha-ra* is often identified with the sex drive (which embraces human physical appetites in general as well as aggressive desires). Frequently it is portrayed as the force which impels human beings to satisfy their longings. Although it is described as the evil inclination, it is essential to life itself. Thus the **midrash** remarks that if it were not for the *yetzer ha-ra*, no one would build a house, marry, have children, or engage in trade. For this reason Scripture states: 'And God saw everything that He had made and behold, it was very good' (Gen. 1:31). Here 'good' refers to the good inclination; very good to the evil inclination. In this light the *Talmud* relates that the men of the Great Synagogue (Ezra and his colleagues) wanted to kill the *yetzer ha-ra*, but the evil inclination (who is here personified) warned them that this would result in the destruction of the world. As a result, he was imprisoned, and they subsequently put out his eyes so that he would not be able to entice men to incest. (Yoma 69b)

According to the rabbis, human beings are engaged in a continual struggle against the *yetzer ha-ra*. In this quest the Torah serves as the fundamental defence. Hence the *Talmud* declares that the Torah is the antidote to the poison of the *yetzer ha-ra*. The implication of this passage is that when human beings submit to the discipline provided by the Torah, they are liberated from the influence of the *yetzer ha-ra*. The rabbis state that this is like a king who struck his son and subsequently urged him to keep a plaster on his wound. When the wound is protected in this way the prince can eat and drink without coming to harm. But if he removes the plaster, the wound will grow worse if the prince indulges his appetites. For the rabbis the Torah is the plaster which protects the king's son. (Kidd, 30b)

Rabbinic literature also teaches that this struggle against the *yetzer ha-ra* is unending. All that one can do is to subdue it through self-control – no person can destroy it. Arguably such a view parallels the Christian concept of original sin, yet unlike Christian exegetes, the rabbis interpreted Genesis 2–3 as simply indicating how death became part of human destiny. According to the rabbis death was the direct result of Adam's disobedience. Although they did not teach a doctrine of original sin on this basis, they did accept that 'the wickedness of man was great in the earth, and that every imagination of the thoughts of his heart was only evil continually' (Gen. 6:5). They explain this by positing the existence of the evil inclination within every person.

In the Bible the concept of repentance is of fundamental importance. Throughout the prophetic books sinners are admonished to give up their evil ways and return to God. Thus 2 Kings declares: 'Yet the Lord warned Israel and Judah by the hand of every prophet, and of every seer, saying: "Turn from your evil ways, and keep my commandments and my statutes, in accordance with all the law which I commanded your fathers, and which I sent to you by my servants the prophets"' (2 Kings 17:13). According to Jewish teaching, atonement can only be attained after a process of repentance involving the recognition of sin. It requires remorse, restitution, and a determination not to commit a similar offence. Both the Bible and rabbinic sources emphasize that God does not want the death of the sinner, but desires that he return from his evil ways. Unlike in Christianity, God does not instigate this process through prevenient grace; rather, atonement depends on the sinner's sincere act of repentance. Only at this stage does God grant forgiveness and pardon.

With regard to unwitting offences against ritual law, a sin offering was required in the Biblical period as a sacramental act that restores the relationship between God and the transgressor. Following the destruction of the second Temple in 70 CE, prayer took the place of sacrifice. In addition, fasting, kindly acts, and the giving of charity were also viewed as a means of atonement. In the Jewish yearly cycle, a ten day period (Ten Days of Penitence) is set aside, commencing with *Rosh Hashanah* (New Year) and ending with **Yom Kippur** (Day of Atonement) which is devoted to prayer and fasting. An echo of the ancient scapegoat ritual is observed by some traditional Jews on the eve of the Day of Atonement, whereby an individual's sins are expiated by the death of a white fowl. The Day of Atonement, however, only brings forgiveness for sins committed against God; for sins against others, atonement is granted only after the sinner has made final restitution and sought forgiveness from the offended party.

In the Middle Ages the twelfth-century philosopher Moses Maimonides' discussion of repentance in the *Mishneh Torah* summarizes the rabbinic view. According to Maimonides, when a person sins wittingly or unwittingly and repents of his wrongdoing, he is obliged to confess his sins to God. Now that the Temple is no longer standing, he asserts, repentance itself atones for all sins. True repentance takes place if the sinner has the opportunity of sinning, but refrains from doing so because he has repented. The sinner must confess verbally, and it is praiseworthy for him to do so in public. Whoever is too proud to confess his sins to others, he asserts, but keeps them to himself, is not a true penitent. This, however, does not apply to offences against God where a declaration of sinfulness should be made to him alone. With regard to offences against others, the sinner must make restitution and beg for forgiveness. Here Maimonides maintains that repentance is effected by a resolve to give up the transgression by confession and restitution – mortification plays no role in this process.

Other medieval writers differed regarding the necessity of ascetic actions. In his *Shaare Teshuvah*, for example, the thirteenth-century writer Jonah ben Abraham Gerondi lists twenty factors of sincere repentance, some of which involve self-mortificaion: (l) remorse; (2) relinquishing sin; (3) pain for the sin; (4) affliction of the body through fasting and weeping; (5) fear of the consequences of the sinful act and of repeating it; (6) shame; (7) submission to God; (8) gentleness in future actions; (9) overcoming physical lust through asceticism; (10) the use of the organ with which the sinner transgressed to do good; (11) self-observation; (12) reflection on the suitable appropriate punishment; (13) treating minor sins as major; (14) confession; (15) prayer; (16) compensating the victim; (17) almsgiving; (18) consciousness of sin; (19) refraining from repeating the transgression; (20) leading others away from sinfulness.

In another medieval work Isaac Alfasi (eleventh to twelfth century) outlines twenty-four things which act as a barrier to repentance: (1) slander and gossip; (2) anger; (3) evil thoughts; (4) association with evil people; (5) partaking of food so as to deprive the host

of his share; (6) looking lustfully at women; (7) partaking of the spoils of robbery; (8) sinning with the intention to repent at a later stage; (9) attaining fame at others' expense; (10) separating oneself from the community; (11) holding parents in disgrace; (12) holding teachers in disgrace; (13) cursing the public; (14) preventing the public from performing good acts; (15) leading a neighbour astray; (16) using a pledge obtained from the poor; (17) taking bribes to pervert justice; (18) keeping a lost article that one has found; (19) refraining from preventing one's son from doing evil; (20) eating the spoil of widows and orphans; (21) disagreeing with sages; (22) suspecting the innocent; (23) hating rebuke; (24) mocking Jewish practices.

In the modern world, such speculation about the nature of repentance as well as obstacles toward true remorse have given way to the more simple view that human beings are responsible for their actions and must repent of their sins. For Jews of all religious persuasions, such action is fundamental to the faith. Although non-Orthodox Judaism does not accept Biblical and rabbinic precepts as binding, it nevertheless affirms that all Jews are required to search their ways and make atonement for transgression. The Day of Atonement is designed to remind the Jewish people of this divinely sanctioned task.

SOURCES

Evil Inclination

According to the rabbis, the evil inclination and the good inclination are constantly engaged in conflict. Yet they indicated that if one is not able to control his lustful impulses, he should act as his passion dictates in a distant place:

> R. Ilai said: If a man finds that his evil inclination overmasters him, let him go to a place where nobody knows him, dress and cover himself in black, and act as his passion desires, but let him not profane the name of God in public. Is this a contradiction to the teaching that he who does not spare the honour of his creator had better never have been born, a teaching which R. Joseph interpreted to refer to the man who sins in secret? The solution of the contradiction is to be found in the fact that the second teaching must be regarded as referring to the man who could control his inclination, and the first to the man who cannot possibly do so.
>
> (*Talmud*, *Kiddushin*, 40a in RA, p. 305)

Midrash

For the rabbis, God avidly waits for sinners to repent:

> God said, 'All depends on you. As the lily blooms and looks upward, so when you repent before me, let your heart be directed upward, and then I will bring the Redeemer,' as it says 'I will be as the dew unto Israel; he shall blossom as the lily; that is when he blossoms as the lily' (Hos. 14:5).
>
> (*Midrash Ps.* on 45:1, in RA, p. 330)

Yom Kippur

On *Yom Kippur* the faithful are to repent of their sins and ask God for forgiveness:

> Our God and God of our fathers, hear our prayer; do not ignore our plea. We are neither so brazen nor so arrogant to claim that we are righteous, without sin, for indeed we have sinned.
>
> We abuse, we betray, we are cruel.
>
> We destroy, we embitter, we falsify.
>
> We gossip, we hate, we insult.
>
> We jeer, we kill, we lie.
>
> We mock, we neglect, we oppress.
>
> We pervert, we quarrel, we rebel.
>
> We steal, we transgress, we are unkind.
>
> We are violent, we are wicked, we are xenophobic.
>
> We yield to evil, we are zealots for bad causes.
>
> We have ignored your commandments and statutes, but it has not profited us. You are just, we have stumbled. You have acted faithfully, we have been unrighteous. What can we say to you; what can we tell you? You know everything, secret and revealed.
>
> You know the mysteries of the universe, the secrets of everyone alive. You probe our innermost depths. You examine our thoughts and desires. Nothing escapes you, nothing is hidden from you.
>
> May it therefore be your will, Lord our God and God of our fathers, to forgive us all our sins, to pardon all our iniquities, to grant us atonement for all our transgressions.
>
> We have sinned against you unwillingly and willingly,
>
> And we have sinned against you by misusing our minds.
>
> We have sinned against you through sexual immorality,
>
> And we have sinned against you knowingly and deceitfully.

We have sinned against you by wronging others,

And we have sinned against you by deriding parents and teachers.

And we have sinned against you by using violence.

We have sinned against you through foul speech,

And we have sinned against you by not resisting the impulse to evil.

For all these sins, forgiving God, forgive us, pardon us, grant us atonement.

We have sinned against you by fraud and by falsehood,

And we have sinned against you by scoffing.

We have sinned against you by dishonesty in business,

And we have sinned against you by usurious interest.

We have sinned against you by idle chatter,

And we have sinned against you by haughtiness.

We have sinned against you by rejecting responsibility,

And we have sinned against you by plotting against others.

We have sinned against you by irreverence,

And we have sinned against you by rushing to do evil.

We have sinned against you by false oaths,

And we have sinned against you by breach of trust.

For all these sins, forgiving God, forgive us, pardon us, grant us atonement.

(Conservative Prayer Book for Rosh Hashanah and Yom Kippur,
in MRHYK, pp. 377–381)

DISCUSSION

1. Discuss how the concept of sin is understood within Orthodoxy as opposed to the non-Orthodox branches of Judaism.

2. Discuss the notion of the *yetzer ha-tov* (good inclination) and the *yetzer ha-ra* (evil inclination) in rabbinic Judaism. Is such a doctrine consistent with a modern understanding of the psyche?

FURTHER READING

Cohen, Abraham, *Everyman's Talmud: The Major Teachings of the Rabbinic Sages*, Schocken, 1995.

Cohon, Samuel S., *Essays in Jewish Theology*, Behrman House, 1987.

Feldman, Daniel, *The Right and the Good: Halakhah and Human Relations*, Jason Aronson, 1999.

Hoenig, Samuel, *The Essence of Talmudic Law and Thought*, Jason Aronson, 1993.

Jacobs, Louis, *A Jewish Theology*, Behrman House, 1989.

Kushner, Harold, *How Good Do We Have to Be: A New Understanding of Guilt and Forgiveness*, Little, Brown, 1996.

Lamm, Norman, *The Shema: Spirituality and Law in Judaism*, Jewish Publication Society, 1998.

Lewittes, Mendell, *Jewish Law: An Introduction*, Jason Aronson, 1993.

Neusner, Jacob, *Tzedakah: Can Jewish Philanthropy Buy Jewish Survival?*, UAHC, 1997.

Schimmel, Solomon, *The Seven Deadly Sins: Jewish, Christian and Classical Reflections on Human Psychology*, Oxford University Press, 1997.

Sears, David, *Compassion for Humanity in the Jewish Tradition*, Jason Aronson, 1998.

Siegel, Seymour (ed.), *Conservative Judaism and Jewish Law*, KTAV, 1977.

Tamari, Meir, *With All Your Possessions: Jewish Ethics and Economic Life*, Jason Aronson, 1998.

Warshofsky, Mark, *Jewish Living: A Guide to Contemporary Reform Practice*, UAHC Press, 2000.

CHAPTER 66

The Chosen People

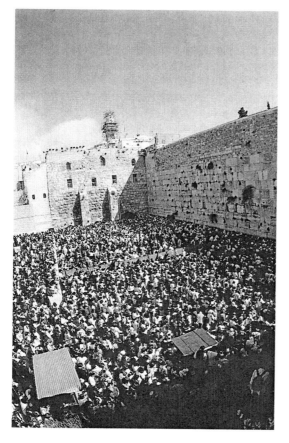

Figure 66 Jewish women praying at the Western Wall, Jerusalem. Copyright David Rose.

The concept of Israel as God's chosen people has been a constant feature of Jewish thought from Biblical times to the present. In the Bible the Hebrew root '*bhr*' (to choose) denotes the belief that God selected the Jewish nation from all the other peoples. As the Book of Deuteronomy relates: 'For you are a people holy to the Lord your God: the Lord your God has chosen you to be a people for his own possession out of all the

peoples that are on the face of the earth' (Deut. 7:6). According to Scripture this act was motivated by divine love: 'It was not because you were more in number than any other people that the Lord set his love upon you and chose you, for you were the fewest of all peoples; but it is because the Lord loves you' (Deut. 7:7–8). Such love for Israel was later echoed in the synagogue liturgy, especially in the prayer for holy days, which begins: 'Thou hast chosen us from all peoples; thou has loved us and found pleasure in us and hast exalted us above all tongues; thou hast sanctified us by thy commandments and brought us near unto thy service, O king, and hast called us by thy great and holy name.'

Through its election Israel has been given an historic mission to bear divine truth to humanity. Thus, before God proclaimed the Ten Commandments on Mount Sinai, he admonished the people to carry out this appointed task:

> You have seen what I did to the Egyptians, and how I bore you on eagles' wings, and brought you to myself. Now, therefore, if you will obey my voice, and keep my covenant, you shall be my own possession among all peoples; for all the earth is mine, and you shall be to me a kingdom of priests and a holy nation. (Exod. 19:4–6)

God's choice of Israel thus carries with it numerous responsibilities. As Genesis proclaims: 'For I have chosen him, that he may charge his children and his household after him to keep the way of the Lord by doing righteousness and justice' (Gen. 18:19).

Divine choice demands reciprocal response. Israel is obligated to keep God's statutes and observe his laws. In doing so, the nation will be able to persuade the nations of the world that there is only one universal God. Israel is to be a prophet to the nation, in that it will bring them to salvation. Yet despite this obligation, the Bible asserts that God will not abandon his chosen people even if they violate the covenant. The wayward nation will be punished, but God will not reject them: 'Yet for all that, when they are in the land of their enemies, I will not spurn them, neither will I abhor them so as to destroy them utterly and break my covenant with them: for I am the Lord their God' (Lev. 26:44).

In rabbinic sources the Biblical doctrine of the chosen people is a constant theme. While upholding the belief that God chose the Jews from all peoples, the rabbis argued that their election was due to an acceptance of the Torah. This conviction was based on Scripture: 'If you will hearken to my voice, indeed, and keep my covenant, then you shall be my own treasure from among all the peoples (Exod. 19:5). According to the **rabbis**, the Torah was offered first to the other nations of the world, but they all rejected it because its precepts conflicted with their way of life. Only Israel accepted it. According to one tradition, this occurred only because God suspended a mountain over the Jewish people, threatening to destroy the nation if they refused: 'If you will accept the Torah, it will be well with you, but if not, here you will find your grave.' The dominant view, however, was that the Israelites accepted God's law enthusiastically. For this reason Scripture states that the Jewish people declared: 'All that the Lord has spoken we will do (Exod. 24:7), showing a willingness to obey God's decrees without knowledge of their contents.

Rabbinic Judaism asserts that there is a special relationship between the children of Israel and God based on love – this is the basis of the allegorical interpretations in rabbinic sources of the Song of Songs, and is also expressed in the *Talmud* by such sayings as: 'How beloved is Israel before the Holy One, blessed be He; for wherever they were exiled the *Shekhinah* (divine presence) was with them.' Rabbinic literature also emphasizes that God's election of the Jewish people is due to the character of the nation and of the patriarchs in particular; according to the *Talmud*, mercy and forgiveness are characteristic of Abraham and his descendants.

In the Middle Ages the Jewish claim to be God's chosen people was disputed by the Church which saw itself as the true Israel. In response philosophers such as **Judah Halevi** in the twelfth century maintained that the entire Jewish people was endowed with a special religious sense. According to Halevi, this faculty was first given to Adam, and then passed on through a line of representatives to all the Jewish people. In consequence, the Jewish people was able to enter into communion with God. Further, because of this divine influence, the election of Israel implies dependence on special providence which sustains the people of Israel, while the remainder of the human race is subject to the general workings of the laws of nature and general providence.

Like Halevi, other Jewish philosophers emphasized Israel's special role in God's plan of salvation. Earlier in the tenth century in *The Book of Beliefs and Opinions*, **Saadiah Gaon** discusses God's promise that the Jewish nation would continue to exist as long as the heavens and the earth. Only Israel, Saadiah insists, is assured of redemption and will be included in the resurrection of the dead. According to Abraham ibn Daud, only Israel is privileged to receive prophecy. For Maimonides, the Jewish faith is the one true revelation which will never be superseded by another divine encounter. Among these Jewish thinkers the doctrine of election was stressed largely as a reaction to oppression by the non-Jewish world. Forced to withdraw into the imposed confines of the ghetto, Jews sought consolation from the belief that despite their sufferings they are God's special people whom he loves above all others.

The concept of Israel's chosenness is also a major theme of medieval kabbalistic thought. According to the *kabbalah*, the Jewish people on earth has its counterpart in the *Shekhinah* in the *sefirotic* realm – the *sefirah Malkhut* is known as the 'community of Israel' which serves as the archetype of the Israelite people on earth. For the kabbalists, Israel's exile mirrors the cosmic disharmony in which the *Shekhinah* is cast into exile form the Godhead. The drama of Israel's exile and its ultimate restoration reflects the dynamic of the upper worlds. In later *Habad* mysticism the Jew has two souls: the animal soul and the divine soul. This divine soul is possessed only by Jews, and even the animal soul of Israel is derived from a source which is an admixture of good and evil. The animal souls of gentiles on the other hand derive from an unclean source. For this reason, no gentile is capable of acting in a completely good fashion.

During the Enlightenment the Jewish people underwent a major transformation – no longer was the community confined to a ghetto existence. This alteration in Jewish existence challenged the concept of Jewish uniqueness. At the end of the eighteenth century the Jewish philosopher Moses Mendelssohn argued that the intellectual content of Judaism is identical with the religion of reason. In response to the question, 'Why should one remain a Jew?', he responded that Jewry has been singled out by the revelation on Mount Sinai. For this reason it was compelled to carry out a divinely appointed mission to the peoples of the earth.

Subsequently this conception has remained a central teaching of the various branches of the Jewish religious community. In this regard, a number of thinkers have sought to defend this doctrine despite its seeming insularity. In their view, the Biblical concept of the election of Israel does not imply the assumption of superiority; rather, the relation between the Jewish people and their God is natural. Further, it is alleged that the doctrine of closeness is not of a special people who must be served. Rather, Judaism impels individuals to serve others. In the view of the prophets, the Jewish nation is to be dedicated to service. It is also asserted that the doctrine of election has nothing to do with the notion of racial superiority. Jewish particularism is not exclusive in orientation. Anyone can become a Jew by accepting the tenets of the faith. In this regard, it is pointed out that some of the most important Jewish figures of the past were converts.

Again, supporters note that the choice was reciprocal in character: God chose Israel and Israel chose God. This was the basis of the covenant between God and Israel:

> You have declared this day concerning the Lord that He is your God, and that you will walk in his ways, and keep his statutes and his commandments and his ordinances, and will obey his voice; and the Lord has declared this day concerning you that you are a people for his own possession, as He has promised you, and that you are to keep all his commandments, that he will set you high above all nations. (Deut. 26:17–18)

Within **Reform Judaism** the notion of Jewish mission was developed stressing the special message of God which is to be passed on to all the nations. As the Pittsburgh Platform of 1885 explained:

> We recognize in Judaism a progressive religion, ever striving to be in accord with the postulates of reason. We are convinced of the utmost necessity of preserving the historical identity with our great past. Christianity and Islam being the daughter-religions of Judaism, we appreciate their mission to aid in the spreading of monotheistic and moral truth. We acknowledge that the spirit of broad humanity of our age is our ally in the fulfilment of our mission, and therefore we extend the hand of fellowship to all who co-operate with us in the establishment of the reign of truth and righteousness among men. (Dan Cohn-Sherbok, *Modern Judaism*, Macmillan, 1996, p. 83)

Nonetheless, within the various branches of non-Orthodox Judaism a number of writers have expressed considerable unease about the claim that the Jews constitute a divinely chosen people. The rejection of this traditional doctrine derives from universalistic and humanistic tendencies; unlike traditionalists, progressive Jews believe that Jews are inherently no different from the rest of humanity. Although the Jewish community has a unique history, they believe, this does not imply that God has selected the nation as his very own. Instead, the God of Israel is also the Lord of history who loves all people and guides the destiny of humanity to its ultimate conclusion.

SOURCES

Rabbis

According to rabbinic literature, God chose Israel to be his special people:

'You shall be holy unto me, for I, the Lord, am holy. Even as I am holy, so you be holy. As I am separate, so be you separate. And I have severed you from the other peoples that you should be mine. If you sever yourselves from the other peoples, then you belong to me: but if not, then you belong to Nebuchadnezzar and his fellows.' R. Eliezer said: 'How can we know that a man must not say, "I have no desire to eat pig, I have no desire to have intercourse with a woman whom I may not marry": but he must say, "Yes, I would like to do these acts, but what can I do? My father who is in heaven has forbidden them." Because it says, "I have severed you from among the nations to be mine." He who is separated from iniquity receives to himself the Kingdom of heaven.'

(*Sifre* 93d in RA, p. 105)

'You shall be holy unto me, for I the Lord am holy, and I have severed you from other peoples that ye should be mine' (Lev. 20:26). R. Yudan in the name of R. Hama b. Hanina and R. Berechiah in the name of R. Abbahu said: If God had separated the other nations from you, there would have been no hope for survival for these nations, but he separated you from the nations. If a man picks out the fair from the foul, he comes and picks again, but if he picks the foul from the fair, he does not come to pick again.

(*Pes. R.* 69b in RA, p. 105)

Prayer Book

The *Kiddush* for the Sabbath refers to God's choice of Israel as his people:

Blessed art thou, O Lord our God, king of the universe, who has hallowed us by thy commandments and hast taken pleasure in us, and in love and favour hast given us thy holy Sabbath as an inheritance, a memorial of the creation – that day being also the first of the holy convocations, in remembrance of the departure from Egypt. For thou hast chosen us and hallowed us above all nations, and in love and favour hast given us thy holy Sabbath as an inheritance. Blessed art thou, O Lord who hallowest the Sabbath.

(*Daily Prayer Book* in DPB, p. 409)

Saadiah Gaon

According to the tenth-century Jewish philosopher Saadiah Gaon, God chose the Jews from all peoples and bestowed the law upon them:

The first of his acts of kindness towards his creatures was the gift of existence, i.e. his act of calling them into existence after they had been non-existent, as he said to the men of distinction among them, 'Everyone that is called by my name, and whom I have created for my glory (Isa. 43:7). Thereafter he offered them a gift by means of which they are able to obtain complete happiness and perfect bliss, as is said, 'Thou makest me to know the path of life; in thy presence is fullness of joy, in thy right hand bliss for evermore' (Ps. 16:11). This gift consists of the commandments and prohibitions which He gave them.

When faced with this statement, the first impulse of reason will be to object that God should have been able to bestow upon men perfect bliss and to grant them everlasting happiness without imposing upon them commandments and prohibitions. Moreover, it would seem that in this way his goodness would have been more beneficial to them, seeing that they would have been free from the necessity of making any laborious effort. My answer to this objection is that, on the contrary, the order instituted by God, whereby everlasting happiness is achieved by man's labours in fulfilment of the Law, is preferable. For

reason judges that one who obtains some good in return for work which he has accomplished enjoys a double portion of happiness in comparison with one who has not done any work and receives what he receives as a gift of grace. Reason does not deem it right to place both on the same level. This being so, our creator has chosen for us the more abundant portion, namely, to bestow welfare on us in the shape of reward, thus making it double the benefit which we could expect without an effort on our part, as is said, 'Behold, the Lord God will come as a Mighty One, and his arm will rule for him; behold, his reward is with him, and his recompense before him'.

(Isa. 40:10)

Judah Halevi

In the *Kuzari*, Judah Halevi argues that the basis of the Jewish faith is the belief that God chose the Jews and guides his people through their history:

The Rabbi: I believe in the God of Abraham, Isaac and Israel, who led the Israelites out of Egypt with signs and miracles; who fed them in the desert and gave them the Land, after having made them traverse the sea and the Jordan in a miraculous way; who sent Moses with his law, and subsequently thousands of prophets who confirmed his law by promises to those who observed, and threats to the disobedient. We believe in what is contained in the Torah – a very large domain . . .

In this way I answered thy question. In the same strain Moses spoke to Pharaoh, when he told him 'The God of the Hebrews sent me to thee' – viz. the

God of Abraham, Isaac and Jacob. For the story of their life was well known to the nations, who also knew that the Divine power was in contact with the Patriarchs, caring for them and performing miracles for them. He did not say: 'The God of heaven and earth' nor 'my creator and thine sent me'. In the same way God commenced his speech to the assembled people of Israel: 'I am the God whom you worship, who hath led you out of the land of Egypt'; he did not say 'I am the creator of the world and your creator'.

(*Kuzari* in TJP, pp. 33–35)

Reform Judaism

In the Statement of Principles for Reform Judaism adopted at the 1999 Pittsburgh Convention of the Central Conference of American Rabbis, the Reform movement expressed its commitment to Israel; here the emphasis is on the nation's determination to join together with other Jews to witness to God's presence:

We are Israel, a people aspiring to holiness, singled out through our ancient covenant and our unique history among the nations to be witnesses to God's presence. We are linked by that covenant and that history to all Jews in every age and place.

We are committed to the *mitzvah* of love for the Jewish people, and to the entirety of the community of Israel. Recognizing that all Jews are responsible for one another, we reach out to all Jews across ideological and geographic boundaries.

(*CCAR Statement of Principles*, in www.ccarnet.org/platforms/principles)

DISCUSSION

1. Does the concept of chosenness imply the superiority of the Jewish people?

2. Is the doctrine of the chosen people still viable in the modern world?

FURTHER READING

Almog, S., Reinharz, Jehuda, Shapira, Anita (eds), *Zionism and Religion*, University Press of New England, 1998.

Cohn-Sherbok, Dan, *The Jewish Faith*, SPCK, 1993.

Eisen, Robert, *Gersonides on Providence, Covenant and the Chosen People: Study of Medieval Jewish Philosophy and Biblical Commentary*, State University of New York, 1995.

Frank, Daniel (ed.), *People Apart: Chosenness and Ritual in Jewish Philosophical Thought*, State University of New York, 1993.

Gillman, Neil, *Shattered Fragments: Reconverting Theology for the Modern Man*, Jewish Publication Society, 1992.

Jacobs, Louis, *Principles of the Jewish Faith*, Vallentine Mitchell, 1964.

Jacobs, Louis, *A Jewish Theology*, Behrman House, 1973.

Novak, David, *The Election of Israel: The Idea of the Chosen People*, Cambridge University Press, 1995.

Roth, Cecil, Wigoder, Geoffrey, *Encyclopedia Judaica*, Coronet, 2002.

Trepp, Leo, *A History of the Jewish Experience: Eternal Faith, Eternal People*, Behrman House, 1996.

Wyschograd, Michael, *The Body of Faith: God and the People of Israel*, Jason Aronson, 1996.

CHAPTER 67

The Promised Land

Figure 67 Jerusalem showing Omar mosque, 1843, hand-coloured engraving from lithographs, The Holy Land. Artist: Roberts, David: 1796–1864: English. Copyright The Art Archive/Bibliothèque des Arts Décoratifs Paris/Dagli Orti.

Throughout history the Jewish people have longed for a land of their own. In Genesis God called Abraham to travel to Canaan where he promised to make him a great nation: 'Go from your country and your kindred and your father's house to the land that I will show you. And I will make of you a great nation' (Gen. 12:1–2). This same declaration was repeated to his grandson Jacob who, after wrestling with God's messenger, was renamed Israel (meaning 'he who struggles with God'). After Jacob's son Joseph became vizier in Egypt, the Israelite clan settled in Egypt for several hundred years. Eventually Moses led them out of Egyptian bondage, and the people settled in the Promised Land. There they established a monarchy, but due to the corruption of the nation, God punished his chosen people through the instrument of the foreign powers who devastated the northern kingdom in the eighth century BCE and the southern kingdom two centuries later.

Though the Temple lay in ruins and Jerusalem was destroyed, Jews who had been exiled to Babylonia had not lost their faith in God. Sustained by their belief that God would deliver them from exile, a number of Jews sought permission to return to their former home. In 538 BCE King **Cyrus** of Persia allowed them to leave. Under the leadership of Joshua and Zerubbabel, restoration of the Temple began. After the destruction of the First Temple, the nation had strayed from the religious faith of their ancestors. To combat such laxity, the prophet Nehemiah asserted that the community must purify itself; in this effort he was joined by the priest Ezra. Although religious reforms were carried out, the people continued to abandon the Torah, and the Temple was destroyed a second time in the first century CE by the Romans.

After Jerusalem and the Second Temple were devastated, the Jews were bereft of a homeland. The glories of ancient Israel had come to an end, and the Jews were destined to live among the nations. In their despair the nation longed for a messianic figure of the House of David who would lead them back to Zion. Basing their beliefs on prophecies in Scripture, they foresaw a period of redemption in which earthly life would be transformed and all nations would bow down to the one true God. Such a vision animated rabbinic reflection about God's providential plan for his chosen people.

According to rabbinic speculation, this process would involve the coming of a messianic figure, **Messiah ben Joseph**, who would serve as the forerunner of the second Messiah. The second Messiah would bring back all the exiles to Zion and complete earthly existence. Eventually at the end of the messianic era, all human beings would be judged: the righteous would enter into heaven whereas the wicked would be condemned to eternal punishment. This eschatological vision served as a means of overcoming the nation's trauma at suffering the loss of its sacred home and institutions.

In the early rabbinic period some Jews believed that Jesus would usher in the period of messianic redemption. Although mainstream Judaism rejected

such claims, the Jewish community continued to long for deliverance, and in 132 CE the military leader, Simon Bar Kochba, was acclaimed by many Jews as the Davidic Messiah. When the rebellion he led was crushed, Jews put forward the year of redemption until the fifth century. In about the middle of this century another messianic pretender, Moses from Crete, declared he would lead Jewish inhabitants from the island back to their homeland. After this plan failed, Jews continued to hope for a future return and their aspirations are recorded in a number of midrashic collections.

In the ninth century the Jewish theologian Saadiah Gaon attempted to determine the date of the final redemption on the basis of Scriptural texts. In addition, during this period a number of pseudo-Messiahs appeared, and the traveller Eldad Ha-Dani brought news from Africa of the ten lost tribes which further stimulated messianic longing. Such messianic speculation continued into the medieval period. Many Jews viewed the year of the First Crusade (1096) as a year of deliverance: when Jews were slaughtered during this period, their suffering was viewed as the birth pangs of the Messiah. In later years the same yearning for a return to Zion was expressed by Jews who continued to be persecuted by the Christian population. Medieval Jews, like their ancestors, yearned for release from the bondage of exile, and in their misery looked to God's promises of messianic fulfilment as the means of deliverance.

The early modern period witnessed this same aspiration for messianic redemption. During the sixteenth and seventeenth centuries various messianic treatises were produced, and in the next century the tradition of messianic calculation was continued by numerous rabbinic scholars. During this century several false Messiahs also appeared, claiming to bring about a new age. In the middle of the seventeenth century the Cossack rebellion that devastated Polish Jewry heightened Jewish yearning for deliverance, and in 1665 the arrival of Shabbatai Zevi electrified the Jewish world. Claiming to be the Messiah, he attracted a large circle of followers; however, his conversion to Islam evoked widespread despair.

With the apostasy of Shabbatai Zevi, the Jewish preoccupation with messianic calculation diminished: many Jews became disillusioned with messianic anticipation and belief in the Messiah receded in significance. Yet despite this shift in orientation, a number of religious Jews continued to believe in the coming of the Messiah and linked this yearning to an advocacy of Zionism. Paralleling these religious aspirations to establish a Jewish settlement in the Holy Land prior to the coming of the Messiah, modern secular Zionists encouraged such a development in order to solve the problem of anti-Semitism. In *The Jewish State* the foremost Zionist leader Theodor Herzl argued that the only solution to Judaeophobia is for the Jewish people to reconstitute themselves in their own country.

The Zionist movement, however, was met with considerable opposition within the Jewish community. Ultra-Orthodox critics of Zionism believed the creation of a Jewish state was a betrayal of traditional Judaism. It is forbidden, they asserted, to accelerate the coming of the Messiah through human effort. At the opposite end of the spectrum Reform Judaism attacked Zionism as misguided utopianism. According to these progressives, only emancipation could serve as a solution to the Jewish problem – Zionism is a reactionary delusion. In place of a national homeland, they promoted assimilation as a remedy to anti-Jewish sentiment.

Nevertheless, the Zionist cause gained increasing acceptance in the Jewish world. The first steps towards creating a Jewish homeland were taken at the end of the nineteenth century with the first Zionist Congress. Subsequently, Zionists attempted to persuade the British government to permit the creation of a Jewish home in Palestine. Although Britain eventually approved of such a plan, the British government insisted that the rights of the Arab population be protected. After World War One British representatives attempted to oversee this policy but were met with considerable opposition by militant Zionists. In 1939 a White Paper was published which set limits on the number of Jewish emigrants who could be allowed into Palestine. The Jewish population rejected this policy and inaugurated a campaign of terror against the British. After World War Two the creation of a Jewish state was approved by the United Nations. Despite such an official endorsement, this plan was rejected by the Arabs. In subsequent years Arabs and Jews have engaged in a series of conflicts. Arab–Israeli antagonism thus continues to undermine the Jewish quest for a homeland in the land of their ancestors.

This saga of Jewish aspiration for a homeland reveals the utopian aspects of the nation's yearning. Through four millennia, Jewry was guided by the belief that it was possible to create God's kingdom on earth. In ancient Israel, the state was to be a theocracy. Continually the prophets reminded the nation of its divine obligations. With the destruction of Jerusalem and the Temple, the desire for a Jewish home was transformed into an eschatological vision of messianic redemption in Zion. The Jews were to return triumphantly with the Messiah at their head. As time passed, this dream faded, yet the longing for a Jewish home did not diminish. Increasingly Jewry came to believe that this eternal quest could be realized only through the labours of the Zionists. The early Zionists were infused with hope and enthusiasm. Their task was to create a Jewish society which would be a light to the nations. Now that the state of Israel has become a reality, a number of Jewish writers have stressed that the Jewish nation should not lose sight of the moral and spiritual dimensions of the Jewish tradition. As the Jewish people face a new century, they argue, the nation must attempt to reconcile the political, social and economic concerns of everyday life with an idealistic vision of God's kingdom on earth.

SOURCES

Cyrus

The Book of Ezra records Cyrus' decree allowing the exiles in Babylonia to return to their homeland:

> Concerning the house of God at Jerusalem, let the house be rebuilt, the place where
> sacrifices are offered, and burnt-offerings are brought . . . let the gold and silver vessels

of the house of God which Nebuchadnezzar took out of the Temple that is in Jerusalem and brought to Babylon, be restored and brought back to the Temple which is in Jerusalem . . . let the governor of the Jews and the elders of the Jews rebuild this house of God on its site.

(Ezra 6:3–7)

Psalms of Solomon

The Psalms of Solomon extol the messianic king who will rebuild the land and draw all nations to Zion:

He shall gather together a holy people
whom he shall lead in righteousness.
And he shall judge the tribes of the people
that has been sanctified by the Lord his God . . .
And he shall divide them according to their tribes
upon the land.
And neither sojourner nor alien shall sojourn
with them any more.
He shall judge peoples and nations
in the wisdom of his righteousness. Selah.
The people of the nations shall serve him
under his yoke:
He shall glorify the Lord openly in all the earth;
And he shall purge Jerusalem
making it holy as of old,
So that nations shall come from the ends of the earth
to see his glory.

(Ps. Solomon 17)

Messiah ben Joseph

In their depictions of the Messiah, the rabbis formulated the doctrine of a second Messiah, the son of Joseph, who would precede Messiah ben David:

And the land shall mourn, every family apart; the family of the house of David apart, and their wives apart (Zechariah 12:12) . . . What is the cause of this mourning? R. Dosa and our teachers differ on the point. One said, The cause is the slaying of the evil inclinations. It is well with him who said the cause is the slaying of Messiah ben Joseph, for that agrees with the verse (Zechariah 12:10), 'And they shall look upon him who they have pierced, and they shall mourn for him as one mourneth for his only son.'

(Sukkah 52a)

Yehudai hai Alkalai

In the nineteenth century the religious Zionist Yehudai hai Alkalai argued in *Minhat Yehuda* that the Messiah will be preceded by the return of the Jewish nation to its ancestral land:

This new redemption will be different; our land is waste and desolate, and we shall have to build houses, dig wells, and plant vines and olive trees . . . We are, therefore, commanded not to attempt to go at once and all together in the Holy Land . . . the Lord desires that we be redeemed in dignity; we cannot, therefore, migrate in a mass, for we should then have to live like Bedouin, scattered in tents all over the fields of the Holy Land. Redemption must come slowly. The land must, by degrees, be built up and prepared.

(Yehuda hai Alkalai, *The Third Redemption*, in I, p. 101)

In Alkalai's view, Hebrew will become the language for ordinary life in Palestine:

I wish to attest to the pain I have always felt at the error of our ancestors, that they allowed our Holy Tongue to be so forgotten. Because of this our people was divided into seventy peoples; our one language was replaced by the seventy languages of the lands of exile. If the Almighty should indeed show us his miraculous favour and gather us into our land, we would not be able to speak to each other and such a divided community could not succeed.

(Yehuda hai Alkalai, *The Third Redemption*, in I, p. 102)

DISCUSSION

1. Discuss the biblical view that the Jewish people have a divine right to the land of Israel.

2. In what ways has Zionism altered the traditional understanding of the place of the Messiah in the return of the Jewish people from exile?

FURTHER READING

Chapman, Colin, *Whose Promised Land?*, Lion, 2002.

Cohn-Sherbok, Dan, *Israel: The History of an Idea*, SPCK, 1992.

Cohn-Sherbok, Dan, El-Alamai, Dawoud, *The Palestine–Israeli Conflict*, Oneworld, 2002.

Day, John (ed.), *King and Messiah in Israel and the Ancient Near East*, Continuum, 1998.

Drane, John, *Introducing the Old Testament*, Lion, 2000.

Erlich, Avi, *Ancient Zionism: The Biblical Origins of the National Idea*, Free Press, 1994.

Finkelstein, Norman, *Image and Reality of the Israel–Palestine Conflict*, Verso, 2001.

Gottwald, Norman, *The Politics of Ancient Israel*, Westminster John Knox, 2000.

Herzog, Chaim, *The Arab–Israeli Wars: War and Peace in the Middle East*, Vintage Books, 1983.

La Guardia, Anton, *Holy Land, Unholy War*, John Murray, 2002.

Pardes, Ilana, *The Biography of Ancient Israel*, University of California Press, 2002.

Potok, Chaim, *Wanderings: Chaim Potok's History of the Jews*, Fawcett Books, 1987.

Soggin, J. Alberto, *An Introduction to the History of Israel and Judah*, SCM, 1999.

Thomas, Baylis, *How Israel Was Won: A Concise History of the Arab–Israeli Conflict*, Lexington Books, 1999.

Whitelam, Keith, *The Invention of Ancient Israel: The Silencing of Palestinian History*, Routledge, 1997.

Wilson, Robert, *Prophecy and Society in Ancient Israel*, Augsburg Fortress, 1980.

CHAPTER 68

Prayer

Figure 68 Jewish men praying at the Western Wall, Jerusalem. Copyright David Rose, London.

According to the Jewish tradition, human beings are able to communicate with God individually or collectively; in response, God answers the prayers which are addressed to him. In Scripture He is portrayed as a personal Deity who created human beings in his image; as a consequence, they are able to attain this exalted position. In the Bible the word most frequently used for such communication is '*tefillah*' – it is derived from the Hebrew root which means to think, entreat, or judge. In its reflexive verbal form it has the sense of judging oneself.

The Bible itself lists more than eighty examples of both formalized and impromptu worship. Initially no special prayers were required for regular prayer, but later worship services became institutionalized through sacrifices and offerings. In Biblical times sacrifice was made to God to obtain his favour or atone for sin. The Canaanites sacrificed human beings (2 Kings 3:27), but the story of the binding of Isaac (Gen. 22:1–19) teaches God's displeasure with this type of sacrificial act. In ancient Israel three types of sacrifice were offered in the Temple: animal sacrifice (*zerah*), made as a burnt offering for sin, meal offerings (*minhah*), and libations. The rituals and practices prescribed for the Temple sacrifice are set down in Leviticus chapters 2 and 23 and Numbers chapters 28 and 29.

The *Mishnah* states that priests serving in the Second Temple participated in a short liturgy comprising the **Shema** (Deut. 6:4), the Ten Commandments, and the Priestly Blessing (Num. 6:24–6). During this period the entire congregation began to pray at fixed times, and an order of prayers has been attributed to the men of the Great Assembly. Regular services were held four times daily by the delegations of representatives from the twenty-four districts of the country. These services were referred to as: *shaharit* (morning), *musaf* (additional), *minhah* (afternoon), and *neilat shearim* (evening).

Several orders of prayers coexisted until Gamaliel II produced a regularized standard after the destruction of the Second Temple in 70 CE. Prayers then officially replaced the sacrifices that could no longer be made. This new ritual, referred to as 'service of the heart' was conducted in the synagogue. The core of the liturgy included the prayer formula 'Blessed be You', the *Shema*, and the *Amidah* (also known as *tefillah*) originally consisting of eighteen benedictions. On special occasions (such as the Sabbath and festivals), an additional *Amidah* was included. Ideally prayers were recited by a *minyan* (quorum of ten men). However if such a number did not exist, certain prayers had to be omitted including the *kaddish*, *kedushah* and the reading of the Law. The *alenu* prayer, originating from the New Year liturgy, and the *kaddish* were the two concluding prayers of all services.

During the worship service portions of the Pentateuch and the Prophets were recited, and this became normal practice by the time of the Mishnah. By the end of the talmudic period the prayer service was supplemented by liturgical hymns (*piyyutim*). These compositions were produced in Palestine as well as Babylonia from *geonic* times until the twelfth century. The Palestinian rite itself was distinguished by a triennial cycle of readings of the Pentateuch, a recension of the benedictions of the *Amidah*, and an introductory blessing before the recitation of the *Shema*. The Babylonian rite was first recorded in *Seder Rav Amram* by Amram Gaon in the ninth century – this work serves as the official ordering of prayers with their legal requirements. Such an act of setting down liturgical arrangements led to the dissolution of the ban against committing prayers to writing, and in the tenth century the first authoritative prayer book (*siddur*) was edited by Saadiah Gaon.

Among Jewish mystics mystical cleaving to God (*devekut*) in prayer is of fundamental importance. For the early kabbalists of Provence *devekut* was the goal of the mystical way. According to Isaac the Blind, the principal task of the mystics and of they who contemplate on his name is, 'And you shall serve him and cleave to him' (Deut. 13:4). This, he argued, is a central principle of the Torah and of prayer, and of blessings, to harmonize one's thought above, to conjoin God in his letters and to link the ten *sefirot* to him. For the thirteenth-century philosopher and kabbalist Nahmanides, *devekut* is a state of mind in which one constantly remembers God and his love, to the point that when a person speaks with another, his heart is not with them at all but is still before God. In his view, whoever cleaves in this way to his creator becomes eligible to receive the Holy Spirit. For Nahmanides, the true *hasid* is able to attain such a spiritual state. *Devekut* does not completely eliminate the distance between God and human beings – it denotes rather a state of beatitude and intimate union between the soul and its source.

In ascending the higher worlds, the path of prayer paralleled the observance of God's commandments. Yet unlike the *mitzvot*, prayer is independent of action and can become a process of meditation. Mystical prayer, accompanied by meditative *kavvanot* (intention) focusing on each prayer's kabbalistic content, was a feature of the various systems of *kabbalah*. For the kabbalist, prayer is seen as the ascent of man into the higher realm where the soul can integrate with the higher spheres. By using the traditional liturgy in a symbolic fashion, prayer repeats the hidden processes of the cosmos. At the time of prayer, the hierarchy of the upper realms is revealed as one of the names of God. Such disclosure is what constitutes the mystical activity of the individual in prayer, as the kabbalist concentrates on the name that belongs to the domain through which his prayer is passing. The *kavvanah* involved in mystic prayer is seen as a necessary element in the mystery of heavenly unification which brought the divine down to the lowest realm and tied the *sefirot* to each other and the *Ayn Sof*. As the *Zohar* explains, both the upper and lower worlds are blessed through the man who performs his prayer in a union of action and word, and thus effects a unification.

In the nineteenth century *Hasidim* incorporated kabbalistic ideas in their understanding of prayer. According to Hasidic thought, the kabbalistic type of *kavvanot* brings about an emotional involvement and attachment to God. In *Hasidism*, prayer is understood as a mystical encounter with the divine in which the human heart is elevated towards its ultimate source. Frequently the act of prayer was viewed as the most important religious activity. Thus R. Shneur Zalman of Lyady, the founder of *Habad Hasidism*, wrote in the eighteenth century: 'For although the forms of the prayers and the duty of praying three times a day are rabbinic, the idea of prayer is the foundation of the whole Torah. This means that man knows God, recognizing his greatness and his splendour with a serene and whole mind, and an understanding heart.' In *Habad Hasidism* prayer involves the contemplation of the kabbalistic scheme in which God's infinite light proceeds through the entire chain of being. The devout should reflect on this until their hearts are moved in rapture.

The advent of the Enlightenment in the same century brought about major changes in Jewish life. In 1801 the Jewish communal leader Israel Jacobson initiated a programme of reform: the consistory under his leadership introduced reforms to the Jewish worship service including singing, hymns and addresses as well as prayers in German. In 1810 he built the first Reform Temple. In his address at the dedication ceremony, he stated: 'Our ritual is still weighed down with religious customs which must be rightly offensive to reason as well as to our Christian friends. It desecrates the holiness of our religion and dishonours the reasonable man to place a value upon such customs.'

Subsequently other temples were established in which innovations were made to the liturgy, including prayers and sermons in German as well as choral singing and organ music. The central aim of these early reformers was to adapt Jewish worship to contemporary aesthetic standards. For these innovators, the informality of the traditional service seemed foreign and undignified, and they therefore insisted on greater decorum, more unison in prayer, a choir, hymns and musical responses, as well as alterations in prayers and the length of the service. When **Reform Judaism** spread to the United States, such reformers continued to promote liturgical change based on both aesthetic and theological criteria, resulting in the publication of a variety of prayer books. Typical of the changes introduced by these Reformers was an altered wording to a number of prayers in the traditional liturgy.

SOURCES

Shema

The *Shema* is a central prayer of the Jewish liturgy: it is made up of three passages: Deuteronomy 6:4–9; Deuteronomy 11:13–21; Numbers 15:37–41. Recited every day, the first paragraph contains the phrase: 'Hear, O Israel, the Lord is our God, the Lord is One':

Hear, O Israel, the Lord is Our God, the Lord is One. Blessed be his name, whose glorious kingdom is for ever and ever.

And thou shalt love the Lord thy God with all thine heart, and with all thy soul, and with all thy might. And these words, which I command thee this day, shall be upon thine heart: and thou shalt teach them diligently unto thy children, and shalt talk of them when thou sittest in thine house, and when thou walkest by the way, and when thou liest down, and when thou risest up. And thou shalt bind them for a sign upon thine hand, and they shall be for frontlets between thine eyes. And thou shalt write them upon the door-posts of thy house, and upon thy gates.

(*Shema* in DPB, p. 119)

Reform Judaism and Mission

The Reform prayer book emphasizes the role of the Jewish people in carrying out God's mission on earth:

The sense of being chosen impressed itself deeply on the soul of our people. And yet they did not consider themselves superior to other nations, for they knew that all humans are God's children. It was not their lineage but the possession of Torah that made them a choice people. For centuries they stood alone in upholding divine truth and the way of Torah in a world steeped in ignorance, superstition and cruelty. Yet they always believed that others, too, might be chosen, if only they would choose the way of God.

Only one privilege did they claim, that of serving God and his truth. And with that privilege came an exacting responsibility: 'You, of all the families of the earth, have known me best; therefore I will hold you all the more accountable for your iniquities.'

Israel gave birth in time to other religions that have brought many to God, but our responsibility continues, for our mission remains unfulfilled. It will continue until the earth is full of the knowledge of the Lord as the sea-bed is covered by water.

(*Prayer concerning mission,*
in GP:NUPB, p. 704)

Prayer for Settling in Israel

The Reconstructionist movement has emphasized the importance of Israel in the life of the Jewish people. This prayer is to be recited for those making *aliyah*:

May the one who blessed our ancestors, Abraham, Isaac, and Jacob, Sarah Rebekah, Rachel, and Leah, bless _____ who is making *aliyah* to *Eretz Yisrael* (together with his/her family) in order to establish a home there. May he/she journey there in peace and settle safely in the Land of Zion. May

he/she find blessing and success in all he/she undertakes there. 'Whoever among you (wishes to settle there), may the God of Israel be with that person – let him/her go up to the Land!'

(*Prayer for Making Aliyah,*
in KH, p. 692)

Humanistic Worship

Adopting a non-theistic approach, the Humanistic movement celebrates Jewish festivals focusing on their humanistic dimension. This reading for *Yom Kippur* emphasizes the importance of memory:

We live with our memories. We cannot escape them. They have made their comfortable home within our brain and leave reluctantly. Good memories are easy to recall. Our conscious mind invites them to seize our attention and to comfort us with pleasant nostalgia. Bad memories are more difficult to find. They are banished to the underworld of our mind. They emerge without permission to make us relive old pain and old agony.

We are condemned to remember. It is the very nature of the human condition. Because we

remember, we have culture. Because we remember, we have tradition. Because we remember, we are able to learn from our past. Even if we wanted to stop remembering, we could not stop. Even if we desired to forget our past, it would insist on intruding. We cannot be the creatures of our evolutionary past who lived from moment to moment with the assault of conscious memory. Our past stays with us vividly. We must learn how to live with it.

(*Prayer*
in C, p. 226)

DISCUSSION

1. What are the major differences between worship in ancient Israel and the synagogue liturgy?

2. Does it make sense to pray if one does not believe in a supernatural Diety?

FURTHER READING

Cohen, Jeffrey, *Blessed You Are: A Comprehensive Guide to Jewish Prayer*, Jason Aronson, 1997.

Cohn, Gabriel, Fisch, Harold (eds), *Prayer and Judaism*, Jason Aronson, 1996.

Donin, Hayim Halevy, *To Pray as a Jew: A Guide to the Prayer Book and the Synagogue Service*, HarperCollins, 1991.

Green, Arthur, Holtz, Barry (eds), *Your Word is Fire: Hasidic Masters on Contemplative Prayer*, Jewish Lights, 1973.

Hammer, Reuven, *Entering Jewish Prayer*, Random House, 1995.

Hoffman, Lawrence, *The Way into Jewish Prayer*, Jewish Lights, 2000.

Idelsohn, A.Z., *Jewish Liturgy and Its Development*, Dover, 1995.

Isaacs, Ronald, *Every Person's Guide to Jewish Prayer*, Jason Aronson, 1997.

Kadish, Seth, *Kavvana: Directing the Heart in Jewish Prayer*, Jason Aronson, 1997.

Nulman, Macy, *Encyclopedia of Jewish Prayer*, Kuperard, 1995.

Rosenberg, Arnold, *Jewish Liturgy as Spiritual System*, Jason Aronson, 2000.

Steinsaltz, Adin, *Guide to Jewish Prayer*, Random House, 2002.

Wagner, Jordan Lee, *The Synagogue Survival Kit*, Jason Aronson, 1997.

CHAPTER 69

Love and Fear of God

· Pphetia Jfaic ·

uuuc
deferr
ignu.s
aheuu
aut uu
quetu
uu vu
auuet
vafta
liquid
Sodou
mourt
verbi
papuu
pls ci
ttuou
oūs.
uemi.
guuu
huuot
coufu
hetoe

Iho Jfaie filii Xuuos, Caput, j.

Figure 69 The Prophet Isaiah hidden in a tree trunk, from 1526 French manuscript Bible. Copyright The Art Archive/ Bibliothèque Municipale Valenciennes/Dagli Orti.

Within the Jewish tradition, the love of God is of central importance. Thus Deuteronomy declares: 'You shall love the Lord your God with all your heart and with all your soul and with all your might' (Deut. 6:5). In the *Mishnah* this verse is quoted to demonstrate that human beings must love God not only for the good that befalls them, but for evil as well. This explanation is based on an interpretation of three expressions in this verse: 'with all your heart' means with both the good and evil inclinations; 'with all your soul' means even if God takes away your soul through martyrdom; 'with

all your might' means with all your wealth (Ber. 9:5). According to the *Mishnah*, the injunction to love God involves being faithful even if this requires the loss of one's wealth or one's life.

The **midrash** comments on this Biblical text. Concerning the phrase 'You shall love the Lord your God', the *Sifre* on Deut. 32 states:

> Do it out of love. Scripture distinguishes between one who does it out of love and one who does it out of fear. Out of love, his reward is doubled and again doubled. Scripture says: 'You shall fear the Lord your God: you shall serve him and cleave to him' (Deut. 10:20). A man who fears his neighbour will leave him when his demands become too troublesome, but you do it out of love. For love and fear are never found together except in relation to God.

Here the *Sifre* maintains that love and fear are incompatible in human relations, but not with regard to the love of God. The *Sifre* also points out that loving God involves convincing others to love God just as Abraham did when he brought unbelievers under the wings of the *Shekhinah*. Commenting on the verse, 'And these words which I command you this day shall be upon your heart (Deut. 6:6), the *Sifre* explains: 'Why is this said?' Because it is said: "You shall love the Lord your God with all your heart", and I do not know in what way God is to be loved, therefore it says: "Take these to heart and in this way you will come to recognize God and cleave to his ways".' Here loving God is understood as cleaving to his commandments.

In these rabbinic sources, loving God is perceived as living according to his decrees. Among medieval Jewish thinkers, however, stress was placed on mystical love. Thus in *The Book of Beliefs and Opinions* the ninth-century Jewish philosopher Saadiah Gaon asks how is it possible to have knowledge of God, much less love him, since we have not perceived him with our senses. In response, he asserts that certain statements are believed as true even though they cannot be proved on empirical grounds. According to Saadiah, it is possible to acquire knowledge of God through rational speculation and the miracles afforded by Scripture. Hence truth about God is able to mingle with the human spirit.

Again, in *Duties of the Heart* the eleventh-century Jewish philosopher Bahya ibn Pakuda sees the love of God as the final goal – this is the aim of all virtues. However, the only way is through fear of him. For Bahya such fear involves the abstinence from worldly desires. According to Bahya the love of God is the soul's longing for the creator. When human beings contemplate God's power and greatness, they bow before his majesty until God stills this fear. Individuals who love God in this fashion have no other interest than serving him. With complete faith and trust they accept all sufferings. In this regard Bahya quotes the saint who used to proclaim at night: 'My God! Thou hast made me hungry and left me naked. Thou has caused me to dwell in night's darkness and hast shown me thy power and might. Yet even if thou wouldst burn me in fire I would continue only to love thee and rejoice in thee.' Having depicted such love for God, Bahya asks whether human beings are capable of attaining such heights. In response he stresses that only a few individuals are capable of sacrificing their wealth or lives for God's sake.

In his code of Law the twelfth-century Jewish philosopher Moses Maimonides discusses the love of God in relation to the nature of the universe. According to Maimonides, one who truly loves God serves him not out of an ulterior motive but disinterestedly. When a person loves God, he automatically carries out the divine commandments: this state is like being lovesick, unable to get the person he loves out of his mind, pining constantly when he stands, sits, eats or drinks. Like Bahya, Maimonides asserts that not everyone is able to attain such a state of pure love. Rather, God can be loved only in proportion to the knowledge one has of him.

In kabbalistic literature the love of God plays a major role. Concerning the verse, 'You shall love the Lord your God', the *Zohar* states that human beings are here commanded to cleave unto God with selfless devotion. In the writings of later kabbalists the theme of the love of God was further elaborated. Thus, the sixteenth-century writer Elijah de Vidas in his *Reshit Hokhmah* argues that it is impossible for human beings to love a disembodied spirit. Here the love of God must refer to something which is embodied. Since God as *Ayn Sof* (Infinite) has no body, human love of the divine must be understood as love of the *Shekhinah* (God's presence). For de Vidas, the *Shekhinah* is in no way apart from God; rather God manifests himself through the *Shekhinah* in order to provide human beings with something tangible they can grasp so as to rise above worldly desires. Subsequently among Hasidic Jews, joy in God's service was conceived as central to the love of God; in addition, it was at times understood in the form of martyrdom.

In Scripture there are also numerous references to the fear of God. Often allusions to the love and fear of God are intermingled: they express a particularly intense relationship with the Divine. Frequently the fear of God refers to piety and moral worth. Thus in the Book of Job, Job is described as 'blameless and upright, one who feared God and turned away from evil' (Job 1:1). In rabbinic literature the Hebrew terminology for such awesome reverence is *yirat shamayim* (the fear of heaven).

Among medieval theologians a distinction is drawn between *yirat ha-onesh* (fear of punishment) and *yirat ha-romemut* (fear in the presence of the exalted majesty of God). Concerning these two types of fear, the twelfth-century Jewish philosopher Abraham ibn Daud argued in *Emnunah Ramah* that the reference to fear in Deut. 10:20 is to the fear produced by his greatness, not to the fear of harm. In *Duties of the Heart* the eleventh-century Jewish philosopher Bahya ibn Pakuda draws a similar distinction. Only *yirat ha-romemut* can lead to the pure love of God. A person who attains this degree of reverence will neither fear nor love anything other than the creator.

In mystical sources this distinction is also maintained. The *Zohar*, for example, stresses that there are three types of fear: two of these have no proper foundation but the third is the main foundation of fear. A man may fear God in order that his sons may live and not die or because he is afraid of some punishment to be visited upon his person or his wealth, and because of it he is in constant fear. But it follows that such a person's fear has no proper foundation. There is another man who fears God because he is terrified of punishment in the next world. Both these types of fear do not belong to the main foundation of fear and its root meaning. The fear which does have a proper foundation is when a person fears his master because he is a great and mighty ruler, the foundation of all worlds, and all before him are counted as naught.

In his *Ikkarim* the fifteenth-century Jewish philosopher Joseph Albo defines fear as the receding of the soul and the gathering of all her powers into herself, when she imagines some fear-inspiring thing. But there is another type of fear in which the soul is awestruck not because of any fear of harm, but because of the person's unworthiness in the face of majesty. This is the highest form of fear. Because human beings are usually unable to reach this state, he argues, the Torah establishes punishments to coerce obedience to God. Both types of fear are therefore necessary – the lower to subdue a person's wayward nature, and the higher as an authentic response to God's greatness and power.

In *Reshit Hokhmah* Elijah de Vidas argues that the fear of God is the gate through which every servant of the Lord must pass; it is a necessary condition for loving God and doing his will. Basing his views on kabbalistic doctrine, de Vidas maintains that since human beings are created after the pattern of the upper world, all acts have a cosmic effect. Good deeds cause the divine grace to flow through all worlds, whereas evil deeds arrest this flow and bring about a flaw in the domain of the *sefirot*: the fear of sin thus has cosmic significance. Further, de Vidas contends that human sin prevents the transgressor's entry into Paradise. Mortals should therefore be apprehensive about their fate, and in particular the horrors of hell which await evildoers.

In the eighteenth century the Italian kabbalist **Moses Luzzatto** in *The Path of the Upright* maintained that the fear of sin should be identified with the higher type of fear (*yirat ha-romemut*) rather than with the fear of punishment. The latter means fear of transgressing a divine precept because of physical or spiritual punishment. Such fear is only suitable for the ignorant and for women. Men of learning, however, are able to reach a higher type of fear which consists in refraining from sin through the recognition of God's glory. Such fear is difficult to attain since it requires knowledge of God and the worthlessness of the human being. Only through deep contemplation can the pious achieve such a state.

Among the *Hasidim* the fear of God is viewed as complementary to the love of God. Basing his views on kabbalistic notions, the nineteenth-century thinker Zevi Elimelech Spira in his *Bene Yisaskhar* argues that effort is required to reach this state. Again, Levi Yitzhak of Berditchev in *Kedushat Levi* draws a distinction between the lower fear of sin, and the higher fear where one is overwhelmed by God's majesty. In this state a person has no self-awareness. Yet, he continues, this higher fear can only be attained as a product of the lower fear. In the Lithuanian *musar* movement of the nineteenth century, however, the fear of punishment occupies a more central place: it is viewed as essential for those who struggle to reach perfection.

In modern times, there has been less speculation about the different types of fear of God. This is in part due to the fact that the belief in punishment in the hereafter has been discarded by a large number of Jews. Such a shift has occurred because punishment as retaliation in a vindictive sense is generally rejected. In this light earlier discussions about the distinction between lower and higher types of fear have ceased to be relevant; as the fear of future punishment has lost its hold on Jewish consciousness, divine retribution seems no longer credible. Nonetheless, the higher type of fear which is evoked by an awareness of one's insignificance in the face of God's majesty still remains a feature of Jewish spirituality. As in the past, Jewish writers continue to view such fear as an essential preliminary to the love of God.

SOURCES

Midrash

According to the rabbis, the Jewish people have no terror of God; only when they sin do they fear the Lord:

'Before Israel sinned, the appearance of the glory of the Lord was a burning fire at the head of the mountain in the sight of all Israel' (Exodus 24:17). R. Abba b. Kahana said: Seven divisions of fire could not terrify Israel, but after they had sinned, they could not look even on the face of the intermediary; they feared to approach him, as it says, 'They were afraid to come at night to Moses for his face shone' (Exod. 34:30) . . . Before David sinned, he wrote 'The Lord is my light and my salvation: whom shall I fear?' (Ps. 27:1). But after he had sinned, it says, 'I will come upon him while he is weary, and will make him afraid' (2 Sam. 17:2). Before Solomon sinned, he ruled over the demons. After he sinned, he brought sixty warriors to protect his couch from the terror of night. As it says, 'Behold, Solomon's bed; sixty mighty men are about it of the mighty men of Israel' (Song of Songs 3:7).

(*Pes. R.* 69a in RA, p. 110)

Philo

According to the first-century Jewish philosopher Philo, the soul is to take delight in God:

The name of 'Eden' means 'luxuriance', symbol of a soul whose eyesight is perfect, disporting itself in virtues, leaping and skipping by reason of abundance of great joy, having set before it, as an enjoyment outweighing thousands of those that men deem sweetest, the worship and service of the Only Wise One. After taking a sheer draught of this bright joy, a member indeed of Moses' fellowship, not found among the indifferent, spake aloud in hymns of praise, and addressing his own mind cried, 'Delight in the Lord' (Ps. 37:4), moved by the utterance to an ecstasy of the love that is heavenly and divine, filled with loathing for those interminable bouts of softness and debauchery amid the seeming and so-called good things of mankind, while his whole mind is snatched up in holy frenzy by a divine possession, and he finds his gladness in God alone.

(Philo, *Noah's Work as a Planter* in TJP, pp. 76–77)

Eleazar ben Judah of Worms

In *Secret of Secrets* the medieval writer Eleazar ben Judah of Worms discussed the root of the fear of God:

It is not that he fears punishment in this world or in the next but rather he is afraid that he may not be perfect before God whom he loves. When a good deed presents itself to him and he finds it very difficult to perform, he nonetheless performs it, just as Abraham did when he bound his son on the altar, as it is written, 'For now I know that you are a God-fearing man' (Genesis 22:12).

(Eleazar ben Judah, *Secret of Secrets* in JM, 91)

Moses Luzzatto

For the eighteenth-century Jewish writer Moses Luzzatto, there are two types of fear:

It is necessary to state at the outset that there are two types of fear, one that is extremely easy to acquire, and another that is extremely difficult to acquire and, when attained, is an evidence of moral perfection. There is the fear of punishment, and there is the sense of awe. It is with the latter that we should identify the fear of sin . . .

The way to attain this sense of awe is to realize the following two veritable facts: first, that the Divine Presence exists everywhere in the universe; and second, that God exercises his providence over everything, both great and small. Nothing is hidden from his sight. Nothing is too great or too small for him to see. He beholds and discerns equally all things, whether trivial or important . . .

When a man is convinced that, wherever he is, he always stands in the presence of God, blessed be He, he is spontaneously imbued with fear lest he do anything wrong, and so detract from the exalted glory of God. 'Know what is above thee', said our sages, 'a seeing eye and a hearing ear, and all thy deeds written in a book'.

(Moses Luzzatto, *Path of the Upright*, in WJ, p. 450)

Baal Shem Tov

According to the founder of *Hasidism*, the Baal Shem Tov, *devekut* (cleaving to God) is of supreme importance in the spiritual quest:

It should be of indifference to him if he be considered as a person of little knowledge or as one who is knowledgeable in the entire Torah. The means for attaining this is *devekut*, cleaving to God, since the preoccupation with *devekut* leaves one no time to think of such matters, being constantly concerned with linking himself to the realm on high, to God, praised be He. In whatever act he performs in the service of God, he should consider that he thereby brings delight to his creator, praised be He, rather than for his own benefit . . .A person should not think to himself that he is greater than his neighbour because his service has reached the level of *devekut*, for he is only like other creatures who were formed to serve God, and God who endowed him with intelligence also endowed his neighbour with intelligence.

(*The Will of the Besht*, in JM, pp. 176–177)

Mystics of Bet El

At the beginning of the eighteenth century a circle of those who during prayer used kabbalistic meditation on the Godhead was established in Jerusalem:

In Bet El joy was attained by no artificial means, but by silent meditation, by introspection in an atmosphere in which music blended with men's thoughts, indeed a forgetfulness of externals. Each man's eyes were turned inwards. Seeking to mine the wealth of his own soul, he found there the soul of the universe. Amazed at his own discovery of this hidden treasure, the mystic pursues his course upwards until he obtains the ecstasy enthroned.

(Ariel Bension, *The Zohar in Moslem and Christian Spain*, in JM, p. 177)

DISCUSSION

1. Discuss the rabbinic view that one who truly loves God serves him not out of an ulterior motive but disinterestedly.

2. Why is it that the doctrine of Hell is no longer a major feature of Jewish theology?

FURTHER READING

Buber, Martin, *I and Thou*, Scribner, 2000.

Gillman, Neil, *The Way into Encountering God in Judaism*, Jewish Lights, 2000.

Goldstein, Niels Elliot, *Forests of the Night: The Fear of God in Early Hasidic Thought*, Jason Aronson, 1996.

Gordis, Daniel, *God Was Not in the Fire: The Search for a Spiritual Judaism*, Touchstone, 1997.

Hartman, David, *Love and Terror in the God Encounter: The Theological Legacy of Rabbi Joseph B. Soloveitchik, Vol. 1*, Jewish Lights, 2001.

Isaacs, Ronald, *Close Encounters: Jewish Views About God*, Jason Aronson, 1996.

Koltach, Alfred (ed.), *What Jews Say about God*, Jonathan David, 1999.

Kushner, Harold, *Who Needs God*, Fireside, 2002.

Raphael, Melissa, *The Female Face of God in Auschwitz*, Routledge, 2003.

Solomon, Lewis, *Jewish Spirituality: Revitalizing Judaism for the Twenty-First Century*, Jason Aronson, 1997.

Steinstaltz, Adin, Hanegbi, Yehuda (eds), *The Candle of God: Discourses on Chasidic Thought*, Jason Aronson, 1999.

Stone, Ira, *Seeking the Path to Life, Theological Meditations on God, the Nature of the Jewish People, Love, Life*, Jewish Lights, 1995.

CHAPTER 70

Messiah

Figure 70 The Messiah entering Jerusalem. Venice Haggadah, 1629. Coloured engraving. Copyright Beth Hatefutsoth Photo Archive.

The term 'Messiah' is an adaptation of the Hebrew *Ha-Mashiah* (the Anointed), a term frequently used in Scripture. Initially in the Book of Samuel the view was expressed that the Lord had chosen David and his descendants to reign over Israel to the end of time (2 Sam. 7; 23:1,3,5). In addition it was held that this figure had been granted dominion over all nations. Thus 2 Samuel 22:50–51 declares:

> For this I will extol thee, O Lord, among the
>   nations, and sing praises to thy name.
> Great triumphs he gives to his king,
>   and shows steadfast love to his anointed,
>   to David, and his descendants forever.

Here David is 'the anointed' in the sense that he was consecrated for a divine purpose. However, it was not only Israelites who would become God's emissaries. Second Isaiah, for example, described the Persian Cyrus as the Lord's anointed (Isa. 45:1). This early biblical doctrine thus presupposes that David's position would endure throughout his lifetime and would be inherited by a series of successors (including non-Israelites) who would carry out God's will.

With the fall of the Davidic empire after Solomon's death, there arose the view that the house of David would eventually rule over the two divided kingdoms as well as neighbouring peoples. Such an expectation paved the way for the vision of a transformation of earthly life. During the Second Temple period, the idea of eschatological salvation became an animating force in Jewish life. During this time there was intense speculation about the nature of the Messiah. In the

Book of Zechariah, for example, two messianic figures – the high priest and the messianic king – are depicted. Later, in the Dead Sea sect, these two figures also played an important role and were joined by a third personage, the prophet of the last days. These three messianic roles correspond to the three major functions of a future Jewish state in which kingship, priesthood and prophecy will exist side by side.

Yet despite such a proliferation of messianic figures, it was the Davidic Messiah who came to dominate Jewish thought. In the *Sibylline Oracles* he is portrayed in utopian terms. According to tradition, this king–Messiah will put an end to all wars on earth, make a covenant with the righteous and slay the wicked. The Psalms of Solomon extol the messianic king who will rebuild the land and draw all nations to Zion. Such a conception served as the basis for subsequent rabbinic reflection about messianic redemption, the ingathering of the exiles, and salvation in the world to come.

As time passed, the rabbis elaborated the themes found in the Bible and Jewish literature of the Second Temple period. In the *midrashim* and the *Talmud* they formulated an elaborate eschatological scheme divided into various stages. Some scholars emphasized that the prevalence of iniquity would be a prelude to the messianic age. Yet despite such dire predictions, the rabbis believed that the prophet **Elijah** would return prior to the coming of the Messiah to resolve all earthly problems. An illustration of this belief is found in the *Talmud* where the Aramaic word *teku* is used whenever a religious question cannot be resolved. Literally the word means 'let it remain undecided', but the term was interpreted as a phrase meaning: 'The Tishbite (Elijah) will resolve difficulties and problems'. As the forerunner of the Messiah, Elijah will announce his coming from the top of Mount Carmel: it will be the king–Messiah of Israel who will bring about the end of history and the advent of God's kingdom on earth.

In their depictions of the Messiah, the rabbis formulated the doctrine of **another Messiah**, the son of Joseph, who would precede the king–Messiah, the Messiah ben David. According to legend, this Messiah would engage in battle with **Gog and Magog**, the enemies of Israel, and be slain; only after this would the Messiah ben David arrive in his glory. With the coming of this second Messiah, the dispersion of Israel will cease and all exiles will return from the four corners of the earth to the Holy Land with God at their head. Clouds of glory shall spread over them, and they will come singing with joy on their lips.

In rabbinic literature, there is frequent speculation about the Days of the Messiah. In their descriptions of the messianic age, the rabbis stressed that the Days of the Messiah will be totally unlike the present world. On the length of this epoch, the rabbis differed. The first- to second-century sage Rabbi Eliezer, for instance, stated that the Days of the Messiah will be forty years; his contemporary Dosa said it will last four hundred years; Rabbi Jose the Galilean said in the same century that it would last three hundred and sixty years. In another rabbinic passage, it was taught that the world will endure six thousand years; two thousand in chaos; two thousand under the law; and two thousand during the messianic age. Despite such disagreements there was a general acceptance among the sages that at the end of this era a final judgement will come upon all humankind. Those who are judged righteous will enter into heaven (*Gan Eden*) whereas the wicked will be condemned to hell (*Gehenna*).

The destruction of the Temple and the city of Jerusalem in the first century CE intensified Jewish longing for the coming of the Messiah who would bring about the restoration of the kingdom. In this milieu, a Jewish sect emerged during the years following Herod's death, which believed that Jesus, a carpenter from Galilee, would usher in the era of messianic redemption. Attracting adherents from among the most marginalized sectors of Jewish society, Jesus soon aroused hostility and was put to death. Nonetheless, his disciples believed that he had risen from the dead and would return to reign in glory.

Although mainstream Judaism rejected such claims, the Jewish community continued to long for divine deliverance, and in 132 CE a messianic revolt was led by Simeon bar Kochba. This rebellion was inspired by the conviction that God would empower the Jews and when it failed the year of deliverance was put forward until the fifth century. In about 448 a messianic figure named Moses appeared in Crete, declaring he would lead the Jews across the sea to Judea. After his plan failed, Jews continued to engage in messianic speculation and their reflections are recorded in a number of midrashic works of the next few centuries. In the ninth century the scholar Saadiah Gaon calculated the date of final redemption on the basis of biblical texts. During these centuries of heightened messianic awareness, a number of pseudo Messiahs including Abu Isa al-Isphani (eighth century), Serene (eighth century), and Yudghan (eighth century) appeared on the scene.

During the time of the crusades, Jewish aspirations for the coming of the Messiah intensified. Initially the date of the First Crusade (1096) was viewed as the year of messianic deliverance. When the massacres of this year occurred, the Jewish community envisaged this tragedy as the birth pangs of the Messiah. In the next two centuries a number of Jewish writers attempted to determine the date of deliverance on the basis of verses in the Book of Daniel. Also during this period several would-be Messiahs appeared in the Jewish world. Previously such figures came from Asia Minor, Babylonia and Persia, but with the shift of Jewry to Mediterranean countries pseudo-Messiahs also emerged in western Europe. The most important false Messiah of this period was David Alroy (twelfth century) who, even after his death, was viewed by his followers as the Redeemer of Israel. In subsequent centuries messianic calculators continued to speculate about the year of deliverance and return of the exiles to the Holy Land on the basis of scriptural texts. Frequently they relied on kabbalistic forms of exegesis in their computations. Mystical works of this era such as the *Zohar* also contained speculations about the advent of the Messiah. In the thirteenth century another messianic figure, Abraham Abulafia, appeared on the scene; although he attracted a wide circle of followers, he also aroused considerable hostility from the scholarly community.

During the fourteenth and fifteenth centuries, the Jewish community continued to anticipate the coming of the Messiah despite his failure to appear in 1348 and 1403 as predicted. These centuries witnessed the production of messianic treatises, and various scholars speculated about the year of his arrival. This tradition of messianic speculation was continued in the sixteenth century by numerous sages, and at this time several false Messiahs appeared on the Jewish scene such as David Reuveni and Solomon Molko in the sixteenth century. Undaunted by the failure of these would-be Messiahs, messianic calculators of the seventeenth century persisted in their investigations. Eventually the Cossack rebellion of 1648 which devastated Polish Jewry heightened the belief that the coming of the Messiah was close at hand. In 1665 the arrival of the self-proclaimed messianic king, Shabbatai Zevi, was announced by his disciple Nathan of Gaza. Throughout the world, Jewry was electrified. Yet when Shabbatai converted to Islam, rather than face death, his apostasy evoked widespread disillusionment.

With the conversion to Islam of Shabbatai Zevi in the seventeenth century, the Jewish preoccupation with messianic calculation diminished: the longing for the Messiah who would lead the Jewish people to the Holy Land and bring about the end of history seemed a distant hope. Instead, eighteenth- and early nineteenth-century Jewry hailed the breaking down of the ghetto walls and the elimination of social barriers between Jews and Christians. In this milieu the belief in the kingdom of God inaugurated by the Messiah-king receded in importance. In its place the clarion call for liberty, equality and fraternity signified the dawning of a golden age for the Jewish people.

Within Reform Judaism in particular, the doctrine of messianic redemption was radically modified in the light of these developments. In the nineteenth century Reform Jews tended to interpret the new liberation in the Western world as the first step towards the realization of the messianic dream. For these reformers messianic redemption was understood in this-worldly terms. No longer, according to this view, is it necessary for Jews to pray for a restoration in *Eretz Israel* (the Land of Israel); rather Jews should view their own countries as Zion and their political leaders as bringing about the messianic age. Secular Zionists, on the other hand, saw the return to Israel as the legitimate conclusion to be drawn from the realities of Jewish life in Western countries, thereby viewing the state of Israel as a substitute for the Messiah himself. There has thus been a major transformation of Jewish thought in the modern world. In the past Jews longed for the advent of a personal Messiah who would bring about the messianic age and the ultimate fulfilment of human history. Although this doctrine continues to be upheld by a number of devout Orthodox believers, it has been eclipsed by a more secular outlook on the part of most Jews.

SOURCES

Book of Samuel

In the Book of Samuel the notion of redemption through a divinely appointed agent was explicitly expressed. Here David is depicted as the anointed in the sense that he was consecrated for a divine purpose:

> Now these are the last words of David:
> The oracle of David, the son of Jesse,
> . . . the anointed of the God of Jacob . . .
> The God of Israel has spoken,
> The Rock of Israel has said to me:
> When one rules justly over men,
> ruling in the fear of God . . .
> Yea, does not my house stand so with God?
> For he has made with me an everlasting covenant,
> ordered in all things and secure. (2 Samuel 23:1,3,5)

Of similar significance are the verses in Samuel where Nathan the prophet assured the king that his throne would be established for ever and that his throne would be secure forever. Speaking to David about the construction of the Temple, he stated:

> Thus says the Lord of hosts, I took you from the pasture, from following the sheep, that you should be prince over my people Israel; and I have been with you wherever you went, and have cut off all your enemies from before you; and will make for you a great name, like the name of the great ones of the earth. And I will appoint a place for my people Israel, and will plant them, that they may dwell in their own place . . . (2 Samuel 7:8–10)

The Two Messiahs

As a hero the Messiah ben Joseph will be mourned by the Jewish people. As the *Talmud* states:

> And the land shall mourn, every family apart; the family of the house of David apart, and their wives apart (Zechariah 12:12) . . . what is the cause of this mourning. Rabbi Dosa and our teachers differ on the point. One said, 'The cause is the slaying of the Messiah ben Joseph, and another said, The cause is the slaying of the evil inclination. It is well with him who said the cause is the slaying of the Messiah ben Joseph, for that agrees with the verse (Zechariah 12:10), 'And they shall look upon him who they have pierced, and they shall mourn for him as one mourneth for his only son.' (*Sukkah* 52a, JM, p. 48)

In his final struggle against the nation's enemies, God will himself act on behalf of Israel. Thus in the *midrash*, the rabbis maintain that:

> There are four shinings forth: the first was in Egypt, as it is written (Psalm 80:1), 'Give ear, O Shepherd of Israel, thou that leadest Joseph like a flock, thou that art enthroned upon the cherubim, shine forth'; the second was at the time of the giving of the Law, as it is written (Deut. 33:2), 'He shone forth from Mount Paran'; the third will take place in the days of Gog and Magog, as it is written (Psalm 94:1), 'Thou God to whom vengeance belongeth, shine forth'; the fourth will be in the days of the Messiah (ben David) as it is written (Psalm 50:2), 'Out of Zion, the perfection of beauty, shall God shine forth.' (*Siphre*, Deut. 34:3, JM, p. 48)

With the coming of the Messiah ben David, the dispersion of Israel will cease; all exiles will return from the four corners of the earth to the Holy Land. Thus Simeon ben Yohai proclaimed:

> Come and see how beloved is Israel before the Holy One, blessed is he; for wherever they went into exile the *Shekhinah* (God's presence) was with them. They went into exile in Egypt, and the *Shekhinah* was with them, as it is written (1 Sam. 2:27), 'Did I indeed reveal myself unto the house of thy father when they were in Egypt?' They went into exile in Babylonia, and the *Shekhinah* was with them, as it is written (Isaiah 43:14), 'For your sake I was sent to Babylonia.' Likewise, when they shall be redeemed in the future, the *Shekhinah* will be with them, as it is written (Deut. 30:3), 'Then the Lord thy God will return with thy captivity'. It does not say 'will bring back thy captivity' but 'will return with thy captivity' – teaching that the Holy One, blessed is he, returns with them from the places of exile. (*Megillah* 29a, JM, pp. 50–51)

The Sibylline Oracles

The *Sibylline Oracles* contain a variety of messianic ideas. Book II describes the confrontation between God and the anti-Messiah Beliar; here the Lord is victorious, bringing about the transformation of nature:

> From the stock of Sebaste Belair shall come in later time and shall raise the mountain heights and raise the sea, the great fiery sun and the bright moon, and he shall raise up the dead and shall perform many signs for men: but they shall not be effective in him. Nay, but he deceives mortals, and many shall he deceive, Hebrews faithful and elect and lawless too, and other men who have never yet listened to the word of God. But at whatsoever time the threatened vengeance of the Almighty God draws near, and fiery energy comes through the swelling surge to earth, and burns up Beliar and the overweening men, even all who have put their trust in him, then the world shall be under the domination of a woman's hands obeying her every behest. Then when a widow shall reign over the whole world and cast both gold and silver into the godlike deep, and the brass and iron of shortlived man cast into the sea, then the elements of the world one and all shall be widowed, what time God whose dwelling is in the sky shall roll up the heaven as a book is rolled. And the whole firmament in its varied forms shall fall on the divine earth and on the sea: and then shall flow a ceaseless cataract of raging fire, and shall burn land and sea, and the firmament of heaven and the stars and creation itself it shall cast into one molten mass and clean dissolve. (*Sibylline Oracles*, Book III 63–87 in TJM, p. 41)

The Prophet Elijah

According to the Book of Malachi, God will send his prophet Elijah before the Day of the Lord:

Behold, I will send you Elijah the prophet before the great and terrible day of the Lord comes. And he will turn the hearts of the fathers to their children and the hearts of the children to their fathers, lest I come and smite the land with a curse. (Malachi 4:5–6)

The *Talmud* indicates that Elijah is expected to solve difficult legal problems prior to the coming of the Messiah:

If the fourteenth (of *Nisan*) falls on the Sabbath, everything (that is leavened) must be removed before the Sabbath; and heave-offerings, whether unclean, or doubtful, or clean must be burnt . . . This is the ruling of Rabbi Judah ben Eliezer of Bartotha, which he stated in the name of Rabbi Joshua. But they said to him: 'Clean heave-offerings should not be burnt, lest persons be found who need to eat them (before the Passover).' . . . He retorted: 'Then on your reasoning even those in doubt should not be burnt, lest Elijah come and declare them clean.' They said to him: 'It has long been assured to Israel that Elijah will come neither on the eve of the Sabbath, nor on the eve of festivals on account of the trouble.' (*Pesahim* 13a, JM, pp. 46–47)

Elijah's role in the messianic era will be to certify that ritual uncleanliness of families which suffered from mixed marriages or forbidden unions, and also grant permission to hitherto excluded peoples from marrying Jews. Moreover, Elijah's task will be to bring back to the Jewish people those who had been wrongfully excluded from the community. All this is to be done in anticipation of the coming of the Messiah:

Rabbi Joshua said: I have received a tradition from Rabban Johanan ben Zakkai, who heard from his teacher, and his teacher from his teacher, as a *halakhah* given to Moses from Sinai, that Elijah will come not to declare unclean or clean (families in general), to remove afar or bring nigh (in general), but to remove afar those (families) that were brought nigh by force and to bring nigh those (families) that were afar by force. The family of Beth-Zerepha was in the land beyond Jordan, and the sons of Zion removed it afar by force. And yet another (family) was there, and the sons of Zion brought it nigh by force. The like of these Elijah will come to declare unclean or clean, to remove afar or to bring nigh. Rabbi Judah (ben Bathyra) says: To bring nigh but not to remove afar. Rabbi Ishmael says: To bring agreement where there is a matter for dispute. And the sages say: Neither to remove afar nor to bring nigh, but to make peace with the world, as it is written (Malachi 4:5): 'Behold I will send you Elijah the prophet . . . And he shall turn the heart of the fathers to the children, and the heart of the children to their fathers.' (*Eduyyot* 8:7, JM, p. 47)

Gog and Magog

According to Simeon ben Yohai, the war with Gog and Magog was one of the most terrible evils to befall humanity, yet viciousness in the family is worse:

Viciousness in man's own household is worse than the war with Gog and Magog. For it is said (Psalm 3:1), 'A Psalm of David, when he fled from Absalom his son'; and next it is written (Psalm

3:1), 'Lord, how many are mine adversaries become! Many are they that rise up against me.' Now in regard to the war with Gog and Magog it is written (Psalm 2:1), 'Why are the nations in an uproar? And why do the peoples mutter in vain?' – but it is not written, 'How many are mine adversaries become!' (*Berakhoth* 7b, JM, p. 49)

DISCUSSION

1. Discuss the reasons for the Jewish rejection of Jesus as the Messiah.

2. Is the concept of the Messiah still viable today?

FURTHER READING

Charlesworth, James (ed.), *The Messiah: Developments in Earliest Judaism and Christianity*, Fortress, 1992.

Cohn-Sherbok, Dan, *The Jewish Messiah*, T. and T. Clark, 1997.

Gubbay, Lucien, *Quest for the Messiah*, Sussex, 1990.

Jacobs, Louis, *A Jewish Theology*, Behrman House, 1973.

Klausner, Jacob, *The Messianic Idea in History*, London, 1956.

Ravitsky, Aviezer, *Messianism, Zionism and Jewish Religious Radicalism*, University of Chicago Press, 1996.

Saperstein, Marc (ed.), *Essential Papers on Messianic Movements and Personalities in Jewish History*, New York University Press, 1992.

Sarachek, J., *The Messianic Ideal in Medieval Jewish Literature*, New York, 1932.

Scholem, Gershom, *The Messianic Idea in Judaism*, New York, 1971.

Scholem, Gershom, *Shabbetai Zevi: The Mystical Messiah*, Routledge and Kegan Paul, 1973.

Silver, Abba Hillel, *A History of Messianic Speculation in Israel*, Gloucester, Mass, 1978.

Urbach, Ephraim, *The Sages*, Harvard University Press, 1987.

CHAPTER 71

Afterlife

Figure 71 Heaven and Hell, fifteenth-century Bolognese School, from Church of St Petronius, Bologna, Italy. Artist unknown. Copyright The Art Archive/Pinacoteca Nazionale Bologna/Dagli Orti.

Though there is no explicit reference to the hereafter in the Hebrew Bible, a number of expressions are used to refer to the realm of the dead. In Psalms 28:1 and 88:5 *bor* refers to a pit. In Psalm 6:5 as well as in Job 28:22 and 30:23, *mavet* is used in a similar sense. In Psalm 22:15 the expression *afar mavet* refers to the dust of death. In Exodus 15:12 and Jonah 2:6 the earth (*eretz*) is described as swallowing up the dead, and in Ezekiel 31:14 the expression *eretz tachtit* refers to the

nether parts of the earth where the dead dwell. Finally, the word *sheol* is frequently used to refer to the dwelling of the dead in the nether world. In addition, the words *ge ben hinnom, ge hinnom* and *ge* are used to refer to a cursed valley associated with fire and death where, according to Jeremiah, children were sacrificed as burnt offerings to Moloch and Baal. In later rabbinic literature the word ordinarily used for hell (*Gehenna*) is derived from these names.

Though these passages point to a Biblical conception of an afterlife, there is no indication of a clearly defined concept. It was only later in the Graeco-Roman world that such a notion began to take shape. The idea of a future world in which the righteous would be compensated for the ills they suffered in this life was prompted by a failure to justify the ways of God by any other means. According to Biblical theodicy individuals were promised rewards for obeying God's law and punishments were threatened for disobedience. As time passed, however, it became clear that life did not operate in accordance with such a tidy scheme. In response to this dilemma the rabbis developed a doctrine of reward and punishment in the hereafter. Such a belief helped Jews to cope with suffering in this life, and it also explained, if not the presence of evil in the world, then at least the value of creation despite the world's ills.

Given that there is no explicit belief in eternal salvation in the Bible, the rabbis of the post-Biblical period were faced with the difficulty of proving that the doctrine of resurrection of the dead is contained in Scripture. To do this they employed methods of exegesis based on the assumption that every word in the Torah was transmitted by God to Moses. Thus, for example, Eleazar, the son of R. Jose (second century) claimed to have refuted the sectarians who maintained that resurrection is not a Biblical doctrine:

I said to them: 'You have falsified your Torah . . . For you maintain that resurrection is not a Biblical doctrine, but it is written (in Numbers 15:31ff.), "Because he has despised the word of the Lord, and has broken his commandment, that person shall be utterly cut off; his iniquity shall be upon him." Now seeing that he shall be utterly cut off in this world, when shall his iniquity be upon him? Surely in the next world.' (San. 90b)

According to rabbinic Judaism, the World-to-Come (*Olam HaBa*) is divided into several stages. First, there is the time of messianic redemption. According to the *Talmud* the Messianic Age (*Yemot HaMashiah*) is to take place on earth after a period of calamity, and will result in a complete fulfilment of every human wish. Peace will reign throughout nature; Jerusalem will be rebuilt; and at the close of this era, the dead will be resurrected and rejoined with their souls, and a final judgement will come upon all mankind. Those who are judged righteous will enter into heaven (*Gan Eden*) which is portrayed in various ways in rabbinic literature. One of the earliest descriptions of Gan Eden is found in the *midrash Konen*:

The *Gan Eden* at the east measures 800,000 years (at ten miles per day or 3650 miles per year). There are five chambers for various classes of the righteous. The first is built of cedar, with a ceiling of transparent crystal. This is the habitation of non-Jews who become true and devoted converts to Judaism. They are headed by Obadiah the prophet and Onkelos the proselyte, who teach them the Law. The second is built of cedar, with a ceiling of vine silver. This is the habitation of the penitents, headed by Manasseh, king of Israel, who teaches them the law.

The third chamber is built of silver and gold, ornamented with pearls. It is very spacious, and contains the best of heaven and of earth, with spices, fragrance, and sweet odours. In the centre of this chamber stands the Tree of Life, 500 years high. Under its shadow rest Abraham, Isaac, and Jacob, the tribes, those of the Egyptian exodus, and those who died in the wilderness, headed by Moses and Aaron. There are also David and Solomon, crowned and Chileab, as if living,

attending on his father, David. Every generation of Israel is represented except that of Absalom and his confederates. Moses teaches them the Law, and Aaron gives instruction to the priests.

The Tree of Life is like a ladder on which the souls of the righteous may ascend and descend. In a conclave above are seated the Patriarchs, the Ten Martyrs, and those who sacrificed their lives for the cause of his sacred Name. These souls descend daily to the *Gan Eden* to join their families and tribes, where they lounge on soft cathedrals studded with jewels. Everyone, according to his excellence, is received in audience to praise and thank the ever-living God; and all enjoy the brilliant light of the *Shekhinah*. The flaming sword, changing from intense heat to icy cold, and from ice to glowing coals, guards the entrance against living mortals. The size of the sword is ten years. The souls on entering paradise are bathed in the 248 rivulets of balsam and attar.

The fourth chamber is made of olive-wood and is inhabited by those who have suffered for the sake of their religion. Olives typify bitterness in taste and brilliancy in light (olive oil), symbolizing persecution and its reward. The fifth chamber is built of precious stones, gold and silver, surrounded by myrrh and aloes. In front of the chamber runs the river Gihon, on whose banks are planted shrubs affording perfume and aromatic incense. There are couches of gold and silver and fine drapery. This chamber is inhabited by the Messiah ben David, Elijah and the Messiah of Ephraim (Joseph). In the centre are a canopy made of the cedars of Lebanon, in the style of the tabernacle, with posts and vessels of silver; and a settee of Lebanon wood with pillars of silver and a seat of gold, the covering thereof of purple. (ICJ, p. 28)

Conversely, those who are judged wicked are condemned to eternal punishment. In one of the most elaborate descriptions of this place of punishment, Moses is depicted as guided by an angel through *Gehenna*:

When Moses and the angel of Hell entered Hell together, they saw men being tortured by the angels of destruction. Some sinners were suspended by their hair and their breasts by chains of fire. Such punishments were inflicted on the basis of the sins that were committed: those who hung by their eyes had looked lustfully upon their neighbours' wives and possessions; those who hung by their ears had listened to empty and vain speech and did not listen to the Torah; those who hung by their tongues had spoken foolishly and slanderously; those who hung by their hands had robbed and murdered their neighbours. The women who hung by their hair and breasts had uncovered them in the presence of young men in order to seduce them. (LJ, pp. 310–313)

On the basis of this scheme of eternal salvation and damnation – which was at the heart of rabbinic theology throughout the centuries – it might be expected that modern Jewish theologians would attempt to explain contemporary Jewish history in the context of traditional eschatology. This, however, has not happened: instead many Jewish writers have set aside doctrines concerning messianic redemption, resurrection, final judgement and reward for the righteous and punishment for the wicked. This shift in emphasis is in part due to the fact that the views expressed in the narrative sections of the *midrashim* and the **Talmud** are not binding. While all Jews are obliged to accept the divine origin of the Law, this is not so with regard to theological concepts and theories expounded by the rabbis. Thus it is possible for a Jew to be religious and pious without accepting all the central beliefs of mainstream Judaism. Indeed, throughout Jewish history there has been widespread confusion as to what these beliefs are.

The doctrine of the **resurrection of the dead** has in modern times been largely replaced in both Orthodox and non-Orthodox Judaism by the belief in the **immortality of the soul**. The original belief in resurrection was an eschatological hope bound up with the rebirth of the nation in the Days of the Messiah, but as this messianic concept faded into the background so also did this doctrine. For most Jews the physical resurrection is simply inconceivable in the light of a scientific understanding of the world. The late Chief Rabbi of Great Britain, Dr Joseph Herman

Hertz, for example, argued that what really matters is the doctrine of the immortality of the soul. Thus he wrote:

> Many and various are the folk beliefs and poetical fancies in the rabbinic writings concerning Heaven, *Gan Eden* and Hell, *Gehinnom*. Our most authoritative religious guides, however, proclaim that no eye hath seen, nor can mortal fathom, what awaiteth us in the Hereafter; but that even the tarnished soul will not forever be denied spiritual bliss. (ICJ, p. 28)

In the Reform community a similar attitude prevails. A well-known statement of the beliefs of Reform Judaism contends that Reform Jews:

> reassert the doctrine of Judaism that the soul is immortal, grounding this belief on the divine nature of the human spirit, which forever finds bliss in righteousness and misery in wickedness. We reject as ideas not rooted in Judaism the belief in bodily resurrection and in *Gehenna* and *Eden* as eternal punishment or reward. (ICJ, p. 28)

Traditional rabbinic eschatology has thus lost its force for a large number of Jews in the modern world, and in consequence there has been a gradual this-worldly emphasis in Jewish thought. Significantly, this has been accompanied by a powerful attachment to the state of Israel. For many Jews the founding of the Jewish state is the central focus of their religious and cultural identity. Jews throughout the world have a deep admiration for the astonishing achievements of Israelis in reclaiming the desert and building a viable society, and great respect for the heroism of Israel's soldiers and statesmen. As a result, it is not uncommon for Jews to equate Jewishness with Zionism, and to see Judaism as fundamentally nationalistic in character. Whereas the rabbis put the belief in the hereafter at the centre of their religious life, modern Jewish thinkers have largely abandoned such an other-worldly outlook. Although a number of contemporary Jews still continue to embrace some form of immortality, this is far removed from the elaborate doctrine of the hereafter as formulated in traditional rabbinic sources.

SOURCES

Talmud

The *Talmud* contains speculation about the Days of the Messiah (also referred to as 'The World to Come'). This passage contains a depiction how the land will be divided:

And the division in the World to Come will not be like the division in this world. In this world, should a man possess a cornfield, he does not possess an orchard; should he possess an orchard he does not possess a cornfield. But in the World to Come, there will be no single individual who will not possess land in mountain, lowland, and valley.

(Bavva Batra 122a in TJM, p. 51)

Resurrection of the Dead

According to the rabbis, the doctrine of the resurrection of the dead is contained in Scripture:

Whence do we know resurrection from the Torah? From the verse, 'Then shall Moses and the children of Israel sing this song unto the Lord' (Exodus 15:1). Not 'sang', but 'sing' is written. Since Moses and the children of Israel did not sing a second time in this life, the text must mean that they will sing after resurrection. Likewise it is written, 'Then shall Joshua build an altar unto the Lord God of Israel' (Joshua 8:30). Not 'build' but 'shall build' is stated. Thus resurrection is intimated in the Torah.

(Sanhedrin 91b in TJM, p. 53)

The Holocaust and the Future Life

In considering the religious implications of the Holocaust, a number of Orthodox thinkers have viewed the terrible events of the Nazi era as part of the unfolding of God's eschatological plan. For Sha'ar Yashuv Cohen, who has served as Chief Rabbi of Haifa, the Holocaust should be seen as part of the birth pangs of the Messiah initiating the redemption of the Jewish people:

I conclude from this that we are all living in a generation too sublime for human comprehension. We cannot understand the suffering we have endured, and we have similar difficulty in fathoming the salvation and redemption we have received. If we know how to believe, how to trust in the Lord, and how to appreciate those who regarded all this suffering as a prelude to the 'beginning of the flowering of our redemption' – then the *Hester Panim* (hiding of the face) of the Holocaust will be transformed into the magnificent revelation of miracles in our time, before our eyes.

May it be the will of the one who assured us 'Even when they are in the land of their enemies, I will neither reject nor abhor them, to destroy them and to break my covenant with them' (Lev. 26:44) to fulfil his promise. May it be his will that the Holocaust and the wars for *Eretz Israel* will constitute the entire measure of the birth pangs of the Messiah, and that from now on we will receive the salvation and the consolation of the Holy One, blessed be He, for the people of Israel, and witness the complete redemption, speedily in our days.

(Sha'ar Yashuv Cohen, '*Hester Panim* in the Holocaust versus the Manifest Miracles in our Generation', in HT, p. 101)

Immortality of the Soul

As the modern Jewish writer Louis Jacobs explains, for most modern Jews the concept of the resurrection of the dead has been replaced by the doctrine of the immortality of the soul:

The general tendency among modern Jews who do believe in an after-life is to place the stress on the immortality of the soul rather than on the resurrection of the dead. We can see why this should be so. Already in the Middle Ages . . . the difficulties of the purpose of the resurrection and in the idea of a body inhabiting eternity were recognised. In more recent years some Jewish thinkers have tried to defend the doctrine of the resurrection and to prefer it, in fact, to that of the immortality of the soul. The argument runs that the doctrine of immortality is Greek, not Jewish, and that it fails to consider the survival of the whole person. To prefer the doctrine of the resurrection to that of immortality on the grounds that the latter is Greek is to overlook the evidence that the doctrine of the resurrection in all probability is Persian in origin. Why should this matter? It is all a question of studying ideas which have come into Judaism from without to see how a viable Jewish theology can be constructed. One can see the point about the whole human personality surviving but, unless we are prepared to accept the biological details of an actual recomposition of the physical body, we are still affirming a version of the immortality of the soul even when we affirm the doctrine of the resurrection. To speak of a spiritual body or an especially refined body is really to use only different words for the same thing. We ought to be frank enough to admit that all the speculations regarding life here on earth after the resurrection simply do not 'ring a bell' for us whereas the more spiritual interpretation of a Maimonides does.

(Louis Jacobs, *A Jewish Theology*, in JT, pp. 318–319)

DISCUSSION

1. In what ways has a belief in the afterlife provided a consolation for Jewish suffering through the centuries?

2. Is belief in life after death consonant with a scientific world view?

FURTHER READING

Cohn-Sherbok, Dan, *Holocaust Theology: A Reader*, Exeter University Press, 2002.

Gershom, Yonassan, *Jewish Tales of Reincarnation*, Jason Aronson, 1999.

Jacobs, Louis, *A Jewish Theology*, Behrman House, 1973.

Pinson, Dov Ber, *Reincarnation and Judaism: The Journey of the Soul*, Jason Aronson, 1999.

Raphael, Simcha Paul, *Jewish Views of the Afterlife*, Jason Aronson, 1996.

Sonsino, Rifat, Syme, Daniel, *What Happens After I Die: Jewish Views of Life after Death*, UAHC Press, 1990.

Spitz, Elie Kaplan, *Does the Soul Survive?: A Jewish Journey to Belief in Afterlife, Past Lives and Living with Purpose*, Jewish Lights, 2000.

Wexelman, David, *The Jewish Concept of Reincarnation and Creation: Based on the Writings of Rabbi Chaim Vital*, Jason Aronson, 1998.

Wright, J. Edward, *The Early History of Heaven*, Oxford University Press, 2000.

CHAPTER 72

Community Life

Figure 72 Jews at prayer in Richmond, London. Copyright David Rose.

Through the centuries Jews have been organized as a distinct group. In ancient Israel they were a Hebrew clan; subsequently, as they changed from a nomadic to an agricultural existence, they settled in towns. In consequence their leadership became urbanized: elders were responsible for administering justice, and towns were organized in territorial or tribal units. During the Babylonian exile the emergence of Jewish institutions established the pattern for later communal development throughout the diaspora. As early as the second century BCE Jews in Alexandria formed their own

corporation with a council (*gerousia*) which conducted its affairs in conformity with Jewish law, built synagogues, and sent taxes collected for the Temple to Jerusalem. Throughout the Roman Empire, Jews were judged by their own courts according to Jewish law – this system established the basis for legal autonomy that characterized Jewish life for the next two millennia.

With the destruction of the Second Temple in 70 CE, Jewish life underwent a major transformation. In Israel the patriarchate together with the Sanhedrin served as the central authority. In Babylonia the *exilarch* was the leader of the community along with the heads of rabbinical academies (*geonim*). In its daily life Jewry was bound by the *halakhah* (Jewish law), and synagogues, law courts, schools, philanthropic institutions and ritual baths constituted the framework for communal life. In North Africa and Spain, the *nagid* was the head of the community. Later in the medieval period, communal leadership in the Franco-German region was exercised by rabbinical authorities, and daily existence was regulated by traditional law. As in Babylonia, a wide range of institutions dealt with all aspects of community affairs, and taxes were raised to provide for a wide range of needs: ransoming captives, providing hospitality to Jewish visitors, visiting the sick, caring for the elderly, collecting dowries for poor brides, maintaining widows, and supervising Jewish baths. As elsewhere in the Jewish world, the focus of the community was the synagogue which served as the centre for Jewish worship and study.

To regulate Jewish life, communal statutes (*takkanot ha-kahal*) were stipulated by the community's constitution. These were amplified by special ordinances and enactments. To ensure their enforcement, a court (*bet din*) was presided over by a panel of judges (*dayyanim*). In certain cases they excommunicated individuals, or in the case of Jews who informed on fellow Jews, they passed sentences of death. The community's head (*parnas*) was recognized by secular or Church authorities as the representative of the Jewish populace. He and the local rabbi were frequently designated as *Magister Judaeorum* (Master of the Jews) or *Judenbischof* (Bishop of the Jews). From the fourteenth century, Polish Jewry gained dominance in Eastern Europe, and communal autonomy was often invested in the Jewish community of a central town which had responsibility for smaller communities in the region. In Poland–Lithuania the Council of the Four Lands functioned as a Jewish parliament. By contrast in the Ottoman Empire, authority was vested in a chief rabbi (*hakham bashi*) who was recognized as the Jewish community's representative. Each province of the Empire had its own chief rabbi, and in Egypt this office replaced the *nagid.*

With the advent of the Enlightenment in the nineteenth century, the traditional pattern of Jewish life was transformed. Previously Jews were unable to opt out of the community. However, with full civil rights, Jews became full members of the wider community and membership in the Jewish community was voluntary. In modern times Jews have adjusted communal life to contemporary demands throughout the diaspora, and in Israel new forms of association have emerged. In contrast with previous centres where Jewish religious life was uniform in character, the community has fragmented into a number of differing religious groupings, each with its own character.

At the far right of the religious spectrum traditional **Orthodoxy** has attempted to preserve the religious beliefs and practices of the Jewish faith. From the late eighteenth century Orthodox Judaism opposed changes to Jewish existence brought about by the Enlightenment and the innovations advanced by Reform Jews. In essence, Orthodoxy is synonymous with rabbinic Judaism as it developed through the centuries. Orthodox Jewry accepts the Torah as divinely revealed, and the process of rabbinic expansion of Biblical law as guided by God's providence.

From the very beginning of the modern age Orthodox Jews rejected the values of the Enlightenment and proclaimed a ban of excommunication against Reformers. Such an approach was advocated by Mosheh Sofer of Pressburg (eighteenth to nineteenth century) and was characteristic of Hungarian Orthodoxy as well as eastern European Jewry. In addition, it found expression in the anti-Zionist *Agudat Israel* movement. Other Orthodox leaders, however, attempted to integrate traditional Judaism and modern values. Such figures as the nineteenth-century thinkers Samson Raphael Hirsch and Azriel Hildesheimer, as well as members of the Breuer and Carlebach families, formed the Neo-Orthodox movement from which centrist Orthodoxy later emerged in the West. A similar development occurred in eastern Europe and can be traced from Elijah Gaon of Vilna (eighteenth century), Hayyim of Volozhin (eighteenth to nineteenth century) and the Berlin and Soloveichik families to Isaac Jacob Reines (nineteenth to twentieth century) and Abraham Isaac Kook (nineteenth to twentieth century).

In the United States the Orthodox movement underwent enormous growth with the arrival of Orthodox scholars, heads of *yeshivot* and Hasidic leaders during the first half of the twentieth century. From 1944 *Torah Umesorah* organized a network of Hebrew day schools and *yeshivot* throughout the country. Today there are almost forty *yeshivot* for advanced talmudic studies. The most important Orthdox rabbinic institutions are Yeshivah University in New York and the Hebrew Theological College in Chicago. The largest Orthodox synagogue body is the Union of Orthodox Jewish Congregations of America. As elsewhere, Orthodoxy in the USA is divided into two distinct groups: traditionalists and modernists. The institutions of Orthodox traditionalists include: the Union of Orthodox Rabbis, the Rabbinical Alliance, and *Agudat Israel*. Modern Orthodoxy's religious leadership on the other hand is found in the Rabbinical Council of America. Elsewhere in the diaspora Orthodox Judaism constitutes the largest religious body. In France, for example, several traditional *yeshivot* have merged alongside the old-fashioned *École Rabbinique*. In Great Britain a large network of congregations is maintained by the United Synagogue. Parallel with this body is the Federation of Synagogues and the Spanish and Portugese Jews Congregation. On the traditional right is the Union of Orthodox Hebrew Congregations and the *yeshivah* community of Gateshead.

In Israel Orthodoxy is the formally organized religious body of the state. Rabbinical courts exercise exclusive jurisdiction in matters of personal status and the Orthodox religous judges are presided over by the two Chief Rabbis (*Sephardi* and *Ashkenazi*). At the local level Orthodox religious councils cater to religious needs: the provision of ritual baths, burial facilities, registration of marriages, care of synagogues, and the promotion of religious education. In addition, a state religious school system run on Orthodox lines exists alongside the state school system. Within the government Orthodox religious parties represent both religious Zionists and the non-Zionist *Agudat* camp.

Within the Orthodox camp **Hasidism** plays an important role. Founded by Israel ben Eliezer (Baal Shem Tov) in the eighteenth century as a reaction against arid rabbinism, the Hasidic movement spread to southern Poland, the Ukraine and Lithuania. This popular mystical movement was initially condemned by Orthodox leaders such as the Gaon of Vilna in the eighteenth century; eventually, however, it became a major force in Jewish life. Prior to World War Two hundreds of Hasidic dynasties flourished in eastern Europe, but after the Holocaust most of the remaining leaders (*rebbes*) escaped to Israel and the United States. Today the best known groups (named after their town of origin) are: *Belz, Bobova, Gur, Klausenburg-Zanz, Lubavich, Satmar* and *Vizhnits*. Each of these groups preserves its traditions, including a distinctive type of dress worn by noblemen in the eighteenth century. Like the Orthodox generally, the *Hasidim* adhere to traditional Jewish practices as codified in the *Code of Jewish Law*.

Moving to the centre of the religious spectrum, **Conservative Judaism** constitutes one of the major developments in modern Jewish life. Founded by Zacharias Frankel in the middle of the nineteenth century, it advocates a middle of the road stance in which traditional Jewish law is observed, but modified according to contemporary needs. According to Frankel, Judaism should be understood as an evolving religious way of life. In the United States, this ideology was propounded by the Jewish Theological Seminary founded in 1956. Later its president Solomon Schechter, founded the United Synagogue as the movement's lay organization. From 1940 to 1972 the Seminary was headed by Louis Finkelstein; during this time a West Coast affiliate of the Seminary (the University of Judaism) was established in Los Angeles. Through its rabbinical body (the Rabbinical Association) and its synagogual association (the United Synagogue of America), the movement grew in strength and founded a variety of innovative institutions including a camping programme (*Ramah* as well as United Synagogue Youth), radio and TV programmes, Solomon Schechter Day Schools, and New York's Jewish Museum. In 1972 Finkelstein was succeeded by Gerson D. Cohen who introduced far-reaching changes, including the ordination of women. By 1985 830 congregations were affiliated to the United Synagogue of America with a membership of 1,250,000. Elsewhere, the movement is represented by the World Council of Synagogues. An offshoot of the Conservative movement, **Reconstructionist Judaism**, has also made an important impact on Jewish life. This new religious body was founded by Mordecai Kaplan who rejected supernaturalism and instead propounded a new view of Judaism. Currently, Reconstructionist Judaism has its headquarters at the Rabbinical College in Pennsylvania; affiliated congregations are organized in the Federation of Reconstructionist Congregations.

On the far left of the religious spectrum is Reform Judaism. At the beginning of the nineteenth century the communal leader, Israel Jacobson, initiated a programme of educational and liturgical reform. Following this initiative, Reform temples were established in Germany and elsewhere. The central aim of the early Reformers was to adapt Jewish worship to contemporary aesthetic standards. For these innovators, the informality of the traditional service seemed foreign and undignified, and they therefore insisted on greater decorum, more participation in prayer, a choir and hymns as well as alterations in prayers and the length of the service. Despite the criticisms of the Orthodox, the Reform movement underwent considerable growth, and during the nineteenth century a series of Reform synods took place in Europe.

In the United States **Reform** first appeared in Charleston, South Carolina in 1824. In subsequent years German immigrants founded a number of congregations throughout the country. Under the leadership of Isaac Mayer Wise the first Conference of American Reform Rabbis took place in Philadelphia in 1869; this was followed in 1873 by the founding of the Union of American Hebrew Congregations. Two years later Wise established the Hebrew Union

College, the first American rabbinical seminary. In 1885 the principles of the Reform movement were formulated by a group of rabbis in the Pittsburgh Platform. In 1889 the Central Conference of American Rabbis was established with Isaac Mayer Wise as president. Dissatisfaction with the Pittsburgh Platform led to the adoption of a more traditionalist position (the Columbus Platform) in 1937. In recent years Reform Judaism has undergone further development: by 1980, 739 congregations were affiliated with the Union of American Hebrew Congregations; during the latter half of the twentieth century the Jewish Institute of Religion in New York combined with the Hebrew Union College and branches were established in Los Angeles and Jerusalem. Elsewhere Reform Judaism is represented in South Africa, Asia, Australia, and Europe; these congregations are affiliated with the World Union for Progressive Judaism. In addition to these movements, **Humanistic Judaism** was founded in the 1960s by Rabbi Sherwin Wine in Detroit, Michigan. Currently it has become an international movement with branches throughout the world. A further alternative to Jewish existence is fostered by the growing Jewish Renewal movement.

SOURCES

Orthodox Judaism

Orthodox Judaism continues the traditions of previous centuries, insisting that modern Jews must embrace the central principles of the Jewish faith as it developed through the centuries:

> Traditionally Jewish life centred around the observance of the law. It was an article of faith that the Torah was given to Moses in its entirety by God. Therefore it must be true in every particular. In handing down the Torah, Moses acted like a scribe, writing from dictation, and thus the whole Pentateuch is literally the word of God. This conviction sustained the Jewish community through many disasters, from the loss of the Temple in 70 CE, through the experience of exile and during periods of persecution and massacre. Together with the oneness of God, it was an essential element of the Jewish creed.
>
> Today, the findings of Biblical criticism and the general scepticism of the times have undermined this view of the Torah. Nonetheless, some remain faithful. The Orthodox define themselves as those who remain true to the doctrine that the Torah is from Heaven. This has enormous practical consequence on their day-to-day way of life since they follow not only the provision of the Pentateuch, but also all the manifold details of the Oral Law.

(In SIJ, p. 25)

Hasidism

In the modern world, *Hasidism* has become an important force in Jewish life:

The most prominent group among the Orthodox are the *Hasidim*. The word *hasidim* means 'the pious' and the *Hasidim* are known for their spiritual devotion. They are immediately recognizable. The men are bearded and wear side-curls which are twisted and tucked behind their ears. They are invariably dressed in black – large black hat worn over small black skull-cap, black jacket, plain black trousers and black shoes and socks. Their shirts are white, buttoned up to the neck and worn without a tie. Issuing forth from the waistband of their trousers are the ritual fringes which are attached to their undergarments. These are generally discreetly tucked into trouser pockets. On the Sabbath, they are even more resplendent. The weekday jacket is exchanged for a long black silk coat, and instead of the everyday trilby a magnificent fur hat may be worn.

Female dress is perhaps less distinctive. In common with all the Orthodox, the women follow the rules of modesty. Their skirts cover their knees; their sleeves are extended over their elbows and their necklines are cut high. The married women wear wigs. This is because, according to the law, once a woman is married, she must conceal her hair so she is no longer a temptation to other men . . .

Hasidism arose in the early eighteenth century in eastern Europe. Its founder, Israel ben Eliezer (1700–60) who was known as the Baal Shem Tov (the Master of the Good Name) stressed personal piety and mystical worship. In Europe it centred around the courts of the various spiritual leaders, the *tzaddikim*, who were believed to have extraordinary powers. When a *tzaddik* died, he was succeeded in the early days by his most prominent disciple. Subsequently, however, it became a hereditary position and was passed down to son, son-in-law or grandson . . . The *tzaddik* is believed to have a special relationship with God. His prayers protect his followers, miracles are not unknown and stories of his saintliness are circulated. He is the spiritual leader of his community and the greatest honour for his disciples is to sit at his Sabbath meal and to share in his leftovers. Hasidic worship is characterized by intense joy.

(In SIJ, pp. 27–28)

Conservative Judaism

Conservative Judaism is one of the major movements in modern Judaism:

Among religious Jews, the great theological divide is between the Orthodox and the non-Orthodox. Non-Orthodox Judaism arose in response to Jewish participation in mainstream, secular civilization. Increasingly, western European Jews were uncomfortable with the traditional services; many could no longer read Hebrew and some of the ancient doctrines and practices were felt to have no relevance to modern life. Initially liturgical changes were made. Hymns and prayers were offered in German; choral singing was introduced and the services were conducted with less enthusiasm and more decorum. Later, in the mid-nineteenth century, an attempt was made to study the tradition with no religious presuppositions. Taking note of advances in Biblical scholarship, many Jews found they could no longer believe that the entire Written and Oral Torah was handed down complete and perfect by God to Moses on Mount Sinai.

Conservative Judaism is essentially an American phenomenon. It arose in reaction to what were perceived as the radical excesses of the Reform movement. It stands midway between the certainties of Orthodoxy and the liberties of Reform. Less than half of all

American Jews affiliate with a synagogue. Of those who do, the largest number join the Conservative movement; the Reform attracts the next biggest group and the Orthodox, although both visible and committed, comes a lagging third. Since the United States has the largest Jewish community in the world, the Conservative movement influences a large number of people – possibly as many as a million and a half.

Today Conservative Judaism covers a wide variety of beliefs and considerable tensions exist between members of the Rabbinical Assembly, the official association for Conservative rabbis. Nonetheless, in a recent statement, a measure of agreement was reached: 'We accept the results of modern scholarship. We agreed that historical development of the tradition had taken place, and that the tradition continues to develop. We all agreed on the indispensability of the *halakhah* (Jewish law) for Conservative Jews, but a *halakhah* which responds to changing times and changing needs.'

(In SIJ, pp. 29–30)

Reconstructionist Judaism

Reconstructionist Judaism is an offshoot of Conservative Judaism and has played an important role in American Jewish life:

Reconstructionism is a new movement which grew out of Conservative Judaism. It was founded by Mordecai Kaplan (1881–1983) who for many years taught at the Conservative Jewish Theological Seminary. He believed that Judaism is a religious civilization not a divinely revealed religion. He defined God not as a supernatural being, but as 'the sum of all the animating, organizing forces and relationships which are forever making a cosmos out of chaos'. Thus Reconstructionism, like Conservative Judaism, retains many traditional Jewish practices, but differs from its parent movement in explaining its theological beliefs in this-worldly terms. Today the movement supports its own rabbinical training college and has established a small network of synagogues.

(In SIJ, p. 30)

Reform Judaism

Reform Judaism is one of the largest movements worldwide:

The Reform movement arose in early nineteenth-century Germany. Having had the benefit of a Western secular education and mixing freely with gentiles, these German Jews were embarrassed by the traditional worship services. They created a liturgy which was more dignified and more in keeping with Western ideas. They called their houses of worship temples rather than synagogues; they preferred to pray in German rather than Hebrew and they emphasized the ethical and universal ideals of Judaism. They no longer yearned for the restoration of sacrifice in the Jerusalem Temple and they were not comfortable with may of the traditional laws concerning food, clothing and day-to-day living.

As in Conservative Judaism, there are many shades of opinion to be found among Reform Jews. In 1885 a group of American rabbis produced what was called the Pittsburgh Platform . . . These early Reform leaders saw themselves as the spiritual descendants of the Biblical prophets, calling the people back to a more ethical way of life and dispensing with all the old rituals and ceremonies which obstructed rather than contributed to holiness. In recent years the Reform movement has become more traditional. In Western society generally, there is a greater interest in ethical roots, and Reform Jews have not been immune to this.

(In SIJ, pp. 30–31)

Humanistic Judaism

Humanistic Judaism was founded in the 1960s by Rabbi Sherwin Wine:

> Humanistic Judaism is a recent offshoot of the Reform movement. It was founded by Rabbi Sherwin Wine (b. 1928) and it extols the humanistic aspects of Judaism. Like the Reconstructionists, Humanistic Jews abandoned belief in a supernatural deity and, in its manifesto, the Humanistic Federation declares: 'The natural universe stands on its own, requiring no supernatural intervention . . . Judaism, as the civilization of the Jews, is a human creation.'
>
> (In SRJ, p. 32)

DISCUSSION

1. How did the Enlightement in the nineteenth century transform Jewish life?

2. Discuss the fragmentation of the Jewish community into conflicting ideological groupings in the contemporary world.

FURTHER READING

Cohn-Sherbok, Dan, *Modern Judaism*, Macmillan, 1996.

Cohn-Sherbok, Dan and Lavinia, *The American Jew*, Eerdmans, 1995.

Eleazar, Daniel, Geffen, Rela, *The Conservative Movement in Judaism*, State University of New York, 2000.

Gillman, Neil, *Conservative Judaism: The New Century*, Behrman House, 1993.

Greene, Laura, Wesson, Lisa, *I am an Orthodox Jew*, Henry Holt and Co., 1979.

Helmreich, William, *The World of the Yeshiva: An Intimate Portrait of Orthodox Jewry*, KTAV, 2000.

Hirsch, Ammiel, Reinman, Yosef, *One People, Two Worlds: A Reform Rabbi and An Orthodox Rabbi Explore the Issues that Divide Them*, Schocken Books, 2002.

Meyer, Michael, *Response to Modernity: A History of the Reform Movement in Judaism*, Oxford University Press, 1990.

Raphael, Mark, *Profiles in American Judaism*, HarperCollins, 1988.

Sklare, Marshall, *Conservative Judaism*, Schocken, 1972.

Steinsaltz, Adin, *Teshuvah: A Guide for the Newly Observant Jew*, Jason Aronson, 1996.

CHAPTER 73

Jewish Education

Figure 73 Yeshiva University, 1948, year of the establishment of the Jewish State of Israel. Yeshiva University is the oldest and most comprehensive educational institute under Jewish auspices in America and one of the top 50 research universities. Copyright, the Office of Communications and Public Affairs, Yeshiva University.

According to the tradition, it is the duty of parents to educate their children. Thus, Deuteronomy 6:7 declares of Biblical laws: 'And you shall teach them diligently to your children, and shall talk of them when you sit in your house, and when you walk by the way, and when you lie down and when you rise.' In addition, Scripture repeatedly refers to a father's obligation to tell his children about the Exodus from Egypt: 'You may tell in the hearing of your son and of your son's son how I have made sport of the Egyptians and what signs I have done among them' (Exod. 10:2); 'And you shall tell your son on that day, "It is because of what the Lord did for me when I came out of Egypt"' (Exod. 13:8); 'When your son asks you in the time to come, "What is the meaning of the statutes and the ordinances which the Lord our God has commanded

you?" then you shall say to your son, "We were Pharaoh's slaves in Egypt; and the Lord brought us out of Egypt with a mighty hand"' (Deut. 6:20–21). In addition to such parental obligations, it was the duty of the Levites to teach the people: 'They shall teach Jacob thy ordinances, and Israel the law' (Deut. 33:10).

Hence from the earliest period the study of the traditions was of fundamental importance. For this reason Scripture contains numerous references to the process of learning. The Book of Joshua, for example, states: 'This book of the law shall not depart out of your mouth, but you shall meditate on it day and night, that you may be careful to do according to all that is written in it' (Joshua 1:8).

Again, the Book of Proverbs contains various references to the process of education: 'He who spares the rod hates his son' (Prov. 13:24); 'Train up a child in the way he should go, and when he is old he will not depart from it' (Prov. 22:6).

When the ancient Israelites returned from the Babylonian exile, the Bible records that Ezra gathered the people and taught them the law (Nehemiah, Chapter 8). When the nation heard his words, they were profoundly moved and vowed to observe the religious practices and festivals of their ancestors, such as the pilgrim festivals, the New Year celebration, and the Day of Atonement. According to the rabbis, it was Ezra who instituted the Torah reading on Monday and Thursday when the people attended local markets.

In the **rabbinic era** sages continued this process of education. Thus Judah ben Tema declared: 'Five years old (is the age) for (the study of) the Bible, ten years old for the *Mishnah*, thirteen for (the obligation to keep) the commandments, fifteen years old for *Gemara* (rabbinic commentary on the *Mishnah*)' (*Avot*, 5:21). According to Jewish law, parents are obliged to begin a child's education at the earliest possible time; as soon as a child begins to speak he must be taught the verse: 'Moses commanded us a law, as a possession for the assembly of Jacob' (Deut. 33:4). During this period Simeon ben Shetah (first century CE) established schools and urged parents to send their sons to them. However, it was Joshua ben Gamla (first century CE) who is credited with creating a formal system of education. About him the *Talmud* declares: 'May Joshua ben Gamla be remembered for good, for had it not been for him, the Torah would have been forgotten from Israel' (BB, 21a). Prior to Joshua ben Gamla, only those with fathers were taught the tradition, whereas those without fathers were deprived of instruction.

To remedy this situation Joshua ben Gamla decreed that teachers had to be engaged in each locality at the community's expense and all children were to be given an education. Later the *Talmud* stipulated the size of classes: one teacher was permitted to handle up to twenty-five students; if students exceeded this number an assistant was to be hired. More than forty students required two teachers.

Although the *Talmud* does not provide a systematic programme of study, it emphasizes the importance of parental instruction: 'One who does not teach his son an occupation, teaches him to be a brigand'. Among the duties imposed on the fathers is the obligation to

teach his son the Torah. As in Babylonia such instruction in the Law was carried out in the Palestinian academy. Initially it was founded in Javneh after the destruction of the Temple in 70 CE. According to tradition, Johanan ben Zakkai arranged to have himself smuggled out of the city in a coffin; he was then brought before the Roman commander, Vespasian, and requested permission to found a centre of learning. This institution took over from the Great Sanhedrin. Subsequently other academies flourished under Johanan ben Zakkai's disciples. In the second century following the devastation of central and southern Palestine during the Bar Kochba revolt, many scholars emigrated and the Javneh academy was transferred to Galilee.

In Babylonia schools of higher learning were established in the first century CE. In the next century under the leadership of Rav Shila and Abba bar Abba, the **academy** of Nehardea became the Babylonian spiritual centre, maintaining contact with the Palestinian Jewish community. When Rav returned to Babylonia from Palestine, he founded another academy at Sura in 220 CE. In 259 CE the Nehardea academy was destroyed; under Judah ben Ezekiel it was transferred to Pumbedita where it remained for the next five hundred years. From then it functioned in Baghdad until the thirteenth century. These academies attracted students from throughout the Jewish world; twice a year during the months of *Adar* and *Elul* individual study sessions (*kallah*) were held for large audiences.

During the period between the completion of the **Talmud** (sixth century CE) and the Enlightenment, the majority of male Jews received some sort of education. This was generally limited to the study of sacred texts; however, in some periods secular subjects were also included. In twelfth- and thirteenth-century Spain, for example, Jewish scholars engaged in secular studies. In this context the medieval *talmudist* Joseph ibn Aknin argued that there is no contradiction between studying sacred works and such subjects as logic, rhetoric, arithmetic, geometry, astronomy, music, science and philosophy.

Prior to Jewish emancipation, the typical pattern of Jewish education involved a teacher with several students who studied religious texts – this was known as a *heder* (room). Although these study circles were not schools in the modern sense, they did have some parallels. Students were able to graduate from one teacher to another as they progressed in their education. In some communities there was a formally structured *Talmud Torah* which had several classes; here too the subjects of study were exclusively religious. Most students were exposed to several years of such formal education before they went to work; only a few were able to have an extensive educational training.

In the nineteenth century organized **yeshivot** (rabbinic academies) emerged in **eastern Europe** in such centres as Tels, Ponevezh and Slobodka as well as at *Hasidic* centres. In these colleges students progressed from one level to another; the best students often went on to a lifetime of Torah study. Throughout the subject matter was the *Talmud* and *halakhah* – secular studies were not permitted. With the emancipation of Jewry, however, many Jews became proficient in other fields of study, including languages, mathematics, and the sciences. This marked the beginning of the *Haskalah* (Enlightenment) movement. In most cases such secular investigation was done secretly, particularly in eastern Europe.

However, in western Europe new types of schools were founded with combined religious and secular education. In the nineteenth century the neo-Orthodox thinker Samson Raphael Hirsch formulated the principles of such an educational system in his *Torah im Derekh Eretz*. Eventually even eastern European *yeshivot* broadened their curriculum to include ethics (*musar*) as a result of the influence of the *Musar* movement. The Alliance Israélite Française also advanced the combination of religious and secular studies in new schools in North Africa and the Middle East.

Once Jews were permitted to study at secular schools, there was a growing need for supplementary Jewish education. In most cases *heders* or *Talmud Torah* schools were held in the afternoon or on Sundays. In some cases Jewish day schools were established to provide a more extensive Jewish education. By the middle of the twentieth century, there was an increasing awareness that such supplementary Jewish education was inadequate, and the number of day schools proliferated. In the United States the Orthodox *Torah U-Meshorah* day school network expanded from 100 schools prior to World War Two to the current

number of 600. In addition, both the Conservative and Reform movements have established religious day schools. In other countries day schools have been encouraged by the Zionist movement. In Yiddish circles day schools were also founded, but most have either closed or amalgamated with other schools.

During the period of emancipation non-Orthodox rabbinical seminaries were established in the United States. Thus, in the last quarter of the nineteenth century the Reform seminary, the Hebrew Union College, and the Conservative Jewish Theological Seminary were created on the pattern of their predecessors in Berlin and Breslau. At this time New York's Yeshiva University was founded on neo-Orthodox lines; its curriculum combines religious with secular studies. Eventually all these seminaries developed graduate schools in a wide range of fields including Jewish education, communal service, sacred music, Biblical studies, and rabbinics.

Until the period of the Enlightenment, Jewish education was limited to the education of male Jews. However, as Jews assimilated into Western society, the education of women became a priority. Thus in 1917 Sara Schnirer, with the encouragement of a number of Orthodox rabbis, established the Beth Jacob Orthodox system in which women were provided with an official educational programme, although these institutions refused to teach *Mishnah* and *Talmud*. By contrast, the Stern College for Women in Yeshiva University provides a wide range of courses including talmudic study. In the Conservative, Reform, Reconstructionist and Humanist movements, the education of women has been a fundamental principle, and in the last few decades all of these religious bodies have ordained women as rabbis.

In recent years there has also been a large growth in traditional *yeshivot* for post-high school students, particularly in Israel and the United States. In addition, a considerable number of *yeshivah* graduates have gone on to spend several years studying in *kollels* (advanced institutes for *Talmud* study), and Jewish studies have become an integral part of university and college studies since World War Two. Throughout the world, Jewish studies departments have been created where thousands of Jewish as well as non-Jewish students are able to take courses in a wide range of Jewish subjects.

SOURCES

Rabbis

According to the rabbis, study was a religious duty; yet knowledge of sin was more important:

A man may learn *halakhot, midrashim, haggadot*, but if he has no fear of sin, he has nothing. It is like a man who says to his neighbour, 'I have a thousand measures of corn, wine and oil.' His neighbour says to him, 'Have you storehouses in which to put them? If yes, you have all, if no, you have nothing.' So with the man who has learnt everything; only if he has the fear of sin is it all his.

(Exodus R., Mishpatim, 30 in RA, p. 177)

Academies

The sages maintained that the academies in which the oral law was debated originated in Biblical times:

R. Hama b. Hanina said: Our ancestors were never left without the Scholars' Council. In Egypt they had the Scholars' Council, as it is said: Go and gather the elders of Israel together (Exodus 3:16); in the desert they had the Scholars' Council, as it is said: Gather for me seventy men of the elders of Israel (Numbers 11:16); our father Abraham was an elder and a member of the Scholars' Council.

(Talmud, Yoma, 28 in SRJ, p. 70)

Head of the Academy

The head of each academy was the *Rosh Yeshiva*:

R. Joseph was 'Sinai' while Rabbah was an 'uprooter of mountains'. When the time came that one should be *Rosh Yeshivah*, they sent to ask: Who should be preferred, Sinai or the Uprooter of Mountains. The answer came back: Sinai, because everyone needs to know the authentic traditions. But R. Joseph would not accept the position . . . so Rabbah remained *Rosh Yeshivah* for twenty-two years.

(Talmud, Berakoth, 64 in SRJ, p. 72)

Talmud

The Jerusalem *Talmud* was compiled at the end of the fourth century CE and the Babylonian *Talmud* during the sixth century CE. Both record the discussions of the *Amoraim* on the *Mishnah* and are vast repositories of Jewish law, theology, ethics, and legend:

Rav Judah said in Rav's name: The Holy One, blessed be He, did not create a single thing in all this world which has no purpose. He created the snail as a remedy for a scab; the fly as an antidote to the hornet; the mosquito (crushed) for a serpent (sting); a serpent as a remedy for a boil, and a spider as a remedy for a scorpion (sting). A serpent is a remedy for a boil. What is the treatment? One black and white serpent should be taken, boiled to a pulp and then rubbed in.

(Talmud, Shabbat 77 in SRJ, p. 75)

Education in Eastern Europe

Jewish education began at the *heder* or elementary school where Jewish texts were studied by young boys as described by the eighteenth-century Jewish philosopher Solomon Maimon:

I should now describe the general state of Jewish schools. Usually the school is housed in a small smoky hut and the children sit either on benches or on the bare earth. The schoolmaster, in a dirty shirt, sits on the table and grips between his knees a bowl in which he beats tobacco into snuff with a huge pestle like the club of Hercules. At the same time he asserts his authority over the children. In each corner, the undermasters give lessons and rule their small charges quite as tyrannously as the master himself.

(Solomon Maimon, *Autobiography,* in SRJ, p. 124)

Yeshivah

After *heder* families sent their sons to a *yeshivah* as described by the novelist Isaac Bashevis Singer:

He explained that he was returning to Beshev for his fourth year. The *yeshivah* there was small with only thirty students and the people in the town provided board for them all . . . The students at the *yeshivah* studied in pairs . . . The two friends, sharing a lectern in the corner of the study house, spent more time talking than learning . . . The friends met twice each day; in the morning they studied the *Gemara* and the commentaries, and in the afternoon the legal codes and their glossaries.

(Isaac Bashevis Singer, *Yentl the Yeshivah Boy* in SRJ, p. 124)

Samson Raphael Hirsch

Critical of Reform Judaism, the Orthodox scholar Samson Raphael Hirsch denounced the establishment of a Reform seminary. Writing a letter to its founder, Zacharias Frankel, he stated:

1. What will revelation mean in the proposed seminary? Orthodox Judaism teaches the divine origin of the whole Bible . . .

2. What will the Bible mean in the proposed seminary? Orthodox Judaism teaches the divine origin of the whole Bible . . .

3. What will tradition mean in the proposed seminary? For Orthodox Judaism tradition has its origin in God as much as does the written word. Everything in the *Talmud* has the same value and the same origin as the words of the Bible . . .

4. What will rabbinic law and custom mean in the proposed seminary? Orthodox Judaism teaches that it is a divine obligation never to depart from the law and even customs carry the same obligations as vows.

(In SRJ, p. 138)

DISCUSSION

1. Explain the nature of traditional religious education prior to Jewish emancipation in the nineteenth century.

2. How have the non-Orthodox branches of Judaism altered the process of Jewish education in the modern world?

FURTHER READING

Abrams, Judith, Steinsaltz, Adin, *Learn How to Use the Talmud, the Steinsaltz Edition*, Jason Aronson, 1995.

Adron, Isa (ed.), *A Congregation of Learners: Transforming the Synagogue indto a Learning Community*, UAHC Press, 1995.

Goldman, Israel, *Lifelong Learning Among Jews: Adult Education in Judaism from Biblical Times to the Twentieth Century*, KTAV, 1975.

Gurock, Jeffrey, *The Men and Women of Yeshiva*, Columbia University Press, 1992.

Helmreich, William, *The World of the Yeshiva*, Yale University Press, 1986.

Neusner, Jacob, *Classical Judaism: Learning*, Peter Lang, 1993.

Neusner, Jacob (ed.), *The Academy and Traditions of Jewish Learning*, Garland Science, 1993.

Ritterband, P., *Jewish Learning in American Universities*, Indiana University Press, 1994.

Rosenzweig, Franz, Glatzer, Nahum (eds), *On Jewish Learning*, University of Wisconsin Press, 2002.

Rubin, Devora, *Daughters of Destiny: Women Who Revolutionized Jewish Life and Torah Education*, Mesorah Publications, 1988.

Shapiro, Marc, *Between the Yeshiva World and Modern Orthodoxy*, Littman Library, 2002.

CHAPTER 74

The Jewish Calendar

Figure 74   Rosh Hashanah. Copyright David Rose, London.

In the Jewish religion the act of creation is the starting point of year one in the calendar. According to tradition the first work of chronology is the *Seder Olam*, attributed to the second-century sage Yose ben Halafta. In this work the calculation is based on Biblical genealogical tables, the length of lives recorded in Scripture, and the creation of the world in six days: on this reckoning the year of creation was 3761 BCE. The Jewish calendar itself is based on a lunar year of twelve months (of twenty-nine or thirty days). The year is thus approximately 354 days. The shortage of eleven days between lunar and solar years is made up by adding a thirteenth month in certain years. In 356 CE the patriarch Hillel II introduced a permanent calendar based on mathematical and astrological calculations – this calendar has remained in force with only minor modifications.

The names of the months in the Jewish year are of Babylonian origin. In the pre-exilic books they are generally identified by their numerical order.

Regarding the days themselves, they begin at sunset and end at nightfall on the following day: as a result the Sabbath begins at sundown on Friday and ends the next night with the appearance of three stars. This same pattern also applies to all holy days. The Hebrew date is normally given by indicating the name of the month first, then the date, followed by the year. When the year is written in Hebrew, it is usual to omit the thousands.

In recent times there have been a number of attempts at calendar reform so as to arrange a calendar with the same number of days in each month. This would result in a uniform pattern so that the same date would fall on the same day of the week each year. In addition, the year would be divisible into two equal halves and four quarters. The central objection to such an alteration is that it would disturb the regularity of a fixed Sabbath after every six working days – if the reform were carried out, it would fall on a different day each year.

(1)	*NISAN*		
		Shabbat ha-Gadol	This Sabbath takes place before Passover.
	14th	The Fast of the First-Born	A fast is observed on this day by every male first-born in gratitude for God's deliverance at the time of the Exodus.
	15th–22nd	Passover	This eight-day festival commemorates God's redemption of the Israelites from Egyptian bondage. It is also referred to as the Festival of Unleavened Bread – this term refers to the unleavened bread which the Israelites baked in their hurried departure.
	16th	The Counting of the *Omer*	The Israelites were commanded to count forty-nine days from the second day of Passover (when the *Omer* was brought to the Temple). The fiftieth day was celebrated as the wheat harvest.
	17th–20th	*Hol-Hamoed*	The intermediate days of Passover and *Sukkot*. They are observed as semi-holy days.
	23rd	*Isru Hag*	The day after the festival of Passover.
(2)	*IYYAR*		
	5th	*Yom ha-Atzmaut*	Israel Independence Day commemorates the proclamation of Israel's independence on 5th *Iyyar*, 1948.

	Second, Fifth and Seventh (Days of the Week)	During the months of *Iyyar* and *Marheshvan* these days are kept as fast days to atone for any sins committed on the preceding Passover or *Sukkot*.
14th	Second Passover	The *Paschal* lamb was to be sacrificed only on 14th *Nisan*. Those who were not able to make this sacrifice because they were in a state of impurity or a long way from home, could make this offering on 14th *Iyyar*.
18th	*Lag Ba-Omer*	The period between Passover and *Shavuot* was frequently a time of tragedy. During the time of Akiva a plague occurred among his disciples and only ceased on 18th *Iyyar* (33rd of the *Omer*). This day subsequently became known as the Scholars' Feast. The Day itself is a day of joy. In Israel pilgrims go to Meron where Simeon ben Yochai is buried.
28th	*Yom Yerushalaim*	Jerusalem Re-unification Day
(3) SIVAN		
3rd–5th	Three Days of Bordering	This day commemorates the days when Israelites prepared themselves for the revelation on Mount Sinai.
6th–7th	*Shavuot*	This festival is celebrated after seven weeks have been counted from the bringing of the *Omer* on the second day of Passover. It commemorates the giving of the Torah on Mount Sinai.
8th	*Isru Hag*	The day after *Shavuot*.
(4) TAMMUZ		
17th	The Fast of the 17th of *Tammuz*	This fast commemorates the day when the walls of Jerusalem were breached by the Romans, as well as other disasters.

(5) *AV*

		The Sabbath of the 'Vision'	The Sabbath before *Tishah B'Av*
	9th	**Tishah B'Av**	This fast commemorates the day on which the First Temple was destroyed by Nebuchadnezzar, and the Second Temple by Titus.
		The Sabbath of 'Comfort Ye'	The Sabbath after *Tishah B'Av*.
	15th	The 15th of *Av*	This was a joyous day in ancient times when the people participated in a wood offering

(6) *ELUL* (The time of preparation for the Solemn Days)

(7) *TISHRI*

	1st–10th	Ten Days of Penitence	This period begins with *Rosh Hashanah* and concludes with *Yom Kippur*. It is time for religious reflection and penitence.
	1st and 2nd	*Rosh Hashanah*	The **New Year** festival inaugurates the beginning of the spiritual year. It is observed for two days.
	3rd	The Fast of Gedaliah	This fast commemorates the assassination of Gedaliah the Governor of the Jews appointed by Nebuchadnezzar
	10th	**Yom Kippur**	The Day of Atonement is the most solemn day of the Jewish Year. Jews are commanded to fast and atone for their sins.
	15th–21st	*Sukkot*	This festival commemorates God's protection of the Israelites in the wilderness. Booths are built during this festival to symbolize the temporary shelter used by the Israelites in their wanderings.
	17th–21st	*Hol Hamoed*	These intermediate days of the festival are observed as semi-holy days.

21st	*Hoshanah Rabbah*	This name is given to the seventh day of *Sukkot* since seven circuits are made around the Torah while *Hoshanah* prayers are recited.
22nd and 23rd	*Shemini Atzeret*	This festival is observed following *Sukkot*. The annual cycle of Torah readings is completed and begun again on this day. For this reason the festival is also known as *Simhat Torah*. Outside Israel, where two days of *Shemini Atzeret* are observed, *Simhat Torah* is kept only on the second day.
23rd	*Simhat Torah*	On this festival the Torah is completed and recommenced.
24th	*Isru Hag*	The day after *Sukkot*.
(8) *MARHESHVAN*		
	Second, Fifth and Seventh	During *Iyyar* and *Marheshvan* these days are kept by some as fast days to atone for sins committed during *Sukkot*.
(9) *KISLEV* 25th–2nd or 3rd of *Tevet*	**Hanukkah**	This festival is celebrated for eight days. It commemorates the re-dedication of the Temple by Judah Maccabee after the Seleucids were defeated in 165 BCE.
(10) *TEVET* 10th	The Fast of the 10th of *Tevet*	This day commemorates the siege of Jerusalem by Nebuchadnezzar.
(11) *SHEVAT* 15th	New Year for Trees	This joyous festival is celebrated in Israel by the planting of trees.
	Sabbath relating to the *Shekels*	This Sabbath takes place before or on the lst of *Adar*.

(12) *ADAR*

	The Sabbath of 'Remember'	This Sabbath takes place before *Purim*.
13th	The Fast of Esther	This fast commemorates Queen Esther's fast before she asked Ahasuerus to revoke his decree against the Jews.
14th	**Purim**	This festival commemorates the defeat of Haman's plot to destroy the Jewish people. It is a joyous occasion during which the Scroll of Esther is read.
15th	*Shushan Purim*	This festival commemorates the victory of the Jews of Shushan.
	The Sabbath of the Red Heifer	This Sabbath occurs on the first or second Sabbath after Purim.
	The Sabbath of the Month	This Sabbath occurs before or on the lst of *Nisan*.

SOURCES

The Cycle of the Jewish Year

As Jews living in the diaspora, two calendars regulate our lives, the civil and the Jewish . . . Every day of the week points toward *Shabbat* – day of rest, day of joy, day of holiness. Each year begins in the fall with *Rosh Hashanah*. The blast of the *shofar* ushers in the New Year, announcing the season of repentance. *Yom Kippur* follows with its day-long fast and majestic liturgy. We confess our sins and become reconciled with God so that we can begin the new year free from accumulated guilt. Then *Sukkot*, the joyous celebration of the harvest, reminder of the ancient journey of our people to the land of Israel, arrives rich with agricultural symbolism.

However, soon fall becomes winter, and the dark nights are illuminated by the brightly burning lights of *Hanukkah*, recalling for us the heroic Maccabees and our people's long struggle to remain Jewish. As winter nears its end, we read the *Purim* story from the *Megilah*, and we revel in the miracle of our physical survival despite the numerous attempts to destroy us.

Spring liberates the world from the grip of winter, and we recall our liberation from Egyptian bondage. We gather at the *Pesach* table to recite the *Haggadah*, to eat the symbolic foods, and to renew our commitment to the liberation of all humanity. From Passover we count seven weeks to *Shavuot*. During this period, on *Yom HaShoah*, we mourn the death of six million Jews slaughtered by the Nazis, but our grief gives way to rejoicing when we join in the celebration of Israel's rebirth on *Yom Ha-Atzmaut*. The counting ends with *Shavuot*, the festival which celebrates revelation . . .

Summer is soon upon us, and on *Tishah B'Av* we recall the tragic destructions of the Temples and two periods of sovereignty over the Land of Israel and lament the historic suffering of our people. Then, the dark mood turns to anticipation as we enter the month of *Elul* and prepare again to greet the New Year with *Rosh Hashanah.*

(In GS, pp. 5–6)

New Year

According to the Bible, the New Year was to be observed as a holy day accompanied by the sound of the *shofar*:

In the seventh month, on the first day of the month, you shall observe complete rest, a holy day commemorated with loud blasts. (Leviticus 23:24)

In the seventh month, on the first day of the month, you shall observe a holy day; you shall not work at your occupations. You shall observe it as a day when the *shofar* is sounded. (Numbers 29:1)

On the first day of the seventh month, Ezra the priest brought the Torah before the assembly, both men and women and all who could understand, and he read from it facing in front of the Water Gate from early morning till noon. (Nehemiah 8:2–3)

Yom Kippur

The Day of Atonement is to be observed as a time of penitence and prayer:

For on this day atonement shall be made for you to cleanse you of all your sins; you shall be clean. It shall be a Sabbath of complete rest for you and you shall practise self-denial; it is a law for all time. (Leviticus 16:30–31)

Mark, the tenth day of this seventh month is the Day of Atonement . . . For it is the Day of Atonement on which expiation is made on your behalf before the Lord your God . . . Do no work whatever; it is a law for all time, throughout the generations in your settlements. It shall be a Sabbath of complete rest for you and you shall practise self-denial; on the ninth of the month at evening from evening to evening, you shall observe this your Sabbath. (Leviticus 23:27–28; 31–32)

On the tenth day of the same seventh month you shall observe a sacred occasion when you shall practise self-denial. (Numbers 29:7)

Pilgrim Festivals

Scripture decrees that the Jewish people shall observe the three pilgrim festivals as a sign of divine deliverance:

Three times a year you shall hold a festival for me. You shall observe the Feast of unleavened bread – eating unleavened bread for seven days as I have commanded you – at the set time in the month of *Aviv*, for in it you went forth from Egypt; and the feast of the harvest, of the first fruits of your work, of what you sow in the field; and the Feast of Ingathering at the end of the year when you gather in the results of your work from the field.

(Exodus 23:14–16)

Hanukkah

According to the Book of Maccabees, the festival of *Hanukkah* shall be observed to commemorate the victory of the Jewish people over their enemies. The *Talmud* explains the nature of the festival:

Now on the twenty-fifth of the ninth month, which is called the month of *Kislev*, in the 148th year, they rose up in the morning and offered sacrifice according to the law upon the new altar of burnt offerings, which they had made. At the very season and on the very day that the gentiles had profaned it, it was dedicated with songs, citherns, harps and cymbals . . . And so they kept the dedication of the altar eight days . . . Moreover, Judah and his brethren, with the whole congregation of Israel, ordained that the days of the dedication of the altar should be kept in their season from year to year for eight days, from the twenty-fifth day of the month of *Kislev*, with mirth and gladness.

(1 Maccabees, 4:52–59)

What is *Hanukkah*? For the rabbis have taught: Commencing with the twenty-fifth day of the month of *Kislev*, there are eight days upon which there shall be neither mourning nor fasting. For when the Hellenists entered the Temple, they defiled all the oil that was there. It was when the might of the Hasmonean dynasty overcame and vanquished them that, upon search, only a single cruse of undefiled oil, sealed by the High Priest, was found. In it was oil enough for the needs of a single day. A miracle was wrought and it burned eight days. The next year they ordained these days a holiday with songs and praises.

(*Talmud, Shabbat* 21b in GS, p. 89)

Rosh Hodesh

Traditionally Jews celebrated the New Moon every month:

The months of the Hebrew calendar are determined by the recurring phases of the moon; the new month begins when the new moon appears. From the earliest times, the lunar month was far more than a measuring device for Jews . . . The *Mishnah* describes in detail the procedure by which the new month was fixed in the days before the destruction of the Temple. That catastrophe, combined with the development of a scientifically calculated calendar in the *Talmudic* period, served to diminish the significance of *Rosh Hodesh*, reducing it to a minor festival. Its observance today is generally limited to its proclamation in certain synagogues on the preceding *Shabbat* and to some liturgical changes in the service on the day of *Rosh Hodesh*.

(In GS, p. 101)

Purim

The Book of Esther describes Purim as a commemoration of the defeat of Haman:

> The rest of the Jews, those in the king's provinces, likewise mustered and fought for their lives . . . That was on the thirteenth day of the month of *Adar*, and they rested on the fourteenth day and made it a day of feasting and merrymaking.
>
> (Esther 9:16–19)

Tishah B'Av

Tishah B'Av is a day of mourning commemorating tragic events in the history of the Jewish people:

> *Tishah B'Av* (the 9th of *Av*) has been a traditional day of mourning which commemorates major tragic events of the past – the destruction of the First Temple by the Babylonians in 587 BCE and of the Second Temple by the Romans in 70 CE, and the expulsion from Spain in 1492. Tradition has assigned additional subsequent major tragedies to the ninth of *Av*. The day's special liturgy which has developed from the Biblical book of Lamentations recalls the pain and suffering of the Jewish people.
>
> (In GP: NUPB, p. 103)

DISCUSSION

1. In what ways does the Jewish spiritual year commence with *Rosh Ha-Shanah* in the seventh month of *Tishri*?

2. How does the traditional belief in the year of creation in 3761 BCE conflict with a scientific understanding of the origin of the universe?

FURTHER READING

Black, Naomi (ed.), *Celebration: The Book of Jewish Festivals*, Jonathan David, 1989.

Greenberg, Irving, *The Jewish Way: Living the Holidays*, Simon and Schuster, 1993.

Isaacs, Ronald, *Sacred Seasons: A Sourcebook for the Jewish Holidays*, Jason Aronson, 1997.

Isaacs, Ronald, *Every Person's Guide to the High Holy Days*, Jason Aronson, 1998.

Schach, Stephen, *The Structure of the High Holiday Services*, Jason Aronson, 2002.

Schauss, Hayyim, *The Jewish Festivals: A Guide to Their History and Observance*, Schocken, 1996.

Strassfeld, Michael, *The Jewish Holidays: A Guide and Commentary*, Harper Resource, 1985.

Waskow, Arthur, *Seasons of Our Joy: Handbook of Jewish Festivals*, Simon and Schuster, 1986.

Witty, Abraham, Witty, Rachel, *Exploring Jewish Tradition: A Transliterated Guide to Everyday Practice and Observance*, Doubleday, 2001.

Wood, Angela, *Jewish Festivals*, Heinemann, 1996.

Zevin, Shelomoh Yosef *et al.*, *The Festivals in Halachah: An Analysis of the Development of the Festival Laws*, Mesorah, 1986.

Places of Worship

Figure 75 Interior of synagogue. Artist: Polak, K.J. Copyright The Art Archive/Israel Museum Jerusalem/Dagli Orti.

Scripture relates that Moses made a portable shrine (sanctuary) following God's instructions (Exodus Chapters 25–7). This structure travelled with the Israelites in the desert and it was placed in the centre of the camp in an open courtyard 1,000 cubits by 50 cubits in size. The fence surrounding it consisted of wooden pillars from which a cloth curtain was suspended. Located in the eastern half of the courtyard, the sanctuary measured 30 cubits by 10 cubits. At its end stood the Holy of Holies, which was separated by a veil hanging on five wooden pillars on which were woven images of the cherubim. Inside the Holy of Holies was the Ark of the Covenant, the table on which the shewbread was placed, the incense altar, and the *menorah* (candelabrum). In the courtyard there was also an outer altar on which sacrifices were offered, as well as a brass laver for priests.

Eventually this structure was superseded by the **Temple**, which was built by Solomon in Jerusalem in the tenth century BCE. Standing within a royal compound which also consisted of the palace, a Hall of Judgement, the Hall of Cedars, and a house for Solomon's wife, the Temple was 60 cubits long, 20 cubits wide, and 30 cubits high. The main part of the Temple was surrounded by a three-storey building divided into chambers with storeys connected by trapdoors – these were probably storerooms for the Temple treasures. The main building consisted of an inner room – the Holy of Holies – on the west, and an outer room measuring 20 by 40 cubits on the east. Around the Temple was a walled-in compound. At the entrance to the Temple stood two massive bronze pillars (Jachin and Boaz).

Within the Holy of Holies stood the Ark which contained the Two Tablets of the Covenant with the Ten Commandments. In the outer room stood an incense altar, the table for the shewbread, and ten lampstands made of gold. In front of the Temple stood a bronze basin supported by twelve bronze cattle. A bronze altar also stood in the courtyard, which was used for various sacrifices.

From the time of Solomon's reign, the Temple served as the site for prayer and the offering of sacrifices to God. In addition to the communal sacrifices made daily, there were communal sacrifices offered on the Sabbath, festivals, and the New Moon. The Temple was also the site to which the *Omer* (the first barley measure harvested on the second day of Passover) and the first fruits were brought on *Shavuot*. On Passover all families were required to come to Jerusalem to offer the paschal sacrifice. In the sixth century BCE, however, the Temple was destroyed by the Babylonians when they invaded the country. After the exile in the sixth century BCE, Jews in Babylonia established a new institution for public worship – the **synagogue** (meaning 'assembly' in Greek). There they came together to study and pray. On their return to Jerusalem in the latter part of the sixth century BCE, the Jewish populace continued to gather in synagogues as well as offer sacrifice in the Temple. Thus the synagogue developed alongside the Second Temple.

In the synagogue itself, there are a number of elements which parallel the ancient Tabernacle and the Temple. First, there is the Holy Ark – this is symbolic of the Holy of Holies, the most important part of the Sanctuary and the Temple. The Ark itself is located on the wall which faces toward Jerusalem so that Jews are able to pray in the direction of the Temple in Jerusalem. Second, the eternal light hangs before the Ark – this represents the lamp which burned continually in the Sanctuary. The third major element in the synagogue is the Torah (Five Books of Moses) which are placed in the Ark. The Torah is written in Hebrew by a scribe who uses a special ink on parchment. A breastplate covers the Torah, and over it hangs a pointer which is used for the chanting or recitation of the Torah. There are two rollers on which the Torah Scroll is wrapped. In addition, various ornaments, usually in silver, adorn the Scroll: these are symbolic of the ornaments of the High Priest in Temple times. A fourth feature of the synagogue is the platform (or *bimah*) which was in previous times used only for the reading of the Law and the Prophets, as well as for rabbinical sermons. Finally, there is a separation between men and women, usually in the form of a balcony where women are seated during the service.

According to tradition, there were about 400 synagogues in Jerusalem when the Second Temple was destroyed. Although this figure may be exaggerated, there is considerable evidence of synagogue building in the Jewish world during the Second Temple period. The earliest concrete evidence comes from Egypt in the third century BCE; two centuries later the Jewish philosopher Philo referred to the presence of synagogues in Rome. In addition, the Book of Acts mentions Paul's presence in synagogues in Damascus, Asia Minor and Cyprus. By the fifth century CE it was widely attested that wherever Jews lived, they built structures which became the focus of Jewish life and thought. Unlike the Temple, where ritual was carried out exclusively by priests, the only requirement for synagogue worship was the presence of a quorum (*minyan*) of ten men – any service could be led by a lay person. This shift away from Temple hierarchy marked a fundamental democratization of Jewish life. Both *halakhic* and *aggadic* sources testify to the importance of this institution: all synagogues were perceived as partaking of the holiness of the Temple. For this reason it became customary for men to cover their heads when worshipping in the synagogue.

From the third to the eighth century CE, over 100 synagogues existed in Israel, largely in Galilee. In general they followed several prototypes: the most common was the basilica form which consisted of a long hall divided by two rows of pillars into a central nave and two aisles. During this period it does not appear that there was a separate seating area for women. These buildings were impressive structures which dominated the surrounding Jewish settlement – frequently they were located at the highest point in a town or near a source of water. The interiors were usually unadorned so that worshippers would not be distracted from prayer. At a certain stage, mosaic floors were introduced which contained geometrical designs and later depictions of Biblical stories, as well as mythological figures drawn from the surrounding cultures.

In the Middle Ages the synagogue dominated Jewish life. In most communities it was located at the centre of the Jewish quarter. Three times a day men attended services, and frequently the local rabbinic court convened there. Classes took place in the sanctuary or in an annexe, and oaths as well as banns of excommunication were pronounced in its environs. In addition, communal offices, the ritual bath, a library, a hospice for travellers and a social hall were located in synagogue rooms or adjacent buildings. Throughout this period synagogue architecture was influenced by Romanesque and Gothic styles, and special sections for women became common. The readers' platform in the centre of the building together with the Ark served as the focal points for the structure. Because synagogues were not permitted to be higher than neighbouring churches, many European synagogues were built with the floors below street level to maximize their height.

In the early modern period synagogues were constructed in western European ghettos (such as Venice); in Poland wooden synagogues influenced synagogue architecture throughout eastern Europe. In Muslim countries synagogues were modest in scale in accordance with Muslim law. From the nineteenth century, however, major innovations were introduced by reformers. Influenced by church architecture, Reform synagogues (temples) were large, imposing buildings containing organs. The section for women was abolished, and decorum during the service was emphasized. Head coverings and prayer shawls for men were also abandoned, although they have in recent years reappeared, and the reader's platform was shifted from the centre to the area in front of the Ark. Yet despite such changes Reform temples, together with Orthodox synagogues, have reassumed the role of the social centre. Both generally contain social halls used for a wide variety of activities, classrooms for religious schooling, and offices for administrative staff. Thus, no matter what their form, synagogues continue to dominate Jewish life and serve as the religious focus of the community in contemporary society.

SOURCES

Temple

Despite God's determination to destroy the Temple, He expressed regret for this action:

In the hour when God determined to destroy the Temple, He said, 'So long as I was in its midst, the nations could not touch it; now I will hide my eyes from it, and I will swear that I will not connect myself with it until the end; then the enemy can come and destroy it.' At once God swore with his right hand, and drew it back, as it is said, 'He drew back his right hand on account of the enemy' (Lam. 2:3). Then the enemy entered the Temple and burnt it. When it was burnt, God said, 'Now I have no dwelling-place in the land; I will withdraw my *Shekhinah* from it, and ascend to my former place', as it is said, 'I will go and return to my place till they acknowledge their sins' (Hosea 5:15). Then the Lord wept, and said, 'Woe is me, what have I done? I caused my *Shekhinah* to descend because of Israel, and now that they have sinned, I have returned to my former place. Far be it from me that I should be a laughing stock to the nations and a scorn to men.' Then *Metatron* came, and fell on his face, and said, 'I will work, but thou must not weep'. Then God said, 'If thou sufferest me not to weep, I will go to a place where thou hast no power to enter, and I will weep there', as it is said, 'My soul shall weep in secret places' (Jer. 13:7). Then God said to the angels of the service, 'Come, we will go, you and I, and we will see what the enemy has done to my house.' So God and the angels of the service set forth, and Jeremiah went in front of them. When God saw the Temple, He said, 'Assuredly, that is my house, and that is my place of rest, into which the enemy has come and worked his will.' Then God wept and said, 'Woe is me for my house. Where are you, my sons? Where are you, my priests? Where are you, my friends? What can I do to you? I warned you, but you did not repent.' Then God said to Jeremiah, 'I am today like a man who had an only son, and he set up for him the marriage canopy, and he died under it. Do you not grieve for me and my sons? Go, call Abraham and Isaac and Jacob and Moses from their graves, for they know how to weep.' Then Jeremiah said, 'I do not know where Moses is buried.' God said, 'Go to the border of the Jordan, and lift up your voice and cry: 'Son of Amram, stand up, and see how the enemy has devoured your flock.' So Jeremiah went to the cave of Macpelah, and he said to the patriarchs, 'Arise, for the time has come when you are summoned before God'. They said, 'Why?' He replied 'I know not', because he was afraid lest they should say, 'So it is in your days that this evil has befallen our sons.' Then Jeremiah went, and stood by the border of Jordan, and cried, 'Son of Amram, arise, the time has come that you are summoned before God.' He said, 'Why is it today more than on other days that I am summoned before God?' Jeremiah replied, 'I do not know.' Then Moses left Jeremiah, and went to the angels of the service, for he knew them ever since the giving of the Law. He said to them, 'You ministers of God on high, do you know at all why I am summoned before God?' They said, 'Do you not know that the Temple is laid waste, and Israel driven into exile?' Then Moses cried and wept till he came to the patriarchs. Then they, too, rent their clothes, and they laid their hands on their heads, and they wept and cried till they came to the gates of the Temple. When God saw them, He 'called to weeping and to mourning and to baldness and to girding with sackcloth' (Isa. 22:12) . . . Then they all went weeping from one gate of the Temple to another, as a man whose dead lies before him. And God mourned.

(*Lam. R.*, Introduction 24, f. 6b in RA, p. 68)

Synagogue

God's presence was manifest in the synagogue as He was in the ancient Temple:

> 'My love is like a gazelle' (Song of Songs. 2:9). As the gazelle leaps from place to place, and from fence to fence, and from tree to tree, so God jumps and leaps from synagogue to synagogue to bless the children of Israel.
>
> (*Numbers R., Naso*, 11:2 in RA, p. 18)

Modern Synagogue

Modern Jews continue to worship in the synagogue as they did in past ages. Across the religious spectrum – from Orthodox Judaism to Reform – the synagogue continues to be the spiritual centre of Jewish life:

> In the liturgy of the synagogue the Jewish people has written its spiritual autobiography. For a score of centuries each generation has, in turn, added its own distinctive chapter to this book, which contains memories of time past and promises for the future, praise and

lamentation, ethical teaching, and mystical vision. A people possessed by its God is the author of this book.

We are that people still. There are divisions among us; some are matters of principle and others relate to style. And yet, at root, we remain united in our yearning for transcendence, in our hope for peace and human friendship. All of us, in our reflective moments continue to look beneath the surface of our lives, hoping for light, strength, eternal – or at least durable – purpose. Our people's modes of worship are many and various, but we are at one in attempting through worship to express our deepest selves.

Worship is more than an act of cognition; it is a turning of the whole being toward that which we affirm as ultimately real and valuable. Humble in the face of a spiritual reality whose essence we cannot 'know', we speak in metaphors. Our 'truth' is a truth of the heart not less than of the mind. The 'facts' we assert are those of the hopeful spirit. But we believe that the spiritual reality within us corresponds to a spiritual Reality beyond us, and in worship we hope to bring the two realities into communion.

(In GP: NUPB, p. xi)

DISCUSSION

1. How does the synagogue reflect the ancient Temple in Jerusalem?

2. Compare and contrast the traditional synagogue with Reform temples.

FURTHER READING

Donin, Hayim Halevy, *To Pray as a Jew: A Guide to the Prayer Book and the Synagogue Service*, Basic Books, 1991.

Eisenberg, Azriel, *Synagogue Through the Ages: An Illustrated History of Judaism's House of Worship*, Bloch, 1973.

Gutmann, Joseph, *The Synagogue: Studies in Origins, Archaeology and Architecture*, KTAV, 1974.

Hammer, Reuven, *Entering Jewish Prayer: A Guide to Personal Devotion and the Worship Service*, Schocken, 1995.

Idelsohn, Abraham, *Jewish Music: Its Historical Development*, Dover, 1992.

Kadish, Sharman, *Places of Worship: Synagogues*, Heinemann, 1999.

Kraeling, Carl, *The Synagogue*, KTAV, 1979.

Levine, Joseph, *Rise and Be Seated: The Ups and Downs of Jewish Worship*, Jason Aronson, 2000.

Levine, Lee, *The Ancient Synagogue*, Yale University Press, 2000.

Mann, Jacob, *The Bible as Read and Preached in the Old Synagogue*, Vol. 1, KTAV, 1970.

Wagner, Jordan Lee, *The Synagogue Survival Kit*, Jason Aronson, 2001.

CHAPTER 76

Worship

Figure 76 Women praying at the Western Wall, Jerusalem. Copyright David Rose, London.

For the Jewish people, prayer has served as the vehicle by which they have expressed their joys, sorrows and hopes: it has played a major role in the religious life of the Jewish nation, especially in view of the successive crises and calamities in which they have been involved throughout their history. In such situations Jews continually turned to God for assistance. Thus in the Torah the patriarchs frequently addressed God

through personal prayer. **Abraham**, for example, begged God to spare Sodom since he knew that by destroying the entire population he would destroy the righteous as well as the guilty (Gen. 18: 23–33). At Beth-El Jacob vowed, 'If God will be with me, and will keep me in this way that I go, and will give me bread to eat and raiment to put on . . . then shall the Lord be my God' (Gen. 38:20–21).

Later **Moses**, too, prayed to God. After Israel had made a golden calf to worship, Moses begged God to forgive them for this sin (Exod. 32:31–32). **Joshua** also turned to God for help. When the Israelites went to conquer the city of Ai, their attack was repulsed; in desperation Joshua prayed to God for help in defeating Israel's enemies (Jos. 7:7). Later in the prophetic books, the prophets also offered personal prayers to God, as did the Psalmist and others. This tradition of prayer continued after the canonization of Scripture, and as a consequence prayer has constantly animated the Jewish spirit. Through personal encounter with the Divine, Jews have been consoled, sustained, and uplifted.

In addition to personal prayer, Jews have throughout history turned to God through communal worship. In ancient times Jewish communal worship centred on the **Temple** in Jerusalem. Twice daily – in the morning and afternoon – the priests offered prescribed sacrifices while the Levites chanted psalms. On Sabbaths and festivals additional services were added to this daily ritual. At some stage it became customary to include other prayers along with the recitation of the Ten Commandments and the **Shema** (Deut. 6:4–9, 11, 13–21; Num. 15:37–41) in the Temple service.

With the destruction of the Second Temple in 70 CE, sacrificial offerings were replaced by the prayer service in the synagogue, referred to by the rabbis as *avodah she-ba-lev* (service of the heart). To enhance uniformity, they introduced fixed periods for daily prayer which corresponded with the times sacrifices had been offered in the Temple. The morning prayer (*shaharit*) and afternoon prayer (*minhah*) correspond with the daily and afternoon sacrifice. Evening prayer (*maariv*) corresponds with the nightly burning of fats and limbs. By the completion of the *Talmud* in the sixth century, the essential features of the synagogue service were established, but it was only in the eighth century that the first prayer book was composed by Rav Amram, Gaon of Sura.

In the order of service the first central feature is the *Shema*. In accordance with the commandment 'You shall talk of them when you lie down and when you rise' (Deut. 6:7), Jews are commanded to recite this prayer during the morning and evening service. The first section (Deut. 6:4–9) begins with the phrase '*Shema Yisrael*' ('Hear, O Israel: the Lord our God is one Lord'). This verse teaches the unity of God, and the paragraph emphasizes the duty to love God, meditate on his commandments and impress them on one's children. In addition it contains laws regarding the *tefillin* and the *mezuzah*. *Tefillin* consist of two black leather boxes containing scriptural passages which are bound by black leather straps on the arm and forehead in accordance with the commandment requiring that 'you shall bind them as a sign upon your hand, and they shall be as frontlets between your eyes' (Deut. 6:8). They are worn by men during morning prayer except on the Sabbath and festivals. The *mezuzah* consists of a piece of parchment containing two paragraphs of the *Shema* which is placed into a case and affixed to the right-hand side of an entrance. Male Jews wear an undergarment with fringes (the smaller *tallit*) and a larger *tallit* (prayer shawl) for morning services. The prayer shawl used is made of silk or wool with black or blue stripes with fringes (*tzitzit*) at each of the four corners.

The second major feature of the synagogue service is the *Shemoneh Esreh* (Eighteen Benedictions or *Amidah*). These prayers were composed over a long period of time and received their full form in the second century. They consist of eighteen separate prayers plus an additional benediction dealing with heretics which was composed by the sage Samuel the Younger at the request of Rabban Gamaliel in the second century. The first and last three benedictions are recited at every service; the thirteen other prayers are recited only on weekdays. On Sabbaths and festivals they are replaced by one prayer dealing with the Holy Day. They consist of the following:

1. Praise for God who remembers the deeds of the patriarchs on behalf of the community.
2. Acknowledgement of God's power in sustaining the living and his ability to revive the dead.
3. Praise of God's holiness.
4. Request for understanding and knowledge.
5. Plea for God's assistance to return to him in perfect repentance.
6. Supplication for forgiveness for sin.
7. Request for deliverance from affliction and persecution.
8. Petition for bodily health.
9. Request for God to bless agricultural produce so as to relieve want.
10. Supplication for the ingathering of the exiles.
11. Plea for the rule of justice under righteous leaders.
12. Request for the reward of the righteous and the pious.
13. Plea for the rebuilding of Jerusalem.
14. Supplication for the restoration of the dynasty of David.
15. Plea for God to accept prayer in mercy and favour.
16. Supplication for the restoration of the divine service in the Temple.
17. Thanksgiving for God's mercies.
18. Request for granting the blessing of peace to Israel.

On special occasions a number of special prayers are added to these benedictions.

From earliest times the Torah was read in public gatherings; subsequently regular readings of the Torah on Sabbaths and festivals were instituted. In Babylonia the entire Torah was read during the yearly cycle; in Palestine it was completed once every three years. The Torah itself is divided into fifty-four sections, each of which is known as the 'order' or 'section' (*sidrah*). Each section is subdivided into portions (each of which is called a *parashah*). Before the reading of the Torah in the synagogue, the Ark is opened and the Scroll (or Torah Scrolls) are taken out.

The number of men called up to the reading varies: on Sabbaths there are seven; on *Yom Kippur* six; on festivals five; on *Rosh Hodesh* and *Hol Hamoed*, four;

on *Purim*, *Hanukkah* and fast days, three; and on Sabbath afternoons and Monday and Thursday mornings (when the first *parashah* of the forthcoming *sidrah* is read), three. In former times those who were called up to the Torah read a section of the weekly *sidrah*; subsequently an expert in Torah reading was appointed to recite the entire *sidrah* and those called up recited blessings instead. The first three people to be called up are: *Cohen* (priest), *Levi* (priest), and *Yisrael* (member of the congregation).

After the reading of the Torah, a section from the prophetic books (*Haftarah*) is recited. The person who is called up for the last *parashah* of the *sidrah* reads the *Haftarah* – he is known as the *maftir*. The section from the Prophets parallels the content of the *sidrah*. Once the Torah scroll is replaced in the Ark, a sermon is usually delivered based on the *sidrah* of the week.

Another central feature of the synagogue service is the **Kaddish** prayer. Written in Aramaic, it takes several forms in the prayer book and expresses the hope for universal peace under the kingdom of God. There are five main forms:

1. Half *Kaddish* recited by the reader between sections of the service.
2. Full *Kaddish* recited by the reader at the end of a major section of the service.
3. Mourners' *Kaddish* recited by mourners after the service.
4. Scholars' *Kaddish* recited after the reading of *talmudic midrashic* passages in the presence of a *minyan* (quorum of ten men).
5. Expanded form of the mourners' *kaddish* which is recited at the cemetery after a burial.

A further feature of the service is the *Hallel* consisting of Psalms 113–118. In the *talmudic* period it was known as the 'Egyptian *Hallel*' because the second psalm (114) begins with the words: 'When Israel went forth from Egypt'. (This designation was used to distinguish this group of psalms from another psalm (136) – the 'Great *Hallel*' – which is recited on the Sabbath and festivals during the morning service.) The complete *Hallel* is recited on the first two days of Passover, on both days of *Shavuot*, on the nine days of *Sukkot*, and the eight days of *Hanukkah*. Part of the *Hallel* is recited on the intermediate days (*Hol Hamoed*), and the last two days of Passover.

Since the thirteenth century the three daily services have concluded with the recitation of the **Alenu** prayer which proclaims God as king over humanity. In all likelihood it was introduced by Rav in the third century CE as an introduction to the *malhuyot*, the section recited as part of the *musaf* service for *Rosh Hashanah*. In the Middle Ages this prayer was the death-song of Jewish martyrs. The first part of this prayer proclaims God as king of Israel; the second anticipates the time when idolatry will disappear and all human beings will acknowledge God as king of the universe.

The traditional liturgy remained essentially the same until the Enlightenment. At this time reformers in central Europe altered the worship service and introduced new prayers into the liturgy in conformity with current cultural and spiritual developments. Influenced by Protestant Christianity, these innovators decreed that the service should be shortened and conducted in the vernacular as well as in Hebrew. In addition they introduced Western melodies to the accompaniment of a choir and organ and replaced the chanting of the Torah with a recitation of the *sidrah*. Prayers viewed as anachronistic were abandoned (such as the priestly blessing given by *Cohanim*, the *Kol Nidre* prayer on the Day of Atonement, and prayers for the restoration of the Temple and the reinstitution of sacrifice). Further, prayers of a particularistic character were amended so that they became more universalistic in scope.

The Conservative movement also produced prayer books in line with its ideology. In general the Conservative liturgy followed the traditional *siddur* except for several differences: (1) prayers for the restoration of sacrifice were changed; (2) the early morning benediction thanking God that the worshipper was not made a woman was altered; (3) prayers for peace were altered to include all of humanity; (4) in general the *yekum purkah* prayer for schools and sages in Babylonia was omitted; (5) *Cohanim* (priests) usually did not recite the priestly benediction; (6) the *Amidah* was not usually repeated except on high holy days. More radical alterations to the Jewish liturgy have occurred in the Reform, Reconstructionist and Humanistic movements.

In recent times all groups across the Jewish spectrum have produced new liturgies (such as those that commemorate Holocaust Remembrance Day, Israel Independence Day and Jerusalem Reunification Day). Moreover, a wide range of occasional liturgies exist for camps, youth groups and *havurot* (informal prayer groups). Among non-Orthodox denominations there is a growing emphasis on more egalitarian liturgies with gender-free language and an increasing democratic sense of responsibility. Thus prayer and worship continue to be of vital importance to the Jewish people, yet there have occurred a variety of alterations to its

SOURCES

Abraham

When God planned to destroy Sodom, Abraham prayed for its inhabitants:

Then Abraham drew near, and said, 'Wilt thou indeed destroy the righteous with the wicked? Suppose there are fifty righteous within the city; wilt thou then destroy the place and not spare it for the fifty righteous who are in it? Far be it from thee to do such a thing, to slay the righteous with the wicked, so that the righteous fare as the wicked! Far be it from thee! Shall not the Judge of all the earth do right?' And the Lord said, 'If I find at Sodom fifty righteous in the city, I will spare the whole place for their sake.' Abraham answered, 'Behold, I have taken upon myself to speak to the Lord, I who am but dust and ashes. Suppose five of the fifty righteous are lacking? Wilt thou destroy the whole city for lack of five?' And he said, 'I will not destroy it if I find forty-five there.' Again, he spoke to him and said, 'Suppose forty are found there.' He answered, 'For the sake of forty I will not do it.' Then he said, 'Oh let not the Lord be angry, and I will speak. Suppose thirty are found there.' He answered, 'I will not do it, if I find thirty there.' He said, 'Behold, I have taken upon myself to speak to the Lord. Suppose twenty are found there.' He answered, 'For the sake of twenty I will not destroy it.' Then he said, 'Oh let not the Lord be angry, and I will speak again but this once. Suppose ten are found there.' He answered, for the sake of ten I will not destroy it.'

(Genesis 18:23–32)

Moses

After the ancient Israelites had sinned, Moses prayed to God to forgive them for their transgression:

So Moses returned to the Lord and said, 'Alas, this people have sinned a great sin; they have made for themselves gods of gold. But now, if thou wilt forgive their sin – and if not, blot me, I pray thee, out of thy book which thou hast written.' But the Lord said to Moses, 'Whoever has sinned against me, him will I blot out of my book. But now go, lead the people to the place of which I have spoken to you; behold, my angel shall go before you. Nevertheless, in the day when I visit, I will visit their sin upon them.'

(Exodus 32:31–32)

Joshua

Determined that the ancient Israelites would be able to conquer their enemies, Joshua prayed to God for assistance:

Then Joshua rent his clothes, and fell to the earth upon his face before the ark of the Lord until the evening, he and the elders of Israel; and they put dust upon their heads. And

Joshua said, 'Alas, O Lord God, why hast thou brought this people over the Jordan at all, to give us into the hands of the Amorites, to destroy us? Would that we had been content to dwell beyond the Jordan! O Lord, what can I say, when Israel has turned their backs before their enemies. For the Canaanites and all the inhabitants of the land will hear of it, and will surround us, and cut off our name from the earth; and what will thou do for thy great name?'

(Joshua 7:6–9)

Temple Worship

Once the ancient Israelites had established a monarchy, Solomon constructed a Temple for worship:

The house which King Solomon built for the Lord was sixty cubits long, twenty cubits wide, and thirty cubits high. The vestibule in front of the nave of the house was twenty cubits long, equal to the width of the house, and ten cubits deep in front of the house. And he made for the house windows with recessed frames . . . The inner sanctuary he prepared in the innermost part of the house, to set there the ark of the covenant of the Lord. The inner sanctuary was twenty cubits wide, and twenty cubits high; and he overlaid it with pure gold.

(1 Kings 6:2–4, 19–20)

nature within all branches of the Jewish faith.

Shema

The *Shema* prayer is one of the central prayers of the Jewish worship service:

Hear, O Israel: The Lord is our God, the Lord is one. And thou shalt love the Lord thy God with all thine heart, and with all thy soul, and with all thy might, and these words which I command thee this day, shall be upon thine heart: and thou shalt teach them diligently unto thy children, and shalt talk of them when thou sittest in thine house, and when thou walkest by the way, and when thou liest down, and when thou risest up. And thou shalt bind them for a sign upon thine hand, and they shall be for frontlets between thine eyes. And thou shalt write them upon the doorposts of thy house, and upon thy gates.

(*Shema* in DPB, pp. 117–119)

Kaddish

The mourners' *Kaddish* is recited at the end of the synagogue service:

Magnified and sanctified be his great name in the world which he hath created according to his will. May He establish his kingdom during your life and during your days, and during the life of all the house of Israel, even speedily and at a near time, and say ye, Amen.

Let his great name be blessed for ever and to all eternity.

Blessed, praised and glorified, exalted, extolled and honoured, magnified and lauded be the name of the Holy One, blessed be He; though He be high above all the blessings and hymns, praises and consolations, which are uttered in the world; and say ye, Amen.

May there be abundant peace from heaven, and life for us and for all Israel; and say ye, Amen.

He who maketh peace in his high places, may he make peace for us and for all Israel; and say ye, Amen.

(*Kaddish* in DPB, p. 213)

Alenu

The *Alenu* prayer concludes the synagogue service:

It is our duty to praise the Lord of all things, to ascribe greatness to him who formed the world in the beginning, since he hath not made us like the nations of other lands, and hath not placed us like other families of the earth, since he hath not assigned unto us a portion as unto them, nor a lot as unto all their multitude. For we bend the knee and offer worship and thanks before the supreme king of kings, the Holy One, blessed be He, who stretched forth the heavens and laid the foundations of the earth, the seat of whose glory is in the heavens above, and the abode of whose might is in the loftiest heights. He is our God; there is none else: in truth He is our king; there is none besides him; as it is written in his Torah, And thou shalt know this day, and lay it to thine heart, that the Lord He is God in heaven above and upon the earth beneath: there is none else.

(*Alenu* in DPB, pp. 209–211)

DISCUSSION

1. Discuss the nature of worship in the ancient Temple.

2. What changes have been made to the nature of the liturgy in the various non-Orthodox branches of Judaism?

FURTHER READING

Cohen, Jeffrey, *Blessed Are You: A Comprehensive Guide to Jewish Prayer*, Jason Aronson, 1993.

Cohn, Gabriel, Fisch, Harold (eds), *Prayer in Judaism: Continuity and Change*, Jason Aronson, 1996.

Donin, Hayim Halevy, *To Pray as a Jew: A Guide to the Prayerbook and the Synagogue Service*, Basic Books, 1991.

Hammer, Reuven, *Entering Jewish Prayer*, Schocken, 1995.

Hoffman, Lawrence, *The Way into Jewish Prayer*, Jewish Lights, 2000.

Idelsohn, A.Z., *Jewish Liturgy and Its Development*, Dover, 1995.

Isaacs, Ronald, *Every Person's Guide to Jewish Prayer*, Jason Aronson, 1997.

Jacobs, Louis, *Hasidic Prayer*, Littman Library, 1993.

Martin, Bernard, *Prayer in Judaism*, Basic Books, 1968.

Nulman, Macy, *Encyclopedia of Jewish Prayer*, Jason Aronson, 1993.

Petuchowski, Jacob, *Understanding Jewish Prayer*, KTAV, 1972.

Reif, Stefan, *Judaism and Hebrew Prayer*, Cambridge University Press, 1995.

Steinsaltz, Adin, *A Guide to Jewish Prayer*, Schocken, 2002.

Weiss, Avraham, *Women at Prayer: A Halakhic Analysis of Women's Prayer*, KTAV, 2001.

CHAPTER 77

The Sabbath

Figure 77 Sabbath observance. Copyright David Rose, London.

Genesis 2:1–3 declares 'The heaven and the earth were finished, and all the host of them. And on the seventh day God finished his work which he had done, and he rested on the seventh day from all his work which he had done. So God blessed the seventh day and hallowed it, because on it God rested from all his work which he had done in creation.' This passage serves as the basis for the decree that no work should be done on the Sabbath. During their sojourn in the wilderness

of Zin, the Israelites were first commanded to observe the Sabbath. They were told to work on five days of the week when they should collect a single portion of *manna*; on the sixth day they were instructed to collect a double portion for the following day which was to be a 'day of solemn rest, a holy sabbath of the Lord' (Exod. 16:23). On the seventh day when several individuals made a search for manna, the Lord stated: 'How long do you refuse to keep my commandments and my laws? See! The Lord has given you the Sabbath, therefore on the sixth day he gives you bread for two days; remain every man of you in his place, let no man go out of his place on the seventh day' (Exod. 16:28–29).

Several weeks later God revealed the Ten Commandments, including prescriptions concerning the Sabbath day:

> Remember the Sabbath day, to keep it holy. Six days you shall labour, and do all your work, but the seventh day is a Sabbath to the Lord your God; in it you shall not do any work, you, or your son, or your daughter, your manservant, or your maidservant, or your cattle, or the sojourner who is within your gates; for in six days the Lord made heaven and earth, the sea, and all that is in them, and rested on the seventh day; therefore the Lord blessed the Sabbath day and hallowed it' (Exod. 20:8–11).

The Book of Deuteronomy contains a different version, emphasizing the exodus from Egypt:

> Observe the Sabbath day, to keep it holy, as the Lord your God commanded you. Six days you shall labour, and do all your work; but the seventh day is a Sabbath to the Lord your God; in it you shall not do any work . . . You shall remember

that you were a servant in the land of Egypt, and the Lord your God brought you out thence with a mighty hand and an outstretched arm; therefore the Lord your God commanded you to keep the Sabbath day (Deut. 5:12–15).

According to the Book of Exodus, the Sabbath is a covenant between Israel and God:

> Say to the people of Israel, 'You shall keep my Sabbaths, for this is a sign between me and you throughout your generations, that you may know that I, the Lord, sanctify you . . . Therefore the people of Israel shall keep the Sabbath, observing the Sabbath throughout their generations as a perpetual covenant (Exod. 31:12,16).

By the time the Sanhedrin began to function, the observance of the Sabbath was regulated by Jewish law. Following the injunction in Exodus 20:10, the primary aim was to refrain from work. In the Five Books of Moses only a few provisions are delineated: kindling a fire (Exod. 35:3); ploughing and harvesting (Exod. 23:12); carrying from one place to another (Exod. 16:29). Such regulations were expanded by the rabbis who listed thirty-nine categories of work (which were involved in the building of the Tabernacle). According to the *Mishnah* they are:

> 1. sowing; 2. ploughing; 3. reaping; 4. binding sheaves; 5. threshing; 6. winnowing; 7. sorting; 8. grinding; 9. sifting; 10. kneading; 11. baking; 12. shearing sheep; 13. washing wool; 14. beating wool; 15. dyeing wool; 16. spinning; 17. sieving; 18. making two loops; 19. weaving two threads; 20. separating two threads; 21. tying; 22. loosening; 23. sewing two stitches; 24. tearing in order to sew two stitches; 25. hunting a deer; 26. slaughtering; 27. flaying; 28. salting; 29. curing a skin; 30. scraping the hide; 31. cutting; 32. writing two letters; 33. erasing in order to write two letters; 34. building; 35. pulling down a structure; 36. extinguishing a fire; 37. lighting a fire; 38. striking with a hammer; 39. moving something.

In the *Talmud* these categories were discussed and expanded to include within each category a range of activities. In order to ensure that individuals did not transgress these prescriptions, the rabbis enacted further legislation which serve as a fence around the Law. Yet despite such ordinances, there are certain situations which take precedence over Sabbath prohibitions. Witnesses of the New Moon, for example, who were to inform the Sanhedrin or *Bet Din* of this occurrence were permitted to do so on the Sabbath. Other instances include circumcision on the Sabbath; dangerous animals may be killed; persons are permitted to fight in self-defence; anything may be done to save a life or assist a woman in childbirth.

The Sabbath itself commences on Friday at sunset. A little while before sunset, **Sabbath candles** are traditionally lit by the woman of the house who recites the blessing: 'Blessed are you, O Lord our God, King of the universe, who has hallowed us by your commandments and commanded us to kindle the Sabbath light'.

In the synagogue, the service preceding Friday *maariv* takes place at twilight. Known as *Kabbalat Shabbat*, it is a late addition dating back to the sixteenth century when kabbalists in Safed went out to the fields on Friday afternoon to greet the Sabbath queen. In kabbalistic lore the Sabbath represents the *Shekhinah* (divine presence). This ritual is rooted in the custom of Hanina (first century CE) who, after preparing himself for the Sabbath, stood at sunset and said: 'Come, let us go forth to welcome the Sabbath', and that of Yannai (third century CE) who said: 'Come Bride! Come bride!' On the basis of such sentiments Solomon Alkabets composed the Sabbath hymn **Lekhah Dodi** which has become a major feature of the liturgy. In the Sephardi rite Psalm 29 and *Lekhah Dodi* are recited, whereas the Ashkenazi rite is composed of Psalms 95–99, *Lekhah Dodi* and Psalms 92–93. The Reform prayerbook offers a variety of alternative services including abridged versions of these psalms and the entire *Lekhah Dodi*. The Reconstructionist service commences with Biblical passages, continues with an invocation and meditation on the Sabbath, and proceeds to a reading of psalms and *Lekhah Dodi*.

Traditionally, when the father returns home from the synagogue, he blesses the children. With both hands placed on the head of a boy, he says: 'May God make you like Ephraim and Manasseh', and for a girl says: 'May God make you like Sarah, Rebekah,

Rachel and Leah'. In addition, he recites the priestly blessing. Those assembled then sing **Shalom Aleichem** which welcomes the Sabbath angels. At the Sabbath table the father recites the **kiddush** prayer over a cup of wine:

> Blessed are you, O Lord our God, King of the universe, who has sanctified us by your commandments and has taken pleasure in us, and in love and favour has given us your holy Sabbath as an inheritance, a memorial of the creation, that day being the first of the holy convocations, in remembrance of the Exodus from Egypt. For you have chosen us and hallowed us above all nations, and in love and favour have given us your holy Sabbath as an inheritance. Blessed are you, O Lord, who sanctifies the Sabbath.

This is followed by the washing of the hands and the blessing of bread. The meal is followed by the singing of table hymns (**zemirot**), and concludes with the Grace after Meals (*Birkhat ha-Mazon*). This, which Jews are obligated to recite after every meal, originally consisted of three paragraphs in which worshippers thank God for sustenance, the land and the Torah, and pray for the restoration of the Temple. Subsequently a fourth paragraph was added which contains the words: 'Who is good and does good'. Subsequently short prayers beginning with 'the All Merciful' were added. On the Sabbath an additional prayer is included dealing with the Sabbath day.

On Sabbath morning the liturgy consists of a morning service, a reading of the Torah and the *Haftarah*, and the additional service. In the service itself, introductory prayers prior to the *Shema* differ from those of weekdays, and the *Amidah* is also different. Seven individuals are called to the reading of the Law, and an eighth for a reading from the prophets. (In the Reform movement the worship is abridged and has no additional service.) On returning home, the morning *Kiddush* and the blessing over bread are recited followed by the Sabbath meal and then the Grace after Meals. In the afternoon service the Torah is read prior to the *Amidah*. Three persons are called to the Torah, and the first portion of the reading of the Law for the following week is recited. Customarily three meals are to be eaten on the Sabbath day; the third meal is known as the *Seudah Shelishit*. It should take place just in time for the evening service. At the end of the Sabbath, the evening service takes place and is followed by the *Havdalah* service.

The **Havdalah** ceremony marks the conclusion of the Sabbath period. It consists of four blessings. Three are recited over wine, spices and lights, and the service concludes with the *Havdalah* blessing. In the *Sephardi*, *Ashkenazi* and Yemenite rites, the blessings are similar, but the introductory sentences are different. The *Ashkenazi* rite contains Biblical phrases with the term 'salvation'; the *Sephardi* requests the granting of bountifulness and success; the Yemenite prays for a successful week. The final blessing opens with the phrase, 'Blessed are you, O Lord our God, King of the universe, who distinguishes'; it is followed by a series of comparisons between the holy and the profane, light and darkness, Israel and the nations, between the seventh day and the six days of the week. The hymn *Ha-Mavdil* follows the *Havdalah* ceremony and asks for forgiveness of sins and for the granting of a large number of children. A number of customs, including filling a cup and extinguishing the *Havdalah* candle in wine poured from it, are associated with the *Havdalah* ceremony. Within Reform Judaism an alternative *Havdalah* service incorporates additional readings with traditional blessings.

SOURCES

Lighting the Sabbath Candles

Traditionally, the woman of the house lights the Sabbath candles:

> Blessed art thou, O Lord our God, king of the universe, who hast hallowed us by thy commandments, and commanded us to kindle the Sabbath lights.
>
> (In DPB, p. 345)

Lekhah Dodi

The *Lekhah Dodi* prayer is recited in anticipation of the coming of the Sabbath:

Come, my beloved, with chorus of praise,
Welcome Bride Sabbath, the Queen of days.

'Keep and Remember'! – in one divine word,
He that is one, made his will heard;
One is the name of him, one is the Lord!
His are the fame and the glory and praise!

Sabbath, to welcome thee, joyous we haste;
Fountain of blessing from ever thou wast –
First in God's planning, thou fashioned the last,
Crown of his handiwork, chiefest of days.

City of holiness, filled are the years;
Up from thine overflow! Forth from thy fears!
Long hast thou dwelt in the valley of tears,
Now shall God's tenderness shepherd thy ways.

Rise, O my folk, from the dust of the earth,
Garb thee in raiment beseeming thy worth;
Nigh draws the hour of Bethlehemite's birth,
Freedom who bringeth, and glorious days.

Wake and bestir thee, for come is thy light!
Up! With thy shining, the world shall be bright;
Sing! For thy Lord is revealed in his might –
Thine is the splendour his glory displays!

'Be not ashamed', saith the Lord, 'nor distressed;
Fear not and doubt not. The people oppressed,
Zion, my city, in thee shall find rest –
Thee, that anew on thy ruins I raise'.

'Those that despoiled thee shall plundered be,
Routed all those who showed no ruth;
God shall exult and rejoice in thee,
Joyful as bridegroom with bride of youth'.

Stretch out thy borders to left and to right;
Fear but the Lord, whom to fear is delight –
The man, son of Perez, shall gladden our sight,
And we shall rejoice to the fullness of days.

> Come in thy joyousness, Crown of thy Lord;
> Come, bringing peace to the fold of the word;
> Come where the faithful in gladsome accord,
> Hail thee as Sabbath-bride, Queen of the days.
>
> Come where the faithful are hymning thy praise;
> Come as a bride cometh, Queen of days!
>
> (In DPB, pp. 357–359)

Family Blessings

Traditionally, it has been the custom of the father to bless his children:

For sons:

May God give you the blessings of Ephraim and Manasseh

For daughters:

May God give you the blessings of Sarah, Rebecca, Rachel, and Leah.

For all:

May the Lord bless you and guard you. May the Lord show you favour and be gracious to you. May the Lord show you kindness and grant you peace.

(In SSS, p. 723)

Eishet Hayil

Traditionally the husband recites a proverb in praise of his wife:

A good wife, who can find? She is precious far beyond rubies. Her husband trusts in her, and he shall lack nothing thereby. She renders him good and not evil all the days of her life. She opens her hand to the needy and extends her hand to the poor. She is robed in strength and dignity and cheerfully faces the future. She opens her mouth with wisdom; her tongue is guided by kindness. She tends to the affairs of her household and eats not the bread of idleness. Her children come forward and bless her; her husband, too, and praises her: 'Many women have done superbly, but you surpass them all'. Charm is deceitful and beauty is vain, but a God-revering woman is much to be praised. Give her honour for the fruit of her hands; wherever people gather, her deeds speak her praise.

(In SSS, p. 725)

Shalom Aleichem

The song *Shalom Aleichem* is sung on Sabbath eve:

> We wish you peace, attending angels, angels of the most sublime,
> the king of kings, the Holy One praised be He.
>
> Come to us in peace, angels of peace, angels of the most sublime,
> the king of kings, the Holy One praised be He.
>
> Bless us with peace, angels of peace, angels of the most sublime,
> the king of kings, the Holy One praised be He.
>
> Take your leave in peace, angels of peace, angels of the most sublime,
> the king of kings, the Holy One praised be He.

(In SSS, p. 723)

Kiddush

The *Kiddush* blesses God who creates the fruit of the vine.

Blessed are you, the source of life, our God, sovereign of all worlds, who has set us apart with your *mitzvot* and taken pleasure in us, and the holy *Shabbat* with love and favour made our possession, a remembrance of the work of Creation. For it is the first of all the holy days, proclaimed, a symbol of the Exodus from Egypt. For you have called to us and set us apart to serve you, and given us to keep in love and favour, your holy *Shabbat*. Blessed are you, the source of wonder, who sets apart *Shabbat*.

(In KH, p. 118)

Zemirot

After the Sabbath meal, those gathered sing Sabbath songs:

Tranquillity and joy, light for all the Jews; *Shabbat* with its delights are blessings that we choose. We celebrate *Shabbat* with glee and testify that God created land and sea, man and beast, earth and sky. Our eternal God decreed that we should sanctify *Shabbat* all day in celebration; in its holiness He delights, as it recalls the goal of his creation. Come before him in prayer on this day; then eat your food in joy, for God accepts what you do, what you say. You shall celebrate with two *hallot* and wine; on tasty foods in abundance shall you dine. For those who enjoy *Shabbat* many joys are held in store, and redemption will be theirs forevermore.

(In SSS, p. 730)

Havdalah

The final service for *Shabbat* is *Havdalah*:

Praised are you, Lord our God, king of the universe, who has endowed all creation with distinctive qualities, distinguishing between sacred and secular time, between light and darkness, between the people Israel and other people, between the seventh day and the six working days of the week. Praised are you, Lord, who distinguishes between sacred and secular time.

(In SSS, p. 701)

DISCUSSION

1. What is the nature of work according to the rabbinic tradition? Exemplify this conception with specific contemporary examples.

2. How has Sabbath observance been modified within the different non-Orthodox branches of Judaism?

FURTHER READING

Benyosef, Simcha, Lurya, Mosheh, *Living the Kabbalah: A Guide to the Sabbath and Festivals in the Teachings of Rabbi Rafael Moshe Luria*, Continuum, 1999.

Cooper, David, *The Handbook of Jewish Meditation Practices: A Guide for Enriching the Sabbath and Other Days of Your Life*, Jewish Lights, 2000.

Elkins, Dor Peretz (ed.), *A Shabbat Reader: Universe of Cosmic Joy*, UAHC Press, 1998.

Ginsburg, Eliot, *The Sabbath in the Classical Kabbalah*, State University of New York, 1989.

Heschel, Abraham Joshua, *The Sabbath*, Farrar Straus Giroux, 1975.

Hoffman, Lawrence (ed.), *My People's Prayerbook, Vol. 14: Traditional Prayers, Modern Commentaries – Seder K'riyat Hatorah*, Jewish Lights, 2000.

Isaacs, Ronald, *Every Person's Guide to Shabbat*, Jason Aronson, 1998.

Kobre, Faige, *A Sense of Shabbat*, Torah Aura Productions, 1990.

Neuman, Jacob, *The Talmud of the Land of Israel, Vol. 3: Shabbat*, University of Chicago Press, 1991.

Neuwith, Yehoshau, *Shemirath Shabbat: A Guide to the Practical Observance of Shabbat*, Volume 2, Feldheim, 1989.

Perelson, Ruth, *An Invitation to Shabbat: A Beginner's Guide to Weekly Celebration*, UAHC Press, 1997.

CHAPTER 78

Special Sabbaths

Figure 78 Special Sabbaths. Copyright David Rose, London.

In the Jewish tradition, a number of Sabbaths are of importance in the Jewish calendar. Three are linked to the beginning of a month: *Shabbat Mevarekhim* (Sabbath before a New Moon); *Shabbat Mahar Hodesh* (*Sabbath on the eve of a New Moon*); and *Shabbat Rosh Hodesh* (Sabbath coinciding with the beginning of a month). Other special Sabbaths are *Shabbat Shuvah* (Sabbath during the Ten Days of Penitence between

Rosh Hashanah and the Day of Atonement); *Shabbat Hol Hamoed* (Sabbath during the Intermediate Days of *Sukkot*); *Shabbat Bereshit* (when the new Torah reading commences); *Shabbat Hanukkah* (Sabbath during *Hanukkah*); *Shabbat Shirah* (Sabbath when the Song of Moses is recited); four Sabbaths during the spring (*Shekalim, Zakhor, Parah, Ha-Hodesh*); *Shabbat ha-Gadol* (Sabbath before Passover); another *Shabbat Hol Hamoed* (Sabbath during the Intermediate Days of Passover); *Shabbat Hazon* (Sabbath before *Tishah B'Av*; and *Shabbat Nahamu* (Sabbath after *Tishah B'Av*). In the Reform movement only a few of these Sabbaths are recognized.

These special Sabbaths are observed in various ways:

Shabbat Mevarekhim (The Sabbath of Blessing). On this Sabbath before a New Moon, worshippers using the Ashkenazi liturgy recite *yehi ratson*, a formula based on the sage Rav's prayer that 'it will be God's will to renew the coming month for good service', with four '*yehi ratson*' expressions of hope that it will be God's intention to re-establish the Temple, rescue his people from all afflictions and disasters, maintain Israel's sages, and grant a month of good tidings. In both rites the service continues with the prayer, 'He who performs miracles', an announcement of the date of the New Moon, and a benediction. The Torah and *Haftarah* are the portions of the week.

Shabbat Mahar Hodesh. This Sabbath, which falls on the eve of the New Moon, has a Biblical origin (1 Sam. 20:18). The Torah reading is for the week. The *Haftarah* (1 Sam. 20:18–42) depicts the covenant between Jonathan and David on the eve of the New Moon.

Shabbat Rosh Hodesh. In the Sabbath service which falls on the New Moon the *Hallel* is recited after the morning service; in the additional service *Amidah*, the

Attah Yatsarta sequence replaces *Tikkanta Shabbat.* The Torah reading is that for the week and the *maftir* (additional reading) is Numbers 28:9–15. The *Haftarah* is Isaiah 66:1–24.

Shabbat Shuvah (The Sabbath of Return). The origin of the name of this Sabbath is derived from the opening words of the *Haftarah*: 'Return (*shuvah*), O Israel, to the Lord your God.' Since this Sabbath occurs during the Days of Penitence, it is also known as *Shabbat Teshuvah* (Sabbath of Repentance). The Torah reading is that prescribed for the week, and the *Haftarah* is either Hosea 14:2–10; Joel 2:15–27 in the Ashkenazi rite, or Hosea 14:2–10; Micah 7:18–20 in the Sephardi rite (in the diaspora *Ashkenazim* read Micah 7:18–20 before the Joel passage).

Shabbat Hol Hamoed Sukkot. In the service for this Sabbath which occurs during the intermediate days of **Sukkot**, the *Hallel* and the book of Ecclesiastes are read after the morning service. In some traditional congregations *piyyutim* (religious poems) are recited. The reading for the day is Exodus 33:12–34:26 and a selection from Numbers 29; the *Haftarah* is Ezekiel 38:18–39:16.

Shabbat Bereshit (The Sabbath of Genesis). The origin of the name of this Sabbath is derived from the opening words of the Book of Genesis which are included in the reading of the Law for this Sabbath (which follows the *Simhat Torah* festival: 'In the beginning (*bereshit*) God created'. On this Sabbath the annual reading cycle of the Torah commences with Genesis 1:1–6:8 and the *Haftarah* is that for the week. Included among those who are called to the Torah is the person chosen as 'bridegroom of Genesis' on *Simhat Torah*. He normally provides a festival meal to which all are invited after the Sabbath morning service.

Shabbat Hanukkah. This Sabbath takes place during the **Hanukkah** festival. After the morning service, the *Hallel* is recited. The Torah reading from the first scroll is that for the week; the *maftir* (additional reading) from the second scroll is from Numbers 7:1–17. If the Sabbath also falls on the eighth day of *Hanukkah* the weekly portion is Genesis 41:1–44:17 and the *maftir* is Numbers 7:54–8:4. If this Sabbath coincides with the New Moon, Numbers 28:9–15 is recited from a third scroll before *maftir*. The *Haftarah* is Zechariah 2:14–4:7 (1 Kings 7:40–50 for second Sabbath); if it

is New Moon, verses from Isaiah 66:1–24 are added in some communities).

Shabbat Shirah (The Sabbath of the Song). The origin of the name of this Sabbath is the song that Moses and the Israelites sang at the Red Sea (Exod. 15:1–18) which is included in the Torah reading. In some congregations special religious poems are also recited. The Torah reading is the weekly portion (Exod. 13:17–17:16). The *Haftarah* is Judges 4:4–5:31 among *Ashkenazim*, and Judges 5:1–31 among *Sephardim*. In traditional communities a special form of cantillation is reserved for this song. Ashkenazi worshippers stand while this song is read, but not *Sephardim*. In Moroccan communities a liturgical poem referring to the eight Biblical songs sung by Moses, Miriam, Joshua, Deborah and other Israelites is recited. Western Sephardi congregations have a double reading of the song to a traditional melody, and Exodus 14:30–15:18 is chanted before and as part of the Torah reading. Orthodox congregations of the United Synagogue in England have borrowed this Sephardic tune for their own cantillation of the song. *Ashkenazim* elsewhere use a traditional eastern European mode.

Shabbat Shekalim (The Sabbath of the *Shekel* Tax). The origin of the name of this Sabbath which precedes or coincides with the New Moon *Rosh Hodesh Adar* is derived from the *Mishnah* which states that 'on the first day of *Adar* they gave warning of the *shekel* dues'. The *maftir* (additional reading) concerns the half-*shekel* levy which was used to support the Sanctuary. In some congregations special religious poems are recited; the Torah reading is that for the week and the *maftir* is Exodus 30:11–16. The *Haftarah* is 2 Kings 12:1–17 among *Ashkenazim*, and 2 Kings 11:17–12:17 among *Sephardim*. In some congregations the rabbi urges that contributions be made to religious institutions in Israel.

Shabbat Zakhor (The Sabbath of Remembrance). On this Sabbath before *Purim*, the *maftir* (additional reading) emphasizes the obligation to 'remember what Amalek did to you' (since traditionally Haman was a descendant of Amalek). During the service special religious poems are read in some synagogues. The Torah reading is that of the week and the *maftir* is Deuteronomy 25:17–19. The *Haftarah* is 1 Samuel 15:2–34.

Shabbat Parah (Sabbath of the Red Heifer). This Sabbath precedes *Shabbat ha-Hodesh*. The *maftir* (additional reading) deals with the red heifer whose ashes were used for purification. Special poems are recited on this Sabbath, and the Torah portion is that of the week; the *maftir* is Numbers 19:1–22. The *Haftarah* is Ezekiel 36:16–38 among *Ashkenazim*, and Ezekiel 36:16–36 among *Sephardim*.

Shabbat ha-Hodesh (The Sabbath of the Month). The origin of the name for this Sabbath is derived from the opening words of the *maftir* (additional reading): 'This month (*ha-Hodesh*) shall mark for you the beginning of the months'. This Sabbath precedes or coincides with *Rosh Hodesh Nisan* (the month when Passover takes place). In some congregations special religious poems are recited. The Torah portion is that for the week, and the *maftir* is Exodus 12:1–20. The *Haftarah* is Ezekiel 45:16–46:18 among *Ashkenazim*, and Ezekiel 45:18–46:15 among *Sephardim*.

Shabbat ha-Gadol (The Great Sabbath). The origin of the name of this Sabbath is uncertain but it may derive from the last verse of the *Haftarah*: 'Lo, I will send the prophet Elijah to you before the coming of the awesome (*gadol*), fearful day of the Lord' (Mal. 4:5). This Sabbath precedes Passover. Religious poems are read in some congregations, and the rabbi usually gives a lecture on Passover and preparations for the holiday. In the afternoon a portion of the *Haggadah* (Passover prayer book) is recited. The Torah reading is that of the week, and the *Haftarah* is Malachi 3:4–24.

Shabbat Hol Hamoed Pesah. This Sabbath takes place during the intermediate days (*Hol Ha-Moed*) of *Pesach*. In the service the *Hallel* and Song of Songs are recited after the morning service. In some synagogues special religious poems are also recited. The Torah reading is Exodus 33:12–34:26, and the *maftir* (additional reading) is Numbers 28:19–25. The *Haftarah* is Ezekiel 37:1–14.

Shabbat Hazon (The Sabbath of Prophecy). The origin of the name of this Sabbath, which precedes the ninth of *Av*, is derived from the *Haftarah* which refers to Isaiah's vision (*hazon*) about the punishments which will be inflicted on Israel. The Torah portion is Deuteronomy 1:1–3:22; the *Haftarah* is Isaiah 1:1–27. During the service the rabbi or a learned Jew chants the *Haftarah*. Congregants are to attend synagogue in plainer clothes than normal. The Ark, in some congregations, is covered by a weekday or dark-coloured curtain. Among *Ashkenazim* the *Lekhah Dodi* hymn is sung on Friday night to the tune of the *Eli Tziayyon* elegy.

Shabbat Nahamu (The Sabbath of Comfort). The origin of this name is derived from the opening words of the *Haftarah*: 'Comfort (*nahamu*), O comfort my people'. The Torah reading is Deuteronomy 3:23–7:11 which includes the Ten Commandments and the first paragraph of the *Shema*. The *Haftarah* is Isaiah 40:1–26.

SOURCES

Sabbath before a New Moon

On *Shabbat Rosh Hodesh*, the following prayer is recited:

> Our God, our ancients' God
> take pleasure in our rest
> and bring renewal to us
> on this day of *Shabbat*,
> with this coming of the New Moon.
> May it be for goodness and for blessing, for joy and for happiness, for healing and for rest,
> for sustenance and for support, for life and for peace,
> for forgiveness, pardon, and atonement
> between us and any we have wronged.

For you have brought your people Israel close to your service,
and made known to them the holiness of your *Shabbat*,
and fixed their practice of celebrating *Rosh Hodesh*.
Blessed are you, Wise One,
who sanctifies *Shabbat*,
Israel, and the renewal of the moon.

(In KH, p. 310)

The Sabbath in *Sukkot*

During the Sabbath in *Sukkot* the following is recited to commemorate the importance of this festival:

The Lord brought you into a good land, a land with streams and springs and lakes issuing from plain and hill, a land where you may eat food without scarcity, where you will lack nothing.

Take care lest you forget the Lord your God and fail to keep his commandments. When you have eaten and are satisfied, and have built fine houses to live in, and your herds and flocks have multiplied, and your silver and gold have increased, and everything you own has prospered, beware lest your hearts grow haughty and you forget the Lord your God, and you say to yourselves: My own power and the might of my hand have won all this for me. Remember that is the Lord your God who gives you the power to prosper.

And now, O Israel, what is it that the Lord your God demands of you? It is to revere the Lord your God, to walk always in his paths, to love him and to serve the Lord your God with all your heart and soul, keeping his laws and commandments . . . He upholds the cause of the orphan and the widow, and loves the strangers, providing them with food and clothing. You too must love the stranger, for you were strangers in the land of Egypt.

May our observance of this festival of *Sukkot* inspire us with gratitude for the wondrous gifts that are ours, and fill us with the resolve to share them with all who are in need. Let us hold precious one another, and the world which provides us with sustenance and beauty. And let a song of thanksgiving be on our lips to the creator and Sustainer of life.

(In GP, p. 395)

The Sabbath in *Hanukkah*

The festival of *Hanukkah* has importance religious significance for the Jewish people:

With greatful hearts we remember your protection, when tyrants sought to destroy your people and to uproot the religion of Israel. We take pride in the valour of the Maccabees, their faith in you, their devotion to your law which inspired them to deeds of heroism. We commemorate the rededication of your sanctuary, the consecration of its altar to your worship, and celebrate the rekindling of the eternal light, whose rays shone forth out of the encircling darkness as the symbol of your presence and the beacon light of your truth for all the world.

Be with us now – with us and our children. Make us strong to do your will. Help us to understand and proclaim the truth, that not by might and not by power, but by your spirit alone can we prevail. Grant to each person and every nation the blessings of liberty, justice and peace. Let injustice and oppression cease, and hatred, cruelty, and wrong pass away, so that all human beings may unite to worship you in love and devotion.

Bless, O God, the *Hanukkah* lights, that they may shed their radiance into our homes and our lives. May they kindle within us the flame of faith and zeal, that, like the Maccabees of old, we battle bravely for your cause. Then shall we be worthy of your love and our blessing, O God, our Shield and our Protector.

(In GP, p. 397)

The Sabbath in *Pesach*

Passover commemorates the significance of human freedom:

Let every living soul bless your name, O Lord our God, and let every human spirit acclaim your majesty, for ever and ever.

Through all eternity you are God; we have no king but you.

God of all ages, ruler of all creatures, Lord of all the living, all praise to you. You guide the world with steadfast love, your creatures with tender mercy. You neither slumber nor sleep; you awaken the sleeping and arouse the dormant. You give speech to the silent, freedom to the enslaved, and justice to the oppressed.

In every generation you have redeemed our people from the house of bondage.

Our God and God of our people. You have been our help in all ages; your mercy and kindness are with us still. May the House of Israel show its love for you by labouring for the day when freedom shall be the heritage of all your children.

(In GP, p. 405)

The Sabbath before *Yom Ha-Atzmaut*

During the Sabbath service before *Yom Ha-Atzmaut*, Jews celebrate the renewal of Jewish life in Israel:

Today we turn our thoughts to the land of Israel. It is the cradle of our faith, a land hallowed by memories of kings and prophets, of poets and sages. In all the ages of our history, and in all the lands of our dispersion, we have remembered it with love and longing, saying with the Psalmist:

If I forget you, O Jerusalem,
let my right hand wither.
Let my tongue cleave to the roof of my mouth
if I do not remember you,
if I do not set Jerusalem
above my highest joy.

(In GP, p. 412)

DISCUSSION

1. Explain why the New Moon was important in ancient times?

2. Discuss the concept of forgiveness in Judaism. How does it compare with the Christian understanding of forgiveness and repentance?

FURTHER READING

Bokser, Ben Zion, *Prayer Book: Weekday, Sabbath, and the Festival*, Behrman House, 1996.

Falk, Marcia, *The Book of Blessings: New Jewish Prayers for Daily Life, the Sabbath, and the New Moon Festival*, Beacon, 1999.

Greenberg, Sidney, Levine, Jonathan (eds), *Siddur Hadash: A New Prayer Book for Sabbath and Festival Mornings*, Hartmore House, 1992.

Hoffman, Lawrence (ed.), *My People's Prayer Book, Vol. 1: Traditional Prayers, Modern Commentaries – The Shema and Its Blessings*, Jewish Lights, 1997.

Hoffman, Lawrence (ed.), *My People's Prayer Book, Vol. 2: Traditional Prayers, Modern Commentaries*, Jewish Lights, 1998.

Hoffman, Lawrence (ed.), *My People's Prayer Book, Vol. 3: Traditional Prayers, Modern Commentaries – P'sukei D'zimrah (Morning Psalms)*, Jewish Lights, 1999.

Hoffman, Lawerence (ed.), *My People's Prayer Book, Vol. 4: Traditional Prayers, Modern Commentaries – Seder K'riyat Hatorah (Shabbat Torah Service)*, Jewish Lights, 2000.

Hoffman, Lawrence (ed.), *My People's Prayer Book, Vol. 5: 'Birkhot Hashachar' (Morning Blessings) – Traditional Prayers, Modern Commentaries*, Jewish Lights, 2001.

Schauss, Hayyim, *The Jewish Festivals: A Guide to Their History And Observance*, Schocken, 1996.

Shendelman, Sara, Davis, Avram, *Traditions: The Complete Book of Prayers, Rituals, and Blessings for Every Jewish Home*, Hyperion, 1998.

Singer, S., *Sabbath and Holidays Prayer Book*, Hebrew Publishing Co., 1925.

CHAPTER 79

Pilgrim Festivals

Figure 79 Pesach. Copyright David Rose, London.

According to the Book of Deuteronomy, Jews are to celebrate three pilgrim festivals each year: 'Three times each year shall all your males appear before the Lord your God at the place which He will choose, at the feast of unleavened bread, at the feast of weeks, and at the feast of booths' (Deut. 16:16). On the basis of this commandment large numbers of pilgrims went to Jerusalem during the First and Second Temple periods from throughout the Holy Land and Babylonia. There they assembled in the Temple area to offer sacrifice and pray to God.

The first of these festivals is Passover, which is celebrated for eight days (seven in Israel) from the 15th to the 22nd of *Nisan*. The various names for this festival illustrate its different dimensions.

1. *Pesach* (Passover). The term is derived from the account of the tenth plague in Egypt when first-born Egyptians were killed, whereas God 'passed over' the houses of the Israelites (whose door posts and lintels were sprinkled with the blood of the paschal lamb). This term is also applied to the Passover sacrifice which

took place on the 14th of *Nisan*; its flesh was roasted and eaten together with unleavened bread and bitter herbs.

2. *Hag ha-Matzot* (The Festival of Unleavened Bread). This term refers to the unleavened bread baked by the Israelites on their departure from Egypt. In accordance with God's command to Moses and Aaron while the people were in Egypt, no leaven was to be eaten during future Passover celebrations, nor was it to be kept in the house. All vessels used for leavening must be put away, and their place taken by a complete set used only for Passover. Although no leaven may be eaten during this period, the obligation to eat *matzah* applies only to the first two nights during the *seder* service.

3. *Zeman Herutenu* (The Season of our Freedom). This term designates the deliverance from Egyptian slavery and the emergence of the Jewish people as a separate nation.

4. *Hag ha-Aviv* (The Festival of Spring). This name is used because the month of *Nisan* is described in Scripture as the month of *Aviv*, when ears of barley begin to ripen. In accordance with the Biblical command, a measure of barley (*Omer*) was brought to the Temple on the second day of Passover. Only when this was done could food be made from the new barley harvest.

In preparation for Passover, Jewish law stipulates that all leaven must be removed from the house. On the night before the 14th of *Nisan* a formal search is made for any remains of leaven. This is then put aside and burned on the following morning. The first night of Passover is celebrated in the home ceremony referred to as the *Seder*. This is done to fulfil the Biblical commandment to relate the story of the Exodus to one's son: 'And you shall tell thy son on the day, saying: "It is because of what the Lord did for me when I came out of Egypt"' (Exod. 13:8). The order of the service dates back to Temple times. During the ceremony celebrants traditionally lean on their left sides – this was the custom of freemen in ancient times.

The symbols placed on the *seder* table serve to remind those present of Egyptian bondage, God's redemption, and the celebration in Temple times. They consist of:

(1) Three *matzot*: these three pieces of unleavened bread are placed on top of one another, usually in a special cover. The upper and lower *matzot* symbolize the double portion of *manna* provided for the Israelites in the wilderness. The middle *matzah* (which is broken in two at the beginning of the *seder*) represents the 'bread of affliction'. The smaller part is eaten to comply with the commandment to eat *matzah*. The larger part is set aside for the *afikoman*, which recalls Temple times when the meal was completed with the eating of the *paschal* lamb. These three *matzot* also symbolize the three divisions of the Jewish people: *Cohen, Levi and Yisrael*.

(2) Four cups of wine: according to tradition, each Jew must drink four cups of wine at the *seder*. The first is linked to the recital of *kiddush*; the second with the account of the Exodus and the Blessing for Redemption; the third with the Grace after Meals; and the fourth with the *Hallel* and prayers for thanksgiving. These cups also symbolize four expressions of redemption in Exodus 6:6–7.

(3) The cup of Elijah: this cup symbolizes the hospitality awaiting the passer-by and wayfarer. According to tradition, the Messiah will reveal himself at the Passover, and Malachi declared that he will be preceded by Elijah. The cup of Elijah was also introduced because of the doubt as to whether five cups of wine should be drunk rather than four.

(4) Bitter herbs: these symbolize the bitterness of Egyptian slavery.

(5) Parsley: this is dipped in salt water and eaten after the *Kiddush*. It is associated with spring.

(6) *Haroset*: this is a mixture of apples, nuts, cinnamon and wine. It is a reminder of the bricks and mortar that Jews were forced to use in Egypt.

(7) Roasted shankbone: this symbolizes the *paschal* offering.

(8) Roasted egg: this commemorates the festival sacrifice in the Temple.

(9) Salt water: this recalls the salt that was offered with all sacrifices. It also symbolizes the salt water of the tears of the ancient Israelites.

At the *seder*, the *Haggadah* details the order of service. It is as follows:

1. The *Kiddush* is recited.
2. The celebrant washes his hands.
3. The parsley is dipped in salt water.
4. The celebrant divides the middle *matzah* and sets aside the *afikoman*.
5. The celebrant recites the **Haggadah narration**.
6. The participants wash their hands.
7. The blessing over bread is recited.
8. The blessing over *matzah* is recited.
9. Bitter herbs are eaten.
10. The *matzah* and *marror* are combined.
11. The meal is eaten.
12. The *afikoman* is eaten.
13. Grace after Meals is recited.
14. The *Hallel* is recited.
15. The service is concluded.
16. Hymns and songs are sung.

The second pilgrim festival – **Shavuot** – is celebrated for two days on the 6th and 7th of *Sivan*. The word 'Shavuot' means 'weeks' – seven weeks are counted from the bringing of the *omer* on the second day of *Pesah* (Lev. 23:15). The festival is also referred to as Pentecost, a Greek word meaning 'fiftieth', since it was celebrated on the fiftieth day. Symbolically the day commemorates the culmination of the process of emancipation which began with the Exodus at Passover. It is concluded with the proclamation of the Law at Mount Sinai. Liturgically, the festival is also called *Zeman Mattan Toratenu* (the Season of the Giving of our Torah). This name relates to events depicted in Exodus Chapters 19–20.

During the Temple period farmers set out for Jerusalem to offer a selection of first ripe fruits as a thank-offering. In post-Temple times, the emphasis shifted to the festival's identification as the anniversary of the giving of the Law on Mount Sinai. In some communities it is a practice to remain awake during *Shavuot* night. In the sixteenth century Solomon Alkabets and other kabbalists began the custom of *tikkun* in which an anthology of Biblical and rabbinic material was recited. Today in those communities where this custom is observed, this lectionary has been replaced by a passage of the *Talmud* or other rabbinic literature. Some congregations in the diaspora read a book of psalms on the second night. Synagogues themselves are decorated with flowers or plants, and dairy food is consumed during the festival. The liturgical readings for the festival include the Ten Commandments preceded by the liturgical poem *Akdamut Millin* on the first day, and *Yetsiv Pitgam* before the *Haftarah* on the second day. The Book of Ruth is also recited. In many communities this festival marks the graduation of young people from formal synagogue education (or confirmation in Reform temples). In Israel, agricultural settlements hold a First Fruits celebration on *Shavuot*.

The third pilgrim festival – **Sukkot** – is also prescribed in the Bible: 'On the fifteenth day of this seventh month and for seven days is the feast of tabernacles to the Lord (Lev. 23:34). Beginning on the 15th of *Tishri*, it commemorates God's protection of the Israelites during their sojourn in the desert. Leviticus commands that Jews are to construct booths during this period as a reminder that the people of Israel dwelt in booths when they fled from Egypt (Lev. 23:42–43).

During this festival a *sukkah* (booth) is constructed and its roof is covered with branches of trees and plants. During the festival, meals are to be eaten inside the *sukkah*. Leviticus also declares that various agricultural species should play a part in the observance of this festival: 'And you shall take on the first day the fruit of goodly trees, branches of palm trees, and boughs of leafy trees, and willows of the brook; and you shall rejoice before the Lord your God seven days (Lev. 23:40). In compliance with this prescription the four species are used in the liturgy: palm, myrtle, willow and citron. On each day of the festival the *lulav* (palm branch) is waved in every direction before and during the *Hallel* – this symbolizes God's presence throughout the world. Holding the four species Jews make one circuit around the Torah which is carried onto the *bimah* (platform) on each of the first six days. During this circuit, **hoshanah** prayers are recited. On the seventh day of *Sukkot* (*Hoshanah Rabba*) seven circuits are made around the Torah while reciting *hoshanah* prayers. During the service the reader wears a white *kittel* (robe).

In conformity with Leviticus 23:36, 'On the eighth day you shall hold a holy convocation . . . it is a solemn assembly', *Shemini Atzeret* and *Simhat Torah* are celebrated on the same day (or on separate days in the diaspora). No work is permitted at this time. On *Shemini Atzeret* a prayer for rain is recited, and the reader wears a white *kittel*. Ecclesiastes is recited at the end of the morning service on *Shabbat Hol Hamoed* (or on *Shemini Atzeret* if it falls on the Sabbath). The ninth day of *Sukkot* is *Simhat Torah*. On this joyous day the reading of the Torah is completed and recommenced. The Torah scrolls are taken out of the Ark and members of the congregation carry them in a procession around the synagogue.

SOURCES

Festival Lights for Passover, *Shavuot* and *Sukkot*

Before kindling the lights on the eve of the festival in the home, the following prayer is recited:

> Lord of the universe, I am about to perform the sacred duty of kindling the lights in honour of the festival. And may the effect of fulfilling this commandment be that the stream of abundant life and heavenly blessing flow in upon me and mine; that thou be gracious unto us, and cause thy presence to dwell among us.
>
> Father of mercy, O continue thy lovingkindness unto me and my dear ones. Make me worthy to (rear my children so that they) walk in the way of the righteous before thee, loyal to thy Torah and clinging to good deeds. Keep thou far from us all manner of shame, grief, and care; and grant that peace, light, and joy ever abide in our home. For with thee is the fountain of life; in thy light do we see light. Amen.
>
> Blessed art thou, O Lord our God, king of the universe, who hast hallowed us by thy commandments, and hast commanded us to kindle the festival light.
>
> (In DPB, p. 797)

Searching for Leaven for Passover

On the eve of the day before Passover a search for leaven is made in the house. Before the search the following is recited:

> Blessed art thou, O Lord our God, king of the universe, who hast commanded us concerning the removal of leaven.

After the search, the following is said:

> May all leaven in my possession both that which I have seen and that which I have not seen or not removed be annulled and deemed as dust of the earth.

On the following morning, the following is said:

> May all leaven in my possession, whether I have seen it or not, or whether I removed it or not, be annullled and deemed as dust of the earth.

Four Questions

The youngest person at the Passover *seder* asks the four questions about the meaning of Passover:

Why is this night different from all other nights? On all other nights we eat either leavened or unleavened bread. Why, on this night, do we at only unleavened bread? On all other nights, we eat all kinds of herbs. Why, on this night, do we eat especially bitter herbs. On all other nights, we do not dip herbs in any con-diment. Why, on this night, do we dip them in salt water and haroses? On all other nights, we eat without special festivities. Why, on this night, do we hold this *seder* service?

(Four Questions
in TUH, p. 18)

Haggadah Narration

The story of the Egyptian oppression is recounted during the Passover meal:

It is well for all of us whether young or old to consider how God's help has been our unfailing stay and support through ages of trial and persecution. Ever since He called our father Abraham from the bondage of idolatry to his service of truth, He has been our guardian; for not in one country alone nor in one age have violent men risen up against us, but in every generation and in every land, tyrants have sought to destroy us; and the Holy One, blessed be He, has delivered us from their hands . . .

After Joseph died, and all his brethren, and all that generation. Now there arose a new king over Egypt, who knew not Joseph. And he said unto his people: 'Behold, the people of the children of Israel are too many and too mighty for us; come, let us deal wisely with them, lest they multiply, and it come to pass, that when there befalleth us any war, they also join themselves unto our enemies, and fight against us, and get them up out of the land.' Therefore they set over them taskmasters to afflict them with burdens. And they built for Pharaoh store-cities, Pithom and Raamses. But the more the Egyptians afflicted them, the more the Israelites multiplied, and the more they spread abroad.

And the Egyptians dealt ill with us, and afflicted us, and laid upon us cruel bondage. And we cried unto the Lord, the God of our fathers, and the Lord heard our voice and saw our affliction and our toil and our oppression. And the Lord brought us forth out of Egypt, with a mighty hand and with an outstretched arm and with great terror and with signs and with wonders.

(In TUH, pp. 24–26)

Counting of the *Omer*

From the eve of the second day of Passover, through the evening before *Shavuot*, the days are counted as follows after the evening *Amidah*:

On the second day of *Pesah* in ancient times, our ancestors brought the first sheaf of barley reaped that season as an offering to God. From that day, they began counting the days and weeks of *Shavuot*, when they would celebrate the beginning of the wheat harvest by offering the loaves made of the first wheat. Even after the Temple was destroyed and offerings were no longer brought, they continued to count the days from *Pesah* to *Shavuot* in accordance with the Biblical injunction.

And you shall count from the day after the Sabbath, from the day that you brought the sheaf of the wave offering; seven full weeks shall they be; continuing fifty days to the day after the seventh Sabbath; then you shall present a cereal offering of new grain to the Eternal.

Thus our ancestors linked *Pesah* and *Shavuot* as occasions for thanking God for the fruits of the field. So do we thank God for the renewal of life which all nature proclaims at this season.

(In KH, pp. 674–675)

Shavuot

The festival of *Shavuot* commemorates the giving of the law on Mt Sinai. In the youth service for *Shavuot*, Humanistic Jews celebrate the importance of Jewish culture:

When most of our ancestors moved away from their farms and left the land of Israel, the holiday of *Shavuot* took on new meaning.

The rabbis declared that the writing of the Torah began on *Shavuot*. The Torah was the first Hebrew book that was ever written. A new harvest of good books was added to the harvest of wheat and barley.

Jewish books, like Jewish farming, are part of Jewish culture. A culture includes all the things a living people tries to do in order to stay alive, in order to be happy. Jewish culture includes all the things the Jewish people tries to do in order to stay alive, in order to be happy. The name for Jewish culture is Judaism.

Yahadut is a Hebrew word which means 'Judaism'. *Shavuot* is the holiday of *Yahadut*, the feast of Judaism.

(In C, p. 282)

Meditation for *Sukkot*

The following prayer is recited in the *Sukkah* on the first night of *Sukkot*:

May it be thy will, O Lord my God and God of my fathers, to let thy divine presence abide among us. Spread over us the tabernacle of thy peace in recognition of the precept of the Tabernacle which we are now fulfilling, and whereby we establish in fear and love the unity of thy holy and blessed name. O surround us with the pure and holy radiance of thy glory, that is spread over our heads as the eagle over the nest he stirreth up: and thence bid the stream of life flow in upon thy servant (thy handmaid). And seeing that I have gone forth from my house abroad, and am speeding the way of thy command-ments, may it be accounted unto me as though I had wandered far in thy cause. O wash me thoroughly from mine iniquity, and cleanse me from my sin. Keep me in life, O Lord; bestow upon me the abundance of thy blessings; and to such as are hungry and thirsty give bread and water unfailingly. Make me worthy to dwell trustingly in the covert of thy shadowing wings at the time when I part from the world. O deal graciously with us in the decree to which thou settest thy seal, and make us worthy to dwell many days upon the land, the holy land, ever serving and fearing thee. Blessed be the Lord for ever. Amen and Amen.

(in ADPB, p. 315)

Hoshanot

During *Sukkot*, the *Hoshanot* are recited as part of the Torah service. A Torah scroll is brought to the lectern, and the reader chants:

> *Hosha na!*
> For your sake, our God, *Hosha na!*
> For your sake, our Creator, *Hosha na!*
> For your sake, our Redeemer, *Hosha na!*
> For your sake, our Teacher, *Hosha na!*

A procession is formed around the synagogue. The *lulav* and *etrog* are carried and the following is said:

> For the sake of your all-embracing truth,
> for the sake of your binding covenant,
> for the sake of your greatness and your beauty,
> for the sake of your divine decree,
> for the sake of your heavenly splendour,
> for the sake of your wise assembly,
> for the sake of your sign and remembrance,
> for the sake of your heavenly love,
> for the sake of your timeless good,
> for the sake of your indivisibility,
> for the sake of your consoling glory,
> for the sake of your learning's light,
> for the sake of your majestic sovereignty,
> for the sake of your name's victory,
> for the sake of your sublime mystery,
> for the sake of your omnipotence,
> for the sake of your praise eternal,
> for the sake of your complete and utter holiness,
> for the sake of your supernal justice,
> for the sake of your redeeming and abundant love,
> for the sake of your *Shekhinah's* presence,
> save us, please,
> for the sake of your thunderous praises,
> save us please!
>
> (In KH, pp. 646–648)

DISCUSSION

1. Is it plausible that God sent the plagues to free the ancient Israelites from Egyptian bondage?

2. Is the account of the Exodus supported by Biblical scholarship?

FURTHER READING

Cohen, Jeffrey, *1001 Questions and Answers on Pesach*, Jason Aronson, 1996.

Donin, Hayim, *To Be a Jew: A Guide to Jewish Observance in Contemporary Life*, Basic Books, 1991.

Goodman, Philip (ed.), *Shavuot Anthology*, Jewish Publication Society, 1992.

Goodman, Philip (ed.), *The Sukkot/Simhat Torah Anthology*, Jewish Publication Society, 1992.

Green, Leona, *The Traditional Egalitarian Passover Haggadah*, Norlee Publishing, 2002.

Isaacs, Ron, *Every Person's Guide to Shavuot*, Jason Aronson, 1999.

Isaacs, Ron, *Every Person's Guide to Sukkot, Shemini Atzeret and Simhat Torah*, Jason Aronson, 2001.

Mohr, Tara, Spector, Catherine, Arisfeld, Sharon (eds), *The Women's Passover Companion: Women's Reflections on the Festival of Freedom*, Jewish Lights, 2003.

Reinman, Yaakov Yosef, *The Passover Haggadah*, Cis Communications, 1995.

Rubenstein, Jeffrey, *The History of Sukkot in the Second Temple and Rabbinic Periods*, Brown Judaica Studies, 1995.

Schauss, Hayyim, *The Jewish Festivals: A Guide to Their History and Observance*, Schocken, 1996.

Wolfson, Ron, *The Art of Jewish Living: The Passover Seder*, Jewish Lights, 1996.

CHAPTER 80

New Year and Day of Atonement

Figure 80 Morning of the Day of Atonement, poem, from Hebrew prayer book, Germany, *c.* 1320–35 (Mich 619 folio r). Copyright The Art Archive/Bodleian Library Oxford/ The Bodleian Library.

In ancient times the Jewish New Year (*Rosh Hashanah*) took place on one day; it is presently observed for two days, both in Israel and the diaspora, on the lst and 2nd of *Tishri*, marking the beginning of the Ten Days of Penitence which ends on the Day of Atonement (*Yom Kippur*). The term '*Rosh Hashanah*' occurs only once in Scripture (Ezek. 40:1). Nonetheless, this festival has three other Biblical designations: (1) *Shabbaton* –

a day of solemn rest to be observed on the first day of the seventh month; (2) *Zikhron Teruah* – memorial proclaimed with the blast of a horn (Lev. 23:24); and (3) *Yom Teruah* – 'a day of blowing the horn' (Num. 29:1). Later the rabbis referred to the New Year as *Yom ha-Din* (the Day of Judgement, and *Yom ha-Zikkaron* (the Day of Remembrance).

According to the *Mishnah* all human beings will pass before God on the New Year; the *Talmud* expands this idea by stressing the need for self-examination. In rabbinic literature each person stands before the throne of God, and judgement on every person is entered on the New Year and sealed on the Day of Atonement. The tractate *Rosh Hashanah* in the *Talmud* declares that, 'there are three ledgers opened in heaven: one for the completely righteous who are immediately inscribed and sealed in the Book of Life; another for the thoroughly wicked who are recorded in the Book of Death; and a third for the intermediate, ordinary type of person whose fate hangs in the balance and is suspended until the Day of Atonement' (*RH* 16b). In this light, *Rosh Hashanah* and *Yom Kippur* are also called *Yamim Noraim* (Days of Awe).

On *Rosh Hashanah* the Ark curtain, reading desk and Torah Scroll mantles are decked in white, and the rabbi, cantor and person who blows the *shofar* (ram's horn) all wear a white *kittel* (robe). In the synagogue service the *Amidah* or the *musaf* service contains three sections relating to God's sovereignty, providence and revelation: *Malkhuyyot* (introduced by the *Alenu* prayer) deals with God's rule; *Zikhronot* portrays God's remembrance of the ancestors of the Jewish people when he judges each generation: **Shofarot** contains verses relating to the *shofar* (ram's horn) and deals with the revelation on Mount Sinai and the messianic age. Each introductory section is followed by three verses from the Torah, three from the Writings; three from the Prophets, and a final verse from the Torah. On the first and second day of *Rosh Hashanah* the Torah readings concern the birth of Isaac (Genesis 12:1–34) and the binding of Isaac or *Akedah* (Genesis 22:1–24). The *Haftarah* for the first day is 1 Samuel 1:29–2:10 which depicts the birth of Samuel, who subsequently dedicated his life to God's service. On the second day the *Haftarah* deals with Jeremiah's prophecy (Jer. 31:2–20) concerning the restoration of Israel.

On both days of *Rosh Hashanah* (except when the first is on the Sabbath) the *shofar* is blown at three points during the service; thirty times after the reading of the Law; thirty times during *musaf* (ten at the end of the three main sections); thirty times after *musaf*, and ten before *alenu*. In the liturgy there are three variants of the blowing of the *shofar: tekiah* (a long note); *shevarim* (three tremulous notes); and *teruah* (nine short notes). According to Maimonides, the *shofar* is blown to call sinners to repent. As he explains in the *Mishneh Torah:* 'Awake you sinners, and ponder your deeds; remember your creator, forsake your evil ways, and return to God.' In the Ashkenazi rite the *U-Netanneh Tokef* prayer concludes the service on a hopeful note as congregants declare that, 'Repentance, prayer and charity can avert the evil decree.'

Traditionally it was a custom to go to the sea-side or the banks of a river on the afternoon of the first day (or on the second day if the first falls on a Sabbath). The ceremony of *Tashlikh* symbolizes the casting of one's sins into a body of water. The prayers for *Tashlikh* and three verses from the Book of Micah (Mic. 7:18–20) express confidence in divine forgiveness. In the home after *Kiddush* a piece of bread is dipped in honey followed by a piece of apple, and a prayer is recited that the year ahead may be good and sweet. It is also a custom to eat the new season's fruit on the second night of *Rosh Hashanah* to justify reciting the *Sheheheyanu* benediction on enjoying new things. The *hallah* loaves baked for this festival are usually round or have a plaited crust shaped like a ladder to represent hopes for a good round year, or to direct one's life upward to God.

The Ten Days of Penitence begin with the New Year and last until the Day of Atonement. This is considered the most solemn time of the year when all are judged and their fate determined for the coming year. During the Ten Days a number of additions are made to the liturgy, especially in the morning service.

Selihot (penitential prayers) are recited during the morning service, and various additions are made to the *Amidah* and the reader's repetition of the *Amidah*. The reader's repetition is followed by the **Avinu Malkenu** prayer. In some synagogues it is customary to recite Psalm 130:1 in the morning service. It is also traditional to visit the graves of close relatives at this time. The Sabbath between the New Year and the Day of Atonement is *Shabbat Shuvah*.

The holiest day of the Jewish calendar is the Day of Atonement which takes place on the 10th of *Tishri*. Like other major festivals its observance is prescribed in Scripture: 'On the tenth day of this seventh month is the Day of Atonement; and you shall afflict yourselves. It shall be to you a sabbath of solemn rest, and you shall afflict yourselves; on the ninth day of the month, beginning at evening, from evening to evening' (Lev. 23:27,32). According to the sages, afflicting one's soul involved abstaining from food and drink. Thus every male over the age of thirteen and every female over twelve is obliged to fast from sunset until nightfall the next evening. Sick people, however, may take medicine and small amounts of food and drink; similarly, those who are ill may be forbidden to fast.

During the day normal Sabbath prohibitions apply, but worshippers are to abstain from food and drink, marital relations, wearing leather shoes, using cosmetics and lotions, and washing the body except for fingers and eyes. The rabbis stress that the Day of Atonement enables human beings to atone for sins against God; however, regarding transgressions committed against others, pardon cannot be obtained unless forgiveness has been sought from the persons injured: as a consequence, it is customary for Jews to seek reconciliation with anyone they might have offended during the year. Previously lashes (*malkot*) were administered in the synagogue to impart a feeling of repentance, but this custom has largely disappeared. The *kapparot* ritual still takes place before the Day of Atonement among Sephardi and Eastern communities as well as among some *Ashkenazim*. During this ceremony a fowl is slaughtered and either eaten before the fast or sold for money which is given to charity – its death symbolizes the transfer of guilt from the person to the bird that has been killed. In many congregations Jews substitute coins for the fowl, and charity boxes are available at the morning and afternoon services before *Yom Kippur.*

Customarily Jews were able to absolve vows on the eve of *Yom Kippur*. In addition, afternoon prayers are recited earlier than normal, and the *Amidah* is extended by two formulas of confession (*Ashamnu* and *Al Het*). Some pious Jews immerse themselves in a *mikveh* (ritual bath) in order to undergo purification before the fast. In the home a final meal (*seudah mafseket*) is eaten, and prior to lighting the festival candles, a memorial candle is kindled to burn throughout the day. Further, leather shoes are replaced by non-leather shoes or slippers. The prayer shawl (*tallit*) is worn throughout all the services, and a white curtain (*parokhet*) adorns the synagogue Ark and scrolls of the Law. The reader's desk and other furnishings are also covered in white. Among *Ashkenazim*, rabbis, cantors and other officiants also wear a white *kittel*.

On *Yom Kippur* five services take place. The first, **Kol Nidre** (named after its introductory declarations), takes place on *Yom Kippur* eve. Except for the extended *Amidah*, each service has its own characteristic liturgy. In all of them, however, the confession of sins (*viddui*) is pronounced – shorter confessions as well as longer ones are in the first person plural to emphasize collective responsibility. In some liturgies there are also confessions of personal transgressions. Of special importance in the liturgy is the *Avinu Malkenu* prayer in which individuals confess their sins and **pray for forgiveness**.

In most congregations the *Kol Nidre* (declaration of annulment of vows) is recited on the eve of *Yom Kippur*. Among the Orthodox it was a custom to spend the night in the synagogue reciting the entire Book of Psalms as well as other readings. Among *Sephardim* and Reform Jews the memorial prayer is recited on *Kol Nidre*. In addition to *selihot* and other hymns, the morning service includes a Torah reading (Leviticus Chapter 16) describing the Day of Atonement ritual in the Sanctuary, and a *maftir* (additional) reading (Num. 29:7–11) concerning the festival sacrifices. The *Haftarah* (Isa. 57:14–58:14) describes the fast that is required. The *Ashkenazim* (including Reform Jews) then recite memorial prayers (*yizkor*). Among Sephardi Jewry and eastern communities, the *Hashkavah* service is repeated.

Before the *musaf* service a special prayer (*Hineni He-Ani Mi-Maas*) is recited. A number of liturgical hymns are also included in the reader's repetition of the *Amidah*, including the *U-Netanneh Tokef* passage. Interpolated in among the *selihot* and confessions toward the end of *musaf* is the *Elleh Ezkerah* martyrology. Based on a medieval *midrash*, this martyrology describes the plight of the Ten Martyrs who were persecuted for defying Hadrian's ban on the study of Torah. In some rites this part of the service has been expanded to include readings from Holocaust sources. In the afternoon service Leviticus Chapter 18 is read, dealing with prohibited marriages and sexual offences; the *Haftarah* is the Book of Jonah.

Before the concluding service (*neilah*), the hymn *El Nora Alilah* is chanted among *Sephardim*. This part of the liturgy is recited as twilight approaches. During this time hymns such as *Petah Lanu Shaar* serve to remind congregants that the period for repentance is nearly over. In many congregations the Ark remains open and worshippers stand throughout the service. Worshippers ask God to inscribe each person for a good life and to seal them for a favourable fate. *Neilah* concludes with the chanting of *Avinu Malkenu*. This is followed by the *Shema*, the threefold recital of *Barukh Shem Kevod Malkhuto*, and a sevenfold acknowledgement that the Lord is God. The *shofar* is then blown, and the congregants recite *La-Shanah ha-Baah Bi-Yerushalayim* (Next Year in Jerusalem). After the service concludes it is customary to begin the construction of the booth (*sukkah*).

SOURCES

Shofaroth for *Rosh Hashanah*

On *Rosh Hashanah*, the *shofar* is sounded in remembrance of the revelation on Mount Sinai; its stirring sound is to awaken the people to their dedication to God:

Thou didst reveal thyself in a cloud of glory unto thy holy people in order to speak with them. Out of heaven thou didst make them hear thy voice, and wast revealed unto them in clouds of purity. The whole world trembled at thy presence, and the works of creation were in awe of thee, when thou didst thus reveal thyself, O our king, upon Mount Sinai to teach thy people the Torah and command-ments, and didst make them hear thy majestic voice and thy holy utterances out of flames of fire. Amidst thunders and lightnings thou didst manifest thyself to them, and while the *shofar* sounded thou didst shine forth upon them; as it is written in thy Torah. And it came to pass on the third day, when it was morning, that there were thunders and lightnings, and a thick cloud upon the mount, and the sound of the *shofar* exceeding loud; and all the people that were in the camp trembled. And it is said, And the sound of the *shofar* waxed louder and louder; Moses spake, and God answered him by a voice. And it is said, And all the people perceived the thunderings and the lightnings, and the sound of the *shofar*, and the mountain smoking: and when the people saw it, they were moved and stood afar off.

And in thy Holy Words it is written, saying, God is gone up with a shout, the Lord with the sound of a *shofar*. and it is said, With trumpets and sound of *shofar* shout joyously before the king, the Lord. And it is said, Blow the *shofar* on the new moon, in the time appointed, for our day of festival: for it is a statute for Israel, a decree of the God of Jacob. And it is said, Praise ye the Lord. Praise God in his sanctuary: praise him in the firmament of his power. Praise him for his mighty acts: praise him according to his abundant greatness. Praise him with the blast of the *shofar*. praise him with the harp and the lyre. Praise him with the timbrel and dance: praise him with stringed instruments and the pipe. Praise him with the clear-toned cymbals: praise him with the loud-sounding cymbals. Let everything that hath breath praise the Lord. Praise ye the Lord.

(In DPB, pp. 883–886)

Avinu Malkeinu

On *Rosh Hashanah* the congregation prays for forgiveness before the Ark:

Our father, our king

Avinu malkeinu (our father, our king), we have no king but you.
Avinu malkeinu, help us for your own sake.
Avinu malkeinu, grant us a blessed New Year.

Avinu malkeinu, annul all evil decrees against us.
Avinu malkeinu, annul the plots of our enemies.
Avinu malkeinu, frustrate the designs of our foes.
Avinu malkeinu, rid us of tyrants.
Avinu malkeinu, rid us of pestilence, sword, famine, captivity, sin and destruction.

Avinu malkeinu, forgive and pardon all our sins.
Avinu malkeinu, ignore the record of our transgressions.

Avinu malkeinu, help us return to you fully repentant.
Avinu malkeinu, send complete healing to the sick.
Avinu malkeinu, remember us with favour.

Avinu malkeinu, inscribe us in the book of happiness.
Avinu malkeinu, inscribe us in the book of deliverance.
Avinu malkeinu, inscribe us in the book of prosperity.
Avinu malkeinu, inscribe us in the book of merit.
Avinu malkeinu, inscribe us in the book of forgiveness.

Avinu malkeinu, hasten our deliverance.
Avinu malkeinu, exalt your people Israel.
Avinu malkeinu, hear us; show us mercy and compassion.
Avinu malkeinu, accept our prayer with favour and mercy.
Avinu malkeinu, do not turn us away unanswered.

Avinu malkeinu, remember that we are dust.
Avinu malkeinu, have pity for us and for our children.

Avinu malkeinu, act for those slain for your holy name.
Avinu malkeinu, act for those who were slaughtered for proclaiming your unique
  holiness.
Avinu malkeinu, act for those who went through fire and water to sanctify you.
Avinu malkeinu, act for your sake if not for ours.
Avinu malkeinu, answer us though we have no deeds to plead our cause; save us with
  mercy and lovingkindness.

(In M, pp. 153–154)

Kol Nidrei

The *Kol Nidrei* prayer is recited on the evening of *Yom Kippur*.

By authority of the court on high and by the authority of this court below, with divine
consent and with the consent of this congregation, we hereby declare that it is permitted
to pray with those who have transgressed.

All vows and oaths we take, all promises and obligations we make to God between this
Yom Kippur and the next we hereby publicly retract in the event that we should forget
them, and hereby declare our intention to be absolved of them.

(In M, p. 353)

Prayer for Forgiveness

During the *Yom Kippur* service, Jews pray for forgiveness for previous transgressions:

We have sinned against you unwillingly and willingly,
And we have sinned against you by misusing our minds.
We have sinned against you through sexual immorality,

And we have sinned against you knowingly and deceitfully.
We have sinned against you by wronging others,
And we have sinned against you through prostitution.
We have sinned against you by deriding parents and teachers.
And we have sinned against you by using violence.
We have sinned against you by not resisting the impulse to evil.

For all these sins, forgiving God, forgive us, pardon us, grant us atonement.

We have sinned against you by fraud and by falsehood,
And we have sinned against you by scoffing.
We have sinned against you by dishonesty in business.
And we have sinned against you by usurious interest.
We have sinned against you by idle chatter, And we have sinned against you by
   haughtiness.
We have sinned against you by rejecting responsibility,
And we have sinned against you by plotting against others.
We have sinned against you by irreverence,
And we have sinned against you by rushing to do evil.
We have sinned against you by false oaths,
And we have sinned against you by breach of trust.

For all these sins, forgiving God, forgive us, pardon us, grant us atonement.

(In M, pp. 379–381)

Moral Failure

In the *Yom Kippur* service, moral failure is confessed:

We have sinned against you by being heartless,
And we have sinned against you by speaking recklessly.
We have sinned against you openly and in secret,
And we have sinned against you through offensive talk.
We have sinned against you through impure thoughts,
And we have sinned against you through empty confession.
We have sinned against you purposely and by mistake,
And we have sinned against you by public desecration of your name.
We have sinned against you through foolish talk,
And we have sinned against you wittingly and unwittingly.

For all these sins, forgiving God, forgive us, pardon us, grant us atonement.

We have sinned against you through bribery,
And we have sinned against you through slander.
We have sinned against you through gluttony.
And we have sinned against you through arrogance.
We have sinned against you through wanton glances,
And we have sinned against you through effrontery.

We have sinned against you by rashly judging others.
And we have sinned against you through selfishness.
We have sinned against you through stubbornness,
And we have sinned against you through gossip.
We have sinned against you through baseless hatred,
And we have sinned against you by succumbing to dismay.

For all these sins, forgiving God, forgive us, pardon us, grant us atonement.

(In M, pp. 407–408)

DISCUSSION

1. If judgement is made concerning every person on the New Year and sealed on the Day of Atonement, can human beings redeem themselves from a harsh decree?

2. Discuss the concept of repentence and forgiveness in the Jewish tradition.

FURTHER READING

Cohen, Jeffrey, *1,001 Questions and Answers on Rosh Hashanah and Yom Kippur*, Jason Aronson, 1997.

Davis, Avrohom, *The Metsudah Interlinear Machzor: Yom Kippur*, Metsudah, 2002.

Eisemann, Moshe, *The Machzor Companion – Rosh Hashanah and Yom Kippur: The Themes of the High Holy Days Machzor*, Mesorah, 1993.

Elkins, Dov Peretz (ed.), *Moments of Transcendence: Inspirational Readings for Rosh Hashanah*, Jason Aronson, 1992.

Goodman, Philip (ed.), *The Rosh Hashanah Anthology*, Jewish Publication Society, 1992.

Goodman, Philip (ed.), *The Yom Kippur Anthology*, Jewish Publication Society, 1992.

Harlow, Jules (ed.), *Mahzor for Rosh Hashanah and Yom Kippur*, United Synagogue of Conservative Judaism, The Rabbinical Assembly, 2000.

Sorscher, Moshe, Auman, Kenneth, Sharfman, Solomon, *Companion Guide to the Rosh Hashanah Service: Featuring Selected Transliterations and Explanations of Prayers*, Judaica Press, 1998.

Scherman, Nosson (ed.), *The Complete Artscroll Machzor Rosh Hashanah*, Mesorah, 1985.

Scherman, Nosson, Goldwurm, Hersh (eds), *Rosh Hashanah: Its Significance, Laws and Prayers*, Mesorah, 1989.

Soloveitchik, Joseph Dov, Lustiger, Arnold, *Before Hashem You Shall Be Purified: Rabbi Joseph B. Soloveitchik on the Days of Awe*, Ohr Publishing, 1998.

CHAPTER 81

The Days of Joy

Figure 81 Book of Esther, miniature scroll, late eighteenth to early nineteenth century Italian. Copyright The Art Archive/ Szapiro Collection Paris/Dagli Orti.

In the Jewish calendar there are a number of joyous festivals on which Jews are permitted to follow their daily tasks:

(1) **Hanukkah**. This festival (meaning 'dedication') is celebrated for eight days beginning on 25th of *Kislev* – it commemorates the victory of the Maccabees over the Seleucids in the second century BCE. At this time the Maccabees engaged in a military struggle with the Seleucids who had desecrated the Temple of Jerusalem. After a three-year struggle (165–163 BCE),

the Maccabees under Judah Maccabee conquered Jerusalem and rebuilt the altar. According to Talmudic legend, one day's worth of oil miraculously kept the menorah burning in the Temple for eight days. *Hanukkah* commemorates this miracle.

The central observance of this festival is the kindling of the festive lamp on each of the eight nights. This practice gave this holiday the additional name of *Hag ha-Urim* (Festival of Lights). In ancient times this lamp was placed in the doorway or in the street outside; subsequently the lamp was placed inside the house. The lighting occurs after dark (except on Friday evenings when it must be done before the kindling of the Sabbath lights). The procedure for lighting the *Hanukkah* candles is to light one candle (or oil lamp) on the first night, and an additional candle each night until the last night when all eight candles are lit. The kindling should go from left to right. An alternative Talmudic tradition not in practice anymore prescribes that the eight candles are lit on the first night, seven on the second night, and so forth. These candles are lit by an additional candle called the *shammash* (serving light). In addition to this home ceremony, candles are lit in the synagogue.

In the synagogue liturgy this festival is commemorated by the recitation of the *Al ha-Nissim* prayer in the *Amidah*, and Grace after Meals. In the morning service the *Hallel* is recited, and a special reading of the Law takes place on each day of the holiday. In both the home and the synagogue the hymn *Maoz Tsur* is sung in the Ashkenazi communities; the *Sephardim* read Psalm 30 instead. During *Hanukkah* it is customary to hold parties which include games and singing. The most well-known game involves a *dreydel* (spinning top). The *dreydel* is inscribed with four Hebrew letters (*nun, gimmel, he, shin*) on its side – this is an acrostic for the phrase '*nes gadol hayah sham*' (a great miracle happened here). During *Hanukkah* it is customary to eat *latkes* (potato pancakes) and *sufganiyyot* (doughnuts). In modern Israel the festival is associated with national heroism, and a torch is carried from the traditional burial site of the Maccabees at Modiin to various parts of the country.

(2) Another festival of joy is **Purim** celebrated on 14th of *Adar* to commemorate the deliverance of Persian Jewry from the plans of Haman, the chief minister of King Ahasuerus. The name of this holiday is derived from the Akkadian word '*pur*' (lots) which refers to Haman's casting of lots to determine a date (13th *Adar*) to destroy the Jewish people (Esth. 3:7–14). In remembrance of this date the Fast of Esther is observed on 13th of *Adar*, named after the fast Queen Esther proclaimed before she interceded with the king. On the next day *Purim* is celebrated as the Feast of Lots which Mordecai, Esther's cousin, inaugurated to remember the deliverance of the Jewish people (Esth. 9:20ff.). The 15th of *Adar* is *Shushan Purim* since the conflict between the Jews and Haman's supporters in ancient Susa did not cease until the 14th, and Ahasuerus allowed the Jews an extra day to overcome their foes. This means that the deliverance could only be celebrated a day later (Esth. 9:13–18).

The laws regarding the observance of *Purim* are specified in the tractate *Megillah* in the *Talmud*. In the evening and morning services the Esther scroll is chanted to a traditional melody. In most congregations *Purim* resembles a carnival – children frequently attend the reading from the scroll in fancy dress, and whenever Haman's name is mentioned, worshippers stamp their feet and whirl noisemakers (*greggers*). In the *Amidah* and Grace after Meals a prayer of thanksgiving is included; however, the *Hallel* psalms are excluded. During the afternoon a special festive meal takes place including such traditional dishes as *Hamentashen* (Haman's hats) – triangular buns or pastries filled with poppyseed, prunes, dates, etc. It is usual for parents and relatives to give children money (*Purim gelt*). On *Purim* it is customary to stage plays, and in *yeshivot* students mimic their teachers. In modern Israel parades take pace with revellers dressed in *Purim* costumes.

(3) **Rosh Hodesh** is another festival of joy which occurs with the **New Moon** each month. Since the Jewish calendar is lunar, each month lasts a little more than twenty-nine days. Because it was not possible to arrange the calendar with months of alternative length the Sanhedrin declared whether a month had twenty-nine or thirty days. If this outgoing month had twenty-nine days, the next day was *Rosh Hodesh*. When a month had thirty days, the last day of the outgoing month and the first day of the new month constituted *Rosh Hodesh*. In early rabbinic times, the Sanhedrin was responsible for determining the day of the New Moon on the basis of eye witnesses who had claimed to see the new moon. Only in the fourth century was a permanent calendar fixed by Hillel II.

During the period of the First Temple, *Rosh Hodesh* was observed with the offering of special sacrifices, the blowing of *shofars*, feasting and a rest from work. By the end of the sixth century BCE *Rosh Hodesh* became a semi-holiday. Eventually even this status disappeared, and *Rosh Hodesh* became a normal working day except for various liturgical changes. The liturgy for *Rosh Hodesh* includes the *Yaaleh Ve-Yavo* prayer, read in the *Amidah* and in Grace after Meals, which asks God to remember his people for good, for blessing and for life. In the morning service the *Hallel* psalms of praise are recited. The Bible reading is from Numbers Chapter 28 which describes the Temple service for the New Moon. An additional service is also included, corresponding to the additional sacrifice which was offered on the New Moon.

(4) A further joyous festival is the New Year for Trees (**Tu Bi-Shevat**) which takes place on the 15th of *Shevat*. Although this festival is not referred to in the Bible, it appeared in the Second Temple period as a fixed cut-off date for determining the tithe levied on the produce of fruit trees. Once the Temple was destroyed, the laws of tithing were no longer applicable. As a result, this festival took on a new character. Wherever Jews resided, it reminded them of their connection with the Holy Land. During the fifteenth century, a number of new ceremonies and rituals were instituted by the mystics of Safed. Due to the influence of Isaac Luria, it became customary to celebrate the festival with gatherings where special fruits were eaten and hymns and readings from Scripture were recited. Among the fruits eaten on *Tu Bi-Shevat* were those of the Holy Land. In modern Israel new trees are planted during this festival.

(5) Another joyous occasion is the 15th of *Av* which was a folk festival in the Second Temple period. At this time bachelors selected their wives from unmarried maidens. According to the *Mishnah*, on both this day and the Day of Atonement, young girls in Jerusalem dressed in white garments and danced in the vineyards where young men selected their brides. In modern times this festival is marked only by a ban on eulogies or fasting. In the liturgy the *Tahanun* prayer is not recited after the *Amidah*.

(6) The final festival is **Israel Independence Day** – this is Israel's national day, which commemorates the proclamation of its independence on the 5th of *Iyyar*

1948. The Chief Rabbinate of Israel declared it a religious holiday and established a special order of service for the evening and morning worship. This service includes the *Hallel*, and a reading from Isaiah (Isa. 10:32–11:12). The rabbinate also suspended any fast which occurs on the day, the recital of the *Tahanun* prayer, and mourning restrictions of the *Omer* period. In Israel the preceding day is set aside as a day of remembrance for soldiers who died in battle. *Yizkor* prayers (including the *Kaddish*) are recited then, and next-of-kin visit the military cemeteries. At home memorial candles are lit, and Psalm 9 is recited in many synagogues.

SOURCES

Hanukkah Candle Lighting

On each of the eight nights of *Hanukkah*, candles are lit, one the first night, two the second, adding one candle each subsequent night:

> Praised are you, Lord our God, king of the universe whose *mitzvot* add holiness to our life and who gave us the *mitzvah* to light the lights of *Hanukkah*.

> Praised are you, Lord our God, king of the universe who accomplished miracles for our ancestors in ancient days, and in our time.

> These lights we kindle to recall the wondrous triumphs and the miraculous victories wrought through your holy *kohanim* for our ancestors in ancient days at this season. These lights are sacred through all the eight days of *Hanukkah*. We may not put them to ordinary use, but are to look upon them and thus be reminded to thank and praise you for the wondrous miracle of our deliverance.

> Rock of Ages, let our song praise your saving power.
> You amid the raging throng were our sheltering tower.
> Furious they assailed us, but your help availed us.
> And your word broke their sword when our own strength failed us.

> (In SSS, p. 243)

Purim

The Book of Esther describes the festival of *Purim* in ancient times:

> The rest of the Jews, those in the king's provinces, likewise mustered and fought for their lives . . . That was on the thirteenth day of the month of *Adar*; and they rested on the fourteenth day and made it a day of feasting and merrymaking. (But the Jews in Shushan

mustered on both the thirteenth and fourteenth days, and so rested on the fifteenth and made it a day of feasting and merrymaking.) That is why village Jews, who live in unwalled towns, observe the fourteenth day of the month of *Adar* and make it a day for merrymaking and feasting, and as a holiday and an occasion for sending gifts to one another.

(Esther 9:16–19)

Blessing of the New Moon

The first of the month (*Rosh Hodesh*) is celebrated as a special day, and once the new moon is clearly visible in the heavens – usually from the 7th to the 14th of the month – prayers are said outside.

Rabbi Yohanan: Whoever blesses the new moon at the proper time is considered as having welcomed the presence of the *Shekhinah*.

Halleluyah. Praise the Lord from the heavens. Praise him, angels on high. Praise him, sun and moon and all shining stars. Praise him, highest heavens. Let them praise the glory of the Lord at whose command they were created, at whose command they endure forever and by whose laws nature abides.

Praised are you, Lord our God, king of the universe whose word created the heavens, whose breath created all that they contain. Statutes and seasons He set for them that they should not deviate from their assigned task. Happily, gladly they do the will of their creator, whose work is dependable. To the moon He spoke: renew yourself, crown of glory for those who were borne in the womb, who also are destined to be renewed and to extol their creator for his glorious sovereignty. Praised are you, Lord who renews the months.

David, king of Israel, lives and endures.

Shalom aleikhem
Aleikhem Shalom.

May good fortune be ours, and blessing be for the whole house of Israel.

(In SSS, p. 705)

Tu Bi-Shevat

The festival of *Tu Bi-Shevat* is a spring festival and is celebrated as a time of the planting of trees:

> On *Tu Bi-Shevat*
> When spring comes
> An angel descends, ledger in hand,
> and records each bud, each twig, each tree,
> And all our garden flowers.
> From town to town, from village to village,
> The angel makes a winged way,
> Searching the valleys, inspecting the hills,
> Flying over the desert
> And returns to heaven.

> And when the ledger will be full
> Of trees and blossoms and shrubs,
> When the desert is turned into a meadow
> And all our land is a watered garden,
> Messianic days will be with us.
>
> (In KH, p. 810)

Israel Independence Day

Israel Independence Day is a time of rejoicing for the creation of the State of Israel in the Holy Land:

> Blessed is the match consumed in kindling flame.
> Blessed is the flame that burns in the heart's secret places. Blessed is the heart with strength to stop its beating for honour's sake.
> Blessed is the match consumed in kindling flame.
>
> For Zion's sake I will not keep silence; for Jerusalem's sake I will speak out, until her right shines forth like the sunrise, her deliverance like a blazing torch.
>
> Let the wilderness and the thirsty land be glad, let the desert rejoice and burst into flower.
>
> The people who walked in darkness have seen a great light. On those who dwelt in a land dark as death, a light has dawned.
>
> Blessed is the Lord our God, ruler of the universe, for giving us life, for sustaining us, and for enabling us to reach this joyous day.
>
> Give thanks to the Lord, for He is good;
> For his love is everlasting!
>
> So let them say whom the Lord has redeemed, whom He has redeemed from the oppressor's hand:
>
> For his love is everlasting!
>
> He gathered them out of every land, from east and west, from north and south:
>
> For his love is everlasting!
>
> Some were lost in desert wastes; hungry and thirsty, their spirit sank within them. So they cried to the Lord in their trouble, and He rescued them from their distress:
>
> For his love is everlasting!
>
> He brought them out of darkness, dark as death, and broke their chains:
>
> For his love is everlasting!
>
> He turns wilderness into flowing streams, parched lands into springs of water. There He gives the hungry a home, where they build cities to live in. They sow fields and plant vineyards and reap a fruitful harvest.
>
> Give thanks to the Lord, for He is good; for his love is everlasting!
>
> (In GP, pp. 590–592)

DISCUSSION

1. How have the festivals of *Hanukkah* and *Purim* reinforced the Jewish belief in the victory of the Jews over their enemies?

2. How has Israel Independence Day supplemented other joyous occasions in stressing God's providential care of his people?

FURTHER READING

Buxbaum, Yitzhak, *A Person is Like a Tree: A Sourcebook for Tu Beshvat*, Jason Aronson, 1999.

Cohen, Jeffrey, *500 Questions and Answers on Chanukah*, Jason Aronson, 2003.

Elon, Ari, Hyman, Naomi, Waskow, Arthur (eds), *Trees, Earth, and Torah: A Tu'B'Shvat Anthology*, Jewish Publication Society of America, 1999.

Goodman, Philip, *Purim Anthology*, Jewish Publication Society of America, 1988.

Isaacs, Ronald, *Every Person's Guide to Purim*, Jason Aronson, 2000.

Randall, Ronnie, *Festival Cookbooks: Jewish Festivals Cookbook*, Hodder Wayland, 2001.

Schauss, Hayyim, *Jewish Festivals: From Their Beginnings to Our Own Day*, UAHC Press, 1969.

Schauss, Hayyim, *The Jewish Festivals: A Guide to Their History and Observance*, Schocken, 1996.

Wood, Angela, *Jewish Festivals*, Heinemann, 1996.

CHAPTER 82

Fasts

Figure 82 Fast days: boys sitting on the floor and praying on the Ninth of *Av*, in the Belem synagogue, Brazil, 1981. Photo: Abraham Isaac Amzalak, Brazil. Copyright Beth Hatefutsoth Photo Archive, courtesy of Abraham Isaac Amzalak.

In the ritual of the First Temple, fasting was a permanent feature; in addition, the death of a national leader (such as King Saul) could initiate a day-long fast (2 Sam. 12) or even a weekly fast (1 Sam. 31:13). The purpose of such fasting was manifold. Its most widely attested function was to avert or terminate calamities. Fasting also served as a means of obtaining divine forgiveness.

In the Bible there is no record of specific fast days in the annual calendar (except for the Day of Atonement). Fixed fast days were first mentioned in the post-exilic period by the prophet Zechariah who declared: 'Thus says the Lord of hosts: The fast of the fourth month, and the fast of the fifth, and the fast of the seventh, and the fast of the tenth, shall be to the houses of Judah seasons of joy and gladness, and cheerful feasts' (Zech. 8:19). According to tradition, these fasts commemorate the events which resulted in the destruction of the Temple: the 10th of *Tevet* – the beginning of the siege of Jerusalem; the 17th of

Tammuz – the breaching of the walls; the 9th of *Av* – the destruction of the Temple; the 3rd of *Tishri* – the assassination of Gedaliah (the Babylonian-appointed governor of Judah). Thus the practice of fasting, which was a spontaneous phenomenon in the period of the First Temple, later entered the calendar as a recurring event in commemoration of historical calamities.

Jewish sources lay down a series of prescriptions to regularize the process of fasting. During the First Temple period the devout offered sacrifices, confessed sins and uttered prayers. From the Second Temple period onward, public fasts were also accompanied by a reading from Scripture. On solemn fasts four prayers (*shaharit, hazot, minhah, ad neilat shearim*) were recited as well as *maariv*. The *Amidah* of the fast day consisted of twenty-four benedictions (the normal eighteen, plus six others) and the liturgy was elaborated with passages of supplications (*selihot*) and prayers for mercy. During the service, the *shofar* was sounded, accompanied by horns. In the Temple the blowing of *shofarot* and trumpets was performed differently from other localities. Prayers were normally uttered in the open, and all the people tore their clothes, wore sackcloth, and put ashes or earth on their heads. Holy objects were also humiliated. It was not uncommon to cover the altar with sackcloth and the Ark, containing the Torah scrolls, was frequently taken into the street and covered with ashes. During the mass assembly, one of the elders rebuked the people for their failings, and the affairs of the community were scrutinized. It was normal for young children and animals to fast as well. (The sages, however, exempted young children and animals, the sick, those obliged to preserve their strength, and pregnant and nursing women.)

Ordinary fast days lasted during the daylight hours; important fasts were twenty-four hours in length. Fasts were held either for one day or, on some occasions, for a series of three or seven days. In some cases, fasts were held on Sabbaths and festivals – but it was normally forbidden to fast on these days. So as not to mar the celebration of joyful events in Jewish history, Hananiah ben Hezekiah ben Garon (first century CE) formulated a Scroll of Fasting which lists thirty-five dates on which a public fast should not be proclaimed. Eventually, however, this list was abrogated. It was customary to hold fast days on Mondays and Thursdays. After the destruction of the Second Temple, individuals took upon themselves to fast every Monday and Thursday; Jewish law specifies that in such cases these persons should fast. It was also possible to fast for a certain number of hours. On some occasions, the fast was only partial, and those who fasted refrained only from meat and wine.

According to tradition, fast days fall into three categories:

A. FASTS DECREED OR REFERRED TO IN THE BIBLE

1. The Day of Atonement (**Yom Kippur**) is to be a fast day in accordance with the declaration: 'You shall afflict your souls'. This is done so that individuals may be cleansed from sin (Lev. 16:29–31; 23:27–32; Num. 29:7ff.).

2. The Ninth of *Av* (**Tishah B'Av**) was the day when Nebuchadnezzar destroyed the Temple in 586 BCE and Titus later devastated the Second Temple in 70 CE). The *Mishnah* also decrees that on this day God declared that the older Israelites should not enter the Promised Land (Num. 14:28ff.). Betar was captured in 135 CE, and Jerusalem was ploughed up on Hadrian's decree. Like *Yom Kippur* this fast is observed for a complete day, beginning at sunset on the eighth day of *Av* and ending at nightfall on the ninth. As a sign of mourning neither meat, drink, nor wine should be consumed from the first day of *Av* until noon on the tenth, except on the Sabbath and on a *Seudat Mitzvah* (a meal in honour of a religious act). In the synagogue service the Ark curtain and coverings are removed; congregants take off their shoes and sit on low chairs. During the morning service *tefillin* and *tallit* are not worn but are put on during the afternoon service. At the evening and morning services a number of elegies (*kinot*) are recited, which are connected with tragic events in the history of the Jewish people. The Torah reading at the morning service is taken from Deuteronomy 4:25–40), which deals with God's forgiveness of penitents. The *Haftarah* (Jer. 8:13–9:23) predicts the punishment which will befall the kingdom of Judah. At the afternoon service the Torah and *Haftarah* readings are the same as on other fast days.

During the seven weeks between *Tishah B'Av* and *Rosh Hashanah* the *Haftarah* portions are taken from the Book of Isaiah, containing messages of consolation.

3. The Seventeenth of *Tammuz* commemorates the breaching of the walls of Jerusalem. This occurred on 9th of *Tammuz* in the First Temple period (2 Kings 25:3–4) and in Second Temple times they were breached by the Romans on 17th of *Tammuz*. In addition, the *Mishnah* records that other disasters took place on 17th of *Tammuz*: Moses broke the tablets of stone on which the Ten Commandments were inscribed when he saw the ancient Israelites worship the golden calf; the communal burnt offerings ceased when Jerusalem was besieged; a Syrian officer, Apostomos, burnt the Torah Scrolls and set up an idol in the Temple. The fast of 17th of *Tammuz* begins at sunrise on the day itself (rather than the previous night). In the morning service, Exodus 32:22–24 and 34:1–10 are read; in the afternoon, these passages are repeated and, among *Ashkenazim*, followed by a *Haftarah* taken from the Book of Isaiah (Isa. 55:6–56:8).

4. The 10th of *Tevet* is a fast commemorating the commencement of the siege of Jerusalem by Nebuchadnezzar (2 Kings 25:1). This fast begins at dawn and lasts until nightfall. The liturgy for the day includes the penitential prayers (*selihot*) and a reading from Exodus (parts of Exodus Chapters 32 and 34) which deals with the worship of the golden calf and Moses' prayer for forgiveness for the nation. In the afternoon service the same passage is read with the addition of a *Haftarah* from Isaiah Chapters 55 and 56. In Israel, 10th of *Tevet* is observed as a day of remembrance of the six million Jews who died at the hands of the Nazis in the Holocaust.

5. The Fast of Gedaliah takes place on 3rd of *Tishri* to commemorate the fate of Gedaliah, the governor of Judah who was assassinated on this day. Fasting takes place from dawn to dusk and penitential hymns (*selihot*) are recited during the morning service. (If the fast falls on a Sabbath, it is observed the next day.)

6. The Fast of Esther takes place on 13th of *Adar* (the day before *Purim*).

B. FASTS DECREED BY THE RABBIS

1. Those who are especially pious are encouraged to fast during the Ten Days of Penitence and for as many days as possible during the month of *Elul*.

2. The first Monday and Thursday, and the following Monday after Passover and *Sukkot* are to be observed as fast days.

3. *ShOVaVIM Tat* (initial letters of the first eight weekly Bible portions of the Book of Exodus) is observed during the winter months of January and February.

4. A fast is observed during the Three Weeks of Mourning between 17th of *Tammuz* and 9th of *Av*.

5. 7th of *Adar* is a traditional date of the death of Moses; it is observed by members of the burial society who fast prior to their annual banquet held on the evening of that day.

6. *Yom Kippur Katan* is a fast day which takes place on the last day of each month.

7. The Fast of the First-Born takes place on 14th of *Nisan* to commemorate the sanctification of the first-born who were saved during the time of the last plague of Egypt.

8. Days commemorating calamitous events in the history of the Jewish nation.

C. PRIVATE FASTS

1. The anniversary of the death of a parent or teacher.

2. Grooms and brides fast on their wedding days.

3. Fasting occurs to prevent the consequences of nightmares taking place.

4. Fasting takes place if a Torah Scroll is dropped.

SOURCES

Yom Kippur

During *Yom Kippur* the faithful fast as a sign of remorse for their sinful actions of the previous year:

Grant us compassion from your abundant store of compassion. For you do not desire destruction, as your prophet Isaiah declared: 'Seek the Lord while He may be found, call to him while He is near. Let the wicked man abandon his ways, and the evil man his thoughts. Let him return to the Lord who will have compassion for him, let him return to our God who freely forgives.' Forgiving God, you are gracious and compassionate, patient, abounding in kindness and faithfulness. You desire the return of the wicked, not their death, as you have proclaimed through your prophet Ezekiel: 'As I live, says the Lord God, I do not desire the death of the wicked, but that he abandon his ways and live. Turn, turn from your wicked ways, for why should you die, House of Israel?' And it is written: 'Do I desire the death of the wicked? Do I not prefer that he abandon his ways and live? . . . I do not desire anyone's death. Turn then, and live.' For you pardon and forgive the House of Israel in every generation. But for you we have no king who pardons and forgives.

(In M, p. 717)

Tishah B'Av

The service for *Tishah B'Av* recalls the suffering of the Jewish people:

In the presence of eyes
which witnessed the slaughter,
which saw the oppression
the heart could not bear, and as witness the heart
that once taught compassion
until the days came to pass that crushed human feeling,
I have taken an oath: To remember it all,
to remember, not once to forget!
Forget not one thing to the last generation
when degradation shall cease,
to the last, to its ending,
when the rod of instruction
shall have come to conclusion.
An oath: Not in vain passed over
the night of the terror.
An oath: No morning shall see me at
flesh-pots again.
An oath: Lest from this we learned nothing.

(In GP, p. 573)

Yom Ha-Shoah

Yom Ha-Shoah is a day of remembrance of the horrors of the Holocaust:

The twenty-seventh day of *Nisan* is the day on which Jews throughout the world formally recall the six million Jews of Europe who were tortured and murdered during the Second World War because they were Jews. It is a time when we recall the splendour of their lives, as well as the terror of their deaths. Countless memoirs and diaries written by survivors plead and demand that we remember the details of how they were degraded, brutalized, and killed. We recall part of what they witnessed, part of the horrors that they suffered, in order to remember them and to remind others. On this day, and not on this day alone, we perpetuate their testimony, recalling the words of Ignacy Schipper, who perished at Maidanek: 'Nobody will want to believe us, because our disaster is the disaster of the entire civilized world . . . We will have the thankless job of proving to a reluctant world that we are Abel, the murdered brother.'

(In SSS, p. 828)

DISCUSSION

1. Should one forgive all those who have transgressed against one regardless of their offence?

2. Is it healthy for the Jewish people to focus on past suffering?

FURTHER READING

Cohen, Jeffrey, *1001 Questions and Answers on Rosh Hashanah and Yom Kippur*, Jason Aronson, 1997.

Domnitch, Larry, *The Jewish Holidays: A Journey Through History*, Jason Aronson, 2000.

Goldman, Ari, *Being Jewish: The Spiritual and Cultural Practice of Judaism Today*, Simon and Schuster, 2000.

Greenberg, Irving, *The Jewish Way: Living the Holidays*, Simon and Schuster, 1993.

Isaacs, Ronald, *Sacred Seasons: A Sourcebook for the Jewish Holidays*, Jason Aronson, 1997.

Schauss, Hayyim, *The Jewish Festivals: A Guide to Their History and Observance*, Schocken, 1996.

Schweid, Eliezer, *The Jewish Experience of Time: Philosophical Dimensions of the Jewish Holy Days*, Jason Aronson, 2000.

Segal, Eliezer, *Holidays, History and Halakhah*, Jason Aronson, 2001.

Strassfeld, Michael, *The Jewish Holidays: A Guide and Commentary*, Harper Resource, 1985.

Tov, Eliyahu Ki, Landesman, David, *The Book of Our Heritage: The Jewish Year and its Days of Significance*, Feldheim, 1997.

Witty, Abraham, Witty, Rachel, *Exploring Jewish Tradition: A Transliterated Guide to Everyday Practice and Observance*, Doubleday, 2001.

CHAPTER 83

Life Cycle Events

Figure 83 Bar Mitzvah. Copyright David Rose, London.

In Scripture the first commandment is to be fruitful and multiply (Gen. 1:28). In Biblical times childbirth took place in a kneeling position (1 Sam. 4:19) or sitting on a special birthstool (Exodus Chapter 1). Scriptural law imposes various laws on ritual purity and impurity on the mother: if she gives birth to a boy she is considered ritually impure for seven days; for the next thirty-three days she is not allowed to enter the Temple precincts or handle sacred objects. For the mother of a girl, the number of days are respectively fourteen and sixty-six. According to Jewish law, if a woman in childbirth is in mortal danger, her life takes precedence over that of the unborn child – only when over half of the child's body has emerged from the birth canal is it considered to be fully human.

In ancient times the birth of a child was accompanied by numerous superstitious practices, including the use of amulets to ward off the evil eye. After the birth, family and friends gathered nightly to recite prayers to ward off evil spirits such as Lilith, the female demon who allegedly attempts to kill off all newborn children. Among German Jews, it was frequently the practice for parents of a son to cut off a strip of swaddling in which the child was wrapped during his circumcision; this is known as the *wimple*, and is kept until his bar mitzvah, when it is used for tying the scroll of the Law. From the medieval period Ashkenazi mothers visited the synagogue after the birth of a child to recite the *Gomel* blessing (which expresses gratitude to God) as well as other prayers. It is also the custom for the congregation to recite the *Mi She-Barakh* prayer for the welfare of the mother and the child.

The naming of a new-born child takes place on one of two occasions: a baby boy is named at the circumcision ceremony; a baby girl is named in the synagogue on the first time the Torah is read after her birth. The Hebrew form of the individual's name consists of the individual's name followed by '*ben*' (son) or '*bat*' (daughter) of the father. This form is used in all Hebrew documents as well as for the call to the reading of the Torah. In modern times it is still the practice to give a child a Jewish name in addition to a secular one. Ashkenazi Jews frequently name the child after a deceased relative; Sephardi Jews after someone who is still alive. Alternatively, a Hebrew name may be selected which is related to the secular name either in meaning or sound, or the secular name may be transliterated in

Hebrew characters. Traditionally it was the custom to change the name of a person at the time of a serious illness; according to the rabbis, changing the name is a way of misleading the angel of death. On this basis, it became the custom to add a further name to the ill person's – from that point the individual was known by his original name, together with the new one.

The custom of redeeming first-born male children is based on the Biblical prescription that first-born sons should be consecrated to the Temple. Just as first fruits and first-born animals had to be given to the priests, so first-born male children were dedicated to God. The obligation to redeem first-born sons from this service is referred to in Numbers 3:44–51: redemption is to take place by payment of five shekels to a priest. Detailed laws concerning the **Redemption of the First-Born** (*Pidyon ha-Ben*) are presented in the *Mishnah* tractate *Bekhorot*, and expanded in the talmudic commentary on the passage. According to this legislation, the sons of priests and *Levites* are exempt from redemption, as are first-born sons whose mother is the daughter of either a priest or *Levite*. In the *geonic* period, a ceremony was instituted in which the father of the child declares to the priest on the thirty-first day after its birth that the infant is the first-born son of his mother and the father and that, as a father, he is obliged to redeem him. The priest then asks the father if he prefers to give his son to the priest or redeem his son, and the father hands the priest the required amount. The father then recites a blessing concerning the fulfilment of the precept of redeeming the child, and another expressing gratitude to God. This procedure has served as the basis for the ceremony since the Middle Ages.

According to Jewish law, all male children are to undergo **circumcision**, in accordance with God's decree, and as a sign of the covenant between God and Abraham's offspring. As Genesis Chapter 17 relates:

> God said to Abraham . . . 'This is my covenant which you shall keep between me and you and your descendants after you; every male among you shall be circumcised. You shall be circumcised in the flesh of your foreskins, and it shall be a sign of the covenant between me and you' (Gen. 17:9–11).

Jewish ritual circumcision involves the removal of the entire foreskin. It is to be performed on the eighth day after the birth of the child by a person who is properly qualified (*mohel*). Jewish law specifies that this ceremony can be performed even on the Sabbath, festivals, or the Day of Atonement; however, postponement is allowed if there is any danger to the child's health. The laws regulating this procedure are derived from Biblical sources as well as rabbinic enactments. Traditionally the ceremony is to take place in the presence of a quorum of ten adult Jewish men (*minyan*). On the morning of the eighth day, the infant is taken from the mother by the godmother who hands him to the *sandak* (godfather). The *sandak* then carries the child into the room where the circumcision is to take place and hands him to the individual who places the child on a chair called the Chair of Elijah. Another person then takes him from the Chair of Elijah and passes him to the child's father who puts him on the lap of the godfather who holds the boy during the ceremony. The circumcision is performed by a *mohel*; formerly blood was drawn orally by the *mohel* but today an instrument is used. The infant is then handed to the person who will hold him during the ceremony of naming, and the ceremony concludes with a special blessing over a cup of wine, followed by the naming of the child.

At thirteen a boy attains the age of Jewish adulthood; from this point he is accounted as part of a *minyan* (the quorum for prayer). According to the *Mishnah*, the thirteenth year is when a boy should observe the commandments. The term **bar mitzvah** ('son of a commandment') occurs five times in the Babylonian *Talmud*, but in all cases it is used merely to refer to someone obliged to fulfil Jewish law. The *Talmud* stipulates that male adolescence begins at the age of thirteen years and a day; nonetheless a boy is able to participate in religious ceremonies at an earlier age as long as he can appreciate their meaning. However, by the Middle Ages, a Jewish minor's participation in religious rituals had become limited. *Ashkenazim*, for example, allowed a boy to wear *tefillin* only after he was thirteen; in addition, he was not allowed to be called to the reading of the Law until then. Sephardi congregations also imposed similar restrictions.

The essentials of the bar mitzvah ceremony involve prayer with *tefillin* for the first time, and reading from the Torah. Among east European *Ashkenazim*, a boy was normally called to the reading of the Torah on the first Monday or Thursday after his thirteenth birthday; then he would recite the Torah blessings and chant some verses from the weekly *sidrah*. In western Europe, on the other hand, a thirteen-year-old boy would be called to the reading at Sabbath morning services where he would recite the Torah blessings, chant a portion of the Law (*maftir*), and read from the Prophets. This has now become a universally accepted practice. Once the bar mitzvah boy had completed the second Torah blessing, his father would recite a special prayer – *Barukh She-Pataroni*.

In both Ashkenazi and Sephardi communities the bar mitzvah ceremony included a discourse (*derashah*) by the bar mitzvah boy which demonstrates his knowledge of rabbinic sources. In time other practices became part of the bar mitzvah ceremony; some boys chanted the entire weekly reading; others were trained as prayer leaders; some conducted the Sabbath eve service on Friday night as well as the Sabbath morning service. In some Western communities the bar mitzvah boy reads a special prayer standing before the rabbi or the Ark. In modern times it is usual for the rabbi to address the bar mitzvah boy after the reading of the law.

Initially a bar mitzvah meal for family and friends was held after the weekday morning service, or a *seudah shelishit* (third meal) was consumed after the Sabbath afternoon service. Subsequently this was expanded into a *Kiddush* (blessing over wine and bread) at the Sabbath morning service, followed by a family meal. Today there is frequently a bar mitzvah reception on a more lavish scale. Among Oriental Jews other variations of such festivities take place. In many Eastern Sephardi communities, Hebrew poems (*piyyutim*) are composed for this occasion. In the nineteenth century Reform Judaism substituted a confirmation ceremony for both boys and girls in place of bar mitzvah; however, as time passed, most Reform congregations have instituted bar mitzvah as well. Since 1967 both Orthodox and non-Orthodox bar mitzvahs have taken place at the Western Wall in Jerusalem.

Unlike bar mitzvah there is no legal requirement for a girl to take part in a religious ceremony to mark her religious majority (at the age of twelve years and a day). Nonetheless, a ceremonial equivalent of bar mitzvah has been designed for girls. In Orthodoxy this was the innovation of Jacob Ettliner in the nineteenth century, and subsequently spread to other lands. In the late nineteenth century it was approved by Joseph Hayyim ben Elijah al-Hakam of Baghdad, who formulated various regulations, including the holding of a banquet and the wearing of a new dress so that the bat mitzvah girl could recite the *Sheheheyanu* benediction.

In the early twentieth century the Conservative scholar Mordecai Kaplan pioneered the bat mitzvah ceremony in the USA as part of the synagogue service, and since then this has become widely accepted by many American communities. In non-Orthodox communities, a twelve-year-old girl celebrates her coming of age on a Friday night or during the Sabbath morning service where she conducts the prayers, chants the *Haftarah*, and in some cases reads from the Torah and delivers an address. In Orthodox synagogues, however, the bat mitzvah's participation in the services is more limited. At a women's *minyan*, however, she is called to the reading of the Torah and may even chant one of the portions, together with the *Haftarah*.

Outside the USA the bat mitzvah ceremony takes various forms. In Reform congregations it is in line with the American pattern. Orthodox girls, however, do not participate in the synagogue service; rather a bat mitzvah's father is called to the Torah on the appropriate Sabbath morning and recites the *Barukh She-Pataroni* benediction. His daughter then recites the *Sheheheyanu* prayer, and the rabbi addresses her in the synagogue or at a *Kiddush* reception afterwards. Alternatively, the ceremony takes place at home or in the synagogue hall on a weekday. In Britain and South Africa the procedure is different; bat mitzvah girls must pass a special examination enabling them to participate in a collective ceremony.

SOURCES

Circumcision

After the performance of circumcision, a prayer is recited over the the goblet of wine:

> Praised be Thou, O Lord our God, king of the universe, who hast created the fruit of the vine.
>
> Praised be Thou, O Lord our God, king of the universe, who hast sanctified the well beloved (Isaac) from the womb and hast set thy statute in his flesh, and hast sealed his offspring with the sign of the holy covenant. Therefore, because of this, O living God, our portion and our rock, deliver from destruction the dearly beloved of our flesh, for the sake of the covenant Thou hast set in our bodies. Praised be Thou, O Lord our God, who hast made the covenant.
>
> Our God and God of our fathers, preserve this child to his father and to his mother, and let his name be called in Israel . . . son of . . . Let the father rejoice in his offspring, and let the mother be glad with her children; as it is written: 'Let thy father and thy mother rejoice, and let her that bore thee be glad'. And it is said: 'And I passed by thee, and I saw thee weltering in thy blood, and I said unto thee: "In thy blood thou shalt live". Yea, I said: "In thy blood thou shalt live."' And it is said: 'He hath remembered his covenant for ever, the word which He commanded to a thousand generations; (the covenant) which he made with Abraham, and his oath unto Isaac, and confirmed the same unto Jacob for a statute, to Israel for everlasting covenant.' And it is said: 'And Abraham circumcised his son Isaac when he was eight days old, as God commanded him.' O give thanks unto the Lord; for He is good; for his loving kindness endureth for ever. The little child . . ., may he become great. As he has been entered into the covenant, so may he be introduced to the study of the Law, to the nuptial canopy, and to good deeds.

(H, pp. 34–36)

Redemption of the First Born

The guests wash their hands for the meal, are seated, and pronounce the blessing over bread. Then the father brings his first-born son, holding in his hands coins or articles and says to the priest who is seated:

> This, the first-born son of mine, is the first-born of his mother, and the Holy One, praised be He, has bidden to redeem him; as it is said (Numbers 18:16): 'And their redemption-money – from a month old shalt thou redeem them – shall be, according to thy valuation, five *shekels* of silver, after the *shekel* of the sanctuary – the same is twenty *gerahs*.' And it is said again (Exodus 13:2): 'Sanctify unto me all the first-born, whatsoever openeth the womb among the children of Israel, both of man and of beast, it is mine.'

(H, p. 52)

Bar Mitzvah

The following prayer is for a *bar-mitzvah*:

May He who blessed our ancestors Abraham, Isaac and Jacob, bless this youth who was called up today in honour of God and in honour of the Torah, and to give thanks for all the good that God has done for him. As a reward for this, may the Holy One, praised be He, keep him and grant him life. May He incline his heart to be perfect with him, to study his Law, to walk in his ways, to observe his commandments, statutes and judgements. May he be successful and prosperous in all his ways, and may he find grace and mercy in the eyes of God and man. May his parents deserve to raise him up to the study of the Law, to the nuptial canopy and to good deeds.

(H, p. 54)

DISCUSSION

1. Do traditional life-cycle events illustrate the patriarchal character of the Jewish tradition?

2. Is circumcision a barbaric rite?

FURTHER READING

Cardin, Nina Beth, *The Tapestry of Jewish Time: A Spiritual Guide to Holidays and Life-Cycle Events*, Behrman House, 2000.

Cohen, Eugene, *Guide to Ritual Circumcision and Redemption of the First-Born Son*, KTAV, 1984.

David, Jo, Syme, Daniel, *The Book of the Jewish Life*, UAHC Press, 1997.

Davis, Judith, *Whose Bar/Bat Mitzvah is This, Anyway?: A Guide for Parents Through a Family Rite of Passage*, St Martins, 1998.

Geffen, Rela (ed.), *Celebration and Renewal: Rites of Passage in Judaism*, Jewish Publication Society, 1993.

Goldman, Ari, *Being Jewish: The Spiritual and Cultural Practice of Judaism Today*, Simon and Schuster, 2000.

Goldman, Ronald, *Questioning Circumcision: A Jewish Perspective*, Vanguard, 1997.

Gollaher, David, *Circumcision: A History of the World's Most Controversial Surgery*, Basic Books, 2000.

Greenberg, Melanie, *Blessings: Our Jewish Ceremonies*, Jewish Publication Society of America, 1995.

Gutmann, J., *The Jewish Life Cycle*, Brill, 1987.

Isaacs, Ronald, Olitzky, Kerry (eds), *Sacred Moments: Tales from the Jewish Life Cycle*, Jason Aronson, 1995.

Lieberman, Dale, *Witness to the Covenant of Circumcision: Bris Milah*, Jason Aronson, 1997.

Romberg, Henry, *Bris Milah: A Book about the Jewish Ritual of Circumcision*, Feldheim, 1982.

Rossel, Seymour, Cutter, William, *A Spiritual Journey: The Bar Mitzvah and Bat Mitzvah Handbook*, Behrman House, 1996.

Schulweis, Harold, *Finding Each Other in Judaism: Meditations on the Rites of Passage from Birth to Immortality*, UAHC Press, 2001.

Waskow, Arthur, Berman, Phyllis, *A Time for Every Purpose Under Heaven: The Jewish Life Spiral as a Spiritual Path*, Farrar Straus Giroux, 2002.

CHAPTER 84

Marriage

Figure 84 Bride and groom under the *huppah* (marriage canopy) at Bevis Marks, London. Copyright, David Rose, London.

According to tradition, marriage is God's plan for humanity, as illustrated by the story of Adam and Eve in the Book of Genesis. In the Jewish faith it is viewed as a sacred bond as well as a means to personal fulfilment. It is more than a legal contract, rather an institution with cosmic significance, legitimized through divine authority. The purpose of marriage is to build a home, create a family and thereby perpetuate society. Initially Jews were allowed to have more than one wife, but this was banned in Ashkenazi countries with the decree of Rabbenu Gershom in 1000. In

modern society, all Jewish communities – Sephardic and Ashkenazic – followed this ruling.

In the Bible marriages were arranged by fathers: Abraham, for example, sent his servant to find a wife for Isaac (Gen. 24:10–53), and Judah arranged the marriage of his first-born son (Gen. 38:6). When the proposal of marriage was accepted by the girl's father (or elder brother in his absence), the nature and amount of the *mohar* (payment by the groom) was agreed. By Second Temple times, there was a degree of choice in the selection of a bride – on 15th of *Av* and the Day of Atonement, young men could select their brides from among the girls dancing in the vineyards.

According to tradition, a period of engagement preceded marriage itself. The ceremony was a seven-day occasion for celebration during which love songs were sung in praise of the bride. In the talmudic period a major development occurred concerning the *mohar* – since it could be used by the father of the bride, a wife could become penniless if her husband divorced or predeceased her. As a result the *mohar* evolved into the formulation of a marriage document (**ketubah**) which gave protection to the bride. In addition, the act of marriage changed from being a personal civil procedure to a public religious ceremony which required the presence of a *minyan* (quorum) and the recitation of prayers.

In Biblical and talmudic times marriage occurred in two stages: betrothal and *Nissuin*:

1. Betrothal: The concept of betrothal has two stages: (a) the commitment of a couple to marry as well as the terms of financial obligations (*shiddukhin*), and (b) a ceremony establishing a nuptial relationship independent of the wedding ceremony (*kiddushin* or *erusin*). An early instance of *shiddukhin* is found in Genesis 34 where the term '*mohar*' is used for a sum of money the father of the groom is to pay the father of the bride. During the *talmudic* period, this term was not used; instead the *Talmud* stipulates that negotiations should take place between the respective parents concerning financial obligations. The term for such negotiations is *shiddukhin* (an Aramaic word meaning 'tranquillity'). The terms agreed upon were written in a document called a *shetar pesikta*; the amount given to the son was called *nedunyah*. From the medieval period to the present the prenuptial agreement was itself divided into two stages: a verbal understanding (*vort*) was made, followed by a ceremony (*kinyan*) symbolizing the acceptance of the obligation to marry. This normally occurred at a meal; the act of accepting was accomplished by taking an object (usually the corner of a handkerchief). The second stage involved the writing in a document (*tenaim*) of the terms undertaken. In addition, the *tenaim* designated the date and place of the nuptial ceremony. The ceremony of the *tenaim* concludes with the mothers of the bride and

groom breaking a pottery dish. This ceremony is frequently celebrated with a dinner, and during the following period the bride and groom exchange gifts.

In the Bible the betrothal or nuptial ceremony which takes place prior to the wedding is referred to as '*erusin*': in the rabbinic period the sages who outlined this procedure called it *kiddushin* to indicate that the bride is forbidden to all men except her husband. According to the *Mishnah*, the bride could be acquired in marriage in three ways: by money, deed or intercourse. Traditionally the method involved placing a ring on the bride's finger. At this stage the groom declared: 'Behold, you are consecrated unto me with this ring according to the law of Moses and of Israel.' Then the blessing over wine was recited:

> Blessed are you, O Lord our God, King of the Universe, who has hallowed us by your commandments, and has commanded us concerning forbidden marriages; who has forbidden unto us those who are betrothed, but has sanctioned unto us such as are wedded unto us by the rite of the nuptial canopy and the sacred covenant of wedlock.

After this ceremony the bride continued to remain in her father's house until the stage of *nissuin*.

2. *Nissuin*: During the second stage of the procedure for marriage the seven blessings (*sheva berakhot*) are recited:

> Blessed are you, O Lord our God, King of the Universe, who creates the fruit of the vine.
> . . . Who has created all things to your glory.
> . . . Creator of man.
> Who has made man in your image, after your likeness . . .
> . . . made she who was barren (Zion) be glad and exult when her children are gathered within her in joy. Blessed are you, O Lord, who makes Zion joyful through her children.
> O make these loved companions greatly to rejoice, even as of old you did gladden your creatures in the Garden of Eden. Blessed are you, O Lord, who makes bridegroom and bride to rejoice.

. . . Who has created joy and gladness, bridegroom and bride, mirth and exultation, pleasure and delight, love, brotherhood, peace and fellowship. Soon may there be heard in the cities of Judah and in the streets of Jerusalem, the voice of joy and gladness, the voice of the bridegroom and the voice of the bride, the happy sound of bridegrooms from their canopies, and of youths from their feasts of song. Blessed are you, O Lord, who makes the bridegroom to rejoice with the bride.

From the Middle Ages, it became customary for Ashkenazi Jewish communities to postpone the betrothal ceremony until immediately prior to the *nissuin* wedding ceremony – this also became customary among Sephardi Jews. In Hasidic communities, however, the traditional *tenaim* ceremony is still usually observed.

According to Jewish law, a marriage cannot be contracted in certain instances. Prohibited marriages are divided into two classes: permanent and temporary.

1. Permanent prohibitions: Leviticus Chapters 18 and 29 outline types of relationships between relatives which are not permitted for marriage, including a man's parents, stepmother, sister, granddaughter, aunt, daughter-in-law, sister-in-law, stepdaughter, step-granddaughter, and wife's sister (during his wife's lifetime). Other prohibited liaisons include the following cases: (a) if a husband has divorced his wife and she remarried and was subsequently divorced or became a widow, he may not remarry her; (b) a wife who had willingly committed adultery is prohibited to her husband as well as the adulterer. If she was raped she is prohibited to her husband if he is a priest (*Cohen*); (c) a woman is not allowed to marry anyone who represented her in her divorce case or witnessed her husband's death; (d) a priest is not allowed to marry a divorcee, a widow, or a harlot; (e) a *mamzer* (child of an illegitimate or incestuous relationship) may not marry a Jewish man or woman but only a fellow *mamzer* or a convert; (f) mixed marriage is forbidden.

2. Temporary prohibitions: Some marriages are prohibited only for limited periods such as: (a) a widow or divorcee may not remarry within ninety days of her husband's death or after receiving a bill of divorce (*get*); (b) a person may not marry within the thirty-day period of mourning; a widower must wait until three festivals have occurred (unless he has no children or he has young children who need the care of a mother); one is not allowed to marry a pregnant woman, or a nursing woman until the child is twenty-four months; (c) a woman may not marry for a third time if her two successive husbands died due to accidents; (d) a married woman is not allowed to marry a second husband; she may only do so if she receives a bill of divorce.

Prior to the wedding itself, the bride is to immerse herself in a ritual bath (*mikveh*) usually on the evening before the ceremony. To facilitate this the wedding date is determined so that it does not occur during her time of menstruation, or the following week. In some Sephardi and Eastern communities this event is a public celebration. In most Sephardi communities a special celebration for the bride also takes place on the evening of the wedding. Referred to as the '*hinnah*', women friends and family come to the house of the bride, whose hands are painted with red henna. Yemeni women dress the bride in splendid clothes and jewellery to the accompaniment of singing, and then apply the henna. The aim of this ceremony is to ward off the evil eye.

On the Sabbath before the wedding in Ashkenazi communities, the groom is called to the reading of the Law and is showered with candies during the reading of the Torah blessings. In Sephardi and Eastern communities, the groom's Sabbath takes place on the Sabbath after the wedding. During the ceremony itself it is customary to shower the couple with rice and confetti. In some Ashkenazi circles, the bride when reaching the marriage canopy (*huppah*) is led around the groom seven times. The ceremony itself can be held anywhere, but from the Middle Ages the synagogue or synagogue courtyard was commonly used. It also became customary to hold it in the open air to symbolize God's promise to Abraham to make his descendants as numerous as the stars. Eventually, however, it has become customary to hold the ceremony in a hall.

In modern times the Orthodox wedding ceremony normally follows a uniform pattern based on traditional law. Normally the groom signs the *ketubah*. If this takes place before evening, the afternoon service takes place and the groom who is fasting recites the *Yom Kippur* confession. He is then led to the bride and covers her face with her veil; the couple are led next to the marriage canopy (*huppah*) with their parents walking with the groom and the bride (or the fathers accompanying the groom and the mothers the bride). According to custom those leading the couple carry lighted candles. When the participants are under the canopy the rabbi recites the blessing over wine and the *erusin* blessing. Then the bride and groom drink from the cup. The groom then recites the traditional formula: 'Behold you are consecrated unto me with this ring according to the law of Moses and of Israel'. He then puts the ring on the bride's right index finger.

To demonstrate that the act of marriage consists of two ceremonies, the *ketubah* is read prior to the *nissuin* ceremony. The seven blessings are then recited over a second cup of wine. The ceremony concludes with the groom stepping on a glass and breaking it. After the ceremony the bride and groom are led into a private room for *yihud* (seclusion). At the end of the wedding meal, the Grace after Meals is recited, and is followed by another reading of the Seven Blessings.

Within Conservative and Reform Judaism the wedding service follows this traditional pattern with varying alterations. In most cases the custom of the groom covering the bride's face before the ceremony, the procession to the *huppah* with candles, and the *yihud* observance are omitted. In addition both movements have introduced a double ring ceremony in which the bride also puts a ring on the groom's finger (either with or without reciting the relevant blessing). The Reform ceremony is frequently accompanied by additional readings.

In the Orthodox community, the laws of ritual purity (*niddah*) are observed. Sexual intercourse even between married couples may only take place when the woman is ritually clean. During her menstrual period and for seven full days afterwards, a woman is forbidden to her husband. At the end of that time she must visit the ritual bath (*mikveh*) and immerse herself completely. Then they can resume marital relations. These laws are generally ignored by the non-Orthodox.

SOURCES

Wedding Ceremony

After the rabbi takes his place under the *huppah*, the bridegroom is led by his father and mother to the *huppah*. The rabbi then says:

> May he who cometh be blessed.
>
> He who is supremely mighty;
> He who is supremely praised;
> He who is supremely great;
> May He bless this bridegroom and bride.

After the bride is led by her parents to the *huppah*, the rabbi says:

> May she who cometh be blessed
>
> Mighty is our God.
> Auspicious signs, and good fortune.
> Praiseworthy is the bridegroom.
> Praiseworthy and handsome is the bride.

The rabbi then fills a goblet of wine, and recites two benedictions:

> Praised be Thou, O Lord our God, king of the universe, who hast created the fruit of the vine.

> Praised be Thou, O Lord our God, king of the universe, who hast sanctified us with thy commandments, and hast commanded us concerning forbidden connections, and hast forbidden us those who are merely betrothed, but hast allowed to us those lawfully married to us through *huppah* and betrothal. Praised be Thou, O Lord our god, who sanctifiest Thy people Israel through *huppah* and betrothal.

The bride and bridegroom drink from the winecup. The rabbi then says to the groom:

> . . . (*name of groom*): Do you of your own free will and consent, take . . . (*name of bride*) to be your wife; and do you promise to love, honour and cherish her throughout life. If so, answer yes.

The rabbi then says to the bride:

> . . . (*name of bride*): Do you of your own free will and consent, take . . . (*name of groom*) to be your husband, and do you promise to love, honour and cherish him throughout life? If so, answer yes.

The rabbi then appoints two witnesses, who must not be related to either the groom or the bride, to witness the betrothal.

Rabbi to groom:

> You will now betroth the bride, in the presence of these two witnesses, by placing this ring upon the forefinger of her right hand, and say to her in Hebrew:

> *Hare at Mekudeshet Li Betabaat Zu, Kedat Moseh Veyisrael*

> Behold, thou art betrothed to me with this ring, in accordance with the Law of Moses and Israel.

> (In H, pp. 15–17)

Ketubah

According to tradition, the *ketubah* is read during the wedding ceremony:

On the (first) day of the week, the . . . day of the month . . . , in the year five thousand, six hundred and . . . since the creation of the world, the era according to which we are accustomed to reckon here in the city of (*name of city, state and country*), how (*name of bridegroom*), son of (*name of father*), surnamed (*family name*), said to this virgin (*name of bride*), daughter of (*name of father*), surnamed (*family name*): 'Be thou my wife according to the law of Moses and Israel, and I will cherish, honour, support and maintain thee in accordance with the custom of Jewish husbands who cherish, honour, support and maintain their wives in truth. And I herewith make for thee the settlement of virgins, two hundred silver *zuzim*, which belongs to thee, according to the law of Moses and Israel; and (I will also give thee) thy food, clothing and necessaries, and live with thee as husband and wife according to universal custom.' And Miss (*name of bride*), this virgin, consented and became his wife. The wedding outfit that she brought unto him from her father's house, in silver, gold, valuables, wearing apparel, house furniture, and bedclothes, all this (*name of bridegroom*), the said bridegroom accepted in the sum of one hundred silver pieces, and (*name of bridegroom*), the bridegroom, consented to increase this amount from his own property with the sum of one hundred silver pieces, making in all two hundred silver pieces. And thus said (*name of bridegroom*), the bridegroom: 'The responsibility of this marriage contract, of this wedding outfit, and of this additional sum, I take upon myself and my heirs after me, so that they shall be paid from the best part of my property and possession that I have beneath the whole heaven, that which I now possess or may hereafter acquire. All my property, real and personal, even the mantle on my shoulders, shall be mortgaged to secure the payment of this marriage contract, of the wedding outfit, and of the addition made thereto, during my lifetime and after my death, from the present day and forever.' (*Name of bridegroom*), the bridegroom, has taken upon himself the responsibility of this marriage contract, of this wedding outfit and the addition made thereto, according to the restrictive usages of all marriage contracts and the additions thereto made for the daughters of Israel, in accordance with the institution of our sages of blessed memory. It is not to be regarded as a mere forfeiture without consideration or as a mere formula of a document. We have followed the legal formality of symbolic delivery between (*name of bridegroom*), the son of . . . , the bridegroom, and (*name of bride*), the daughter of . . . , this virgin, and we have used a garment legally fit for the purpose, to strengthen all that is stated above.

(In H, pp. 17–20)

DISCUSSION

1. In what ways is Jewish marriage perceived as vital to Jewish survival?

2. Has intermarriage threatened the future of Judaism?

FURTHER READING

Cohen, J. Simcha, *Intermarriage and Conversion: A Halakhic Solution*, KTAV, 1987.

Cowan, Paul, Cowan, Rachel, *Mixed Blessings: Marriage Between Jews and Christians*, Doubleday, 1987.

Crohn, Joel, Markman, Howard, Blumberg, Susan, Levine, Janice, *Beyond the Chuppah – a Jewish Guide to Happy Marriages*, Jossey Bass Wiley, 2001.

Friedland, Ronnie, Case, Edmund, *The Guide to Jewish Interfaith Family Life: An Interfaithfamily.com Handbook*, Jewish Lights, 2001.

Gold, Michael, *God, Love, Sex, and Family: A Rabbi's Guide for Building Relationships That Last*, Jason Aronson, 1998.

Lamm, Maurice, *The Jewish Way in Love and Marriage*, Jonathan David, 1991.

Rapp, Lea Bayers, *Mazel Tov: The Complete Book of Jewish Weddings*, Citadel Press, 2002.

Sandmel, Samuel, *When a Jew and Christian Marry*, Fortress, 1977.

Satlow, Michael, *Jewish Marriage in Antiquity*, Princeton University Press, 2001.

Silverstein, Alan, *It All Begins With a Date: Jewish Concerns about Intermarriage*, Jason Aronson, 1995.

Syme, Daniel, *The Jewish Wedding Book*, Pharos Books, 1991.

CHAPTER 85

Divorce

The *Get*

"On the _____ day of the week, the _____ day of the month of _____ in the year _____ from the creation of the world according to the calendar reckoning we are accustomed to count here, in the city _____, which is located on the river _____, and situated near wells of the water, I, _____, the son of _____, who today am present in the city _____, which is located on the river_____, and situated near wells of water, do willingly consent, being under no restraint, to release, to set free and put aside thee, my wife _____, daughter of _____, who art today in the city of _____, which is located on the river _____, and situated near wells of water, who has been my wife from before. Thus do I set free, release thee, and put thee aside, in order that thou may have permission and the authority over thy self to go and marry any man thou may desire. No person may hinder thee from this day onward, and thou are permitted to every man. This shall be for thee from me a bill of dismissal, a letter of release, and a document of freedom, in accordance with the law of Moses and Israel."

Figure 85 Jewish Bill of Divorce, or *get*.

Biblical law specifies the procedure for divorce. According to the Book of Deuteronomy, 'When a man takes a wife and marries her, if then she finds no favour in his eyes because he has found some indecency in her, he writes her a bill of divorce and puts it in her hand and sends her out of his house' (Deut. 24:1). This verse stipulates that the power of divorce rests with the husband, and the act of divorce must be in the form of a legal document. Among early rabbinic scholars there was disagreement as to the meaning of the term 'indecency': the School of Shammai interpreted it as referring to unchastity, whereas the School of Hillel understood the term more widely. Nonetheless, in two instances it was not permitted for divorce to take place: (1) if a man claimed that his wife was not a virgin at the time of marriage and his charge was disproved (Deut. 22:13–19); or (2) if he raped a virgin whom he later married (Deut. 22:28–29). Conversely, a man

was not allowed to remarry his divorced wife if she had married another person and had been divorced or widowed (Deut. 24:2–4). Nor could a priest marry a divorced woman (Lev. 21:7).

In the Talmudic period, the law of divorce underwent considerable development, including the elaboration of various situations under which the court could compel a husband to divorce his wife if she remained barren over a period of ten years, if the husband contracted a loathsome disease, if he refused to support her or was not in a position to do so, if he denied his wife her conjugal rights, or if he beat her despite the court's warnings. In such cases the *Talmud* states that the husband is coerced by the court only to the extent that he would in fact want to divorce his wife.

The bill of divorce (*get*) is to be drawn up by a scribe following a formula based on mishnaic law. This document is written almost entirely in Aramaic on parchment. Once it has been given to the wife, it is retained by the rabbi who cuts it in criss-cross fashion so that it cannot be used a second time. The husband then gives the wife a document (*petor*) which affirms that he has been divorced, and may remarry. The wife is permitted to remarry only after ninety days, so as to ascertain whether she was pregnant at the stage of divorce. This document must be witnessed by two males over the age of thirteen who are not related to each other or to the divorcing husband and wife.

The traditional procedure is based on the *Code of Jewish Law*. The officiating rabbi initially asks the husband if he gives the **bill of divorce** (*get*) of his own free will without duress and compulsion. After receiving the writing materials from a scribe, he instructs the scribe to write a *get*. The *get* is written, and the witnesses must be present during the writing of the first line; the witnesses as well as the scribe then make a distinguishing mark on the *get*. When the *get* is completed and the ink is dry, the witnesses read the *get*. The rabbi then questions the scribe to ensure that the document was written by him on the instruction of the husband. Turning to the witnesses, the rabbi asks if they heard the husband instruct the scribe to write the *get*, as well as observed him writing it. In addition, the rabbi questions the witnesses about their signatures on the bill of divorce. Finally, the rabbi asks the husband if the *get* was given freely. The wife is then asked if she freely accepts the *get*.

Rabbi: 'Are you accepting this *get* of your own free will?'
Wife: 'Yes.'
Rabbi: 'Did you bind yourself by any statement or vow that would compel you to accept this *get* against your will?'
Wife: 'No.'
Rabbi: 'Perhaps you have unwittingly made such a statement that would nullify the *get*. In order to prevent that, will you kindly retract all such declarations?'
Wife: 'I revoke all such statements that may nullify the *get*, in the presence of the witnesses.'

The rabbi tells the wife to remove all jewellery from her hands and hold her hands together with open palms upward to receive the bill of divorce. The scribe holds the *get* and gives it to the rabbi. The rabbi then gives the *get* to her husband; he holds it in both hands and drops it into the palms of the wife and states: 'This be your *get* and with it be you divorced from this time forth so that you may become the wife of any man.' When the wife receives the bill of divorce, she walks with it a short distance and returns. She gives the *get* to the rabbi who reads it again in the presence of the witnesses; the rabbi then asks the scribe and the witnesses to identify the *get* as well as the signatures. Following this, the rabbi states: 'Hear all you present that Rabbenu Tam has issued a ban against all those who try to invalidate a *get* after it has been delivered.' The four corners of the *get* are cut, and it is placed in the rabbi's files. The husband and wife receive written statements certifying that their marriage has been dissolved in accordance with Jewish law.

It is customary for the husband and wife to be present during the divorce proceedings, but if this is not possible Jewish law stipulates that an agent can take the place of either party. The husband may appoint an agent to deliver the *get* to his wife; if this agent is unable to complete this task, he has the right to appoint another one, and the second agent yet another. The wife can also appoint an agent to receive the *get*. Thus it is possible for the entire procedure to take place without the husband or wife seeing one another; this is sometimes done to avoid the emotional strain of the husband and wife meeting each other if a bitter divorce has occurred.

In certain instances a *get* of benefit (*get zikkui*) may be arranged. Jewish law stipulates that the woman's consent to a divorce is not necessary, and the *get* can be given to her against her will. However, the ordinance of Rabbenu Gershom (tenth to eleventh century) prohibits divorcing a woman without consent. According to Talmudic scholars, a benefit can be conferred upon an individual even when that person is not present. That is, if the procedure can bring about a benefit for an individual, it is logical to assume that this person would give his or her consent if he or she knew about it. In the case of civil divorce, it can be assumed that if the husband and wife have already obtained a divorce from the secular authorities, she has given consent to divorce. In such a case, the rabbinical court (*bet din*) can appoint an agent to receive the *get* for her even without her consent. Here the wife would be receiving a benefit because she would be able to remarry according to the *halakhah* without risking being considered an adulteress. In such instances the procedure of divorce is the same, except that instead of giving the bill of divorce to the wife, the husband gives the *get* to an agent who is appointed by the court.

Throughout history a number of modifications have been made to divorce legislation. In the Middle Ages Rabbenu Gershom brought about a fundamental change in the law of divorce among Ashkenazim as well as some Sephardi communities. In an enactment (*takkanah*), he decreed that a husband may not divorce his wife without her consent. This *takkanah* in essence made the rights of the wife nearly equivalent to those of the husband: from this time forth divorce could only be by mutual consent. Later *halakhists* strengthened this enactment by stating that any writ of divorce issued in violation of this ruling was null and void. Some time later Jacob Tam decreed that in certain emergencies the *takkanah* requiring mutual consent could be set aside, such as in the case of a woman who apostasized and left the Jewish community.

Yet despite such modifications, certain difficulties still remain about the granting of a *get*. Since it is the husband who must give the bill of divorce to his wife, if he cannot be located, this presents an insurmountable obstacle. Similarly in the diaspora rabbinic scholars have no authority to compel a husband to comply with their instructions. In both cases the wife has the status of being an *agunah* (a 'tied' woman) who is not able to remarry according to traditional Jewish law. In order to vitiate this difficulty the Rabbinical Assembly of the Conservative movement proposed a *takkanah* calling for the insertion of a clause in the marriage contract whereby both groom and bride in grave circumstances agree to abide by the decision of the religious court (*bet din*) of the Conservative movement:

> And both together agreed that if this marriage shall be dissolved under civil law, then either husband or wife may invoke the authority of the *bet din* of the Rabbinical Assembly and the Jewish Theological Seminary of America or its duly authorized representatives, to decide what action by either spouse is then appropriate under Jewish matrimonial law, and if either spouse should fail

to honour the demand of the other or to carry out the decision of the *bet din* or its representatives, then the other spouse may invoke any and all remedies available in civil law and equity to enforce compliance with the *bet din*'s decision and this solemn obligation.

Another solution proposed by the Conservative movement involves an antenuptial agreement signed by the bride and groom:

> On the . . . day of . . . , 20 . . . , corresponding to . . . 57 . . . , in . . . , the groom, Mr . . . , and the bride, Mrs . . . , of their own free will and accord entered into the following agreement with respect to their intended marriage.

The groom made the following declaration to the bride:

> I will betroth and marry you according to the laws of Moses and Israel, subject to the following conditions: (a) If our marriage be terminated by decree of the civil courts and if by expiration of six months after such a decree I give you a divorce according to the laws of Moses and Israel (a *get*), then our betrothal (*kiddushin*) and marriage (*nissuin*) will have been valid and binding. (b) But if our marriage be terminated by decree of civil court and if by expiration of six months after such a decree I do not give you a divorce according to the laws of Moses and Israel (a *get*) then our betrothal (*kiddushin*) and marriage (*nissuin*) will have been null and void.

This document gives authority to the *bet din* to annul the marriage *ab initio* in the case where there is a refusal to authorize a *get*.

In a later enactment the Rabbinical Assembly of the Conservative movement invoked the power that the Talmudic rabbis had to annul marriages. The formula ('You are betrothed unto me with this ring, according to the laws of Moses and Israel') is interpreted by the rabbis in the *Talmud* to imply that every bride and groom contract a marriage subject to the approval of rabbinical authorities. If the rabbinical authorities remove their approval then the marriage is null and void *ab initio*. Since this power was invoked in ancient times when the husband acted in an unjust manner, it was felt that in later times the power could be invoked again to resolve the problem of the *agunah*.

Within Reform Judaism the traditional practice of granting a bill of divorce has been abandoned. Instead civil divorce is regarded as valid. For this reason there has been no attempt within Reform Judaism to formulate a policy dealing with the status of the *agunah*.

SOURCES

Bill of Divorce

A typical bill of divorce is as follows:

> On the . . . day of the week, the . . . day of the month of . . . in the year . . . from the creation of the world according to the calendar reckoning we are accustomed to count here, in the city . . . which is located on the river . . . and situated near wells of water, I . . . the son of . . . who today am presently in the city . . . which is located on the river . . . and situated near wells of water, do willingly consent, being under no restraint, to release, to set free, and put aside you, my wife . . . , daughter of . . . , who is today in the city of . . . , which is located on the river . . . and situated near wells of water, who has been my wife from before. Thus I do set free, release you, and put you aside, in order that you may have permission and the authority over yourself to go and marry any man you may desire. No person may hinder you from this day onward, and you are permitted to every man. This shall be for you from me a bill of dismissal, a letter of release, and a document of freedom, in accordance with the laws of Moses and Israel.
>
> (In JF, p. 202)

DISCUSSION

1. Are women treated unfairly in a Jewish divorce?

2. Discuss the problems regarding the position of an *agunah*.

FURTHER READING

Broyde, Michael, *Marriage, Divorce, and the Abandoned Wife in Jewish Law: A Conceptual Understanding of the Agunah Problems in America*, KTAV, 2001.

Feld, Merle, *A Spiritual Life: A Jewish Feminist Journey*, State University of New York, 2000.

Frankiel, Tamar, *The Voice of Sarah: Feminine Spirituality and Traditional Judaism*, Bloch, 1997.

Heschel, Susannah, *On Being a Jewish Feminist*, Random House, 1995.

Jaffe-Gili, Ellen, *The Jewish Woman's Book of Wisdom: Thoughts from Prominent Jewish Women on Spirituality, Identity, Sisterhood, Family and Faith*, Citadel Press, 1998.

Katch, Elise Edelson, *The Get: A Spiritual Memoir of Divorce*, Health Communications, 2001.

Levitt, Laura, *Jews and Feminism: The Ambivalent Search for Home*, Routledge, 1997.

Netter, Perry, *Divorce Is a Mitzvah: A Practical Guide to Finding Wholeness and Holiness When Your Marriage Dies*, Jewish Lights, 2002.

Reuven, P. Bulka, *Jewish Divorce Ethics: The Right Way to Say Goodbye*, Ivy League Press, 1992.

Riskin, Shlomo, *Women and Jewish Divorce: The Rebellious Wife, the Agunah, and the Right of Women to Initiate Divorce in Jewish Law, a Halakhic Solution*, KTAV, 1988.

Ruttenberg, Danya (ed.), *Yentl's Revenge: The Next Wave of Jewish Feminism*, Seal, 2001.

Schneider, Susan Weidman, *Jewish and Female: Choices and Changes in Our Lives Today*, Simon and Schuster, 1984.

Seltzer, Sanford, *When There is No Other Alternative: A Spiritual Guide for Jewish Couples Contemplating Divorce*, UAHC, 2000.

CHAPTER 86

The Home

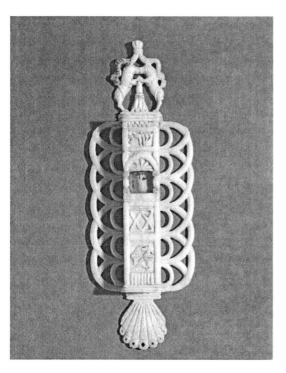

Figure 86 Mezuzah (doorpost), Italian bone, fifteenth century. Copyright The Art Archive/Jewish Museum London/ Eileen Tweedy.

In Judaism religious observance in the home is of fundamental importance. According to the sages, it is (to use Ezekiel's terminology) a *mikdash me-at* (a minor sanctuary). Like the synagogue, it continues various traditions of the ancient Temple. The Sabbath candles, for example, recall the Temple *menorah* and the dining table symbolizes the altar. Most significantly, within the home, family life is sanctified. As head of the family, the father is to exercise authority over his wife and children. He is obligated to circumcise his son, redeem him if he is the first-born, teach him Torah, marry him off and teach him a craft. Further,

he is required to serve as a role model for the transmission of Jewish ideals to his offspring.

Regarding Jewish women, the prevailing sentiment is that the role of the wife is to bear children and exercise responsibility for family life. According to the *halakhah*, womanhood is a separate status with its own specific sets of rules, obligations and responsibilities. In terms of religious observance, women were classed as slaves and children, disqualified as witnesses, excluded from the study of the Torah and segregated from men. Moreover, they were regarded as ritually impure for extended periods of time. In general, they were exempted from time-bound commands; as a result they were not obliged to fulfil those commandments which must be followed at a particular time (such as the recitation of prayer). The purpose of these restrictions was to ensure that their attention and energy be directed toward completing their domestic duties. In the contemporary period, however, a growing number of women have agitated for equal treatment – in consequence, the role of women has undergone a major transformation. Nonetheless, there has been a universal recognition in all branches of Judaism that the Jewish wife should continue to play a central role in the home.

Children are expected to carry out the commandment to honour (Exod. 20:12) and respect (Lev. 19:3) their parents. For the rabbis, the concept of honour refers to providing parents with food, drink, clothing and transportation. Respect requires that a child does not sit in his parent's seat, nor interrupt them, and takes their side in a dispute. The *Talmud* extols such treatment: 'There are three partners in man, the Holy One, blessed be He, the father, and the mother. When a man honours his father and mother, the Holy One blessed be He, says, "I will ascribe (merit) to them as though I had dwelt among them and they had honoured me"' (*Kid.* 30b).

The Jewish tradition teaches that domestic harmony is the ideal of home life. The *Talmud* specifies the guidelines for attaining this goal: 'A man should spend less than his means on food, up to his means on clothes, and more than his means in honouring wife and children because they are dependent on him.' Such harmony is to be attained through give and take on the part of all, as well as through the observance of Jewish ritual which serves to unify the family. The Jewish home is permeated with sanctity when the family lives in accordance with God's commandments.

Symbols of the Jewish religion characterize the Jewish home, beginning with the *mezuzah* on each doorpost. In Scripture it is written that 'these words' shall be written on the doorposts (*mezuzot*) of the house (Deut. 6:4–9; 11:13–21). This prescription has been understood literally: these two passages must be copied by hand on a piece of parchment, put into a case, and affixed to the doorpost of every room in the house.

The first of these passages from Deuteronomy contains the *Shema* as well as the commandments to love God, study the Torah, express the unity of God, wear *tefillin*, and affix a *mezuzah*. The second passage connects prosperity with the observance of God's commandments. The *mezuzah* itself must be written by a scribe on parchment – the scroll is rolled and put into a case with a small opening through which the word *Shaddai* (Almighty) is visible. The *mezuzah* is placed on the upper part of the doorpost at the entrance in a slanting position. The following conditions should be met in placing the *mezuzah* on every right-hand entrance, according to Maimonides:

1. The room into which the doorway leads should be at least four by four cubits.
2. The doorway should have doorposts on both sides.
3. The doorway should serve as an entrance into a room with a ceiling.
4. The door should have a lintel.
5. The doorway should have doors that open as well as close.
6. The doorway should be at least forty inches high and sixteen inches wide (though many authors do not regard this as necessary).
7. The room must be for ordinary residence.

8. The room should be for human dwelling.
9. The room should be used as a dignified dwelling.
10. The room should be for continued habitation.

When the *mezuzah* is placed on the doorpost, a benediction is recited. Traditional Jews touch the *mezuzah* with their hand while entering or leaving the home.

Other home ritual objects of major importance are the Sabbath candles. At least two candles should be used in honour of the dual commandment to remember and observe the Sabbath day (Exod. 20:8; Deut. 5:12). This ceremony is performed before sunset on the eve of Sabbaths (as well as festivals), symbolizing light and joy. Lighting the candles is normally the task of the wife, but it may be done by any member of the family.

At the beginning of the Sabbath the *Kiddush* prayer is recited over wine prior to the evening meal. It consists of two sections: the blessing over the wine and the benediction of the day. The introductory Biblical passages which precede this prayer are Genesis 1:31 and 2:1–3. The blessing for wine is then recited, followed by the benedictions for the sanctification of the day. The blessing which follows includes the assertion that Israel was made holy through God's commandments, that it was favoured by having been given the Sabbath as an inheritance in remembrance of creation, and that the Sabbath is the first of the holy convocations and commemorates the Exodus from Egypt. This is followed by a sentence whose form is reminiscent of the festival *Kiddush*. The festival *Kiddush*, which is also recited at home, consists of the blessing over wine as well as the blessing over the day; this is followed by the recitation of the *sheheheyanu* prayer ('Blessed are you, Lord our God, King of the universe, who has kept us alive, sustained us, and brought us to this season'). Wine goblets reserved for this occasion are frequently made of silver and bear an inscription such as, 'Observe the Sabbath day and keep it holy'. It is usual for participants to wash their hands after the *Kiddush* is recited.

Before meals on the Sabbath as well as on ordinary days, a blessing over food is recited. Over food the blessing is, 'who brings forth bread from the earth'; over wine, 'who creates the fruit of the vine'; over fruit, 'who creates the fruit of the tree'; over vegetables, 'who creates the fruit of the ground'. Alternatively, there is a more general blessing for things for which there are no specific blessings: 'By whose word all things were brought into being'.

After the meal is completed a Grace after Meals is recited. This prayer, *Birkat ha-Mazon*, comprises a series of blessings and prayers. Structurally the Grace consists of four benedictions interspersed with various prayers and petitions. The first blessing praises God for sustaining his creatures with food; the second is a national expression of thanks for deliverance from Egypt, God's covenant with his chosen people, and the land which he gave to them; the third asks God to provide Israel with relief from want and humiliation, and to vindicate his people by restoring Jerusalem; the fourth blessing acknowledges the benefits for which God is to be thanked. This is followed by a series of petitions which invoke 'the Compassionate One' (*Ha-Rahaman*).

The cycle of the year provides various opportunities for home observances. On Passover normal dishes are replaced. Traditional law excludes the use of all domestic utensils, crockery and cutlery. As a result sets are kept especially for this holiday. The *seder* itself is observed on the first two nights of Passover. The purpose of this festival is to commemorate the redemption of the Jewish people from slavery. During the service the *Haggadah* (Prayer Book) is read, and a special *seder* dish is prepared which includes a roasted hard-boiled egg symbolizing the Temple sacrifice, a roasted bone symbolizing the *paschal* lamb, bitter herbs symbolizing bitter oppression, *charoset* reminiscent of the mortar prepared by the Israelites in making brick, parsley in imitation of the *hors d'oeuvres* of Roman nobility, and salt water representing the tears shed by the Israelites in bondage. During the *seder* participants eat *matzot* (unleavened bread) and drink four glasses of wine. Prayers and narratives are recited before and after the meal. In recent times revised versions of the *Haggadah* have been composed for various non-Orthodox communities.

On *Sukkot* it is customary to dwell in a temporary structure (*sukkah*) built for the festival in a yard, garden or balcony. It is covered by foliage through which the stars can be seen at night. All the meals which take place during this festival should be eaten in the *sukkah* if possible. During *Hanukkah* a festival lamp is kindled at home on each day of the festival in memory of the victory of the Maccabees over the Seleucids. In ancient times a lamp was put in the doorway or even in the street outside; in modern times it is placed within the home. The custom is to light a candle on the first night and an additional candle for each night until the last night when eight candles are kindled. On *Purim* families frequently exchange gifts and enjoy a festive meal.

Life cycle events also provide an occasion for special observances in the home. At the birth of a male child, a *Shalom Zakhor* gathering takes place on the Friday night after the birth; the circumcision ceremony takes place on the eighth day; and the redemption of the first-born on the thirty-first day. All these occasions are times for festivity. Similarly *bar* and *bat mitzvah* are times of festivity in the home. Again, during the week after a marriage, a nightly feast is held where the Seven Benedictions are recited. Finally, at the time of mourning, friends and visitors come to the home during the seven days of mourning (*shivah*) where a *minyan* recites the morning and evening prayers.

In contemporary society Orthodox Judaism continues to carry out these home activities; however, within the various branches of non-Orthodox Judaism modifications have been made to those traditions, and a number of home festivities have been eliminated because they are no longer viewed as spiritually meaningful. Nonetheless there is a universal recognition among Jewry that the home is central to Jewish existence and survival.

SOURCES

Dedication of a New House

When one builds or buys a house, he should pronounce these verses from the Psalms:

> Lord, who shall sojourn in Thy Tabernacle?
> Who shall dwell upon Thy holy mountain?
> He that walketh uprightly, and worketh righteousness,
> And speaketh truth in his heart.
> That hath no slander upon his tongue,
> Nor doeth evil to his fellow,
> Nor taketh up a reproach against his neighbour;
> In whose eyes a vile person is despised,
> But he honoureth them that fear the Lord;
> He that sweareth to his own hurt, and changeth not;
> He that putteth not out his money on interest,
> Nor taketh a bribe against the innocent.
> He that doeth these things shall never be moved.

(Psalm 40 in H, pp. 55–56)

Sabbath Candles

It is the obligation of a woman to light candles for *Shabbat*. When the candles are lit, she recites the blessing:

> Praised are you, Lord our God, king of the universe whose *mitzvot* add holiness to our lives and who gave us the *mitzvah* to kindle *Shabbat* light.

(In SSS, p. 715)

Kiddush

On the Sabbath evening, the Kiddush is recited at home:

> And there was evening and there was morning – the sixth day. The heavens and the earth, and all they contain, were completed. On the seventh day God completed the work which He had been doing. He ceased on the seventh day from all the work which He had done. Then God blessed the seventh day and called it holy, because on it He ceased from all his work of creation.
>
> Praised are you, Lord our God, king of the universe who creates fruit of the vine.
>
> Praised are you, Lord our God, king of the universe whose *mitzvot* add holiness to our lives, cherishing us through the gift of his holy *Shabbat* granted lovingly, gladly, a reminder of creation. It is the first among our days of sacred assembly recalling the Exodus from Egypt. Thus you have chosen us, endowing us with holiness, from among all peoples by granting us your holy *Shabbat* lovingly and gladly. Praised are you, Lord who hallows *Shabbat*.

(In SSS, p. 727)

DISCUSSION

1. In what ways does Jewish life centre around the home?

2. Are home rituals anachronistic in the modern world?

FURTHER READING

Bial, Morrison, *Liberal Judaism at Home: The Practice of Modern Reform Judaism*, UAHC Press, 1971.

Broner, E.M., *Bringing Home the Light: A Jewish Woman's Handbook of Rituals*, Council Oak Books, 1999.

Diamant, Anita, *Choosing a Jewish Life: A Handbook for People Converting to Judaism and for Their Family and Friends*, Schocken, 1998.

Donin, Hayim, *To Be a Jew: A Guide to Jewish Observance in Contemporary Life*, Basic Books, 1991.

Hoffman, Lawrence, *The Journey Home: Discovering the Deep Spiritual Wisdom of the Jewish Tradition*, Beacon Press, 2002.

Levitt, Laura, *Jews and Feminism: The Ambivalent Search for Home*, Routledge, 1997.

Reuben, Stephen Carr, *Raising Jewish Children in a Contemporary World: The Modern Parent's Guide to Creating a Jewish Home*, Prima, 1992.

Schauss, Hayyim, *The Jewish Festivals: A Guide to Their History and Observance*, Dimensions, 1996.

Schwartz, Richard, *Judaism and Vegetarianism*, Lantern Books, 2001.

Shire, Michael, *To Life! L'Chaim! Prayers and Blessings for the Jewish Home*, Francis Lincoln, 2000.

Syme, Daniel, *The Jewish Home: A Guide for Jewish Living*, UAHC Press, 1988.

Trepp, Leo, *The Complete Book of Jewish Observance*, Simon and Schuster, 1986.

Witty, Abraham, Witty, Rachel, *Exploring Jewish Tradition: A Transliterated Guide to Everyday Practice and Observance*, Doubleday, 2001.

CHAPTER 87

Dietary Laws

Figure 87 Rabbinic certificate of *kashrut* on boxes of matzos from a Jewish delicatessen. Copyright David Rose, London.

According to the Jewish tradition, food must be ritually fit (*kosher*) if it is to be eaten. The Bible declares that laws of *kashrut* (dietary laws) were given by God to Moses on Mount Sinai: thus Jews are obligated to follow this legislation because of its divine origin. Nonetheless, various reasons have been adduced for observing these prescriptions. Allegedly forbidden foods are unhealthy; that is why they are forbidden. Another justification is that those who refrain from eating particular kinds of food serve God even while eating, and thereby attain an elevated spiritual state.

Indeed, some of these laws – such as refraining from eating pork – have gained such symbolic significance that Jews were prepared to sacrifice their lives rather than violate God's decree. In this way these martyrs demonstrated their devotion to the Jewish faith.

The laws concerning which animals, birds and fish may be eaten are contained in Leviticus Chapter 11 and Deuteronomy 14:3–21. According to Scripture, only those animals which both chew the cud and have split hooves may be eaten. Such animals include domestic animals like cows and sheep. No similar formula is stated concerning which birds may be consumed; rather a list is given of forbidden birds such as the eagle, the owl and the raven. Although no reasons are given to explain these choices, it has been suggested that forbidden birds are in fact birds of prey; by not eating them human beings are able to express their abhorrence of cruelty as well as the exploitation of the weak over the strong. Regarding fish, the law states that only fish which have both fins and scales are allowed. Again, no reason is given to support this distinction; however, various explanations have been proposed, such as the argument that fish that do not have fins and scales frequently live in the depths of the sea, which was regarded as the abode of the gods of chaos – on this basis the law constitutes a protest against idolatry.

A further category of *kashrut* deals with the method of killing animals for food (*shehitah*). Although the Torah does not offer details of this procedure, the *Talmud* states that this method has divine authority because it was explained by God to Moses on Mount Sinai. According to tradition, the act of slaughter must be done with a sharpened knife without a single notch, since that might tear the animal's food pipe or windpipe.

Numerous other laws govern this procedure, and a person must be trained in the law if he is to be a *shohet* (slaughterer). According to scholars such as Maimonides (twelfth century), the central idea underlying the laws of ritual slaughter is to give the animal as painless a death as possible. Judaism does not require that the devout become vegetarians, but when animals are killed for food this must be done so as to cause the least amount of suffering possible.

Another feature of ritual slaughter is the concern that no animal is eaten if it has a defect; in such cases it is referred to as '*terefah*' (meaning 'torn'). The prohibition against *terefah* is based on Exodus 22:31: 'You shall be men consecrated to me; therefore you shall not eat any flesh that is torn by beasts in the field; you shall cast it to the dogs'. This prescription is elaborated in the *Mishnah* where the rabbis decree that *terefah* refers not only to the meat of an animal torn by wild beasts, but to any serious defect in an animal or bird's organs. In this section of the *Mishnah* such defects are listed in detail. On the basis of this law, the *shohet* is obliged to examine the lungs of an animal after it has been slaughtered to ensure that no defect is found. Similarly, if any irregularity is found in an animal which has been slaughtered, it should be taken to a rabbi to determine if it is *kosher*. In the preparation of meat, it is important that adequate salting takes place. This prescription is based on the Biblical prohibition against blood. Although it is theoretically possible to extract a large quantity of blood from meat, the process can be aided by salting it. While being salted, meat is soaked in cold water for half an hour – this softens the texture of the meat and makes it easier for salt to extract the blood. The meat is then put on a sloping draining board so that the water drains away. Subsequently salt is placed on the meat and left for an hour. The meat is then rinsed in water three or four times.

Another restriction concerning ritual food is the prohibition against eating milk and meat together. This stipulation is based on Exodus 23:19: 'Thou shalt not boil a kid in its mother's milk'. According to the rabbis, this rule refers not only to the act of boiling a kid in its mother's milk, but to any combination of meat and milk. Tradition stipulates that it is forbidden to cook meat and milk together. Later, this prohibition was expanded to eating milk and meat products at the same time. Eventually the law was introduced that dairy dishes should not be eaten after a meal until a stipulated period of time had passed. The required amount of time has varied according to local custom: some Jews wait three hours; others six. Meat, on the other hand, may be eaten after dairy products; nonetheless, it is usual to wash the mouth out beforehand.

A number of explanations have been given to account for this prohibition. According to Maimonides, it is because a mixture of milk and meat cannot be digested easily; in addition, the practice of cooking meat in milk was a pagan practice which was forbidden to the Israelites. Another explanation is that meat represents death whereas milk symbolizes life: life and death must be kept apart. Others maintain that this prohibition serves as a reminder to make distinctions in life – in this way the thinking of a Jew is sharpened.

Not only should milk and meat products not be consumed at the same time, dairy food should not be cooked in meat utensils, and vice versa. Thus it is the usual practice for Jewish households to have two sets of dishes and cutlery reserved for milk and meat.

Meat dishes are known in Yiddish as *fleishig*, milk dishes are *milchig* (milky). Food as well as utensils that are neither *fleishig* nor *milchig* are referred to as *parave*. A pot in which forbidden (*terefah*) food has been cooked should not be used for cooking *kosher* food until it is thoroughly scoured. Here the principle is that the taste of the forbidden food remains in the pot itself, but the pot can be made *kosher* by boiling water in it. If a utensil has been used for forbidden food on a naked flame or in a fire, it can be made *kosher* by heating it over a fire. China, however, cannot be made *kosher* since it is so thoroughly absorbent that the *terefah* cannot be eliminated; on the other hand, a number of contemporary authorities argue that Pyrex dishes can be made ritually fit.

In formulating these regulations, the principle of neutralization is that *terefah* food becomes neutralized in a ratio of one to sixty. Thus if a piece of *terefah* meat is cooked in a pot of *kosher* meat and can no longer be identified, it is *kosher* as long as there is sixty times as much *kosher* meat as *terefah*. Another rule maintains that if food is cooked in a utensil that was used for *terefah* more than twenty-four hours previously, the food is *kosher*. Here the principle is that when *terefah* food has been in a utensil for twenty-four hours or longer its taste becomes flawed and cannot contaminate food later cooked in that object.

Although the Bible does not attempt to explain the origin of these various dietary laws, it does associate them with holiness in three passages: (1) Exodus 22:31: 'You shall be consecrated to me: therefore you shall not eat any flesh torn by beasts in the field; you shall cast it to the dogs'; (2) Leviticus 11:44–45: 'For I am the Lord your God: consecrate yourselves therefore, and be holy, for I am holy. You shall not defile yourselves with any swarming thing that crawls upon the earth. For I am the Lord who brought you up out from the land of Egypt, to be your God; you shall therefore be holy, for

I am holy'; (3) Deuteronomy 14:21: 'You shall not eat anything that has died of itself; you may give it to the alien who is within your towns, that he may eat it, or you may sell it to a foreigner; for you are a people holy to the Lord your God. You shall not boil a kid in its mother's milk.'

Similarly, the rabbis of the *Talmud* and *midrash* explored the rationale of the system of *kashrut*. Generally they believed that observance of such laws aids the development of self-disicipline and moral conduct. Maimonides argued in *The Guide for the Perplexed* that the laws of *kashrut* teach mastery of the appetites as well as discipline. In addition, he feels that all forbidden foods are unwholesome. Subsequently, other writers have suggested that there is a humanitarian basis to these laws as reflected in the revulsion to blood, the requirement that an animal be killed painlessly, and the rule that only herbivorous animals be eaten.

Until modern times the rules of *kashrut* were universally practised by Jewry. Yet in the nineteenth century the Reform movement in Germany broke with tradition, decreeing that the dietary laws were connected with Temple ritual and thus not integral to the Jewish tradition. On this basis the Pittsburgh Conference of the Reform movement declared in its statement of principles that the laws of *kashrut* 'fail to impress the modern Jew with the spirit of holiness . . . their observance in our days is apt rather to obstruct than to further modern spiritual elevation'. For this reason, most Reform Jews have largely ignored the prescriptions of the dietary system. Conservative Judaism, however, adheres to the laws of *kashrut*, although allowance is made for personal selectivity. Orthodox Judaism, on the other hand, strictly follows the tradition, and in recent years the observance of the dietary laws has undergone a revival in various Jewish communities, particularly in the State of Israel.

SOURCES

Prohibitions

The *Shulkhan Arukh* specifies the wide range of forbidden foods:

> 1. Blood which is found in eggs is prohibited. Furthermore, at times, the entire egg may be prohibited. Therefore, eggs should be checked before being used for cooking.

2. The blood of fish is permitted. However, it is forbidden if it is collected in a receptacle, lest it create a wrong impression. Since this is the reason for the prohibition, if the blood is clearly recognizable as coming from fish – e.g. it is served with scales – it is permitted to be used.

3. (Once blood leaves a person's body, it is forbidden. Therefore, if a person with bleeding gums) bites into a loaf of bread and some blood is left on the bread, the portion with the blood must be cut off and disposed of. However, during the week, one is allowed to suck the blood from the gums, since it has not left the body.

4. Sometimes blood will be discovered together with milk – i.e. when the animal was milked, blood came out together with the milk. A competent rabbinic authority should be consulted concerning this matter.

5. Meat and milk are forbidden to be cooked together; we are prohibited both to eat and to benefit from the combination. Therefore, if an entity (i.e. a pot, dish, or food) becomes forbidden because of a mixture of milk and meat, a rabbinic authority must be consulted. At times, it may be forbidden to benefit from the object, while at times benefit may be permitted.

6. Two Jews who are familiar with each other may not eat at the same table if one is eating meat and the other dairy products, unless they make a clear thing of distinction – e.g. each will eat only on his individual table mat or they place an article which would not usually be placed on the table between them (for the purpose of separation). They should take care not to drink from the same vessel, because particles of food may become stuck to it. This prohibition applies even if the two (are feuding and) are careful not to use the other's property.

7. Surely, precautions should be taken not to eat from one loaf of bread for both dairy and meat meals. Similarly, separate dishes should be set aside for salt; one for salt that is used together with meat meals, and another for dairy meals. At times, food is dipped into the salt and small particles remain.

8. It is customary to mark the knives used for milk products and, similarly, other utensils for dairy, so they do not become interchanged (with those used for meat).

9. A person who eats meat or a dish cooked with meat may not eat dairy products for six hours.

10. One may eat dairy products after eating food which contains neither meat nor fat from meat, but was cooked in a pot used to cook meat. This applies even if the pot was not thoroughly clean.

11. It is permitted to eat meat immediately after eating dairy products, as part of a second meal. However, one must wash one's hands or check to see that none of the dairy products are stuck to them. Similarly, one must clean one's teeth and wash one's mouth.

12. A person who wants to eat meat after eating dairy products must remove all pieces of bread that were eaten together with the dairy products from the table. It is forbidden to eat dairy products on the same tablecloth upon which meat was eaten. The converse also applies.

(*Shulkhan Arukh*, in KSO, pp. 201–203)

DISCUSSION

1. What was the purpose of the dietary laws?

2. Is the system of *kashrut* spiritually significant in the modern world?

FURTHER READING

Bailey, Stephen, *Kashrut Tefillin Tzitzit: Studies in the Purpose and Meaning of Symbolic Mitzvot Inspired by the Commentaries of Rabbi Samson Raphael Hirsch*, Jason Aronson, 2000.

Goldman, Marcy, *A Treasury of Jewish Holiday Baking*, Doubleday, 1998.

Mann, Gil, *How to Get More Out of Being Jewish Even If: A. You Are not Sure You Believe in God; B. You Think Going to Synagogue is a Waste of Time, C. You Think Keeping Kosher is Stupid, D. You Hated Hebrew School, or E. All of the Above*, Leo and Sons, 2002.

Marks, Gil, *The World of Jewish Entertaining: Menus and Recipes for the Sabbath, Holidays, and Other Family Celebrations*, Simon and Schuster, 1998.

Paraiso, Aviva, *Jewish Food and Drink*, Hodder Wayland, 1988.

Randall, Ronnie, *Festival Cookbooks: Jewish Festival Cookbook*, Hodder Wayland, 2001.

Solomon, Judith, *The Rosh Hodesh Table: Foods at the New Moon*, Bloch, 1997.

Waskow, Arthur, *Down-To-Earth Judaism: Food, Money, Sex, and the Rest of Life*, Quill, 1997.

Waskow, Arthur *et al.*, *Seasons of Our Joy: A Modern Guide to the Jewish Holidays*, Beacon Press, 1990.

CHAPTER 88

Death and Mourning

Figure 88 Service at Alderney Road Cemetery, London, on 1 June 1997, to mark the Tercentenary of the Synagogue. Copyright Peter Fisher, London.

Concerning death the Bible declares that human beings will return to the dust of the earth (Gen. 3:19). According to Scripture, burial – especially in a family tomb – was the normal procedure for dealing with the deceased (Gen. 47:29–30; 49:29–31; 1 Kings 21:19). In a number of Biblical passages human beings are depicted as descending to a nether world (*sheol*) where they live a shadowy existence – only in the later books of the Bible is there any illusion to resurrection (such as in Dan. 12:2)

The rabbis of the *Talmud* decreed that death occurs when respiration has stopped. However, with the development of modern medical technology, this definition has been subject to alteration. Today it is now possible to resuscitate those who previously would have been regarded as dead: thus the modern rabbinic scholar Mosheh Sofer in his *responsum* declares that death is considered to have occurred when there has been respiratory and cardiac arrest. Another *halakhist*, Mosheh Feinstein, however, has ruled that a person is considered to have died with the death of his brain stem. Despite such disagreements, it is generally accepted that a critically ill person who hovers between life and death is alive. It is forbidden to hasten the death of such an individual by any positive action; nonetheless, it is permitted to remove an external obstacle which may be preventing his death.

Jewish law accepts that no effort should be spared to save a dying patient; in this regard the *Talmud* lays down that a change of name may avert the evil decree, and hence the custom developed of altering the formal name of an individual who is seriously ill. Yet despite such an attitude, traditional Judaism fosters an acceptance of death when it is inevitable. The *Tzidduk ha-Din* prayer which is recited by mourners at the funeral service describes God as a righteous judge and accepts the finality of his decrees. On his deathbed, the dying person is to recite a prayer accepting God's will:

> I admit before you, God, my God and God of my ancestors, that my cure and my death are in your hands. May it be your will that you heal me with a complete healing. And if I die, may my death be an atonement for the sins, transgressions, and violations which I have sinned, transgressed, and violated before you. And set my portion in the Garden of Eden, and let me merit the world to come reserved for the righteous. Hear, O Israel, the Lord our God, the Lord is One.

The Jewish tradition maintains that utmost regard should be shown for the dying person. Such an individual is not to be left alone. When informing someone who is dying of the duty to confess sins, he should be told: 'Many have confessed, but have not died; and many who have not confessed have died. And many who are walking outside in the market-place have confessed. By the merit of your confessing, you live. All who confess have a place in the world to come.' All those who are present at the moment of death should recite the blessing: 'Blessed be the true judge'; relatives are to recite the prayer, *Tzidduk ha-Din*. The arrangements for care of the body and burial are referred to as *hesed shel emet* (true kindness), because they are made on behalf of those who are unable to reciprocate.

Once death has been determined, the eyes and

mouth are closed, and if necessary the mouth is tied shut. The body is then put on the floor, covered with a sheet, and a lighted candle is placed close to the head. Mirrors are covered in the home of the deceased, and any standing water is poured out. A dead body is not to be left unattended, and it is considered a *mitzvah* (good deed) to sit with the person who has died and recite psalms. An individual who watches over a person who has died is exempt from prayers and wearing *tefillin*.

The burial of the body should take place as soon as possible. No burial is allowed to take place on Sabbath or the Day of Atonement, and in contemporary practice it is considered unacceptable for it to take place on the first and last days of pilgrim festivals. After the members of the burial society have taken care of the body, they prepare it for burial; it is washed and dressed in a white linen shroud. The corpse is then placed in a coffin or on a bier before the funeral service. Traditional Jews only permit the use of a plain wooden coffin, with no metal handles or ornaments. The deceased is then borne to the grave face upwards; adult males are buried wearing their prayer shawl – one of the fringes having been removed or marred so as to render the prayer shawl unfit. In some Eastern communities, the dead person's *tefillin* are also buried with him. A marker should be placed on a newly filled grave, and a tombstone should be erected and unveiled as soon as permissible (either at the end of the thirty-day mourning period in Israel, or after eleven months have elapsed in the diaspora). A limb severed or amputated from a person who is still alive should also be buried – this is true also of bodies on which autopsies or dissections have been carried out.

Among Reform Jews, burial practice differs from that of the Orthodox. Embalming and cremation are usually permitted, and Reform rabbis commonly officiate at crematoria. Burial may be delayed for several days, and the person who has died is usually buried in normal clothing without a prayer shawl. No special places are reserved for priests, nor is any separate arrangement made for someone who has committed suicide or married out of the faith.

Despite differences in procedure between Ashkenazi and Sephardi Jews, there are a number of common features of the burial service: in both rites mourners rend their garments, and Biblical and liturgical verses are chanted by the rabbi as he leads the funeral procession to the cemetery. It is customary to stop on the way, allowing mourners to express their grief. Often a eulogy is given either in the funeral chapel or as the coffin is lowered into the grave, which the male mourners help to fill with earth. Memorial prayers and a special mourners' *Kaddish* are recited; mourners present words of comfort to the bereaved; and all wash their hands before leaving the cemetery.

The Jewish tradition provides a special framework for mourning which applies to males over the age of thirteen and females over the age of twelve who have lost a father or mother, husband or wife, son or daughter, brother or sister. From the moment that death takes place until the burial, the mourners are exempt from positive commandments (praying, reciting grace after meals, wearing *tefillin*, etc.); in addition a mourner is not allowed to participate in festival meals or engage in pleasurable activities. Instead, he must rend a garment – this is done (depending on custom) on receiving the news of death, just prior to the funeral, or after the funeral. Once the burial has taken place, mourners are to return to the home of the deceased or where the mourning period will be observed, and consume a meal consisting of bread and a hard-boiled egg which should be provided by others.

The mourning period, known as *shivah* (seven), lasts for seven days beginning with the day of burial. During this time mourners sit on the floor or on low cushions or benches and are forbidden to shave, bathe, go to work, study the Torah (except subjects related to mourning), engage in sexual relations, wear leather shoes, greet others, cut their hair, or wear laundered clothing. Through these seven days, it is customary to visit mourners – in some places it is the practice to bring prepared food. Those comforting mourners are not to greet them but rather offer words of consolation. On the Sabbath which falls during the *shivah*, it is forbidden to make a public display of mourning; in some communities mourners do not occupy their normal seats in the synagogue. Among the *Sephardim*

members frequently sit near the mourners for part of the service.

Shivah concludes on the morning of the seventh day and is followed by mourning of a lesser intensity for thirty days known as *sheloshim* (thirty). At this time mourners are not permitted to cut their hair, shave, wear new clothes or attend festivities. Some traditions consider that the *sheloshim* constitutes the full mourning period for relatives other than parents. Mourning for parents should take place for nearly a year, and mourners are not supposed to shave or cut their hair after *sheloshim*. Those who mourn are not permitted to attend public celebrations or parties. Mourners are to recite *kaddish* daily throughout the period of mourning – in the case of those whose mourning continues for a year, it is at times customary to recite *Kaddish* till one month or week before the anniversary of death. If the holy days and festivals of *Rosh Hashanah*, Day of Atonement, *Sukkot*, Passover or *Shavuot* intervene, the *shivah* is terminated; if a burial takes place during the middle days (*Hol Hamoed*) or *Sukkot* or Passover, the laws of *shivah* take effect once the festival ends.

If one hears of the death of a relative while other mourners are observing *shivah*, the person may end his *shivah* with these individuals. However, if news arrives within thirty days after death, *shivah* must be observed in its entirety. On the other hand, if the news arrives after thirty days, mourners are required to observe only a brief period of mourning. When news arrives of a parent's death, the mourner shall rend his garment; however if he learns of the death of another relative after thirty days, he need not do so, although he is to recite the blessing of *Tzidduk ha-Din*. If the deceased was a violator of God's law or had committed suicide (unless it was the result of insanity), the laws of mourning are not carried out. It is a general practice to mark the anniversary of the death of a relative (*yartzeit*) by reciting the *Kaddish*, a memorial prayer, studying the Torah, chanting the *Haftarah* (reading from the Prophets), and igniting memorial lights.

SOURCES

Memorial Service

At the end of the Memorial service, the following prayer is recited:

Father of mercy, in whose hands are the souls of the living and the dead, may thy consolation cheer us as we remember on this holy day our beloved and revered kinsfolk who have gone to their rest, our dear parents the crown of our head and our glory, whose desire it was to train us in the good and righteous way, to teach us thy statutes and thy commandments, and to instruct us to do justice and to love mercy. We beseech thee, O Lord, grant us strength to be faithful to their charge while the breath of life is within us. And may their souls repose in the land of eternal life, beholding thy glory and delighting in thy goodness.

And now, O good and beneficent God, what shall we say, and what shall we speak unto thee? Our needs are many, our knowledge slender. Shame covers us as the remembrance of all thy love for us rises within our minds. O turn this day in loving-kindness and tender mercy to the prayers of thy servants who pour out their souls before thee. May thy lovingkindness not depart from us. Give us our needful sustenance, and let us not be in want of the gifts of flesh and blood. Remove from us all worry and grief, distress and fear, shame and contempt. Let thy grace be with us, that we may rear our children to keep thy commandments and to fulfil thy will all the days of their life. O God, take us not hence in the midst of our days. Let us complete in peace the number of our years. Verily we know that our strength is frail, and that thou hast made our days in limited measure. Help us, O God of our salvation, to bear ourselves faithfully and blamelessly during the years of our pilgrimage. And when our end draws nigh and we depart this world, be thou with us, and may our souls be bound up in the bond of eternal life with the souls of our parents and of the righteous who are ever with thee. Amen and Amen.

(Memorial prayer in H, pp. 183–184)

DISCUSSION

1. What is the purpose of rituals concerning mourning?

2. What are the arguments for and against cremation?

FURTHER READING

Aiken, Lisa, *Why Me God? A Jewish Guide for Coping and Suffering*, Jason Aronson, 1998.

Brener, Anne, *Mourning and Mitzvah: A Guided Journal for Walking the Mourner's Path Through Grief to Healing*, Jewish Lights, 1993.

Dorff, Elliot, *Matters of Life and Death*, Jewish Publication Society of America, 1998.

Grollman, Earl, *Living With Loss, Healing With Hope: A Jewish Perspective*, Beacon Press, 2000.

Heilman, Samuel, *When a Jew Dies: The Ethnography of a Bereaved Son*, University of California Press, 2001.

Lamm, Maurice, *The Jewish Way in Death and Mourning*, Jonathan David, 2000.

Palatnik, Lori, *Remember My Soul: A Guided Journey Through Shiva and the Thirty Days of Mourning for a Loved One*, Leviathan, 1998.

Reimer, Jack (ed.), *Jewish Insights on Death and Mourning*, Syracuse University Press, 2002.

Rozwaski, Chaim, *Jewish Meditations on the Meaning of Death*, Jason Aronson, 1994.

Silverman, William, *When Mourning Comes: A Book of Comfort for the Grieving*, Jason Aronson, 1990.

Solomon, Lewis, Raphael, Simcha Paul, *The Jewish Book of Living and Dying*, Jason Aronson, 1999.

Solomon, Lewis, *The Jewish Tradition and Choices at the End of Life: A New Judaic Approach to Illness and Dying*, University Press of America, 2001.

Sonsino, Rifat, Syme, Daniel, *What Happens After I Die?: Jewish Views of Life After Death*, UAHC Press, 1990.

Swirsky, Michael (ed.), *At the Threshold: Jewish Meditations on Death*, Jason Aronson, 1995.

Weiss, Abner, *Death and Bereavement: A Halakhic Guide*, Mesorah, 2001.

Wolfson, Ron, *A Time to Mourn, a Time to Comfort*, Jewish Lights, 1995.

Zlotnik, Dov (ed.), *The Tractate 'Mourning': (Semachot) Regulations Relating to Death, Burial and Mourning*, Yale University Press, 1977.

CHAPTER 89

Jewish Ethics

Figure 89 Ethics – kindness to animals. Copyright, David Rose, London.

In the Jewish faith ethical values are of primary concern. For Jews moral action is fundamental – it is through the rule of the moral law that God's kingdom can be realized. From ancient times the synagogue liturgy concluded with a prayer in which this hope was expressed:

> May we speedily behold the glory of thy might,
> when thou wilt remove the abominations from
>   the earth,
> and the idols will be utterly cut off;

when the world will be perfected under the
  kingdom of the Almighty,
and all the children of flesh will call upon thy
  name;
when thou wilt turn unto thyself all the wicked of
  the earth.

This is the goal of the history of the world in which God's chosen people have a central role. In this context the Jewish people have a historical mission to be a light to the nations. Through Moses God addressed the people and declared: 'You have seen what I did to the Egyptians, and how I bore you on eagles' wings, and brought you unto myself. Now therefore, if you will obey my voice and keep my covenant, you shall be my own possession among all people; for all the earth is mine, and you shall be to me a kingdom of priests and a holy nation (Exod. 19:4–6). Election was to be a servant of the Lord; to proclaim God's truth and righteousness throughout the world. Being chosen meant duty and responsibility – it was a divine call which persisted through all ages and embraced the whole earth.

In this quest Judaism did not separate religion from life; instead Jews were called to action, to turn humankind away from violence, wickedness, and falsehood. It was not the hope of bliss in a future life but the establishment of the kingdom of justice and peace that was central to the Jewish faith. Moral action is thus at the heart of the religious tradition. The people of Israel as a light to the nations reflects the moral nature of God. Each Jew is to be like the creator mirroring the divine qualities revealed to Moses: 'The Lord, the Lord, a God merciful and gracious, slow to anger, and abounding in steadfast love and faithfulness, keeping steadfast love for thousands, forgiving iniquity and transgression and sin' (Exod. 34:6–7).

God as a moral being demands moral living, as the Psalms declare: 'The Lord is righteous; He loves righteous deeds' (Ps. 11:7): 'Righteousness and justice are the foundation of his throne' (Ps. 97:2): 'Thou has established equity; thou hast executed justice and righteousness' (Ps. 99:4). Given this theological framework, Jews are directed to obey the revealed will of God, which serves as the basis of the covenantal relationship between God and the Jewish nation.

In the Bible, deeds and events involving moral issues can be found in abundance: the punishment of Cain for murdering his brother, the violence of the generation that brought on the flood, the early prohibition against murder, the hospitality of Abraham and his pleading for the people of Sodom, the praise of Abraham for his moral attitudes, the condemnation of Joseph's brothers, Joseph's self-restraint in the house of Potiphar, Moses' intercessions on the side of the exploited.

But it is pre-eminently in the legal codes of the Torah that we encounter moral guidelines formulated in specific rules. The Decalogue (Ten Commandments) in particular illustrates the centrality of moral action in the life of the Jew. The first commandments are theological in character, but the last six deal with relationships between human beings. The first commandment describes God as the one who redeemed the Jews from Egypt; the one who forbade the worship of other deities and demands respect for the Sabbath and the divine name. These commandments are expressions of the love and fear of God; the remaining injunctions provide a means of expressing love of other human beings. The Decalogue thus makes it clear that moral rules are fundamental to the Jewish religion.

Such ethical standards were repeated in the prophetic books. The teachings of the prophets are rooted in the Torah of Moses. The prophets saw themselves as messengers of the divine word: their special task was to denounce the people for their transgressions and call them to repentance. In all this they pointed to concrete moral action as the only means of sustaining the covenantal relationship with God. The essential theme of their message was that God demands righteousness and justice.

Emphasis on the moral life was reflected in the prophetic condemnation of cultic practices that were not accompanied by ethical concern. These passages illustrate that ritual commandments are of instrumental value – morality is intrinsic and absolute. The primacy of morality was also reflected in the prophetic warning that righteous action is the determining factor in the destiny of the Jewish nation. Moral transgressions referred to in such contexts concern exploitation, oppression, and the perversion of justice. These sins have the potential to bring about the downfall of the nation.

The Book of Proverbs reinforces the teaching of the Torah and the prophets; wisdom is here conceived as a capacity to act morally; it is a skill that can be learned. Throughout Proverbs dispositional traits are catalogued: the positive moral types include the *tzaddik* (righteous person), the *hakham* (wise person), and the *yashar* (upright person); evil characters include the *rasha* (evil person), the *kheseil* (fool), the *letz* (mocker), and the *peti* (simpleton). Thus here as in the rest of the Bible, the moral life is seen as the basis of the Jewish faith. Theology is defined in relation to practical activity – it is through moral activity that humanity encounters the Divine.

Rabbinic literature continued this emphasis on ethical action. Convinced they were the authentic expositors of Scripture, the rabbis amplified Biblical law. In their expansion of the commandments, rabbinic exegetes differentiated between the laws governing human relationships to God (*bain adam la-makom*), and those that concern human relationships to others (*bain adam la-havero*). As in the Biblical period, rabbinic teachings reflected the same sense of the primacy of morality. Such texts as the following indicate rabbinic priority:

> He who acts honestly and is popular with his fellow creatures, it is imputed to him as though he had fulfilled the entire Torah.

> Hillel said: 'What is hateful to yourself, do not do to your fellow man. This is the entire Torah, the rest is commentary.'

> Better is one hour of repentance and good deeds in this world than the whole life of the world-to-come.

In the classic texts of Judaism, then, moral behaviour is the predominant theme. By choosing the moral life, the Jew is able to complete God's work of creation. To accomplish this task the rabbis formulated an elaborate system of traditions, which were written down in the *Mishnah*, subsequently expanded in the **Talmud**, and eventually codified in the *Code of Jewish Law*. According to traditional Judaism, this expansion of the pentateuchal law is part of God's revelation. Both the Written Law and the Oral Law are binding on Jews for all time. Such a conviction implies that the entire corpus of moral law is an expression of the divine will and must be obeyed.

For Jews the moral law is absolute and binding. In all cases it was made precise and specific – it is God's word made concrete in the daily life of the Jew. The commandment to love's one's neighbour embraces all humanity. In the *Code of Jewish Law* the virtues of justice, honesty and humane concern are regarded as central to community life; hatred, vengeance, deceit, cruelty, and anger are condemned as anti-social. The Jew is instructed to exercise lovingkindness towards all: to clothe the naked, to feed the hungry, to care for the sick, and to comfort the mourner. By fulfilling these ethical demands, the Jewish people are able to help bring about God's kingdom on earth in which exploitation, oppression and injustice are eliminated.

Such a system of ethics – as enshrined in the Bible and in rabbinic literature – embodies a number of essential characteristics. First, there is an intensity of passion about the moral demands made upon human beings. For sins of person greed, social inequity, and deceit, the prophets denounced the people and threatened horrific catastrophes. Such shrill denunciations of iniquity continued through the ages as the rabbis attempted to stir the Jewish people from their spiritual slumber.

Second, Jewish ethics require that each person be treated equally – Biblical and rabbinic sources show a constant concern to eliminate arbitrary distinctions between individuals so as to establish a proper balance between competing claims. On the basis of the Biblical view that everyone is created in the image of God, the Torah declares that false and irrelevant distinctions must not be introduced to disqualify human beings from the right to justice. The fatherhood and motherhood of God implies human solidarity; the Torah rejects the idea of different codes of morality for oneself and others, for the great and the humble, for rulers and ruled. Further, since all of humanity is created in the image of God, Judaism maintains that there is no fundamental difference between Jew and non-Jew. God's ethical demands apply to all.

A third characteristic of Jewish morality is its emphasis on human motivation. The Jewish faith is not solely concerned with actions and their consequences; it also demands right intention. As the rabbis explained: 'The Merciful One requires the heart.' While it is true that Judaism emphasizes the importance of moral action, the Jewish faith also focuses attention on rightmindedness: inner experiences – motives, feelings, dispositions, and attitudes – are of supreme moral significance. For this reason, the rabbis identified a group of negative commandments in the Torah involving thought. The following are representative examples:

> Thou shalt not take vengeance, nor bear any grudge against the sons of your own people (Lev. 19:18).

> There are six things which the Lord hateth . . . a heart that devises evil plans (Prov. 6:16, 18).

Take heed lest there be a base thought in your heart (Deut. 15:9).

In the *Mishnah* the rabbis elaborated on this concern for the human heart:

> Rabbi Eliezer said, '. . . be not easily moved to anger' (*Mishnah, Sayings of the Fathers* 2:15).

> Rabbi Joshua said, 'The evil eye, the evil inclination, and hatred of his fellow creatures drives a man out of the world' (*Mishnah, Sayings of the Fathers* 2:16).

> Rabbi Levitas of Yavneh said, 'Be exceedingly lowly of spirit' (*Mishnah, Sayings of the Fathers* 4:4).

A fourth dimension of Jewish morality concerns the traditional attitude to animals. Since God's mercy and goodness extend to all creatures, 'a righteous person should show consideration to animals' (Ps. 145:9; Prov. 12:10). According to the Jewish religion, human beings are morally obliged to refrain from inflicting pain on animals. Thus the Pentateuch stipulates that assistance be given to animals in distress even on the Sabbath: 'You shall not see your brother's ass or his ox fallen down by the way and withhold your help from them; you shall help him to lift them up again' (Deut. 22:4). In rabbinic Judaism this same theme was reflected in various *midrashim.*

A final aspect of Jewish ethics is its concern for human dignity. The Jewish faith continually emphasizes the respect due to all individuals. This concept, found in various laws in the Torah, was developed by the rabbis who cautioned that one must be careful not to humiliate or embarrass others. Maimonides (twelfth century), for example, wrote:

> A man ought to be especially heedful of his behaviour towards widows and orphans, for their souls are exceedingly depressed and their spirits low, even if they are wealthy. How are we to conduct ourselves toward them? One must not speak to them otherwise than tenderly. One must show them unvarying courtesy; not hurt them physically with hard toil nor wound their feelings with harsh speech.

> (Shubert Spero, *Morality, Halakha and the Jewish Tradition,* KTAV, 1983, p. 160)

Throughout the Biblical and rabbinic tradition, then, moral behaviour is a predominant theme. Continually the Jewish people have been God's suffering servant, yet inspired by a vision of God's reign they have been able to transcend their own misfortunes. The Jewish tradition points to God's kingdom as the goal and hope of humanity; a world in which all peoples shall turn away from iniquity and injustice. This is not the hope of bliss in a future life, but the building up of the divine kingdom of truth and peace on earth.

SOURCES

Josephus

The first-century historian Josephus emphasized the importance of welcoming non-Jews to the Jewish faith:

The consideration given by our legislator to the equitable treatment of aliens also merits attention. It will be seen that he took the best of all possible measures at once to secure our own customs from corruption, and to throw them open ungrudgingly to any who elect to share them. To all who desire to come and live under the same laws with us, he gives a gracious welcome, holding that it is not family ties alone which constitute relationship, but agreement in principles of conduct. On the other hand, it was not his pleasure that casual visitors should be admitted to the intimacies of our daily life.

(*Josephus, Against Apion,* in WI, p. 139)

According to Josephus, Jewish law respects the humanity of all persons:

The duty of sharing with others was inculcated by our legislator in other matters. We must furnish fire, water, food to all who ask for them, point out the road, not leave a corpse unburied, show consideration even to declared enemies. He does not allow us to burn up their country, or to cut down their fruit trees, and forbids even the despoiling of fallen combatants. He has taken measures to prevent outrage to prisoners of war, especially women. So thorough a lesson has he given us in gentleness and humanity that he does not overlook even the brute beasts, authorizing their use only in accordance with the Law, and forbidding all other employment of them. Creatures that take refuge in our houses, like suppliants, we are forbidden to kill. He would not suffer us to take the parent birds with their young, and bade us even in an enemy's country to spare and not to kill the beasts employed in labour. Thus, in every particular, he had an eye to mercy, using the laws I have mentioned to enforce the lesson, and drawing up for transgressors other penal laws admitting of no excuse.

(*Josephus, Against Apion*, in WI, p. 139)

Talmud

According to the rabbis, one should share in another's difficulties and help those in need:

If the community is in trouble, a man must not say, 'I will go to my house, and eat and drink, and peace shall be with thee, O my soul'. But a man must share in the trouble of the community, even as Moses did. He who shares in its troubles is worthy to see its consolation.

(*Talmud, Taanit*, 11a, in WI, p. 183)

Rabbi Elazar saw an impoverished colleague approaching, so he let a coin drop to the ground. When the other wished to return it, Rabbi Elazar said: 'I lost it some time ago and despaired of finding it. It is therefore legally yours'.

(*Jerusalem Talmud, Baba Metzia*, 2, in WI, p. 185)

Charity knows neither race nor creed.

(*Talmud, Gittin*, 61a, in WI, p. 184)

Midrash

Rabbinic sources concern both human morality and the treatment of animals:

If men make a sea voyage, and take cattle with them, should a storm arise, they jettison the animals to save mankind, because people do not love animals as much as they love human beings. Not so is God's love. Just as He is merciful to man, so is He merciful to the beasts. You can see this from the story of the Flood. When man sinned, and God determined to destroy the world, He treated man and beast alike. But when He was reconciled, He was reconciled to both, and He pitied both, man and beast alike, as we read in the narrative, 'God remembered Noah and the animals that were with him in the ark (Gen. 8:1).

(*Tanh., Noah*, 17a, in WI, p. 236)

Solomon ibn Gabirol

For the eleventh-century Jewish philosopher, Solomon ibn Gabirol, envy is a cardinal sin:

> Envy is to men like bodily ailments – it leads to consumption.
>
> I have not seen one who hurts himself more than does the envious person; his mourning is unceasing, his soul grieves, his intellect deteriorates and his heart is disquieted.
>
> Everybody can eat with satisfaction except the man who envies good fortune; for he is only pleased with the misfortune (of others).
>
> Every enmity has the possibility of cure, except the enmity of him who hates thee from envy.
>
> Envy not thy brother for what he has; he enjoys his life whilst thou art sated with vexation and unrest.
>
> Thou hast sufficient revenge of the envious person that he grieves over thy happiness and good fortune.
>
> (Solomon ibn Gabirol, *The Choice of Pearls*, in WI, p. 292)

Bahya ibn Pakuda

The eleventh-century Jewish philosopher, Bahya ibn Pakuda, in *Duties of the Heart* insisted on the importance of mutual aid:

> We assert, as a truth generally recognized, that if anyone benefits us, we are under an obligation of gratitude to him in accordance with his intent to help us. Even if he actually falls short, owing to some mishap which prevents his benefiting us, we are still bound to be grateful to him, since we are convinced that he has a benevolent disposition toward us and his inteniton is to be of use to us.
>
> (Bahya ibn Pakuda, *Duties of the Heart*, WI, p. 317)

Moses Maimonides

According to the twelfth-century Jewish philosopher Moses Maimonides, charity should be given without any consideration of benefit to oneself:

Whoever closes his eyes against charity is called, like the idol-worshipper, impious . . . Whoever gives alms to the poor with bad grace and surly looks, though he bestow a thousand gold pieces, all the merit of his action is lost. He must give with a good grace, gladly, sympathizing with the mendicant in his trouble. If a poor man solicit alms of you and you have nothing to give him, console him with words. It is forbidden to upbraid the poor, or raise the voice against him, since his heart is broken and crushed . . . Woe, then, to the person who shames the poor man! Be to him, rather, like a parent whether with funds or kindly words.

There are eight degrees in alms-giving, one lower than the other. Supreme above all is to give assistance to a fellowman who has fallen on evil times by presenting him with a gift or loan, or entering into a partnership with him, or procuring him work, thereby helping him to become self-supporting. Next best is giving alms in such a way that the giver and recipient are unknown to each other. This is, indeed, the performance of a commandment from disinterested motives; and it is exemplified by the institution of the chamber of the silent which existed in the Temple where the righteous secretly deposited their alms and the respectable poor were secretly assisted.

Next in order is the donation of money to the charity fund of the community, to which no contribution should be made unless there is confidence that the administration is honest, prudent, and efficient.

Below this degree is the instance where the donor is aware to whom he is giving the alms, but the recipient is unaware from whom he received them. The great sages, for example, used to go about secretly throwing money through the doors to the poor. This is quite a proper course to adopt and a great virtue where the administrators of a charity fund are not acting fairly.

Inferior to this degree is the case where the recipient knows the identity of the donor, but not vice versa. For example, the great sages would sometimes tie sums of money in linen bundles and throw them behind their backs for poor men to pick up, so that they should not feel shame.

The next four degrees in their order are: the man who gives money to the poor before he is asked; the man who gives money to the poor after he is asked; the man who gives less than he should, but does it with good grace; and lastly, he who gives grudgingly.

(Moses Maimonides, *Mishneh Torah*, in WI, pp. 369–370)

DISCUSSION

1. What are the underlying principles of Jewish ethics?

2. Discuss the treatment of animals in the Jewish tradition.

FURTHER READING

Benyosef, Simcha, *The Beginning of Wisdom*, KTAV, 2001.

Blumenthal, David, *The Banality of Good and Evil: Moral Lessons from the Shoah and Jewish Tradition*, Georgetown University Press, 1999.

Borowitz, Eugene, Schwartz, Frances Weinman, *The Jewish Moral Virtues*, Jewish Publication Society of America, 1999.

Cohen, Abraham, *Everyman's Talmud: The Major Teachings of the Rabbinic Sages*, Schocken, 1995.

Dorff, Elliot, *To Do Right and Good: The Jewish Approach to Modern Social Ethics*, Jewish Publication Society of America, 2002.

Flancbaum, Louis, *'And You Shall Live By Them': Contemporary Jewish Approaches to Medical Ethics*, Mirkov, 2001.

Freund, Richard, *Understanding Jewish Ethics*, Vol. II, Edwin Mellen, 1993.

Kaplan, Kalman, Schwartz, Matthew (eds), *Jewish Approaches to Suicide, Martyrdom and Euthanasia*, Jason Aronson, 1998.

Maimonides, Moses, *Ethical Writings of Maimonides*, Dover, 1983.

Pava, Moses, Levine, Aaron, *Jewish Business Ethics: The Firm and Its Stakeholder*, Jason Aronson, 1999.

Pies, Ronald, *The Ethics of the Sages: An Interfaith Commentary on Pirkei Avot*, Jason Aronson, 1999.

Rosner, Fred, *Biomedical Ethics and Jewish Law*, KTAV, 2001.

Rosner, Fred (ed.), *Pioneers in Jewish Medical Ethics*, Jason Aronson, 1997.

Roth, John, Grob, Leonard, Hass, Peter (eds), *Ethics After the Holocaust*, Paragon, 1999.

Sherwin, Byron, *Jewish Ethics for the Twenty-First Century: Living in the Image of God*, Syracuse University Press, 2000.

Sherwin, Byron, Cohen, Seymour, *Creating an Ethical Jewish Life: A Practical Introduction to Classic Teachings on How to Be a Jew*, Jewish Lights, 2001.

Telushin, Joseph, *The Book of Jewish Values: A Day-By-Day Guide to Ethical Living*, Bell Tower, 2000.

CHAPTER 90

Conversion

Figure 90 *Mikvah* at Kingsbury synagogue in London. Copyright Peter Fisher, London.

Though there is no formal term for the process of conversion in the Hebrew Bible, there are several Biblical terms which are suggestive of such an act: *hityahed* is used to describe persons who are said to have converted to Judaism for fear of the Jews; *amilam* (Ps. 118:10–12) may well refer to the circumcision of foreign nations; *nilvah* (Isa. 56:3) refers to the alien who has joined himself to the Lord. Such terms as these illustrate that conversion was practised during the Biblical period in order to assimilate conquered peoples as well as those who came to live within the Israelite community.

During the *tannaitic* and *amoraic* periods (100 BCE– 600 CE), conversion was frequently extolled by various rabbinic authorities. According to Elazar, for example, conversion was viewed as part of God's salvationist scheme: 'The Holy One, blessed be He, dispersed the people of Israel among the nations in order that they might acquire proselytes'. According to Hoshiah, God acted righteously towards Israel when he scattered them among the nations. In another passage in the *Talmud* it is asserted that the proselyte is dearer to God than the Israelite since he has come of his own accord, while the Israelites are believers as a result of the miracles exhibited on Mount Sinai. Resh Lakish noted that the person who oppresses the convert is as one who oppresses God. In the *midrash* it is maintained that it is never too late to convert: to teach this, Abraham did not enter the covenant until he was 99, when he was circumcised. As with Abraham, so every Israelite had the obligation to bring men under God's wings. In another *midrash*, we read that God loves proselytes exceedingly: 'So spoke the Holy One: "I owe great things to the stranger in that he has left his family and his father's house, and has come to dwell amongst us; therefore I order in the Law: Love the stranger"' (*Num. R., Naso,* 3, 2–4).

This positive attitude to proselytes is echoed by the historian Josephus who, in *Against Apion*, describes the openness of Hellenistic Judaism to converts: 'The consideration given by our legislator (Moses) to the equitable treatment of aliens also merits attention. To all who desire to come and live under the same laws as us he gives a gracious welcome' (p. 210). As a result of such openness to converts, a number of gentiles converted to Judaism during the early rabbinic period. However, the rise of Christianity led to the cessation of Jewish missionizing. Nevertheless, during the Talmudic and post-Talmudic period occasional conversions did take place in accordance with rabbinic law. Eventually the regulations governing conversion were drawn together and edited by Joseph Caro, the compiler of the *Shulkhan Arukh*, which since its publication in 1565 has served as the authoritative *Code of Jewish Law.*

In the section *Yoreh Deah*, the requirements for conversion as laid down in the *Talmud* and other codes are outlined in detail. When one presents himself as a candidate for conversion he is asked: 'What motivates you? Do you know that, in these days, Jews are subject to persecution and discrimination, that they are hounded and troubled?' If he replies: 'I know this and yet I regard myself as unworthy of being joined to them,' he is accepted immediately. The root principles of the faith, namely the unity of God and the prohibition of idol worship, are expounded to him at considerable length. He is taught, too, some of the simpler

and some of the more difficult commandments, and he is informed of the punishment involved in violating the commandments. Similarly, he is told of the rewards of observing them, particularly that by virtue of keeping the commandments, he will merit the life of the World-to-Come. He is told that no one is considered wholly righteous except those who understand and fulfil the commandments. Further, he is told that the World-to-Come is only intended for the righteous. If he finds these doctrines acceptable, he is circumcised immediately. After his circumcision has completely healed, he undergoes ritual immersion: three learned Jews stand by while he is in the water and instruct him in some of the easy and some of the difficult commandments. In the case of a female proselyte, Jewish women accompany her and supervise her immersion. The three learned male Jews remain outside the *mikvah* and give the convert instruction while she is in the water.

Concerning the candidate's motives, the *Shulkhan Arukh* states: 'When the would-be proselyte presents himself, he should be examined lest he be motivated to enter the congregation of Israel by hope of financial gain or social advantage or by fear. A man is examined lest his motive be to marry a Jewish woman and a woman is questioned lest she have similar desires toward some Jewish man.' If no unethical motive is found, the candidate is told of the heaviness of the yoke of the Torah and how difficult it is for the average person to live up to the commandments of the Torah. This is done to give the candidate a chance to withdraw if he so desires. If the candidate goes through all this and is not dissuaded, and it is apparent that his motives are of the best, he is accepted. Once a person is circumcised and ritually immersed, he is no longer a non-Jew although he continues to be under suspicion until he proves by his righteous living that he is worthy of respect. The central feature of these regulations governing the traditional conversion procedure is the emphasis on joining the Jewish community and accepting the Law – conversion is viewed as a legal rite of passage through which the convert takes his place within the Jewish community.

Up until the present day the procedure outlined in the *Shulkhan Arukh* has been rigorously followed. Within modern Orthodox Judaism, the emphasis is on living a Jewish way of life within the community. For this reason converts are meticulously given extensive religious instruction before conversion takes place. Although Conservative Judaism follows these legal requirements, Reform Judaism has departed from the traditional practice in a variety of ways. Emphasizing the universalistic mission of Judaism, Reform Jews very early in their history abrogated the necessity of ritual immersion for converts. On the question of circumcision, opinion was at first divided. In 1869 the Pittsburgh Conference took no definite stand, but a particular case of conversion without circumcision brought this question to the forefront of rabbinic debate. As a result, the Reform rabbinate decreed in 1892 that any rabbi, with the concurrence of two associates could accept into the Jewish faith any 'honourable and intelligent person, without any initiating rite'. The only requirements were that the person freely seek membership, that the candidate be of good character, and be sufficiently acquainted with the faith and practices of Judaism. In addition, the candidate was required to give evidence of sincere desire to worship only the God of Judaism, to live by God's laws, and to adhere in life and death to the sacred cause of Israel.

In 1927 the Central Conference of American Rabbis published a handbook for conversion along these lines. Among the questions asked of the candidate were queries about his voluntary acceptance of the Jewish faith, his pledge of loyalty to Judaism, his determination to cast in his lot with that of the Jewish people, his promise to lead a Jewish life, and to rear his children as Jews.

In 1961 the Central Conference of American Rabbis issued a revised version of the conversion service paralleling the 1927 format which was later updated. Unlike the traditional conversion procedure, the Reform service indicates that definite religious commitment is necessary in order to be accepted. The convert must state that he seeks admittance to the Jewish faith. While he is not under an obligation to profess that he worships 'only the One and Eternal God', as in the 1892 procedure, the service makes it clear that conversion to Judaism essentially entails the acceptance of religious belief. For this reason the service is conducted in the synagogue, and throughout the service the convert is told that conversion to Judaism is a religious act performed in God's presence. Thus, both explicitly and implicitly, conversion to Reform Judaism is con-

strued as primarily a religious ceremony expressing the convert's particular religious convictions, rather than as an affirmation of his willingness to accept the yoke of Jewish law as in Orthodoxy.

In modern times the vast majority of conversions have been performed by Reform and Conservative rabbis, particularly in the United States. In accordance with previous practice most Reform rabbis (unlike Conservative rabbis) do not require circumcision or immersion in the ritual bath. Instead a course of study and a ceremony are required. In addition, Reform Judaism – unlike Orthodoxy – encourages conversion to Judaism for purposes of marriage; in this way, reformers believe, the Jewish faith will be strengthened in times of increasing secularlism. In most places Orthodox Judaism refuses to accept the validity of either Reform or Conservative conversions. If asked to conduct a religious service (such as a wedding for non-Orthodox converts) or to register as Jews in Israel, Orthodox rabbis frequently require a new conversion under Orthodox auspices. According to Orthodoxy, non-Orthodox conversion is not valid because it does not take place according to the *halakhah* (Jewish law), nor is there an insistence that the convert live an Orthodox lifestyle; further, Orthodox Judaism insists that since non-Orthodox rabbis are not entitled to sit on a *bet din* (rabbinical court), any non-Orthodox procedure is not legally valid. Faced with such a lack of recognition, Conservative rabbis (as well as a few Reform rabbis) stress that they do follow the *halakhah* of Orthodox conversion, yet this has not persuaded Orthodoxy to accept their converts.

The issue of conversion has been further complicated in recent years by the decision of the American Reform rabbinate to adopt patrilineal descent as a criterion of Jewishness. According to this stance, a child born of a marriage between a Jewish father and a non-Jewish mother who is religiously observant is considered a Jew without undergoing conversion. Following this decree, Reconstructionist Judaism has adopted the same policy. This is radically different from the position of traditional Judaism, which maintains that a child of a non-Jewish mother is not Jewish, as stipulated by talmudic law – 'Your son by an Israelite woman is called your son, but your son by a heathen woman is not called your son'. In this view, a child who is born of a Jewish mother is considered Jewish regardless of the religion of the father, whereas the child born of a Jewish father and a non-Jewish mother is not recognized as a Jew.

In response to this new understanding of Jewish descent, Orthodoxy has repudiated the stance of Reform and Reconstructionist Judaism, and the Rabbinical Assembly of the Conservative movement has reaffirmed its adherence to the traditional interpretation of Jewishness. Both Orthodox and Conservative Judaism argue that the concept of patrilineal descent undermines the *halakhah* as well as the concept of *Kelal Yisrael* (the belief that all Jews are part of a communal body). As a result, the Jewish community is deeply divided about who is Jewish, which individuals require conversion, and what procedures should be employed to grant Jewish status to those who wish to convert to the Jewish faith.

SOURCES

Modern Conversion

Traditionally rabbis have initially tried to discourage a non-Jew who asks to convert. On the most obvious level, it may have been dangerous, even life-threatening, to offer to help such a person become a Jew. At the same time, though, attempts to dissuade them serve another purpose, to make them re-examine their decision, not to take it lightly. A candidate for conversion must be warned of the possibility of persecution and of the rigours of accepting the *mitzvot*. With such knowledge placed before him, a potential convert who stays the course will be someone who is genuinely eager to become a Jew.

The process leading to conversion begins with a period of study. Orthodox and Conservative converts are urged to spend some time living under the strictures that govern the life of a traditionally observant Jew. The level of commitment required of a convert will be same as that expected of a Jew by birth; a Reform rabbi will expect a convert to live up to the same standard of practice as a Reform Jew, a Reconstructionist rabbi that of a Reconstructionist, and so on. Rabbis of all denominations of Judaism will require study of Jewish history, lore, and religious practice. The Orthodox rabbinate, which is more stringent regarding the level of observance of its converts, refuses to recognize conversions performed by anyone other than the Orthodox.

(In EJCG, pp. 175–176)

DISCUSSION

1. Why is Judaism not a missionizing religion?

2. Are converts treated equally to those born into the Jewish faith?

FURTHER READING

Berkowitz, Allan, Moskovitz, Patti (eds), *Embracing the Convenant: Converts to Judaism Talk About Why and How*, Jewish Lights, 1996.

Cohen, J. Simcha, *Intermarriage and Conversion: A Halakhic Solution*, KTAV, 1987.

Epstein, Lawrence, *The Theory and Practice of Welcoming Converts to Judaism*, Edwin Mellen, 1992.

Epstein, Lawrence, *Conversion to Judaism: A Guidebook*, Jason Aronson, 1994.

Epstein, Lawrence (ed.), *Readings on Conversion to Judaism*, Jason Aronson, 1995.

Epstein, Lawrence, *Questions and Answers on Conversion to Judaism*, Jason Aronson, 1998.

Forster, Brenda, Tabachnik, Joseph, *Jews By Choice: A Study of Converts to Reform and Conservative Judaism*, KTAV, 1991.

Kukoff, Lydia, *Choosing Judaism*, UAHC Press, 1981.

Lamm, Maurice, *Becoming a Jew*, Jonathan David, 1991.

Lester, Julius, *Lovesong: Becoming a Jew*, Henry Holt and Co., 1988.

Lifland, Yosef, *Converts and Conversion to Judaism*, Gefen Publishing House, 2001.

Myowitz, Catherine Hall, *Finding a Home for the Soul: Interviews with Converts to Judaism*, Jason Aronson, 1995.

Weiss, Bernice, Silverman, Sheryl, *Converting to Judaism – Choosing to Be Chosen: Personal Stories*, Simcha, 2000.

Glossary

Adam Kadmon: primeval man

Adar: twelfth month of the Jewish year

Adon Olam: poem which begins, 'Lord of eternity'

Afar Mavet: dust of the earth

Afikoman: part of the middle *matzah*

Agudat Israel: anti-Zionist movement

Agunah: married woman whose husband's death is suspected or whose husband refuses to give her a *get*

Akdamut Millin: liturgical poem ('introduction')

Akedah: the binding (of Isaac)

Alenu: prayer at the end of a service

Al ha-Nissim: prayer ('for the miracles')

Al Het: prayer ('for the sin')

Amidah: the eighteen benedictions ('standing')

Amilam: circumcision of foreign nations

Amoraim: Palestinian sages (200–500 CE)

Ani Maamin: prayer which begins 'I believe'

Ashamnu: prayer ('we have trespassed')

Ashkenazic: originating in Eastern Europe

Asiyah: *kabbalistic* realm ('making')

Attah Yatsarta: prayer ('you have desired')

Atzilut: kabbalistic realm ('emanation')

Av: fifth month of the Jewish year

Avinu Malkenu: prayer ('our father our king')

Avodah She-ba-lev: service of the heart

Avon: crookedness

Avot: sayings of the fathers

Ayin: nothingness

Ayn Sof: the Infinite

Bain Adam la-Havero: laws governing human relationships with each other

Bain Adam la-Makom: laws governing human relations with God

Baraita: teachings not included in the *Mishnah*

Bar Mitzvah: male adolescent ceremony ('son of the commandment')

Barukh Shem Kevod Malkhuto: prayer ('blessed is the name of his holy kingdom')

Barukh She-Petaroni: prayer ('blessed be he who has relieved me')

Bat: daughter

Bat Mitzvah: female adolescent ceremony ('daughter of the commandment')

Bereshit: 'In the beginning'

Beriyah: kabbalistic realm ('creation')

Besht: Israel ben Eliezer (also known as the Baal Shem Tov)

Bet Din: rabbinic court

Bhr: 'to choose' in Hebrew

Bimah: platform

Binah: God's wisdom

Birkhat ha-Mazon: Grace after Meals

Bor: pit

Cantor: chanter

Cohen: priest

Creatio Ex Nihilo: creation from nothing

Dayyan: judge

Derashah: discourse

Devekut: mystical cleaving to God

Diaspora: outside Israel

Dreydel: *Hanukkah* top

Einsatzgruppen: mobile killing battalions used by the Nazis

Elilim: non-entities

Eli Tziayyon: prayer ('lament, O Zion')

Elleh Ezkerah: martyrology ('these things I remember')

El Nora Alilah: hymn

Elohim: God

Elul: sixth month of the Jewish year

Eretz: earth

Eretz Israel: land of Israel

Eretz Tachtit: nether parts of the earth

Erusin: stage in betrothal

Exodus Rabbah: *midrash* on Exodus

Fleishig: meat foods

Gan Eden: Garden of Eden (or heaven)

Gaon: head of a Babylonian academy
Ge: cursed valley associated with fire and death
Gehinnom: Hell
Gemara: rabbinic discussions on the *Mishnah*
Genesis Rabbah: *midrash* on Genesis
Gerousia: council
Get: bill of divorce
Get Zikkui: *get* of benefit
Ghetto: residential area where Jews were confined
Gomel: blessing ('he who makes recompense')
Greggar: noisemaker
Habad: *Hasidic* movement whose name is based on
    the initials of the words *hokhmah* (wisdom); *binah*
    (understanding); and *daat* (knowledge)
Haftarah: prophetic reading
Haganah: Israeli defence force
Haggadah: Passover prayer book
Hag ha-Aviv: Festival of Spring
Hag ha-Matzot: Festival of Unleavened Bread
Hag ha-Urim: Festival of Lights
Hakham: wise person
Hakham Bashi: chief rabbi
Halakhah: Jewish law
Hallel: Psalms 113–118
Hamantashen: *Purim* cakes ('Haman's hats)
Ha-Mashiah: Messiah ('the anointed')
Hanukkah: festival of lights ('dedication')
Ha-Rahaman: the Compassionate One
Haroset: paste of fruit, spices, wine and *matzah* eaten
    at the Passover *seder*
Hashgahah: divine action
Hashkavah: memorial prayer ('cause us to lie down')
Hasid: pious person
Hasidism: mystical Jewish movement founded in the
    eighteenth century
Haskalah: Jewish Enlightenment
Havdalah: service at the end of the Sabbath and festivals
Havurot: informal prayer groups
Hazot: noon service
Heder: school for children
Hesed Shel Emet: true kindness
Het: to miss, to fail
Hineni He-Ani Mi-Maas: prayer
Hinnah: bride's party before a wedding
Hityahed: convert to Judaism who converts for fear of
    the Jews
Hokhmah: God's wisdom

Hol Hamoed: intermediate days of a festival
Holocaust: destruction of the Jewish people between
    1939 and 1945 in Europe
Hoshanah: prayer ('save, I pray')
Hoshanah Rabbah: seventh day of *Sukkot*
Humanistic Judaism: Non-supernaturalistic and
    humanistically orientated movement
Huppah: marriage canopy
Isru Hag: day after the festival of Passover, *Shavuot* or
    Tabernacles
Iyyar: second month of the Jewish calendar
Judenbischof: bishop of the Jews
Kabbalah: Jewish mysticism
Kallah: study session
Kapparot: atonements
Karaism: anti-rabbinic sect
Kashrut: dietary laws
Kavvanot: intention
Kedushah: holiness prayer
Kehillot: Jewish communal bodies
Kelal Yisrael: community of Israel
Keter: God's will
Ketubbah: marriage contract
Ketuvim: Writings (third section of the Hebrew Bible)
Kheseil: foolish person
Kiddush: sanctification prayer
Kiddushin: stage in betrothal
Kinot: elegies
Kislev: ninth month of the Jewish calendar
Kittel: robe
Kodashim: holy things
Kollel: advanced institute for *Talmud* study
Kol Nidre: evening service which starts the Day of
    Atonement ('all vows')
Kosher: ritually fit food
Kristallnacht: German onslaught on Jewish property
    which took place on 9th to 10th November 1938
Lag Ba-Omer: scholars' feast
La-Shanah ha-Baah bi-Yerushalayim: 'Next year in
    Jerusalem'
Latkes: potato pancakes
Lekhah Dodi: Sabbath hymn ('come, my beloved')
Letz: mocker
Levite: priest
Lulav: palm branch (used on *Sukkot*)
Maariv: evening service
Maftir: reader of the *Haftarah*

Malkhuyyot: prayer dealing with God's rule

Malkot: lashes

Mamzer: child of an incestuous or adulterous relationship

Manna: food provided by God in the desert

Maoz Tsur: hymn for *Hanukkah* ('rock of ages')

Mappah: glosses of Moses Isserles on the *Shulkhan Arukh*

Marheshvan: second month of the Jewish year

Maror: bitter herbs

Marranos: Jews who converted to Christianity (in Spain and Portugal)

Maskilim: followers of the Jewish Enlightenment

Matzah: unleavened bread used for Passover

Mavet: death

Megillah: scroll

Mekhilta: *midrash* on Exodus

Menorah: candelabrum

Merkavah: divine chariot

Messiah: God's chosen leader

Mezuzah: box fixed to the doorpost of a Jewish home

Midrash: rabbinic commentary on Scripture

Midrash Rabbah: *midrash* on the Pentateuch and the Five Scrolls

Mikdash me-at: minor sanctuary

Mikveh: ritual bath

Milchig: milk foods

Minhah: meal offering (or afternoon service)

Minyan: quorum of ten men

Mi She-Barakh: prayer ('he who blessed')

Mishnah: compendium of the Oral Torah

Mitnaggedim: Rabbinic opponents of the Hasidim

Mitzvah: commandment

Moed: season

Mohar: payment by the groom

Mohel: official who performs a circumcision

Musaf: additional service

Musar: movement of return to traditional ethics founded in the modern period

Nagid: head of Spanish or North African community

Nahamu: 'comfort'

Nashim: women

Nedunyah: money given to the son on betrothal

Neilah: concluding service

Neilat Shearim: evening service

Neviim: Prophets (second section of the Hebrew Scriptures)

Nezikim: damages

Nilvah: alien who has joined himself to the Lord

Nisan: first month of the Jewish year

Nissuin: second stage in the marriage procedure

Olam: eternity

Olam ha-tikkun: world of perfection

Olam ha-tohu: world of the void

Omer: barley offering

Ophanim: lower order of angels

Orthodoxy: Torah-observant Judaism

Parashah: Torah portion

Parnas: head of the community

Parokhet: white curtain

Paschal: Passover

Pesach: Passover festival

Peshah: breach

Petah Lanu Shaar: hymn ('open the gate for us')

Peti: simpleton

Petor: divorce document

Pidyon ha-Ben: redemption of the first-born

Piyyutim: hymns

Proselyte: convert

Pur: lot

Purim: feast of Esther

Purim gelt: *Purim* coins

Purim Shoshan: 15th of *Adar*

Rabbi: teacher

Rasha: evil person

Rebbe: Hasidic leader

Reconstructionist Judaism: modernizing movement founded by Mordecai Kaplan

Reform Movement: progressive modernizing movement

Responsa: answers to specific legal questions

Rosh Hashanah: New Year

Rosh Hodesh: 1st of the month

Sabbath: seventh day

Sandak: godfather

Sanhedrin: central rabbinic court in ancient times

Seder: Passover ceremony at home

Sefirah Malkhut: heavenly archetype of the community of Israel

Sefirot: divine emanations

Selihot: penitential prayers

Sephardi: originating in Spain or North Africa

Seudah Mafseket: final meal

Seudah Mitzvah: meal in honour of a religious act

Seudah Shelishit: third meal

Shabbat Bereshit: Sabbath when the new Torah reading begins ('Sabbath of Genesis')

Shabbat ha-Gadol: Great Sabbath

Shabbat ha-Hodesh: Spring Sabbath ('Sabbath of the month')

Shabbat Hanukkah: Sabbath during *Hanukkah*

Shabbat Hazon: Sabbath before *Tishah B'Av* ('Sabbath of Prophecy')

Shabbat Hol Hamoed: Sabbath during *Sukkot* or Passover season

Shabbat Mahar Hodesh: Sabbath of the eve of a New Moon

Shabbat Mevarekhim: Sabbath before a New Moon

Shabbat Nahamu: Sabbath after *Tishah B'Av*

Shabbaton: day of solemn rest

Shabbat Parah: Spring Sabbath ('Sabbath of the Red Heifer')

Shabbat Rosh Hodesh: New Moon Sabbath

Shabbat Shekalim: Spring Sabbath ('Sabbath of the *Shekel* Tax')

Shabbat Shirah: Sabbath when the Song of Moses is recited

Shabbat Shuvah: Sabbath between *Rosh Hashanah* and *Yom Kippur* ('Sabbath of Return')

Shabbat Teshuvah: Sabbath of Repentance

Shabbat Zakhor Rakhor: Spring Sabbath ('Sabbath of Remembrance')

Shaddai: Almighty

Shaharit: morning service

Shalom Aleikhem: hymn ('peace be to you')

Shalom Zakhor: birth celebration gathering

Shammash: serving light for *Hanukkah*

Shavuot: Festival of Weeks

Sheheheyanu: blessing ('who has preserved us')

Shehitah: ritual slaughter

Shekhinah: divine presence

Sheloshim: thirty days of mourning

Shema: prayer ('Hear, O Israel')

Shema Yisrael: Hear, O Israel

Shemini Atzeret: final day of the festival of *Sukkot*

Shemoneh Esreh: *Amidah*

Sheol: place of the dead

Shetar Pesikta: betrothal document

Sheva Berakhot: seven blessings

Shevarim: three tremulous notes sounded on the *shofar*

Shevat: eleventh month of the Jewish year

Shiddukhin: pre-marital arrangements

Shivah: seven days of mourning

Shofar: ram's horn

Shofarot: prayer relating to the ram's horn

Shohet: slaughterer

ShOVaVIM Tat: optional fasts in January or February

Shulkhan Arukh: *Code of Jewish Law*

Shushan Purim: festival of the victory of the Jews of Shushan

Shuvah: prayer ('return')

Siddur: traditional prayer book

Sidrah: section of the Torah reading

Sifra: *midrash* on Leviticus

Sifrei: *midrash* on Numbers and Deuteronomy

Simhat Torah: Festival of the Rejoicing of the Law

Sitra Ahra: demonic realm ('the other side')

Sivan: third month of the Jewish year

Sufganiyyot: doughnuts

Sukkah: booth

Sukkot: Feast of Tabernacles

Synagogue: place of worship

Tahanun: prayer ('supplication')

Takkanah: enactment

Takkanot ha-Kahal: communal statutes

Tallit (larger): prayer shawl

Tallit (smaller): fringed undergarment

Talmud: compilation of the legal discussions based on the *Mishnah*

Talmud Torah: Jewish school

Tammuz: fourth month of the Jewish year

Tanakh: Hebrew Bible

Tanna: Jewish sages (70–200 CE)

Tashlikh: casting away sin

Tefillah: prayer (also the *Amidah*)

Tekiah: long note sounded on the *shofar*

Teku: 'let it remain undecided'

Tenaim: betrothal document

Terefah: not *kosher* ('torn')

Teruot: nine short notes sounded on the *shofar*

Tevet: tenth month of the Jewish year

Tikkanta Shabbat: prayer

Tikkun: cosmic repair

Tishah B'Av: ninth of *Av*

Tishri: seventh month of the Jewish year

Tohorot: purity

Tohu u vohu: 'without form' (void)

Torah: Law (or Pentateuch)

Torah She-Be-Al Peh: Oral Law
Torah She-Bi Ketav: Written Law
Tosefta: additions to the *Mishnah*
Tu Bi-Shevat: New Year for Trees
Tzaddik: righteous person
Tzidduk ha-Din: prayer ('justification of the judgement')
Tzimtzum: contraction of the Godhead into itself
Tzitzit: fringes
U-Netanneh Tokef: prayer ('let us declare the mighty importance')
Viddui: confession
Vort: verbal betrothal agreement
Wimple: swaddling clothes
Yaaleh Ve-Yavo: prayer ('may our remembrances rise and come')
Yamim Noraim: Days of Awe
Yartzeit: anniversary of a death
Yashar: upright person
Yehi Ratson: prayer ('it will be God's will')
Yekum Purkah: prayer for schools and sages
Yemot Hamashiah: Days of the Messiah
Yeshivah: college
Yetsirah: *kabbalistic* realm ('formation')
Yetsiv Pitgam: liturgical prayer

Yetzer ha-Ra: evil inclination
Yetzer ha-Tov: good inclination
Yihud: seclusion
Yirat ha-onesh: fear of punishment
Yirat ha-romemut: fear in the presence of God
Yirat Shamayim: fear of heaven
Yisrael: Jewish people
Yizkor: memorial prayers
Yom ha-Atzmaut: Israel Independence Day
Yom ha-Din: Day of Judgement
Yom ha-Zikkaron: Day of Remembrance
Yom Kippur: Day of Atonement
Yom Kippur Katan: Small Day of Atonement
Yom Teruah: Day of blowing of the *shofar*
Zeman Herutenu: Season of our Freedom
Zeman Mattan Toratenu: Season of the Giving of our Torah
Zemirot: hymns
Zeraim: seeds
Zevah: animal sacrifice
Zikhronot: prayer ('proclamation of God's remembrance')
Zikhron Teruah: memorial proclaimed with a horn
Zionism: movement for a Jewish homeland in Israel
Zohar: medieval mystical work

Reference Bibliography

ATLASES

Barnavi, Eli (ed.), *A Historical Atlas of the Jewish People*, London, Hutchinson, 1992.
Cohn-Sherbok, Dan, *Atlas of Jewish History*, London, Routledge, 1994.
De Lange, Nicholas, *Atlas of the Jewish World*, Oxford, Phaidon, 1984.
Friesel, Efyatar, *Atlas of Modern Jewish History*, New York, Oxford University Press, 1990.

DICTIONARIES AND ENCYCLOPEDIAS

Abramson, Glenda (ed.), *The Blackwell Companion to Jewish Culture*, Cambridge, Ma, Blackwell, 1989.
Brisman, Shimeon (ed.), *A History and Guide to Judaic Bibliography*, Cincinnati, Hebrew Union College Press and New York, Ktav, 1977.
Cohn-Sherbok, Dan, *The Blackwell Dictionary of Judaica*, Oxford, Blackwell, 1992.
Cohn-Sherbok, Dan, *A Concise Encyclopedia of Judaism*, Oxford, Oneworld, 1999.
Encyclopedia Judaica, Jerusalem, Keter, 1972.
The Jewish Encyclopedia, New York, Funk and Wagnalls, 1901–1906.
Kantor, Mattis, *The Jewish Time Line Encyclopedia*, Northvale, NJ, Jason Aronson, 1989.
Shamir, Ilana and Shavit, Shlomo, *Encyclopedia of Jewish History*, Israel, Massada, 1986.
Shunami, Shlomo, *Bibliography of Jewish Bibliographies*, Jerusalem, Magnes Press, Hebrew University, 1965, Supplement, 1975.
Waxman, Meyer, *A History of Jewish Literature*, New York, Thomas Yoseloff, 1960.
Werblowsky, R.J. and Wigoder, Geoffrey, *The Encyclopedia of the Jewish Religion*, Jerusalem, Massada, PEC, 1966.
Wigoder, Geoffrey, *Dictionary of Jewish Bibliography*, Jerusalem, Jerusalem Publishing House, 1991.
Wigoder, Geoffrey (ed.), *The Standard Jewish Encyclopedia*, New York, Facts on File, 1992.

ELECTRONIC TEXTS

Bar-Ilan's Judaic Library: Torah Education Software.
Davka Corporation publish the CD-Rom Judaic Classic Library including a comprehensive set of classic Jewish texts in Hebrew and Aramaic including the Soncino *Talmud*, the Soncino *Midrash Rabbah*, the new CD-Rom *Bible*, *The Encyclopedia of Judaism* and *Dictionary of Jewish Bibliography*.
Encyclopedia Judaica on CD-Rom obtainable through Davka Corporation.
Oxford University Press and Brill publish the texts of the Dead Sea Scrolls on CD-Rom.

JOURNALS IN JEWISH STUDIES

CCAR Journal
Conservative Judaism
Hebrew Union College Annual
Holocaust and Genocide Studies
Humanistic Judaism
Jewish Journal of Sociology
Jewish Law Annual
Jewish Quarterly
Jewish Quarterly Review
Jewish Social Studies
Journal of Halakha and Contemporary Society
Journal of Jewish Studies
Journal of Jewish Thought and Philosophy
Judaism
Midstream
Modern Judaism
Reconstructionist Judaism
Tradition

Judaism on the Internet

The World Wide Web (WWW) is now of enormous help in exploring all aspects of Judaism. Thus, readers are strongly urged to make use of this important resource when reading this book as well as the *Judaism Website Companion* which is located on www.routledge.com/textbooks/0415236614.

In the *Judaism Website Companion* students are frequently encouraged to look up material on the World Wide Web to enhance their understanding of all aspects of the tradition. There are two major ways of accessing material. The first is by using a search engine, such as Google.com, to find information. This is easily done by first typing in www.google.com. This will access the search engine. It is then possible to find a wealth of material by simply typing in the relevant words, such as 'jewish mysticism', 'jewish theology', 'jewish law', etc. You will be able to find a vast quantity of information about every topic mentioned in *Judaism: History, Belief and Practice* simply by using any of the major search engines (Google.com, Yahoo.com, Altavista.com, etc.). Of course not every website is of equal value, and you will need to exercise discretion in determining what information is useful.

If possible, you should ask for advice from teachers or experts in the field.

The second method of accessing data is by going directly to a website. There are so many websites dealing with Judaism on the web that it would be impossible to list them all. However, you will be able to find these websites by first using a search engine to locate material on a specific subject. For example, if you want to locate the website of Jewish magazines, you should first go to Google.com, and type in 'Jewish magazines'. This will provide you with information about relevant websites. You can then go directly to these websites from Google by clicking on the mouse, or you can type in the website addresses. You should also be aware that it is possible to locate a vast quantity of illustrations, pictures, photographs, etc. by going to a search engine, such as Google.com. Then, when you type in the relevant words, such as '*kabbalah*', you will find an enormous quantity of images which will greatly aid your comprehension of Judaism. The World Wide Web is therefore of enormous help, and you should make every use of it as you read through this book as well as the *Judaism Website Companion*.

Index

CPSIA information can be obtained
at www.ICGtesting.com
Printed in the USA
FFOW01n0713041116
29016FF